[CONNECTIONS]
English Language Arts

7

Teacher Wraparound Edition, Resources, and Assessments

PERFECTION LEARNING®

Editorial Director:	Sue Thies
Editors:	Andrea Stark, John T. Ham
Proofreading Coordinator:	Sheri Cooper
Art Director:	Randy Messer
Designer:	Emily Adickes
Cover:	Mike Aspengren

Reviewers:

Danielle Emery, M.Ed.
Secondary ESL Coordinator
Lewisville, Texas, ISD
Lauri Garbo, M.Ed.

English Department
Gulf Coast High School
Collier County School District, Florida

Jennifer Martin
Instructional Strategist
Greenville, Texas ISD

Carmel McDonald
Instructional Coach
Paragon Charter Academy
Jackson, Michigan

Kendall Mott
DL Spanish Instructor
Region 5 Education Service Center
Beaumont, Texas

Debora L Stonich, M.Ed., Curriculum and Instruction
Owner/Instructor ESL for Business Professionals
and Graduate Students

Jen Joy Yocum
Teacher, English Language Arts
Paragon Charter Academy
Jackson, Michigan

Acknowledgments:

pp. 396–397, "Why Do We Hurt Each Other?" is reprinted courtesy of StopBullying.gov.   pp. 401–402, "The Man Who Fell from Heaven" by G. J. Boekenoogen, from Folklore and Mythology Electronic Texts. Translated by D. L. Ashliman, copyright 2014. Used by permission.   pp. 405–406, "Direct Marketer Agrees to Pay $8 Million for Deceiving Consumers" is reprinted courtesy of the United States Federal Trade Commission, www.ftc.gov.   pp. 426–428, "Robbie," copyright © 1950 and renewed 1977 by Isaac Asimov; from I, ROBOT by Isaac Asimov. Used by permission of Bantam Books, an imprint of Random House, and Doubleday, an imprint of the Knopf Doubleday Publishing Group, divisions of Penguin Random House LLC. All rights reserved.   pp. 432–433, From "Money for Morality" by Mary Arguelles as appeared in Newsweek, October 28, 1991. Used by permission of the author.   pp. 499–500, "Geoffrey's Tale" by Andrew Galloway, from Calliope magazine, © by Carus Publishing Company. Reproduced with permission. All Cricket Media material is copyrighted by Carus Publishing Company, d/b/a Cricket Media, and/or various authors and illustrators. Any commercial use or distribution of material without permission is strictly prohibited. Please visit http://www.cricketmedia.com/info/licensing2 for licensing and http://www.cricketmedia.com for subscriptions.

Please visit our website at: www.perfectionlearning.com

When ordering this book, please specify:
ISBN: 978-1-5311-2719-0 or **R7346**
ebook ISBN: 978-1-5311-2720-6 or **R7346D**

2 3 4 5 6 7 EPAC 25 24 23 22 21 20

Printed in the United States of America

Contents

Wraparound Teacher Support

CONNECTIONS
English Language Arts

Connections: English Language Arts provides the foundation for success through its unique approach to high-quality, complex texts.

The Connections program guides students in the close reading process as they:

- engage in close reading of complex fiction and nonfiction texts, all related to an Essential Question.
- learn and apply English language arts skills through authentic practice using complex texts.
- develop a deeper understanding of texts through multiple readings.
- respond by organizing, evaluating, and synthesizing textual evidence in writing, speaking, and listening activities.
- demonstrate proficiency through project-based assessments, standardized exams, and performance tasks.

UNIT OPENER

- The **Essential Question** guides reading, writing, speaking, and listening throughout the unit.
- Opening activity engages students in Essential Question to develop context for the selections and skills.

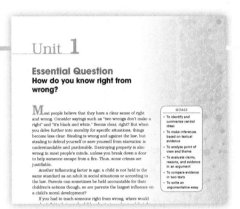

ESSENTIAL QUESTIONS

	GRADE 6	GRADE 7	GRADE 8
Unit 1	How Are Friendships Built and Broken?	How Do You Know Right From Wrong?	What Are the Benefits and Challenges of Living in a Diverse Society?
Unit 2	How Do People Deal with Difficulties?	Can You Trust What You Hear, See, and Read?	What Does Humanity's Future Hold?
Unit 3	What Power Do Words Have?	How Is Technology Shaping Society?	Why Do We Tell Stories?
Unit 4	Why Should You Protect Earth and Its Creatures?	What Does History Tell Us About Ourselves?	What Informs Your Decisions?

Chapter at a Glance

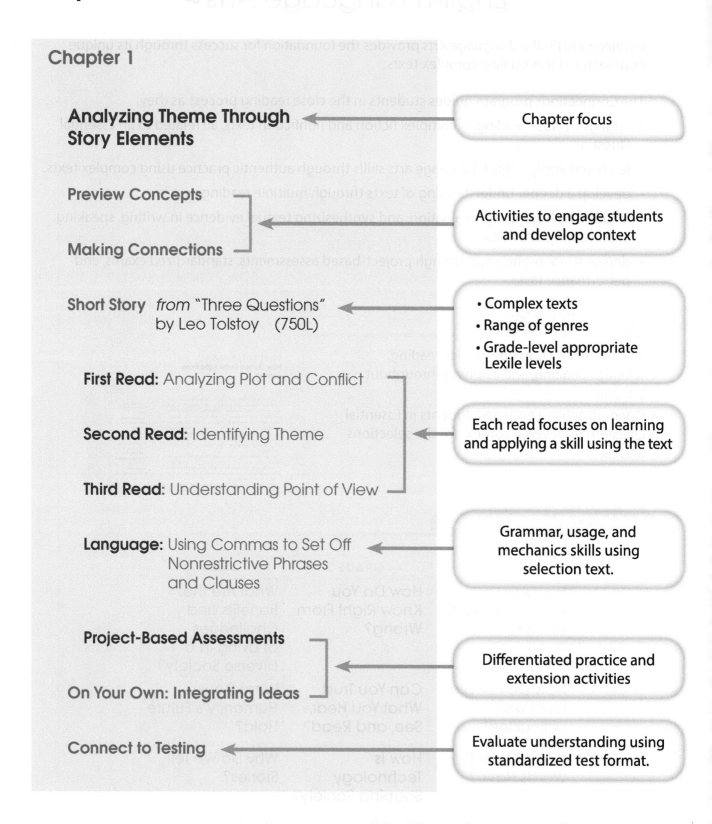

Chapter 1

Analyzing Theme Through Story Elements
— Chapter focus

Preview Concepts

Making Connections
— Activities to engage students and develop context

Short Story *from* "Three Questions" by Leo Tolstoy   (750L)
- Complex texts
- Range of genres
- Grade-level appropriate Lexile levels

First Read: Analyzing Plot and Conflict

Second Read: Identifying Theme

Third Read: Understanding Point of View
— Each read focuses on learning and applying a skill using the text

Language: Using Commas to Set Off Nonrestrictive Phrases and Clauses
— Grammar, usage, and mechanics skills using selection text.

Project-Based Assessments

On Your Own: Integrating Ideas
— Differentiated practice and extension activities

Connect to Testing
— Evaluate understanding using standardized test format.

Close Reading Process

- **Three close readings of each selection** move students from comprehending key ideas to synthesizing and connecting themes across texts.

- Each close read develops a specific skill, allowing students to practice through reading, writing, speaking, and listening activities.

- Throughout each close read, scaffolded activities help students navigate complex texts.

FIRST READ   KEY IDEAS & DETAILS

Discover **what** the text says by applying comprehension skills, such as making predictions, connecting to ideas and personal experience, making inferences, evaluating details, and monitoring comprehension.

> **First Read:** Citing Textual Evidence to Support Inferences
>
> The following excerpt is from Christopher Paul Curtis's novel *Bud, Not Buddy*.
>
> Objective: As you read the excerpt, underline words and phrases that help you make inferences about the setting (when and where the action is taking place), the situation, and the relationship between the two main characters. Use the My Thoughts box to record your inferences.

SECOND READ   CRAFT & STRUCTURE

Explore **how** the author uses text structures, literary elements, figurative language, and literary devices to create meaning.

> **Second Read:** Analyzing Characters
>
> Follow along with the text as your teacher reads the excerpt aloud.
>
> Objective: As you read, notice and underline dialogue and other details that explain what Bud and Bugs are like. In the My Thoughts column, write a word or phrase that explains the characteristic your underlined sentence reveals.
>
> **Focus on Analyzing Characters**
>
> Authors develop and reveal their characters in various ways. The process of developing characters is called *characterization*. The list below shows ways that authors use characterization to create

THIRD READ   INTEGRATE KNOWLEDGE & IDEAS

Explain **why** one or more texts convey a specific meaning; support with analysis, evaluation, and synthesis of ideas and evidence.

> **Third Read:** Analyzing Dialogue
>
> Listen as two of your classmates read the text aloud, taking the parts of the two main characters.
>
> Objective: Listen for words and phrases that make the characters sound as if they are actually living in 1936 during the Great Depression. Draw a box around words that reflect a regional difference in vocabulary, grammar, and pronunciation.

Research-Based 5-Step Approach

*"*Literary analysis is indeed a process where there is no right or wrong answer. This empowers students to be passionate about their topics and, most importantly, encourages them to look beyond the words on the page.*"*

—Edutopia, *George Lucas Educational Foundation*

". . .If students take time to ask themselves these questions while reading and become skillful at answering them, there'll be less need for the teacher to do all the asking. For this to happen, we must develop students' capacity to observe and analyze.*"*

—Nancy Boyles, *Educational Leadership*

*"*The point of the questions is to guide students to think about the text in effective ways.*"*

—Tim Shanahan, *shanahanonliteracy.com*

1. ESTABLISH PURPOSE

- Direct student attention during the reading
- Provide clear objective for identifying textual evidence

First Read: Citing Textual Evidence to Support Inferences

The following excerpt is from Christopher Paul Curtis's novel *Bud, Not Buddy.*

Objective: As you read the excerpt, underline words and phrases that help you make inferences about the setting (when and where the action is taking place), the situation, and the relationship between the two main characters. Use the My Thoughts box to record your inferences.

excerpt
Bud, Not Buddy

2. DEVELOP QUESTIONS

- Both teacher- and student-generated questions guide students' reading.
- Questioning strategies supported through reading objectives, note-taking and suggestions, and presentation slides

Text-Based Discussion Questions

1. What did you feel was the most suspenseful image in the story? Why? Support your answer with evidence.

2. What words or phrases best describe the character of the man Jack?

Slide 1

3. DISCOVER EVIDENCE

- Students respond to text-based questions by highlighting, annotating, and notetaking.
- Objective directs students' attention during their reading.

> 1   Something stepped on <u>a little stick</u>. As soon as the <u>twig</u> cracked my eyes snapped open and I was wide awake. I held my breath and kept as still as I could. Whatever it was that was sneaking up on me knew I'd woked up 'cause it stopped
> 5   moving and kept as still as it could too. Even though my head was still under my blanket, I could feel two eyes staring at me real hard, and I knew these weren't critter eyes, these eyes made the hair on the back of my neck raise up the way only human bean eyes can do.
> 10   Without wiggling or jiggling around too much under

4. ANALYZE & EVALUATE

- "Focus On" activities require students to organize, analyze, and evaluate their evidence.
- Activities develop and strengthen the targeted skills.

FIRST RESPONSE: KEY IDEAS AND DETAILS
Return to the sentences you underlined. Which one sentence from this excerpt do you feel creates the most suspenseful visual image? Write your choice in your response journal. Be prepared to defend your sentence selection and be ready to explain what you picture in your mind when you read that sentence.

TECH-CONNECT
Submit your sentence selection to your class website or tweet your sentence (include the line number and your initials) to your teacher.

Focus on Suspenseful Details
When defending your ideas about the most suspenseful sentence, return to the passage and analyze the sentences you underlined during the first read. Evidence to support your choice of the most suspenseful sentence should be based on what the text says—not on personal feelings. Compare the following sentences:

Not Based on What the Text Says (Nonexample)	Based on What the Text Says (Textual Evidence) (Good Example)
I think the most suspenseful sentence is the one about the knife because I saw a movie about a serial killer that scared me.	The most suspenseful sentence in the paragraph is *The knife had done almost everything it was brought to that house to do, and both the blade and the handle were wet* because the word *wet* implies that there is blood on the knife.
My teacher's example:	
My example:	

5. RESPOND & SHARE

Through writing, speaking, and listening activities, students:

- share ideas and perspectives,
- engage in active discourse, and
- refine their own thoughts and perspectives.

Write Analyze how Neil Gaiman uses sensory description to establish the mood and setting and to introduce the man Jack. Use details from the text to support your answer.

Write your paragraph on a separate sheet of paper or compose it using a word processing program. Double-space if typing or write on every other line if writing on a piece of paper. This will make it easier to mark your revisions.

Speak and Listen In groups of three or four, conduct a peer review of your paragraph about sensory imagery. Follow these steps:

Extension Activities

LANGUAGE

- Use the selection text to teach a specific skill in context.
- Each lesson covers important grammar, usage, and mechanics skills.
- PowerPoint slides offer additional support through extended practice and collaboration.

Language: Using Commas

Read the following paragraph from the excerpt. Underline where the author uses commas and a colon. Can you explain the reason why each is needed to communicate effectively?

The toddler's room was at the very top of the house. The man Jack walked up the stairs, his feet silent on the carpeting. Then he pushed open the attic door, and he walked in. His shoes were black leather, and they were polished to such a shine that they looked like dark mirrors: you could see the moon reflected in them, tiny and half full.

DIFFERENTIATION

Project-Based Assessments provide opportunities for differentiation and extension.

- Easy-to-use rubrics set clear objectives.
- Differentiated project options meet the needs of students with various abilities.
- Two projects in each chapter provide flexibility and grouping opportunities.

On Your Own: Integrating Ideas activities enhance and extend learning through online research and resources.

Project-Based Assessments

Pictorial Presentation

Create a pictorial presentation of the events in Chapter 1 of Neil Gaiman's *The Graveyard Book*.

- You may create either a digital presentation using PowerPoint, a video, or a storyboard (digital or hand drawn) of each scene.
- Use a minimum of six images, presented in order, with captions briefly explaining each scene. Include pictures to reflect what you predict happens when the man Jack arrives at the graveyard mentioned at the end of the excerpt.
- Be sensitive to avoid overly graphic images because your audience includes other students and your teacher.

Ideas to help you in your research for this presentation:

- Read the rubric below carefully so you know what is expected of you from the beginning.
- Plan your images before you begin so you can search more effectively.
- Use keywords such as *graveyard*, *The Graveyard Book*, or *fog* when conducting a search. (These words are only suggestions. You may use other keywords for your search.)
- Refine your search by clicking on Videos or Images.
- Once you find an image you like, save the image or capture a screen shot of it. Paste that image into your presentation and crop it. If you pause a video, you can capture an image as if it were a still shot.
- Challenge your technology skills by using filmmaking software such as FinalCut or iMovie, if it is available.

Assessment

- Assesses students' understanding of the academic vocabulary and skills practiced within the chapter.
- Questions represent DoK levels 1, 2, and 3.

Connect to Testing

In this chapter, you practiced using evidence from a reading passage to support your conclusions about a suspenseful image from the story. You were asked to point to specific words and sentences in the text that supported your ideas. When you take assessments, you will be tested on your ability to support your ideas by using textual evidence. Here is an example of this type of question.

1. Read this statement and the directions that follow.

   The man Jack is a supernatural creature of the night.

   Choose the sentence from the text that best supports the conclusion.
   A. *The man Jack was, above all things, a professional, or so he told himself, and he would not allow himself to smile until the job was completed.*
   B. *The man Jack walked up the stairs, his feet silent on the carpeting. Then he pushed open the attic door, and he walked in.*
   C. *The man Jack's eyes were accustomed to the dim moonlight, so he had no desire to turn on an electric light. And light was not that important, after all. He had other skills.*

PERFORMANCE TASKS

- Provides alternative assessment.
- Questions challenge students to integrate ideas from multiple texts.
- Tasks culminate with a writing assignment.

Practice Performance Task

A performance task evaluates your ability to comprehend selections of literature and informational text and then demonstrate your knowledge in writing. The task may begin with several multiple-choice or short-answer questions on key vocabulary and the main ideas of the passage(s). The task culminates with a writing assignment. Complete the following performance task based upon selections from Unit 1.

Source #1

Read the following excerpt from *Genreflecting: A Guide to Reading Interest in Genre Fiction* from Chapter 5 of this unit.

Terror of the unknown haunts us all. Some readers avoid the horror genre; others delight in being frightened. The emotional and spiritual response to reading horror stories—true fright—must be evoked for the tale to be successful. This reaction may be labeled an "affective fallacy" in academic jargon, but it is, nevertheless, a truly <u>visceral</u> reaction. The appeal of horror is not to the intellect, however staunchly the reader thinks he can distinguish between reality and fantasy.

1. What is the meaning of the word *visceral* as used in the text?
   A. related to literature
   B. extremely frightened
   C. unreal or fake
   D. emotional, not intellectual

2. Which phrases from Source #1 best help the reader understand the meaning of the word *visceral*? Choose all that apply.
   A. *Terror of the unknown haunts us all.*
   B. *others delight in being frightened*

SUMMATIVE ASSESSMENTS

- Feature multiple-choice and open-response questions.
- Unit Assessments test student mastery of the skills and strategies presented in each unit.
- End-of Course assessments evaluate student mastery of the skills and strategies presented in all four units.

Unit 1 Summative Assessment
`Unit 1 (p. 1)`

Name _____ Date _____

Vocabulary

Directions: Circle the letter of the word that best completes the sentence.

1. The fact that the concert is free should _____ interest in attending.
   a. entrance   b. insinuate
   c. heighten   d. accustom

2. The teacher _____ on the student in the

9. The antagonist was a(n) _____ character that caused chaos and pain throughout the story.
   a. inimical   b. arose
   c. staunch   d. evoked

End-of-Course Assessment
`(p. 1)`

Name _____ Date _____

Directions: Read the excerpt and answer the questions that follow.

Unless It Moves the Human Heart: The Craft and Art of Writing
Roger Rosenblatt

In his book Roger Rosenblatt recreates discussions that took place in his writing classes at Stony Brook University in the winter and spring of 2008.

1 "But you're always saying good readers make good writers," says Robert. "So where does the making come in?"

2 "Where was it for you? Every one of you has read something at an early age that made

Writing Workshop

- Focuses on an essential writing type:
  - argumentative
  - informational
  - literary analysis
  - narrative
  - or research.
- Writing Prompt connects the selections within the unit.
- Guides students step-by-step through the Writing Process.
- Lessons feature targeted language skills to build and improve writing skills.
- Students work cooperatively in pairs or small groups to generate ideas.
- Organizers assist students in collecting research, drafting, editing, revising, and publishing.
- Peer reviews provide valuable learning exchanges.

Writing a Personal Narrative

Fear has its use but cowardice has none.
–Mohandas Gandhi

In Chapters 1–5, you read a variety of fictional stories, a nonfiction narrative, and an educational text on classifications within the horror genre. In this section, you will apply what you've learned by writing your own personal narrative about a scary experience.

> **CONNECT TO ESSENTIAL QUESTION**
> What about the situation created your fear?

WRITING PROMPT

One of the major challenges in a person's life is overcoming fear. Think about a time when you were truly frightened. Try to remember when, where, and who was involved. Write a personal narrative (a story from your own life) in which you explain why this experience is significant and what you learned. Use thoughtful description, realistic dialogue, and careful pacing so that your reader will understand your fear. The narrative should also contain an *allusion*, or a reference, to one of the stories covered in this unit. Your personal narrative should be three to five typed pages, double-spaced, using standard Times New Roman 12-point font.

The Writing Process

Brainstorm

Fear is a response to physical and emotional dangers. The little voice in the brain that screams "No!" is protecting you from legitimate threats. Read through the table below. Underline fears you have experienced. Make a note about when you felt this fear. Consider how your physical fear may be linked to an emotional one.

> **CONNECT TO ESSENTIAL QUESTION**
> How does fear play an important role in our lives?

Emotional Fears	Physical Fears
Abandonment	Accidents
Being disliked or hated	Animals (in general or a specific one)
Being forgotten (or ignored)	
Being laughed at	Bees, bugs, spiders
Change	Being a victim
Commitment	Being poor
Criticism	Cemeteries
Disorder or chaos	Confined spaces
Failure	Death
Falling in love	Disease or germs
New experiences	Fire
Loneliness	Ghosts or spirits
Losing control	Heights
Making a mistake	The night/the dark
Making an important decision	Pain
Responsibility	People (or a specific person)
	Public speaking
	Storms
	Violence
	Water

Generate Ideas

A good narrative has certain characteristics. First, it must tell an interesting story. The structure will probably be chronological order, but that doesn't mean you can't play with the timeline by adding flashbacks or foreshadowing. These elements can add interest to your writing.

Descriptive details will draw your reader into your story. Details include a clear setting and well-drawn characters. Another characteristic of a good narrative is interesting dialogue. Since a narrative is based on real events, you may not remember every word that was spoken. You may have to recreate conversations based on your own memories and the recollections of others.

Teacher Planning Tools, ELL Resource, and Digital Resources

TEACHER PLANNING TOOLS

- Guide to Integrating Technology
- Lesson Plan Template
- Pacing Guide

DIGITAL ELL TEACHER RESOURCE

- Extensive support for teaching ELLs at different language acquisition levels, including strategies for sheltered instruction
- Ideas for teaching close reading, vocabulary, and reading passages in Connections
- Sentence frame handouts, graphic organizers, and revision and proofing checklists
- Links and page references are provided within the ELL Support ideas in Wraparound Teacher Edition.

CLASSROOM PRESENTATION TOOLS

- Presentations to support Vocabulary, Text-based Discussion Questions, Language lessons, and "Focus On" skill lessons.
- Resources available are marked with this icon in the teacher text. Links are provided in the e-book or see inside front cover to download presentations.

Lesson Plan Template		
Teacher:	**Class:**	**Text:**

Classroom Demographics: Briefly describe the students in the class and any special needs or adaptations.

Overall Chapter Objectives: What are the key standards for the chapter?

First Read: Key Ideas and Details
Students should have the opportunity to struggle with the text within a predetermined time limit. Keep the purpose simple. What does the text say? What are the main ideas?

Purpose for Reading:

Standard(s) Covered:

First Response:

Text-Based Discussion Questions:

Writing or Speaking/Listening Activity

Name _____

Text Structures

Claim/Reasons
Purpose: to convince the reader that an idea is right or true Claim = idea the writer is arguing for Reasons = facts and examples that support the claim

Signal Words and Phrases		
also	for instance	so that
an example	for this reason	this proves
another reason	in order to	this supports
as a result	reasons for	therefore
because	should/should not	thus
first	since	

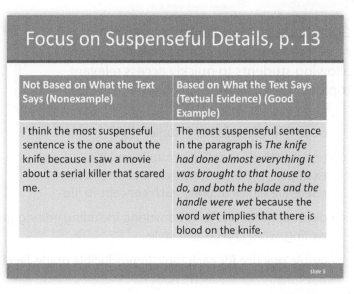

Focus on Suspenseful Details, p. 13

Not Based on What the Text Says (Nonexample)	Based on What the Text Says (Textual Evidence) (Good Example)
I think the most suspenseful sentence is the one about the knife because I saw a movie about a serial killer that scared me.	The most suspenseful sentence in the paragraph is *The knife had done almost everything it was brought to that house to do, and both the blade and the handle were wet* because the word *wet* implies that there is blood on the knife.

Slide 5

Using *Connections: Writing & Language*

An easy-to-use reference and instructional resource, *Connections: Writing & Language* is designed to complement *Connections: English Language Arts* with writing and language support.

- Pacing guides align lessons from *Connections: Writing & Language* to specific chapters and lessons in *Connections: ELA*, simplifying lesson design and standards alignment

- PowerPoint minilessons enable in-depth writing and language instruction and practice in whole group or small group settings

- Language and composition practice books incorporate hundreds of activities for practice and remediation

- Assessments pinpoint students' strengths and weaknesses

WRITING

Each writing genre is focused on the critical elements of good writing and includes

- student models of common structural elements

- strategies, questions, and guidelines for planning, focusing, and organizing ideas

- guidelines and suggestions for drafting each section of writing

- ways to identify improvement areas and shape the final product through editing and revising

- using language to energize and clarify writing

- rubrics for self-evaluation

- mentor texts and student models

Drafting the Introduction

The introduction to a composition has two main goals. The first is to arouse your reader's interest and make him or her want to read on. The second is to state clearly the main idea of the composition. In the following introduction on the subject of snorkeling, the sentence stating the main idea is in blue type.

| Introduction | Imagine the feeling of suddenly having all of your weight lifted from you. You glide along almost without effort. You feel the coolness of water around you. You see the brilliant colors of fish swimming past you, and the sounds of the world outside are muffled. These are just a few of the pleasures of snorkeling. For those who have mastered the basic techniques, however, the pleasures are even greater. Instead of simply gliding and observing, an experienced snorkeler can keep busy underwater with several interesting activities. |
| Main Idea | |

LANGUAGE

Grammar, usage, and mechanics chapters are numbered and broken into small sections, allowing students to quickly access relevant topics and examples. Each chapter includes

- a QuickGuide defining chapter terms and page references for each topic

- topics with clear definitions followed by examples, model writing excerpts, and handy reference tables to bring each concept to life

---

QuickGuide

21 A   Sentence Fragments   **page 297**

A **sentence fragment** is a group of words that does not express a complete thought.

21 B   Run-On Sentences   **page 300**

Two or more independent clauses that are joined without adequate punctuation form a **run-on sentence**. A **splice** is a type of run-on sentence.

- direct applications to good writing including editing guidelines, revising for more powerful writing, word choice, and style.

- ample practice for each topic (reproducible grade-level practice books)

READING, SPEAKING, AND LISTENING

Connections: Writing & Language also supports students as they develop their reading, speaking, and listening skills.

- **Close reading** helps students create meaning from texts as they define the purpose for each read, ask questions, identify patterns, analyze evidence, and share their insights with others.

- **Word Study** reinforces skills and strategies for building a more powerful vocabulary and using words that clearly communicate meaning.

- **Speaking and Listening** provides quick reference on strategies for speaking formally and informally, listening actively, and collaborating in groups.

Listening Actively

You have probably heard countless conversations—in real life, on television, or in the movies. No doubt you focused on *what* was being said, but did you also think about *how* it was said—and how the message was received? Did the speaker look relaxed, excited, or nervous? Did the listener look interested, distracted, or bored? Were the two people really listening to each other?

Hearing means that you are receiving sound waves. On the other hand, *listening* is an act you do on purpose. Active listening requires specific skills and a positive attitude. When listening actively, you don't just hear the words that are being spoken, you understand the meaning of what the other person is saying. Whether you are listening to a friend's story, a teacher's lecture, or candidates' political debate, the following techniques will help you listen actively.

Stay Focused

The most common obstacle to listening is a lack of focus. Everyone's mind wanders sometimes. Consider this: the brain processes words at the rate of more than 500 per minute. Yet most speakers communicate at 125 to 250 words per minute. In other words, you think more quickly than a speaker talks. Listening actively will help you stay focused on the speaker. The more you focus, the better you will become at evaluating, analyzing, and understanding what was said. Here are tips to help you stay focused:

✓ Look at the speaker and put yourself in his or her place.
✓ Use body language that indicates active listening, such as facing the speaker, keeping your arms uncrossed, leaning slightly forward, nodding to show you understand, and showing interest on your face.
✓ Do not think about something else while trying to listen.
✓ Remove distractions: Turn off your cell phone or music. Remove headphones.

Listen for Key Words

Often, a speaker will clue you in when he or she is about to say something important. The word *however*, for example, usually means the person is about to make an exception to what was just said. The phrase *for example* signals that the speaker is about to provide an actual situation or story that could help you better understand. You can repeat important words in your mind to help you stay focused.

Respond Appropriately

The best way to show a speaker that you were listening is to respond to them. Many times, this means holding back your opinions until the speaker has finished talking. Refrain from interrupting or jumping in with your own ideas. Listen to understand the

PRACTICE ACTIVITIES

Grade-level practice activities reinforce skills in

- grammar
- usage
- mechanics
- vocabulary
- spelling
- sentence structure
- word choice
- revising and editing writing

Name _____ Date _____

CHAPTER 15 **Adjectives and Adverbs**

Using Adverbs to Add Interest

◆ Rewrite the following sentences, adding an adverb or adverbs to make them more interesting. <u>Underline</u> your adverbs and draw an arrow from each one to the word or words it modifies.

1. The common house cat is attracted by the sound of a can opener.

   _____

   _____

2. These animals like a bowl of milk.

   _____

   _____

3. A cat will claw.

   _____

   _____

4. They may purr.

   _____

   _____

5. The cat will leap for moving objects.

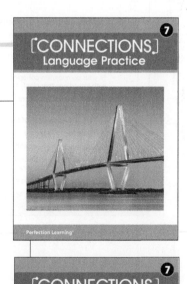

[CONNECTIONS] 7
Language Practice

Perfection Learning®

[CONNECTIONS] 7
Composition Practice

Perfection Learning®

LESSON PLANNING & INSTRUCTIONAL SUPPORT

Connections: Writing & Language Teacher Guide and the Digital ToolKit provide planning guidance and instructional support including

- PowerPoint minilessons on writing and language
- guided instruction
- warm-up activities
- differentiation strategies
- collaborative learning activities
- workplace applications

Suggested activities for Guided Instruction and Guided Practice are supported by PowerPoint minilessons.

Informational Writing Checklist   Lesson 5.6

Organization, Structure, and Focus

✓ Do you have an interesting introduction that states the main idea of the composition and previews what is to follow?

✓ Does your composition have unity? That is, do all your sentences relate to the main idea?

✓ Is your composition coherent? That is, are your ideas arranged logically with transitions that clarify the relationships among them?

✓ Do you have a strong conclusion that follows from and supports your main ideas?

Content and Development of Ideas

✓ Are your ideas clear and interesting?

✓ Is your main idea well defined and focused?

✓ Have you identified enough points to support your main idea with relevant facts, definitions, quotations, and other supporting information?

✓ Have you added depth to your ideas by in

Organizing Your Information   Lesson 5.3

During the organizing stage, you arrange your facts and details in a logical order. A **logical order** is an arrangement that your readers will be able to follow clearly. The table below lists some types of order.

Type	Description
Chronological Order	Information is presented in the order in which events occurred.
Sequential Order	Information is presented in the order in which events occur.
Order of Importance	Information is given in order of importance, interest, size, or degree.
Developmental Order	Information is arranged to lead up to a conclusion.
Comparison/Contrast	Information is arranged to point out similarities and differences.

12

LESSON 1.3 FINDING & LIMITING A SUBJECT (pages 3–7)

Objectives

- To identify and practice strategies for finding a subject to write about
- To develop strategies for choosing and limiting a subject

Guided Instruction

Slide 8: Planning: Finding a Subject
Slide 9: Focusing: Limiting a Subject

CREATE INTEREST Comedians, critics, and others often make lists, such as the ten best movies of the year or ten reasons to wear a bow tie. Direct students to find a list on a topic that interests them. Then have them use the list to propose one or more possible topics for writing.

INTEREST INVENTORY Have students begin to explore their own interests by listing five words that they think best describe them. Invite interested students to explain orally or in writing why those words describe them.

FREEWRITING Have students try freewriting for t setting such as a library n a noisy, public place such street corner. Ask them to see how the setting affected te students to identify the h they prefer to do their

LESSON PLANNER

Lesson Planners align lessons from *Connections: Writing & Language* to specific chapters and lessons in *Connections: ELA* simplifying lesson design and standards alignment.

Lesson Planner

Connections: English Language Arts Grade 7	Connections: Writing & Language Handbook	Time needed
Introduction to Course		
Close Reading and Annotating Texts, pp. xxii–6	Chapter 31: Close Reading SB: pp. 418–439 TG: p. 290	2 days (3 days with Writing and Language)
Unit 1		
Introduction to Unit 1, p. 7		1 day
Chapter 1 Chapter Opener and First Read, pp. 8–15 (Summarizing a Text)		2–3 days
Second Read, pp. 15–17 (Understanding Technical Terms)		1 day
Third Read, pp. 17–20 (Identifying Claims, Reasons, and Details)		2 days
Language: Prefixes, Suffixes, and Root Words, pp. 20–22	Chapter 30: Prefixes and Suffixes SB: pp. 413–416 TG: p. 282	
Project-Based Assessment: Roundtable Discussion p. 23 Argumentative Essay, p. 24 On Your Own, p. 25	Chapter 33: Speaking Effectively; Listening Actively SB: pp. 459–464 TG: p. 308 Chapter 6: Argumentative Writing SB: pp. 92–117 TG: p. 46	*2–4 days per project (3–5 days with Writing and Language)
Connect to Testing, pp. 26–28		½ day
		Total: 7½ days
Chapter 2 Chapter Opener and First Read, pp. 29–36 (Analyzing Plot and Conflict)		2–3 days
Second Read, pp. 36–37 (Identifying Theme)		1 day
Third Read, pp. 38–39 (Understanding Point of View)		1 day

Lesson Planner

Connections: English Language Arts Grade 7	Connections: Writing & Language Handbook	Time needed
Chapter 3 Chapter Opener and First Read, pp. 46–52 (Making Inferences)		2–3 days
Second Read, pp. 53–55 (Understanding Structure and Purpose)		1 days
Third Read, pp. 56–57 (Determining Point of View)		1–2 days
Language: Sentence Structure, pp. 57–58	Chapter 20: Kinds of Sentence Structure SB: pp. 293–295 TG: p. 176	
Project-Based Assessment: Digital Presentation, p. 58 Roundtable Discussion, pp. 59–60 On Your Own, p. 60	Chapter 10: Evaluating Sources SB: pp. 187–188 TG: p. 90 Chapter 33: Speaking Effectively; Listening Actively SB: pp. 459–464 TG: p. 308	*2–4 days per project
Connect to Testing, pp. 61–63		1 day
		Total: 7 days
Chapter 4 Chapter Opener and First Read, pp. 64–71 (Summarizing Central Ideas)		2–3 days
Second Read, pp. 71–72 (Understanding Figurative Language)		½ days
Third Read, pp. 72–74 (Determining Points of View)		2 days
Language: Connotations and Denotations, pp. 74–75	Chapter 32: Words That Communicate Clearly SB: pp. 456–457 TG: p. 296	
Project-Based Assessment: Pictorial Presentation, p. 75 Literary Analysis, p. 76 On Your Own, p. 77	Chapter 8: Writing About Literary Texts SB: pp. 148–165 TG: p. 74	*2–4 days per project (4–6 days with Writing and Language)
Connect to Testing, pp. 78–80		1 day
		Total: 6½ days

See inside the front cover for details on how to download this pacing guide.

ASSESSMENT

Extensive assessment resources include

- pretests, chapter, and end-of-course tests
- rubrics
- student models

STUDENT MODELS & RUBRICS ARGUMENTATIVE WRITING

Read the information in the box and follow the directions.

> Many people enjoy a trip to the zoo to look at animals of all kinds. But some people are against zoos. They believe animals should live freely in the wild. Do you think zoos are a good idea?

Directions: Write an essay expressing your opinion on the question and backing up your opinion with persuasive facts, examples, and reasons. If you like, you may organize your argument as a letter to the president.

- After you're done writing, proofread for grammar, usage, and mechanics errors.
- Check for misspelled words, mistakes in punctuation and capitalization, and incorrect sentence structure.

Student Model: Score 4

Dear President,

Many people have been having second thoughts about keeping animals in zoos. Some people say yes because a zoo provides "not only a protective environment for these animals but also breeding programs." However, some people say no because "no zoo environment can duplicate the freedom of an animal's natural environment." Here is what I think.

First, zoos can help animals live longer. Out in the wild all animals have some sort of enemy, and a lot of times the enemy is man! Zoos keep animals safe and give them the proper diet and nutrition that they need. This will keep the animals healthy and strong.

Next, zoos give animals proper breeding. In other words there will be more of that species to populate. If there are too few of one species, then they may not find each other to breed. Zoos will help animals get together with the right mate to breed with.

CHAPTER 6 TEST ARGUMENTATIVE WRITING RUBRIC

Writing Test Rubric

	4	3	2	1
Focus, Structure, & Organization	The writing has unity and focus; the organization is clear with a strong introduction that presents an engaging claim, a body with supporting examples and reasons, and a conclusion with a clincher statement that ties up the argument; coherence is maintained throughout with transitions.	The writing is mostly unified and may exhibit some lack of focus; the organization is clear, but the main claim may lack interest, a few supporting examples and reasons may seem out of place, and the conclusion may simply repeat the main claim; some transitions may be missing.	The writing is not completely unified, and there is a lack of focus; the organization is not clear because it lacks a clearly stated claim or because supporting examples are not connected to the main claim with reasons; many transitions are missing.	The writing lacks unity and focus; the organization is unclear and hard to follow; there are no transitions to connect ideas.
Content & Development of Ideas	Ideas are clear and interesting and exhibit depth of thought; examples are connected to the claim through sound reasons and valid rhetorical appeals.	Ideas are mostly clear and interesting and exhibit some depth of thought; some examples may not be connected to the claim or may lack sound reasons or valid appeals.	Ideas are unclear or uninteresting and many lack depth of thought; many examples are not connected to the claim, and most lack sound reasons and valid appeals.	Ideas are unclear, lack interest, and lack depth of thought; examples do not support the claim and lack sound reason and valid appeals.
Language Use: Voice, Word Choice, & Sentence Fluency	The voice is authoritative and confident; words are specific; sentences flow smoothly and vary in structure and length.	The voice may be a bit authoritarian or lack confidence; some words may be general or overused; most sentences vary and flow smoothly.	The voice may be authoritarian or lack confidence; many words are overly general; many sentences lack variety or are choppy.	The voice is authoritarian or lacks confidence; most words are overly general; sentences lack variety and are choppy.
Conventions	Punctuation, usage, and spelling	There are only a few errors in	There are several errors in	There are many errors.

Connections Digital

Enhance instruction, increase engagement, and improve collaboration.

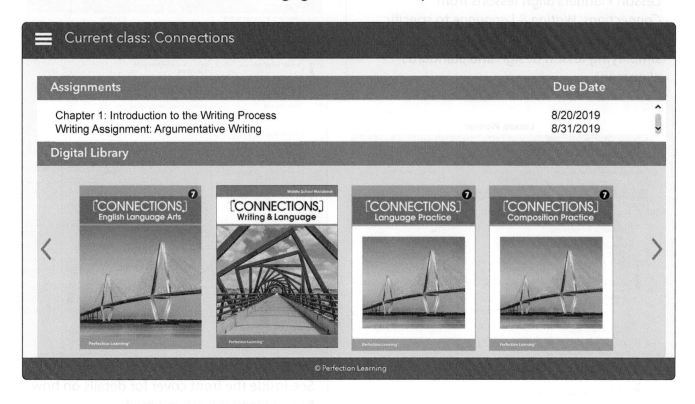

DIGITAL STUDENT EDITIONS

The digital student editions include

- interactive responses and digital submission to writing prompts and graphic organizers

- text annotation and note-capturing tools

- collaborative learning opportunities through real-time shared responses and discussion forums

- student submission of completed work

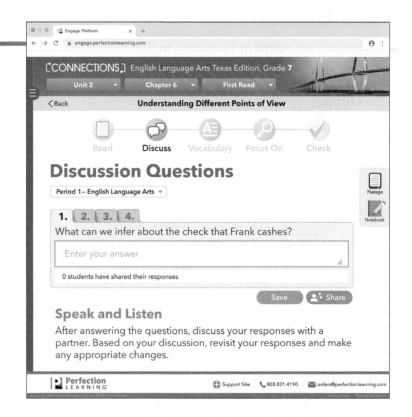

DIGITAL TEACHER RESOURCES

The digital teacher editions include

- access to assignment generator and grade book

- reporting on completed student work

- links to all resources including teacher editions, online videos, websites, and lesson PowerPoints

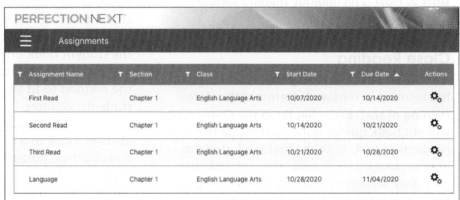

ONLINE PRACTICE & ASSESSMENT

Through the *Connections* digital platform, educators can assign

- skill check quizzes

- project-based writing assignments

- grammar, usage, and mechanics practice

- chapter, unit, and summative tests

- teacher-created writing assignments incorporating links, uploaded documents, and other sources

- group projects

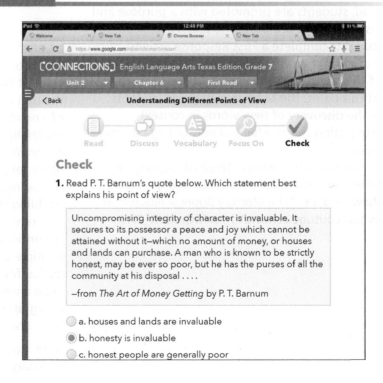

Close Reading in *Connections*

The selections chosen for *Connections* represent a blend of fiction and informational text in a variety of genres. Each selection was evaluated using a three-part model for measuring text-complexity, as well as its literary and historical significance.

The selections within each unit all relate to an Essential Question. The Essential Questions for Grade 7 are

Unit 1: How do you know right from wrong?

Unit 2: Can you trust what you hear, see, and read?

Unit 3: How is technology shaping society?

Unit 4: What does history tell us about ourselves?

Close Reading

The emphasis on using textual evidence has resulted in renewed interest in the close reading of text. Each chapter in the *Connections* student book guides students through three close readings of text. With the first read, students are encouraged to discover the text without prefatory discussion or notes, although a purpose for reading is given. It is recommended that students complete this first read on their own so that they have an opportunity to encounter, and even struggle with, the text. During this first read, students are prompted with a purpose and instructions to annotate the text. After reading, students complete a First Response activity, recording their initial reaction and observations of the text based upon the purpose for reading. At this point, the teacher may guide students in the discovery of new words in context, integrating the teaching of vocabulary into the lesson.

To illustrate the importance of focusing on different elements of a text with multiple reads, show students "The Monkey Business Illusion" at <www.youtube.com/watch?v=IGQmdoK_ZfY>.

First Read The goal of the first read is to ask, *What does this say?* or *What does this mean?* The "Focus on" activities help students identify the key ideas and details (Reading Standards 1–3). Students learn and practice the skills of summarizing, inferring, and using textual evidence through writing and speaking activities. Concepts are often presented visually in graphic organizers for enhanced comprehension. After previewing the text with students, encourage them to read the text on their own. However, if a text is especially challenging, read the text aloud and have students follow along.

Second Read During the second read, students reread the selection, hear the text read aloud, or read it with a partner. Note that the student book often suggests that students listen as the text is read aloud. Again, adapt the method to fit the type of text and your students' abilities. Depending upon the difficulty of the text, the lesson may concentrate on main ideas or move to a deeper analysis of the craft and structure (Reading Standards 4–6). At this stage, the questions to ask are *How does the writer communicate meaning? What techniques does the writer use to convey main ideas in a convincing manner or beautiful way?* Students discover how language, structure, and point of view create meaning in a text.

Third Read With the third read, the lesson may return to Standards 4–6 or move on to connect the chapter themes to another text within the unit or to a text read outside class. (Integration of Knowledge and Ideas, Standards 7–9). Readers are challenged to ask, *Why is this text meaningful or convincing? How does this text connect to other texts? What can I learn from this text?* At this point, students understand the text at a level enabling them to make connections among several different texts. They have the knowledge base to confidently evaluate arguments and analyze multiple interpretations of a story. Another option for the third read is to have students focus in on a smaller section of the passage, perhaps a paragraph or a page. See the side channel support throughout this Teacher Guide for ideas.

Note: Page 6 of the student book includes a summary of the process for the three reads.

Lesson for Introducing Close Reading

Before beginning the *Connections* curriculum, explain to students that close reading is about noticing. It's about zooming in closer to a short portion of text. It's about asking questions, making observations, and drawing conclusions. Finally, close reading is about stepping back and seeing the whole picture more clearly. Use the following lesson to introduce close reading.

Practice Close "Watching"

Show a commercial that evokes discussion. The following possibilities can be found on YouTube. If any of the links are broken, search by the topic to find new options. Be sure to view the videos before sharing them.

- Commercial in which dogs find their way into a supermarket to buy Doritos. https://youtu.be/MNRAdrB9TSs

- Jim Gaffigan's Chrysler commercial about being a great dad. <https://youtu.be/VwX8uBPtnto>

- Toy commercial that targets boys: Nerf Vortex Commercial <https://youtu.be/cFRsvv_LoC4>

- Toy commercial that breaks gender stereotypes and encourages girls to engage in play related to science and engineering skills. <https://youtu.be/Ch8EweOfhcc>

1. Instruct students to watch and closely observe the commercial.

   Write *First View—What?* where all can see. Ask, *What did you notice? What is the story? What is the purpose? What does this mean? What is unclear? What is directly stated? What is implied?* Display student answers. Ask students to support their ideas by referencing what they saw in the video. Use follow-up questions that require students to provide evidence: *What did you see that supports your idea? Can you show me where that is in the video?*

2. Show the clip again. Write *Second View—How?* on the board and ask, *How does the writer accomplish his/her purpose? What do the creators use to accomplish their purpose? Music or visuals? Words? Story?* Again, use good follow-up questions that encourage students to return to the commercial to find evidence.

   Student answers at this point may lead to a discussion concerning methods of persuasion, such as appeals to emotion (pathos), logic (logos), or ethics/character (ethos).

3. Watch the clip a third time. Write *Third View— Why or why not?* on the board. Ask, *Why is this or isn't this an effective commercial? What specific elements make it effective (or not effective)? What other advertisements have you seen with the same theme? Have you seen other commercials that use this idea or method of persuasion more effectively? Why was it more (or less) effective?*

   Explain to students that the skills they learned during this close "viewing" of a commercial is the same process they will use as they closely read the texts in their student books.

Practice Annotating Text

Provide students copies of the Tips for Close Reading (p. xxvi) and Annotating a Text handouts (pp. xxv–xxvi). Read through the descriptions of the three reads and the instructions for marking a text. Read aloud the first paragraph of the excerpt from "Three Questions". Using a think-aloud strategy, model how to mark the first paragraph of text. Encourage students to mark the rest of the passage on their own. You may choose to annotate the text as a class. Have students form pairs and share their annotations. Then have each pair share one or two examples with the larger group.

Ask students how informational text differs from fiction. *(It communicates through information and ideas, not events and characters. We often read it to gain information instead of for entertainment.)* Ask students how they might read or mark informational text differently from texts of fiction. Using the Annotating a Text handout, read through the examples concerning how to mark informational text and model how to annotate the first paragraph. Assign the rest of the text as independent practice.

Name _____ Date _____

Tips for Close Reading

Close reading is the careful reading and rereading of a text. With each reading, your understanding of the text should increase. The goal is to understand the main ideas of the text and also to analyze the words and techniques the writer uses to communicate. In the end, you will be able to step back and critically evaluate the text as a whole.

First Reading   Focus on *What?*

What are the main ideas?

Ask: What is this mostly about? Which ideas are most important?

What message is the author trying to share?

What words or phrases stand out as important?

Second Reading: Focus on *How?*

How does the way the writer communicates support his or her purpose?

Ask: How do details develop the main idea?

What special types of language (figurative language, repetition, rhyme) does the writer use to create meaning?

From what point of view is this story told?/Who is narrating the story?

How do the sentences/paragraphs in the text relate, or fit together? How does the structure of the text emphasize the ideas? Do I see causes/effects? problems/solutions? claims/reasons?

Third Reading: Focus on *Why* or *Why not?*

Why is this text important or meaningful to me—or to others?

Ask: What can I learn from this text that will help me understand the world?

What can I learn that will make me a better writer?

Why is (or why isn't) this informational text convincing? Why is (or why isn't) this work of literature meaningful?

How does this text connect to other texts? Where have I seen this theme before? How do other presentations of this text (movie, recording, etc.) communicate the theme in similar or different ways?

Annotating a Text

Annotating a text means "marking a text as you read." Annotating keeps you focused and improves your understanding of the main ideas. Think of annotating a text as talking to the text as you read. You might agree with some points the author makes, you might have questions about the meanings of words, or you might connect the writer's ideas with your own experiences.

Mark fiction/literature by:

- underlining words and phrases that describe the characters
- circling repeated ideas
- starring (*) important scenes or dialogue
- marking confusing parts or unfamiliar words with a question mark (?) so you can return to them later
- writing questions about what you read in the margin
- writing personal connections to the text (This reminds me of . . . .)
- writing a short summary of what happens on a page or in a chapter

Directions: Read and mark the following excerpt.

The Three Questions
by Leo Tolstoy, translated by L. and A. Maude

When the King approached, the hermit was digging the ground in front of his hut. Seeing the King, he greeted him and went on digging. The hermit was frail and weak, and each time he stuck his spade into the ground and turned a little earth, he breathed heavily.

The King went up to him and said: "I have come to you, wise hermit, to ask you to answer three questions: How can I learn to do the right thing at the right time? Who are the people I most need, and to whom should I, therefore, pay more attention than to the rest? And, what affairs are the most important, and need my first attention?"

The hermit listened to the King, but answered nothing. He just spat on his hand and recommenced digging.

"You are tired," said the King, "let me take the spade and work awhile for you."

"Thanks!" said the hermit, and, giving the spade to the King, he sat down on the ground.

When he had dug two beds, the King stopped and repeated his questions. The hermit again gave no answer, but rose, stretched out his hand for the spade, and said:

"Now rest awhile—and let me work a bit."

But the King did not give him the spade, and continued to dig. One hour passed, and another.

Annotating a Text (continued)

Mark nonfiction/informational text by:

- underlining main ideas
- circling key words and ideas that repeat throughout the text
- drawing arrows to show relationships between ideas (cause and effect/problem and solution)
- marking confusing parts or unfamiliar words with a question mark (?) so you can return to them later
- placing an exclamation point (!) by something that affects you
- writing questions in the margin
- writing personal connections to the text (This reminds me of . . . .)

Directions: Read and mark the following text.

Our Brains Are Wired for Morality: Evolution, Development, and Neuroscience
by Jean Decety and Jason M. Cowell
edited by Paul Glimcher

How do we distinguish good from evil, right from wrong, just from unjust, and vice from virtue? An obvious answer is that we have learned to do so through socialization, that is, our behaviors were shaped from birth onward by our families, our preschools, and almost everything we contacted in our environments. Morality is an inner sense of rightness about our behavior and the behavior of others. How we feel, think, and act about the concepts of "good" and "bad" are all parts of our morality. For example, hitting another person for any reason is seen as bad, while sharing something we like with another child who is sad is considered good. Morality is so deeply rooted in the fabric of our everyday lives that it seems hard to imagine a society without any moral rules. Indeed, observations made by scientists who study different societies around the world have shown that, despite cultural and individual differences, all human beings have some sense of right and wrong.

When we use the word "morality" we are generally talking about ideas of justice, fairness and rights, and the rules we have about how people should treat one another. Consider the following: as a reward for finishing your homework, you have been given 10 marbles that you really like. You are then told about a poor child who would not be able to get any marbles, even though he did his homework too. However, you have the option to give some of your marbles to the poor child. What would you choose to do? . . .

[CONNECTIONS]
English Language Arts
7

PERFECTIONLEARNING®

Teacher Wraparound Edition

How to Use This Teacher Guide

The side columns and bottom channels on each page support the contents of the student book and include:

- vocabulary lists for each selection with definitions and example sentences.
- academic vocabulary definitions.
- text-based discussion questions that teach students to use evidence to support conclusions about the text.
- ideas for integrating language lessons on grammar, usage, and punctuation.
- lesson support for reading, writing, and speaking and listening activities, as well as project-based assessments.
- answers for all activities in the student book.
- support for teaching English language learners and struggling readers
- suggestions for remediation

Editorial Director: Sue Thies
Editors: Andrea Stark, John T. Ham
Proofreading Coordinator: Sheri Cooper
Art Director: Randy Messer
Designers: Tobi Cunningham, Emily Adickes
Contributors: Carmel McDonald, Jen Yocum

Reviewers:

Karen Dierks
Media Specialist, ESL certified
ELA and Social Studies
Shawnee Mission Schools
Overland Park, Kansas

Danielle Emery, M.Ed.
Secondary ESL Coordinator
Lewisville, Texas, ISD

Lauri Garbo, M.Ed.
English Department
Gulf Coast High School
Collier County School District, Florida

Carmel McDonald
Instructional Coach
Paragon Charter Academy
Jackson, Michigan

Matthew T. Meldrum
Secondary Language Arts Curriculum
   Specialist
Austin Independent School District
Austin, Texas

Lisa Scribellito Milligan, MA.Ed.
Special Education/Reading
   /ELL Teacher Ed
White High School
Jacksonville, Florida

Kendall Mott
DL Spanish Instructor
Region 5 Education Service Center
Beaumont, Texas

Shelli Shaw
Instructional Officer for Secondary
   Reading Intervention
Katy Independent School District
Katy, Texas

JoAnn Williams
Secondary ELA/Reading Interventionist
Alief Independent School District
Houston, Texas

Contents

3

Teacher Wraparound Edition

A Note About Text Complexity

The Table of Contents for this teacher guide indicates the Lexile levels for the texts used in this curriculum. This quantitative evaluation is just one of three factors used when considering text complexity.

Quantitative evaluations, such as Lexile scores, measure numbers of letters in a word, word frequency, and number of words in a sentence. These objective measurements are compiled by computer software.

Qualitative factors of a text include such elements as layout, purpose and meaning, text structure, language features, and knowledge demands.

Quantitative and qualitative elements describe the complexity inherent in the text and were considered as the texts were chosen for each unit. The third factor of text complexity, reader and task considerations, requires the professional judgment of teachers to provide the support needed to ensure the success of their students as readers.

TEACHING READING STRATEGIES

Remind struggling readers to use strategies to help them comprehend complex texts in each unit. Display these tips in the classroom:

- Preview the text before you read. Consider the title, section heads, and any graphics or pictures. Make predictions.

- Adjust your reading speed based on your purpose for reading. Skim text to find big ideas. Slow down to grasp details. Close reading is slower reading.

- Mark the text as you read. Underline main ideas and write questions in the margins. "Talk back" to the text.

- Visualize events, places, and information in your mind.

- Monitor your comprehension. Go back and reread if needed. Connect what you don't understand to what you do understand.

4

5

Teaching Close Reading: This introductory page sets a purpose for multiple close reads of a complex text, the foundation of the structure of each chapter in the book.

To illustrate the importance of focusing on different elements of a text with multiple reads, show students "The Monkey Business Illusion" at <https://youtu.be/IGQmdoK_ZfY>. When first viewed, students will focus on counting the number of passes made. However, they will often not even notice the gorilla that appears in the background. They will also not notice that the curtain changes colors. In the same way, complex texts are so packed with meaning that understanding requires a reader to look at different elements during multiple reads.

A handout of this content is also found on page xvi of this teacher edition.

Suggestions for practicing close reading with commercials can be found on page xv.

Another way to practice close reading is to have students analyze song lyrics. Display the lyrics and play the song as students listen and follow along. Suggested songs include "Brave" by Sara Bareilles," "Mean" by Taylor Swift, "Man in the Mirror" by Michael Jackson, or "Let It Go" by Idina Menzel. Guide class discussion by asking the questions for each of the three reads on the handout on page 6 of the student book. Note students' observations on the displayed copy of the lyrics. Add another layer to the lesson by showing a music video of the song and asking students to identify how the visuals support or extend the ideas in the lyrics.

Annotating Text: Within the directions for Making Connections and the First Read and sometimes the Second and Third Reads for every selection in *Connections*, students are provided specific instructions regarding what to look for and how to annotate the text as they read. Use the annotations that are marked in the Student Book insert to guide your discussions.

Read, Reread, and Read Again

Welcome to *Connections!* Think about an amazing movie you have seen—one you couldn't stop thinking about when you left the theater. Have you talked about the movie with your family or friends? Have you watched the movie again after first seeing it in the theater? Do you see something new each time you watch it?

Complex texts are like movies. You can't grasp all of the details in one read. Each time you read, you'll discover something new.

Connections will encourage you to develop a habit of reading a text several times. With each read, you will dive deeper into the text. You'll move from key ideas and details to discovering how authors create meaning by using special types of language to communicate their thoughts. With each read of the selections in *Connections*, you will be asked to focus on a central question: *What? How? Why* or *Why Not?*

First Read Focus on *What?*

What are the key ideas?

Ask: What is this mostly about? Which ideas are most important?

Who is writing and why are they writing?

What words or phrases stand out as important?

Second Read Focus on *How?*

How does the writer support his or her purpose?

Ask: How do details develop the central idea?

What special types of language (figurative language, repetition, rhyme) does the writer use to create meaning?

How do the sentences/paragraphs in the text relate, or fit together? How does the structure of the text emphasize the ideas? Do I see causes/effects? problems/solutions? claims/reasons?

Third Read Focus on *Why* or *Why not?*

Why is this text important or meaningful to me—or to others?

Ask: What can I learn from this text that will help me understand the world?

What can I learn that will make me a better writer?

Why is (or why isn't) this nonfiction text convincing? Why is (or why isn't) this work of literature meaningful?

How does this text connect to other texts? Where have I seen this theme before? How do other presentations of this text (movie, artwork, etc.) or ideas in this text communicate the theme in similar or different ways?

Learning to read and reread texts for meaning will make you a confident, successful reader as you encounter ever more challenging texts.

6

ELL Support: Close Reading See Teaching Close Reading in the *Connections* ELL Teacher Resource (p. 15) for ideas on adapting this lesson for Beginning, Intermediate, and Advanced ELLs.

Unit 1

Essential Question
How do you know right from wrong?

Most people believe that they have a clear sense of right and wrong. Consider sayings such as "two wrongs don't make a right" and "it's black and white." Seems clear, right? But when you delve further into morality for specific situations, things become less clear. Stealing is wrong and against the law, but stealing to defend yourself or save yourself from starvation is understandable and pardonable. Destroying property is also wrong in most people's minds, unless you break down a door to help someone escape from a fire. Thus, some crimes are justifiable.

Another influencing factor is age; a child is not held to the same standard as an adult in social situations or according to the law. Parents can sometimes be held accountable for their children's actions though, so are parents the largest influence on a child's moral development?

If you had to teach someone right from wrong, where would you begin? At what age do children begin to understand that they have a choice between good and evil? In fact, how do people in general learn about what is the right thing to do versus the wrong thing? How do they decide what to do when faced with a moral dilemma—like whether to tell a lie to protect someone they love?

In this unit, you will explore the question: How do you know right from wrong? You will explore the morality of people's actions and decisions. Activities will provide opportunities to write, speak, and debate about right and wrong. You will also read and discuss issues related to the ethical treatment of animals. As you work through this unit, you may make surprising discoveries about the nature of right and wrong and how point of view impacts ideas about morality.

> ### GOALS
> - To identify and summarize central ideas
> - To make inferences based on textual evidence
> - To analyze point of view and theme
> - To evaluate claims, reasons, and evidence in an argument
> - To compare evidence in two texts
> - To write an argumentative essay

ELL Support: Preview Unit 1 Essential Question See the _Connections_ ELL Teacher Resource (p. 32) for ideas on adapting this lesson for Beginning, Intermediate, and Advanced ELLs.

Unit 1

Essential Question: How do you know right from wrong?

Introduction

Goals: Have students read through the goals and mark any words that are unfamiliar. Discuss the meanings of any academic vocabulary within the goals that students marked as unfamiliar. Consider posting the Unit Goals.

Introduction Suggestions
Kick off the unit with one or more of the following activities:

- Ask students to think about a time they did something kind, helpful, or supportive for another person. How did it feel? Invite volunteers to describe their experiences.

- What does it mean to "put yourself in another person's shoes"? Is it difficult or easy? Explain.

- Share the following quote from Mark Twain's _The Adventures of Huckleberry Finn:_ "What's the use you learning to do right when it's troublesome to do right and ain't no trouble to do wrong, and the wages is just the same?" Have volunteers explain what the quote means to them. Then ask students whether they agree or disagree: _Is it really harder to do right than wrong? Do people pay any price for doing wrong? Do we always get the same results whether we do right or wrong?_

- Invite students to offer their opinions about what the "right thing" to do is in each of the situations described below. Encourage them to explain their responses.
  - You find a wallet with $10 and no identification.
  - You find $10 on the ground.
  - You notice a ring on the sidewalk.
  - You see a couple of kids bullying another student.
  - You see some kids copying another student's paper.

- Debate the following question: _Is it always easy to tell what is right or wrong?_

 Gr7U1Opener.pptx

Chapter 1

Identifying Key Ideas and Details

Our Brains Are Wired for Morality: Evolution, Development, and Neuroscience
by Jean Decety and Jason M. Cowell

Introduction

Chapter Goals: Have students read through the goals and mark any unfamiliar words. Discuss the meanings of any unfamiliar academic vocabulary within the goals. Consider posting the Chapter Goals.

Preview Academic Vocabulary: Read and discuss the meanings of the academic vocabulary.

affix: *a word part added to the beginning or end of a word.* By adding the <u>affix</u> *sub-* to the word *marine*, we get *submarine*.

antonym: *a word that means the opposite of another word. Cruelty* is an <u>antonym</u> of *kindness*.

claim: *the writer's or speaker's opinion which he/she is attempting to prove is true; the central idea of an argument.* His <u>claim</u> is that global warming is irreversible.

evidence: *data, examples, and facts used to prove a claim.* The ability of chimpanzees to learn sign language is <u>evidence</u> of their intelligence.

reason: *a statement that explains why a claim should be accepted as true.* One <u>reason</u> to be a vegetarian is that eating vegetables offers more health benefits than eating meat.

root word: *a base word that contains a word's basic meaning.* The <u>root word</u> of both *portable* and *porter* is *port*, meaning "to carry."

Chapter 1

Identifying Key Ideas and Details

Preview Concepts

Who is your favorite superhero? Who is your superhero's villain or nemesis? What are the differences between the hero and the villain that identify them as good and bad? Write a response below.

Share your answers with a partner. Then discuss the following question:

- Which two qualities are the most important for the hero to possess to be considered a good guy? Why?

> **CHAPTER GOALS**
>
> In this chapter you will
> - develop a summary.
> - determine the meaning of technical terms.
> - identify claims and support.
> - participate in a roundtable discussion or write an argumentative essay.

> **PREVIEW ACADEMIC VOCABULARY**
>
> affix
> antonym
> claim
> evidence
> reason
> root word
> suffix
> synonym

ELL Support: Academic Vocabulary See <u>Teaching Vocabulary in the ELL Teacher Resource (p. 18)</u> for ideas for teaching vocabulary throughout *Connections*.

To help students learn the academic vocabulary on p. 8, group the vocabulary into the following categories: affix, root word, and suffix; claim, evidence, and reason; antonym and synonym. Explain the words in each category and give examples of each term in each category to support understanding (e.g., *international*: identify *inter-* as the prefix, *nation* as the root word, and *-al* as the suffix. Then write the word *submarine* on the board and ask students to identify the prefix, root, and suffix. Repeat with the other categories of academic vocabulary words. For Beginning and Intermediate speakers, provide additional adaptations for difficult vocabulary as needed. For example explain that *affix* is the first or the last part of a word.

Making Connections

Read the following moral dilemma.

You have witnessed a man rob a bank, but then, he did something completely unusual and unexpected with the money. He donated it to an orphanage that was struggling to take care of the children. With this money, the orphanage could keep its doors open and continue taking care of the needy children. Would you:

    a. Call the police and report the robbery, even though they would likely take the money away from the orphanage, or

    b. Do nothing?

1. With a partner, discuss what you would do. Explain reasons for your choice of action.

2. What does your choice say about your moral beliefs or what is right and wrong?

3. What does your choice say about your belief in laws vs. your belief in fairness?

4. Do you think your ability to choose between right and wrong is something you learned from your family and society or it is something that developed in your brain over time? Or is it both?

> **MAKING CONNECTIONS**
>
> In this passage you will be reading a text that presents a claim about the human brain and morality.

---

suffix: *a word part added to the end of a word.* Detachable *and* understandable *both end with the* <u>suffix</u> *–able meaning "given to" or "able to."*

synonym: *a word that has the same meaning as another word.* Truthfulness *is a* <u>synonym</u> *for* honesty.

⌕ Gr7Ch1Vocabulary.pptx

Preview Concepts: Extend the discussion about superheroes by asking students about how recent movies about superheroes have portrayed flawed superheroes. Emphasize this point by showing clips of the old *Batman* television show and newer *Batman* movies. What does this say about our culture's view of good and bad or right and wrong?

Another way to extend the discussion is to point out to students that decisions about right and wrong can be tricky. Ask them: *What might you do if you saw somebody copying from another student? Or what might you do if you saw somebody going through another student's backpack? Who could be hurt by your action—or inaction? What consequences might come from your action—or inaction? And what if your impression of wrongdoing was incorrect?* Invite students to share their ideas about one of these situations and the potential consequences.

Making Connections: Take a poll of students' responses to the moral dilemma presented by the Robin Hood-esque bank robbery. Ask them whether they were surprised by the number of students who said they would report the robbery (or would not). Encourage them to share their reactions to questions 1 through 4, as well as their discussion with a partner.

ELL Support: Preview Concepts Explain, act out, show pictures, and use realia to explain the vocabulary from p. 8 (*hero, superhero, villain, nemesis*). Model how to turn questions into answers by using the question: *Who is your favorite superhero?* and indicating how the pronouns and order of words change when making a statement: *My favorite superhero is . . . .* Group students in multilevel pairs. Provide sentence frames for both prompts:

- My favorite superhero is . . . .
- The superhero is good because . . . .
- The villain is bad because . . . .
- The superhero and villain are different because . . . .
- A hero must have/be . . . and . . . to be considered a good guy.
- A hero must have/be . . . because . . . .

Chapter 1 (continued)

Lesson Support

First Read: Summarizing a Text

Before Reading: Read the first paragraph and access background knowledge. Ask students what they expect from this genre—an article from a science journal. Remind students of fix-up strategies to use when reading complex text. Tell students that during the close reading process the first read of a text focuses on identifying key ideas or what the text is mainly about. Explain to students that finding and underlining main ideas will help them understand a selection. In nonfiction, the central idea is the overall focus of the text. The term *main idea* refers to the key ideas of smaller sections of the overall text such as paragraphs. Supporting details support these main points with facts (data or statistics), reasons, examples, or events. Read the objective and then have students read and annotate the text. If students need extra support use a think-aloud strategy to model reading and annotating the first paragraph of the excerpt. Then have students read the rest of the text on their own.

Preview Vocabulary: Preview unfamiliar vocabulary to aid comprehension. Or instead have students circle unfamiliar words as they complete the first read. After the first read, guide students to determine the words' meanings using the context. Encourage students to support their responses with evidence and then confirm their initial definitions with a dictionary. Words that students might find difficult include:

socialization: *the process through which a child's behavior is shaped by family and environment.* The socialization of a child begins at a very young age.

morality: *beliefs about what is right behavior and what is wrong behavior.* My sense of morality would not let me leave the injured man stranded by the side of the road.

flourish: *blossom and succeed.* With the support of family and friends, most children will flourish.

First Read: Summarizing a Text

The following article comes from *Frontiers for Young Minds*, an online science journal. The authors are a professor of psychology and psychiatry and a developmental neuroscientist. In other words, one is an expert on how the mind works, and the other is an expert on how the brain develops. Before you read, consider the style of writing you expect from this informational genre.

Objective: As you read, underline the key idea of each paragraph. Write questions you have about morality in the My Thoughts column.

—— First Read
---- Second Read
—— Third Read

excerpt

Our Brains Are Wired for Morality: Evolution, Development, and Neuroscience

by Jean Decety and Jason M. Cowell, edited by Paul Glimcher

	My Thoughts

1   How do we distinguish good from evil, right from wrong, just from unjust, and vice from virtue? An obvious answer is that we have learned to do so through socialization, that is, our behaviors were shaped from birth onward by our families,

5   our preschools, and almost everything we contacted in our environments. Morality is an inner sense of rightness about our behavior and the behavior of others. How we feel, think, and act about the concepts of "good" and "bad" are all parts of our morality. For example, hitting another person for any

10 reason is seen as bad, while sharing something we like with another child who is sad is considered good. Morality is so deeply rooted in the fabric of our everyday lives that it seems hard to imagine a society without any moral rules. Indeed, observations made by scientists who study different societies

15 around the world have shown that, despite cultural and individual differences, all human beings have some sense of right and wrong.

    When we use the word "morality" we are generally talking about ideas of justice, fairness and rights, and the rules we

10   Chapter 1 • Unit 1   ©Perfection Learning® • No Reproduction Permitted

ELL Support: First Read Explain the title of the passage thoroughly using gestures and emphasis so students understand the authors' main point before reading: *Our brains (point to head) are made to be moral, to know the difference between right and wrong. The authors will look at this idea through the science of evolution, which is the study of how people and animals and plants change over time.* (Display an image of the classic evolutionary chart March of Progress.) *They will look at this idea through development or how things grow and change.* (Reference evolution pictures.) *And they will look at this idea through neuroscience or the study of the brain* (point to head). Encourage students to write notes in English or in their home language that reiterate the main point next to the title. Have multilevel pairs or small groups read the article aloud. Then have these groups identify the main ideas, putting those ideas in their own words in the My Thoughts column.

20 have about how people should treat one another. Consider the
   following: as a reward for finishing your homework, you have
   been given 10 marbles that you really like. You are then told
   about a poor child who would not be able to get any marbles,
   even though he did his homework too. However, you have

25 the option to give some of your marbles to the poor child.
   What would you choose to do? Most children would naturally
   share some of their marbles with a poor child and would also
   be surprised if another child received more than 10 marbles
   after doing the same amount of homework! This shows that

30 children understand both fairness and justice. As humans,
   when we consider how we or others should share something
   we have been given, we tend to take into account both how
   much of a reward someone deserves for the "work" they did
   and whether rewards are evenly split between individuals.

35   Humans are an extremely social species. We are dependent
   on each other and cannot survive and flourish without
   interacting with others. Newborns only survive to adulthood if
   given enough care, and societies succeed through cooperation.
   Almost all of our actions and thoughts are about others or are

40 in response to others. We cooperate with and help people who
   are not related to us at a level that is unmatched in the animal
   kingdom.[1] Since humans are, by nature, both helpful and
   selfish, we think that morality evolved to support our helpful
   social interactions with others and control our somewhat

45 selfish tendencies.
      However, it would be misleading to see morality as only
   a result of evolution. Although some human traits, like skin
   color, are determined by our genes alone, morality is quite

[1] Tomasello, M., and Vaish, A. 2013. *Origins of human cooperation and morality.* Annu. Rev. Psychol. 64:231–55. doi: 10.1146/annurev-psych-113011-143812

My Thoughts

---

genes: *the basic, hereditary parts of a person's cellular makeup that determine his or her development.* My genes determined that I look like my mother, think like my father, and act like myself.

virtue: *righteousness.* His colleagues all admire his virtue and goodness.

vice: *wickedness; weakness.* Temptation leads him to vice—and trouble.

evolution: *the process by which changes in plants and animals happen over time.* Scientists believe that evolution has caused the human sense of smell to become less keen as we no longer depend on it for survival.

After Reading: Use the following questions to check comprehension.

Text-Based Discussion Questions

1. How does the article define morality? *"Morality is an inner sense of rightness about our behavior and the behavior of others." Lines 6–9 "Ideas of justice, fairness, rights and the rules we have about how people should treat one another. Lines 19–20*

2. According to the article, what shapes human morality? *Our morality is shaped by our genes and our environment, including our family and our society.*

3. Why is morality important? *Morality regulates how we behave and how we treat others. It helps to control our selfish tendencies. In these ways, morality helps to keep society running smoothly.*

4. What causes moral rules and values to change? What examples did the authors provide of how morals change over time? *As society's attitudes change, so do moral rules and values. Examples of this include bullfighting and slavery.*

5. Why do the writers include references to the work of other scientists by using numbered footnotes? *Referring to other people's research gives validity to the author's ideas by providing corroborating evidence. The writers also avoid plagiarism by acknowledging the work of other scientists.*

 Gr7Ch1Read1.pptx

Lesson Support

6. Background Information: As students read this chapter, they will be learning about how humans' brains are wired for morality. They may not know that the teen brain is a work in progress. In many ways, our brains don't reach maturation until the early twenties. This fact is ironic considering that teens are near peak in terms of physical fitness and strength, as well as mental capacity. What changes are taking place in the teen brain? The cortex is the thin outer layer of the brain where thought and memory processes are located. The volume of the cortex is made up of gray matter. The amount of gray matter in the cortex peaks during adolescence, reaching its adult level in the early twenties. Various parts of the cortex develop at different rates. Basic functions, such as information processing of the senses and movement control, develop first. Impulse control and planning mature later. The fact that a teen's brain is changing doesn't mean it's not effective, but it does mean that teens are more likely to act impulsively and misread social cues and emotions. On the other hand, studies have shown that the adolescent brain is better suited to learn than the adult brain.

Tech-Connect Suggestion: Students who are interested in learning more about brain networks that play a role in influencing moral decision-making might check out a related article: "How Your Brain Makes Moral Judgments" at cnn.com.

		My Thoughts

different in that it is also determined both by our nature and

50 the society in which we live. Many moral rules and values vary

between different cultures and also change over time. For

instance, bull fighting is seen as a cruel form of entertainment

or even as animal torture in North America and most European

countries, but it is still very popular in Spain and Colombia

55 where it is considered a form of expression, despite the

obvious suffering of the animals. An example of a shift in

morality over time is our attitude toward slavery. Most people

in the world today think that it is immoral to own slaves but

that was not the case a century ago.

60   Thus, our morality has been formed over thousands of

years from the combination of both our genes and our culture,

rather than just one or the other. This genetic and cultural

evolution has shaped our brains to care for others, react to

those who try to harm us, and to create moral rules that help

65 us to live together successfully.[2]

        There are three main lines of evidence that support the

view that our brains are wired for morality. (1) The "building

blocks" of morality have been observed in non-human animals,

(2) even very young babies appear to exhibit some **basic**

70 **moral evaluations**, and (3) the parts of the brain involved in

moral judgments are beginning to be identified.

CITATION: Decety J and Cowell J (2016) Our Brains are Wired for Morality: Evolution, Development, and Neuroscience. Front Young Minds. 4:3. doi: 10.3389/frym.2016.00003
Copyright © 2016 Decety and Cowell

[2] Decety, J., and Wheatley, T. 2015. *The Moral Brain: A Multidisciplinary Perspective.* Cambridge: MIT Press.

basic moral evaluations: considered to be an early form leading to mature morality in babies and involves basic appraisals of the social interactions of others

FIRST RESPONSE: KEY IDEAS AND DETAILS

Based on your first read of the article, what do the authors believe about the way people make moral decisions? Write your answer in your journal. Share your answer with a partner.

TECH-CONNECT

Post your response on your class website, according to your teacher's instructions, or tweet it to your teacher.

Focus on Summarizing a Text

A good summary explains the key ideas in an article without repeating the entire article. Writing a summary is a little like packing a suitcase. You can't include everything you want to, so you have to decide what's the most important. Sometimes it isn't easy!

When summarizing, use the following guidelines:

- Be objective. Do not include your personal opinions.

- Include only essential information. If you remove the information and it doesn't change the passage's overall meaning, it is probably not essential.

- Use your own words to retell the central idea.

You identified sentences containing key ideas during the First Read, so let's pack the summary suitcase. In the left-hand box below, write the sentences with the most important ideas you underlined during the First Read. In the "suitcase" on the right, rewrite these sentences in your own words. Not every key idea will fit. Remember to be objective, restating what the author says without changing the meaning.

Key Ideas	My Summary
1. An obvious answer is that we have learned to do so through socialization, that is, our behaviors were shaped from birth onward by our families, our preschools, and almost everything we contacted in our environments.	
2. When we use the word "morality" we are generally talking about ideas of justice, fairness, rights, and the rules we have about how people should treat one another.	

FIRST RESPONSE: KEY IDEAS AND DETAILS

Please note that students are encouraged to have a response journal in which to complete the First Response activities in this curriculum. For this activity, you may have students post their responses on the class website or tweet them to you. Before students answer the First Response question, encourage them to think about factors that, according to the authors, determine a person's moral rules and values: family, society (school, friends, groups), and genes.

Focus on Summarizing a Text:

Possible Answers to Key Ideas Column in Chart:

See answers on Student Book insert page to the left and on the following page.

 Gr7Ch1Read1.pptx

ELL Support: First Response Reword the First Response question as *How do people make decisions between right and wrong?* If students still do not understand, continue to offer synonyms for key words in the question until they comprehend.

Focus on Summarizing a Text Remind students that they can use their notes and underlined sentences to fill in the Key Ideas column. Have students work in multilevel pairs to write summaries together. Provide the central idea and sentence frames to guide multilevel pairs in writing their summaries:

- In "Our Brains Are Wired for Morality," the authors explain how people learn what is right and what is wrong.

- One way people learn this is . . . .

- Another way people learn this is . . . .

Chapter 1 (continued)

Lesson Support

Possible Answers to My Summary Column:

1. Most people would say our morality is shaped from birth through our family and the society in which we live.

2. Experiments show that even young children understand prevailing moral concepts of fairness and justice.

3. Because humans are social creatures, morality developed to support positive relations.

4. Morality changes from culture to culture and evolves throughout the centuries.

5. Morality is shaped by both our genes and our culture.

6. Three lines of evidence show that morality is built into our brains.

Key Ideas	My Summary
3. Since humans are, by nature, both helpful and selfish, we think that morality evolved to support our helpful social interactions with others and control our somewhat selfish tendencies.	
4. . . .Morality is quite different in that it is also determined by both our nature and the society in which we live. Many moral rules and values vary between cultures and also change over time.	
5. Thus, our morality has been formed over thousands of years from the combination of both our genes and our culture, rather than just one or the other.	
6. There are three main lines of evidence that support the view that our brains are wired for morality.	

ELL Support: Focus on Summarizing a Text Use the chart created for ELL Support on the bottom of p. 7 and gestures to ensure students understand the concepts of right, wrong, and learning. You may also adapt the exercise by providing the key ideas to the students and having them write simple summaries.

Write Based on the graphic organizer on the previous page, write a summary of the article. Your summary should include the authors' beliefs about the source of morality. Here are some sentence frames to help you get started. Use specific evidence from the article in your answers.

- In "Our Brains Are Wired for Morality," the authors describe . . . .
- They state that morality is shaped by . . . .
- But they believe it is also . . . .
- They support this position by referring to . . . .

CONNECT TO ESSENTIAL QUESTION

Criminals receive jail sentences based on the severity of their crimes. How do you decide which wrong acts are worse than others? Or what a fitting punishment is?

Second Read: Understanding Technical Terms

Objective: Read the article a second time with a partner, taking turns reading paragraphs. Circle words and phrases that are confusing or unfamiliar. Underline context clues that help you infer the meaning of these unfamiliar or unclear terms.

Focus on Understanding Technical Terms

This article includes many scientific terms. Articles about scientific or historical topics often include technical terms that are important to understand the topic. Sometimes an article includes footnotes that define key terms. Always use this feature when reading challenging texts with technical terms.

One way to figure out the meaning of unfamiliar words and phrases is to use context clues. Context clues are the words and phrases that surround the unfamiliar word. Context clues have four main types:

Synonym: another word or phrase has a similar meaning to the unfamiliar word.

> The frigid wind slipped through the gaps in the makeshift shelter, making an *icy* current of air swirl around our feet.

Antonym: another word or phrase has an opposite or contrasting meaning to the unfamiliar word.

> The new tiger at the zoo was wary of emerging from the den at first, but she soon became more *trusting* of her surroundings.

Inference: the word's meaning is not directly stated but can be figured out by the context.

> The castaway's *gaunt, skeletal frame* and *lack of energy* showed him on the brink of starvation.

ELL Support: Second Read Explain to students that they should only circle words and phrases that are part of the key idea in each paragraph. This will limit the vocabulary to the essential words and to a manageable list for students to learn.

Write: Help students identify the central idea of the passage using the sentence frame provided *Possible response: In "Our Brains Are Wired for Morality," the authors describe factors that determine our moral values.* Have them continue with the additional sentence frames, adding a few important details to round out their summary.

Connect to Essential Question: Point out that our legal system provides some sentencing guidelines. Allow time to discuss reasons why justice may not always be meted out fairly despite such guidelines.

Second Read: Understanding Technical Terms

Before Reading: Read the first four sentences of the passage aloud with students. Point out the words *virtue, socialization, environments,* and *morality.* Help them to identify context clues that reveal the word meanings. (virtue: *inferred from the antonym* vice; socialization: *defined in context;* morality: *defined in context*) Ask students to read the text with a partner.

After Reading: Use the following questions to check comprehension.

Text-Based Discussion Questions

1. Based on the final paragraph, what is the overall purpose for this section? *This section introduces concepts about morality that lead up to the central claim in the final paragraph—that our brains are wired for morality.*

2. If the authors' main purpose for the entire article is to show how our brains are wired for morality, why do they provide evidence for the idea that morality is affected by our culture and environment? *Although the authors' focus is on the brain and morality, they want to present evidence for the idea that morality is also determined by environment. They are anticipating the readers' objections and questions by fairly presenting other theories before focusing on their own.*

Focus on Understanding Technical Terms: Ask students to identify which context clue(s) helped them define the four words in the chart on page 16. *Possible answers:* morality: *definition in context;* tendencies, culture, genetic: *inference.*

Chapter 1 *(continued)*

Lesson Support

Answers to Chart:

See answers on Student Book insert page to the right.

Reflect: Invite students to explain how they knew, at an early age, when they had done something wrong. Do they believe their experience is better evidence for the idea that morality is shaped by their environment or for the idea that their brain is wired for morality?

 Gr7Ch1Read2.pptx

Definition: the unfamiliar word is defined in the sentence (or in a nearby sentence).

> A <u>speedometer</u>, *an instrument for measuring a vehicle's speed,* comes standard in vehicles today, and the idea of measuring speed has been around since early Romans estimated their speed and distance by marking the wheels of their chariots and counting the revolutions.

REFLECT

What is your earliest memory of knowing you did something wrong?

Fill in the following table, first with your own definition and then confirm the definition by checking a dictionary. At the bottom, use the blank spaces for any words or phrases you identified in the article that are not listed in the table.

Word(s)	What I think it means from the context and my background knowledge	Dictionary definition
morality		the standards of conduct that are generally accepted as right or wrong
tendencies		inclinations toward particular characteristics or behaviors
culture		the customs, arts, social institutions, and achievements of a particular nation, people, or other social group
genetic		relating to genes or heredity; physical characteristics passed from a parent to offspring

©Perfection Learning® • No Reproduction Permitted

ELL Support: Understanding Technical Terms Once students complete their second read and have identified all the key unknown words, they can work in multilevel pairs or small groups to record them in the graphic organizer and look up any remaining words in an online dictionary: http://learnersdictionary.com/. Students can then organize the words into categories, using a <u>Word Web graphic organizer from the ELL Teacher Resource (p.50)</u>. Doing so will help students more easily learn the vocabulary because many are related words.

Speak and Listen: Place students in multilevel pairs or small groups. Provide sentence frames for students to respond to the prompts. Sentence frames are also provided as a student reproducible in the ELL Digital Resource.

- The most important word in the passage is . . . .
- This is the most important word because . . . .

(Speak and Listen Share your answers to the definitions chart with a partner. Discuss the following questions:

1. Which word or phrase is most important to understanding the passage's key ideas? Why?
2. Why would the authors be interested in whether morality has evolved or is cultural?

Third Read: Identifying Claims, Reasons, and Evidence

The authors state, "There are three main lines of evidence that support the view that our brains are wired for morality." This sentence explains what the authors intend to prove: that morality is built into the brain. During this read, you will read another excerpt from the same article.

Objective: Reread the final paragraph of the first excerpt on page 12. Then read the three headers from the article below. How do the headers help you understand and predict what this article is about? As you read, think about the following questions:

- What reasons do the authors give to support the ideas that "our brains are wired for morality"?
- What evidence do they use to support their reasons?

Underline sentences that state the authors' reasons that support their central claim. Then double underline sentences that provide evidence to support the reasons.

TECH-CONNECT

Search online for one of the words used in the passage. Click on three links for websites and notice how the word is used in context. Add this new information to your knowledge of how to use the unfamiliar word.

——— Reasons

=== Evidence

excerpt

Our Brains Are Wired for Morality: Evolution, Development, and Neuroscience

by Jean Decety and Jason M. Cowell

My Thoughts

1 **Building Blocks of Morality in Non-Human Species**

Natural observations of animals in the wild and research in laboratories show us that a number of "building blocks" of moral behavior can be found in animals. For instance,
5 many animals exhibit behaviors that benefit other members of their species. Such prosocial behaviors (meaning behaviors that are good for others), like helping each other and caring

(Speak and Listen

1. *Answers will vary: The topic of the entire passage is the development of morality; therefore, the most important word is morality.*

2. *Understanding that morality is both evolved and cultural helps to explain the universality of morality, as well as the many variations in the world of moral rules and values.*

Third Read: Identifying Claims, Reasons, and Evidence

Before Reading: Preview this new passage by reading through the introduction and objective. Read the final paragraph of the first excerpt on page 12. Discuss the answer to the question *How do the headers help you understand and predict what this article is about?*

Read the first paragraph aloud and model how to underline the authors' reasons and evidence. Then have students read the rest of the text on their own.

- The authors are interested in the idea of morality evolving because they . . . .

Remind advanced students that they can create their own sentence frames from the words in the questions.

Third Read: Confirm that students understand that they are reading a new section of the article. As necessary, review the main ideas from the first section of the article. Also review the academic vocabulary *claim, evidence,* and *reasons.* Use the graphic organizer on pp. 19–20 to review these concepts and to preview the main ideas in the passage.

Chapter 1 *(continued)*

Lesson Support

After Reading: Use the following questions to check comprehension.

Text-Based Discussion Questions

1. How do the facts about the moral behaviors of babies support the idea that morality is inborn? *The environment is not an influence on young babies, who have not yet had an opportunity to interact with society; therefore, some basis for morality is likely inborn or genetic in humans.*

2. Why might empathetic and collaborative behavior in animals suggest that our brains are wired for morality? *These rudimentary signs of morality, which are not influenced by human environment, suggest a genetic, evolutionary wiring of our brains that sustains survival.*

 Gr7Ch1Read3.pptx

Tech-Connect Suggestion: Instruct students to go to https://kids.frontiersin.org/article/10.3389/frym.2016.00003 and read the digital copy of the article, including the abstract. Point out the digital features of the product. Encourage students to click on the words linked to the glossary and also to click on the numbered references. Point out the visuals included in the article. Ask them to analyze how these features help them better understand the text.

---

for offspring, have been seen in rodents and primates. Rats will help other distressed rats that have been soaked with

10 water, and [they] will also choose to help a cage mate that is in distress before obtaining a food reward. Chimpanzees will help each other and share with each other, but only when they benefit from the sharing, as long as the costs are minimal and the needs of the other chimpanzees are clear. Chimpanzees

15 also collaborate and form alliances in fights or when hunting. Capuchin monkeys have even been shown to react in a negative way when they see other monkeys being treated unfairly. . . .

Evidence for Moral Behavior in Babies

When we see early signs of morality in young babies,

20 this provides strong evidence for the evolutionary roots of morality, because babies have not yet had much time to be influenced by their environment. Psychologists who study human development have shown that human babies enter the world ready to pay attention and respond to social stimuli,

25 such as voices and faces, and that babies begin forming social relationships during the first year of life. Young children provide comfort and assistance to both other children and adults in emotional distress. For instance, when they see their mothers in pain, 18-month-old toddlers show comforting

30 behaviors (such as hugging, patting, and sharing toys). As infants develop and become more able to analyze what is going on around them, they even have the ability to recognize when a person in their environment is treating another person badly. At a young age, infants are quickly able to figure

35 out whether the consequence of a behavior is good or bad, suggesting that their genes are involved and that experience and learning are not the only causes of moral development. . . .

My Thoughts

18   Chapter 1 • Unit 1   ©Perfection Learning® • No Reproduction Permitted

---

ELL Support: Third Read Students will benefit from reading the digital article with glossary. Go to https://kids.frontiersin.org/article/10.3389/frym.2016.00003.

The Role of The Brain in Morality

...An area of the brain called the ventromedial prefrontal
40 cortex has been found to be important for certain aspects of
human morality. If this brain region is damaged early in life
(before 5 years of age), the person is more likely to break
moral rules or inflict harm on others, suggesting that the
ventromedial prefrontal cortex helps us to understand what
is and is not moral. Patients who have damage to this brain
45 region or who have had it removed also tend to experience
less **empathy**, embarrassment, and guilt than people without
damage to this region.

empathy: the ability to understand others' feelings

My Thoughts
_____
_____
_____
_____
_____
_____
_____
_____
_____

Focus on Identifying Claims, Reasons, and Evidence

A claim is a statement or assertion that something is true. A
claim is based on an opinion and is sometimes directly stated and
other times must be inferred. Authors support their claims with
reasons that explain why their opinion is valid. Reasons should be
"sound." This means that the reasons are logical. They fit with the
claim being made.

In a strong argument, reasons are then supported by
evidence. Evidence includes facts (statistics or data) and opinions
and testimony from experts. Evidence should be relevant and
sufficient. *Relevant* means the evidence is clearly connected to the
reason. *Sufficient* means there is enough evidence to prove that the
claim is true.

Fill in the chart below. The reasons are listed. Fill in the
evidence from the article.

> **CONNECT TO ESSENTIAL QUESTION**
>
> How do expectations for understanding right from wrong change with age?

Claim: Our brains are wired for morality.	
Reasons	**Evidence**
1. The "building blocks" of morality have been observed in non-human animals.	• Rats help other rats that have been soaked with water. • Chimpanzees will collaborate. • Capuchin monkeys react negatively to unfair treatment of other monkeys.

continued on next page

Focus on Identifying Claims, Reasons, and Evidence:

> **Sample Answers to Chart:**
>
> See answers on Student Book insert page to the left.

 Gr7Ch1Read3.pptx

Connect to Essential Question:
Discuss the fact that children don't begin to understand abstract qualities like right and wrong until they are older. Parents teach the difference between good and bad behavior by rewards and punishments that change unwanted behavior—such as putting a child in time-out when they hits another child. When a child is old enough, she is able to understand for herself that some behaviors are right and wrong. However, young children are not always expected to recognize when they break a "moral rule."

ELL Support: Third Read Have students form multilevel pairs or small groups to paraphrase the three reasons in the chart in simple sentences. For example: 1. Animals show some morality. 2. Even babies show some moral understanding. 3. Parts of our brain control moral decisions. Then help students identify the paragraphs that correlate to each reason so they can identify and record evidence in the chart.

Use pictures, pantomime, and Total Physical Response (See ELL Teacher Resource, page 18) to summarize the main events in each paragraph. For example, show pictures or videos of rats and chimpanzees and use pantomime and simple sentences: *Rats help each other. One rat is wet. The other rat helps. Chimpanzees help each other. Chimpanzees share food.* Show videos of rats helping each other: https://youtu.be/leHLL4vcbCc and babies helping adults: https://youtu.be/2BYJf2xSONc.

Chapter 1 *(continued)*

Lesson Support

Speak and Listen: Invite students to share the results of their discussion. Then vote on these questions: 1. Which reason (of the three) is the strongest? 2. Did the authors convince you that our brains are wired for morality? Extend the activity by asking students to find another scientific article that supports or contradicts the central claim of the article.

Language: Prefixes, Suffixes, and Root Words:

Give students 5 minutes to brainstorm with partners an additional example (or examples) for each of the prefixes, suffixes, and roots in the table. Invite them to share their findings. Then review the four sentences and the meanings of the underlined words on page 22. Point out the value of combining strategies to determine the meanings of underlined words (i.e., using context clues along with word roots and affixes).

 Gr7Ch1Language.pptx

Claim: Our brains are wired for morality.	
Reasons	**Evidence**
2. Even very young babies appear to exhibit some basic moral evaluations.	• Babies show comforting behaviors. • Babies respond to social stimuli early. • Babies differentiate consequences.
3. The parts of the brain involved in moral judgments are beginning to be identified.	• The ventromedial prefrontal cortex appears to impact morality. • Damage/removal of the ventromedial prefrontal cortex undermines moral behavior. • Damage/removal undermines empathy, guilt reactions.

Speak and Listen With a partner, share your answers to the claims and evidence chart. Use the following questions in your discussion.

1. Which reasons have the strongest evidence?
2. Does some evidence seem weaker than other evidence? Identify the strongest evidence.
3. What evidence do you think could have been added to strengthen a particular reason?

If you add or change information in your chart based on your discussion, use a different color pen or pencil.

Language: Prefixes, Suffixes, and Root Words

Earlier in the chapter, you learned about using context clues to determine word meanings. Another way to figure out unfamiliar word meanings is to analyze word parts and their meanings.

A root word is the base word. It contains the basic meaning of the word. A prefix is a word part added to the beginning of a word that changes its meaning. A suffix is a word part added to the end of a word that changes its meaning. Knowing what common prefixes and suffixes mean can help you figure out a word's meaning.

ELL Support: Language Studying root words, prefixes, and suffixes is an excellent way for students to learn and expand their English vocabulary. Have students create a deck of index cards with a word part on one side and examples on the back. Students might begin with the word parts in the chart and may use an online dictionary to find additional examples. Students can also add word meanings to the cards and use them as flashcards. Additionally, students can join with a partner to play one of the following games with the flashcards:

Match It One student lays out all his/her cards with roots up, and the other student lays out his/her cards with the examples side up. Students take turns identifying the matching pair, one from each set.

War Each student holds his/her deck of cards in his/her hands, and both students flip over a card. The first student to name the correct root or example for each card wins both cards. Play continues until one student wins all the cards.

Look at the charts below to become familiar with a few common roots, prefixes, and suffixes.

Root	Meaning	Example
aqua	water	aquarium
bio	life	biography
gen	birth, kind	generate, genre
graph	writing	graphic
hydr	water	hydrate
luc	light	translucent
log/logue	word, study	dialogue, biology
omni	all	omniscient
phil	love	philanthropy
struct	build	construct
vid/vis	see	video, visual

Prefix	Meaning	Example
auto-	self	autobiography
co-	joint, together with others	cooperate
dis-	not, none	disinterest
mis-	wrongly	misspeak
sub-	under, below	submarine
un-, non-	not, opposite of	unbelievable, nonsense

Suffix	Meaning	Example
-able	capable of	achievable
-al	relating to or characterized by	three-dimensional
-ic	having characteristics of	Celtic
-ion	act or process, condition	calculation
-ology	study of	geology

continued on next page

Tech-Connect Suggestion: For more information about moral behavior in animals, students can listen to a podcast by Frans de Waal, a biologist who works with primates: https://n.pr/V8IGKp or search for *Do Animals Have Morals* at www.npr.org.

Sort It! Students work together with one set of cards and sort them by categories that they devise. Students can share their categories and words with the class.

Chapter 1 *(continued)*

Lesson Support

Answers to Questions:

1. <u>collaborate</u>: *work together with others* (*co-*: "together with other"); context also gives insight into the word meaning

2. <u>nonhuman</u>: *not human* (non = not)

3. <u>evolution</u>: *the process of evolving* (*-tion*: process); context also provides insight

4. <u>cultural</u>: *relating to culture* (*-al*: relating to*)

Read these sentences from the article and use the information in the charts to determine the word meanings.

1. Chimpanzees also <u>collaborate</u> and form alliances in fights or when hunting.

2. The "building blocks" of morality have been observed in <u>non-human</u> animals.

3. This genetic and cultural <u>evolution</u> has shaped our brains to care for others, react to those who try to harm us, and to create moral rules that help us to live together successfully.

4. Indeed, observations made by scientists who study different societies around the world have shown that, despite <u>cultural</u> and individual differences, all human beings have some sense of right and wrong.

Project-Based Assessments

Roundtable Discussion

Participate in a roundtable discussion on the following question, based on your reading of the chapter text.

Is morality mostly learned from social interactions, or is it built into our genes?

In a roundtable discussion, all students are equal and everyone participates. Arrange your seats in a circle so that all participants can see one another. The teacher or a discussion leader may sit in the middle. Come to the discussion with an open mind and be prepared for a challenge! You will be evaluated on the following:

Expectations for Discussion	
Listening	**Speaking**
Listen respectfully.	Speak at least two times.
Look at speaker.	Ask questions.
Follow text references.	Explain and give reasons to support your opinion.
Take notes on what the speaker is saying.	Refer to the text to support conclusions.
Write follow-up questions.	Use a tone of voice and language appropriate for an open exchange of ideas.
Reflect on what others say and be open to changing your mind based on new evidence.	Invite comment.

As you participate in the discussion, you will need to support your conclusions with details from the passage. In your response journal, create the following chart to refer to during the discussion.

Detail from the text	How it supports your opinion

Assessment

Project-Based Assessments

Roundtable Discussion: Ask students to paraphrase, or restate in their own words, the roundtable question. (*Possible paraphrase: Are our moral values and rules determined by our environment—family, friends, and groups—or by our genes?*) Then review the expectations for participating in a roundtable discussion. Point out that skills required for listening under the Expectations for Discussion are very much like those required of college students in their classes.

Make sure students understand that the chart for their response journal should be completed in advance of the roundtable discussion. They may want to review the guidelines, which should help them to work toward the highest score.

One idea to help students monitor their participation in the discussion is to give them tokens or chips. Each student gets his or her own color or puts his or her initials on the tokens. Whenever a student participates in the discussion, he or she plays a token in the center of the table. This is a visual reminder that everyone should be participating. (No hogs or logs.)

ELL Support: Roundtable Discussion Have students form multilevel pairs or small groups. Provide sentence frames for students to use in their chart and then during the discussion:

- People learn morality from social interactions/their genes.

- For example, the text says, " . . . ."

- This quote shows that . . . .

Note: Reproducible handouts with sentence frames for this and other activities for this unit can be found in the ELL Teacher Resource (p. 34).

Chapter 1 *(continued)*

Assessment

Project-Based Assessments

Argumentative Essay: Students can use the chapter selection as a model for their own essays. Like the article, their essays should include a claim, their central idea (about whether humans are by nature more or less moral than animals). Their claim should be supported by reasons and evidence. Additionally, their essays should include quotations and evidence from the chapter selection.

Instructions for a Roundtable Discussion

1. The discussion leader (or teacher) begins by asking the following question:

> Is morality mostly learned from social interactions or is it built into our genes?

2. Allow each member a chance to reply to the question.
3. Take notes on comments you disagree with or have questions about. Record what was said and who said it.
4. Go around the circle again and allow everyone to ask a follow-up question or make a comment. Questions should be directed to the person who made the original comment. Try phrasing your questions and comments in this way:
   - Explain what you mean by . . . .
   - I agree/disagree with ____ because . . . .
   - Why do you think . . . .?
5. Close the discussion by having everyone respond to the following question:

> Which aspects of morality seem to be inborn, and which ones are learned?

REFLECT
Why do people sometimes do the wrong thing even when they know it is wrong?

Use the following guidelines for your roundtable discussion.	
To receive the highest score, the discussion must meet all of these criteria.	During the discussion, you should • listen carefully when others are speaking and make notes about what they say. • offer thoughtful feedback and encourage everyone to participate. • share reasonable opinions and support your opinion with examples from the text. • demonstrate an understanding of the text. • speak to the question or point in a clear, concise manner.

Argumentative Essay

Write an essay in which you argue whether humans are by nature more or less moral than animals.

Use these steps to help you:

1. Write a central idea statement that includes your claim about whether humans are more or less moral than animals.
2. Develop an outline to organize your main reasons to support your claim. Include direct quotations and evidence from the article.
3. Write your essay. Include an introduction and conclusion.

ELL Support: On Your Own Activity 1: Organize students into multilevel groups and have them work together to create a sketch of the trolley problem. Circulate to assist as necessary. Each student in the group should participate in drawing and adding details. Students can also add speech and thought bubbles to practice language and writing.

For the writing portion of the activity, provide students with the following sentence frame. Allow students time to discuss their opinions in their multilevel groups.

- It is/is not morally acceptable (right) to pull the lever to save five people because . . . .

4. Ask two classmates to read your essay and give feedback. Revise your essay based on their suggestions.
5. Check your essay for mistakes in grammar, usage, spelling, and punctuation.

Use the following guidelines for your argumentative essay.	
To receive the highest score, the discussion must meet all of these criteria.	Your argumentative essay • makes a claim about whether humans are by nature more or less moral than animals. • supports the claim with more than one reason. • includes support in the form of direct quotations and evidence from the article. • includes an introduction and a conclusion. • is clearly organized with good transitions between sentences and paragraphs. • uses correct grammar, word usage, punctuation, and spelling.

On Your Own: Integrating Ideas

1. Experts in morality often talk about the "trolley problem." Imagine this situation: A runaway trolley, or train, is about to hit five people who are stuck on the tracks. You are standing nearby. You can pull a lever that will switch the tracks so the trolley changes direction. But if the trolley switches tracks, it will hit a single person. Is it morally acceptable to pull the lever in order to save the five people? What if you have to push a single person in front of the trolley to stop it? Discuss the trolley problem with a small group.

2. The question of whether morality is more built-in or learned is only one example of a larger question in science. The debate is often called "nature versus nurture." Watch the About.com video "What Is Nature Vs. Nurture?" on YouTube and discuss it with friends or family members.

On Your Own: Integrating Ideas:
Activity 1: Students could create a cartoon strip or other visualization about the "trolley problem."

ELL Support: On Your Own Activity 2: Have students watch the Nature vs. Nurture video together: https://youtu.be/J9731MLLs_E. Then provide these sentence frames for them to summarize the ideas in the video and discuss their own opinions:

• Nature is . . . .

• Nurture is . . . .

• People are formed more by nature/nurture because . . . .

Chapter 1 *(continued)*

Assessment

Connect to Testing: This Connect to Testing section focuses on summarizing a text, determining word meanings from context, and analyzing claims, reasons, and evidence in an argument.

Encourage students to work in pairs to choose the correct answers to the questions and then to compare their answers with those of another pair of students. If there is disagreement, encourage the groups to try to reach a consensus as they discuss the reasons for their choices.

Answers to Connect to Testing Questions:

1. **Part A:** A. (DoK 1)

   Part B: D. (DoK 2)

Connect to Testing

In this chapter, you practiced summarizing a text; determining word meanings from context; and analyzing claims, reasons, and evidence in an argument. When you take assessments, you will be tested on these skills. Answer the following questions.

1. **Part A:** Read this sentence from the text. Then answer the question that follows.

   > Psychologists who study human development have shown that human babies enter the world ready to pay attention and respond to social <u>stimuli</u>, such as voices and faces, and that babies begin forming social relationships during the first year of life.

   What is the meaning of *stimuli* as it is used in the text?

   A. things that are seen or heard

   B. rules that govern behavior

   C. parents or other caretakers

   D. method of decision-making

   Part B: Which words or phrases from the text in Part A best help the reader understand the meaning of the word *stimuli?*

   A. *Psychologists who study human development*

   B. *ready to pay attention*

   C. *begin forming social relationships*

   D. *such as voices and faces*

EXPLANATION

Remediation: Connect to Testing Review responses with students. For questions 4 and 5, model how to use the text to answer each question.

2. **Part A:** Which of the following best summarizes the central claim of the text in this chapter?

   A. Morality is an inner sense of right and wrong.

   B. Humans are an extremely social species.

   C. Morality evolved to support social behaviors.

   D. The human brain is set up to understand right and wrong.

   Part B: Provide two examples of textual evidence to support your answer to Part A.

3. Which of the following quotations is evidence used by the authors to support the central claim of the article?

   A. *How we feel, think, and act about the concepts of "good" and "bad" are all parts of our morality.*

   B. *For instance, bull fighting is seen as cruel form of entertainment or even as animal torture in North America and most European countries, but it is still very popular in Spain and Colombia . . .*

   C. *This genetic and cultural evolution has shaped our brains to care for others, react to those who try to harm us, and to create moral rules that help us to live together successfully.*

   D. *For instance, when they see their mothers in pain, 18-month-old toddlers show comforting behaviors (such as hugging, patting, and sharing toys).*

4. Read the following paragraph from the excerpt in the chapter. Then answer the questions that follow.

   > However, it would be misleading to see morality as only a result of evolution. Although some human traits, like skin color, are determined by our genes alone, morality is quite different in that it is also determined both by our nature and the society in which we live. Many moral rules and values vary between different cultures and also change over time. For instance, bull fighting is seen as a cruel form of entertainment or even as animal torture in North America and most European countries, but it is

   continued on next page

Answers to Connect to Testing Questions:

2. **Part A:** D. (DoK 2)

   Part B: The central claim of the passage is "There are three main lines of evidence that support the view that our brains are wired for morality." The authors also write "we think that morality evolved to support our helpful social interactions with others . . ." This also supports the idea that morality is something innate that has evolved and is not merely learned from social interactions. (DoK 2)

3. D. Choice A explains the concept of morality. It is incorrect. Choice B is incorrect as well; it describes how judgments may differ, not whether they are guided by an inborn sense of morality. Choice C states that morality is a result of both genes and culture but does not provide evidence for either cause. Choice D is the best answer because it asserts that toddlers, who have not had time to learn morality, still act kindly because a moral sense is part of human nature. (DoK 2)

   (continued)

ELL Support: Using Connect to Testing and Assessments See the *Connections* ELL Teacher Resource (p. 22) for ideas on adapting this section for ELLs.

Chapter 1 *(continued)*

Assessment

Answers to Connect to Testing Questions:

4. **Part A:** B. (DoK 2) The paragraph clarifies the authors' belief that morality is both cultural and genetic, not that they disagree with what others say, so choice A is incorrect. Choice C is incorrect because the paragraph does not suggest that any culture is more moral than another; instead, it says that values are different. It says values change over time, not necessarily that societies become more moral. Choice D is also incorrect. The paragraph uses bullfighting as an example of differing values, not as a larger point about animal treatment. Choice B is the best answer because the paragraph focuses on the role cultures play in shaping the moral instincts people are born with.
   Part B: A. (DoK 2)

5. **Part A:** A. Choice B, *difficulties*, does not fit the context of something that is "helpful," so it is incorrect. Choice C is not correct because morality is the set of rules, not something that supports the rules. Choice D can be eliminated because *benefits* does not fit the context. Choice A is the best answer because the word *relations* fits the best in this context, as morality promotes our better instincts in how we get along with others. (DoK 1)
   Part B: D., E. Based on the context, the words "social" and "with others" provide clues to the meaning of the word *interactions*. (DoK 2)

still very popular in Spain and Colombia where it is considered a form of expression, despite the obvious suffering of the animals. An example of a shift in morality over time is our attitude toward slavery. Most people in the world today think that it is immoral to own slaves but that was not the case a century ago.

Part A: What is the key idea of this paragraph?

A. Some people argue that morality is purely genetic, but the authors disagree.

B. Humans are naturally moral, but cultures decide what behavior is moral.

C. Some cultures are more moral than others, and cultures become more moral over time.

D. The way a culture treats animals is key to understanding the culture's morality.

Part B: Which of the following provides the best evidence for the answer to Part A?

A. *morality is quite different in that it is also determined both by our nature and the society in which we live.*

B. *For instance, bull fighting is seen as a cruel form of entertainment or even as animal torture in North America and most European countries*

C. *An example of a shift in morality over time is our attitude toward slavery.*

D. *Most people in the world today think that it is immoral to own slaves but that was not the case a century ago.*

5. Read this sentence from the text. Then answer the question that follows.
   Since humans are, by nature, both helpful and selfish, we think that morality evolved to support our helpful social <u>interactions</u> with others and control our somewhat selfish tendencies.

Part A: What is the meaning of *interactions* as it is used in the text?

A. relations

B. difficulties

C. rules

D. benefits

Part B: Which of the following provides the best evidence for the answer to Part A? Choose two.

A. *by nature*

B. *morality evolved to support*

C. *helpful social*

D. *with others*

E. *somewhat selfish tendencies*

Connections • © Perfection Learning®

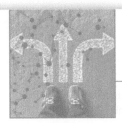

Chapter 2

Analyzing Theme Through Story Elements

Preview Concepts

Conflict is the struggle the characters in a story must overcome. Conflict makes a story interesting, moves the plot, adds suspense, and reveals the true personalities of the characters.

With a partner, study the following types of conflict found in stories. Then identify examples of this conflict from books or stories you have read. If you have studied other types of conflict, add them to the first row.

Main Types of Conflict in a Story	
person vs. person	Harry Potter vs. Voldemort
person vs. nature	
person vs. self	

CHAPTER GOALS

In this chapter you will

- analyze how conflicts interact in the story.
- identify the theme of a story.
- understand the point of view of a character in a story.
- rewrite a story from a different point of view.

PREVIEW ACADEMIC VOCABULARY

conflict

first-person point of view

narrator

point of view

theme

third-person limited point of view

third-person omniscient point of view

Chapter 2

Analyzing Theme Through Story Elements

The Three Questions
by Leo Tolstoy

Introduction

Chapter Goals: Have students read through the goals and mark any words that are unfamiliar. Discuss the meanings of any academic vocabulary within the goals that students marked as unfamiliar. Consider posting the Chapter Goals.

Preview Academic Vocabulary: Read and discuss the meanings of the academic vocabulary.

conflict: *a problem, struggle, or obstacle faced by a character or characters.* The main character's central <u>conflict</u> is the struggle against injustice.

first-person point of view: *the perspective of a story told by a character in the story.* The story is told from the <u>*first-person point of view*</u> by a character named Jim Hopkins.

narrator: *a character/speaker who tells the story.* The story's <u>narrator</u> is the best friend of the main character.

point of view: *the perspective from which a story is told.* The story is told from the <u>point of view</u> of the main character, Virginia.

theme: *the central idea or message of a literary text, developed through the characters and conflicts.* The <u>theme</u> of this author's books is always *Treat your neighbors kindly.*

third-person limited point of view: *the perspective of a story told by an outside narrator who offers the thoughts of only one character.* Hilda's world, and only Hilda's world, is revealed in this story told in <u>*third-person limited point of view*</u>.

ELL Support: Preview Concepts Confirm that students understand *plot, personalities,* and *characters.* Give simple definitions. Say: *Plot is the events in a story. An exciting plot has lots of interesting events.* Ask students to name a familiar movie or book. Use sketches and pantomime to tell a few central events. Say: *Personality is the way a person acts and thinks. I have a calm and happy personality. Do you have a calm personality? a happy personality? What is your personality?* Ask more advanced students to describe the personalities of the people in the book or movie you previously discussed. *Characters are the people (or animals) in a story.* Ask students to name the characters from the book or movie previously discussed.

Before students fill in the chart on p. 29, explain that the abbreviation *vs.* stands for *versus,* which means "against." Draw examples of conflicts from stories with which students are familiar.

Chapter 2 *(continued)*

Introduction

third-person omniscient point of view: *the perspective of a story told by an all-knowing narrator who reports the thoughts of many characters.* Readers come to know an entire family in this novel, which is told from a *third-person omniscient point of view*.

Gr7Ch2Vocabulary.pptx

Preview Concepts: Direct students to the chart, Main Types of Conflict in a Story. Invite them to suggest additional types of conflict. *Possible response: person versus society; person versus fate; person versus technology* Ask them why people enjoy reading about characters' struggles, problems, and obstacles. *Possible response: Conflict is exciting. It makes us take sides and root for certain characters. Conflict is suspenseful and keeps us wondering how the struggles will end. Will the characters overcome obstacles, problems, and struggles? Or will they give up?* Invite students to use the chart to discuss story conflicts with their partners.

Making Connections: "The Wise King" was published in Kahlil Gibran's book, *The Madman*, in 1918. Students may be surprised to learn that Gibran (1883–1931) was a best-selling twentieth-century American poet. A Syrian immigrant, he came to the United States in 1895 with his mother and siblings. Gibran's most famous work is *The Prophet* (1923), which has sold millions of copies.

Possible Responses:

1. The conflict is between the king and his bewitched subjects who have been maddened by a witch.

2. The king allows himself to be poisoned so that he can remain in sync with his people.

3. The king is wise and benevolent. He realizes that the only way to retain the loyalty of his people is to join his fate with theirs.

4. A king's destiny depends on his people. Sometimes, none of a person's choices are good. Sometimes, circumstances can be difficult.

Tech-Connect Suggestion: Kahlil Gibran's *The Madman* is in the public domain. It can be read online at Gutenberg Press.

30   Grade 7 • Chapter 2

Making Connections

Read the following story.

> Once there ruled in the distant city of Wirani a king who was both mighty and wise. And he was feared for his might and loved for his wisdom.
>
> One night when all were asleep, a witch entered the city, and poured seven drops of strange liquid into the city well, and said, "From this hour he who drinks this water shall become mad."
>
> Next morning all the inhabitants, save the king and his lord **chamberlain**, drank from the well and became mad, even as the witch had foretold. The people in the narrow streets and in the market places began to whisper to one another, "The king is mad. Our king and his lord chamberlain have lost their reason. Surely we cannot be ruled by a mad king. We must dethrone him."
>
> That evening the king drank from a goblet full of water from the well. He gave it to his lord chamberlain to drink as well.
>
> And there was great rejoicing in that distant city of Wirani, because its king and its lord chamberlain had regained their reason.
>
> —"The Wise King" by Kahlil Gibran

chamberlain: a manager of a royal household

With a partner or small group, answer the following questions.

1. What is the conflict in the story?

2. How is the conflict resolved?

3. What is the king like? How does his reaction to the conflict reveal his character?

4. Use your answers to questions 1–3 to write an explanation of the theme.

> **MAKING CONNECTIONS**
>
> In this chapter you will analyze conflicts in a story to understand its theme.

30   Chapter 2 • Unit 1   ©Perfection Learning® • No Reproduction Permitted

---

ELL Support: Academic Vocabulary See Teaching Vocabulary in the ELL Teacher Resource (p. 18) for ideas to use for teaching vocabulary throughout *Connections*.

Making Connections Use pantomime and sketches to act out the story as you read it aloud. To check comprehension when you are done, have students act out the story for you. Have students form multilevel pairs or small groups to respond to the questions. Ask the following support questions in addition to the questions on page 30.

1. What is the problem? Who causes the problem? Who has the problem?

2. How is the problem solved? Who solves it?

3. What does the king do to solve the problem? What does this show about the kind of person the king is?

4. What is the main idea the author is developing through this story?

Connections   •   © Perfection Learning®

First Read: Analyzing Plot and Conflict

Leo Tolstoy was a Russian author who is best known for his complex and sprawling novels *War and Peace* (1869) and *Anna Karenina* (1877) that explore truth and morality. Today Tolstoy is still considered one of the greatest writers of all time. In this story, a king longs to make good decisions so he asks the advice of a hermit.

Objective: As you read, think about how the actions of the characters move the plot forward. Draw arrows in the text from an action that results in a reaction.

—— First Read

---- Second Read

—— Third Read

excerpt
The Three Questions
by Leo Tolstoy
translated by L. and A. Maude

My Thoughts

1   When the King approached, the **hermit** was digging the ground in front of his hut. Seeing the King, he greeted him and went on digging. The hermit was frail and weak, and each time he stuck his spade into the ground and turned a little

5   earth, he breathed heavily.

The King went up to him and said: "I have come to you, wise hermit, to ask you to answer three questions: How can I learn to do the right thing at the right time? Who are the people I most need, and to whom should I, therefore, pay

10   more attention than to the rest? And, what **affairs** are the most important, and need my first attention?"

The hermit listened to the King, but answered nothing. He just spat on his hand and recommenced digging.

The hermit doesn't stop digging to focus on the King's questions.

"You are tired," said the King, "let me take the spade and

15   work awhile for you."

"Thanks!" said the hermit, and, giving the spade to the King, he sat down on the ground.

When he had dug two beds, the King stopped and

hermit: one that retires from society and lives in solitude especially for religious reasons
affairs: matters of concern

ELL Support: First Read Have students form multilevel pairs or small groups to create a comic strip version of the story. Pause at the end of each paragraph and allow time for students to sketch an image of what is happening in the scene. To assist students in identifying the key plot points of each paragraph ask: *Who is in this scene? What are they doing? Why? What are they saying?* Before students begin, show an image of a traditional hermit and a king from the Internet so students understand who the characters are. An illustrated version of the story can also be found at https://www.plough.com/en/topics/culture/short-stories/the-three-questions.

First Read: Analyzing Plot and Conflict

Before Reading: Read aloud the introduction and objective. Remind students that a story's plot includes a conflict. Characters act to resolve that conflict. Some character actions cause other characters to react. Other character actions cause events to happen. In both cases, the actions of characters are moving the plot forward. Explain that during the first read, students should think about how the actions of the characters move the plot forward.

Preview Vocabulary: Preview unfamiliar vocabulary to aid comprehension. Ask students to circle unfamiliar words as they complete the first read of a text. After the first read, guide students to determine the words' meanings using the context. Encourage students to support their responses with evidence. Have students confirm their initial definitions with a dictionary. Words that students might find difficult include:

frail: *weak; fragile.* The old man looked <u>frail</u>, but he was strong.

recommence: *continue; begin again.* After vacation, we will <u>recommence</u> our study of the Renaissance.

feebly: *weakly; frailly.* Because of her illness, she walked <u>feebly</u>.

threshold: *doorstep; entrance.* She rang the bell, and then waited patiently at the <u>threshold</u>.

execute: *kill; put to death.* They will <u>execute</u> the man for his crime.

ambush: *trap; surprise attack.* The thieves planned an <u>ambush</u> of the caravan.

After Reading: Use the following questions to check comprehension.

Text-Based Discussion Questions

1. What do the king's questions to the hermit show about him? *They show that he wants to be a good ruler and to do what is right for his people. They show his desire for improvement.*

2. Why did the king likely turn to the hermit for advice? *The hermit is known for his wisdom and lack of interest in material things; therefore, he is likely to be honest and not self-interested.*

3. What words best describe the king? *compassionate, curious*

Chapter 2 (continued)

Lesson Support

About the Author: In 1865, Leo Nicolayovich Tolstoy (1828–1910) wrote: "If I were told that what I shall write will be read in twenty years by the children of today and that they will weep and smile over it and will fall in love with life, I would devote all my life and all my strength to it."

Tolstoy wrote from his youth into old age. His first publication, an autobiographical work, came out in 1852, when he was twenty-six years old. His great epic novel, *War and Peace*, appeared in 1865, followed by *Anna Karenina* in 1878. After this second celebrated novel, Tolstoy's work turned more religious and philosophical.

Tolstoy was born on August 18, 1828, to wealthy parents. His mother died when he was two years old, his father seven years later. After a raucous young adulthood, Tolstoy joined the army in 1851 during the Crimean War. At the end of the decade, he returned to the family estate. In 1862, he married Sonya Behrs, and together they had thirteen children. Tolstoy's writing brought him tremendous literary success, yet he fought depression most of his life. During his later years, Tolstoy became increasingly more religious and tried to follow the teachings of Jesus Christ by living a simple life.

As a boy, Tolstoy's brother had told him a legend about a magical green stick that could destroy evil in men's hearts. The stick was said to be buried in a spot in a nearby forest. At his death, Tolstoy asked to buried near that spot.

repeated his questions. The hermit again gave no answer, but

20 rose, stretched out his hand for the spade, and said:

"Now rest awhile—and let me work a bit."

But the King did not give him the spade, and continued to dig. One hour passed, and another. The sun began to sink behind the trees, and the King at last stuck the spade into the

25 ground, and said:

"I came to you, wise man, for an answer to my questions. If you can give me none, tell me so, and I will return home."

"Here comes someone running," said the hermit, "let us see who it is."

30 The King turned round, and saw a bearded man come running out of the wood. The man held his hands pressed against his stomach, and blood was flowing from under them. When he reached the King, he fell fainting on the ground moaning feebly. The King and the hermit unfastened the

35 man's clothing. There was a large wound in his stomach. The King washed it as best he could, and bandaged it with his handkerchief and with a towel the hermit had . . . So the King, with the hermit's help, carried the wounded man into the hut and laid him on the bed. Lying on the bed the man closed his

40 eyes and was quiet; but the King was so tired with his walk and with the work he had done, that he crouched down on the threshold, and also fell asleep. . .

"Forgive me!" said the bearded man in a weak voice, when he saw that the King was awake and was looking at him.

45 "I do not know you, and have nothing to forgive you for," said the King.

"You do not know me, but I know you. I am that enemy of yours who swore to revenge himself on you, because you

My Thoughts
The King thinks the hermit is wise but is frustrated because he won't answer the King's questions.
The King sees the stranger as a man in need.

executed his brother and seized his property. I knew you had
50 gone alone to see the hermit, and I resolved to kill you on
your way back. But the day passed and you did not return.
So I came out from my ambush to find you, and I came upon
your bodyguard, and they recognized me, and wounded me. I
escaped from them, but should have bled to death had you not
55 dressed my wound. I wished to kill you, and you have saved my
life. Now, if I live, and if you wish it, I will serve you as your most
faithful slave, and will bid my sons do the same. Forgive me!"

The King was very glad to have made peace with his enemy
so easily, and to have gained him for a friend . . .
60 Having taken leave of the wounded man, the King went
out into the porch and looked around for the hermit. Before
going away he wished once more to beg an answer to the
questions he had put. The hermit was outside, on his knees,
sowing seeds in the beds that had been dug the day before.
65 The King approached him, and said:

"For the last time, I pray you to answer my questions, wise
man."

"You have already been answered!" said the hermit, still
crouching on his thin legs, and looking up at the King, who
70 stood before him.

"How answered? What do you mean?" asked the King.

"Do you not see," replied the hermit. "If you had not
pitied my weakness yesterday, and had not dug those beds for
me, but had gone your way, that man would have attacked
75 you, and you would have repented of not having stayed with
me. So the most important time was when you were digging
the beds; and I was the most important man; and to do me
good was your most important business. Afterwards when that

My Thoughts
The man hated the King, but changed his mind after the King saved his life.
The King views the man as a friend.

Tech-Connect Suggestion: Students can view black-and-white movie footage of Tolstoy on his eightieth birthday, strolling, riding a horse in the countryside, driving in a carriage, and meeting family at a train stop. The vintage pictures also provide glimpses of Russia in 1908, a fitting backdrop to the images of Tolstoy. Go to www.openculture.com/2014/05/vintage-footage-of-leo-tolstoy.html or go to openculture.com and search for Tolstoy footage.

Chapter 2 *(continued)*

Lesson Support

FIRST RESPONSE: KEY IDEAS AND DETAILS

Invite students to share their First Response answers. Encourage them to revisit this preliminary response after a second reading.

Focus on Analyzing Plot and Conflict:

Answers to Action/Reaction Chart:

See answers on Student Book insert page to the right.

Gr7Ch2Read1.pptx

Tech-Connect: To help your students practice following oral instructions, explain how to post their first response to your class website or to Twitter. Another option is to have students turn to another student and explain how to do this.

---

man ran to us, the most important time was when you were

80 attending to him, for if you had not bound up his wounds he would have died without having made peace with you. So he was the most important man, and what you did for him was your most important business. Remember then: there is only one time that is important—Now! It is the most important time

85 because it is the only time when we have any power. The most necessary man is he with whom you are, for no man knows whether he will ever have dealings with anyone else: and the most important affair is, to do him good, because for that purpose alone was man sent into this life!"

FIRST RESPONSE: KEY IDEAS AND DETAILS

What is the story mainly about? What further questions do you have after reading? Write your answers and questions in your response journal. Share your answer with a partner.

Post your response on your class website, according to your teacher's instructions, or text or tweet it to your teacher.

Focus on Analyzing Plot and Conflict

Stories have different elements, including character, plot, conflict, and setting. These story elements work together to create the central idea, or in literature, the theme. Plot is often a series of actions and reactions. One event causes a second event, which results in another event and on it goes.

Fill in the following graphic organizer with the king and hermit's actions and reactions during the story. The first action is done for you.

King's Action/Reaction	Hermit's Action/Reaction
1. The king asks the hermit three questions.	2. The hermit says nothing and continues digging.
3. The king offers to dig for the hermit so he can rest.	4. The hermit accepts.
5. The king asks the questions again.	6. The hermit does not answer.

34   Chapter 2 • Unit 1   ©Perfection Learning® • No Reproduction Permitted

---

ELL Support: Focus on Analyzing Plot and Conflict To assist students in completing the conflict chart, place them in multilevel pairs or small groups and answer the following questions: What is the king's first problem? How is this a conflict with himself? What problem does the hermit cause for the king? What is the problem between the wounded man and the king?

Students can refer to their comic strip versions of the story created during the First Read (p. 31) to find the scene that answers these questions. Use the following sentence frames as they respond:

- The king wants to know . . . .
- This is a problem for him because . . . .
- The hermit makes a problem for the king. The hermit . . . .
- The wounded man has a problem with the king. The wounded man . . . .

34   Grade 7 • Chapter 2   Connections • © Perfection Learning®

King's Action/Reaction	Hermit's Action/Reaction
7. The king asks once more.	8. The hermit says he sees a man running toward them.
9. The king helps the wounded man who reveals that he is the king's enemy. The king asks his questions again.	10. The hermit tells the king the important time is now, the important person is the one you are with, and the important matter is being good to that person.

Conflict is important to a story because it moves the plot forward and adds suspense to the story. To understand conflict in a story, ask: What is the character(s) struggling with? Many times there is more than one conflict.

CONNECT TO ESSENTIAL QUESTION

Is seeking revenge a justified action?

Conflicts in the story	Type of conflict (person v. person, person v. self, person v. nature)	Resolution
1. The king is struggling with how to know what is the right thing to do.	(person vs. self)	The king learns that the right thing is to be present in the current moment and to show kindness to the people he is with.
2. He struggles with the hermit not telling him what the right thing is.	(person vs. person)	The hermit finally tells the king why he didn't tell him the answers; the hermit wanted the king to experience the answers for himself.
3. A secondary conflict is the struggle between the king and his enemy.	(person vs. person)	Because the king saves the life of the man who is his enemy, the man's attitude is changed and the men are reconciled.

Answers to Action/Reaction Chart:

See answers on Student Book insert page to the left.

Chapter 2 *(continued)*

Lesson Support

Speak and Listen: Encourage students to reread the hermit's final words to the king, which help to explain how the conflicts and resolutions of the story interact.

Reflect: Ask students: Was the king wise to go to the hermit for advice? Why or why not? What might the author be suggesting about whom to choose for advice? *The author may be suggesting that the best advisors are impartial and altruistic, not looking for an advantage for themselves.*

Tech-Connect Suggestion: For the Second Read, have students listen to an online audiobook of the story. Several can be found on YouTube.

Second Read: Identifying Theme

Before Reading: Use the following strategies to conduct a teacher-led interactive read aloud:

- Before reading, access background knowledge by asking students to describe a person in their lives who, like the Hermit, is good at helping them answer difficult questions.

- During reading, display the text and read it aloud. Model annotating the text as described under the objective on page 36.

- After reading, discuss the following questions in a think-pair-share.

After Reading: Use the following questions to check comprehension.

Text-Based Discussion Questions

1. In what way is "The Three Questions" like a fable? *It is brief; the plot is simple; it includes a limited number of characters; it could take place "anywhere"; it conveys a lesson, message, or moral.*

2. What words best describe the story's style? *simple, minimal, plain*

3. What is the effect of this simple style? *The style makes the reader focus on the meaning and the message of the story.*

Extend the discussion by asking students if the story could also be considered a parable or an allegory.

Speak and Listen Share your answers to the conflict chart with a partner. Then answer the following question:

How do the different conflicts interact? For example, how does the resolution of the king's conflict with his enemy impact the resolution of the other conflicts in the story? How does the conflict create suspense?

> **REFLECT**
> _____
> When you need advice, to whom do you go?

Second Read: Identifying Theme

Read the story a second time or listen as your teacher reads it aloud.

Objective: Think about how the plot reveals the theme. Underline lines from the text that reveal the theme. Write two or three questions you have in the My Thoughts column.

Focus on Identifying Theme

Identifying theme leads to a deeper understanding of literature. Study the following explanation of a theme.

What is theme?
Theme
• is the central idea of a story, poem, or other piece of writing.
• is stated as a sentence that expresses a general, universal truth explored by the author.
• is usually inferred rather than directly stated.
Theme is NOT
• the topic. Examples: love, friendship, war.
• a summary of what happens.
• the purpose.
• the moral.
• the conflict or problem.

Use these steps to determine theme:
1. Summarize the plot, paraphrasing the events in logical order. Write a short description of the events in the story.
2. Identify the conflicts in the story, including the central problem or obstacle the main character is trying to overcome. How do the conflicts resolve?
3. Consider how the main character changes. The theme is often revealed through changes in the main character. Consider what lesson the main character learned or how his or her thinking about life changed.
4. Look for repeated ideas throughout the passage.

Remember, all of the above must be supported by evidence from the text. Longer stories, poems, and novels may have more than one theme.

ELL Support: Second Read Support students' fluency and listening development by having them listen and follow along to the story read aloud on YouTube: https://youtu.be/cxA4-2ylqgc

Focus on Identifying Theme Place students in multilevel pairs or small groups. Remind students to use their completed summary and conflict charts as they respond to items 1 and 2 on p. 36. Provide the following questions and sentence frames for students to respond to items 3 and 4:

3. How does the king change? What is he like at the beginning of the story? What is he like at the end? What lesson does the king learn?

- At the beginning of the story, the king . . . .
- At the end of the story, the king . . . .
- The king learns . . . .

Fill in the chart below to help you identify the theme in the passage. Some sentence starters are included for you.

Steps to finding theme	Your response
1. Summarize the plot. Write a short description of the events in the story from beginning to end.	See sidebar to the right.
2. Identify the conflicts. (See your answers to the First Read.) What central problem or obstacle is the king trying to overcome? How does the conflict resolve?	The king is trying to find answers to his three questions, but the hermit won't answer him. The hermit answers his questions using their experiences together to prove his message.
3. Does the king change or grow throughout the story?	Yes, the king learns through experience the answer to his questions and makes peace with his enemy.
4. What repeated words or ideas do you see?	The king asks the hermit four times to answer his questions; three times the hermit does not answer him. Finally, the hermit points out that the king's questions have already been answered.

Review your responses to 1–4 above. Then finish the following sentence:

The theme of "The Three Questions" is

Life is about being present in the current moment and caring for the people right next to you.

(Speak and Listen Share your theme statements with a partner. Are your statements similar or different? Respectfully explain reasons for your answer. Be open to changing your theme statement based upon your partner's evidence.

REFLECT

What questions related to right and wrong do you struggle with?

Answers to the Chart:

1. A king visits a hermit and asks him to answer three questions. The hermit does not answer, and the king takes over digging for the hermit, who is old and weak. A wounded man runs out of the woods and the king cares for him. When the wounded man wakes up, he reveals that he was going to kill the king. If the king had not stayed to help the hermit dig, the man would have killed the king. Instead, the king's men wounded the man. The man asks for the king's forgiveness. The events of the day reveal the hermit's answer to the king's questions: The right thing to do is to do good right now. The most important person is the person you are with in the current moment. This moment is the only thing we can be sure of.

2.–4. See answers on Student Book insert page to the left.

Gr7Ch2Read2.pptx

(Speak and Listen: Encourage students to read and paraphrase the final three sentences of the story before finalizing their theme statement.

4. What words and phrases are repeated in the story?

- . . . are words and phrases that are repeated in the story.

ELL Support: Speak and Listen Make a list of different story themes, such as love conquers all; power can corrupt; hope supports us through hardship; family is a comfort; follow your conscience; live in the moment. Then have students find the theme that fits "Three Questions." Use images, pantomime, and paraphrasing to help beginning students understand the themes. For example, draw a heart and write: *Love conquers all. = Love solves all problems.*

Chapter 2 *(continued)*

Lesson Support

Third Read: Understanding Point of View

Before Reading: Read the heading "Understanding Point of View" and the objective. Inform students that, in this case, "point of view" isn't referring to whether the story is being told by a first- or third-person narrator. In this case, "understanding point of view" means understanding a character's thoughts and feelings. Thus, during this read, students should look for evidence of what the characters seem to think and feel about each other. Tell students to pay attention not only to what the characters think and say but also to what they do and how they behave. For this read of the text, consider reading the text aloud and asking students to annotate as you read.

After Reading: Use the following questions to check comprehension.

Text-Based Discussion Questions

1. What does the narrator reveal directly about the king's thoughts and feelings? *The narrator does not give direct information about the king's thoughts or feelings.*

2. Based on the king's actions, what can you infer about him as a person and a leader? *Because he seeks the hermit's advice, the king is humble and conscientious. Because he helps the hermit, he is kind and not above manual labor. Also, the fact that he forgives his enemy indicates that he is good and doesn't seek revenge.*

3. Why might the author have used a narrator who does not comment on the king's thoughts and feelings? *Using this point of view causes the reader to experience the events along with the king. We have no idea how the king is feeling about the hermit's actions.*

Focus on Understanding Point of View:

Possible Answers to the Chart:

See answers on Student Book insert page to the right.

 Gr7Ch2Read3.pptx

Third Read: Understanding Point of View

Objective: Read through the story again. Think about how the characters view each other.

Focus on Understanding Point of View

In literature the term *point of view* can have multiple meanings.

First, point of view is the perspective from which a story or poem is told. The story in this chapter is told from a third-person point of view, so readers learn about the characters and events from a narrator outside the story.

The chart below identifies common points of view used in literature along with the related pronouns so you can tell which point of view is being used in a story or poem.

Point of view	Pronouns used
First person—narrator is a character in the story	*I, my, mine*
Second person	*you, your*
Third person limited—narrator is outside the story but only reveals the thoughts of a single character omniscient—narrator reveals the thoughts of multiple characters	*he, she, him, her, it, hers, they*

The second meaning of point of view refers to the opinion or perspective of a character in a story. Readers infer the characters' points of view based on what they say and do and how they respond to other characters in the story.

In the story in this chapter, the events and interactions revolve around the king and the hermit. Complete the graphic organizer below to analyze how the hermit views the king.

The hermit's speech or action(s)	What it shows about how the hermit feels about the king
Seeing the King, he greeted him and went on digging.	The hermit is polite but not intimidated or deferential toward the king.

The hermit's speech or action(s)	What it shows about how the hermit feels about the king
The hermit listened to the King, but answered nothing. He just spat on his hand and recommended digging.	The hermit is attentive but not ready to respond to the king.
"Thanks!" said the hermit, and, giving the spade to the King, he sat down on the ground.	The hermit is grateful for the king's help, but not submissive or flattering.
"Do you not see," replied the hermit. "If you had not pitied my weakness yesterday, and had not dug those beds for me, but had gone your way, that man would have attacked you, and you would have repented of not having stayed with me.	The hermit is respectful and supportive.

Speak and Listen Refer to your answers in the chart, and discuss the following questions with a partner:

- Does the hermit's view of the king change during the story?
- Why does the hermit finally answer the king's questions?

> **REFLECT**
>
> What response would you give to the king's questions?

Write Following your discussion, write a paragraph answering the questions above.

Language: Using Commas To Set Off Nonrestrictive Phrases and Clauses

Restrictive (or essential) phrases or clauses are necessary to understand the meaning of a sentence. They are not set off from the rest of the sentence by commas and often begin with the words *that* or *who*.

> The man who came running out of the trees with a large wound was the King's enemy.

continued on next page

Speak and Listen: Extend this activity by asking students if they think the hermit is a good teacher. Do they learn better when teachers give them answers or when they must search for and experience the answer themselves?

Write: Remind students that readers learn about characters from their words and their actions and from other characters' feelings toward them. Suggest that they keep this in mind as they write their paragraph.

ELL Support: Write Ask multilevel pairs or small groups to underline the correct response in the first sentence below and then complete the second sentence.

1. The king's view of the hermit [changes/does not change].

2. The hermit answers the king in the end because . . . .

Providing these types of example sentences will help Beginning students learn sentence structure.

Chapter 2 *(continued)*

Assessment

Language: Using Commas To Set Off Nonrestrictive Phrases and Clauses:

1. correct

2. correct

3. The ancient castle, which has never been found, might be a legend.

4. Rahul, who wants to be an archaeologist, wrote about the search for Camelot.

5. correct

 Gr7Ch2Language.pptx

Nonrestrictive (or nonessential) phrases or clauses can be taken out of the sentence without affecting its meaning. Nonrestrictive elements should be set off by commas. Read this sentence that has a nonrestrictive element set off by commas.

> The King, puzzled by the hermit's silence, kept digging with the spade.

A clause is nonrestrictive/nonessential if it can be removed from the sentence without changing the basic meaning of the sentence.

Here are some examples of sentences with restrictive and nonrestrictive elements.

> **Restrictive:** A story that was written about King Arthur won first prize.
>
> **Nonrestrictive:** King Arthur, whose adventures were many, may have actually lived during the Dark Ages.

> **Restrictive:** Early medieval monarchs were rulers who were responsible for their people's protection.
>
> **Nonrestrictive:** Early medieval monarchs, who came to power through various means, were responsible for their people's protection.

> **Restrictive:** The girl who played the part of Joan of Arc is Amir's sister.
>
> **Nonrestrictive:** Joan, who is reading a book about Robin Hood, enjoys legends.

Read the following sentences, inserting commas where appropriate. Write correct next to sentences that are correctly punctuated.

1. A hermit is a person who chooses to live alone.

2. In early Christian times a person who lived apart from society in order to focus on his/her devotion to God was a hermit.

3. The ancient castle which has never been found might be a legend.

4. Rahul who wants to be an archaeologist wrote about the search for Camelot

5. The grave discovered by the lost tourists did not contain the body of King Arthur.

Project-Based Assessments

Change the Point of View

The Three Questions is told from an outside narrator's point of view. Rewrite the story from another character's perspective,

---

ELL Support: Change the Point of View Have students form multilevel pairs or small groups. Provide the following sentence frames to use to retell the story from first-person point of view.

- I am . . . .
- I was . . . .
- Next, I . . . .
- Then, I . . . .
- After that, I . . . .
- Finally, I . . . .

using first-person point of view. Make sure the characters are true to their descriptions in the text. Before you begin, think about how the characters interact. Consider how they feel about the events in the story and each other. Follow these steps:

- Add a character's inner thoughts and feelings where appropriate.
- Make sure the main events of the story remain. Stay true to the characters' personalities and emotions. Think about what the king, the hermit, or the wounded man might be thinking when they interact with each other.
- Use the following rubric to guide your writing.

Use the following guidelines for your new point of view story.	
To receive the highest score (4.0), the story must meet all of these criteria.	Your story • is true to the plot, characters, and theme of the passage. • is clearly organized and easy to follow. • uses a variety of sentence types and lengths and has engaging and interesting writing. • contains specific words, creating details that draw the reader into the story. • uses correct grammar, spelling, and punctuation.

In groups of three or four, conduct a peer review of your paragraphs. Follow these steps.

Steps for Peer Review

1. Select a timekeeper. Stick to the time. Each writer gets five minutes.

2. One person begins by reading aloud his or her story while other group members listen.

3. Pause. The same reader reads the story aloud a second time. (Don't skip this step.)

4. The group members listen and write notes or comments.

5. The writer asks, "What part was most clear to you?" Each member responds. Writer jots notes on the draft.

6. The writer asks, "Was there any part that confused you?" Each member responds. Writer jots notes on the draft.

7. Go to the next member in the group and repeat steps 2-6.

As soon as possible after the peer review, make any necessary revisions. Make sure to use proper grammar, punctuation, and spelling.

Project-Based Assessments

Change the Point of View: Students might find it helpful to create a timeline of the story scenes and then try to imagine their character's thoughts and feelings in each scene of the story. Point out that using the first-person point of view requires putting themselves in their character's shoes. Students should be able to answer these questions: What does my character see and hear? What does he feel? What is he thinking (at each point in the story)?

Chapter 2 *(continued)*

Assessment

On Your Own: Integrating Ideas:

Activity 2: During a reading of *The Three Questions* by Jon J. Muth, ask students to comment upon the symbolism of the red kite and the black-and-white pandas. A video of the book is available at https://youtu.be/5pOIYGjjvRc or search YouTube for The Three Questions by Jon Muth.

On Your Own: Integrating Ideas

1. Read more of Leo Tolstoy's stories by searching for his name online at gutenberg.org.
2. Read a children's book *The Three Questions* by Jon J. Muth. Think about how the author transforms the story for the intended audience. You can also find a video of someone reading the book on YouTube.
3. Leo Tolstoy wrote, "Happy families are all alike; every unhappy family is unhappy in its own way." Do you agree or disagree? Go to ted.com and watch a TED talk by Robert Waldinger about a study on happiness done by Harvard researchers.

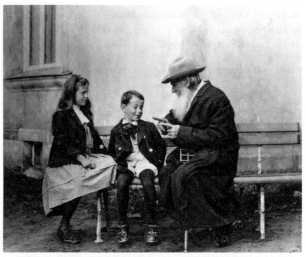

Leo Tolstoy telling a story to his grandchildren.

Connect to Testing

In this chapter, you analyzed story elements, such as conflict, plot, theme, and point of view, and how they interact. When you take assessments, you will be tested on these skills. Answer the following questions.

1. **Part A:** Which statement best expresses a theme of the text?

    A. Treat others well.

    B. Be alert at all times.

    C. Stay close to enemies.

    D. Seek forgiveness.

EXPLANATION

Part B: Support your answer to Part A with at least two details from the text.

Connect to Testing: This Connect to Testing section focuses on analyzing conflict, plot, theme, point of view, and how these element interact.

Encourage students to work in pairs to choose the correct answers to the questions and then to compare their answers with those of another pair of students. If there is disagreement, encourage the groups to try to reach a consensus as they discuss the reasons for their choices.

Answers to Connect to Testing Questions:

1. **Part B:** By helping the hermit dig and helping the wounded man, the king prevented his own death and changed the attitude of his enemy. This supports the theme in Choice A. It is also closely related to the hermit's answer to the king's questions: "the most important affair is, to do him good, because for that purpose alone was man sent into this life!" (DoK 2)

(continued)

Remediation: Connect to Testing Students might find it helpful to read the questions and responses with a partner before answering.

Assessment

Answers to Connect to Testing Questions:

2. C. The king's questions revolve around doing the "right thing at the right time" and deciding "what affairs are the most important." These questions do not show desperation (Choice B) or interest in his legacy (Choice D). Choice A is not far-fetched since the king wants to be sure about his decisions, and this concern could indicate that he doubts his judgment. However, Choice C is the best answer because his questions more clearly show desire to make wise decisions than doubt about his own judgment. (DoK 2)

3. C. A summary should accurately explain the central ideas of a text. Choice A is not true according to the details of the passage. Choice B is not entirely accurate because it is the injured man who learns about forgiveness. Choice D is true but it is a supporting detail and not a central idea. The best choice is C. (DoK 2)

4. **Part A:** The king forgave the wounded man for wanting to kill him in revenge for the death of his brother. (DoK 1)

   Part B: In paragraph 14, the wounded man says, "I wished to kill you, and you have saved my life." For this the man asked forgiveness. (DoK 2)

(continued)

---

2. The king's three questions in the passage reveal his

   A. doubt in his own judgment.

   B. desperation to change his destiny.

   C. desire to make wise decisions.

   D. determination to leave a strong legacy.

3. Which is the best summary of this passage?

   A. A king discovers the value of knowledge by interacting with a hermit.

   B. A king learns a lesson in forgiveness when he visits a hermit's house.

   C. A king learns a lesson about making wise decisions by visiting a hermit.

   D. A king discards his royal rank and helps a hermit with manual tasks.

4. **Part A:** In the excerpt, for what did the king forgive the wounded man?

   Part B: Explain the answer to Part A using evidence from the text.

ELL Support: Using Connect to Testing and Assessments See the *Connections* ELL Teacher Resource (p. 22) for ideas on adapting this section for ELLs.

5. Read this paragraph from the text. Then answer the question that follows.

"Do you not see," replied the hermit. "If you had not pitied my weakness yesterday, and had not dug those beds for me, but had gone your way, that man would have attacked you, and you would have repented of not having stayed with me. So the most important time was when you were digging the beds; and I was the most important man; and to do me good was your most important business. Afterwards when that man ran to us, the most important time was when you were attending to him, for if you had not bound up his wounds he would have died without having made peace with you. So he was the most important man, and what you did for him was your most important business. Remember then: there is only one time that is important—Now! It is the most important time because it is the only time when we have any power. The most necessary man is he with whom you are, for no man knows whether he will ever have dealings with anyone else: and the most important affair is, to do him good, because for that purpose alone was man sent into this life!"

What theme does the author convey in this paragraph? Cite two pieces of textual evidence to support your answer.

5. In this paragraph, the hermit reveals the answer to the king's three questions. The hermit explains, "there is only one time that is important—Now!" He also states, "The most necessary man is he with whom you are," and "the most important affair is, to do him good." The hermit's answers convey the author's message that the present moment, present company, and good works are most important. (DoK 2)

Chapter 3

Understanding Point of View Through Inferences

Zoo Complicated: Are Captive Animals Happy?
by Kathryn Hulick

Introduction

Chapter Goals: Have students read through the goals and mark any words that are unfamiliar. Discuss the meanings of any academic vocabulary within the goals that students marked as unfamiliar. Consider posting the Chapter Goals.

Preview Academic Vocabulary: Read and discuss the meanings of the academic vocabulary.

complex sentence: *a sentence containing an independent clause and one or more subordinate clauses.* An example of a <u>complex sentence</u> is *After the storm ended, the brown horse galloped across the field.*

compound-complex sentence: *a sentence containing at least two independent clauses and one or more subordinate clauses.* An example of a <u>compound-complex sentence</u> is *After the storm ended, the brown horse galloped across the field, and the dappled pony chased after him.*

compound sentence: *a sentence containing two or more independent clauses and no subordinate clauses.* An example of a <u>compound sentence</u> is *The brown horse galloped across the field, and the dappled pony chased after him.*

inference: *a conclusion based on background knowledge and ideas in the text.* From the author's writing, I drew an <u>inference</u> that she loves animals.

point of view: *opinion or perspective on a topic.* The author's <u>point of view</u> about zoos is that they are abusive to animals.

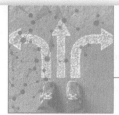

Chapter 3

Understanding Point of View Through Inferences

Preview Concepts

Think about the last time you visited a zoo. Then answer the following questions.

1. Describe the animal enclosures. Were they cages with bars or spaces that imitate the animals' native habitats?

2. Did the animals seem content and happy?

3. Have you ever been to a zoo or petting zoo where the animals did not seem healthy or happy? Describe your experience.

4. Based on your experiences, are zoos important and necessary in teaching the public about animals and protecting endangered animals from extinction, or should the animals be free to live out their lives in the wild?

Discuss your answers with a partner.

©Perfection Learning® • No Reproduction Permitted

CHAPTER GOALS

In this chapter you will

• make inferences.
• analyze the structure of a nonfiction text.
• evaluate an author's point of view.
• create a digital presentation or participate in a roundtable discussion.

PREVIEW ACADEMIC VOCABULARY

complex sentence

compound-complex sentence

compound sentence

inference

point of view

simple sentence

text structures

ELL Support: Academic Vocabulary Organize students into multilevel groups. Have them work together to use their own words to write definitions of the academic vocabulary concepts in their response journal. Additionally, ask students to write their own example of each concept to confirm understanding. Circulate and provide simple definitions or examples as models for students. Groups can compare their definitions and identify similarities and differences. See <u>Teaching Vocabulary in the ELL Teacher Resource (p. 18)</u> for ideas to use for teaching vocabulary throughout *Connections*.

Preview Concepts Have students work in multilevel pairs. Rewrite (or ask advanced students to rewrite) each of the questions on pages 46–47 so that they are appropriate for beginning and intermediate students. Also provide the following sentence frames.

1. Describe the places where the animals live. Are they cages? Or are they like places in the wild?

Connections • © Perfection Learning®

Making Connections

As you read the following passage, underline lines from the text that indicate the author's opinion about zoos.

. . . . in Denmark, the human/animal role of zoos is already being reversed. At Zootopia, BIG, the architecture firm, designed a 300-acre zoo without bars, fences or glass, which it said makes for the "best possible and freest possible environment for the animals." The first phase is scheduled to open in 2019. It's not a preserve—as those who want zoos shut down have called for— but it is an advancement in how people think of holding captive animals. Zootopia's layout would let animals roam land that encircles a doughnut-hole observation center. And though people can walk through tunnels and poke their heads up for a closer look, in this design it's not dangerous animals like the silverback gorilla that are caged, it's the humans.

  —"Do We Need Zoos?" by J. Weston Phippen, *The Atlantic*

1. What is the author's point of view about zoos? What evidence supports your inference?

2. How would people who are against zoos feel about Zootopia? Support your inferences with evidence from the text.

3. How would people who support zoos feel about Zootopia? Support your inferences with evidence from the text.

> MAKING CONNECTIONS
>
> In this chapter you will read an informational article about zoos and infer the author's point of view.

Discuss your answers with a partner. Summarize your discussion in your response journal.

simple sentence: *a sentence containing a single (or compound) subject and single (or compound) verb. An example of a* simple sentence *is The brown horse galloped across the field.*

text structures: *method of organizing information in a text; examples include cause and effect, problem and solution, compare and contrast, and chronological order. In the history book, the main* text structure *used by the author is chronological order.*

Gr7Ch3Vocabulary.pptx

Preview Concepts: After students read through the questions in the Preview Concepts activity, ask them to identify which questions call for an opinion or personal observation. Remind them that a person's opinion about a topic is his or her point of view. *Questions 2 and 3 require reflecting on personal experience to determine whether animals were content or unhappy; both questions involve point of view. Question 4 asks for their opinion/point of view.*

Making Connections:

> **Possible Answers to Questions:**
>
> 1. Students may have different opinions about the author's point of view. Some may say the phrase "it is an advancement in how people think of holding captive animals" indicates a negative attitude toward zoos. Others may point to the phrase "it's not dangerous animals like the silverback gorilla that are caged, it's the humans" and infer that the author is frustrated by those who elevate the "rights" of animals over humans. The final sentence has an ironic tone.
>
> 2. Those who oppose zoos would likely say Zootopia is not a preserve, which is what they favor, but they would likely agree that it is better than traditional zoos with bars and fences.
>
> 3. Those who favor zoos might say it is too open, but they would likely agree that it is better than preserves where it is much harder to observe the animals.

The animals live in . . . . They were . . . .

2. Were the animals happy?

The animals were/were not happy, because . . . .

3. Have you ever seen animals who were not happy or healthy? Tell what that was like.

The animals were not happy or healthy because . . . .

4. Do you think zoos are important? Do they teach people about helping animals? Or should animals live in the wild?

I think zoos are/are not important because . . . . Animals should . . . .

Chapter 3 *(continued)*

Lesson Support

Tech-Connect: The earliest zoos in the U.S. were founded around the middle of the nineteenth century. One of the first zoos—considered to be the first by some—was Central Park Zoo in New York City. Students can find a list of America's oldest zoos at www.worldatlas.com.

They can view a pictorial history of the Central Park Zoo at www.nycgovparks.org. Search for *history of zoos*.

First Read: Making Inferences

Before Reading: Read the introductory paragraph on page 48. Point out that "Zoo Complicated: Are Captive Animals Happy?" presents several questions related to the debate about keeping animals in captivity. However, instead of offering an opinion on the topic, the author presents examples of animals kept in captivity and allows the reader to decide his/her own opinion. This is a different method than typical argumentative essays in which the author clearly argues for a position. Ask students to think about which approach they prefer.

Confirm that students understand the objective. Model how to annotate the first paragraph. Ask students to read the text for the first read on their own.

Preview Vocabulary: Preview unfamiliar vocabulary to aid comprehension. Ask students to circle unfamiliar words as they complete the first read of a text. After the first read, guide students to determine the words' meanings using the context. Encourage students to support their responses with evidence. Have students confirm their initial definitions with a dictionary. Words that students might find difficult include:

species: *a group of plants and animals with common characteristics.* The botanists discovered a new species of orchid deep in the forest.

captivity: *being held or restrained in a confined area.* The lion was trapped and then held in captivity.

psychotherapist: *a trained counselor who treats mental or emotional problems.* The psychotherapist helped the man to see why he often fought with friends.

First Read: Making Inferences

In this article, the author details scenarios featuring zoo animals and asks readers to judge the morality of the actions of the people involved.

Objective: As you read, consider the question: Are the people's actions moral? Underline phrases or sentences in the text that describe how people treat animals. Write questions you have about the animals and their treatment in the My Thoughts column. Think about how the headers help you comprehend the ideas. Use them to make predications about the text.

—— First Read
- - - - Second Read
—— Third Read

excerpt
Zoo Complicated: Are Captive Animals Happy?
by Kathryn Hulick

My Thoughts

1 **Why Zoos?**

We keep animals in zoos or as pets for many reasons. ~~Sometimes~~ the motivation is to rescue an animal or a group of animals. Hawks that fly into windows, black bears that
5 roam through human towns, and harbor seals that swim into propellers often end up in zoos. Other times a species, such as the Asian elephant, is endangered in the wild. Zoo populations help ensure that these rare animals survive. We also keep animals in captivity because we enjoy seeing them
10 and spending time with them.

But do they enjoy spending time with us? Are they happy? Animals likely don't experience emotions the same way we do. But if you have a pet dog at home, you know the difference between a tail-wagging "happy" dog, and a tail-between-the-
15 legs "sad" dog. . . .

Conversations about the way animals should be treated are ongoing. Each of the following stories raises ethical questions. Read them and decide for yourself—did the people involved do the right thing?

Purpose: To introduce the question—should humans keep wild animals in captivity?

ELL Support: First Read Confirm that students understand the animals being discussed by displaying pictures from the Internet of hawks, black bears, harbor seals, Asian elephants, chimpanzees, and orcas. Have volunteers label the images and display them throughout the classroom for the duration of the chapter. Another option is to use a Frayer Model with pictures of each animal.

Students should read the passage in multilevel groups or pairs, pausing at the end of each paragraph to summarize the key ideas and details. Provide a Main Ideas and Supporting Details graphic organizer on page 61 of the *Connections* ELL Teacher Resource for students to use for taking notes. Once students have read and taken notes on the whole article, have them join with another group to share and refine their notes.

Lucy

20   Lucy liked drinking tea and looking in the mirror. But she wasn't human—she was a chimpanzee. Maurice and Jane Temerlin <u>raised Lucy just like a human baby.</u> The chimpanzee began her life with the Temerlins as the subject of research but
25 soon became a daughter. Maurice, who was a psychotherapist, wanted to know how human Lucy would become. <u>She learned sign language</u> and seemed to truly care for her adoptive parents. In his book, *Lucy: Growing Up Human*, he wrote: "If Jane is distressed, Lucy notices it immediately and attempts to comfort
30 her by putting an arm about her, grooming her, or kissing her."

    When Lucy grew up, though, life became difficult for the Temerlin family. An adult chimpanzee is about five times stronger than an adult human, and Lucy got into everything. What's more, she could not live a full life in a human home.
35 Eventually, the human "parents" decided to send Lucy to live with other chimps in the wild. They found a nature reserve in the Gambia, a country in western Africa. Janis Carter, a student who had been helping take care of Lucy, went along to help the chimp adjust.

40   <u>But Lucy didn't have a clue how to live in the wild, and her health suffered during the adjustment.</u> <u>Carter wound up staying with Lucy for years.</u> She ate ants and leaves to show Lucy what to do. She even lived in a cage so Lucy and the other chimpanzees couldn't reach the human objects that distracted
45 them from normal activities like seeking food and shelter.

    Eventually, Lucy did start finding her own food, and Carter moved a short distance away. One year, Lucy went missing. Carter returned from a visit to the United States to join the search. She and members of the reserve staff found Lucy's

My Thoughts

distressed: *troubled; worried.* The veterinarian is <u>distressed</u> with the condition of the horses' barn.

reserve: *a protected area for animals; a preserve.* The elephants roam freely in the <u>reserve</u>.

physiology: *the study of living things and how they function.* Scientists hope to understand the <u>physiology</u> of bats to help wild populations recover from the disease.

concede: *admit; acknowledge something as true.* We <u>concede</u> that our opinion about her illness was wrong and the doctor's diagnosis was correct.

After Reading: Use the following questions to check comprehension.

Text-Based Discussion Questions

1. What are three reasons for keeping animals in a zoo? Are any of these reasons better than others? Explain. *Injured animals can be protected in zoos; zoos can ensure the survival of endangered species; zoos provide an interesting entertainment for humans. Possible response: The first two reasons are the best, as they focus on what is good for the animals rather than what is fun for people.*

2. Why did the Temerlins decide to return Lucy to the wild? *Lucy was becoming too difficult and potentially too dangerous to live with a human family. In captivity, she was being denied the opportunity to live a full life as a chimpanzee.*

3. What made John Jett change his mind about the morality of keeping killer whales in captivity? *John Jett observed that killer whales in captivity had social and health problems; based on his observations, he decided that it is wrong to keep them captive.*

 Gr7Ch3Read1.pptx

Chapter 3 (continued)

Lesson Support

Background Information: Under pressure from animal rights activists that caused attendance at SeaWorld to plummet, the company announced in March 2016 that they would no longer breed killer whales in captivity and were phasing out their orca shows. SeaWorld's orcas will not be returned to the wild. Given that male orcas live up to 60 years and females as long as 100 years, killer whales will likely continue to be a part of SeaWorld for a long time.

50 body. The chimp had spent half her life in a human home and half in the wild.

Do you think it's right or wrong for people to raise chimps in their homes? What could the Temerlins have done differently?

55 . . .

Katina

Katina is a female killer whale, or orca, who lived in the ocean off the coast of Iceland until she was two years old. Now, she lives at SeaWorld in Orlando, Florida, where she
60 regularly performs for huge crowds of excited onlookers. She's easy to work with, knows many tricks, and has had seven calves. Her calf Kalina was the first healthy killer whale born in captivity. "[Katina] was one of the first animals I ever got in the water with," says John Jett, currently a marine mammal
65 scientist at Stetson University. For four years in the 1990s, he was a trainer at SeaWorld. Now, John Jett feels that it is morally wrong to keep killer whales in captivity. "It doesn't work out for the animals and it's never going to work out for the animals," he says. "I think you can put all the money into
70 bigger pools that you want but never recreate the ocean."

Jett explains that killer whales in captivity tend to experience social problems and health problems. For example, captive whales often chew on the concrete edges of their pools or the steel bars that separate different areas. As a result,
75 "most of their teeth are broken, missing, ground down, or drilled out," says Jett. The whales may also float near the top of the pool for long periods. As a result, they may end up with a sunburn or a flopped-over dorsal fin—a common sight on captive male killer whales. Wild whales' fins are almost always
80 straight.

My Thoughts

Purpose: To explain an example of keeping a chimp in captivity so the reader can evaluate the morality of the humans' treatment of an animal.

Of course, life in the wild isn't perfect, either. In fact, a whale in captivity now has about the same chance of surviving the year as a whale in the wild. "Survival of killer whales in captivity has increased over the past 30 years," says
85 Doug DeMaster, Science and Research Director of the Alaska Fisheries Science Center. In addition, research with captive whales has added to our knowledge about their physiology and life history. On several occasions, scientists have used this knowledge to aid wild killer whales in trouble.

90 Jett concedes that parks such as SeaWorld have done some good for killer whales. "We no longer fear them," he says. "People have come to appreciate the need to protect them." However, he feels that the time has come to stop keeping Katina and other whales captive.

95 What do you think? Have you been to a show at SeaWorld or a similar park? Is there any way for these parks to make life more comfortable for killer whales?

My Thoughts

_____
_____
_____
_____
_____
_____
_____
_____

Purpose: To explain the treatment of killer whales in parks so that readers can evaluate whether this is right or wrong.

FIRST RESPONSE: KEY IDEAS AND DETAILS

Based upon your first read of the article, is life in captivity better for wild animals? Support your conclusion with details from the text. Write your answer in your journal.

Focus on Making Inferences

Readers constantly make inferences as they read. An inference is a conclusion not directly stated in the text. It is based on ideas in the story and your own background knowledge. As you read the text, what did you infer about the relationship between captive animals and people? Fill in the chart below.

What the text says	Inference
1. *Maurice and Jane Temerlin raised Lucy just like a human baby.*	Humans can have strong emotional bonds with animals.

continued on next page

TECH-CONNECT

Post your response on your class website or other online site, according to your teacher's instructions.

FIRST RESPONSE: KEY IDEAS AND DETAILS

To make a good case for their own opinion, students should understand the arguments on both sides of the debate. A strong response will offer arguments in support of their own conclusion and also answer the arguments on the other side. The text contains evidence for both sides of the debate.

Focus on Making Inferences:

Ask students to always check that their inferences make sense. They should ask themselves: *Does information from the text back it up? Do the facts add up to this conclusion?*

Answers to Focus on Making Inferences:

See answers on Student Book insert page to the left.

 Gr7Ch3Read1.pptx

Chapter 3 *(continued)*

Lesson Support

▼ **Write:** Before students write their paragraphs, suggest that they reread their response in their journal to the question: *Is life in captivity better for wild animals?*

Reflect: Pets tend to be highly domesticated animals unlike captive chimpanzees or orcas.

What the text says	Inference
2. She [Lucy] learned sign language and seemed to truly care for her adoptive parents.	Chimps' intelligence and emotional connections are similar to those of humans.
3. What's more, she [Lucy] could not live a full life in a human home.	Lucy could not find a mate, have and raise a family of her own, explore the world outside of the Temerlin's home on her own, gather her own food, or have other experiences like wild chimpanzees.
4. Carter wound up staying with Lucy for years. She ate ants and leaves to show Lucy what to do.	Carter cared deeply for Lucy since she stayed with her for so long. Lucy needed help to increase her chances of survival.
5. She's [Katina] easy to work with, knows many tricks, and has had seven calves.	Katina made a good adjustment to life at SeaWorld.
6. Wild whales' fins are almost always straight.	The flopped-over fin of many captive male killer whales is likely a result of maladjustment to living in captivity. Captivity seems to have a negative effect on the health and even the ability of these animals to swim.

▼ **Write** Write a paragraph explaining how returning captive animals to the wild is both necessary and cruel. Refer to specific examples from the article to support your answers.

REFLECT

How does having a pet differ from keeping a wild animal such as a chimp or orca captive?

Remediation: Write Have students create a web with their inference in the middle and facts or other details that support this inference on circles radiating out from the center.

ELL Support: Write Have students form multilevel pairs or small groups to discuss their response before writing. Provide the following sentence frames for students to use when speaking and writing:

- Returning a captive animal to the wild is . . . .
- This example shows that . . . .
- One example that supports this view is . . . .
- Another example that supports this view is . . . .
- This example shows that . . . .
- So returning an animal to the wild is . . . .

Second Read: Understanding Structure and Purpose

Take turns reading the article with a partner. Partner 1 reads paragraph 1. Then partner 2 summarizes the paragraph. Switch roles for paragraph 2. Continue until you have read and summarized the entire passage.

Objective: Notice how the text is divided into three sections with headers. When you and your partner finish reading a section, work together to answer the question: What is the purpose of this section of the text? Write the purpose next to each section.

Focus on Understanding Structure and Purpose

In order to communicate ideas clearly and effectively, authors of nonfiction texts organize their ideas as logically as possible. Understanding text structure can help you be a better reader. Analyzing the structure an author uses to organize information can help you as a reader comprehend complex information. It can help you predict what an author will say next. Text structures also help you understand an author's purpose for writing.

Here are some common ways to structure text:

Description/List: lists or describes information about a topic, such as the amount of technology used in schools.

Cause and Effect: identifies a cause of something and describes its effects, such as the cause and effects of blue light from electronics on people's sleep patterns.

Problem and Solution: identifies a problem and details its solution(s), such as an endangered species and how to save it.

Compare and Contrast: compares and contrasts a topic, such as turtles versus tortoises.

Question/Answer: poses a question and then offers an answer or possible answers in response.

Sequential/Time Order: written in chronological order or a special sequence of events or steps to follow.

Claim/Reasons: makes a claim or takes a position and then explains reasons in support of the claim.

Focus on the first paragraph of the article reprinted on the next page. Underline words and transitions that help you infer the structure the author is using:

ELL Support: Understanding Structure and Purpose On the board create the list of text structures. Then use explanations, synonyms, pantomime, and sketches to explain each text structure. After you explain each text structure, draw an example or sketch next to it on the chart so students have a visual reminder of what the text structure is. Or use the Text Structures handouts in the ELL Teacher Resource (pp. 61–67). Note: explanation in Spanish can be found here: https://www.hoodriver.k12.or.us/cms/lib/OR01000849/Centricity/Domain/873/LA_res_TxtStruc_ORS_Module%20copy.pdf

---

Second Read: Understanding Structure and Purpose

Before Reading: Read the introductory remarks on page 53. With a student volunteer, model the process of reading aloud and summarizing the first two paragraphs. Then read the objective. Point out where each of the three sections of the text ends. Confirm that students understand the objective and that through discussion they must determine and write down the purpose of a section upon finishing it.

In lieu of having students read the passage with a partner, use the following strategies to conduct a teacher-led interactive read aloud:

- Before reading, access background knowledge by asking students to describe a time when they visited a zoo or aquarium. Did the animals seem content and happy? Did they think differently about their visit after reading the passage?

- During reading, display the text and read it aloud. Model annotating the text. Have students turn to a partner and summarize each section after you read it. (See the instructions under the objective on page 53.)

- After reading, discuss the following questions using a think-pair-share strategy.

After Reading: Use the following questions to check comprehension.

Text-Based Discussion Questions

1. In what way is the section called "Lucy" like a biography? *It tells about the life of one creature, an animal instead of a person. It describes important parts of Lucy's life. It begins with her early years and ends with her death.*

2. What is John Jett's point of view about keeping orcas in captivity? How does the author present his views? *He opposes keeping killer whales in captivity. The author presents Jett's views by explaining what Jett thinks and feels and by quoting him.*

Focus on Understanding Structure and Purpose: The header Why Zoos? and the word *reasons* are the most important clues to the structure. Students might also notice the transitional words *sometimes, other times,* and *also.*

Chapter 3 *(continued)*

Lesson Support

Answers to Questions:

1. Claim/Reasons

2. The list gives specific examples of people rescuing animals.

3. This paragraph provides a general discussion of the topic before presenting specific examples of keeping animals in captivity.

(continued)

 Gr7Ch3Read2.pptx

Connect to Essential Question: Ask students whether the Golden Rule (Treat others as you would have others treat you.) should be applied to the treatment of animals as well as people.

Why Zoos?

   We keep animals in zoos or as pets for many reasons. Sometimes the motivation is to rescue an animal or a group of animals. Hawks that fly into windows, black bears that roam through human towns, and harbor seals that swim into propellers often end up in zoos. Other times a species, such as the Asian elephant, is endangered in the wild. Zoo populations help ensure that these rare animals survive. We also keep animals in captivity because we enjoy seeing them and spending time with them.

1. Which text structure is the author using in this paragraph?

> **CONNECT TO ESSENTIAL QUESTION**
>
> Does the same morality for how to treat people apply to the treatment of animals? Why or why not?

2. What is the purpose of the list of animals contained in the third sentence?

3. Why does the author begin her entire article with this paragraph?

ELL Support: Speak and Listen Have students work in multilevel pairs or groups to discuss the questions and then write responses using the following sentence frames:

- The author is using . . . text structure in this paragraph. I know because . . . .

- The purpose of the list of animals in the third sentence is to . . . . (Or The author uses a list because she wants us to understand that . . . .)

- The author begins her article with this paragraph to . . . .

- The purpose of the section Why Zoos? is to . . . . (Or for further support: In this section, the author wants us to understand that . . . .)

- The purpose of the other two sections, Lucy and Katina, are to . . . . (Or for further support: In these sections, the author wants us to understand that . . . .)

Step back and consider the entire excerpt as a whole. How is the entire article structured? To answer this question think about the purpose of the first section as it relates to the rest of the article.

4. What is the purpose of the first section Why Zoos?

5. What is the purpose of the other two sections: Lucy and Katina?

REFLECT

How did domesticated animals become domesticated? Could the same process tame animals that are currently wild?

6. Overall, which text structure does the author use to present her ideas?

Speak and Listen With a partner, analyze the text structures used in the sections Lucy and Katina. Identify how each paragraph is organized and how each one relates to the purpose of that section.

Write Write a paragraph explaining the overall structure of the excerpt and how each section plays a role in the overall purpose.

TECH-CONNECT

Search online for information about Katina the orca. Post three facts about her on your class website.

4. The purpose of the first section is to introduce the topic: the morality of keeping animals captive.

5. The purpose of the other two sections is to give examples that highlight the issues involved in the passage's topic, the morality of keeping animals captive.

6. Overall, the author uses the structure of question and answer. The question is asked in the title: Are Captive Animals Happy?

Speak and Listen: While the "Lucy" section is clearly structured using sequential/time order, "Katina" has a claims/reasons structure that subtly makes an argument against keeping killer whales in captivity.

Write: Students may need help identifying the overall structure as question and answer. Point out that the title is a question. Ask them whether the passage answers that question.

Tech-Connect Suggestion: Students might be interested in learning about the Elephant Sanctuary in Tennessee and the stories behind the elephants that live there now: https://elephants.com/.

• Overall, the author uses the . . . text structure to present her ideas.

ELL Support: Write Have students work in multilevel pairs or small groups to discuss and then write about the structure of the sections. Provide the following sentence frames:

• The section on Lucy uses the text structure . . . .

• The purpose of this section is to . . . . (In this section, the author wants us to understand that . . . .)

• This structure relates to the purpose by . . . . (The structure shows the author's purpose by . . . .)

• The section on Katina uses the text structure . . . .

• The purpose of this section is to . . . . (In this section, the author wants us to understand that . . . .)

• This structure relates to the purpose by . . . . (The structure shows the author's purpose by . . . .)

Chapter 3 *(continued)*

Lesson Support

Third Read: Determining Point of View

Before Reading: Explain that during this read, students will focus on how the author conveys his opinion, or point of view, about keeping animals in captivity. Explain that as they note the author's point of view, they will underline specific words, phrases, and details that suggest or express his opinion. Help students understand how authors choose words to convey point of view by reviewing the difference between connotation and denotation, and that the connotation of a word can be positive, negative, or neutral.

After Reading: Use the following questions to check comprehension.

Text-Based Discussion Questions

1. What does the ending of the section on Lucy suggest about the author's view of what happened? *The section ends with Lucy's death and the comment: "What could the Temerlins have done differently?" This suggests that the author viewed negatively the Temerlins' decision to keep Lucy in their home.*

2. What does the author's choice of John Jett as the main "character" in the section on Katina suggest about the author's view about the issue of keeping killer whales captive? Explain. *John Jett became an opponent of keeping killer whales captive after working at SeaWorld. The fact that the author used somebody who had gone through such a change suggests that she, too, opposes keeping killer whales captive.*

Focus on Point of View: Before students fill in the chart, take a poll about students' impression of the author's view concerning the morality of keeping animals captive. Does the author think animal captivity is a good option—or not?

> **Answers to Determining an Author's Point of View:**
>
> See answers on the Student Book insert page to the right.

 Gr7Ch3Read3.pptx

Third Read: Determining Point of View

Rhetoric is the art of effective persuasive writing and speaking. To convince readers, writer use rhetorical devices including words with positive and negative connotations.

Objective: As you read the article again, consider what the author thinks about keeping animals in captivity. Underline details that suggest the author's point of view, or opinion on the topic.

Focus on Point of View

This passage describes two stories of animals in captivity and then poses questions about the morality of the people's actions. Even though the author does not directly answer the questions about whether keeping animals captive is right or wrong, the author subtly reveals an opinion about the issue. Readers can read between the lines in order to infer whether her point of view is positive, negative, or neutral.

Infer the author's point of view by considering the following:
- the details the author includes
- the details the author leaves out
- words the author chooses to use and their connotations, or the emotions they suggest

Fill in the columns in the following chart.

> **CONNECT TO ESSENTIAL QUESTION**
>
> Some animal shelters have a no-kill policy. Should all shelters have this policy?

Determining an Author's Point of View			
The writer mostly includes details about two animals' situations and their caretakers.	The writer uses these words to describe Lucy: like a human baby, became a daughter, truly care, attempts to comfort	The writer uses these words to describe life in captivity for Lucy: got into everything, could not live a full life in a human home	The writer doesn't say anything about Lucy's cause of death, why Katina was taken from the wild. The writer also does not provide any specific examples of wild animals rescued from the wild to save or improve their lives.
	The writer uses these words to describe Katina: regularly performs, is easy to work with, knows many tricks, has seven calves	The writer uses these words to describe life in captivity for Katina and other orcas: never recreate the ocean, social problems, health problems, broken and damaged teeth, flopped-over fin	

©Perfection Learning® • No Reproduction Permitted

ELL Support: Third Read Confirm that students understand that point of view means the author's overall thoughts and feelings on a topic. Provide the synonym *opinion.* Also, make sure students understand the terms *positive, negative,* and *neutral.* You can use symbols like *plus* and *minus.* You can also use gestures and facial expressions like smiling with thumbs up (positive), frowning with thumbs down (negative), palms down twisting back and forth with a neutral face (neutral). Finally, give some examples of point of view. Say: *I love basketball. I love watching it. I love playing it. I think it's the best sport. My point of view on basketball is very positive. What is your point of view of basketball?* Place students in multilevel pairs or groups to talk about their points of view on basketball or another topic of their choice. Encourage them to use the following sentence frame to respond: My point of view on . . . is positive/negative/neutral. For more advanced students: My point of view on . . . is positive/negative/neutral because . . . .

Connections • © Perfection Learning®

Some examples from the passage are	This makes me think that the writer believes	This makes me think that the writer believes	This makes me think that the writer believes
The Temerlins raised Lucy just like a human baby. Katina at SeaWorld	that the animals are important.	living in captivity is not a favorable condition for wild animals.	most animals in captivity are there for humans to enjoy rather than to rescue them.

Based upon my answers, the author's point of view is

mostly negative toward keeping animals in captivity because people keep animals in captivity for mainly selfish reasons.

Speak and Listen With a partner, discuss the following:
- If Kathryn Hulick were debating the topic of keeping animals in captivity, she would be on the side of . . . .
- I think this because . . . .

Language: Sentence Structure

Sentences in English have four main structures.

Simple: A simple sentence has only one independent clause. An independent clause can stand on its own as a complete thought. In the following examples, independent clauses are underlined.

Example: We keep animals in zoos or as pets for many reasons.

Compound: A compound sentence has at least **two** independent clauses. The clauses are joined by a comma and coordinating conjunction (*and, but, for, nor, or, yet*) or by a semicolon.

Example: An adult chimpanzee is about five times stronger than an adult human, and Lucy got into everything.

Complex: A complex sentence has at least one independent clause and at least one dependent clause. A dependent clause contains a subject and verb but does not express a complete thought. It can't stand on its own. In the following examples, dependent clauses are in (parentheses).

Example: We also keep animals in captivity (because we enjoy seeing them and spending time with them.)

continued on next page

ELL Support: Language Present the following paragraph-by-paragraph summary of the "Lucy" section. Ask students what kind of sentences these are. *(simple sentences)* Have multilevel partners work together to combine the sentences into compound or complex sentences.

1. The Temerlins took Lucy into their home. She was like a daughter.

2. Lucy was difficult to handle as an adult. The Temerlins had to send her to a reserve.

3. Janis Carter stayed with Lucy. She wanted to help Lucy adjust to the wild.

4. Lucy had problems. Janis showed her skills for the wild.

5. Lucy finally stayed at the reserve on her own. She only survived for a while.

Chapter 3 *(continued)*

Lesson Support

Language: Sentence Structure:

1. But Lucy didn't have a clue how to live in the wild, and her health suffered during the adjustment. *(compound sentence)*

2. Carter wound up staying with Lucy for years. *(simple sentence)*

3. She ate ants and leaves to show Lucy what to do. *(simple sentence)*

4. She even lived in a cage so Lucy and the other chimpanzees couldn't reach the human objects that distracted them from normal activities like seeking food and shelter. *(complex sentence)*

Tech-Connect Suggestion: In 2017, Ringling Brothers closed their circus shows, a casualty of protests over the treatment of animals in their acts. Invite students to research the history of the Ringling Brothers circuses and how protests have grown in recent years.

▼**Write:** Remind students that they verbally summarized the passage at the beginning of the second read. They might follow the same procedure and then combine some sentences to create compound, complex, or compound-complex sentences.

 Gr7Ch3Language.pptx

Compound-Complex: A compound-complex sentence has at least two independent clauses and at least one dependent clause.

> Example: The whales may also float near the top of the pool for long periods; as a result, they may end up with a sunburn or a flopped-over dorsal fin, (which is a common sight on captive male killer whales.)

Identify and label each of the sentences in the following paragraph. Notice how using a variety of sentence types makes the writing interesting and helps to emphasize key ideas and de-emphasize lesser ideas.

> But Lucy didn't have a clue how to live in the wild, and her health suffered during the adjustment. Carter wound up staying with Lucy for years. She ate ants and leaves to show Lucy what to do. She even lived in a cage so Lucy and the other chimpanzees couldn't reach the human objects that distracted them from normal activities like seeking food and shelter.

▼**Write** Write a paragraph summarizing the article from the chapter. Use all four sentence types in your writing.

Project-Based Assessments

Digital Presentation

Conduct research and create a digital presentation about an animal rights issue. First, search online using terms such as *animal rights*. The website for the Humane Society of the United States may be helpful in finding topic ideas: www.humanesociety.org. Develop a list of issues and choose one you would like to research.

Next, find reliable sources for your information. Remember, websites that end in *.edu, .gov,* or *.org* usually have more reliable information than sites with many contributors such as Wikipedia. Check the site's About tab to find out if it is maintained by a reliable source, such as a university, government agency, research facility, or other reputable organization.

Gather the following information for your presentation:

- Name and description of the issue
- Cause of the issue
- What and how animals are affected
- Actions taken in the past to address the issue
- Potential solutions to the issue
- Three or more sources used for the project: name of article, website, date

> **TECH-CONNECT**
>
> Download your presentation to a flash drive or email it to yourself so that you can easily access it at school. Be sure to open your files before your presentation, especially when not using your own computer.

ELL Support: Project-Based Assessments An optional project for ELLs is to create a trifold brochure about an animal rights issue using a word processing or design program.

1. Gather the following information for your brochure:

- Name and description of the issue
- Cause of the issue
- What and how animals are affected
- What people and governments have already done to help
- What people and governments should do to help
- Three or more sources used for the project: name of article, website, date

2. Design a brochure with pictures and words. Include a list of sources on the back.

Finally, create an interesting and well-organized computer presentation. Each slide should have both an image or video and text. Read the rubric carefully so you know the expectations of the presentation from the beginning. Practice what you will say with each slide before presenting to the class. If working with a partner(s), decide in advance who will share which slides.

Use the following guidelines for your digital presentation.	
To receive the highest score, the project must meet all of these criteria.	**Your digital presentation** • uses multimedia in a professional way and is appealing both visually and aurally (i.e., to the eye and ear). • contains images or videos that clearly demonstrate understanding of the animal rights issue, its causes and effects, the animals affected, and its potential solutions. • is appropriate for the audience. • demonstrates that you clearly understand the issue. • demonstrates confidence, eye contact, and proper volume. • uses correct grammar, usage, punctuation, and spelling.

Roundtable Discussion

Participate in a roundtable discussion on the following question as posed by the author in the text:

> Did the people in the stories do the right thing by keeping Lucy and Katina in captivity? Why or why not?

In a roundtable discussion all students are equal and everyone participates. Arrange your seats in a circle so that all participants can see one another. The teacher or a discussion leader may sit in the middle. Come to the discussion with an open mind and be prepared for a challenge! You will be evaluated on the following:

Expectations for Discussion	
Listening	**Speaking**
Listen respectfully.	Speak at least two times.
Look at speaker.	Refer to the text to support conclusions.
Follow text references.	Ask questions.
Take notes on what the speaker is saying.	Offer reasons to support your point of view.
Write down follow-up questions.	Be open to other students' comments and questions.

Before the discussion, find two other sources that will help you answer the question. Make a copy or print out the sources. Highlight information that can be used as evidence to support your answer to the discussion question.

Project-Based Assessments

Digital Presentation: Challenge students to use appropriate digital presentation format. Keep text to a minimum. Use bulleted points for easy understanding. Visual aids should enhance and not distract from the text. Encourage students to develop an opening slide that hooks the audience.

Roundtable Discussion: Review and display the expectations for a roundtable discussion. Tell students that they will be rating their own performance using these expectations. If students are participating in such a discussion for the first time, you might want to have a few students model procedures.

Roundtable Discussion Make sure students with limited English language proficiency feel included in the discussion. Provide the following sentence frames for students to use in the discussion:

- I think the people in the story about Lucy did/did not do the right thing because . . . .

- I think the people in the story about Katina did/did not do the right thing because . . . .

Allow time for students to practice their sentences with you or in multilevel pairs before beginning the discussion. Explain that students should monitor (check on) themselves during the discussion and if they need help understanding or participating, they should raise their hand and you or a more advanced student will assist them with paraphrases or sentence frames.

Chapter 3 *(continued)*

Assessment

On Your Own: Integrating Ideas:

Activity 2: Students with an interest in animal emotions could do additional research, using activity 2 as a starting point. Their findings could lead to a classroom debate or discussion of the issue.

Activity 3: Invite volunteers to review *Blackfish*. Encourage them to address whether the director makes a strong case against keeping killer whales in captivity.

Additional Activity: Have students read a news article about SeaWorld's change of policy on keeping killer whales in captivity. Invite volunteers to report on their findings.

Instructions for a Roundtable Discussion

1. The discussion leader (teacher or student) begins by asking the question:

> Did the people in the stories in the text do the right thing by keeping Lucy and Katina in captivity? Why or why not?

2. Allow each member the chance to reply to the question. Members should refer to the chapter text and other research they have conducted in their response.
3. Take notes on comments you disagree with or you have questions about. Write down what was said and who said it.
4. Go around the circle again and allow everyone to ask a follow-up question or make a comment. Questions and comments should be directed to the person who made the original comment. Try phrasing your responses in this way:
   - What did you mean by . . . . ?
   - Can you explain . . . . ?
   - I agree/disagree with . . . . because . . . .
5. Continue the discussion by having everyone respond to the following question, using steps 2–4 above.

> Should humans ever keep wild animals in captivity? Why or why not?

On Your Own: Integrating Ideas

1. Go to Kathryn Hulick's website, kathrynhulick.com, and read the brief article about animal ethics to learn about her viewpoint.
2. In "Zoo Complicated," Hulick claims, "Animals likely don't experience emotions the same way we do." Explore how self-aware animals are by reading her article, "Do Dogs Have a Sense of Self?" Find the article at www.sciencenewsforstudents.org.
3. Watch *Blackfish* (PG-13), a documentary about killer whales in captivity. Then, read SeaWorld's response to the claims in the movie at seaworldcares.com.
4. Conduct research about Jane Goodall, a naturalist who made revolutionary discoveries about chimpanzees and their behavior.

Connect to Testing

In this chapter, you practiced the skills of making inferences, analyzing structure and purpose, and identifying point of view. When you take assessments, you will be tested on these skills. Answer the following questions.

1. **Part A:** Which inference is best supported by the text?

   A. Wild chimpanzees were confused by Lucy's behavior.

   B. The Temerlins' relationship with Lucy was that of scientist and research subject.

   C. The expectation for Lucy's return to the wild was that she would adjust naturally.

   D. The decision to send Lucy to the nature reserve was difficult for the Temerlins.

   Part B: Cite at least two details from the text to support your inference.

2. **Part A:** The author includes the stories about Lucy and Katina in order to

   A. provide illustrations of how animals have been mistreated by humans.

   B. describe two success stories about animals that were rescued from the wild.

   C. provide examples of what can happen when humans keep wild animals captive.

   D. give reasons why people keep animals in zoos.

   Part B: Which of the following lines from the text provides the best evidence to support the answer to Part A?

   A. *Sometimes the motivation is to rescue an animal or a group of animals.*

   B. *We also keep animals in captivity because we enjoy seeing them and spending time with them.*

   C. *Animals likely don't experience emotions the same way we do.*

   D. *Read them and decide for yourself—did the people involved do the right thing?*

continued on next page

Connect to Testing: This Connect to Testing section focuses on making inferences, analyzing structure and purpose, and identifying point of view.

Encourage students to work in pairs to choose the correct answers to the questions and then to compare their answers with those of another pair of students. If there is disagreement, encourage the groups to try to reach a consensus as they discuss the reasons for their choices.

Answers to Connect to Testing Questions:

1. **Part A:** D. (DoK 2)
   Part B: The Temerlins most likely felt sending Lucy to the nature reserve was a difficult decision because she "began her life with the Temerlins as the subject of research but soon became a daughter." Their feelings toward her changed from a clinical point of view to a parental one. The Temerlins "raised Lucy just like a human baby," so sending her away would have been difficult. (DoK 2)

2. **Part A:** C. (DoK 3)
   Part B: D. Choice D clearly explains that the author is providing the stories as examples for the reader to analyze and then decide if the animals were treated humanely. (DoK 2)

(continued)

ELL Support: Using Connect to Testing and Assessments See the *Connections* ELL Teacher Resource (p. 22) for ideas on adapting this section for ELLs.

Chapter 3 *(continued)*

Assessment

Answers to Connect to Testing Questions:

3. The author holds a negative view about keeping animals in captivity. Hulick details how Lucy, a chimpanzee, had difficulty transitioning into the wild after growing up "just like a human baby." Hulick also describes Katina, a killer whale, and her situation by including a former SeaWorld trainer's negative perspective toward killer whale captivity. Hulick writes, "John Jett feels that it is morally wrong to keep killer whales in captivity." Although the article's tone is matter of fact, the author's choice of animal captivity scenarios and including John Jett's perspective suggest a negative point of view on the topic. (DoK 2)

4. **Part A:** C. (DoK 1)
   Part B: D. (DoK 2)

3. Explain how the author's point of view about animals in captivity is expressed in the text. Include evidence from the text to support your points.

4. Read this sentence from the text. Then answer the question that follows.

   In fact, a whale in <u>captivity</u> now has about the same chance of surviving the year as a whale in the wild.

   Part A: What is the meaning of *captivity* as it is used in the text?

   A. The state of being held as a slave

   B. The state of being denied food

   C. The state of being confined

   D. The state of being alive

   Part B: Which of the following phrases from the text best helps the reader understand the meaning of the word *captivity?*

   A. *In fact, a whale*

   B. *About the same chance*

   C. *Of surviving the year*

   D. *As a whale in the wild*

5. Read the following paragraph and then answer the questions that follow.

Lucy liked drinking tea and looking in the mirror. But she wasn't human—she was a chimpanzee. Maurice and Jane Temerlin raised Lucy just like a human baby. The chimpanzee began her life with the Temerlins as the subject of research but soon became a daughter. Maurice, who was a psychotherapist, wanted to know how human Lucy would become. She learned sign language and seemed to truly care for her adoptive parents. In his book, *Lucy: Growing Up Human*, he wrote: "If Jane is distressed, Lucy notices it immediately and attempts to comfort her by putting an arm about her, grooming her, or kissing her."

Part A: Which of the following can be inferred from this paragraph?

A. Lucy was raised by a family with children.
B. Lucy exhibited many human behaviors.
C. Lucy became attached to her adopted parents gradually.
D. Lucy failed as a research subject.

Part B: Cite two pieces of textual evidence to support your answer.

5. **Part A:** B. (DoK 2)
Part B: The paragraph conveys the idea that Lucy displayed human behaviors. For example, two such behaviors include "drinking tea and looking in the mirror." Lucy also "learned sign language" and would comfort Jane Temerlin "by putting an arm about her, grooming her, or kissing her." All of these behaviors are human-like. (DoK 2)

Chapter **4**

Determining Characters' Points of View

The Doll's House
by Katherine Mansfield

Introduction

Chapter Goals: Have students read through the goals and mark any words that are unfamiliar. Discuss the meanings of any academic vocabulary within the goals that students marked as unfamiliar. Consider posting the Chapter Goals.

Preview Academic Vocabulary: Read and discuss the meanings of the academic vocabulary.

> **connotation:** *the positive or negative association suggested by a word.* The word *stubborn* has a negative <u>connotation</u>, but the word *persistent has a positive one.*

> **denotation:** *the literal meaning of a word* Frugal has the <u>denotation</u> of "thrifty," though the word can carry a negative overtone, as in "the frugal meal."

> **figurative language:** *language that goes beyond the literal, appealing to the senses through the use of comparison, exaggeration, imagery, and other devices.* An example of <u>figurative language</u> is this metaphor: The wind was an angry child throwing toys across the yard.

> **metaphor:** *a comparison of two unalike things that does not use* like *or* as. Shakespeare's Romeo often expresses his admiration for Juliet's beauty in <u>metaphors</u>, for example, "Juliet is the sun."

> **point of view:** *opinion or perspective.* The character's words revealed his <u>point of view</u> of the situation.

> **simile:** *a comparison of two dissimilar entities or feelings, using* like *or* as. "My love is like a red, red, rose" is Robert Burns's famous <u>simile</u>.

🖱 **Gr7Ch4Vocabulary.pptx**

Preview Concepts: Many factors determine how different people view a situation or event. A person's age, experience, and background all influence one's perspective. A person's position and responsibility are also factors. Parents,

---

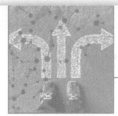

Chapter **4**

Determining Characters' Points of View

Preview Concepts

Think about the last time you asked a parent or teacher for permission, and he or she said no. How did that make you feel? Did you understand the reasons for the refusal? Did you say or do anything in response? Now, put yourself in your teacher's or parent's shoes and imagine their perspective. Write a response below where you explain what happened from your parent's or teacher's point of view.

Now, write a response from your point of view.

Share your answers with a partner and decide if both points of view are reasonable.

CHAPTER GOALS

In this chapter you will

- determine central ideas in a text.
- identify figurative language.
- analyze characters' points of view.
- create a pictorial presentation or write a literary analysis.

PREVIEW ACADEMIC VOCABULARY

connotation

denotation

figurative language

metaphor

point of view

simile

ELL Support: Academic Vocabulary See <u>Teaching Vocabulary (p. 18) in the ELL Teacher Resource</u> for ideas to use for teaching vocabulary throughout *Connections*.

Preview Concepts If necessary, review the idea that point of view is a person's overall thoughts, feelings, or opinions on a topic or situation and that characters are people or animals in a story. Students can create a graphic novel (comic strip) version of the story with thought and speech bubbles to show their own and their parent's or teacher's perspective. Use an online comic strip generator such as storyboardthat.com or makebeliefscomix.com.

Making Connections

The following excerpt is from a short story by Katherine Mansfield. You will be reading another of her stories in this chapter. As you read think about what each of the characters are most concerned about.

> "Dead!" Laura stared at Godber's man.
>
> "Dead when they picked him up," said Godber's man with relish. "They were taking the body home as I come up here." And he said to the cook, "He's left a wife and five little ones."
>
> "Jose, come here." Laura caught hold of her sister's sleeve and dragged her through the kitchen to the other side of the green baize door. There she paused and leaned against it. "Jose!" she said, horrified, "however are we going to stop everything?"
>
> "Stop everything, Laura!" cried Jose in astonishment. "What do you mean?"
>
> "Stop the garden-party, of course." Why did Jose pretend?
>
> But Jose was still more amazed. "Stop the garden-party? My dear Laura, don't be so absurd. Of course we can't do anything of the kind. Nobody expects us to. Don't be so extravagant."
>
> "But we can't possibly have a garden-party with a man dead just outside the front gate."
>
> —"The Garden Party" by Katherine Mansfield

1. What are each of the following characters concerned about?

Godber's man—

Laura—

Jose—

With a partner discuss how the three characters have different points of view about the dead man. Discuss why each person might have a different perspective based on what is important to him or her. Summarize your discussion below.

> **MAKING CONNECTIONS**
>
> In this chapter you will make inferences about characters' points of view based on what they say and do.

teachers, and students often have different perspectives. Sometimes friends or members of different groups see things differently. List factors, invite students to offer other factors, and ask them to explain which they consider most important and why. Invite discussion about the value of understanding the way others see things. Point out that understanding can help to defuse anger and bullying, encourage empathy, and increase cooperation.

Making Connections: After students answer the questions ask them what they learn from the characters' different reactions to news of the dead man. *(They learn whether a character thinks of others or only of himself or herself and whether the character is superficial or deep.)*

1. Godber's man seems most concerned with gossip about the dead man.

2. Laura seems most concerned with doing the right thing.

3. Jose seems most concerned with going about her business and enjoying herself.

ELL Support: Making Connections Before reading, be sure students understand that *concerned* means "worried or interested in." To read the text, assign advanced volunteers a role as you take on the role of narrator. Perform the reading as a readers theater. Use gestures to indicate the setting, the events, and where the dead body is. After reading, provide the following sentence frames for students to use as they discuss the passage:

- Godber's man's point of view of the dead man is . . . because . . . is important to him.

- Laura's point of view of the dead man is . . . because . . . is important to her.

- Jose's point of view of the dead man is . . . because . . . is important to her.

Lesson Support

First Read: Summarizing Central Ideas

Before Reading: Remind students that during the first read of a text they should answer the question *What is this text mostly about?* Then read the introductory material and the objective, making sure students understand the reading task. Use a think-aloud to model how to read and annotate the first few paragraphs and then ask students to read and annotate the rest of the passage on their own.

Preview Vocabulary: Preview unfamiliar vocabulary to aid comprehension. Ask students to circle unfamiliar words as they complete the first read of a text. After the first read, guide students to determine the words' meanings using the context. Encourage students to support their responses with evidence. Have students confirm their initial definitions with a dictionary. Words that students might find difficult include:

postmistress: *a woman in charge of a post office.* The new <u>postmistress</u> runs our post office efficiently.

rage: *a fad or fashion.* Brightly colored socks are the <u>rage</u> this spring.

flagged: *weakened; diminished.* The girl's interest in making bracelets <u>flagged</u> over the summer.

titter: *snicker; giggle.* The mean children <u>tittered</u> when the boy dropped his ice cream cone.

spitefully: *cruelly; hurtfully.* Jim felt angry and tired, so he treated his brother <u>spitefully</u>.

After Reading: Use the following questions to check comprehension.

Text-Based Discussion Questions

1. Why might Mrs. Kelvey have dressed her children so oddly? *She likely had no choice, given her financial circumstances, having no husband to help and forced to work a menial job.*

2. Which words best describe the Kelvey sisters? Their classmates? *The sisters: isolated, aloof, sad. The schoolmates: cruel, mean-spirited.*

First Read: Summarizing Central Ideas

In this Katherine Mansfield story, Isabel and Kezia Burnell proudly show off their new doll house to other children.

Objective: As you read, think about the conflict the narrator describes. Notice any repeated ideas. Underline details that describe the characters' feelings about the dollhouse. Write questions you have about the characters and the conflict in the My Thoughts column.

—— First Read

---- Second Read

excerpt
The Doll's House
by Katherine Mansfield

My Thoughts

1 The Burnell children could hardly walk to school fast enough the next morning. They burned to tell everybody, to describe, to—well—to boast about their doll's house before the school bell rang.

5 "I'm to tell," said Isabel, "because I'm the eldest. And you two can join in after. But I'm to tell first."

Playtime came and Isabel was surrounded. <u>The girls of her class nearly fought to put their arms around her, to walk away with her, to beam flatteringly, to be her special friend.</u> She

10 held quite a court under the huge pine trees at the side of the playground. Nudging, giggling together, the little girls pressed up close. And the only two who stayed outside the ring were the two who were always outside, the little Kelveys. They knew better than to come anywhere near the Burnells.

15 Lil, for instance, who was a stout, plain child, with big freckles, came to school in a dress made from a green art-**serge** table-cloth of the Burnells', with red plush sleeves from the Logans' curtains. Her hat, perched on top of her high forehead, was a grown-up woman's hat, once the property of Miss Lecky,

20 the postmistress. It was turned up at the back and trimmed with a large scarlet quill. What a little **guy** she looked! It was

serge: a strong cloth, usually made of wool
guy: a person who looks odd

66   Chapter 4 • Unit 1   ©Perfection Learning® • No Reproduction Permitted

Remediation: Preview Concept To communicate the idea of putting oneself in another person's shoes, present a few of the following situations and ask students how they think each person would feel.

- Your friend just had her backpack stolen.
- Your neighbor finally got a job.
- Your classmate has been insulted by another student.

	My Thoughts

impossible not to laugh. And her little sister, our Else, wore a long white dress, rather like a nightgown, and a pair of little boy's boots. But whatever our Else wore she would have looked

25 strange. <u>She was a tiny wishbone of a child</u>, with cropped hair and <u>enormous solemn eyes—a little white owl</u>. Nobody had ever seen her smile; she scarcely ever spoke. She went through life holding on to Lil, with a piece of Lil's skirt screwed up in her hand. Where Lil went our Else followed. In the playground, on

30 the road going to and from school, there was Lil marching in front and our Else holding on behind. Only when she wanted anything, or when she was out of breath, our Else gave Lil a tug, a twitch, and Lil stopped and turned round. The Kelveys never failed to understand each other. Now they hovered at

35 the edge; you couldn't stop them listening. When the little girls turned round and sneered, Lil, as usual, gave her silly, shamefaced smile, but our Else only looked.

And Isabel's voice, so very proud, went on telling. The <u>carpet made a great sensation,</u> but so did the beds with real

40 **bedclothes**, and the stove with an oven door.

When she finished Kezia broke in. "You've forgotten the lamp, Isabel."

"Oh, yes," said Isabel, "and there's a teeny little lamp, all made of yellow glass, with a white globe that stands on the

45 dining-room table. You couldn't tell it from a real one."

<u>"The lamp's best of all," cried Kezia.</u> She thought Isabel wasn't making half enough of the little lamp. But nobody paid any attention. Isabel was choosing the two who were to come back with them that afternoon and see it. She chose Emmie

50 Cole and Lena Logan. But when the others knew they were all to have a chance, they couldn't be nice enough to Isabel. One

My Thoughts (sidebar): metaphor

---
bedclothes: the covering (as sheets and blankets) used on a bed

About the Author: Kathleen Mansfield Beauchamp was born in Wellington, New Zealand, on October 14, 1888. She published her first work at Wellington Girls' High School in the *High School Reporter* in 1898. A teacher there remembered her as "surly" and "imaginative to the point of untruth." Her family sailed to England in 1903 where she adopted the name "Katherine Mansfield." In England, Mansfield began writing seriously. She gained recognition as one of the premier modern short story writers of the time and as a pioneer of the avant-garde. Her bohemian personal life was tumultuous, with affairs, a brief marriage, and a divorce. In 1911, she met critic and editor John Middleton Murry who became her longtime companion and eventually her husband. Mansfield met and befriended many of England's literary and intellectual elites of the period, such as Virginia Woolf, D. H. Lawrence, and Bertrand Russell. Suffering from tuberculosis and other illnesses, Mansfield died in 1923.

Tech-Connect: Students can find a variety of statistics and information on bullying at www.stopbullying.gov.

ELL Support: First Read Before reading, review the meaning of *conflict* (problem between character and self, problem between characters, or problem between characters and the world) and *narrator* (person who tells a story). Also, display pictures of dollhouses from the Internet so students have an image of the main item in the story.

Have students read the story in multilevel groups or pairs. As they read, have students pause to sketch images of the characters, setting, and main events. Students can create one picture that they add to as they read the story or a series of pictures to represent each event. Students should label their pictures with the characters' names and other important items (pine trees, schoolyard, etc.). Assist students in sketching the pictures of the Kelvey girls by helping them draw the odd clothing they're wearing and food they're eating. Another option is to have students search online for pictures of clothing, food, and other items that are similar to those described in the story.

Chapter 4 *(continued)*

Lesson Support

by one they put their arms round Isabel's waist and walked her
off. They had something to whisper to her, a secret. "Isabel's
my friend."

55   Only the little Kelveys moved away forgotten; there was
nothing more for them to hear.

    Days passed, and as more children saw the doll's house, <u>the
fame of it spread. It became the one subject, the rage. The one
question was</u>, "Have you seen Burnells' doll's house?" "Oh,

60 ain't it lovely!" "Haven't you seen it? Oh, I say!"

    Even the dinner hour was given up to talking about it.
The little girls sat under the pines eating their thick **mutton**
sandwiches and big slabs of johnny cake spread with butter.
While always, as near as they could get, sat the Kelveys, our Else

65 holding on to Lil, listening too, while they chewed their jam
sandwiches out of a newspaper soaked with large red blobs.

    "Mother," said Kezia, "can't I ask the Kelveys just once?"

    "Certainly not, Kezia."

    "But why not?"

70   "Run away, Kezia; you know quite well why not."

    At last everybody had seen it except them. On that day the
subject rather flagged. It was the dinner hour. The children
stood together under the pine trees, and suddenly, as they
looked at the Kelveys eating out of their paper, always by

75 themselves, always listening, they wanted to be horrid to them.
Emmie Cole started the whisper.

    "Lil Kelvey's going to be a servant when she grows up."

    "O-oh, how awful!" said Isabel Burnell, and she made eyes
at Emmie.

80   Emmie swallowed in a very meaning way and nodded to
Isabel as she'd seen her mother do on those occasions.

    "It's true—it's true—it's true," she said.

My Thoughts

---

mutton: lamb

Then Lena Logan's little eyes snapped. "Shall I ask her?" she whispered.

85   "Bet you don't," said Jessie May.

"Pooh, I'm not frightened," said Lena. Suddenly she gave a little squeal and danced in front of the other girls. "Watch! Watch me! Watch me now!" said Lena. And sliding, gliding, dragging one foot, giggling behind her hand, Lena went over

90   to the Kelveys.

Lil looked up from her dinner. She wrapped the rest quickly away. Our Else stopped chewing. What was coming now?

"Is it true you're going to be a servant when you grow up, Lil Kelvey?" shrilled Lena.

95   Dead silence. But instead of answering, Lil only gave her silly, shame-faced smile. She didn't seem to mind the question at all. What a sell for Lena! The girls began to titter.

Lena couldn't stand that. She put her hands on her hips; she shot forward. "Yah, yer father's in prison!" she hissed, spitefully.

100   This was such a marvelous thing to have said that the little girls rushed away in a body, deeply, deeply excited, wild with joy. Someone found a long rope, and they began skipping. And never did they skip so high, run in and out so fast, or do such daring things as on that morning.

My Thoughts

FIRST RESPONSE: KEY IDEAS AND DETAILS

How are the Kelvey girls different from the rest of the children in the story? Use evidence from the text to support your conclusions. Describe any personal connections to the text.

Focus on Summarizing Central Ideas

To determine the central ideas of a story, think about the following questions:

- What are the main events?
- How do the main characters respond to the main events?
- How do the characters change over the course of the story?

> **TECH-CONNECT**
>
> As instructed by your teacher, send a question you had about the story to Poll Everywhere or post it on your class website.

continued on next page

FIRST RESPONSE: KEY IDEAS AND DETAILS

Help students identify general ways in which people may differ, such as family circumstances, social situations, finances, opportunities, and prospects, as well as food, clothing, and other belongings.

Chapter 4 *(continued)*

Lesson Support

Focus on Summarizing Central Ideas:

Answers to Summarizing Central Ideas:

See answers on Student Book insert page to the right.

 Gr7Ch4Read1.pptx

Trace the characters' actions and reactions to story events by finishing the sentence starters to summarize what happens in each section.

Paragraphs 1–3 (lines 1–14): The narrator describes how excited the Burnell girls are about telling their friends about their new dollhouse.
Paragraphs 4–5 (lines 15–40): The narrator describes Lil as stout and plain and Else as small and pale.
Paragraphs 6–8 (lines 41–54): The other little girls listen to the description of the dollhouse. Isabel proudly describes the dollhouse in great detail.
Paragraph 9 (lines 55–56): The Kelveys move away because no one talks to them.
Paragraphs 10–11 (lines 57–66): The girls talk excitedly about seeing the dollhouse The Kelveys again are left out of the conversations but stay near enough to listen.
Paragraphs 12–16 (lines 67–76): Kezia wonders why the Kelveys can't come to see the dollhouse. Her mother says Kezia knows why they can't come over.

ELL Support: Speak and Listen Have students form multilevel pairs or small groups. Provide the following sentence frames for students to use in their discussion:

- (I think) Kezia wants to show the Kelvey girls her dollhouse because . . . .
- She changed her mind about the Kelvey girls because . . . .
- Another reason she has is . . . .

Paragraphs 17–23 (lines 77–90): The girls gossip about
the Kelveys in a mean-spirited way.

Paragraphs 24–27 (lines 91–99): Lena
taunts the Kelveys, saying their father is in prison.

Lil
just smiles shamefacedly at Lena.

Paragraph 28 (lines 100–104): The girls
run and play excitedly after taunting the Kelveys.

Speak and Listen Share your answers to the sentence starters
above with a partner. Then discuss these questions:

- Why do you think Kezia wants to show her dollhouse to
  the Kelveys?
- Has she changed her mind about them?
- What other reason might she have?
- How do the characteristics of Kezia and the Kelveys
  influence the events in the story?

Second Read: Understanding Figurative Language

Objective: Read the text again. Underline examples of figurative
language, including similes and metaphors.

Focus on Understanding Figurative Language

Figurative language uses comparisons to help readers picture
what is happening or being described. Writers use figurative
language to help readers "see" the story events and characters.
Two main types of figurative language are similes and metaphors.

continued on next page

> **REFLECT**
>
> In a democracy,
> the majority rules,
> but the majority
> is not always
> right. Is there a
> way to fix this
> problem when the
> majority is in the
> wrong? How have
> people addressed
> majority and
> minority disputes
> throughout
> history?

ELL Support: Second Read Use sketches, pictures, and pantomime
to explain the words in the similes and metaphors. For example, point
to your stomach and say *stomach*. Have students repeat. Sketch or
display a picture of a volcano and say *volcano* and *lava*. Have students
repeat. Hold your stomach and make a face like it hurts as you say,
*My stomach feels like a volcano. My stomach hurts. It is burning
because I feel sick.* Repeat with *army, tornado, wishbone,* and *white
owl.*

Be sure students understand the difference between similes and
metaphors by circling *like* and *as* in the definition and example.

Speak and Listen: Point out that young
people are still learning values, often from
their parents. What did Kezia learn from her
mother?

*Possible responses: Kezia may have changed
her mind about the Kelveys, she may want
to show off her dollhouse to everyone, and
she may be curious about them; the Kelveys
are aloof and somewhat mysterious. Also,
Kezia may identify with the Kelveys; her
sister Isabel, who seems to be older, tells her
what to do and the other girls seem to pay
more attention to Isabel.*

Tech-Connect: Students can find
resources and pictures of the writer, her
home, and her garden at the Katherine
Mansfield Birthplace Society website: www.
katherinemansfield.com/about-katherine-
mansfield.

Second Read: Understanding Figurative Language

Before Reading: Remind students that
during the second read of a text, the goal is
to analyze how the author communicates.
How does the author use figurative
language to help readers picture what is
happening? If helpful, revisit the definitions
of metaphor and simile from page 64:

metaphor: *a comparison of two unalike
things that does not use* like *or* as.

simile: *a comparison of two dissimilar
entities or feelings, using* like *or* as.

Examples of figurative language from the text:
"She was a tiny wishbone of a child, with
cropped hair and enormous solemn eyes—a
little white owl."

Text-Based Discussion Questions

1. Why might the author have repeated
   the phrase "silly shame-faced
   smile"? *The author's repetition was
   meant to draw attention to the phrase
   and to have the reader consider its
   meaning: Was Lil feeling shame or were
   her classmates meant to be ashamed
   of themselves? The repetition of "s"
   (alliteration) contributes to this effect.*

2. Lil's younger sister is referred to as
   "Our Else." What might this reference
   mean? *The author is alluding to
   fondness and protectiveness for Else; this
   feeling is reinforced by Lil's watching
   out for her. The reference also suggests
   a familiarity; "Our Else" may be what
   the mother calls her at home.*

Lesson Support

Text-Based Discussion Questions

3. The author writes: "This was such a marvelous thing to have said that the little girls rushed away in a body, deeply, deeply excited, wild with joy." What is implied by describing the girls' behavior as "a marvelous thing to have said"? *The statement is ironic; the girls' comments and behavior were clearly horrible. Also, this statement shows the school girls' point of view about what Lena had said. They are shallow and uncaring toward the Kelveys.*

Focus on Understanding Figurative Language: Ask students why figurative language might help a reader to visualize characters and events. *Possible Answers: Figurative language can capture what a character is like in a few words. Creative, original similes and metaphors tend to stay with readers. However, the overuse of figurative language can drag down literary writing.*

Point out that sound devices like alliteration and repetition can emphasize personal characteristics. An example is the phrase, "silly shame-faced smile."

Answers to Understanding Figurative Language

1. tiny wishbone of a child, metaphor, the small stature of Else

2. a little white owl, metaphor, her smallness and her paleness

Gr7Ch4Read2.pptx

Reflect: Help students generate a list of similes that have become clichés. Post the list. Encourage students to add to the list. Make sure students understand that they should always avoid using clichés in their writing. To make the point, invite students to each write a paragraph that contains as many clichés as possible.

Third Read: Determining Points of View

Before Reading: Read through the objective for the read. Instruct students to read the selection aloud with a partner. Ask: How does the reader learn what the characters feel about each other? *Possible answers: The words and actions of the school girls let the reader know how they*

Simile: a comparison of two things using *like* or *as.*	*Examples:* Her stomach felt like a volcano had erupted and hot lava burned inside.
	He was as hungry as a lion and as impatient as a two-year-old.
Metaphor: a comparison that says one thing is something else.	*Examples:* The army rushed forward, a tornado of destruction.
	The computer with its unknown pass code was an impenetrable fortress.

Read the following sentence from the passage:

She was a tiny wishbone of a child, with cropped hair and enormous solemn eyes—a little white owl.

Analyze the two examples of figurative language in the sentence by using the following formats:

1. The phrase _____ is a figure of speech called a _____. This shows _____.
2. The phrase _____ is a figure of speech called a _____. This emphasizes _____.

> **REFLECT**
>
> Some similes are used so frequently that they become clichés, or overused expressions. A few examples are *as blind as a bat, as easy as pie,* and *as wise as an owl.* What others have you heard or used?

Third Read: Determining Points of View

Read the passage with a partner. Take turns reading paragraphs.
Objective: Think about the following questions:
- How do the characters feel about each other?
- What makes them feel that way?
- How does the narrator feel about the Kelveys? Underline details that help you infer the narrator's attitude.

72   Chapter 4 • Unit 1   ©Perfection Learning® • No Reproduction Permitted

ELL Support: Third Read Have students work in multilevel pairs or small groups to respond to the questions. Provide the following sentence frames to support students:

- . . . feels . . . about . . . .
- She feels this way because . . . .

Before students answer the last question on page 72, remind them that the narrator is the person telling the story. Explain that a narrator uses words that show how he or she feels about the characters and events. Read examples from the text and ask: *What words does the narrator use to describe this character? Are these positive words?* (Smile) *Are these negative words?* (Frown) Use sketches and gestures to show the meaning and connotation of words like *stout, plain, guy, strange, solemn,* and *hover.*

Then provide the following sentence frames to support students in

Focus on Determining Points of View

This passage has a third-person omniscient narrator. *Omniscient* means "all-knowing." This narrator relates information about all of the characters, including their interactions and some of their inner thoughts.

Point of view often refers to the perspective from which the story is told, in this case, the narrator's point of view. But point of view also describes a character's thoughts and feelings about something or someone.

In the passage, the characters are divided into two groups and two different points of view: 1) the Kelveys and 2) all of the other little girls. The narrator's description of the characters and their interactions helps you determine their points of view.

Read the quotation from the passage in the left-hand column of the chart below. Then in the right-hand column, write what the quotation reveals about the character's feelings toward the Kelveys. You may want to return to the passage to read the quotation in context. The first one is completed for you.

> **REFLECT**
>
> Can you think of other stories or movies where the main character is treated unfairly because of his or her social class?

Thoughts, speech, action	What it shows about how the characters feel about each other
1. *When the little girls turned round and sneered, Lil, as usual, gave her silly, shamefaced smile, but our Else only looked.*	**The little girls** They treat the Kelveys with blatant scorn. **The Kelveys** Lil and Else accept the other girls' behavior and do not seem to harbor any grudges or resentment.
2. *At last everybody had seen it except them [the Kelveys].*	**The little girls** They exclude the Kelveys from their social activities. They view the Kelveys as outsiders who do not belong in their company. **The Kelveys** Lil and Else have no expectations to see the dollhouse as they recognize their place in the social order. However, they are curious about the experiences of the other children.
3. *The children stood together under the pine trees, and suddenly, as they looked at the Kelveys eating out of their paper, always by themselves, always listening, they wanted to be horrid to them.*	**The little girls** They view the Kelveys as fodder for their amusement. They enjoy their sense of superiority. **The Kelveys** Lil and Else are excluded from active participation in the other girls' activities, but they still listen to the other girls' conversations.

©Perfection Learning® • No Reproduction Permitted   Chapter 4 • Unit 1   73

---

feel about Lil and Else. As for Lil and Else, only their actions give a clue.

After Reading: Use the following questions to check comprehension.

Text-Based Discussion Questions

1. Near the end of the story, Emmie nods to Isabella "as she'd seen her mother do on those occasions." What does the narrator's explanation show? *The parents have influenced the children to become snobs.*

2. Why do you think the girls were so excited at the end of the story? *They knew that they had done something unacceptable, breaking a moral rule to treat other people well. Even so, it was exciting to them, as breaking a rule can sometimes be.*

3. What motivates the Burrells and the other children to treat the Kelveys with contempt? Support your answer with evidence from the text. *The girls want to be accepted by the Burrells. They have money and nice toys. The Kelveys do not. Line 51 says "they couldn't be nice enough to Isabel." Sometimes to feel included, people think they have to exclude others: "They wanted to be horrid to them." Also, they are following the example of the parents. Kezia asks her mother if she can show the dollhouse to the Kelveys, but her mother refuses.*

Focus on Determining Points of View: The author's omniscient narrator allows her to develop irony—and comment upon the snobbery and bullying of the school girls and their parents.

> **Answers to Analyzing Point of View:**
>
> See answers on Student Book insert page to the left.

 Gr7Ch4Read3.pptx

---

answering the third question:

- The narrator feels . . . about the Kelveys.
- I know this because the narrator uses words like . . . and . . . to describe the Kelveys.

ELL Support: Focus on Determining Points of View Explain to students that different narrators can have different points of view. Remind students that point of view is the person's perspective or way they see the story. Use the Point of View graphic organizer to support the definition and to explain that characters have points of view too. They have thoughts, feelings, and opinions about other characters and events.

Paraphrase the sample answers in the chart above. Instead of *The little girls treat the Kelveys with blatant scorn*, say: *The little girls are mean to the Kelveys. They treat the Kelveys very badly. The Kelveys do not get angry at the girls.*

© Perfection Learning® • Connections   Grade 7 • Chapter 4   73

Chapter 4 (continued)

Lesson Support

Speak and Listen: Help students break down the question about the narrator. Does the narrator say anything positive about the little girls? What words does she use to characterize Lena's final comment? Does the narrator approve of the way the girls behaved?

Write: Remind students to refer to the point of view chart they just completed to help them write this paragraph.

Language: Connotations and Denotations: Studying connotations and denotations is an effective way to develop vocabulary. Suggest that students use the words in item 3 to create a continuum from most negative to most positive. Challenge students to develop additional continuums with other word groups.

1. *Stout* and *plain* have negative connotations.

2. *Fame* has a positive connotation.

3. Possible responses:

prying → snooping → nosy → questioning → curious → inquisitive

horde → gang → bunch → group → committee → team

 Gr7Ch4Language.pptx

Speak and Listen Discuss how the little girls and the Kelveys feel about each other. Refer to your answers from the graphic organizer. Then discuss the following questions:

- How does the narrator feel about the Kelveys and the other girls' behavior? What details support your inference about the narrator's point of view?

Write Write a paragraph comparing and contrasting the points of view of the Kelveys, the little girls, and the narrator. Support your ideas by quoting and paraphrasing lines from the text.

Language: Connotations and Denotations

A word's denotation is its dictionary definition. A word's connotation is the implied or suggested meaning. In other words, the denotation is the literal meaning of a word, and the connotation is the emotional association people have with the word. Words can have neutral, positive, or negative connotations.

> **Example:** *assertive, bossy*
> The word *assertive* has a positive connotation, whereas *bossy* has a negative connotation.

> **Example:** *brat, child*
> Using the word *brat* to describe a child implies the child misbehaves often or is annoying. Using the word *child*, on the other hand, is neutral in that it does not imply a negative or positive connotation.

Read these sentences from the passage. Rewrite the underlined words below and label them *positive*, *negative*, or *neutral* based on their connotations.

1. Lil, for instance, who was a <u>stout</u>, <u>plain</u> child, with big freckles, came to school in a dress made from a green art-serge table-cloth of the Burnells', with red plush sleeves from the Logans' curtains.

2. Days passed, and as more children saw the doll's house, the <u>fame</u> of it spread.

ELL Support: Speak and Listen Before students answer the questions, help them find and reread passages in which the narrator describes the girls' behavior toward the Kelveys. Ask: *What words does the narrator use to describe the girls' words and actions to the Kelveys? Are the narrator's words positive or negative?* Have students work in multilevel pairs or small groups to discuss the questions on p. 74. Be sure students understand that *behavior* means the way someone acts and an *inference* is a guess based on facts, details, or evidence. Provide the following sentence frames to support students:

- The narrator feels the girls' behavior is . . . .

- I know this because the narrator uses words like . . . and . . . to describe the girls' behavior.

Write Instead of writing a paragraph, have ELLs work in multilevel pairs or groups to complete a Venn diagram or have them fold a sheet of paper in half and write the Kelveys' point of view on one

3. Read the following two word groups and write them in order
   from most to least negative connotation.

   curious, nosy, inquisitive, prying, snooping, questioning

   group, gang, horde, bunch, team, committee

Speak and Listen Share your word ranking with a partner.
Discuss the following questions:

- Which word(s) had the most negative connotation for you?

- Which word(s) had the most positive connotation for you?

- Did any of your word rankings match? Why or why not?

Project-Based Assessments

Pictorial Presentation

Create a pictorial presentation of the events in "The Doll's
House."

- Create a pictorial presentation using PowerPoint, a video,
  or a hand-drawn storyboard of each scene.

- Use a minimum of six images, presented in order. Write
  captions under each image to briefly explain the scene.
  Include pictures that reflect what you think happens next
  in the story.

Use the following ideas to help you in your research for this
presentation.

- Read the rubric on page 70 carefully so that you know
  what is expected of you.

- Plan your images before you begin so you can research
  more effectively.

continued on next page

side and the little girls' point of view on the other side. Use these
topics: the exclusion of the Kelveys, the Kelveys' clothes and food, the
dollhouse, Lena's comments at the end.

Language Have students work in multilevel pairs or small groups to
create word webs with related vocabulary, placing neutral words in
the center and words with strong positive or negative connotations
on opposite legs of the web. Tell students to draw a happy face or
a sad face to indicate positive or negative connotations. Have them
share their webs with a partner during the Speak and Listen activity.

Project-Based Assessments—Pictorial Presentation Have
students work in multilevel groups to develop a list of four scenes to
include in their presentation. Then have them create a quick sketch
on an index card for each scene. Finally, have them fold two sheets of
paper in half and tape them together lengthwise into four sections.
On each section of the paper, they can draw a picture of a scene and
write a short caption.

Project-Based Assessments

Pictorial Presentation: Suggest that
students begin by making a list of scenes to
include in their presentation. Instruct them
to fold two sheets of paper into three or
four sections each and number the sections.
Have them use the sections to create a
simple pictorial outline of scenes from the
story to include in their presentation. Then
they can add captions to each section of
their pictorial outline.

Tech-connect Suggestion: Student may
use an online comic or storyboard maker
to create their pictorial presentations.
Suggestions include pixton.com or
storyboardthat.com.

Chapter 4 *(continued)*

Assessment

Project-Based Assessments

Literary Analysis: If students need practice writing essays under timed conditions, have students complete this essay during a class period. Provide them with time guidelines for each step including rereading/annotating the story with the prompt in mind (10 minutes), planning their essay (5 minutes), writing their essay (25 minutes), and editing/proofreading (10 minutes).

- Use key words such as *school playground, children at play,* and *The Doll's House.* These words are suggestions to get you started. Even if you are hand-drawing your images, looking at ideas from the web will help you make your drawings realistic.
- Refine your search by clicking on Videos or Images.
- Once you find an image you like, save it or capture a screenshot of it. Paste that image into your presentation and crop it. If you pause a video, you can capture an image.
- If adding music, consider using "Don't Laugh at Me" by Mark Wills (1998), "The Man in the Mirror" by Michael Jackson (1987), "Coat of Many Colors" by Dolly Parton (1971), or another suitable piece.

	Use the following guidelines for your pictorial presentation.
To receive the highest score (4.0), the project must meet all of these criteria.	Your pictorial presentation • uses images or drawings in a way that captures the events of the story. • contains interesting images that tell the events in the order they happened. • includes images appropriate for the intended audience (not overly graphic or offensive). • includes short, interesting captions that are free from grammar and punctuation errors.

Literary Analysis

An analysis is a careful study of something to learn how its parts are related to the whole. Throughout this chapter, you analyzed details from "The Doll's House." Write a one-page analysis that answers the following question:

> What does "The Doll's House" communicate about how children treat each other?

First, think about the question and write a strong central idea or thesis statement that answers the question. Then think about how you can support your central idea statement using the work you did during the three reads in this chapter. How do the events of the story, the figurative language that describes the children, and the points of view of the characters support your conclusion about the behavior of children in general?

Organize your analysis into an introduction, a body, and a conclusion. Use good transitional phrases (*first, next, also*) to link ideas together. Another option is to present your analysis as an oral critique to the class. Be sure to use eye contact, a natural speaking rate, appropriate volume, and gestures that support your words.

ELL Support: Literary Analysis Have students form multilevel pairs or small groups. Then write the essay as a group, using simple words and sentences. Have students suggest words or ideas as you write the sentences on chart paper. To supply evidence, have students point to and read lines from the story. Demonstrate how to incorporate a quote as evidence. Display the essay as a model for students to use to write future essays. Use the following sentence frames to guide students in writing the group essay:

- The story "The Doll's House" by Katherine Mansfield shows that children can be very . . . .

- First, the Burnell girls . . . . The other girls . . . . The Kelvey girls . . . . This shows . . . .

Use the following guidelines for your literary analysis.	
To receive the highest score (4.0), the essay must meet all of these criteria.	Your literary analysis • has a clear central idea in a well-developed introduction. • clearly explains what the story communicates about how children treat each other. • has a body organized with good transitional words and phrases. • contains ideas that fit together logically to create an understandable whole. • ends with a satisfying conclusion. • maintains a formal style. • uses correct grammar, usage, punctuation and spelling.

On Your Own: Integrating Ideas

1. One commentator writes, "Katherine Mansfield respects children . . . . her attitude is not entirely new, but it is exceedingly rare." Do you agree with this assessment based on "The Doll's House?" Why or why not?
2. Read the rest of "The Doll's House" by Katherine Mansfield. Think about how the adults and children treat the Kelveys.
3. Watch *Charlie and the Chocolate Factory* (2005) or *A Little Princess* (1995) and consider what the main characters have in common with the Kelveys as well as how they differ.
4. Watch *Poor Kids*, a Frontline film focusing on the lives of three girls whose families are struggling with financial ruin. Find it at www.pbs.org on the Frontline page.

On Your Own: Integrating Ideas:

Activity 1: Ask students to consider the following questions to give them a specific focus for their opinion about the quote: What is Katherine Mansfield's attitude toward the Kelveys? Is her attitude toward their schoolmates different? Why?

Activities 3 and 4: Invite volunteers to write movie reviews on the suggested films. Post their reviews for other students to read. If you encounter different perspectives on the films, have a panel discussion to examine disagreements.

- Next, the Burnell girls . . . . The other girls . . . . The Kelvey girls . . . . This shows . . . .

- Last, the Burnell girls . . . . The other girls . . . . The Kelvey girls . . . . This shows . . . .

- The story "The Doll's House" shows that children treat each other . . . . But why? Can children learn . . . ?

On Your Own: Integrating Ideas Encourage students to view one of the films suggested in Activities 3 and 4. Pause often during the viewing of the movie to paraphrase, explain, and summarize. Use sketches, gestures, and simple words and sentences to communicate what is happening in the movie.

Assessment

Connect to Testing: This Connect to Testing section focuses on identifying central ideas, analyzing figurative language, and analyzing point of view.

Encourage students to work in pairs to choose the correct answers to the questions and then to compare their answers with those of another pair of students. If there is disagreement, encourage the groups to try to reach a consensus as they discuss the reasons for their choices.

Answers to Connect to Testing Questions:

1. **Part A:** A. (DoK 2)
   Part B: In the story, the Kelveys are a lower social class than the other girls. They wear secondhand clothing; for instance, Lil "came to school in a dress made from a green art-serge table-cloth of the Burnells', with red plush sleeves from the Logans' curtains." The Kelveys are cruelly teased by the other girls, and Lena actually taunts them by saying that their father is in prison. Therefore, a theme in the passage is how the less fortunate are treated poorly by members of a higher social class. (DoK 2)

(continued)

Connect to Testing

In this chapter, you practiced analyzing central ideas, figurative langauge, and point of view in a passage. When you take assessments, you will be tested on these skills. Answer the following questions.

1. **Part A:** Which statement best expresses a central idea of the text?

   A. Those who are less fortunate are often treated poorly by those from higher social classes.

   B. Children have a greater understanding of actions and their consequences than may be expected.

   C. Girls and boys have natural differences that make them interact with others in dissimilar ways.

   D. Making cruel jokes at another's expense will eventually have repercussions.

   Part B: Support the answer to Part A by explaining at least two details from the text.

ELL Support: Connect to Testing and Assessments See the *Connections* ELL Teacher Resource (p. 22) for ideas on adapting this section for ELLs.

2. Lena's questions to the other girls and to Lil reveal her

    A. confusion and desperation to feel superior.

    B. meanness and desire for attention.

    C. compassion and yearning to be popular.

    D. recklessness and need for control.

3. Explain how Lil and Else view their social status and their reactions to how the other girls treat them. Include evidence from the text to support your points.

4. **Part A:** Which inference is best supported by the text?

    A. The Kelveys have little interest in seeing or hearing about the dollhouse.

    B. Kezia and Isabel have a difficult relationship with each other because of jealousy.

    C. Kezia's mother worries that Kezia will show the Kelveys the dollhouse.

    D. The girls learned their behavior toward the Kelveys from their parents.

continued on next page

2. B. Evidence from the text best supports Choice B. Lena exclaims "Watch! Watch me! Watch me now!" to the other girls as she approaches the Kelveys. The text says she also hisses spitefully at the Kelveys. (DoK 2)

3. Lil and Else both seem to accept their lot in life without anger or bitterness. For example, when the other girls sneer at them, "Lil, as usual, gave her silly, shamefaced smile, but our Else only looked." Lil's reaction to the cruelty of the girls seems to be a "shamefaced smile," while Else is silent throughout the passage. Even when Lena asks Lil about growing up to be a servant, she smiles and doesn't "seem to mind the question at all." Lil and Else have learned to control their responses to social snubs. Lil and Else do not attempt to change the way the other girls treat them; they appear to understand and perhaps accept their low social status as an uncontrollable part of their life. (DoK 2)

4. **Part A:** D. Choice A is incorrect because we can infer that the Kelveys are very interested in seeing the dollhouse because they stand near enough to hear and see the other girls. There is no support for Choices B and C. The best answer is Choice D because when Kezia asks to show the dollhouse to the Kelveys, her mother refuses her. Clearly, the parents are encouraging their children to judge people by their social class. (DoK 2)

(continued)

Remediation: Connect to Testing Read aloud each question with struggling students. Encourage them to restate each stem in their own words. Go over the responses and encourage them to return to the chapter instruction on central ideas, inferences, or point of view when needed.

Chapter 4 *(continued)*

Assessment

Answers to Connect to Testing Questions:

4. **Part B:** When Kezia questions her mother about why she cannot bring the Kelveys to see the dollhouse, her mother responds, "Run away, Kezia; you know quite well why not." It is understood that the Kelveys are not welcome in the Burnells' house because of their lower social status. When the other girls are talking about Lil becoming a servant when she grows up, "Emmie swallowed in a very meaning way and nodded to Isabel as she'd seen her mother do on those occasions." In both these instances, the girls' mothers guide their interactions with the Kelveys. (DoK 2)

5. **Part A:** B. (DoK 2)
   Part B: C. Kezia's desire to invite the Kelveys to see the dollhouse indicates that she has some compassion and pity for them. (DoK 2)

Part B: Cite at least two details from the text to support your inference.

5. **Part A:** What does Kezia feel toward the Kelveys?

   A. confusion

   B. pity

   C. concern

   D. dismay

   Part B: Which of the following excerpts from the text best supports the answer to Part A?

   A. *"The lamp's best of all," cried Kezia. She thought Isabel wasn't making half enough of the little lamp.*

   B. *While always, as near as they could get, sat the Kelveys, our Else holding on to Lil, listening too*

   C. *"Mother," said Kezia, "can't I ask the Kelveys just once?"*

   D. *"Run away, Kezia; you know quite well why not."*

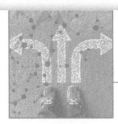

Chapter 5

Analyzing Arguments from Different Texts

Preview Concepts

A good argument supports a central claim with reasons and evidence. The following chart contains a claim and possible reasons to support the claim.

With a partner, identify which of the reasons support the claim, or are relevant to the argument the writer wants to make. Good reasons explain why a reader should agree with the claim.

CHAPTER GOALS

In this chapter you will

- determine an author's purpose in a text.
- analyze the claim, reasons, evidence, and assumptions in an argument.
- evaluate the validity and effectiveness of an argument.
- compare evidence used in two texts.
- write a speech or a letter to the editor.

PREVIEW ACADEMIC VOCABULARY

argument

assumption

claim

evidence

reason

| Claim: Americans should put a "sin" tax on sugary drinks and junk food. ||
Possible reasons	Does it support the claim? (Is it relevant?) Yes or no?
1. People would be forced to make healthier snack choices and thus live healthier lives.	
2. These types of "sin" taxes raise a lot of money, which could be used for better healthcare programs.	
3. "Sin" taxes are not new to America.	
4. Taxes would hurt the companies that make soft drinks and could cost people their jobs.	

Below are several statements related to the reasons above. Decide if any of them could be used as evidence to support the relevant reasons above. Write the number of the reason in the chart next to the evidence. If the evidence is not related to any reason, write none.

5. Denmark had a "fat tax" on junk food that raised about $200 million in one year.
6. Taxes on tobacco and alcohol are (and have been) highly effective in improving public health.
7. With the 18th Amendment in 1920, the government outlawed alcohol, but the amendment was repealed in 1933.

Analyzing Arguments from Different Texts

Why I Am a Vegetarian
by Matthieu Ricard

Vegetarianism
by Judy Krizmanic

Introduction

Chapter Goals: Have students read through the goals and mark any words that are unfamiliar. Discuss the meanings of any academic vocabulary within the goals that students marked as unfamiliar. Consider posting the Chapter Goals.

Preview Academic Vocabulary: Read and discuss the meanings of the academic vocabulary. You may want to review the words *claim, evidence,* and *reason,* which were covered in Chapter 1, because of their importance to Chapter 5.

argument: *a claim along with reasons and evidence in support of a position on a topic.* Her essay makes a strong <u>argument</u> in favor of zoos.

assumption: *a statement accepted without proof.* Everyone does not agree with his <u>assumption</u> that human life is more valuable than animal life.

claim: *the writer's or speaker's opinion which he/she is attempting to prove is true.* She makes a <u>claim</u> in her essay that wild animals are happy in zoos.

evidence: *information, facts, and data used to prove a claim.* The reporter found <u>evidence</u> that some donations did not go to the zoo as promised.

reason: *a statement that explains why a claim should be accepted as true.* The need to save species on the verge of extinction is one <u>reason</u> zoos are necessary.

 Gr7Ch5Vocabulary.pptx

Chapter 5 (continued)

Introduction

Preview Concepts: To check whether a reason supports a claim, students can turn each reason into a subordinate clause with the word *because*. Then they should read this clause with the claim. For example: Americans should put a "sin" tax on sugary drinks and junk food, *because* people would be forced to make healthier snack choices and thus live healthier lives. Does the new sentence make sense? If so, the reason supports the claim.

Answers to Preview Concepts, Page 81:

1. yes
2. yes
3. no
4. no
5. Supports 2
6. Supports 1
7. none

Making Connections

Answers to Making Connections:

1. A vegetarian diet is good for your health.

2. Vegetarian diets can help prevent, treat, or reverse heart disease and cancer.

3. A statistic: Cardiovascular disease kills one million Americans annually and is the leading cause of death in the United States.

4. The argument appears sound and the evidence is relevant. However, students may argue that there is not sufficient evidence provided. More is needed to be more convincing.

Tech-Connect Suggestion: Students with an interest in eating a vegetarian diet might want to check out information on www.choosemyplate.gov. Search for *tips for vegetarians*.

Making Connections

Read the following excerpt. Then answer the questions that follow.

Why go vegetarian? Chew on these reasons.

You'll ward off disease. Vegetarian diets are more healthful than the average American diet, particularly in preventing, treating or reversing heart disease and reducing the risk of cancer. A low-fat vegetarian diet is the single most effective way to stop the progression of coronary artery disease or prevent it entirely. Cardiovascular disease kills 1 million Americans annually and is the leading cause of death in the United States.

—"Why Go Veg?" *from vegetariantimes.com*

1. What implied claim does the author make?

2. What reason does this paragraph develop?

3. Place a a star by evidence used to support the claim. Which piece of evidence is a statistic?

4. With a partner use the following questions to evaluate the paragraph:
   - Is the argument sound? (Is it based on a logical claim and reasons?)
   - Is the evidence relevant? (Does it support the reason?)
   - Is the evidence sufficient? (Is there enough to support the reason?)

> **MAKING CONNECTIONS**
>
> In this chapter you will analyze the effectiveness of arguments related to vegetarianism.

ELL Support: Preview Concepts Have students work in multilevel pairs or small groups. Use visuals and gestures to explain the reasons and evidence. Paraphrase the reasons and evidence. For example:

1. People must make healthier snack choices (pictures of healthy snacks) so they live healthier lives.

2. Taxes are money you pay to the government when you buy something. "Sin" taxes are taxes on bad behaviors. These types of taxes raise a lot of money. (Sketch a dollar sign.) The money can be used to give people better healthcare.

3. "Sin" taxes are not new in America.

4. Taxes on soda makes soda cost more money (pictures of soda). So people buy less soda. Soda companies make less soda (pictures of soda factory). They don't need as many workers.

5. Denmark had a tax on junk food (pictures of junk food). The tax money was $200 million in one year.

The following is an excerpt from a nonfiction book *A Plea for the Animals* by Matthieu Ricard.

Objective: As you read this passage, think about the author's purpose. <u>Underline one sentence that identifies this purpose.</u> Write questions you have about Ricard's views about vegetarianism and eating meat in the My Thoughts column. Consider how the words defined in the footnotes help you comprehend this text.

—— First Read
---- Second Read
—— Third Read

from
A Plea for the Animals
"Why I Am a Vegetarian"
by Matthieu Ricard

My Thoughts

1   My first **Buddhist** teacher, Kangyur Rinpoche, was a very strict vegetarian. I was inspired by him and also by a deep inner reasoning that suddenly became obvious to me. I never hunted in my life, but did go fishing sometimes when I was
5   a little boy in Brittany. When I was 13 years old, a thought bloomed in my mind: "How can I do something like that?" I realized that I was totally avoiding putting myself in the place of the other being. And when I was 20, I gave up eating meat. That was 50 years ago.

10   The heart of the Buddhist path is compassion. That means to value others. If you value others, you value their well-being and are concerned by their suffering.

We can find means to survive without causing suffering to others. In India for example, there are over 400 million
15   vegetarian people who survive well. They are not sacrificing their health or reducing their life span. In fact, even from a selfish standpoint, it is better to be a vegetarian. Many studies have shown that red meat increases the incidence of colon cancer and other illnesses.

My Thoughts column notes:
Note: The central claim is not stated in the text. The inferred claim is People should be vegetarians.

Reason

Reason

Buddhist: one who practices Buddhism, a religion of eastern and central Asia that believes that suffering is inherent in life and that one can be liberated from it by cultivating wisdom, virtue, and concentration

---

6. America has taxes on tobacco (picture of cigarettes) and alcohol (pictures of alcohol). So tobacco and alcohol cost more. So people buy less tobacco and alcohol. People get healthier.

7. In 1920, America made alcohol illegal. In 1933, America ended this law. Alcohol became legal again.

Making Connections Read the article aloud to students, pausing after each sentence to paraphrase and explain it. For example, change *You'll ward off disease* to *You will keep away sickness.* Provide synonyms for words such as *healthful* (healthy), *preventing* (keeping away), *treating* (healing), *reversing* (changing back), *reducing* (lowering), *risk* (chances), *progression* (growth), and *annually* (yearly). Explain coronary artery disease and cardiovascular disease by describing them as serious sicknesses of the heart. Students can use cognates in their first language to understand these words. Fill out a <u>Cause and Effect graphic organizer found in the ELL Teacher Resource (p. 65)</u> as you summarize the main ideas of the article.

Before Reading: Read aloud the introduction and the objective. Remind students that an author can have several purposes for writing, including persuading, entertaining, or informing their readers. Sometimes an author's purpose for writing is clear; other times, it must be inferred from details in the text.

Remind students that during the first read of a text, they should focus on answering the question *What*? In this case, the questions to answer are *What is the author's purpose?* and *What evidence do I have to support my idea about the author's purpose*?

Preview Vocabulary: Preview unfamiliar vocabulary to aid comprehension. Ask students to circle unfamiliar words as they complete the first read of a text. After the first read, guide students to determine the words' meanings using the context. Encourage students to support their responses with evidence. Have students confirm their initial definitions with a dictionary. Words that students might find difficult include:

vegetarian: *a person who eats no meat or meat products.* I fixed a dinner of vegetables and rice for my <u>vegetarian</u> friend.

genocide: *the systematic murder of a group of people because of their race, religion, or ethnic background.* Unfortunately, societies have carried out <u>genocide</u> against minority populations in the twentieth century.

dehumanization: *the act of denying a person or group's human qualities or attributes.* The Nazi's <u>dehumanization</u> of Jews during the Holocaust was frightening.

ethically: *morally; justly.* It is <u>ethically</u> wrong to bully another person.

altruistic: *selfless; humane.* The volunteer received an award for her <u>altruistic</u> activities.

fanatical: *extreme.* They are <u>fanatical</u> about exercise, running five miles every day.

chaotic: *disordered; tumultuous.* After the giant storm, the scene on our street was <u>chaotic</u>.

 Gr7Ch5Vocabulary.pptx

Lesson Support

After Reading: Use the following questions to check comprehension.

Text-Based Discussion Questions

1. What caused Matthieu Ricard to became a vegetarian? *Inspired by a Buddhist teacher, he realized suddenly when he was a teenager that it was wrong to catch fish or to take the life of another creature.*

2. What is Matthieu Ricard calling on people to do? *He is calling on them to give up meat.*

3. According to Ricard, what is the main reason to give up eating meat? *He says that the main reason is to spare the life of other living creatures.*

4. Which sentence in the last paragraph summarizes the reasons in the article? *"A small effort can bring a very big result for animals, for the disadvantaged, for the planet, for our own health."*

Propaganda in Literature: Propaganda, extremely biased writing, is common in advertisements and editorials. It can be an issue in informational text as well, especially when the author's main purpose is to convince the reader about an issue. Propaganda is not necessarily bad, but being on the lookout for propaganda in persuasive writing is a good critical reading skill for students. Examples of propaganda techniques include:

sweeping generalization: a statement that is not adequately supported and speaks for a large group or exaggerated situation. (Example: Football always causes brain trauma.)

bandwagon: an effort to persuade people by calling on them to join others. (Example: More movie stars follow a vegetarian diet than any other diet. Join them!)

loaded words: words that carry strong connotations. (Example: Eating meat causes unbearable suffering.)

Reason

20 However, the main reason to stop eating animals is to spare others' lives. Today, 150 billion land animals and 1.5 trillion sea animals are killed for our consumption. We treat them like rats and vermin and cockroaches to be eliminated. This would be called genocide or dehumanization if they were 25 human beings.

We even go one step further with animals: we **instrumentalize** them. They become objects. They become the pig industry, sausage or meat factories. Ethically you cannot imagine progressing toward a more altruistic or more 30 compassionate society while behaving like this. Eating meat reveals another level of selfishness in terms of fellow human beings. Rich countries consume the most meat: about 200 kilos per year per inhabitant in the USA, compared to about 3 kilos in India. The more the GDP of a country increases, usually so 35 does the amount of meat consumption.

In order to produce one kilo of meat, you need ten kilos of **vegetable protein**. This is at a cost to the poorest section of humanity. With two acres of land, you can feed fifty vegetarians or two meat eaters. The 775 million tons of soy 40 and corn that are used for industrial farming could be used to feed people in need.

The United Nations International Panel on Climate Change, a group that is not particularly fanatical about being vegetarian, recommends that we start by just eating less 45 meat. This is one of the easiest ways to reduce global warming and could make a huge difference to the rate of climate change. The main reason is that industrial farming causes the production of methane. Methane is ten times more active in

Reason

My Thoughts

instrumentalize: to make into an instrument for achieving a goal
vegetable protein: amino acids that are essential for life and found in vegetables

---

ELL Support: First Read Before students read, be sure they understand that Buddhism is a religion and that people who believe in that religion are Buddhists. Explain that most Buddhists are vegetarians. They don't eat meat. Have students read the text in multilevel pairs, pausing at the end of each paragraph to fill in a Main Ideas and Supporting Details graphic organizer found in the ELL Teacher Resource (p. 51). Also, encourage students to take notes and draw sketches in the margins around the article, so they can be sure they understand the topic of each paragraph.

Focus on Identifying Author's Purpose Be sure students understand that an author's purpose is the reason why the author wrote a text. Have students work in multilevel pairs or small groups to complete the chart on pp. 85–86. Also, provide sentence frames for students to use in the charts:

*   The paragraph shows . . . .

*   This connects to the author's main idea because . . . .

	My Thoughts
causing global warming than CO2. It is the second main factor	

50 for global warming before transportation!

It just takes one second to decide to stop. It doesn't create

any huge chaotic changes in our life. It's just that we eat

something else. It's so simple. A small effort can bring a very
big result for animals, *Reason* for the disadvantaged, *Reason* for the planet, *Reason*

55 for our own health. A sensible mind can see this is not an

extreme perspective. This is a most reasonable, ethical, and

compassionate point of view.

FIRST RESPONSE: KEY IDEAS AND DETAILS

What issue is Ricard calling to people's attention? Write your answer in your journal. Be prepared to share your answer in class.

Focus on Identifying Author's Purpose

Writers have a goal when writing. They may wish to persuade, entertain, or inform their audience. The author's purpose may be clear and easy to identify—even directly stated. Or it may be difficult to determine, so the audience must infer it from the details in the text.

Use the following graphic organizer to analyze Ricard's overall purpose and how each paragraph contributes. Three of the cells have been completed for you.

Paragraph 1 (lines 1–9)	Ricard explains his own experience with Buddhism and how this led to his becoming a vegetarian.	It describes his journey to becoming a vegetarian due to his religious beliefs.
Paragraph 2 (lines 10–12)	Buddhism believes in being compassionate to "others" and concerned by their suffering.	This paragraph connects his Buddhists beliefs in valuing others and stopping suffering with his choice to stop eating meat.

continued on next page

Background: About four million people practice Buddhism. Buddhism is a religion based on the teachings of Siddhartha Gautama (c. fifth century BCE), a teacher known as the Buddha, who stressed liberation from the cycle of suffering and rebirth. Buddhism promotes peace and nonviolence. The goal of Buddhism is to achieve enlightenment and the end of suffering (nirvana).

FIRST RESPONSE: KEY IDEAS AND DETAILS

Help students by focusing on the main topic of the article *(eating vegetarian)* and Ricard's main point about the topic *(People should stop eating meat and eat vegetarian).*
Possible journal response: Ricard is calling people's attention to the problems generated by eating meat.

Focus on Identifying Author's Purpose:

Answers to Focus on Identifying Author's Purpose:

See answers on Student Book insert page to the left.

 Gr7Ch5Read1.pptx

Remediation: First Read Struggling students may need additional help focusing on Ricard's main arguments. Underline sentences in the passage that show his arguments. Ask students to reread the first two sentences about identifying author's purpose on page 85 of the Student Book: *Writers have a goal when writing. They may wish to persuade, entertain, or inform their audience.* Have students write down the three basic purposes mentioned in those sentences. *(persuade, entertain, inform)* Have them circle the purpose of Ricard's article. *(persuade)* Then ask the question: *What is Ricard trying to persuade the readers to do? (to stop eating meat)*

Lesson Support

Focus on Identifying Author's Purpose:

Answers to Focus on Identifying
Author's Purpose:

See answers to the chart on Student
Book insert page to the right.

Ricard's purpose for writing is to
convince readers to become vegetarians.

Second Read: Evaluating an Argument

Before Reading: Remind students that
during the second read of a text, they are
exploring how a writer creates meaning. In
this case, students explore how the author
makes his case for vegetarianism.

Read aloud the objective. Make sure
students understand the concepts of *central
claim* and *reason*. Explain that the *central
claim* is the sentence in which the author
states the opinion that the article develops.
Then tell students that *reasons* are logical
statements that say why readers should
accept the author's claim.

After Reading: Use the following
questions to check comprehension.

Text-Based Discussion Questions

1. Which reason did you find most
   convincing? Why? *Answers will vary.
   Encourage students to return to the text
   when responding.*

2. Loaded words are words with strong
   connotations (positive or negative). Using
   loaded words is a persuasive device.
   What loaded words does Ricard use in
   paragraphs 3 through 5? *suffering,
   genocide, dehumanization, ethically,
   altruistic, selfishness. Rats, vermin, and
   cockroaches are also loaded words.*

3. What ideas about animals and humans
   does the writer suggest in the fourth
   paragraph, lines 20–25? *The writer
   suggests that animals should have the
   same value and rights as humans. Yet,
   he also suggests that some animals (rats,
   vermin, cockroaches) are less valuable
   than other animals.*

Section of the Text	Key Idea	Purpose
Paragraph 3 (lines 13–19)	People can survive and thrive without eating meat.	This paragraph supports the central claim by offering a reason: vegetarianism is healthier than eating meat.
Paragraph 4 (lines 20–25)	Eating vegetarian spares the life of innocent creatures.	The author presents his strongest reason for vegetarianism: it is cruel to animals.
Paragraphs 5–6 (lines 26–41)	The production of meat benefits rich countries and hurts poor countries.	These paragraphs present a moral/economic reason to stop eating meat.
Paragraph 7 (lines 42–50)	Eating meat hurts the planet.	These paragraph present another moral/economic reason to stop eating meat.
Paragraph 8 (lines 51–57)	Stopping the practice of eating meat is simple and effective.	This paragraph summarizes the reasons given in the essay and restates the claim. The author is calling the reader to action.

Ricard's purpose for writing is to _____.

Second Read: Evaluating an Argument

Objective: Read the article a second time. As you read, mark the
following in the text:

- Underline the sentence that most clearly reveals the
  central claim of the article. Label it *claim*.

- Underline sentences that give reasons in support of the
  central claim. Write *reason* next to them.

TECH-CONNECT

Search online for
two of the statistics
or facts cited in the
passage. Check if
the information is
derived from reliable
sources.

86   Chapter 5 • Unit 1   ©Perfection Learning® • No Reproduction Permitted

ELL Support: Second Read Before students read, use the
definitions on p. 87 to review *claim, reason,* and *evidence.* Also,
model identifying the claim and the first reason. Use a think aloud
such as: *This is the claim, or the main idea or belief the author has.
This is one of the reasons why the author believes this.* Then have
students reread the article in multilevel pairs or small groups.

- Underline the sentence in the final paragraph that summarizes the four reasons outlined in the rest of the essay.

Focus on Evaluating an Argument

When a writer's purpose is to persuade his audience to think or act a certain way, he builds an argument. An argument usually contains the following elements:

- Claim or position statement: This is what the author wants the reader to believe or to do.
- Reasons: Logical statements that support the claim. Reasons explain why the reader should accept the author's claim.
- Evidence: Facts, data, statistics, and expert opinions that support the reasons.
- Counterargument/alternative explanation: Explains an opposing viewpoint and explains why this viewpoint is not valid.

Analyze Ricard's argument in "Why I Am a Vegetarian" by identifying his reasons and evidence. If Ricard doesn't offer evidence, write *none*.

Claim: Humans should be vegetarians.

Reason 1:
Being a vegetarian is better for one's health.

Evidence:
Many studies have shown that red meat increases the incidence of colon cancer and other illnesses.

Reason 2:
Being a vegetarian is more humane because it spares the lives of animals.

continued on next page

REFLECT

How much meat do you eat in a day? If you are not already a vegetarian, how difficult would it be for you to forgo eating meat?

TECH-CONNECT

This passage is excerpted from *A Plea for the Animals,* which was published in 2016. However, the idea of vegetarianism has existed for centuries. Conduct an Internet search using the phrase *American Vegetarian Society 1850* to discover three facts about vegetarianism in the United States. Post your facts on your class website, according to your teacher's instructions.

Focus on Evaluating an Argument:

After students identify the reasons and evidence, tell them to reread the final paragraph of the essay. Have students check that the four reasons fit into the categories Ricard describes.

If students are ready, extend this lesson by introducing the idea of assumptions in an argument. An assumption is a belief that someone must hold in order to maintain a particular position; something that is taken for granted but that must be true in order for the conclusion to be true. When evaluating an argument, encourage students to look at the author's assumptions. If the author's assumptions are incorrect or if not all readers agree with the author's assumptions, then the argument may not be as effective. Ask students to evaluate Ricard's assumptions about the following:

- All people must be concerned by the suffering of others.
- Animal life and human life are equally valuable.

Answers to Focus on Evaluating an Argument:

See answers on Student Book insert page to the left.

 Gr7Ch5Read2.pptx

Chapter 5 (continued)

Lesson Support

Lesson Suggestion: Challenge students to find counterarguments to the reasons presented in the essay. For example, ask them to think about poorer countries that rely on herding of animals for food and for income. Are these people being selfish or are they just surviving? Raising animals for food is a significant source of income throughout the world. Encourage students to look for additional counterarguments that are not only economic. Whatever one's point of view on a topic, it is helpful to understand the opposing perspective.

▼**Write:** Have students work with a partner to read and evaluate each other's evaluation of the argument.

Evidence:
Today, 150 billion land animals and 1.5 trillion sea animals are killed for our consumption. We treat them like rats and vermin and cockroaches to be eliminated.

Animals are treated as objects because they are raised in huge farms.

Reason 3:
Vegetarianism makes society more equal and is better for the poor.

Evidence:
With two acres of land, you can feed fifty vegetarians or two meat eaters. The 775 million tons of soy and corn that are used for industrial farming could be used to feed people in need.

Reason 4:
Eating vegetables is better for the environment.

Evidence:
Industrial farming causes the production of methane. Methane is ten times more active in causing global warming than carbon dioxide.

> **REFLECT**
>
> Some claims are based on statistics, but the source of the statistics must be considered before accepting them as accurate and unbiased. One reliable source is a government document. What are some other reliable sources?

▼**Write** Write one or two paragraphs answering the following questions:
1. Which reasons are most convincing? Why?
2. Is enough evidence provided to support each reason?
3. Can you think of additional evidence that might weaken or lend support to the reasons?
4. In general, does the argument make sense logically?

ELL Support: Write Students can use the following sentence frames to develop a modified evaluation of the argument.

- The strongest reason to become a vegetarian is . . . .
- This reason is convincing because it is supported by . . . .
- I do/do not think this argument is convincing because . . . .
- The argument is good/is not good because . . . .

Third Read: Comparing and Contrasting Arguments

Read the passage a third time. Then read the following article on the same topic.

Objective: Mark the following as you read.

- Write *claim* next to the author's claim.
- Put a star by any reasons that are similar to ones used by Ricard in the previous text.
- Put a plus sign (+) by new reasons introduced by this text.

CONNECT TO ESSENTIAL QUESTION

People believe in many things from justice to love to equality. What do you believe in? What makes you believe in it?

Vegetarianism
by Judy Krizmanic

Lots of kids today are becoming vegetarians.

My Thoughts

1 What's a vegetarian? Someone who's decided to stop eating meat. Kids do this for a lot of reasons, but the most common is that they think it's wrong to kill animals and eat them.

Claim

5 People have been arguing about vegetarianism for centuries. Most of the arguments have stayed the same: killing a living creature that feels pleasure and pain is wrong, ⭐ especially since we don't need to eat meat to be healthy. ⭐ Other people say that plants and animals are only here so that 10 humans can use them. Or they say it's just the way the world is—that since animals eat other animals, humans should be able to kill animals for food.

Kids argue about the same things today. Ilana Kaplan-Shain, age 13, says, "I don't want to kill something to eat it." ⭐ 15 My friends say it's a stupid reason not to eat meat. Or they say, it's stupid, you kill the plants. But I say, it's my decision. Live with it."

"Most kids who are vegetarian are doing it for ethical reasons," says Danny Seo, age 19, a vegetarian who started 20 his own animal rights and environmental group. Danny gets ⭐

ELL Support: Third Read Have students read the second article in multilevel pairs, pausing at the end of each paragraph to summarize by filling in a Main Ideas and Supporting Details graphic organizer from the ELL Teacher Resource (p. 51). Model identifying the claim and reasons that are similar to the previous article and different from the previous article. As you do so, use a think aloud such as: *This is the claim, or the main idea or belief the author has. This is one of the reasons why the author believes this. This reason is similar to a reason in the other article. This is another reason the author believes this. This reason is new. It is different from the reasons in the other article.* Also, encourage students to take notes and draw sketches in the margins around the article so they can be sure they understand the topic of each paragraph.

Third Read: Comparing and Contrasting Arguments

Before Reading: Remind students that one of the important questions for the third read of a text is *How does this text connect to other texts*?

Explain that during this read, students will compare and contrast the arguments in "Vegetarianism" to the article they read on pages 83–85, "Why I Am a Vegetarian."

Remind students that *comparing* means "noting the similarities between two texts or purposes." *Contrasting* means "noting the differences." Make sure students understand the following process:

- Read "Why I Am a Vegetarian" again.
- As they reread that text, they should revisit its central claim and reasons, keeping them fresh in their minds. Make new notes as needed.
- Then students should return to "Vegetarianism." As students read, they should
  - Identify the author's claim,
  - Put a star by any reasons similar to those in the previous text, and
  - Put a plus sign (+) by new reasons the author provides.

As another option, you can have students use a graphic organizer, such as a Venn diagram, to keep track of similarities and differences between the two passages.

After Reading: Use the following questions to check comprehension.

Text-Based Discussion Questions

1. For what reason do most kids become vegetarians? *They think it is morally wrong to kill and eat animals.*

2. For what reasons do other kids eat meat? *They enjoy the taste, convenience, and traditions; they have been doing it for a long time, as have their families.*

3. What advantages and disadvantages do kids who have become vegetarians find? *Disadvantage: Finding food is a little harder. Advantages: They start new traditions and enjoy new food experiences; they eat with awareness.*

 Gr7Ch5Read3.pptx

hundreds of letters from kids and teens who, as they put it, don't want to eat anything with a face.

Some people don't think about where their neatly plastic-wrapped meat comes from. It's just something to be cooked
25 and eaten. "If pork were called pig and steak were called cow, I think more of the world would be vegetarian," says Matthew McDonough, age 12. Johanna Gidseg is a 10-year-old vegetarian. When she was 6, she went to McDonald's with her dad and sister. "I looked down at my food and said, 'Dad,
30 what's hamburger?' And he said, 'It's beef.' I said, 'What's beef?' He said, 'It's cow.' I said, 'Dad, do I have to eat my hamburger?'" Johanna's been a vegetarian ever since.

But some kids do know where meat comes from, and it doesn't really bother them. Charley Goss, age 9, eats meat:
35 "When I was little, I couldn't imagine meat coming from an animal. I thought it was gross. But I just grew out of it. I don't really pay much attention to it anymore." . . .

Why Aren't There More Vegetarians?

Even with all the reasons that people give for not eating
40 meat (and we haven't gone into all of them), the question still comes up, why aren't there more vegetarians? Julie Kostynick thinks that most people "think meat tastes good and they're just not thinking about the animal and its life." Most people $+$ grow up eating meat—it's what their families have been
45 eating for generations. We're used to it. It's tradition. Some people can't imagine Thanksgiving without a turkey. Andrew Mabey, age 15, acknowledges vegetarian arguments against meat eating, but he says he's not going to change his diet. "Humans have been eating meat for so many years, and
50 they've been doing OK. Life is too short to worry about it."

My Thoughts

Some kids just like the taste of meat. Charley Goss says, "I don't want to eat just vegetables." Some people end up eating meat just because it's more convenient—it's offered just about everywhere. If you're a vegetarian, you'll have a tougher time

55 finding things to eat at Burger King. You also might have to bring your own lunch to school if your cafeteria doesn't serve vegetarian food. On the other hand, it is getting easier to find vegetarian food—just about any restaurant has at least one vegetarian entrée on the menu. . . .

60 But the number of people, including kids, becoming vegetarians is on the rise. There are a lot more vegetarians today than there were 10 years ago. And some kids find being a vegetarian isn't that hard at all. So what if they have to ask whether their soup is made with beef broth? They

65 say it's worth it. They enjoy creating new traditions—like Thanksgiving without the turkey. Being vegetarian opens up a whole new world of food for them. "I'm taking part in something I believe in," says Julie Gerk, a vegetarian. "It feels great to be eating with awareness."

My Thoughts

Focus on Comparing and Contrasting Arguments

Both passages advocate vegetarianism, but they do it in different ways. In order to compare and contrast the two texts, you must bring together, or synthesize, the ideas found in both. Which ideas are similar? Which are different?

Answer the following questions to compare and contrast the claims and evidence used in the two texts. Use textual evidence to support your answers.

1. What is the main claim in Ricard's text?

continued on next page

Focus on Comparing and Contrasting Arguments:

Answers to Comparing and Contrasting Arguments:

1. Ricard believes that vegetarianism saves animals' lives and prevents suffering of animals and humans.

(continued)

Chapter 5 *(continued)*

Lesson Support

Answers to Comparing and Contrasting Arguments:

2. Kids have many reasons to become vegetarians or to remain meat eaters.

3. Ricard's purpose is to persuade his readers to become vegetarians. Krizmanic's purpose is to present reasons why kids become vegetarians or remain meat eaters, although one can infer that her goal is also to persuade kids about the benefits of becoming vegetarians.

4. Ricard uses facts, statistics, and appeals to emotion to support his points. He explains his personal reasons for becoming a vegetarian, but he also cites facts and statistics from sources such as the United Nations International Panel on Climate Change.

5. Krizmanic uses testimonial evidence to support her points. She also states facts about the increasing number of vegetarians.

6. Both texts state facts. Ricard incorporates a personal testimonial about vegetarianism, while Krizmanic includes only testimonials from other sources. Ricard includes more factual information, but Krizmanic primarily uses testimonial evidence. Ricard's intention is to persuade and his bias is obvious; Krizmanic's intentions are not as clear. Her approach is more even-handed. Also, Ricard writes from firsthand experience; Krizmanic does not. It is not clear whether she is or is not a vegetarian.

@ **Gr7Ch5Read3.pptx**

---

2. What is the main claim in Krizmanic's text?

3. How is Ricard's purpose different from Krizmanic's purpose?

TECH-CONNECT

Use an online polling site to compare which argument your classmates believe has more convincing evidence: Ricard's or Krizmanic's. Post your results on your class website.

4. What type of evidence does Ricard use to support his points?

5. What type of evidence does Krizmanic use to support her points? Does she include any counterarguments and evidence against the counterarguments? Is this effective? Why or why not?

6. What similar evidence is used in the two texts?

CONNECT TO ESSENTIAL QUESTION

What do you feel strongly enough about to change your life?

Write Synthesize the ideas from both texts to write a few paragraphs analyzing the arguments presented by the two authors.

Language: Consistent Verb Tenses

Verb tense indicates when an action takes place. The three main verb tenses are present, past, and past perfect.

- Present tense examples: *is, have, eat, make*
- Past tense examples: *was, had, ate, made*
- Past perfect examples: *had been, had had, had eaten, had made* (had/has + past tense of verb)

When writing an essay, a story, or an exam answer, keep your verbs in the same tense. For example, use past tense verbs when writing about historical events for social studies class. Use present tense verbs when summarizing the events in a story and when writing an argument. Only switch to past tense to describe events that actually happened in the past.

Read the following paragraph. Notice how Matthieu Ricard uses present and past tense verbs correctly in the excerpt. Present tense verbs are underlined. Past tense verbs are bold.

My first Buddhist teacher, Kangyur Rinpoche, **was** a very strict vegetarian. I **was inspired** by him and also by a deep inner reasoning that suddenly became obvious to me. I never **hunted** in my life, but **did** go fishing sometimes when I **was** a little boy in Brittany. When I **was** 13 years old, a thought **bloomed** in my mind: "How can I do something like that?" I **realized** that I **was** totally **avoiding** putting myself in the place of the other being. And when I **was** 20, I **gave** up eating meat. That **was** 50 years ago.

The heart of the Buddhist path <u>is</u> compassion. That <u>means</u> to value others. If you <u>value</u> others, you <u>value</u> their well-being and <u>are</u> concerned by their suffering.

Matthieu Ricard begins in the past tense because he is talking about how he was inspired by his first Buddhist teacher to become a vegetarian. This was 50 years ago. He correctly switches to present tense in the second paragraph when he explains the principles of Buddhism, which exist today.

Read the following paragraph. Think about what is happening now and what happened in the past. Consider the underlined verbs. Circle those that are incorrect, and write the correct form in the margin to the right.

But some kids do know where meat <u>comes</u> from, and it <u>didn't</u> really bother them. Charley Goss, age 9, <u>eats</u> meat: "When I <u>am</u> little, I couldn't imagine meat coming from an animal. I <u>think</u> it <u>was</u> gross. We <u>would visit</u> a meat packing plant and <u>see</u> the cattle, the sides of beef hanging in the freezer, and then they <u>would give</u> us a slice of beef lunchmeat to eat. I <u>didn't eat</u> meat for a couple of years. But I just grew out of it. I <u>didn't pay</u> much attention to it anymore."

In small groups, have students discuss the following questions:

- How are the audiences for the two passages different?
- Why does Krizmanic use a different type of evidence than Ricard?
- How are the purposes of the two excerpts different?

Language: Consistent Verb Tenses: Have students analyze the use of verb tenses in a paragraph from one of the excerpts in the chapter. Explain to students that when they write about a work of literature they should use present tense instead of past tense. For example: *Ricard writes about vegetarianism* and not *Ricard wrote about vegetarianism.*

Answers to Language Activity:

Circle the following:

didn't, change to *doesn't*

am, change to *was*

think, change to *thought*

would visit, change to *visited*

see, change to *saw*

would give, change to *gave*

didn't pay, change to *don't pay*

 Gr7Ch5Language.pptx

ELL Support: Language Create a two-column chart on the board or on chart paper with headings as follows: Present Verbs, Past Verbs. Write the present and past tense verbs from the explanation paragraphs on p. 93 in the chart. Complete the first few rows and then have volunteers identify the present tense verbs and their past tense counterparts. Be sure to include the examples of verbs that are in the paragraph, both singular and plural forms. Students can work in multilevel pairs or small groups and use the chart to help them correct the paragraph on the bottom of p. 93.

More advanced students can compare English conjugations with conjugations in their native language. Then they can explain the differences to Beginning learners.

Chapter 5 (continued)

Assessment

Project-Based Assessments

Awareness Speech: You may want to require students to use some kind of multimedia element in their speech, such as a digital presentation, a video, or a graph or chart.

Encourage students to practice their speech with a partner. Another option is to have students record themselves using their cell phones. As they watch themselves, encourage them to evaluate the content and presentation using the following:

Content:

- Introduction gets the audience's attention
- Introduces the problem clearly
- Presents a workable solution based on researched facts
- Uses good transitions between main ideas

Presentation:

- Makes eye contact with audience
- Volume is appropriate
- Rate is not too fast or too slow
- Uses gestures to support ideas

Suggested Listening Activity: Encourage students who are listening to the speeches to evaluate the speaker's argument for logic and clarity. They should also evaluate the use of multimedia, if this is a requirement

Letter to the Editor: Provide copies of letters to the editor from your local or city newspaper. Invite students to find examples of strong evidence or faulty reasoning, such as attacking a person instead of "attacking" an argument (with sound reasoning).

To help students think about a different point of view, ask them to write their letter as if they were a rancher or livestock producer. Encourage them to research facts that would support this point of view.

Visit the Purdue Online Writing Lab to view tips for writing a business letter. Go to https://owl.english.purdue.edu/owl/ and search for *business letter*.

Project-Based Assessments

Awareness Speech

Write a 3-5 minute speech to raise awareness of an issue. Follow these steps to write your speech:

1. Identify a problem or issue at your school that should be addressed or could be changed. Possible ideas might include the following:
   - Availability of junk food
   - Cell phone policy
   - Volunteer opportunities at your school
   - Sports participation policies
   - Mandatory class requirements
2. Plan your speech by introducing the problem, providing facts and information about it, and offering a solution.
3. Conduct research about your topic so that you can add facts to your speech. You may need to interview school administrators, teachers, and other students to gather firsthand information. Use the Internet to learn about policies at other schools.
4. Practice your speech by reading it aloud several times. Make sure you are not tied to your notes. Make eye contact often with your audience. Avoid speaking too quickly. Make your voice interesting by using inflections and pauses effectively.

> **REFLECT**
>
> Why do people sometimes do the wrong thing even when they know it is wrong?

Use the following guidelines for your speech.	
To receive the highest score, the speech must meet all of these criteria.	Your speech • clearly and creatively explains the problem using facts and/or personal examples. • offers a reasonable solution to the problem. • shows evidence of research and demonstrates knowledge of the topic. • is three to five minutes in length. • is free from grammar, spelling, and punctuation errors. • is presented in a professional manner with good vocal variety to communicate ideas.

Letter to the Editor

A letter to the editor is a response to an article that is usually published in the editorial section of a newspaper. Most letters to the editor share an opposing viewpoint of a previously published article. They reference the content of the letter with which the writer disagrees, state why they disagree, and offer evidence to support an alternative point of view. For this project, you will

ELL Support: Project-Based Assessments—Awareness Speech Have students work in multilevel pairs or small groups to create, practice, and deliver a speech together. Students can deliver the speech as one voice or each deliver a part of the speech. Provide sentence frames for an awareness speech:

- I believe the school should consider changing . . . .
- One reason is . . . .
- Another reason is . . . .
- One way to solve this problem is . . . .

If students need practice with informal speaking, stage a live classroom debate as part of the project.

write your own letter to the editor in response to "Why I Am a Vegetarian" or "Vegetarianism."

Follow these steps:

- Read some examples of letters to the editor in your local newspaper or an online newspaper. Think about the evidence the writer uses to support his or her claims.

- Before writing, think about your point of view toward vegetarianism. Provide evidence to support your position or that contradicts evidence presented in the text to which you are responding.

- Use business letter format in a block style and include the following: date, recipient's address (use information for your local newspaper's editor), salutation, body, closing, and signature.

Use the following guidelines for your letter to the editor.	
To receive the highest score, the letter must meet all of these criteria.	**Your letter** • references points made in the passage in this chapter. • clearly explains your point of view. • strongly supports your opinion by presenting reasons and evidence. • contains convincing and effective language and style. • is in business letter format with a header, salutation, body, and closing. • uses correct grammar, usage, punctuation, and spelling.

On Your Own: Integrating Ideas

1. Listen to one of Matthieu Ricard's TED talks, "The Habits of Happiness" or "How to Let Altruism Be Your Guide." Both can be found at www.ted.com.
2. Search online to discover the differences between vegetarians, vegans, and pescetarians. Also find out about the Paleolithic diet and how it compares to a vegan diet.
3. Learn more about teens and vegetarianism by reading Judy Krizmanic's *A Teen's Guide to Going Vegetarian.*
4. Go to www.matthieuricard.org to read an interview with Matthieu Ricard by the Garrison Institute, view some of his photographs, or learn more about his life.
5. Two of the chapters in this unit deal with the human treatment of animals. How has society's attitude toward animals changed in the last century? Why do you think this change has occurred?

On Your Own: Integrating Ideas:

Activity 2: Students might enjoy creating a poster that illustrates similarities and differences among the four diets.

Activity 3: Encourage students to write a review of Judy Krizmanic's book.

ELL Support: On Your Own: Integrating Ideas Have students work in multilevel pairs or small groups to write the letter. Provide the Letter Format Template from the ELL Teacher Resource (p. 55) for students to use. Also, provide the following sentence frames:

- The article "Why I Am a Vegetarian"/"Vegetarianism" is a . . . article. The author's main claim is . . . .

- The author supports this claim with many reasons. For example, ... The author supports this reason with evidence such as . . . .

- The author's argument is strong/weak. The reasons do/do not relate to the argument. The reasons are/are not logical. The evidence does/does not support the reasons. There is/is not enough evidence.

- I believe . . . .

- You should read this article because . . . .

Chapter 5 *(continued)*

Assessment

Connect to Testing: This Connect to Testing section focuses on determining author's purpose, analyzing an argument, and synthesizing information from multiple texts.

Encourage students to work in pairs to choose the correct answers to the questions and then to compare their answers with those of another pair of students. If there is disagreement, encourage the groups to try to reach a consensus as they discuss the reasons for their choices.

Answers to Connect to Testing Questions:

1. D. Choice A is a claim not a fact. Choice B is a fact but it doesn't support a selfish reason. Choice C is an opinion. Choice D is a fact that relates to a selfish reason for being a vegetarian—to live healthier. (DoK 1)

2. A., B., E. In his argument, Ricard assumes that the lives of people and animals have equal value. When he explains that Buddhism values others, he includes both humans and animals. The choices that most nearly support this idea are A, B, and E. (DoK 3)

(continued)

Connect to Testing

In this chapter, you determined an author's purpose and analyzed evidence used in different arguments. When you take assessments, you will be tested on these skills. Answer the following questions.

1. Which of the following facts does Ricard use to support a selfish reason to eat only vegetables?

   A. *We can find means to survive without causing suffering to others.*

   B. *In India for example, there are over 400 million vegetarian people who survive well.*

   C. *They are not sacrificing their health or reducing their life span.*

   D. *Many studies have shown that red meat increases the incidence of colon cancer and other illnesses.*

2. Ricard's central claim is based on the assumption that the lives of animals and people are equally valuable. Which of the following quotations best support Ricard's assumption? (Choose all that apply.)

   A. *If you value others, you value their well-being and are concerned by their suffering.*

   B. *We can find means to survive without causing suffering to others.*

   C. *In India for example, there are over 400 million vegetarian people who survive well.*

   D. *In fact, even from a selfish standpoint, it is better to be a vegetarian.*

   E. *This would be called genocide or dehumanization if they were human beings.*

   F. *The main reason is that industrial farming causes the production of methane.*

ELL Support: Connect to Testing and Assessments See the *Connections* ELL Teacher Resource (p. 22) for ideas on adapting this section for ELLs.

3. Which sentence from "Vegetarianism" **most clearly** explains a central reason in support of vegetarianism?

    A. *killing a living creature that feels pleasure and pain is wrong, especially since we don't need to eat meat to be healthy.*

    B. *If pork were called pig and steak were called cow, I think more of the world would be vegetarian*

    C. *Humans have been eating meat for so many years, and they've been doing OK.*

    D. *Being vegetarian opens up a whole new world of food for them.*

4. **Part A:** Which claim is best supported by "Vegetarianism"?

    A. Many kids become vegetarians because they dislike the taste of meat.

    B. Many kids become vegetarians because they now have more options available outside of their homes.

    C. Many kids become vegetarians because they are concerned for their health.

    D. Many kids become vegetarians because they don't want to kill animals for food.

    Part B: Explain your reasoning for your answer in Part A above. Use textual evidence in your answer.

5. **Part A:** What does Krizmanic convey in paragraph 7 (lines 40–51)?

    A. Most people resist change, so they are unlikely to adopt vegetarianism.

    B. Most people do not question whether it is right to kill animals for meat because eating meat is their custom.

    C. Most people eat meat because they consider animals as lower life-forms and thus, fair game.

    D. Most people blindly follow tradition in all aspects of their lives.

continued on next page

---

3.   A. Choice B expresses an opinion. Choice C states a reason, but it is not an important reason. Choice D is an opinion but not a strong reason. Choice A offers an important moral reason in support of vegetarianism. (DoK 2)

4.   **Part A:** D. (DoK 3) **Part B:** Krizmanic states this directly in the first paragraph and supports it in the second paragraph. In numerous places throughout the article she quotes kids who say that their main reason for not eating meat is that they don't want to kill animals for food. In the end, she adds some additional reasons. (DoK 2)

5.   **Part A:** B. In this paragraph Krizmanic explains a possible reason why more people aren't vegetarians: because they are used to eating meat. The best answer is Choice B. (DoK 1)

(continued)

Chapter 5 *(continued)*

Assessment

Answers to Comparing and Contrasting Arguments:

5. **Part B:** Ricard addresses this point by beginning his article with a story about how he became a vegetarian. He writes, "I realized that I was totally avoiding putting myself in the place of the other being." This idea of putting himself in the animal's place is what many meat eaters fail to do when considering vegetarianism. Ricard also states, "It just takes one second to decide to stop. It doesn't create any huge chaotic changes in our life." This claim counters the argument that people eat meat because it is their custom. (DoK 3)

6. **Part A:** C. (DoK 1) **Part B:** Ricard compares killing animals for food to committing genocide to shock readers and cause them to think of animals as being much like humans. (DoK 3)

Part B: How does Ricard address the answer to Part A in his article? Cite at least two details from the text for support.

6. **Part A:** In paragraph 4, to what does Ricard compare killing animals for food?

   A. regressing society

   B. consuming selfishly

   C. committing genocide

   D. objectifying animals

Part B: Using your answer from Question 6, above, what does Ricard accomplish by using the comparison?

Remediation: Connect to Testing Have students work with a partner to read each question and eliminate incorrect answers.

For question 1, point out that "selfish" refers to a reason that would only help the diner.

For questions 5 and 6, make sure students reread the paragraphs in question.

Writing an Argumentative Essay

> *"To educate a person in the mind but not in morals is to educate a menace to society."*
> — Theodore Roosevelt

In this unit, you read articles and stories related to the theme of right and wrong. This section will lead you step by step to use what you have learned by writing an argumentative text about an issue you believe in.

WRITING PROMPT

In chapter 5, the author of "Why I Am a Vegetarian" explains his personal reasons for choosing vegetarianism and supports these reasons with facts and statistics. What is an issue you feel strongly about and have a personal connection to? Make a claim about the issue in an argumentative essay. Support your claim with strong reasons based on research and on your own personal experience. Include a counterclaim and a response to the counterclaim. Write your essay so that it will appeal to a broad audience beyond just your teachers and classmates. Your argumentative essay should be three to five pages, typed, double-spaced, in standard Times New Roman 12-point font.

Prepare to Write

Read the prompt carefully. Underline key words that explain the requirements of the task. Break it down based on purpose, audience, content, and additional requirements by filling in the chart below.

Purpose	
Audience	
Content Requirements	
Additional Requirements	

Writing an Argumentative Essay

Preview Academic Vocabulary

statistics: *data that represents a piece of information, such as how common something is or how often something is done.* The statistics indicated that obese people have more health problems than people with a healthy weight.

counterclaim: *an opposing claim; a claim that states a different opinion from the one held by the speaker or author.* A counterclaim to the claim that the climate is changing is that the earth is merely experiencing a natural cycle of warming, similar to ones the earth experienced in the past.

transition: *in writing, an indication of a change in thought or idea.* The phrase *on the other hand* indicated that the writer was making a transition from one idea to an opposing one.

audience: *the people who will read a paper.* If your audience for your paper is children, use words that they will understand.

credible: *offering reasonable grounds for being believed.* The source was from a fake news generating website and was not credible.

Prepare to Write: Make sure students understand the requirements for their argumentative essay: find an issue you feel strongly about; make a claim about that issue; use strong reasons from your research and experience; appeal to a broad audience.

Tell students that reading a prompt is a skill they will use in testing situations. They should annotate prompts in the same way they annotate the texts in this chapter—by underlining key words that explain the requirements. Instruct students to pay attention to the type of writing required by the prompt.

 Gr7U1WritingArgumentative.pptx

Brainstorm: Students might consider the following options for a topic:

ELL Support: Prepare to Write Have students work on all the steps of the essay in multilevel pairs or groups. Be sure students understand that an essay is a long, written response with several paragraphs. Explain the words in the chart. Say: *Purpose is the reason for writing. Audience is the people you are writing for. Content Requirements means what the essay has to be about. Additional Requirements means what else the essay needs to include.* Provide questions to support students in completing the chart: *Why are you writing this essay? Who are you writing the essay for? What must the essay be about? What else must the essay include?*

Writing *(continued)*

Lesson Support

- Use of cell phones/smartphones should/should not be limited by parents.
- Teens should/should not be at left home alone.
- Punishments should be automatic for bullying/cyberbullying.
- Teens should/should not be allowed to watch horror movies.
- Teens should/should not be allowed to play violent video games.

Other topics can be found by watching the state or national news or by reading newspapers.

The Writing Process

Brainstorm

The topic of your argumentative essay should be something you feel personally connected to. Think about writing about an issue you or someone you know has experienced.

What struggles have you or someone you know faced and overcome?	What actions have you or someone you know taken to improve health or quality of life?

Complete the table to review some of the big ideas from the passages in this unit. Work independently or with a partner.

	Summary	What claim does the author make?	How could this information be used in an argumentative essay?
"Our Brains Are Wired for Morality: Evolution, Development, and Neuroscience"			

ELL Support: Brainstorm Have students work in their multilevel pairs or small groups. Rephrase the brainstorming questions as follows:

- What problems have you had? How did you solve this problem?
- What problems has someone you know had? How did that person solve this problem?
- What have you done to help others be healthy?
- What has someone you know done to help others be healthy?

Provide the following sentence frames for students to respond to the brainstorming questions:

- I have had problems with . . . . To solve the problem, I . . . .
- My . . . has had problems with . . . . To solve the problem, he/she . . . .

	Summary	What claim does the author make?	How could this information be used in an argumentative essay?
"Three Questions"			
"Zoo Complicated"			
"The Doll's House"			
"Why I Am a Vegetarian"			
"Vegetarianism"			

Brainstorm: Students may find it difficult to identify the "claim" in the two works of fiction from the chapter. Ask them to think about the theme or the truth about life communicated through the characters and conflict.

If students have trouble answering the question *How could this information be used in an argumentative essay?*, then ask follow-up questions:

- What does this text teach you about right and wrong? How could this lesson be applied to other situations?
- What does this text teach about human nature and how humans understand morality?
- Does the text contain any data or statistics that could apply to another topic?
- Does the text contain any memorable stories or quotations that could be used to introduce my topic or inspire the reader in my conclusion?

- To help others be healthy, I . . . . To help others be healthy, my . . . .

If time allows, have students read each other's problems and offer possible solutions.

Before students complete the second brainstorming chart, be sure they understand that these are all the texts they read in the unit. Instruct students to use their notes, graphic organizers, and responses to complete the chart. Model how to fill in the first column.

Writing *(continued)*

Generate Ideas: Point out that the chart suggests a way of thinking about claims/counterclaims. My Opinion is like a claim and A Different Opinion is like a counterclaim. A strong argumentative essay contains evidence, facts, reasons, and other support. However, it should also address counterclaims by stating a differing opinion and then offering arguments against it.

To help students identify ideas for the A Different Opinion column, have pairs of students share their opinions on the topics. Then one student rotates to create a new pair and shares his or her opinion with a new partner. Continue rotating until all the topics are covered with three partners.

Generate Ideas

In order to help you narrow your focus and write a specific claim, explain your opinion about the following controversial topics. Then write a different opinion. This activity will help you consider counterclaims to include in your essay. Fill in the bottom two rows with your own topics.

Topic	My Opinion	A Different Opinion
cyberbullying		
the rise of social media		
teenagers working		
different standards for males versus females		
school uniforms		

©Perfection Learning® • No Reproduction Permitted

ELL Support: Generate Ideas Use gestures, visuals, and explanations to be sure students understand the topics. For example:

Cyberbullying is being mean to people through email, texts, or social media. (Show texts and emails.)

"The rise of social media" means people using social media more and more. (Give examples of social media.)

"Teenagers working" means teens who have jobs. (Give examples of teen jobs.)

"Different standards for males *and* females" means treating men and women differently and unfairly. (Give examples of men getting paid more to do the same job as women.)

School uniforms are the clothes that children wear to school. Uniforms are the same clothes for each child. (Show pictures of school uniforms.)

Connections • © Perfection Learning®

In order to support your ideas about a controversial topic, gather evidence from other sources. Find and read at least four sources on your chosen topic. In your response journal, on notecards, or in a computer file, take detailed notes on your sources. As you record information, always record the source. Keep a list of your sources in the box below. Include the author's name, title of the article or book, website name, publisher, and date of publication.

Sources

1.

2.

3.

4.

Access background knowledge by asking students to share their experiences of cyberbullying, social media, school uniforms, etc. in the country where they previously attended school. Be sensitive to the fact that other cultures have different norms on these issues.

Sources Have students work in their multilevel pairs or small groups. Help students find linguistically accommodated articles on their chosen topic. Newsela is a website that provides articles on a wide range of topics in multiple lexile levels. https://newsela.com*

Generate Ideas: Model how to evaluate a website for bias by pulling up websites and reading the mission statement or About tab. For example on www.heritage.org under the About Heritage tab, it states: "The mission of The Heritage Foundation is to formulate and promote conservative public policies based on the principles of free enterprise, limited government, individual freedom, traditional American values, and a strong national defense." Compare this with the About tab at the Pew Research Center: "We generate a foundation of facts that enriches the public dialogue and supports sound decision-making. We are nonprofit, nonpartisan, and nonadvocacy. We value independence, objectivity, accuracy, rigor, humility, transparency, and innovation." Discuss which ones seems to be less biased?

Also discuss how to identify fake news articles. Some good resources for this include the following:

- "How to Spot Fake News" at www.FactCheck.org

- "Ten Questions For Fake News Detection," PDF for students at thenewsliteracyproject.org. Search for *fake news.*

- www.commonsensemedia.org/Educators include articles and short videos on how to spot fake news. Search for *fake news.* The site also offers tips for educators who want to teach students about media literacy.

Encourage students to ask the following questions about any source:

- Who created this?

- Who is the target audience?

- Who paid for this? or Who gets paid if you click on this?

- Who might benefit or be harmed by this message?

- What is left out of this message that might be important?

- Is this credible (and what makes you think that)?

Writing (continued)

Lesson Support

Encourage students to study the football example closely as a model. It will help them better understand how to move from a topic (football) to a claim→ reason→ evidence→ counterclaim→ response to counterclaim, etc.

Also remind students that reasons explain why the reader should accept or agree with their claim.

Discuss how to use personal testimony in an argumentative essay. Remind students that personal examples and stories appeal to emotion. Emotional appeals can be effective when not overdone. For example, most students have seen commercials asking for money for starving children or abused pets. These commercials appeal to emotions with sad music and emotional language. This should be avoided.

Often a personal story can be used effectively to introduce an argument or in the conclusion to wrap up the writing.

Once you have enough solid information about your topic, write a strong claim. Your claim should make a statement explaining what you want to see changed about the issue you researched. In order to write a strong claim, synthesize the ideas from your research by drawing a conclusion based on the facts and evidence presented by all the sources. Make sure your claim is specific. Then think of strong reasons to support your claim. Support your reasons with evidence, such as facts and personal testimony. Study this example:

> **Claim:** American football is dangerous to players and should be banned in high school.
>
> **Reason 1:** High school football players are at a high risk of injuries, such as concussions.
>
> **Evidence:** Statistics from a study by the Institute of Medicine and guidelines from the American Academy of Neurology.
>
> **Reason 2:** Younger football players often feel motivated to ignore injuries to "get back in the game," and they fear letting their teammates down, so they may make unwise decisions.
>
> **Evidence:** My personal testimony as a football player.
>
> **Counterclaim/Alternative evidence:** Injuries happen in all sports, so it is unfair to single out injuries that occur while playing football.
>
> **Response to counterclaim/alternative evidence:** Out of nine sports, football has the highest number of head injuries, which are potentially more dangerous injuries.

Now synthesize the information from your sources and write your own claim with two strong reasons below.

My claim:

Reason 1:

Reason 2:

ELL Support: Generate Ideas Use the model framework along with sentence frames for ELLs placed in multilevel pairs or small groups.

Claim: My opinion is . . . .

Reason 1: One reason is . . . .

Evidence: This is true because . . . .

Counterclaim: A different opinion is . . . .

Response to counterclaim: This opinion is wrong because . . . .

Reason 2: Another reason is . . . .

Evidence: This is true because . . . .

Before students write, you may want to pick a topic that students are not writing about and work as a class to write a sample essay using the above sentence frames. As you draft the class essay, use a think aloud to narrate your process. For example: *First, we write*

Organize Ideas

Copy this basic outline into your response journal. Use the sentence starters to help you write a basic outline for your essay.

Claim:

I. Introduction
  A. Introduce your topic, capture the reader's interest, use a quote from a text in this unit.
  B. State your claim.

II. The first reason that . . .
  A. Evidence that supports this is . . .
  B. Also, . . .

III. (Counterclaim) Some people may argue that . . .
   However, . . . (Evidence against counterclaim)

IV. Another reason is . . .
  A. Support for this includes . . .
  B. Further evidence proves that . . .

V. Conclusion
  A. In conclusion . . .
  B. Restate your claim in different words.

First Draft

Use your outline to write a draft of your essay. Here are some hints:

- Use to the outline you wrote in your response journal.
- Write quickly. You will revise and proofread later.
- Write on every other line or double-space if working on a computer. This will make it easier to make revisions.
- If you take a break and then return to drafting, reread what you have written before continuing. This will help you continue with your thoughts.
- Mark this paper Draft #1.

REFLECT

As you research your topic, your claim may change based on new information. This is a good thing. It means you are keeping an open mind about your topic and are willing to re-evaluate your opinion as you learn new information.

Organize Ideas: After students write an initial claim and two reasons, they should be able to insert this writing into their outline.

After students develop their basic outline, instruct them to trade drafts with a partner. The partner should rank the reasons and evidence from 1 to 4 based on how logical and relevant each is. The pairs should then meet together to discuss the ranking prior to writing their first drafts. At this point, students may decide to conduct further research to find stronger reasons or evidence for their paper.

Explain to students that the evidence against the counterclaim is also called a *rebuttal*. Some students might want to change the order of their essay so that the rebuttal comes right before their conclusion.

First Draft: Direct students' attention to the second bullet: write quickly; revise and proofread later. During a first draft students should let their thoughts and ideas flow, rather than getting bogged down in revising or correcting punctuation and spelling, which should take place at a later stage.

the introduction, the first paragraph. I introduce my topic. I tell the reader what my topic is. I do this in an interesting way. (Together with students draft a hook.) *Next, I tell a little bit about my topic. What important information does the reader have to know about my topic?* (Together with students draft a second sentence.) *Now I write the last sentence in the introduction paragraph. This sentence should be my claim, my opinion statement.* (Discuss your opinion on the topic and draft a claim statement with students.) Continue the process of narrating your thoughts and actions as you draft topic sentences, include reasons and evidence, present a counterclaim, and summarize the argument in your conclusion.

Writing *(continued)*

Lesson Support

First Peer Review: Students can get so caught up in their own writing that they cannot see issues that require change. Getting a new set of eyes offers an opportunity for an objective review of the paper's interest, flow, logic, etc.

Another idea for the first peer review is to have students use different highlighters to color code a peer's essay for the following elements: claim, reason, evidence. Students should be able to identify these elements easily. If they can't, the writer should edit the text appropriately.

Revision

Having other students and your teacher read your essay will help you improve it. Listen carefully to their questions and comments on your writing. Applying their advice will help you refine your writing.

Here are three ways to revise your paper.

First Peer Review

This review will evaluate whether your ideas are interesting and whether they flow together in a logical order. With a group of two or three people, complete the following steps.

Steps for Peer Review

1. Select a timekeeper. Each writer gets 15 minutes. Respect the time limit.

2. One person begins by reading aloud his or her first paragraph while other members listen.

3. Pause. The same writer reads the first paragraph aloud a second time.

4. The writer asks, "Does the introduction clearly explain my claim and make you want to know more? " Each member responds, as the writer takes notes on his or her draft.

5. The writer reads the entire essay, pauses, and then reads it again.

6. As the writer reads, members take notes.

7. The writer asks, "Did I use strong reasons to support my claim? Did I include effective evidence? Do my key ideas fit together clearly and logically? The writer jots down replies.

8. Repeat Steps 1-7 with the next member of the group who becomes the writer.

REFLECT

The introduction usually has a "hook" to get readers' attention. This hook may be a quote, story, or startling statistic.

ELL Support: First Peer Review Have students work in multilevel pairs or small groups to review their drafts. Highlight the questions in Steps 4 and 7 in the Peer Review on p. 106 that students should use as they read their draft. Provide the following sentence frames for students to use to give feedback to their peers.

(Yes/No), your introduction (clearly explains/does not clearly explain) your claim. Can you explain your claim to me? Can you write that in your paper?

(Yes/No), your introduction (makes me/does not make me) want to read more. Can you start with a question or interesting fact?

(Yes/No), you (used/did not use) strong reasons to support your claim. This reason isn't strong because . . . . What other reasons can you use?

(Yes/No), your ideas (fit/do not fit) together. Can you use connecting words like *because, also, for example*?

Using Transitions

Transitional words and phrases help readers make connections among ideas. As you revise your paper, make sure you have used appropriate transitions between and within paragraphs.

Transitions			
Point to a reason	Identify a conclusion	Show a contrast	Show sequence
because	as a result	although	first, second, third
if	thus	even though	then
since	so	however	next
for this reason	consequently	but	finally
the first reason, another reason	then	on the other hand	before, after, later
	therefore	in contrast	soon
	in conclusion	instead	when

As soon as possible after peer review, revise your draft based on your peers' questions and comments. Mark this paper Draft #2.

Second Peer Review

With a partner, trade essays and use the following checklist to evaluate your partner's essay.

Think big. Look at the draft as a whole.

☐ Has the writer covered everything required by the prompt?
☐ Is the flow between paragraphs smooth or choppy?
☐ Is the point of view consistent throughout?

Think medium. Look at the draft paragraph by paragraph.

☐ Does the introduction hook the reader and make him or her want to read more?
☐ Does each paragraph support the claim with various types of valid evidence?
☐ Are the ideas supported by research?
☐ Did the writer include a valid counterclaim or alternative explanations?

Think small. Look at your draft sentence by sentence.

☐ Which sentences are long and confusing? Short and choppy?
☐ Are any sentences unclear?
☐ Are there errors in spelling, grammar, or usage?

When you finish the steps, mark the version Draft #3.

> **REFLECT**
>
> Reading and revising the same paper over and over again may become tiresome and make you start skipping over words and sentences because they are so familiar. Try reading the essay in reverse to stay focused.

Using Transitions: During the Second Peer Review, have students underline all the transitional words and phrases used in a peer's paper. Tell students that transitions are especially needed between paragraphs. If no transition is provided, the editor should suggest one from the list in the Student Book.

Second Peer Review: The three levels of peer review provide writers with a method for critiquing other students' writing—as well as their own.

ELL Support: Second Peer Review Have students work in new multilevel pairs or small groups to review their drafts. Display these adapted question:

Think Big

Did I answer the prompt question completely?

Did I use connecting words or phrases between sentences and paragraphs?

Is my point of view or thoughts and feelings on the topic the same through the whole essay?

Think Medium

Is my introduction interesting?

Does each paragraph explain my claim with good evidence (facts)?

Did I include information from articles?   *(continued)*

Writing *(continued)*

Lesson Support

Final Peer Review: Encourage students to offer criticism in a positive way that points out strengths while providing advice for improved writing.

Final Peer Review

Ask another student to read your argumentative essay and rate it using the rubric below:

	Use the following guidelines for your argumentative essay.
To receive the highest score, the essay must meet all of these criteria.	Your argumentative essay • makes a claim about a specific topic. • supports the claim with more than one reason. • includes strong evidence that supports the reasons. • relates a personal experience in support of the claim. • includes a counterclaim, along with evidence in response to the counterclaim. • uses transitions to help the reader follow the flow of ideas. • is clearly organized with good transitions between sentences and paragraphs. • uses correct grammar, usage, punctuation, and spelling.

Proofread

As you prepare a final draft, make sure you have included correct grammar and punctuation. Proofread carefully for omitted words and punctuation marks, especially when using direct quotations. If you used a word processing program, run spell-check, but know that it won't catch every error. Proofread again to detect the kinds of errors the computer can't catch.

Final Essay

Share your completed essay with audiences beyond your classroom. Read it to your family and friends. Upload your finished digital copy to your class website. If you have a school or personal blog or website, share it with your readers.

Did I explain the opposite opinion?

Think Small

Which sentences are too long? Which sentences are too short?

Which sentences are unclear?

Is there any other way I can word this?

Did I make any spelling or grammar mistakes?

ELL Support: Proofread Have students work in new multilevel pairs or small groups to review their drafts. Provide them with the proofreading checklist found in the digital resource. For spelling, grammar, and punctuation help, encourage students to use online or digital resources. A search engine will help students identify correct spellings if they type *How do you spell . . . ?*, even when they spell the word incorrectly.

Practice Performance Task

A performance task evaluates your ability to comprehend selections of literature and informational text and then demonstrate your knowledge in writing. The task may begin with several multiple-choice or short-answer questions on key vocabulary and the key ideas of the passage(s). The task culminates with a writing assignment. Complete the following performance task based upon selections from Unit 1.

Source #1

Read the following excerpt from "Our Brains Are Wired for Morality: Evolution, Development, and Neuroscience" by J. Decety and J. Cowell. Then answer the questions that follow.

Humans are an extremely <u>social</u> species. We are dependent on each other and cannot survive and flourish without interacting with others. Newborns only survive to adulthood if given enough care, and societies succeed through cooperation. Almost all of our actions and thoughts are about others or are in response to others. We cooperate with and help people who are not related to us at a level that is unmatched in the animal kingdom [1]. Since humans are, by nature, both helpful and selfish, we think that morality evolved to support our helpful social interactions with others and control our somewhat selfish tendencies.

However, it would be misleading to see morality as only a result of evolution. Although some human traits, like skin color, are determined by our genes alone, morality is quite different in that it is also determined both by our nature and the society in which we live. Many moral rules and values vary between different <u>cultures</u> and also change over time. For instance, bull fighting is seen as a cruel form of entertainment or even as animal torture in North America and most European countries, but it is still very popular in Spain and Colombia where it is considered a form of expression, despite the obvious suffering of the animals. An example of a shift in morality over time is our attitude toward slavery. Most people in the world today think that it is immoral to own slaves but that was not the case a century ago.

continued on next page

Practice Performance Task

The purpose of this section is to prepare students for the types of performance tasks they will be completing on standardized testing. The task requires students to synthesize knowledge gained and skills developed throughout the unit. If used as test prep, review with students the process of answering multiple-choice questions, including eliminating answers that are clearly incorrect.

This performance task could be used as an assessment over Unit 1, instead of the Unit 1 Assessment on pages 451–459. The task may be completed over two class periods by having students complete questions 1–4 and the planning stage of the writing task during one class period and then having them write the essay during the second class period. Another alternative is to assign the writing to be completed at home.

ELL Support: Practice Performance Task Have students work in multilevel pairs or small groups to read, answer questions, and write their essays. Remind students that they have read these texts already. Have students review their notes, graphic organizers, and visuals they created as they read the texts. Ask students to work in their multilevel pairs or groups to summarize the main idea and details of each text. Encourage students to use the writing supports (including the sample class essay) and checklists from the argument essay on this new essay.

Assessment *(continued)*

Lesson Support

Answers to the Practice Performance Task:

1. **Part A:** B. **Part B:** A., B., D. (DoK 1)

2. B. Choice A is the other element that influences morality. The passage contrasts the influence of genes (nature) and culture. It is not correct. Choice E is also clearly incorrect. Choice C describes the elements of a culture that control morality, but these qualities do not define the word *culture*. The best answer is Choice B because *society* and *culture* are similar concepts. (DoK 1)

3. **Part A:** A.

   Part B: D. Choice A is incorrect because the point of the excerpt is that both biology and society play a role in forming morality. Choice B is not a key idea. Choice D is also incorrect because the focus of the passage is not on defining morality. The best choice is C. (DoK 2)

(continued)

Thus, our morality has been formed over thousands of years from the combination of both our genes and our culture, rather than just one or the other. This genetic and cultural evolution has shaped our brains to care for others, react to those who try to harm us, and to create moral rules that help us to live together successfully [2].

1. **Part A:** According to the passage, the word *social* most nearly means
   A. having to do with evolution.
   B. related to relationships.
   C. knowing right and wrong.
   D. fighting for survival.

   Part B: Which of the following lines from the text provide the strongest evidence for your answer to Part A? Choose all that apply.
   A. *dependent on each other*
   B. *without interacting with others*
   C. *only survive to adulthood*
   D. *societies succeed through cooperation*
   E. *Almost all of our actions*

2. The word *cultures* is best explained by which phrase from the passage?
   A. *our nature*
   B. *the society in which we live*
   C. *moral rules and values*
   D. *change over time*

3. **Part A:** Which of the following best summarizes the **key idea** of the passage?
   A. Concepts of right and wrong have been formed through evolutionary changes in our biological makeup and through the communities in which we live.
   B. An understanding of right is wrong is unique to humans and not found in the animal kingdom.
   C. Morality is often based on culture and thus changes depending on where you live.
   D. Morality has to do with caring for others within our own society, protecting ourselves from enemies, and creating standards by which to live.

Part B: Which sentence from the text best supports the answer to Part A?

A. *Newborns only survive to adulthood if given enough care, and societies succeed through cooperation.*

B. *morality evolved to support our helpful social interactions with others and control our somewhat selfish tendencies.*

C. *Most people in the world today think that it is immoral to own slaves but that was not the case a century ago.*

D. *Thus, our morality has been formed over thousands of years from the combination of both our genes and our culture*

Source #2

Read the following passage from the short story "Three Questions" by Leo Tolstoy.

The King approached him, and said:

"For the last time, I pray you to answer my questions, wise man."

"You have already been answered!" said the hermit, still crouching on his thin legs, and looking up at the King, who stood before him.

"How answered? What do you mean?" asked the King.

"Do you not see," replied the hermit. "If you had not pitied my weakness yesterday, and had not dug those beds for me, but had gone your way, that man would have attacked you, and you would have repented of not having stayed with me. So the most important time was when you were digging the beds; and I was the most important man; and to do me good was your most important business. Afterwards when that man ran to us, the most important time was when you were attending to him, for if you had not bound up his wounds he would have died without having made peace with you. So he was the most important man, and what you did for him was your most important business. Remember then: there is only one time that is important—Now! It is the most important time because it is the only time when we have any power. The most necessary man is he with whom you are, for no man knows whether he will ever have dealings with anyone else: and the most important affair is, to do him good, because for that purpose alone was man sent into this life!"

continued on next page

Assessment *(continued)*

Answers to the Practice Performance Task:

4. **Part A:** A. Choice C is not supported by the hermit's words. Choice D is possibly true for the hermit himself, but he is not suggesting that the king must live in poverty. Choices A and B both seem to be correct. However, Choice A is the best choice because the hermit is suggesting that the king should respect everyone not just the weak and needy. (DoK 2)

   Part B: The hermit emphasizes that the king made the right choices because he did what was unselfish and good for the other person. For example, he says "when you were digging the beds; and I was the most important man; and to do me good was your most important business." Later, the hermit explains, "the most important affair is, to do him good, because for that purpose alone was man sent into this life!" (DoK 2)

4. **Part A:** The hermit's response to the King reveals that his point of view of morality is based on

   A. respect for others.

   B. helping the weak and the needy.

   C. paying back those who've wronged you.

   D. living a simple life of poverty.

   Part B: Identify two lines from the text that support the answer to Part A. Explain how these lines provide evidence for the answer.

Your Assignment

WRITING PROMPT

In this unit you read a variety of texts related to the Essential Question: *How do you know right from wrong?* You read informational articles that discussed people's desire to know right and wrong, stories in which characters made good and bad choices, and arguments in which authors developed their point of view on the issues of keeping wild animals in captivity and vegetarianism.

Write an essay in which you bring together ideas about morality from the texts in this chapter as you answer the question: How do you know right and wrong? In your answer, refer to at least three different texts in the unit as support for your conclusions about morality.

To gather ideas for your essay, fill in the following graphic organizer with details from the texts in this unit.

	What does the text say about how we (or the author) know right from wrong?	What does the text say (or imply) about specific actions that are right or wrong?
"Our Brains Are Wired for Morality: Evolution, Development, and Neuroscience"		
"Three Questions"	The hermit tells the King that the current time is the most important time because it is only now in the current moment that we have any power.	

continued on next page

Your Assignment: Make sure students have a clear understanding of the writing prompt by asking these questions:

- What is the purpose of the essay? *(To bring together ideas about morality from the texts in order to answer the question:* How do you know right from wrong?*)*

- How many texts should you use to support your conclusions? *(3)*

Instruct students to annotate the prompt so that they identify the requirements of the assignment before they begin.

 Gr7U1PerformanceTask.pptx

Lesson Support

	What does the text say about how we (or the author) know right from wrong?	What does the text say (or imply) about specific actions that are right or wrong?
"Zoo Complicated"		Keeping wild animals in captivity just for human enjoyment is wrong.
"The Doll's House"		
"Why I Am a Vegetarian"	The author's beliefs about vegetarianism come from his practice of Buddhism, which believes in showing compassion and valuing all creatures.	
"Vegetarianism"		

Your Assignment (continued)

Read the prompt carefully. Underline words that indicate how to write your essay. The rubric on page 116 features the qualities on which your writing will be evaluated. Study the rubric before you begin to write.

Use the organizer below and your answers to the chart on pages 113 and 114 to plan your essay. Make sure your thesis statement is a response to the unit Essential Question. Use evidence from at least three texts in the unit.

Introduction:
Main idea statement (answer to Essential Question):
One way I know right from wrong:
Another way I know right from wrong:
Conclusion:

Assessment *(continued)*

Your writing will be evaluated on the following. Think about each of these points in relation to your writing. Fill in notes about whether you have met the standard or if you need to make revisions.

Reading Comprehension

- How well did you understand the texts?
- Does your essay reflect a correct understanding of the sources?

Writing Expression

- Does your writing address the requirements of the prompt?
- Does your informative essay include a clear thesis statement?
- Is your essay clearly organized with points that fit together logically?
- Does your writing style contain precise, accurate language and content appropriate to the purpose, task, and audience?

Writing Conventions

- Does your writing follow the rules of standard English with few or no errors in grammar, usage, and spelling?

Use the list above to help you revise your essay.

Unit 2

Essential Question
Can you trust what you see, hear, and read?

Sometimes it's hard to know what to trust. Can that shocking headline you just saw online be true? Or is it just "fake news"? Will that alternative medicine really make you healthier, or is that "one weird trick" just a scam? Sometimes you can't even trust your own senses.

When the world seems like it is out to fool you, what can you do? It might be tempting to give up on the idea of truth altogether. If it's impossible to know what is real, then why bother trying? A more powerful way to respond is to become a more critical consumer. Instead of giving in to the lies, you can develop mental habits to help you tell facts from falsehoods and strike back against dishonesty.

Unit 2 will explore issues of trust, truth, and fact-finding. You'll read about the ultimate con man, your tricky brain and eyes, fake news, sketchy medicine, and a society that is not as perfect as it seems. As you read these texts, remember that the truth is out there, even if it's not always easy to find. Sometimes you have to hunt for it.

> **GOALS**
> - To determine central ideas and analyze how they develop
> - To analyze the interactions between individuals, events, and ideas
> - To explore how the structure of a text contributes to its meaning
> - To determine point of view and author's purpose
> - To research how one scientific explanation replaced another
> - To write an explanatory essay comparing two texts

ELL Support: Preview Unit 2 Essential Question See the _Connections_ ELL Teacher Resource (p. 32) for ideas on adapting this lesson for Beginning, Intermediate, and Advanced ELLs.

Unit 2

Essential Question: Can you trust what you see, hear, and read?

Introduction

Goals: Have students read through the goals and mark any words that are unfamiliar. Discuss the meanings of any unfamiliar academic vocabulary. Consider posting the Unit Goals.

Introduction Suggestions

1. Begin class lists (or word webs) of synonyms and antonyms of the word _truth_. As students work through the unit, encourage them to add to both lists. Synonyms might include _accuracy, fact, honesty, reality, nonfiction,_ or _information_. Antonyms might include _lie, dishonesty, disguise,_ or _fiction_. Challenge them to consider the gray area between the synonyms and the antonyms as a place for other words such as _propaganda, marketing,_ or an imaginary concept such as _Santa Claus_.

2. Invite students to do a 1-minute freewrite about a _lie_, either one that they have told or one that was told to them, taking any approach they choose. Have them tuck their writing (or file) into an envelope (or folder) that they will not open until they have finished this unit. Hopefully, they will observe that their thoughts about truth have shifted as a result of their reading and analysis.

3. Have students write a response to one of the following quotations:
   - Three things cannot be long hidden: the sun, the moon, and the truth. —Buddha
   - A lie gets halfway around the world before the truth has a chance to get his pants on. —Winston Churchill
   - The trust of the innocent is the liar's most useful tool. —Stephen King

   Gr7U2Opener.pptx

Tech-Connect Suggestion: Invite students to locate and explore audio and video adaptations of Gwendolyn Brooks's poem "truth." In it, the speaker asks some rhetorical questions about truth and human beings' reactions to it.

Chapter 6

Understanding Different Points of View

Catch Me If You Can
by Frank Abagnale Jr. with Stan Redding

Introduction

Chapter Goals: Have students read through the goals and mark any words that are unfamiliar. Discuss the meanings of any academic vocabulary within the goals that students marked as unfamiliar. Consider posting the Chapter Goals.

Preview Academic Vocabulary: Read and discuss the meanings of the academic vocabulary.

analyze: *to examine or study something in detail for the purpose of interpreting or understanding it.* The biology class studied the bacteria under a microscope to <u>analyze</u> their composition and growth.

evidence: *facts, examples, data, expert opinions, and anecdotes that serve to support an author's claims and reasons in an argument.* The thief was given his freedom because there was not enough <u>evidence</u> to convict him.

inference: *a conclusion or interpretation based on what the text says and also what the reader already knows.* The fashion designer made an <u>inference</u> about what people want to wear next year.

medium: *a means, channel, or system of communication, information, or entertainment; often used in its plural form:* media. The famous author wrote both short stories and screenplays, but film was her preferred <u>medium</u>.

narrator: *a person or character who tells a story.* The <u>narrator</u> in the novel is a twelve-year-old girl named Scout.

Chapter 6

Understanding Different Points of View

Preview Concepts

Name someone you trust. Why do you trust this person? Write your response below. Include two details from your interactions with him or her.

Share your answers with a partner. Based on your discussion, form a definition of *trustworthy* you both agree on. Write your definition in the space below.

CHAPTER GOALS

In this chapter you will:

- cite textual evidence to support an inference about a text.
- analyze how an author develops and contrasts points of view.
- compare and contrast the techniques different media use to tell the same story.

PREVIEW ACADEMIC VOCABULARY

analyze

evidence

inference

medium

narrator

point of view

technique

ELL Support: Academic Vocabulary See <u>Teaching Vocabulary in the ELL Teacher Resource (p. 18)</u> for ideas to use for teaching vocabulary throughout *Connections*.

ELL Support: Making Connections Read the quotations aloud, then work with students to write a paraphrase such as

P. T. Barnum: A true character is priceless. A person who has a true character has peace and joy. Money, land, or houses can't buy this kind of peace and joy. A man who is very honest may be poor, but everyone in the community will want to give him money.

Oscar Wilde: People say that some people are born to lie, just like some people are born to be poets. But they are wrong. Both lying and poetry are arts or take a lot of work. A young man who begins life as a person who tells small lies can grow into a person who tells really big lies.

Making Connections

Read the following excerpts. They express strong points of view about honesty and lying.

> Uncompromising integrity of character is invaluable. It secures to its possessor a peace and joy which cannot be attained without it—which no amount of money, or houses and lands can purchase. A man who is known to be strictly honest, may be ever so poor, but he has the purses of all the community at his disposal . . . .
>
> —from *The Art of Money Getting* by P. T. Barnum

> People have a careless way of talking about a 'born liar,' just as they talk about a 'born poet.' But in both cases they are wrong. Lying and poetry are arts . . . .Many a young man starts in life with a natural gift for exaggeration which, if nurtured . . . might grow into something really great and wonderful.
>
> —from "The Decay of Lying: An Observation" by Oscar Wilde

What is P. T. Barnum's point of view about honesty? Include evidence from the text to support your response.

What point of view about lying is expressed in the second excerpt? Include evidence from the text to support your response.

> **MAKING CONNECTIONS**
>
> The main text in this chapter was written by a man famous for tricking people. Think about the points of view people have of him as well as how he sees himself.

Have students work in multilevel pairs or small groups to answer the questions. Provide the following sentence frames for students to use in their responses:

- Barnum believes that honesty is . . . . For example, he says, " . . . ."
- Wilde believes that lying is . . . . For example, he says, " . . . ."

---

point of view: *an author's opinion or perspective.* From the point of view of this reporter, this disastrous fire could have been avoided.

technique: *the manner in which details are treated by an author or other artist; a writer's way of presenting a story.* The writer's technique of telling the story from the point of view of different characters made the story more interesting.

 Gr7Ch6Vocabulary.pptx

Preview Concepts: As they write their definitions, have pairs of students draw comparisons between their trustworthy persons. Definitions might include words and ideas such as *able to keep secrets, dependable, able to do what is right, faithful, supportive,* or *honest.*

Making Connections:

> **Sample Answers to Questions:**
>
> Barnum considers honesty a virtue that creates peace, joy, and trustworthiness. He values it more than money. The second excerpt expresses the idea that lying is a beneficial skill that can be cultivated.

Extend the discussion about the quotations by having students discuss P. T. Barnum's legacy of promoting freak shows. Do the views expressed by Barnum here seem appropriate for his lifelong vocation?

Tech-Connect Suggestion: Students may enjoy reading "10 Things You May Not Know About P. T. Barnum" at http://histv.co/1hTFT3r, including the fact that he never actually said, "There's a sucker born every minute," even though this statement is often credited to him.

Lesson Support

First Read: Making an Inference

Before Reading: Point out the title of the First Read—Making an Inference. Suggest that making inferences is somewhat like addition. Readers "add up" details from the text, and the sum is their own conclusion. However, it is not like addition in that different readers can make different inferences. Emphasize that all inferences, no matter their differences, must be based on evidence from the text.

Read aloud the introduction and objective. Inform students that the first read will guide them in the process of making and supporting an inference. Explain that during the first read, students should focus on underlining sentences that help them determine whether or not people in the excerpt trust Frank Abagnale.

Preview Vocabulary: Preview the vocabulary to aid comprehension. After the first read, guide students to determine the words' meanings using the context. Encourage students to support their responses with evidence. Have students confirm their initial definitions with a dictionary. Words that students might find difficult include:

immaculately: *in a perfectly clean, neat, manner; with no flaws or mistakes. He tended his lawn so* immaculately *that all the neighbors' lawns looked wild.*

ruefully: *regretfully; mournfully; pitifully. When I scold my dog, he looks at me* ruefully *as if he understands every word.*

wizened: *dry and wrinkled, usually from sun or age.* Point out that the word may evoke the word *wise*, but only by its spelling, not its sense. *Her* wizened *face indicated that she was not as young as her voice on the phone sounded.*

unabashed: *completely honest, undisguised, and out in the open. Even though the candidate was a crook, he had the* unabashed *support of many voters.*

flimflam: *deceptive nonsense; fraud. The phone caller wasn't a real lawyer; her pitch was* flimflam *so I hung up.*

First Read: Making an Inference

Frank Abagnale Jr., the coauthor of the excerpt below, spent the late 1960s and early 1970s pretending to be people he was not, including a doctor, a lawyer, and a government agent. He also stole a great deal of money through many schemes. In this excerpt from the first chapter of his book *Catch Me If You Can*, Frank describes tricking people into thinking he is an airplane pilot. At the time, he was only seventeen years old.

Objective: As you read, underline sentences that suggest whether people trust Frank Abagnale. Record any questions you have about the passage in the My Thoughts column.

—— First Read
---- Second Read
—— Third Read

from
Catch Me If You Can
by Frank Abagnale Jr. with Stan Redding

	My Thoughts

1   A man's alter ego is nothing more than his favorite image of himself. The mirror in my room in the Windsor Hotel in Paris reflected my favorite image of me—a darkly handsome young airline pilot, smooth-skinned, bull-shouldered and

5   immaculately groomed. Modesty is not one of my virtues. At the time, virtue was not one of my virtues.

Satisfied with my appearance, I picked up my bag, left the room and two minutes later was standing in front of the cashier's cage.

10   "Good morning, Captain," said the cashier in warm tones. The markings on my uniform identified me as a first officer, a co-pilot, but the French are like that. They tend to overestimate everything save their women, wine and art.

I signed the hotel bill she slid across the counter, started to

15   turn away, then wheeled back, taking a payroll check from the inside pocket of my jacket. "Oh, can you cash this for me? Your Paris night life nearly wiped me out and it'll be another week before I'm home." I smiled ruefully.

Different

ELL Support: First Read Have students read the text in multilevel pairs, pausing at the end of each paragraph to summarize the story on a Story Map graphic organizer from the ELL Teacher Resource (p. 52). Also, encourage students to draw sketches in the margins around the article or on a separate piece of paper as in a graphic novel so they can be sure they understand the story. Model doing so by taking notes and drawing sketches for the first paragraph. Say as you write: *He likes to look at himself. He likes to pretend he is an airplane pilot. He is not modest (humble) or virtuous (good).* Draw a sketch of a man looking in the mirror and seeing himself as a pilot.

She picked up the Pan American World Airways check and
20 looked at the amount. "I'm sure we can, Captain, but I must
get the manager to approve a check this large," she said. She
stepped into an office behind her and was back in a moment,
<u>displaying a pleased smile. She handed me the check to
endorse.</u>

25 "I assume you want American dollars?" she asked, and
without waiting for my reply counted out $786.73 in Yankee
currency and coin. I pushed back two $50 bills. "I would
appreciate it if you would take care of the necessary people,
since I was so careless," I said, smiling.

30 <u>She beamed.</u> "Of course, Captain. <u>You are very kind,</u>" she
said. "Have a safe flight and please <u>come back to see us.</u>"

I took a cab to Orly, instructing the driver to let me off at
the TWA entrance. I bypassed the TWA ticket counter in the
lobby and presented my FAA license and Pan Am ID card to
35 the <u>TWA operations</u> officer. He checked his manifest. "Okay,
First Officer Frank Williams, **deadheading** to Rome. Gotcha.
Fill this out, please." He handed me the familiar pink form for
nonrevenue passengers and I penned in the pertinent data.
I picked up my bag and walked to the customs gate marked
40 "CREW MEMBERS ONLY." I started to heft my bag to the
counter top but the <u>inspector, a wizened old man with a wispy
mustache, recognized me and waved me through.</u>

A young boy fell in beside me as I walked to the plane,
<u>gazing with unabashed admiration at my uniform with its
45 burnished gold stripes and other adornments.</u>

"You the pilot?" he asked. He was English from his accent.

"Nah, just a passenger like you," I replied. "I fly for Pan Am."

---
deadheading: riding without buying a ticket

My Thoughts

_____
_____
_____
_____
_____
_____
_____
_____
_____

Different

_____
_____
_____
_____
_____
_____
_____
_____
_____
_____
_____
_____

caliber: _degree or level of excellence or quality._ Her poem was outstanding for someone her age, but it was not of the same <u>caliber</u> as a famous poet like Robert Frost.

swindler: _a person who takes money or property by fraud or deceit._ He claimed to be a reputable salesman, but after a few minutes, I realized he was nothing but a <u>swindler</u>.

poseur: _a person who pretends to be what he or she is not; an actor; a fake._ Explain that the word is related to the verb _pose._ The banker looked honest, but he was a <u>poseur</u> who robbed people of their life savings.

After Reading: Use the following questions to check comprehension.

Text-Based Discussion Questions

1. What can we infer about the check that Frank cashes? _We learn that the check is a fake, a "bum-check" as he calls it in line 92._

2. What can you infer about Frank based on his interaction with the cashier? _Answers will vary but may suggest that Frank is a charmer. He knows how to impress people. He is confident._

3. At what moment does the text reveal that Frank is a poseur? _Most students will cite "because I couldn't fly a kite" (line 84) as the turning point in the text._

@ Gr7Ch6Read1.pptx

About the Author: Born in 1948, Frank Abagnale (pronounced AB-bin-yale) blames his parents' divorce for his disillusionment and his life of fraud between the ages of fifteen and twenty-one. In that time, he assumed eight different identities, including a pilot, a doctor, a prison agent, and a lawyer. Eventually, he was arrested in France in 1969 when a flight attendant recognized him and informed the police. He served five years in prison. Upon his release, he worked for the FBI, helping federal authorities investigate other scam artists. He later started his own business, consulting companies about fraud issues. Abagnale is married and lives in South Carolina. The film based on his book was a 2002 blockbuster, directed by Steven Spielberg and starring Leonardo DiCaprio as Abagnale.

Chapter 6 (continued)

Lesson Support

Confessional Literature: This subgenre of autobiography includes work in which the narrator recalls their life and confesses their sins. An early example is *The Confessions of St. Augustine* (ca. C.E. 400), which traces a man's progress from a young sinner to a devout Christian. It is considered a genre of poetry, too, practiced by modern poets such as John Berryman, Sylvia Plath, and Anne Sexton.

Tech-Connect Suggestion: Students may enjoy watching an episode of the 1977 game show *To Tell the Truth* in which three possible Frank Abagnales answer questions from a celebrity panel. At the end of the show, panel members make their guesses and the host says, "Will the real Frank Abagnale please stand up?" It is available here: http://www.historyvshollywood.com/video/frank-abagnale-jr-on-to-tell-the-truth-game-show-1977/.

"You fly 707s?"

I shook my head. "Used to," I said. "Right now I'm on DC-

50 8s." I like kids. This one reminded me of myself a few years

past.

An attractive blond stewardess met me as I stepped aboard

and helped me to stow my gear in the crew's luggage bin.

"We've got a full load this trip, Mr. Williams," she said. "You

55 beat out two other guys for the jump seat. I'll be serving the

cabin."

"Just milk for me," I said. "And don't worry about that

if you get busy. Hitchhikers aren't entitled to anything more

than the ride."

60 I ducked into the cabin. The pilot, co-pilot and flight

engineer were making their pre-takeoff equipment and

instrument check but they paused courteously at my entrance.

"Hi, Frank Williams, Pan Am, and don't let me interrupt you," I

said.

65 "Gary Giles," said the pilot, sticking out his hand. He

nodded toward the other two men. "Bill Austin, number two,

and Jim Wright. Good to have you with us." I shook hands

with the other two airmen and dropped into the jump seat,

leaving them to their work.

70 We were airborne within twenty minutes. Giles took the

707 up to 30,000 feet, checked his instruments, cleared with

the Orly tower and then uncoiled himself from his seat. He

appraised me with casual thoroughness and then indicated his

chair. "Why don't you fly this bird for a while, Frank," he said.

75 "I'll go back and mingle with the paying passengers."

His offer was a courtesy gesture sometimes accorded a

deadheading pilot from a competing airline. I dropped my

My Thoughts

Similar

Similar

Different

Different

Giles point of view

©Perfection Learning® • No Reproduction Permitted

Connections • © Perfection Learning®

cap on the cabin floor and slid into the command seat, very

much aware that I had been handed custody of 140 lives,

80   my own included. Austin, who had taken the controls when

Giles vacated his seat, surrendered them to me. "You got it,

Captain," he said, grinning.

I promptly put the giant jet on automatic pilot and hoped

to [heck] the gadget worked, because I couldn't fly a kite.

85   I wasn't a Pan Am pilot or any other kind of pilot. I was

an impostor, one of the most wanted criminals on four

continents, and at the moment I was doing my thing, putting a

super hype on some nice people. . . .

Oddly enough, I never felt like a criminal. I was one, of

90   course, and I was aware of the fact. I've been described by

authorities and news reporters as one of this century's cleverest

bum-check passers, flimflam artists and crooks, a con man

of Academy Award caliber. I was a swindler and poseur of

astonishing ability. I sometimes astonished myself with some

95   of my impersonations and shenanigans, but I never at any time

deluded myself. I was always aware that I was Frank Abagnale, Jr.,

that I was a check swindler and a faker, and if and when I were

caught I wasn't going to win any Oscars. I was going to jail.

My Thoughts

_____

_____

_____

_____

_____

Frank's point of view

_____

_____

_____

_____

_____

_____

_____

_____

_____

_____

_____

_____

_____

_____

_____

FIRST RESPONSE: KEY IDEAS AND DETAILS

Return to the sentences you underlined. How do other people feel about Frank? How do you know? Write your answers to these questions in your reading journal. Use details from the text in your response.

TECH-CONNECT

Post your First Response answers on your class web page. Compare your answers to those posted by other students.

FIRST RESPONSE: KEY IDEAS AND DETAILS

Students may have underlined phrases and sentences such as *warm tones* (lines 10–11), *displaying a pleased smile* (line 23), *She beamed* (line 30), *waved me through* (line 42), *gazing with unabashed admiration* (line 44), and *grinning* (line 82). All of these details reveal that other people think highly of Frank and even admire him.

Chapter 6 (continued)

Focus on Making an Inference:

Emphasize the action of "reading closely." This means actively reading the text by asking questions, noting key ideas, and making connections. Readers analyze a text by examining its details and explaining how these details contribute to its meaning.

Possible Answers to Chart:

See answers on Student Book insert page to the right.

 Gr7Ch6Read1.pptx

Focus on Making an Inference

After reading the passage, what do you think? Do people trust Frank Abagnale? Analyze the text to find out.

The word *analyze* means "to discover or reveal something through close examination." When you analyze a text, you are reading closely to figure out what the text says and how it says it.

Complete the chart below. In the column on the right, provide the evidence that answers each question. Then at the bottom of the chart, write your conclusion to this question: Do people seem to trust Frank Abagnale?

Question	Evidence
Does the cashier trust Frank?	*"I'm sure we can, Captain."* *displaying a pleased smile* She "beamed" when he gave her a $100 tip.
Does the "wizened old man" at the gate trust Frank?	He recognized Frank and waved him through.
Does Gary Giles, the pilot, trust Frank?	He shook his hand and gave him the control of the plane while he took a break, a "courtesy gesture" common at the time.
Your conclusion: Do people seem to trust Frank?	Yes, three very different people treat him like an airline captain and trust his uniform, his license, and his ID card.

ELL Support: Write Take the opportunity to review the English words and phrases that indicate time and location, not only *before* and *after* but also *during, since, until, when, from, until, at, in,* and *on.* Challenge students to use each one in a sentence that indicates time. Challenge students to work in multilevel pairs or small groups to use each word in a sentence.

You might not realize it, but you just made an inference. An *inference* is "a conclusion based on textual evidence and your prior knowledge." In the chart on the previous page

- your conclusion is about whether people trust Frank.

- the evidence consists of details from the text that support your conclusion.

- your prior knowledge is what you already know. In this case, you already know how people usually act toward someone they trust.

It might seem obvious that the people in the story trust Frank. But Frank never actually says, "These people trusted me." No character openly says, "I trust you, Frank." You as the reader came to the conclusion that people trust Frank, and you supported that conclusion with evidence.

▼Write Frank Abagnale was eventually caught by police. Do you think he wrote this book *before* or *after* his capture? Why do you think this? Support your inference with at least two details from the text.

Second Read: Analyzing Point of View

In literature, the term *point of view* refers to a narrator's or character's thoughts and feelings about something. That "something" can be a person, a place, an action, a series of events, or anything else that a person can have an opinion about.

Objective: Read the passage again. As you read, think about Frank's point of view about his skills as a pilot and Gary Giles's point of view about Frank's skills. Draw boxes around evidence showing each man's point of view.

Focus on Analyzing Point of View

As a narrator, Frank has a point of view about himself and his actions. The details he presents as the author are evidence of that point of view. But it's not just *Frank* who has a point of view about himself. Other characters do too. For example, Gary Giles has a point of view about Frank and his piloting skills.

> **REFLECT**
>
> Think about the first sentence: "A man's alter ego is nothing more than his favorite image of himself." What does Frank mean here by *image*? Do you have a favorite image of yourself? Do you consider that image an *alter ego*, which means "another self"?

> **CONNECT TO ESSENTIAL QUESTION**
>
> In the excerpt, Frank the character is obviously trying to fool people. But what about Frank the narrator, who is telling the story? Do you think he is trustworthy? What evidence do you have for your opinion?

continued on next page

Remediation: Second Read Help students see the difference between the last paragraph and the rest of the excerpt in terms of its tone, content, and point of view. Although the author is still writing in the first-person voice and the past tense, he is looking back on his exploits and commenting on them in a way that is different from the rest of the text. Readers are not along for the ride in this paragraph; they are inside Abagnale's head, "hearing" his thoughts and reflections.

ELL Support: Second Read Have students work in multilevel pairs or small groups to read the story again, identifying points of view. Before they do so, review the concepts of *point of view, narrator,* and *characters* with students. Define the words and give examples from the text.

▼**Write:** Students will infer that Abagnale wrote this book after his capture since he reveals so many incriminating details. He also writes about being "described by authorities and news reporters as one of this century's cleverest" poseurs, which suggests that he has already been discovered.

Second Read: Analyzing Point of View

Before Reading: Review the introduction and the objective with students, making sure they understand the purpose of the second read.

It might be helpful to lead a full-class discussion of the phrase "alter ego" as it is used in the first sentence of the passage. It was first used by 19th-century psychologists to describe a dissociative personality disorder. Perhaps the most famous example in literature is Robert Louis Stevenson's *Strange Case of Dr. Jekyll and Mr. Hyde.* The term "Jekyll and Hyde" has become a commonly used allusion that describes someone who has both good and evil characteristics.

After Reading: Use the following questions to check comprehension.

Text-Based Discussion Questions

1. What two people—or two egos—live inside Frank Abagnale? *Answers will vary but may suggest that one is the poseur and the other is the honest man who reflects on the poseur and knows that he will be caught someday.*

2. What is the blatant lie that Abagnale tells in the excerpt? *He tells both the boy and the pilots that he flies for Pan Am.*

3. Why does the narrator include the detail about the "custody of 140 lives, my own included"? *Answers will likely suggest that this detail makes his charade a matter of life and death. It is dangerous to himself and others in an extremely significant and criminal way.*

Focus on Analyzing Point of View: Clarify the different definitions of the term *point of view.* When studying literature, the term refers to who is telling the story, for example, first-person point of view or third-person point of view. The term can also be used in a more general way to refer to a person's or character's viewpoint or opinion of ideas or events.

Lesson Support

Possible Answers to Chart:

See answers on Student Book insert page to the right.

 Gr7Ch6Read2.pptx

You can analyze Frank's and Gary's points of view about Frank's skills as a pilot. Use the chart below to perform your analysis.

Two Points of View About Frank's Skills as a Pilot	
Frank's point of view about his skills as a pilot: Frank knows that he has no skills and is amazed that he has the ability to kill 140 people, including himself, if he makes a mistake.	Gary's point of view about Frank's skills as a pilot: He trusts that Frank is a real pilot. .
Two pieces of evidence showing Frank's point of view: *I couldn't fly a kite.* He hopes the plane's autopilot can do all the flying for him.	Two pieces of evidence showing Gary's point of view: He gives Frank control of his plane and even leaves the cabin to go talk to passengers. *"You got it, Captain," he said, grinning.*

The point of view of a narrator or character is not always explicit. For example, Gary's point of view might seem obvious through his actions, but nowhere does he explicitly say, "Frank, I know that you have great piloting skills." You as the reader had to infer his point of view.

Third Read: Comparing and Contrasting Presentations

People tell stories through different media, such as books and films. Each medium has different techniques, or methods, for telling that story.

- When a story or a book tells a narrative, its techniques are textual. These techniques can include rambling sentences, brief fragments, interesting similes, odd metaphors, punchy dialogue, long paragraphs—the list goes on and on.

- When a film tells a story, it uses different techniques: lighting, sound, color, camera focus, camera angles, and so on. In a film, everything you see and hear has been carefully chosen to make the audience feel a certain way.

Whether you're reading a text or watching a film, you can analyze how the techniques of each medium work together to tell a story. And if you read a story and watch a film based on it, you can compare how the two media tell their tales.

Watch a scene from the film version of *Catch Me If You Can*. Analyze the techniques the film uses to present events. You should watch it at least three times to gather enough details to complete the chart.

Film Analysis Worksheet of *Catch Me If You Can*
During Viewing
Color Describe the colors in the scene. Are they gray, dark, or washed out? Are they bright, full, or strong? Why do you think the director chose to film the scene this way?
Colors are bright and vibrant.
Point of View Sometimes we see Frank interacting with characters. Other times we see the world from Frank's point of view. How does switching the camera's point of view help to tell the story?
The filmmaker emphasizes Frank's point of view by moving in close during a scene. Examples include the close-up on the stewardess asking "Are you my deadhead?" and the camera zooming in on the plane window and then on Frank's face that shows his fear of flying for the first time.

continued on next page

ELL Support: Third Read Before students view the scene from the film, be sure they understand the film techniques: color, point of view, music, lighting, overall impression. Use the notes and questions that follow each technique in the chart to help students analyze the techniques. If possible, play the film clip with English subtitles, so students understand the dialogue better. Have students work in multilevel pairs or small groups to complete the chart.

Before students reread the text, be sure they understand the literary techniques: rambling (long) sentences, brief fragments (short, incomplete sentences), similes and metaphors (comparisons: Her eyes are stars), punchy dialogue (short, interesting conversations). Have students work in multilevel pairs or small groups to reread the text and complete the chart.

Third Read: Comparing and Contrasting Presentations

Before Reading: Explain that before the third read, students will watch a scene from a movie about Frank Abagnale.

Tell students that they will consider not only what the scene shows but also the techniques used to show it. Explain that *techniques* are like tools in a toolbox. A writer's and filmmaker's toolboxes differ, although some tools might be in both.

Make sure students understand the following process:

- Watch the scene, taking notes in the film analysis worksheet. Three viewings of the scene will produce the best notes.

- If you have the entire movie, begin at 35:22 and end at 40:05. This scene includes a child asking if Abagnale is a pilot and the check-cashing scene.

- A shorter version can be found on YouTube at https://youtu.be/Ow8mG8qutkw. This clip begins with Frank checking in at the airline desk.

- Reread the excerpt on pages 120–123. Students should note places where the text and the movie are similar and different in how each one depicts people, places, and events.

After Reading: Use the following questions to check comprehension.

Text-Based Discussion Questions

1. Is the actor's portrayal of Frank Abagnale similar to or different from how Abagnale describes himself in his autobiography? *It is similar in that both the film and the autobiography portray Abagnale as a smooth con man, although the movie hints at Abagnale's weaknesses, such as his fear when the plane takes off.*

2. How did the filmmaker change the reference to the jump seat from the text? *The stewardess tells him that the jump seat is open, and he makes a joke about remembering which seat is the jump seat. She laughs but doesn't reply.*

Possible Answers to Film Analysis Worksheet:

See answers on Student Book insert page to the left.

Chapter 6 (continued)

Lesson Support

Extend the lesson by showing the movie trailer for *Catch Me If You Can*, which is on YouTube at https://youtu.be/71rDQ7z4eFg. This might give students a better glimpse of the style of the movie and the techniques used by the director.

 Gr7Ch6Read3.pptx

Speak and Listen Suggestion: Have students develop their responses from the film analysis worksheet into a two-minute critique of the movie clip. Encourage students to employ appropriate eye contact, speaking rate, volume, enunciation, a variety of natural gestures, and conventions of language to communicate ideas effectively.

Film Analysis Worksheet of *Catch Me If You Can*

Music As the plane takes off, music begins. What does the music communicate to the viewer? Is it meant to express something about Frank's feelings or situation? Does it try to make the audience feel a certain way? (If it helps, try imagining that same scene without the music.)

Music is upbeat and lively, communicating fun and lightness. It expresses the idea that Frank enjoys his acting while he's doing it. It makes you want to dance or tap your feet.

Lighting As the plane takes off, sunlight moves over Frank's face. This shows the plane is moving. But could the light have any other purposes? (If it helps, try imagining that moment without the light moving.)

The light illuminates Frank's face, which at this point indicates he is afraid. Up to this point in the scene, his face has been a mask of confidence.

After Viewing

Overall Impressions What did you like and dislike about the scene? What emotions did you experience? Do you think the film made you feel what the director wanted you to feel?

Answers will vary.

Objective: Read the text a third time. Write Similar in the My Thoughts column next to details that are similar and Different if the details are different.

©Perfection Learning® • No Reproduction Permitted

Connections • © Perfection Learning®

Focus on Comparing and Contrasting Presentations

Think about the scene from the film and the text. You're ready to compare and contrast the two presentations of these events in Frank's story.

What scene from the text does the clip show?

[blank answer box]

Use the chart below to gather information so you can compare and contrast the text and the scene from the film. The first row and the first column in the second row have been completed for you.

Question	Text	Film
How is Frank presented physically?	Frank describes himself as "bull-shouldered" (large) and "darkly handsome." He sounds like a grown man.	Frank looks slender and brunette. He seems more boyish than adult.
What are Frank's words and reactions as he checks in at the gate?	The passage doesn't describe them, but all interactions prior to that point suggest Frank has been talking and reacting confidently.	Frank appears confident, but he admits that he is not sure which seat is the jump seat because "It's been awhile since I've done this."

continued on next page

Focus on Comparing and Contrasting Presentations:

Answers to Chart:

See answers on Student Book insert page to the left and on page 130.

Remediation: Third Read Remind students that a Venn diagram is a handy graphic organizer to use when comparing and contrasting topics. Provide one for students to record their observations and ideas and help them get started by filling in one detail for each of the two circles (text, movie) and the overlapping area (both).

Question	Text	Film
What does Frank know about the "jump seat"? How do you know?	Frank seems to know all about it as a seat where they accommodate other pilots.	He says, "It's been awhile since I've done this" and asks where the seat is located.
What kinds of things does Frank say to the pilots before takeoff?	He introduces himself, says he works for Pan Am, and politely says that he doesn't want to interrupt them.	Frank's reply is sprinkled with airline terms:"jumping puddles" and "running leapfrog for the weak and weary." He knows enough of the lingo to satisfy the pilots.
How does Frank feel as the plane takes off? What is the evidence?	The text doesn't communicate this information.	Frank's face shows fear as the plane lifts off.
Are there other important similarities or differences you noticed? What are they?	Answers will vary.	Answers will vary.

Speak and Listen Form a small group with three or four classmates and compare charts. Discuss how the text and the film clip are similar and different. Refer to specific sentences and paragraphs in the text. When discussing the film, refer to the information you recorded in your chart.

Write Write a paragraph comparing and contrasting the differences and similarities between the text and the movie. Consider events, characterization, and style of writing/film. Be specific as possible, referring to at least two details in the book and two techniques (such as lighting or music) in the film.

> **CONNECT TO ESSENTIAL QUESTION**
>
> Suppose a friend tells you that he or she recently learned how to fly a plane. Aside from actually seeing your friend fly the plane, what evidence would help you to believe your friend's claim?

Language: Understanding Context Clues

The excerpt uses some words you might not know. Using context clues, or nearby words or sentences, is one way to determine the meaning of unknown words.

The following chart has words from *Catch Me If You Can*. Use context clues to make an inference about the meaning of each word. Then check the dictionary definition to determine whether your inference is accurate. The first row has been completed for you.

Word	My Inference About the Word's Meaning	Context Clues Supporting My Inference	Dictionary Definition
immaculately (line 5)	"perfectly" or "wonderfully"	He looks at himself in a mirror. He says he is not modest. He is satisfied with his appearance. This suggests he groomed himself perfectly.	*Immaculately* means "free from flaws or mistakes."
manifest (line 35)	list of items or people	It is something that the operations officer checked before he let Frank on the plane.	"a list of passengers or cargo for a ship or a plane"

continued on next page

Speak and Listen: Emphasize that students need not reach consensus about their comparisons and contrasts. The activity calls for them only to share and discuss.

Write: Answers will vary but may suggest that the text provides no hints that Abagnale isn't a pilot until line 83. However, in the movie clip there are several hints that Abagnale is not a real pilot. Both portray Abagnale as a smooth huckster, but the movie shows some "cracks" in his smooth-talking act.

Language: Understanding Context Clues:

Answers to Word Chart:

See answers on Student Book insert page to the left and on page 132.

 Gr7Ch6Language.pptx

ELL Support: Speak and Listen and Write Use these sentence frames to help ELLs write their comparison/contrast paragraphs:

- The passage included . . . but the movie did not.
- The movie included . . . but the passage did not.
- Both the movie and the passage show . . . .

Have students work in multilevel pairs or small groups to first discuss their charts then to write their paragraphs.

Note: Reproducible handouts with sentence frames for this and other activities for this unit can be found in the ELL Teacher Resource (p. 36).

Chapter 6 *(continued)*

Assessment

Project-Based Assessments

Introducing Frank Abagnale: For the purposes of this assessment, ask students to be explicit about the lesson or moral that they draw from Abagnale's biography instead of leaving it up to a reader to make an inference. Students may be surprised to learn that after serving less than five years in prison, he began working for the government investigating crimes committed by fraud and scam artists. He soon became a security consultant to banks and businesses, taught at the FBI Academy, and has advised thousands of institutions through his fraud prevention program. Students may conclude that his life shows that people can change.

Word	My Inference About the Word's Meaning	Context Clues Supporting My Inference	Dictionary Definition
adornments (line 45)	Fancy details that show importance	These were on his uniform along with the "burnished gold stripes."	"something added to decorate or make a person more attractive; an ornament"
appraised (line 73)	Looked at someone as if trying to figure them out	The pilot did this to Frank with "casual thoroughness" before he gave him control of the plane.	"to evaluate the worth or status of something or someone; to judge"

Project-Based Assessments

Introducing Frank Abagnale

In the 1970s, law enforcement captured and jailed Frank Abagnale. After several years in prison, Abagnale was released and went on to live a very different kind of life. What did Abagnale do after prison? Does his life offer any lessons?

Imagine you're introducing Frank Abagnale to an audience of people who know nothing about his life. What was Frank like as a young man? What is he doing now? What lesson can we draw from his life?

TECH-CONNECT

Watch other scenes from *Catch Me If You Can* on YouTube. Think about how the movie uses lighting, music, and dialogue to shape the audience's attitude toward Frank Abagnale and his adventures.

ELL Support: Project-Based Assessments Either project is appropriate for ELLs, but the character analysis may be easier for them because they do not have to read and digest more text to write their paragraphs.

Remediation: Project-Based Assessments Students can also learn about Frank Abagnale from listening to a speech he gave circa 2002 that is available on YouTube. It appears in two parts, each of which is about twenty minutes long. The man who introduces Abagnale calls his story "astonishing" and "incredible."

Write a paragraph introducing Frank Abagnale. Follow these steps.

1. Reread the excerpt from *Catch Me If You Can*. Describe the kind of person Abagnale used to be. Use at least two details from the excerpt.

2. Using the Internet or information provided by your teacher, find out what Abagnale has done since leaving prison. Provide at least two details about his life.

3. Explain to your audience what lesson, if any, you think Abagnale's life teaches.

Use the following guidelines for your introduction.	
To receive the highest score (4.0), the introduction must meet all of these criteria.	**Your introduction** • describes and gives details about who Frank Abagnale used to be. • describes and gives details about what Abagnale is doing now. • makes a claim for a lesson people can draw from Abagnale's life. • contains correct grammar, usage, punctuation, and spelling.

Character Analysis

Frank Abagnale's story is real, but *Catch Me If You Can* is not strictly true. As Abagnale later wrote, "I was interviewed by the co-writer only about four times. I believe he did a great job of telling the story, but he also over-dramatized and exaggerated some of the story."

Because the book tells events in story form, you can write about the character Frank Abagnale just as you would any other character. A character analysis describes what a character is like based on what he or she thinks, says, and does.

Write a paragraph in response to the following task.

> In the film, the character Frank Abagnale shows he is unsure of himself. For example, he doesn't know what *deadheading* means. He also doesn't know what or where the jump seat is; the stewardess has to open it for him.

In contrast, the book excerpt presents Frank differently. Write a paragraph responding to these questions:

- In the book, does Frank seem unsure to you? If not, what does he seem to be?

- What does Frank think, say, and do in the book that makes you think this?

continued on next page

Character Analysis: Before students write their analysis, lead a class discussion on the following questions: *Why would a movie director choose to show more weaknesses in Frank's character? What is his goal? Which version of Frank did you find more sympathetic?*

ELL Support: Project-Based Assessments—Character Analysis

Provide students with a list of words or phrases to describe Frank the character in the book as opposed to Frank the character in the movie: *self-assured, overconfident, arrogant, fearless, brave, pushy, unafraid, undaunted, uppity, forceful, audacious, brazen,* or *gutsy.* Suggest that these are all antonyms of *unsure.* Have students work in multilevel pairs or small groups to first discuss their charts and then to write the character analysis. Provide the following sentence frames to guide students in their discussions and writing:

- In the book, Frank is/is not unsure. He is . . . . For example, he says . . . . This shows that he feels . . . because . . . .

- Also, he says . . . . This shows that he feels . . . because . . . .

- Finally, he does . . . . This shows that he feels . . . because . . . .

Chapter 6 *(continued)*

Assessment

On Your Own: Integrating Ideas:

Activity 1: There are two speeches by Abagnale and one interview available on his website. He is a well-known public speaker and lecturer.

Use specific details from the excerpt to support your ideas.

Use the following guidelines for your character analysis.	
To receive the highest score (4.0), the character analysis must meet all of these criteria.	Your character analysis • clearly states what the character Frank is like. • gives examples of what Frank thinks, says, and does that support your statements. • uses linking words and phrases such as *for example, also,* or *in addition.* • is free from grammar, spelling, and punctuation errors.

On Your Own: Integrating Ideas

1. Frank Abagnale has spent several decades teaching both individuals and institutions how to combat fraud. Visit his website Abagnale.com to learn how he turned his life of crime into a business that helps other people. You can also see Frank answer many questions about his life of crime at forum-network.org/lectures/catch-me-if-you-can-frank-abagnales-story/.

2. Frank Abagnale actually has advice for *you* about how to avoid scams. Visit the site news.bbc.co.uk/2/hi/business/4754733.stm to read an interview in which Frank tells how to avoid getting tricked by people like him.

3. In traditional literature, a trickster is a character who cheats or deceives people. Famous tricksters include Coyote in Native American folktales, Anansi the Spider in African folktales, and Loki in Norse mythology. Do some research on the qualities of tricksters, whom they typically come into conflict with, and what often happens to the characters in their stories. Then discuss with a partner: Even though Frank Abagnale is a real person, can you also consider him a literary trickster? Why or why not?

> **REFLECT**
>
> What is the relationship between truth and trust? Is there ever a time when it is okay to lie to a person who trusts you?

ELL Support: On Your Own: Integrating Ideas Activity 3: Have students work in monocultural, multilevel pairs or small groups to use pictures and narration to tell a trickster tale. If students don't know a trickster tale from their country, play one on Youtube: https://www.youtube.com/results?search_query=anansi or find linguistically accommodated versions for students to use: http://americanfolklore.net/folklore/tricksters/. Then show a Compare and Contrast diagram from the ELL Teacher Resource (p. 53) for students to use in comparing Frank Abagnale with a trickster.

Connect to Testing

In this chapter, you supported ideas with text evidence, analyzed different points of view, and compared two presentations of a story. When you take assessments, you will be asked questions related to these skills. Answer the following questions over these skills. Try to answer the first question on your own before reading the explanation below.

1. Read this statement about Frank Abagnale, the narrator and main character of *Catch Me If You Can*.

   > Frank feels pride in his skills at fooling people.

   Which of the following choices from the excerpt is the **best** evidence supporting this statement?

   A. *A man's alter ego is nothing more than his favorite image of himself.*

   B. *I like kids. This one reminded me of myself a few years past.*

   C. *I promptly put the giant jet on automatic pilot and hoped to [heck] the gadget worked, because I couldn't fly a kite.*

   D. *I sometimes astonished myself with some of my impersonations and shenanigans, but I never at any time deluded myself.*

EXPLANATION

continued on next page

Connect to Testing: This Connect to Testing section focuses on using textual evidence, analyzing points of view, and comparing written and movie versions of a topic.

Encourage students to work in pairs to choose the correct answers to the questions and then to compare their answers with those of another pair of students. If there is disagreement, encourage the groups to try to reach a consensus as they discuss the reasons for their choices.

Answers to Connect to Testing Questions:

1. D. Choices A and B are irrelevant to this statement. Choice C expresses a feeling that may be the opposite of pride. Choice D and his claim that he "astonishes himself" with the success of his actions supports the idea of pride in himself. (DoK 2)

(continued)

ELL Support: Connect to Testing and Assessments See the *Connections* ELL Teacher Resource (p. 22) for ideas on adapting this section for ELLs.

Remediation: Connect to Testing Focus attention on questions 1 and 3, which present less reading load yet are good examples of questions about making inferences about characterization. Read each question aloud and have students take turns reading the answer choices. As a group, discuss whether each choice is correct or incorrect until the group reaches consensus about the correct answer.

Chapter 6 (continued)

Assessment

2. **C.** Choices A, B, and D express the pride that Frank feels when he looks in the mirror, when a boy admires his uniform, and when authorities have called him "one of this century's cleverest" crooks. In Choice C, there is a hint of guilt as he calls himself an "imposter," a "wanted criminal," and someone who does bad things to nice people. (DoK 2)

3. **Part A:** B. He is hardly quiet, never nervous in public, and although his actions may seem audacious, he is not boastful in this excerpt. (DoK 2)
Part B: D. In this line of dialogue, he appears to underplay his own needs and to suggest that he is not entitled to any special treatment. (DoK 2)

4. **Part A:** A. Frank admits, "At the time, virtue was not one of my virtues." The older narrator looks back on his younger self with a sharply critical eye. (DoK 2)

(continued)

2. Which excerpt from *Catch Me If You Can* suggests that Frank feels guilty about how he used to fool people?

   A. *The mirror in my room in the Windsor Hotel in Paris reflected my favorite image of me—a darkly handsome young airline pilot. . . .*

   B. *A young boy fell in beside me as I walked to the plane, gazing with unabashed admiration at my uniform. . . .*

   C. *I was an imposter, one of the most wanted criminals on four continents, and at the moment I was doing my thing, putting a super hype on some nice people. . . .*

   D. *I've been described by authorities and news reports as one of this century's cleverest bum-check passers. . . .*

3. **Part A:** Which word **best** describes how the character of Frank behaves around other people?

   A. quiet

   B. humble

   C. nervous

   D. boastful

   Part B: Which of the following best supports your answer to Part A?

   A. *The mirror in my room in the Windsor Hotel in Paris reflected my favorite image of me—a darkly handsome young airline pilot, smooth-skinned, bull-shouldered and immaculately groomed.*

   B. *The markings on my uniform identified me as a first officer, a co-pilot, but the French are like that. They tend to overestimate everything save their women, wine and art.*

   C. *"Oh, can you cash this for me? Your Paris nightlife nearly wiped me out and it'll be another week before I'm home." I smiled ruefully.*

   D. *"Just milk for me," I said. "And don't worry about that if you get busy. Hitchhikers aren't entitled to anything more than the ride."*

4. **Part A:** How does Frank the narrator view his younger self?

   A. Frank sees himself as a better person than he was as a young man.

   B. Frank believes he is exactly the same person he used to be.

   C. Frank feels he is a worse person now than when he was young.

   D. Frank believes he has nothing in common with the person he was.

Part B: In the paragraph below, underline one sentence that supports the answer to Part A.

> A man's alter ego is nothing more than his favorite image of himself. The mirror in my room in the Windsor Hotel in Paris reflected my favorite image of me—a darkly handsome young airline pilot, smooth-skinned, bull-shouldered and immaculately groomed. Modesty is not one of my virtues. At the time, virtue was not one of my virtues.

5. Which of these correctly describes a difference between the written and filmed versions of *Catch Me If You Can*?

   A. The written version uses dialogue showing how people react to Frank. The filmed version does not.

   B. The written version shows Frank tricking his way onto a plane. The filmed version does not.

   C. The filmed version reveals Frank's thoughts as he fools people. The written version does not.

   D. The filmed version shows how Frank feels as the plane takes off. The written version does not.

4. **Part B:** B. *At the time, virtue was not one of my virtues.* (DoK 2)

5. D. (DoK 3)

Chapter 7

Analyzing Central Ideas

Think: Why You Should Question Everything
by Guy Harrison

Introduction

Chapter Goals: Have students read through the goals and mark any words that are unfamiliar. Discuss the meanings of any academic vocabulary within the goals that students marked as unfamiliar. Consider posting the Chapter Goals.

Preview Academic Vocabulary: Read and discuss the meanings of the academic vocabulary.

argument: *a claim along with reasons and evidence in support of a position on a topic.* The teenager's <u>argument</u> that she should have a cell phone was solid, but it did not convince her parents.

central idea: *an idea that an author develops and supports throughout an informational text.* The <u>central idea</u> of the speech was that fear should not motivate our decisions.

claim: *the writer's or speaker's opinion which he/she is attempting to prove is true.* In his opening statement, the attorney made the <u>claim</u> that his client had been framed.

coordinate adjectives: *two or more adjectives of equal importance used to describe the same noun in a sentence.* An example of <u>coordinate adjectives</u> is found in the phrase *old, blue bike*.

connotative meaning: *the positive or negative emotions associated with a word.* Whether you describe your uncle as "thrifty" or "cheap" depends on which <u>connotative meaning</u> you intend.

Analyzing Central Ideas

Preview Concepts

You've probably heard the phrase "Seeing is believing." But what does it actually mean? Explain below what you think the phrase means, using at least one example from your own life.

CHAPTER GOALS

In this chapter you will:

- examine the development of central ideas in a text.
- determine the figurative, connotative, and technical meanings of words.
- analyze the effect of word choice on meaning and tone.
- evaluate the quality of an argument.

PREVIEW ACADEMIC VOCABULARY

argument

central idea

claim

coordinate adjective

connotative meaning

evidence

figurative meaning

reason

technical meaning

tone

ELL Support: Academic Vocabulary See <u>Teaching Vocabulary in the ELL Teacher Resource (p. 18)</u> for ideas to use for teaching vocabulary throughout *Connections*.

Preview Concepts Discuss with students the phrase "Seeing is believing." Have volunteers suggest what they think it means. Confirm that it means "When you see something, you believe it." Have students work in multilevel groups or pairs to discuss examples of when they didn't believe something until they saw it. Provide the following sentence frames for the discussion and students' written responses:

- Seeing is believing means . . . .
- I didn't believe . . . until I saw . . . .

Making Connections Have multilevel pairs or small groups read the paragraph on page 139 and answer the questions. Before they read, display images of the different people mentioned in the quote. Name

Making Connections

Read the following excerpt from a book by a scientist who lived more than one hundred years ago. He talks about the difference between seeing and looking.

> What we do see depends mainly on what we look for. When we turn our eyes to the sky, it is in most cases merely to see whether it is likely to rain. In the same field the farmer will notice the crop, geologists the fossils, botanists the flowers, artists the colouring, sportsmen the cover for game. Though we may all look at the same things, it does not at all follow that we should see them.
>
> —*The Beauties of Nature and the Wonders of the World We Live In* by John Lubbock (1892)

According to Lubbock, how are *seeing* and *looking* related? Why do people *look* at the same thing and *see* something different? Quote a detail from the text that supports your answer.

> **MAKING CONNECTIONS**
>
> In this chapter you will analyze a book excerpt that discusses whether the phrase "seeing is believing" is entirely accurate.

evidence: *data, details, examples, definitions, quotations, and facts that support a claim and reasons in an argument.* Evidence in support of restrictions on new drivers is the high rate of accidents for sixteen- to eighteen-year olds.

figurative meanings: *word meanings that are not literal, which suggest meaning because of associations or comparisons such as metaphors, similes, personification, allusions, etc.* When the teacher called the children "monkeys" and "rabbits," she was using the figurative meanings of those words.

reason: *a statement that explains why a claim should be accepted as true.* If you can't give me a convincing reason to vote against the new law, then I plan to vote for it.

technical meaning: *the meaning of a word as it is used in math or science.* The technical meaning of *core* is the inside of the planet Earth that includes an inner and outer layer made mostly of iron.

tone: *the author's attitude toward his writing.* When the poet wrote about his mother, his tone was respectful and loving, but when he wrote about his father, it was bitter and sarcastic.

Gr7Ch7Vocabulary.pptx

Preview Concepts: Students may be interested to know that the phrase "Seeing is believing," first published in a collection of English proverbs in 1639, probably alludes to the biblical story of St. Thomas (Doubting Thomas), who did not believe that Jesus had risen from the dead until he saw him with his own eyes (John 20:24–29). Jesus replied to Thomas's skepticism by saying, "Blessed are they that have not seen, and have believed."

Making Connections: Most students will understand that Lubbock distinguishes between *looking* and *seeing.* He states that "we all look at the same things," but who we are—and our purpose—determines whether we actually pay attention to crops, fossils, flowers, colors, or ground cover.

Tech-Connect Suggestion: To illustrate Lubbock's quotation, have students locate and observe a painting such as Mary Cassatt's *Red Poppies* or Vincent van Gogh's *Wheat Field.* Ask: *What do you see first— the farmer, the geologist, the botanist, the artist, the hunter? What do you notice or pay attention to?*

the person and have students repeat. Display a picture of a field. Put the field picture in the center and the pictures of the people around it. Then pick up each picture and hold it in front of your chest. Say: *I am a . . . . I look at the field. I see a place I can . . . .* Repeat with all the people. Explain: *Each person looks at the same field. But they see the field differently. They see different things in the field.*

Provide the following sentence frames for student multilevel pairs or small groups to use in their responses:

- Lubbock thinks looking is . . . .
- He thinks seeing is . . . .
- Lubbock thinks looking and seeing are related because . . . .
- People look at the same thing and see different things because . . . .
- For example, Lubbock writes, " . . . ."

Chapter 7 (continued)

Lesson Support

📖 First Read: Analyzing Central Ideas

Before Reading: Remind students that the first read of the close reading process focuses on the central idea of the text or answering the question *What?* Read the introductory paragraph and objective with students. Confirm they understand the reading task. Remind students that sometimes the most important idea in a paragraph is not stated explicitly. They may need to make an inference about the central idea. If that's the case, have them write their inference in the My Thoughts column.

If your class needs extra support, use a think-aloud strategy to model reading and annotating the first few paragraphs of the text. Then have students finish reading the text on their own.

Preview Vocabulary: Preteach unfamiliar vocabulary to aid comprehension or ask students to circle unfamiliar words as they complete the first read of a text. After the first read, guide students to determine the words' meanings using the context. Encourage students to support their responses with evidence. Have students confirm their initial definitions with a dictionary. Words that students might find difficult include:

relays: *to carry forward or transmit, usually as part of a series of steps. When the fire siren relays its message, volunteers from all over town jump into their cars and trucks.*

optic: *of or relating to the eye or sight.* Helen Keller was deprived of both her optic and aural abilities.

monitor: *a screen that accepts and displays information from a computer.* My laptop computer's screen is very small, but I connected it to a big monitor, so I can see much more.

customized: *modified according to one's personal preferences.* My brother's customized wheelchair fits him perfectly and allows him to be independent.

📖 First Read: Analyzing Central Ideas

If you see it with your own eyes, it must be true. Right? Not according to Guy Harrison, an American writer, journalist, and photographer.

Objective: As you read the excerpt, underline the most important idea of each paragraph. Record any questions you have in the My Thoughts column.

—— First Read
---- Second Read
—— Third Read

excerpt
Think: Why You Should Question Everything
by Guy Harrison

My Thoughts

1   Have you heard the old saying, "seeing is believing"? Well, it's often a case of *believing is seeing*. It is well known by researchers that <u>what we think we see can be strongly influenced by images and ideas we have been exposed to</u>

5   <u>previously as well as our own thoughts and imagination.</u> This probably explains why it's the people who already believe in ghosts or UFOs who keep seeing ghosts or UFOs, and why so few nonbelievers do. Seeing things that are not there can happen to anyone <u>because the human brain *constructs* and</u>

Reason

10   <u>*interprets* the visual reality that is around it.</u> What we see is something the brain has produced for us *based on* input it received via the eyes. It's never a 100 percent true and complete reflection of what our eyes are pointed at. For this reason, <u>we can't always be sure about what we think we see.</u>

Claim

15   Yes, that might be an angel that you see up ahead. Or your brain could be showing you an angel that it has mistakenly constructed out of a bush or some other object.

Construct and interpret reality? It sounds crazy when you think about it. We don't really "see" the things we look

20   at? How can this be? Most people probably assume that the brain simply shows us or somehow faithfully relays whatever

140   Chapter 7 • Unit 2   ©Perfection Learning® • No Reproduction Permitted

ELL Support: First Read Before students read, be sure they understand that *construct* means "to build," *interpret* means "to explain the meaning of something," *influence* means "affect," and *exposed to* means "shown." Also, show or sketch pictures of UFOs, ghosts, and angels so students understand the references in the text. Have students read the text in multilevel pairs or small groups, pausing at the end of each paragraph to summarize using a <u>Main Ideas and Supporting Details graphic organizer from the ELL Teacher Resource (p. 51)</u>. Encourage students to take notes and draw sketches in the margins around the article so they can be sure they understand the topic of each paragraph.

images come in through the eyes, but that's just not how it
works. What actually happens is that light patterns enter the
eyes and electrical impulses are sent along optic nerves to
25 the brain. Then the brain *translates* these impulses into visual
information that you "see" in your head. Your brain doesn't
reflect or replay the scenery around you like a mirror or a
camera and monitor would. It provides you with its own highly
edited and customized *sketch* of the scene. Your brain gives
30 you a *version* of what you look at. It's as if your brain comes
up with something like a Hollywood movie production that is
loosely based on what is really going on around you. You are
not watching a video feed; you are watching a docudrama.
The brain takes the liberty of leaving out what it assumes are
35 unimportant details in the scene before your eyes. Just like
memory, this is not necessarily bad most of the time. In fact,
it's necessary in order to avoid information overload. You don't
need to see every leaf in every tree and every blade of grass in
full detail when you look around a park. That would be way
40 too much data. It would clutter your thoughts and make you
less efficient, if not incapacitate you. What you need in order
to walk through a park and function well is to have a general
picture of your surroundings, so that's what your brain gives
you. If you need more detail, then your eyes and brain zoom in
45 and focus on a single leaf or an individual blade of grass.
    It gets weirder. Not only do our brains leave out a
tremendous amount of detail, they also routinely fill in gaps
in our vision with images that you can't possibly "see" or that
maybe don't even exist in reality at all. Your eyes might not
50 be able to track a fast-moving object, for example, so your
brain will sometimes conjure it up and show it to you anyway,

My Thoughts

E

_____

_____

_____

_____

_____

_____

_____

_____

_____

_____

_____

_____

_____

_____

_____

_____

_____

E

_____

_____

_____

_____

_____

_____

docudrama: *a fictionalized film or television program that is based on true events but is presented in a dramatic form.* Because the docudrama combined real footage with filmed scenes, it was difficult to tell reality from fiction.

incapacitate: *to deprive or take away ability or power; to disable.* A broken leg will incapacitate a marathon runner but not a marathon writer.

static: *not moving or changing; stationary.* The artist preferred creating static photographs to dynamic videos.

sleight-of-hand: *pertaining to a trick or deception, often with the hands.* I am not good at card tricks; my sleight-of-hand skills are more like show-your-hand.

extinction: *the condition of no longer being in existence, especially as it applies to a species.* If an enormous comet hit Earth, human beings could face extinction.

skeptics: *people who maintain an attitude of doubt and mistrust about information.* I live in a family of skeptics who question everything they see on the nightly news.

After Reading: Use the following questions to check comprehension.

Text-Based Discussion Questions

1. What is the difference, for Harrison, between looking and seeing? *Answers will vary but may suggest that looking is physical and done with the eyes, whereas seeing is psychological and done with the brain.*

2. According to Harrison, what would happen if we actually saw everything that we could see? *He states that so much data would clutter our thoughts, make us inefficient, and even incapacitate us.*

3. What example does Harrison offer for our brains "filling in gaps"? *He suggests that when people watch magicians perform, their brains fill in missing information.*

 Gr7Ch7Read1.pptx

About the Author: Guy P. Harrison lives in California and is known for his writing about human thought and perception. Born in 1963, he has degrees in history and anthropology from the University of Southern Florida. As a journalist, he has interviewed people as influential as Jane Goodall, Chuck Yeager, and Paul Tibbets.

Remediation: First Read Help students experience the author's lively voice by reading the excerpt aloud as students follow along. Ask them to notice how the author uses *you* to address readers directly and how he uses *we* to make readers feel included in his claims and observations. Have them circle examples of both pronouns as they listen.

Chapter 7 *(continued)*

Lesson Support

Popular Psychology: Psychology is the scientific study of the human mind and its functions, an academic field of study that includes social, behavioral, and cognitive subfields. Mostly, this social science conducts research to advance the treatment of mental problems and/or to solve problems of human activity. During the 1960s, a related field became popular, giving voice to authors, consultants, lecturers, and even entertainers who were *perceived* as psychologists merely because they made observations about humans and offered advice. The term "pop psychology" is somewhat pejorative because these claims are often oversimplified and not based on sound, peer-reviewed research.

figuring that it might be useful to you to see a projected version of reality. The brain also fills in missing elements that "should be there" in static scenes because, again, it can help

55 us to navigate our way through the environment. Magicians have known about this for many years. Even if they don't understand or care about the science behind it, they take full advantage of the way our vision works when they do their sleight-of-hand coin tricks, for example. Again, our brains

60 don't do any of this for a gag or to make fools of us. They do it because it is the most effective and efficient way to function in life most of the time.

   In addition to filling in missing images, our brains also find patterns or connect the dots when we look around. They do

65 this automatically and do it very well. It helps us to see things that otherwise might be difficult or impossible to recognize. It's probably one of the main reasons you and I are alive right now. Like many other animals, our prehistoric ancestors relied on this ability to eat and to avoid being eaten. When they

70 needed to spot well-camouflaged birds and rabbits hiding in the bushes in order to avoid starvation, this ability to see things through clutter was crucial. It was no less important, of course, for them to identify the vague outline of a predator hiding in ambush in order to avoid becoming dinner in the

75 short term and avoid extinction in the long term. . . .

   On one hand, it makes sense for us to see some patterns of things that aren't really there in order to be very good at seeing real ones that matter. On the other hand, we need to be aware of this phenomenon because it can lead

80 to a confident belief in things that are not real or true. . . . Good skeptics understand how the brain often creates false

My Thoughts

E

patterns, so we know to be very cautious when considering claims of UFO sightings, for example, or anything else that is unusual. It only makes sense to be skeptical and ask for

85 additional evidence when people claim to have seen or heard extraordinary things. Maybe they did, maybe they didn't. Given what we now know about the brain, however, are you going to believe someone who tells you she saw a flying saucer or Bigfoot last week? She doesn't have to be lying to be wrong.

90 Anyone with perfect vision can see poorly.

FIRST RESPONSE: KEY IDEAS AND DETAILS
Based on your first reading of the text, what do you think the author *most* wants you to understand about how you see the world? Record your first response in your journal.

My Thoughts

TECH-CONNECT

Post your answer to the First Response question to your class web page or online site as per your teacher's instructions.

Tech-Connect Suggestion: An unabridged audiobook version of *Think: Why You Should Question Everything* is available online at https://www.amazon.com/Think-Why-Should-Question-Everything/dp/B00JQLQH3S.

FIRST RESPONSE: KEY IDEAS AND DETAILS

Sample answer: *Harrison most wants me to understand that just because I think I see something does not mean that I see it accurately. Seeing does not necessarily reveal the truth.*

Lesson Support

Focus on Analyzing Central Ideas:

Explain that each paragraph of an informative text such as this one expresses its own key idea and that all the paragraphs and their key ideas support the central ideas of the entire text.

Before completing the diagram on page 145, students may need further explanation of the following terms:

- **Fact**—information that is real or proven to be true
- **Example**—specific instance of a more general concept
- **Comparison**—showing how a new concept is similar to a concept already understood by the reader

Explain that understanding these types of specific details can help them comprehend difficult texts. Also, as writers, these can help them communicate their ideas clearly.

> **Possible Answers to Diagrams:**
>
> See answers on Student Book insert page to the right.

 Gr7Ch7Read1.pptx

Focus on Analyzing Central Ideas

In an informational text, an author can develop one or more central ideas. A central idea is an idea an author wants readers to understand fully and which the author develops throughout a text. In Guy Harrison's *Think*, the first paragraph clearly states one of the text's central ideas: "The human brain *constructs* and *interprets* the visual reality that is around it." Harrison then develops this idea with key ideas.

The diagram below restates one of *Think*'s central ideas and one of its key ideas. Complete the diagram with key ideas from the third and fourth paragraphs.

> **CONNECT TO ESSENTIAL QUESTION**
>
> Is Harrison suggesting we can't trust *anything* we perceive? Or is his argument subtler than that?

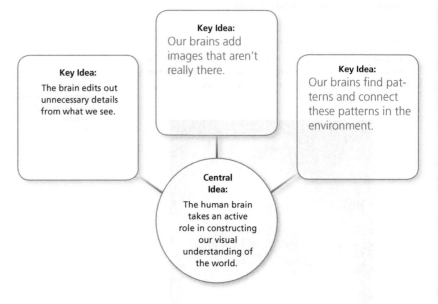

An author further develops central and key ideas with details such as facts, examples, comparisons, and any other information that will help readers understand what the ideas mean.

Remediation: First Read Draw a triangle (or pyramid). Draw two horizontal lines to create three spaces in the triangle. Label the top triangle *Central Idea*. Ask students to identify the central idea of the excerpt. In the center space of the triangle, write three supporting ideas from page 144. Finally, in the bottom space, write the fact, example, and comparison from the web on page 145. Help students understand that individual facts "hold up" supporting ideas and supporting ideas, in turn, hold up the central idea of a text.

ELL Support: Focusing on Analyzing Central Ideas Model how to find the central idea in the text and then the key ideas, paraphrasing them for students: *The human brain builds or creates what we see in the world. The brain cuts out unimportant details so we don't see them.* Have students work in multilevel pairs or small groups to find and paraphrase the other two key ideas. Repeat the process with the graphic organizer work on p. 145.

Consider this key idea: "The brain edits out unnecessary details from what we see." Read the fact. Then find an example and a comparison Harrison uses to develop this idea. These are supporting details. Write your answers in the blank boxes.

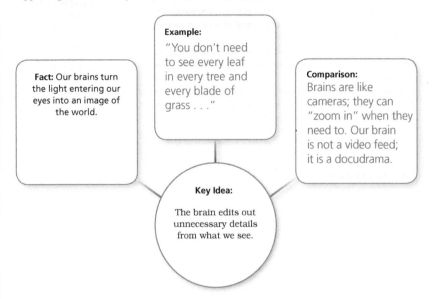

Example:
"You don't need to see every leaf in every tree and every blade of grass . . ."

Fact: Our brains turn the light entering our eyes into an image of the world.

Comparison: Brains are like cameras; they can "zoom in" when they need to. Our brain is not a video feed; it is a docudrama.

Key Idea:
The brain edits out unnecessary details from what we see.

(Speak and Listen With a partner, find a second central idea in *Think*. Discuss how Harrison develops the second central idea with key ideas, facts, examples, and so on.

TECH-CONNECT

We're always glad when our eyes work well, but fooling them can be fun. If you have an interest in optical illusions, check out the site Optics4Kids.org and click on the Optical Illusions box.

Second Read: Determining Word Meanings

When people talk about the meaning of a word or phrase, they usually mean its dictionary definition. But words and phrases can also have technical, connotative, and figurative meanings.

Objective: Reread the text. As you read, circle words or phrases that express ideas in unusual or creative ways.

ELL Support: Second Read Since literal comprehension is a priority, students will find lessons on figurative language challenging. Thus, before students reread the text, help them skim the charts on pp. 146–147 to identify words, phrases, and quotes they should pay attention to as they read. Then have students work in multilevel pairs or small groups to reread the article, placing a star next to any word, phrase, or quote they recognize from the chart.

(Speak and Listen: Have student pairs join with other pairs to share their graphic organizers. Or ask pairs to project their organizers on the whiteboard. Discuss any differences in answers.

Tech-Connect: Other optical illusions sites that are appropriate for this age are https://kids.niehs.nih.gov/games/riddles/illusions/index.htm and https://www.verywell.com/optical-illusions-4020333. The spinning dancer illusion may shock them!

Second Read: Determining Word Meanings

Before Reading: Read with students the introduction and objective. If necessary, review and discuss the definitions and examples of connotative, figurative, and technical meaning provided in the Preview Academic Vocabulary section on pages 138 and 139 of this book.

Tell students that as they read the passage a second time, they should circle any words or phrases that seem to have distinctly technical, connotative, or figurative meanings.

Students may circle words and phrases such as: *an angel mistakenly constructed out of a bush, sketch of the scene, a Hollywood movie production, sleight-of-hand coin tricks, for a gag or to make fools of us, to connect the dots, eat and avoid being eaten, to avoid becoming dinner, avoid extinction, claims of UFO sightings, a flying saucer,* or *Bigfoot.*

After Reading: Use the following questions to check comprehension.

Text-Based Discussion Questions

1. Which words are the most important ones in this text? Give reasons for your choices. *Students may choose words such as* seeing, interpreting, vision, reality, brain, *or* skeptic.

2. Which words name concrete images from the passage? bush, mirror, camera, leaf, tree, grass, coin, birds, rabbits

3. How would Harrison define the word *reality* as he uses it here? *Answers will vary but might suggest that for Harrison,* reality *is the world apart from human perception of it. It has nothing to do with how we see it. It is fixed and true.*

 **Gr7Ch7Read2.pptx**

Lesson Support

Focus on Determining Word Meanings:

Other examples of words that have both technical meanings and more common meanings are *scan, virus, server* (from digital technology); *prime, simplify, ray* (from math); or *matter, wave, volume* (from science).

Possible Answers to Charts:

See answers on Student Book insert page to the right.

Focus on Determining Word Meanings

A word or phrase can have a technical meaning, one used largely in subjects such as math or science. Think about the word *positive*. If you say, "I'm positive I did my homework," this means you're certain. But *positive* also has technical meanings. In science, *positive* can refer to an electrical charge. In math, *positive* describes a number greater than zero.

Sometimes you can find a word's technical meaning in a dictionary, glossary, or footnote. But if you don't have these, you must use context clues.

Read the sentence from the text in the chart below. Use context clues to figure out the underlined word. Then use a dictionary to check the accuracy of your definition.

What actually happens is that light patterns enter the eyes and electrical impulses are sent along <u>*optic*</u> *nerves to the brain.*
What I think the word means: something to do with seeing, as in optical illusion
Context clues: It describes nerves that go from the eyes to the brain.
Dictionary definition: "of or relating to the eye or vision"

A word or phrase might have a connotative meaning, which is the feeling it produces. Connotations range from strongly negative (bad) to strongly positive (good). If a word doesn't evoke much of a feeling, its connotation is neutral.

In the chart on the next page, read the sentence from *Think*. On the line beneath the sentence, say whether *influenced* feels positive, negative, or neutral to you. Then state whether each word that could replace *influenced* has a positive, negative, or neutral connotation.

Remediation: Second Read Tone can be a difficult concept for struggling students. Consider suggesting that *Think* could have been written with a different tone by reading this alternative opening: *Neuroscientists have determined that visual processing in humans is motivated not only by sensory data produced by retinal stimuli such as objects and light but also by physiological components, including linguistics, psychology, and cognition.* Help them see that this sentence has a more distant, objective, formal, scientific tone that is less friendly and accessible than Harrison's book.

Sentence from *Think*	Replacement for *Influenced*	Positive, Negative, or Neutral?
It is well known by researchers that what we think we see can be strongly *influenced* by images and ideas we have been exposed to previously as well as our own thoughts and imagination.	shaped	neutral
	warped	negative
	informed	neutral
	twisted	negative
	guided	positive
Connotation of *influenced:* neutral		

Texts, including nonfiction texts, use figurative language to express ideas in creative ways. Some types of figurative language include the following:

- simile—a comparison that uses the word *like* or *as*
- metaphor—a comparison that says one thing is something else; does not use the word *like* or *as*
- personification—a comparison that gives human qualities to an animal or object

When you encounter figurative language in a text, ask, What does the author really mean by this?

In the table below, identify whether the example is a simile, metaphor, or personification. Then state what the author is actually saying.

Sentence from *Think*	Type of Figurative Language	What the Author Means
Again, our brains don't do any of this for a gag or to make fools of us.	personification	This process is normal and helps us live more efficiently.
You are not watching a video feed; you are watching a docudrama.	metaphor	Your brain takes reality and turns it into something that is fiction based on reality.
It's as if your brain comes up with something like a Hollywood movie production that is loosely based on what is really going around you.	simile	Your brain adds pizzazz, color, drama, costumes, makeup, music, and leaves out details that don't matter, just like movie producers do.

continued on next page

Possible Answers to Charts:

See answers on Student Book insert page to the left.

ELL Support: Second Read Students will be unlikely to identify the connotation or feeling of words without support. Therefore, have students work in multilevel pairs or small groups to use an online or print ELL dictionary to find the definitions of the words in the connotation chart. Then students can discuss with each other and with you how the definition helps them figure out the feeling or connotation of the word.

Chapter 7 *(continued)*

Lesson Support

Speak and Listen: Remind students that the definition of *tone* is "the author's attitude toward his topic or writing." Possible tones: *friendly, informal, conversational.* Evidence: *"Have you heard the old saying," "Yes, that might be an angel that you see up ahead," "It sounds crazy when you think about it," "How can this be?," "It gets weirder,"* and the use of second-person *you.*

Write: Encourage students to use at least one direct quotation in their paragraphs and to cite line numbers in parentheses.

Tech-Connect Suggestion: Many students will associate the term *tone* with music: a steady sound that has qualities such as duration (how long it lasts), pitch, volume, and timbre (quality). Tones are the building blocks of music. Students can hear tones played on a digital piano here: http://www.telacommunications.com/nutshell/music/notes.htm. Explain that in some languages, changing the tone or pitch of a syllable can change its meaning.

Third Read: Evaluating an Argument

Before Reading: Review the introduction and objective with students. Remind them to identify the main claim, one reason, and three pieces of supporting evidence. They also must identify one example of direct address and one rhetorical question.

If helpful, reinforce the concepts of claims, reasons, and evidence before students start reading. Ask pairs to develop reasons for simple claims, such as the following:

- Watching shows on streaming services (Netflix, Hulu, etc.) is better than watching cable TV.
- Cats (or dogs) are better than dogs (or cats).
- The best superhero is . . . .
- A movie everyone should see is . . . .

To support their reasons, have students think of possible facts, examples, statistics, personal experiences, and expert testimony. If time allows, ask pairs to search for websites or online sources that would provide evidence for their claim.

Skilled authors choose words to give their text a certain tone. Tone is like the personality of a text. Texts can have all sorts of tones: friendly, distant, formal, funny, mean, helpful, angry, and so on. Connotative and figurative meanings play a large role in producing a text's tone.

Speak and Listen Discuss with a partner: What is the overall tone of *Think*? What specific words, phrases, or sentences in the text are evidence of this tone?

Write Based on your discussion, write a paragraph describing the tone of *Think*. Refer to specific words, phrases, or sentences from the text to support your claim about the tone.

Third Read: Evaluating an Argument

Because *Think* describes how the brain constructs and interprets what we see, you might think it is an informative text. This isn't entirely true. The excerpt provides information, but that information is part of an argument.

An argument tries to convince readers that an author's viewpoint about a topic is correct. Parts of an argument include claims, reasons, and evidence.

- A claim is a statement the author tries to prove is true. (*Vanilla is better than chocolate.*)
- A reason explains why the readers should agree with the claim. (*Vanilla is more popular than chocolate.*)
- Evidence supports the reason. Evidence comes in many forms: data, details, examples, definitions, quotations, and so on. (*Surveys conducted by the International Ice Cream Association found vanilla to be the most popular flavor.*)

Writers also use rhetorical devices to use emotion to convince their audience. Here are two examples:

- Direct address is when the writer speaks directly to the audience in a familiar or friendly way. The writer does this to establish trust.
- Rhetorical questions are used to make the audience or reader think about an idea. Often rhetorical questions don't have answers but instead are used to make a point.

Objective: Read the text again. In the first paragraph, write a C by the claim and an R by a reason. In paragraphs 2, 3, and 4, write an E by three examples of evidence supporting the claim. Identify an example of direct address and of a rhetorical question.

ELL Support: Speak and Listen and Write Have students work in multilevel pairs or small groups and use these sentence frames to first discuss and then to write about the tone of *Think*. These sentence frames will help ELLs write their paragraphs:

- The tone of *Think* is . . . .
- A detail that shows this tone is . . . .
- An example that shows this tone is . . . .
- A sentence (or phrase) that shows this tone is . . . .
- In conclusion, Harrison is . . . .

Focus on Evaluating an Argument

The subtitle for *Think* is *Why You Should Question Everything*. As you can tell from the subtitle, the entire book is an argument. Harrison wants to convince readers to question *everything*—or at least a lot of things.

The excerpt you read makes a more focused argument than "question everything." Complete the chart below. Locate the reason in the text that supports the given claim, and write that reason in your own words. Read the supporting evidence provided for paragraph 2. Then locate supporting evidence in paragraphs 3 and 4 and restate that evidence.

Claim (Paragraph 1): We can't always be sure about what we think we see.
Reason (Paragraph 1): The brain constructs and interprets the visual reality around us.
Evidence (Paragraph 2, lines 18–46): Our brains don't capture every piece of information, such as every blade of grass or leaf in a park.
Evidence (Paragraph 3, lines 47–63): The brain fills in gaps in our vision.
Evidence (Paragraph 4, lines 64–76): Our brains find patterns and make connections.

Harrison wants people to "question everything." That includes questioning his argument. Focus on one aspect of his argument: the relevance of his evidence, or how well the evidence actually supports the claim.

The chart on the next page restates Harrison's claim, one example of evidence for it, and the relevance of that evidence. Complete the chart by restating a second example of evidence and its relevance.

continued on next page

After Reading: Use the following questions to check comprehension.

Text-Based Discussion Questions

1. What can you infer about Harrison's point of view of ghost and UFO sightings? *Answers will vary but will likely suggest that he does not believe in either since he uses them as examples of times when believing trumps seeing.*

2. Why do you think Harrison refers to his claims as "weirder" in line 46? *Answers may suggest that Harrison assumes that he is challenging people's existing ideas about sight, which means that his assertions are strange or unexpected.*

3. How do you think Harrison would define "perfect vision" (line 90)? *Answers may suggest that for here, Harrison means 20/20 vision that is physically perfect; it does not mean that what is seen is actual reality.*

Focus on Evaluating an Argument:

Possible Answers to Charts:

See answers on Student Book insert page to the left and on page 150.

 Gr7Ch7Read3.pptx

ELL Support: Third Read Before students reread the article, model the process of identifying claim, reasons, and evidence using a think-aloud strategy. Then have students work in multilevel pairs or small groups to analyze the rest of the article.

Chapter 7 (continued)

Lesson Support

Speak and Listen: Sample answers:

- Examples might include politicians, advertisements, speeches, attitudes, diagnoses, habits, norms, and even laws, rules, and processes.

- Why do we do it this way? Is there a better way? What is the real purpose here? Of what am I being convinced? What are they trying to sell me? Is there another way of looking at this?

- Authorities of any kind: teachers, parents, coaches, businesses, politicians, fashion designers, farmers, merchants, doctors

Claim	Evidence	How Relevant Is the Evidence?
We can't always trust what we think we see.	Our brains don't capture every piece of information, such as every blade of grass or leaf in a park.	The evidence is relevant. If our brains don't capture every piece of information, then it's possible they might miss something important. And if we miss something important, then it's possible that we are wrong about what we think we see.
	Our brains fill in gaps in our vision with images that you can't possibly "see" or that don't even exist in reality.	The evidence is relevant because it explains why we can be tricked by magicians.

Speak and Listen

At some point, you've probably heard the phrase "question everything." But what does that even mean? In a group of four or five classmates, discuss these questions:

- What are some real-world examples of "everythings" that could be questioned?

- What sorts of questions should be asked about the examples you mentioned?

- To whom would you ask those questions, and why?

CONNECT TO ESSENTIAL QUESTION

Have you ever been asked to believe something you thought was false? How did you react?

Language: Using Commas with Coordinate Adjectives

Adjectives are words that describe nouns. When two or more adjectives are used to describe one noun, they are called coordinate adjectives. Coordinate adjectives must be separated either by a comma or the word *and*. Read these examples:

He read a <u>fun, lively</u> book.
He read a <u>fun and lively</u> book.

These adjectives both modify the noun *book* in the same way. Neither word carries more weight than the other. *Fun* and *lively* make sense in either order, so a comma is required. (No comma is needed after the final adjective.)

He read a <u>lively, fun</u> book.

Remediation: Third Read Explain that when studying rhetoric, an *argument* does not mean that two opposing sides are having a disagreement. An argument is a logical series of claims and evidence with the purpose of convincing an audience.

If the adjectives are not equally important, they are not considered coordinate. If you reorder the adjectives and the sentence no longer makes sense, then you should *not* put a comma between them.

She loved <u>exciting horror</u> movies.
She loved <u>horror exciting</u> movies. (*incorrect*)
She loved <u>exciting and horror</u> movies. (*incorrect*)

Only the first version of the sentence makes sense. This means that *exciting* and *horror* are not coordinate adjectives, so they should not have a comma between them.

Read the following sentences. If the adjectives in the underlined phrases are coordinate, add a comma where necessary. If the adjectives are not coordinate, write "correct" above the phrase.

1. I went to a <u>small private museum</u> yesterday.

2. The museum was founded by a <u>quirky rich man</u>.

3. The man claims to own <u>many important objects</u> proving that aliens visited Earth.

4. The exhibit included <u>blurry gray photographs</u> of flying saucers.

5. I also saw <u>special plaster casts</u> with shapes labeled "alien footprints."

6. Computer screens showed videos of <u>numerous eyewitness accounts</u>.

7. Finally, there were several <u>large smooth flat rocks</u> with <u>countless odd drawings</u> on them.

8. The museum proved that we still don't have <u>much convincing evidence</u> of alien life.

Language: Using Commas with Coordinate Adjectives:

Answers:

1. correct
2. quirky, rich man
3. correct
4. blurry, gray
5. correct
6. correct
7. large, smooth, flat rocks; correct
8. correct

Tech-Connect Suggestion: Remind students that many word processing programs include grammar-checking functions that will highlight potential errors with commas and adjectives but that they should never accept changes without making their own judgments.

 Gr7Ch7Language.pptx

ELL Support: Language Students may struggle to identify which adjective is "most important" in a sentence. Explain that the most important adjectives are those that are part of the name of a thing or that explain what kind—for example, *eyewitness account* or *private museum*. Model completing the first few items using a think-aloud: *Is a private museum a kind of museum? Yes! So I don't need a comma. The word* private *is more important than* small.

Have students work in multilevel pairs or groups to complete the numbered exercises. Then review them together as a class, explaining how each adjective is or is not important.

Chapter 7 (continued)

Assessment

Project-Based Assessments

Response Essay: This project leads students out of the essay into several other kinds of evidence: memories, lyrics, conversations, anecdotes, videos, memes, etc. Since this is an opinion essay, they do not need to be concerned with reliability of sources; they can be more creative and open-minded about what to include.

Project-Based Assessments

Response Essay

The excerpt from *Think* begins this way: "Have you heard the old saying, 'seeing is believing'? Well, it's often a case of *believing is seeing.*" But what's your opinion? Do you agree that what we believe affects how we understand events? Do you disagree? Or is your response more complex than just "agree" or "disagree"?

Write an essay responding to the idea that "believing is seeing." Use these steps to develop your essay:

1. Brainstorm:

   - Write "believing is seeing" in the center of a blank sheet of paper. Circle the phrase.

   - Record memories from your life that seem relevant to the idea "believing is seeing." These memories could be experiences you've had, conversations with friends and family, song lyrics, Internet videos or memes, and so on.

   - You may also want to speak with classmates or family members about their reactions to the idea that "believing is seeing."

2. Write an opinion sentence declaring what you think about the idea that "believing is seeing." The goal of your essay is to develop your opinion.

3. Think about the best way to develop your opinion. Use the ideas from your brainstorming session. Choose the two most interesting ideas you came up with—ideas you can develop with details, examples, and so on.

4. Write your essay. Try to write at least one full page.

5. Get feedback from a friend. Ask your friend to say which of your two ideas could be improved, and how.

6. Revise your essay based on your friend's feedback.

	Use the following guidelines for your response essay.
To receive the highest score (4.0), the response essay must meet all of these criteria.	Your essay should • clearly state an opinion regarding the idea that "believing is seeing." • contain details that develop and support your opinion about the idea. • be clearly organized, using good transitional words and varying sentence structure. • use correct grammar, usage, and punctuation.

ELL Support: Project-Based Assessments—Response Essay Have students work in multilevel pairs or small groups to discuss their ideas and write their essays. Remind students to review their notes, graphic organizers, and visuals they made as they read the text. Encourage students to use the writing supports from previous argument essays (including the sample class essay from Chapter 5 and their own argument writing from previous chapters). Once students complete a draft, provide them with the Informational Writing Revision Checklist from the ELL Teacher Resource (p. 69) and have students work with new multilevel pairs or small groups to revise and edit their writing.

Use these sentence frames to help students begin their Response Essays:

   - I agree that believing is seeing because . . . .

   - I disagree that believing is seeing because . . . .

Draw a Diagram

Guy Harrison describes the connection between the eyes and the brain in this way: "Light patterns enter the eyes and electrical impulses are sent along optic nerves to the brain." But how the eye works is a little more complicated than that.

In your classroom library, your school library, or on the Internet, research the human eye and what its parts do. Based on your research, draw a diagram of the human eye on an 8.5″ × 11″ sheet of paper. Use markers or colored pencils (if available) to clearly show each part.

Make your diagram large enough to fill the page. Show, label, and describe the functions of these parts:

- the cornea
- the pupil
- the uvea (which includes the iris)
- the lens
- the sclera
- the vitreous humor
- the retina, including a description of its rods and cones cells
- the optic nerve

When finished, show your diagram to a family member or friend outside the class. Use it to educate him or her about the human eye.

Use the following guidelines for your diagram.	
To receive the highest score (4.0), the diagram must meet all of these criteria.	Your diagram • is large enough to fill the entire page. • clearly shows each part of the human eye. • accurately labels each part. • clearly describes the function of each part.

Draw a Diagram: In addition to drawing the diagram, challenge students to use it to explain how the eye works to a much younger student. If possible, display the diagrams so that students can compare and contrast their content, styles, and media.

Another option is to have students use digital drawing software to create the diagram.

- An example of a time that I saw something different from what was real is . . . .

ELL Support: Project-Based Assessments—Draw a Diagram Have students work in multilevel, same-language pairs or small groups to create a diagram of the eye. Encourage students to label and explain the parts of the eye with both English and words from their first language.

Chapter 7 *(continued)*

Assessment

On Your Own: Integrating Ideas:

Activity 1: Harrison's book is also available as an audio book, unabridged and read by George Newbern.

Activity 2: The *NOVA ScienceNOW* episode is narrated by Neil deGrasse Tyson, is fifty-five minutes long, and includes evidence from magic shows.

On Your Own: Integrating Ideas

1. The book *Think: Why You Should Question Everything* includes a section titled "A Thinker's Guide to Unusual Claims and Weird Beliefs." That section includes chapters such as "UFOs," "Conspiracy Theories," and "Ancient Alien Astronauts." If these topics interest you, visit your library and see if they have the book. If your library doesn't have it, ask your librarian if he or she can get you a copy.

2. Guy Harrison is clearly fascinated with how the human brain works. If you have a similar interest, watch the *Nova* documentary titled "How Does the Brain Work?" Go to the website www.pbs.org/wgbh/nova and search for the documentary.

> **REFLECT**
>
> Is there anything you question that you have been told is true?

Connect to Testing

In this chapter, you analyzed central ideas, determined the meanings of words and phrases, and evaluated part of an argument. When you take assessments, you will be asked questions related to these skills and tested over your ability to support your ideas with textual evidence. Below is an example of this type of question. Try to answer the question on your own before reading the explanation below.

1. Which sentence states two central ideas developed in *Think*?

   A. *Have you heard the old saying, "seeing is believing"?*

   B. *It is well known by researchers that what we think we see can be strongly influenced by images and ideas we have been exposed to. . . .*

   C. *Seeing things that are not there can happen to anyone because the human brain constructs and interprets the visual reality that is around it.*

   D. *This probably explains why it's the people who already believe in ghosts or UFOs who keep seeing ghosts or UFOs, and why so few nonbelievers do.*

EXPLANATION

continued on next page

Connect to Testing: This Connect to Testing section focuses on analyzing central ideas, determining word meanings, and evaluating an argument.

Encourage students to work in pairs to choose the correct answers to the questions and then to compare their answers with those of another pair of students. If there is disagreement, encourage the groups to try to reach a consensus as they discuss the reasons for their choices.

Answers to Connect to Testing Questions:

1. C. Choice A does not express a central idea. Choice B is evidence that supports the central claim. Choice D is an example used to support a reason. Choice C expresses the central ideas of the text which are that the brain reinterprets what the eyes see and, as a result, what we see is not always reality. (DoK 2)

ELL Support: Connect to Testing and Assessments See the *Connections* ELL Teacher Resource (p. 22) for ideas on adapting this section for ELLs.

Chapter 7 *(continued)*

Assessment

Answers to Connect to Testing Questions:

2. C. Since *many* is an adjective showing amount, it will always precede other adjectives. In this sentence, *unusual* and *puzzling* can change positions, which indicates that they are coordinate or equal in importance. Therefore, a comma belongs between them but not after *many*. (DoK 1)

3. **Part A:** B. There is no evidence that the tone is worried or paranoid. Although there are two questions, the author is never confused about his topics. He is authoritative but doubtful about people's abilities to "see" by "looking." (DoK 2)
   Part B: D. The tone of this sentence doubts the truthfulness of "someone who tells you" these things. (DoK 2)

4. A. Seeing an angel when one looks at a bush means that he or she has "accidentally made" the angel out of the bush. This common act is not careless, foolish, or poor. (DoK 2)

2. Which of the following sentences is correctly punctuated?

   A. We saw many unusual puzzling rocks from space.

   B. We saw many, unusual puzzling rocks from space.

   C. We saw many unusual, puzzling rocks from space.

   D. We saw many, unusual, puzzling rocks from space.

3. **Part A:** Read these sentences from the second paragraph of *Think*.

   > We don't really "see" the things we look at? How can this be?

   What tone do these sentences convey?

   A. worried

   B. doubtful

   C. paranoid

   D. confused

   Part B: Which sentence from the passage indicates a tone similar to the one identified in Part A?

   A. *Seeing things that are not there can happen to anyone because the human brain constructs and interprets the visual reality that is around it.*

   B. *What you need in order to walk through a park and function well is to have a general picture of your surroundings, so that's what your brain gives you.*

   C. *Like many other animals, our prehistoric ancestors relied on this ability to eat and to avoid being eaten.*

   D. *Given what we now know about the brain, however, are you going to believe someone who tells you she saw a flying saucer or Bigfoot last week?*

4. Read this sentence from *Think*.

   > Or your brain could be showing you an angel that it has mistakenly constructed out of a bush or some other object.

   Which of the following is closest in meaning to the phrase *mistakenly constructed*?

   A. accidentally made

   B. poorly built

   C. carelessly seen

   D. foolishly thought

Remediation: Connect to Testing Focus attention on questions 1 and 4, which are good examples of questions about central ideas and determining meaning from context. Read each question aloud and have students take turns reading the answer choices. As a group, discuss whether each choice is correct or incorrect until the group reaches consensus about the correct answer.

Chapter 8

Determining Author's Purpose

Preview Concepts

In September 2016, only 32% of Americans said they trusted the news media to be accurate and fair. Compare this with 1976, when 72% of Americans felt confident that the news media were doing a good job.

Why do you think trust in the news media has fallen so far since 1976? Did Americans change? Did the media? Or did both change? Write your response below.

Chapter 8

Determining Author's Purpose

The Fact Checker's Guide for Detecting Fake News
by Glenn Kessler

Introduction

Chapter Goals: Have students read through the goals and mark any words that are unfamiliar. Discuss the meanings of any academic vocabulary within the goals that students marked as unfamiliar. Consider posting the Chapter Goals.

Preview Academic Vocabulary: Read and discuss the meanings of the academic vocabulary.

inference: *a conclusion or interpretation based on what the text says and also what the reader already knows.* Because the character was about to go into an old, scary house, I made an <u>inference</u> that there would be something dangerous inside.

point of view: *in nonfiction, an author's opinion or perspective on a topic.* From the <u>point of view</u> of this reporter, this disastrous fire could have been avoided.

purpose: *why an author writes a text or includes certain details and not others; the general goal of an author.* We thought the speaker was going to be funny, but it became clear that her main <u>purpose</u> was to warn us, not to entertain us.

 Gr7Ch8Vocabulary.pptx

ELL Support: Academic Vocabulary See <u>Teaching Vocabulary in the ELL Teacher Resource (p. 18)</u> for ideas to use for teaching vocabulary throughout *Connections*.

Preview Concepts Remind students that *trust* means belief that someone or something is reliable, good, or effective. Also, be sure students understand that *media* means the television, radio, news, and film industry. In this context, *the media* refers to the news media—the news on television, on radio, and in print. Have students work in multilevel groups or pairs to discuss their thoughts about trust in the media. Provide the following sentence frames for the discussion and students' written responses:

• I think trust in the media has fallen because . . . .

• I think Americans changed to become . . . . For example, ...

• I think the media changed to become . . . . For example, ...

Chapter 8 *(continued)*

Introduction

Making Connections: Help students understand the following:

- the "experiment" is the United States itself: a democratic constitutional republic, one of the world's first.

- The experiment was testing whether such a government would work: that people could govern themselves by representation.

- For Jefferson, the most effective "avenue to truth" was a free press.

Tech-Connect Suggestion: Jefferson's letter is available in its entirety at http://www.let.rug.nl/usa/presidents/thomas-jefferson/letters-of-thomas-jefferson/jefl164.php.

Making Connections

Read the following excerpt.

> No experiment can be more interesting than that we are now trying, and which we trust will end in establishing the fact, that man may be governed by reason and truth. Our first object should therefore be, to leave open to him all the avenues to truth. The most effectual hitherto found, is the freedom of the press.
>
> —President Thomas Jefferson

This letter was written in 1804, just twenty-eight years after the signing of the Declaration of Independence. In the first sentence, to what "experiment" is Thomas Jefferson likely referring?

What is this experiment trying to prove?

Jefferson feels the experiment depends on "avenues to truth." What, for him, is the most effective avenue to truth?

> **MAKING CONNECTIONS**
>
> As you read the passage in this chapter, pay attention to how each section of text develops the author's central idea.

First Read: Making an Inference

During the 2016 presidential election, people began talking about "fake news." Fake news refers to stories that look like they come from reliable news outlets but are actually packed with misleading or false information. Readers, assuming the stories are accurate, may share them with friends and family on social media sites such as Facebook and Twitter.

Glenn Kessler is a reporter who works at the *Washington Post*. In this article, he discusses ways to figure out whether a story is "fake news" or not.

Objective: As you read, underline any sentences that suggest what Kessler assumes about his readers. Record any questions you have in the My Thoughts column.

—— First Read
- - - - Second Read
—— Third Read

excerpt
The Fact Checker's Guide for Detecting Fake News
by Glenn Kessler
from *The Washington Post*

My Thoughts

1   Anyone active on social media has <u>probably done this at least once: shared something based on the headline without actually reading the link.</u>

Let's face it, you've probably done this many times.

5   According to a study released in June by computer scientists at Columbia University and the French National Institute, 59 percent of links shared on social media have never actually been clicked.

So the first thing you can do to combat the rise of "fake ~~POV~~ news" is to <u>actually read articles before sharing them.</u> And when you read them, pay attention to the following signs that the article may be fake. There are fake news stories generated by both left-leaning and right-leaning websites, and the same rules apply to both.

This section introduces the idea of fake news and how readers can detect it.

ELL Support: First Read Before students read, be sure they understand that *fake* means "false, untrue, not real." Also, be sure students understand the social media and television references (Facebook, Twitter, ABC News, pop-up ads, etc.), displaying pictures or actual sites to explain the concepts.

Have students read the text in multilevel pairs or small groups, pausing at the end of each paragraph to summarize using a <u>Main Ideas and Supporting Details graphic organizer from the ELL Teacher Resource (p. 51)</u>. Also, encourage students to take notes and draw sketches in the margins around the article so they can be sure they understand the topic of each paragraph.

First Read: Making an Inference

Before Reading: Activate prior knowledge by having students share what they already know about the topic of fake news. Show websites with examples of fake news or clickbait as needed. Remind students that during the first read of a text, they should focus on identifying key ideas or answering the question *What?* Review the introduction and objective with students. Explain that as they think about what Kessler assumes about his readers, they must "read between the lines." To ensure comprehension, model how to read and annotate the first paragraph. Then have students read the rest of the article on their own.

Preview Vocabulary: Preview unfamiliar vocabulary to aid comprehension. Ask students to circle unfamiliar words as they complete the first read. After the first read, guide students to determine the words' meanings using the context. Encourage them to support their responses with evidence and confirm their initial definitions with a dictionary. Words that students might find difficult include:

legitimate: *conforming to rules, standards, or ethics; valid.* I could not tell if the two-for-one sale was <u>legitimate</u> or some kind of scam.

domain: *a subdivision of the Internet, categorized by source, purpose, or country and designated by the last letters in the address.* In general, the *.edu* <u>domain</u> is more trustworthy than the *.com* domain.

absurd: *ridiculous; unreasonable; illogical; impossible.* It's <u>absurd</u> to suggest that the thief could run five miles in ten minutes because that is humanly impossible.

debunks: *exposes the falseness of something; uncovers a sham.* In his lectures, the astronomer <u>debunks</u> the possibility of life on Mars.

biased: *having an inclination or leaning toward one point of view; prejudiced; not neutral.* Some students believed that our principal was <u>biased</u> toward women until she expelled the entire girls' basketball team.

scrutinize: *to examine with extreme care, detail by detail.* The chess player <u>scrutinized</u> every move his opponent made.

Lesson Support

dubious: *questionable; of doubtful promise or integrity.* Being elected class president was a <u>dubious</u> distinction since the office held little power.

fraudster: *a person who engages in cheating, deceit, trickery; an imposter.* The woman was not a medical doctor; she was a <u>fraudster</u> with a stethoscope and a white lab coat.

After Reading: Use the following questions to check comprehension.

Text-Based Discussion Questions

1. Based on evidence in this article, what can you infer about the ABC News site at abcnew.go.com? *It is a legitimate news source that can be trusted.*

2. Based on evidence in this article, what can you infer about websites that end in .co, .uk, or another country code? *These should be checked out first because they indicate the news is being put out by someone in another country.*

3. What can you infer about Kessler from his use of the word *combating* in the last paragraph? *One can infer that he considers the quest for truth in the news media a war, metaphorically speaking.*

Gr7Ch8Read1.pptx

Background Information: Glenn Kessler runs a blog for *The Washington Post* called "Fact Checker" in which he rates statements by politicians and business leaders on a scale of one to four "Pinocchios." One Pinocchio means that the facts have been a little shaded, distorted, or twisted to achieve a purpose. Four Pinocchios means that the statement is a blatant, outright lie. If the statement is true, Kessler may award a rare "Geppetto." Remind students that in general, blogs (regularly updated web pages usually written in conversational style) should never be trusted as legitimate sources of information because anyone can write *anything* in a blog. There is no peer-reviewing, no research necessary, and often little or no oversight.

15 **Determine whether the article is from a legitimate website**

There's ABC News, the television network, with the Web address of abcnews.go.com. And there's ABC News, the fake news website, with the Web address of abcnews.com.co.

20 The use of ".co" at the end of the URL is a strong clue you are looking at a fake news website. (It signifies the Internet country code domain assigned to the country of Colombia.) But there are other signs as well.

Check the 'contact us' page

25 Some fake news sites don't have any contact information, which easily demonstrates it's phony. The fake "ABC News" does have a "contact us" page—but it shows a picture of the controversial Westboro Baptist Church in Topeka, Kan. (An inside joke?) The real television network is based in New York
30 City, housed in a 13-story building on 66th Street.

Examine the byline of the reporter and see whether it makes sense

On the fake ABC News site there is an article claiming a protester was paid $3,500 to protest [Donald] Trump. It's
35 supposedly written by Jimmy Rustling. "Dr. Jimmy Rustling has won many awards for excellence in writing including fourteen Peabody awards and a handful of Pulitzer Prizes," the author biography claims. If that doesn't seem absurd, then how about the fact that he claims to have a Russian mail order bride of
40 almost two months and "also spends 12-15 hours each day teaching their adopted 8-year-old Syrian refugee daughter how to read and write."

All of the details are signs that "Dr. Rustling" is not a real person.

My Thoughts

<u>Each section on pages 160–161 explains a way to evaluate news to determine if it is fake.</u>

160   Chapter 8 • Unit 2   ©Perfection Learning® • No Reproduction Permitted

45 **Read the article closely**

Many fake articles have made-up quotes that do not pass

the laugh test. About midway through the article on the

protest, the founder of Snopes.com—which debunks fake news

on the Internet—is suddenly "quoted," saying he approves of

50 the article. It also goes on to describe Snopes as "a website

known for its biased opinions and inaccurate information they

write about stories on the internet." It's like a weird inside

joke, and in the readers' minds it should raise immediate red

flags.

55 **Scrutinize the sources**

Sometimes fake articles are based on merely a tweet.

The New York Times documented how the fake news

that anti-Trump protesters were bused in started with a

single, ill-informed tweet by a man with just 40 followers.

60 Another apparently fake story, that Trump fed police officers

working protests in Chicago, also started with a tweet—by

a man who wasn't even there but was passing along a claim

made by "friends." The tweeter also has a locked account,

making the "news" highly dubious. Few real news stories are

65 based on a single tweet, with no additional confirmation.

If the article has no links to legitimate sources—or links at

all—that's another telltale sign that you are reading fake news.

Look at the ads

A profusion of pop-up ads or other advertising indicates

70 you should handle the story with care. Another sign is a bunch

of questionable ads or links, designed to be clicked— . . .

"Naughty Walmart Shoppers Who have no Shame at All"—

which you generally do not find on legitimate news sites.

©Perfection Learning® • No Reproduction Permitted

About the Author: Glenn Kessler's career in journalism—writing about politics, economics, airline safety, and Wall Street—has spanned three decades. He served as the chief State Department correspondent for *The Washington Post* for nine years, reporting from dozens of countries and serving three different secretaries of state. He has won numerous awards including two shared Pulitzer Prizes. Currently he lectures at prestigious universities and appears regularly on television and radio as an expert in political truth-telling. A current member of the nonprofit think-tank, Council on Foreign Relations, Kessler has a BA from Brown University and an MA from Columbia University's School of International and Public Affairs. Kessler is a pioneer and expert in global political fact-checking. Find out more at Kessler's website: www.glennkessler.com.

Tech-Connect Suggestion: Glenn Kessler's blog is available here: https://www.washingtonpost.com/news/fact-checker/?utm_term=.1f39dc1b36d7.

Remediation: First Read Read the article aloud, choosing different students to read the content under the heads. Take a few moments after each reader finishes to ask volunteers to summarize what they heard and read. Encourage readers to read slowly and project their voices so that every word is clearly audible.

Lesson Support

FIRST RESPONSE: KEY IDEAS AND DETAILS

After students have written in their journals, encourage individuals to share what they wrote with the whole class. How did students feel about the experience of sharing fake news? Horrified, embarrassed, or maybe they felt it was funny? Perhaps they did it to get a response from other people on social media. Discuss the responsibilities that social media users have to share responsibly and respectfully.

Use search engines to double-check

75   A simple Google search often will quickly tell you if the news you are reading is fake. Our friends at Snopes have also compiled a Field Guide to Fake News Sites, allowing you to check whether the article comes from a fraudster. There is also a website called RealorSatire.com that allows you to post

80   the URL of any article and it will quickly tell you if the article comes from a fake or biased news website.

Combating the spread of fake news begins with you, the reader. If it seems too fantastic, it probably is. <u>Please think</u> **AP POV** <u>before you share.</u>

FIRST RESPONSE: KEY IDEAS AND DETAILS
Glenn Kessler assumes that most readers have accidentally shared a "fake news" story on social media. Have you accidentally shared one? How do you know it was fake news? Was it really an accidental sharing, or did you share it for another reason? Record your response in your journal.

TECH-CONNECT

Post your First Response answers on your class web page. Compare your answers to those posted by other students.

Focus on Making an Inference
Glenn Kessler's "Fact Checker's Guide" describes actions that you, the reader, can take to figure out whether an article is "fake news." But what does Kessler assume about his readers? The article says *you* a lot, so it's fair to think he has assumptions about who *you* are. But he doesn't explicitly say what he thinks about his readers. Is there any textual evidence that can help you figure this out?

Remediation: First Read Help students understand the concepts of intended audience and a writer's assumptions about audience by asking students to circle all the instances of *you* in the text. (There are 14.) Then have students focus on one instance and discuss whom the word *you* refers to. Sometimes *you* refers to any reader in general, and other times the author is referring to a specific group of people.

Complete the activity below. Respond to each quotation by completing each sentence that begins, "This quote assumes that the readers . . . ." The first row has been completed for you.

Quotations from "Fact Checker's Guide"	Assumption About Readers
Anyone active on social media has probably done this at least once: shared something based on the headline without actually reading the link.	This quote assumes that the readers . . . know what social media are; are social media users and possibly active; have possibly shared a link based on the headline alone.
So the first thing you can do to combat the rise of "fake news" is to actually read articles before sharing them.	This statement assumes that the readers . . . don't actually read news articles online.
And when you read them, pay attention to the following signs that the article may be fake.	This statement assumes that the readers . . . take the time to read the entire article to observe the signs that he will describe; actually care if articles are fake.
Combating the spread of fake news begins with you, the reader. If it seems too fantastic, it probably is. Please think before you share.	These statements assume that the readers . . . want to avoid spreading fake news.

▼ Write Based on your analysis of the quotes, write a paragraph describing what Kessler assumes about his readers. Specifically, describe his assumptions about the following:

- readers' experience with social media
- readers' background knowledge about fake news
- readers' belief about whether spreading fake news is good or bad
- what readers want to do about fake news

Focus on Making an Inference:

Possible Answers to Chart:

See answers on Student Book insert page to the left.

▼ **Write:** Guide students to consider the possibility that fake news is spread because people want to spread it, not simply because they do not recognize it. Discuss this question: *Why would someone want to spread news that they know is fake?* Keep track of possible reasons.

Sample response: *Kessler assumes his readers use social media and have accidentally shared at least one fake news story. He also assumes his readers know about fake news and don't want to participate in spreading it. He thinks readers coming across articles that seem "too fantastic" will actually take the time to analyze such articles in the ways he describes. In short, he assumes his readers are thoughtful, responsible people who don't want to spread half-truths or lies.*

ELL Support: Write Have students work in multilevel pairs or small groups and use the following sentence frames first to discuss and then to write about the author's assumptions. Be sure students understand that *assume* means to think something is true without knowing for sure.

- According to Kessler, the people reading his article are . . . .
- Kessler assumes that his readers . . . .
- Kessler thinks his readers are . . . .

Help beginning ELLs by providing possible answers to the sentence starters: use/do not use social media a lot, understand/do not understand fake news, want to/do not want to spread fake news.

Lesson Support

⌒**Speak and Listen:** Once a pair has finished their discussion, have them join with another pair and share again.

Second Read: Analyzing Text Structure

Before Reading: Remind students that during a second read, they are uncovering how a writer communicates his or her ideas by asking the question *How?* In this case, students are focusing on how the different sections of Kessler's article work to develop and communicate his central idea: to help his readers identify fake news and stop spreading it.

Suggest that students focus on the verb phrases *must identify* and *stop it from spreading.* These are two separate yet related actions that the author is trying to convince readers are necessary.

After Reading: Use the following questions to check comprehension.

Text-Based Discussion Questions

1. What does the author really want readers to do to stop fake news from spreading? *The author encourages readers to think before they share. He wants them to be analytical instead of accepting.*

2. Are the headings effective? Why or why not? *Answers may vary. Yes, they are effective because they make each step seem easy and logical; No, because they break up one argument into too many small pieces.*

3. What does the author warn about in the section called Scrutinize the Sources? *The author warns that anyone can tweet anything and start a "fake" news story, and he offers a specific example.*

Focus on Analyzing Text Structure:

If possible, allow students some time to discuss and brainstorm about the metaphor that sections of the text are like house builders with different jobs. The more they explore the metaphor, the richer it will become and the more useful it will be to them as readers and writers.

⌒**Speak and Listen** With a partner, share your description of Kessler's assumptions. If your descriptions differ significantly, figure out why. Are you interpreting the evidence differently? Are you responding to the article from different points of view, and if so, what are they?

Second Read: Analyzing Text Structure

The central idea of Kessler's article can be summed up this way: Readers must identify fake news and stop it from spreading. But how does the article develop this idea?

After the introduction, the article has seven sections, each introduced with a heading. These sections work together to develop the central idea. But what does *work together* mean for a text? And how do these sections work together?

Objective: Read the article a second time. As you finish each major section, answer this question in the My Thoughts box: How does this section help develop the central idea?

Focus on Analyzing Text Structure

Think about the phrase *work together.* Imagine a team of house builders, each with different skills. The plumber gets the water working. The electrician makes sure the lights work. The roofer makes sure rainfall doesn't ruin the walls and floors. Each worker has a job, and they work together to build a house that functions well.

The major sections of Kessler's article are like those workers. Each section has its own job, and they all work together to develop the central idea.

Use the chart below to analyze how each major section relates to the central idea. Use words such as *example, describe, explain,* and *convince.* The first two have been done for you.

Article Section	Purpose of Section
Determine whether the article is from a legitimate website	provides the first step in identifying fake news; explains one way fakers try to deceive readers
Check the 'contact us' page	provides the second step; gives an example of what a fake news source looks like

Remediation: Second Read You can modify this activity for struggling readers by assigning pairs or small groups of students one section of the article to focus on. Have one person in each group read the section aloud as others follow along. Then have a recorder begin to write the purpose based on discussion. Finally, fill in the chart as a whole group by asking each pair or group to report on the purpose of their section.

ELL Support: Second Read Before students reread the article, preview the chart on pp. 164–165, paraphrasing complex words and phrases for understanding. Also, use images of builders (plumbers, electricians, carpenters, etc.) to illustrate the idea of people working together to build a house. Previewing the structure of the chart will help students understand the structure of the text.

Article Section	Purpose of Section
Examine the byline of the reporter and see whether it makes sense	provides another step; explains that taking the time to look up the author might reveal illegitimacy; gives an example
Read the article closely	provides another step; offers an example of bogus information that can be found in the middle of an article
Scrutinize the sources	provides another step; explains and offers examples of how fake news is often started by a single tweet
Look at the ads	provides another step; describes how dubious ads are a warning sign
Use search engines to double-check	provides a final step; provides online resources to check news stories.

Speak and Listen Kessler's article uses subheads to introduce the sections. With a partner, discuss the purpose of these subheads and how each section contributes to the author's central idea.

Write This article was shared on social media platforms such as Facebook and Twitter. Could *this* article be "fake news"? Why or why not? Write a paragraph explaining your reasons in your reading journal.

Possible Answers to Chart:

See answers on Student Book insert page to the left.

Write: Ask students to use the steps outlined in the article to evaluate it. Instruct them to include what they found in their writing.

 Gr7Ch8Read2.pptx

ELL Support: Speak and Listen Have students work in multilevel pairs or small groups to discuss the article. These sentence frames may help students in their discussions:

- These subheads make it easier . . . .
- These subheads help me . . . .
- These subheads show that . . . .

Write Modify this exercise by asking *Is this article news?* or *Is this article fact?* Help students see that the author uses facts to support his opinions but that the article is mostly advice, which is *always* a claim or an opinion, never a fact. Have students work in multilevel pairs or small groups to discuss the article.

Chapter 8 (continued)

Lesson Support

Tech-Connect Suggestion: You may want to have students explore fact-checking sites such as Snopes.com or FactCheck.org. Note that some people claim these sites are biased toward certain political viewpoints. View both sites' About pages. What does this reveal about their purposes and goals? What can a site do to try to be as unbiased as possible?

Third Read: Determining Point of View and Purpose

Before Reading: Have students pair up to discuss the introduction and objective. Help them understand how an author's point of view and purpose are intertwined. Readers' interpretations and analyses tease them apart. Explain that POV and AP inform each other, reflect each other, support each other, and reveal each other.

After Reading: Use the following questions to check comprehension.

Text-Based Discussion Questions

1. Based on this article, how do you think Glenn Kessler would define the term "fake news"? *Fake news is not based on facts; it is made up. However, it looks like it could be real, especially the headline.*

2. What does the author think about inside jokes that he refers to in lines 52 and 53? *He thinks inside jokes are a sign that an Internet site is probably fake or unreliable.*

3. What does the author think of Snopes.com? Give evidence for your answer. *He obviously trusts it to answer the question about whether something is true or fake.*

Focus on Determining Point of View and Purpose:

Possible Answers to Questions:

Kessler's point of view is that fake news should not be spread. His use of negative language such as "combat the rise of 'fake news' " indicates that he takes this "war" seriously.

(continued)

Third Read: Determining Point of View and Purpose

When discussing nonfiction texts, you should distinguish between authors' point of view and their purpose.

- Point of view is the author's opinion about the ideas or events being described. Authors may hold a point of view about an issue because of the way it affects them, in a good way or a bad way. How does the issue of fake news affect a journalist like Glenn Kessler?

- Purpose is the goal the author wants the text to accomplish. Purposes include entertaining or informing readers, convincing readers to take action, and so on. What does Glenn Kessler hope to do by writing this article?

Objective: As you read the article a third time, think about Kessler's point of view and his purpose. Write POV next to a paragraph that most clearly states his point of view. Then write AP next to a paragraph that most clearly states his purpose.

Focus on Determining Point of View and Purpose

Sometimes an author's point of view and purpose are explicit, or clearly stated. Other times, the point of view and purpose are not explicit, and you must infer them.

What is Kessler's point of view regarding fake news? How can you tell? Write your response in the space below. Support your response with details from the text.

REFLECT

Why is accurate news important in a democracy? What would happen to a democracy if accurate news disappeared?

Remediation: Third Read The distinction between point of view and purpose can be challenging for many readers. These sentence stems may help:

- The author feels _____ about her/his topic: _____. *(point of view)*

- This author wants his/her readers to _____. *(purpose)*

ELL Support: Third Read Before reading, use a think-aloud strategy to model identifying a statement that reflects point of view and labeling it POV. For example, say: *I am looking for a sentence that shows what the author thinks about fake news or the people who create fake news. I will know the author's point of view from the words he uses. If he uses positive words, I will know that he likes something. If he uses negative words, I will know he dislikes something. I think that line 38 shows the author's point of view on the fake writer Jimmy Rustling. He uses the word* absurd *to*

What is Kessler's main purpose in writing his article? How can you tell? Write your response in the space below. Support your response with details from the text.

Language: Correcting Misplaced Modifiers

In sentences, a phrase or clause can modify (describe) words, phrases, or clauses. Look at the example sentence below.

> The problem of fake news, <u>which came to prominence in 2016,</u> has existed for as long as journalism itself.

Notice that the phrase "which came to prominence in 2016" modifies the phrase "The problem of fake news." It is important for a modifier to be placed near the words it describes. Otherwise, the sentence might be confusing or make no sense at all. To fix a sentence with a misplaced modifier, just move the modifier closest to the word or phrase it should actually modify.

Study the sentence below.

> We stood and talked about all the fake news <u>in the living room.</u>

The phrase "in the living room" is meant to modify "stood." As written, the sentence suggests "all the fake news" is somehow in the living room. Rewrite the sentence so it is correct.

continued on next page

Possible Answers to Questions:

Kessler's purpose is to convince readers to stop sharing fake news. He wants us to become informed readers who take time to analyze stories before sharing them. The final paragraph indicates this purpose: "Combating the spread of fake news begins with you, the reader" and "Please think before you share."

 Gr7Ch8Read3.pptx

Language: Correcting Misplaced Modifiers: Students will rewrite the sentence this way: *We stood in the living room and talked about all the fake news.*

Gr7Ch8Language.pptx

---

describe Rustling's claim that he won many prizes. The word *absurd is a negative word. It means "completely ridiculous or silly." So the author's point of view on Rustling is negative.* Then use a think-aloud to model identifying a statement that reflects author's purpose.

Then have students work in multilevel pairs or small groups to reread the article, identifying point of view and author's purpose. Next, have students work in the same groups to write their responses on pp. 166–167. Provide the following sentence frames for students to use to complete their paragraphs. These are also included in the ELL Teacher Resource (p. 36).

Kessler's point of view on fake news is . . . . I know this because he uses positive/negative words to describe it. For example, ...

Kessler's purpose for writing the article is . . . . I know this because he . . . . For example, ...

Chapter 8 (continued)

Lesson Support

Answers to Exercises:

The misplaced modifier suggests that "social media sites" are harmful to good decision-making, when the clause actually modifies "fake news stories." It should be written as: *I made the mistake of sharing fake news stories, which are harmful to good decision-making, on social media sites.*

1. In the car, Dana told us how Laura had shared fake news stories.

2. Laura shared stories that were completely false with her friends.

Tech-Connect Suggestion: Sometimes, misplaced or dangling modifiers result in funny sentences. Here are a few examples from http://www.eddiesnipes.com/2011/07/funny-dangling-and-misplaced-modifiers/:

- After a long walk, the wonderful shade tree came into view.

- We saw several blue jays looking out our front window.

- I glimpsed a rat sorting the recyclable materials.

- We saw dinosaurs on a field trip to the natural history museum.

- Abraham Lincoln wrote the Gettysburg address while traveling from Washington to Gettysburg on the back of an envelope.

- My parents bought a dog for my brother named Spot.

- Hanging on the wall, my mom really liked the picture.

Now read this sentence, which also has a misplaced modifier.

> I made the mistake of sharing fake news stories on social media sites, which are harmful to good decision-making.

Explain why the sentence is confusing. Then fix it by rewriting it.

The following sentences contain misplaced modifiers. Rewrite each one, placing the modifier correctly.

1. Dana told us how Laura had shared fake news stories in the car.

2. Laura shared stories with her friends that were completely false.

ELL Support: Language Confirm students' understanding that *modify* means "to describe or tell more about." Explain how the phrases in the sample sentences modify or tell more about a specific noun in each sentence. Use a think-aloud to model completing the first few exercises. Say: *Which words in this sentence are naming something harmful? Are social media sites harmful? Or are fake news stories harmful? Social media sites aren't all bad. Fake news stories are harmful. So I will move the phrase to be close to "fake news stories."*

Have students work in multilevel pairs or groups to complete the items. Then review them together as a class, identifying what each phrase modifies.

3. One story claimed a politician wanted to make his dog a
senator because he had gone insane.

4. Dana used her phone to show evidence that the stories were
fake to Laura.

5. Laura got grumpy at Dana because she does not like being
wrong.

6. Dana told Laura, which is useful, to read Glenn Kessler's
article.

Answers to Exercises:

3. One story claimed a politician who had gone insane wanted to make his dog a senator.

4. Dana used her phone to show Laura evidence that the stories were fake.

5. Because she does not like being wrong, Laura got grumpy at Dana.

6. Dana told Laura to read Glenn Kessler's article, which is useful.

Chapter 8 *(continued)*

Assessment

Project-Based Assessments

Investigative Report: Display the graphic organizer on the board. Remind students of the 5 Ws and the H (*who, what, when, where, why*, and *how*), the building blocks of good news reporting. Remind them to stick to the facts. Also, suggest that they include at least one quotation by an expert to support their main idea.

Tech-connect Suggestion: Have students use Google Docs or another program to keep tract of their notes and sources. One method is to cut and copy URLs into a document and use a different color for information from each source. Remind students not to cut and paste text without using quotation marks around information taken directly from a source. Explain to students that plagiarism is using information word for word from a source without giving credit to the writers of the source. There is also a source chart available on page 217.

Project-Based Assessments

Investigative Report

Write a five-paragraph newspaper report explaining why fake news is a problem.

Make a list of questions the public would want answered. Examples might include the following:

- What is fake news?
- Why do people make it?
- What are its harmful effects?

Then conduct online research using terms such as *fake news*, *effects*, and *society*. Websites that end in *.edu*, *.gov*, or *.org* usually have more reliable information than sites ending in *.com*. Keep track of your source information as you do your research.

Newspaper reports follow an inverted-pyramid structure. The most important ideas come first (the wide part of the pyramid) and lead into less important ideas (the point of the pyramid). Your report will need a catchy headline. Headlines are usually incomplete sentences, such as "How Fake News Harms Our Democracy."

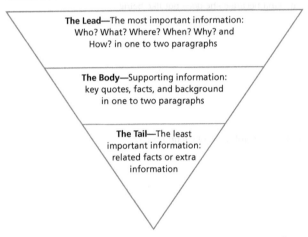

The Lead—The most important information: Who? What? Where? When? Why? and How? in one to two paragraphs

The Body—Supporting information: key quotes, facts, and background in one to two paragraphs

The Tail—The least important information: related facts or extra information

Use a word processing or design program to type your article using newspaper format. Follow these guidelines:

- one-inch margins
- three columns (go to Format/Columns to set up)
- single-spacing, indented first lines of paragraphs, 12-point font (Times)

ELL Support: Project-Based Assessments—Investigative Report Have students work in multilevel pairs or small groups. Reduce the length as needed. Give groups a list of sources that are appropriate to their abilities. Another option is to have students find a news story on social media and use the steps from the article to evaluate it. Newsela (https://newsela.com) provides articles on a wide range of topics and written for varying lexile levels. Help students rewrite an article's headers as questions and instruct them to use the questions as a checklist for evaluating the news story. Encourage students to use the writing supports from previous essays, including the sample class essay from Chapter 5 and their own writing from previous chapters. Once students complete a draft, provide them with Informational Writing Revision Checklists from the ELL Teacher Resource (p. 69) and the Proofreading Checklist (p. 71) and have students work with new multilevel pairs or small groups to revise and edit their writing.

- headline and your byline (example: by Jackie Smith) at the top of the article.
- a picture or image that supports your writing along with a caption; make the text wrap around the picture

Use the following guidelines for your investigative report.	
To receive the highest score (4.0), the investigative report must meet all of these criteria.	Your newspaper report should • have an interesting headline that reveals the main point. • answer important questions in the first two paragraphs. • provide supporting information in the rest of the report. • use correct grammar, usage, punctuation, and spelling.

Compare and Contrast Essay

People show bias when they favor one thing, person, or group over another. Even news articles from reliable sources can show bias. It is important to read news stories from a few sources about any important event. You will get a more complete picture or at least understand why people have different views about the same event. For this project, you will write a four-paragraph essay comparing and contrasting how two news sources report the same event.

In the chart below, the left column lists news sources considered to have a liberal bias. This means the sources generally favor policies that increase the role of the federal government. The right column lists outlets considered to have a conservative bias. In general, these sources favor policies that reduce the role of the federal government.

News Sources with a Liberal Bias	News Sources with a Conservative Bias
The Atlantic (www.theatlantic.com)	*The Economist* (www.economist.com)
The Guardian (www.theguardian.com/us)	The Hill (www.thehill.com)
MSNBC (www.msnbc.com)	*The Fiscal Times* (www.thefiscaltimes.com)
The New York Times (www.nytimes.com)	Fox News (www.foxnews.com)

Follow these steps:
- Visit one site listed in the chart. Find an article on a recent, important event that interests you. Be sure to find an article instead of an editorial. Bookmark the article.

continued on next page

Compare and Contrast Essay:
If students land on two sources that do not differ significantly, they will have more difficulty with this project. If this happens, steer them to look at other sources with the purpose of finding two that differ significantly in their approach or point of view.

Remediation: Project-Based Assessments—Compare and Contrast Essay Find three or four pairs of articles on current events that are appropriate for the age and reading abilities of your students. Articles should represent different points of view on an issue. Allow students to choose from your preselected articles.

Chapter 8 *(continued)*

Assessment

Compare and Contrast Essay:
Draw a graphic organizer to help students understand the organizational pattern of the essay. Here is an example:

Paragraph 1

- Describe events
- Identify sources
- Give your opinion

Paragraph 2

- Describe similarities

Paragraph 3

- Describe differences

Paragraph 4

- Restate opinion from Paragraph 1
- Draw a conclusion

- Visit a site listed in the other column. Find an article on the same event. Again, make sure to find an article, not an editorial. Bookmark the article.
- Print each article. You'll be marking them to identify information for your essay.

As you read each article, do the following:

- Underline at least one sentence that clearly states what each article is reporting on.
- Place a star next to any important information appearing in both articles.
- Draw a box around important information that appears in one article but not the other. (Note: If you find yourself drawing too many boxes, your articles might be reporting on different events. If so, dig back into the sites and look for new articles.)
- Circle words or phrases that suggest some kind of bias. Pay attention to connotations, or words and phrases meant to stir positive or negative feelings in readers.
- In the margins, jot down other thoughts that occur to you as you read.

Now, write your compare and contrast essay. You will write four paragraphs.

- **First paragraph:** Describe the event, identify the sources, and tell your opinion of whether the articles covered the event similarly, differently, or somewhere in-between.

- **Second paragraph:** Describe important similarities. Do the articles present events in the same order? Place the same emphasis on events? Use the same or similar quotations?

- **Third paragraph:** Describe important differences. Do they emphasize different aspects of the event? Does one article have important information the other does not? Do they use words with different connotations to describe the same events?

- **Fourth paragraph:** Restate your opinion regarding the two sources. Then draw a conclusion. If two sources report events similarly, is that always good? Or, if they report events differently, is that necessarily bad? Explain what you think and why.

> **CONNECT TO ESSENTIAL QUESTION**
>
> It's become common for people to say, "The media never tell you the truth." What do you think of this claim? Do you think it's possible to find the truth?

Use the following guidelines for your compare and contrast essay.	
To receive the highest score (4.0), the compare and contrast essay must meet all of these criteria.	Your compare and contrast essay should • introduce the news event and the sources you chose. • state your opinion about whether the sources differ. • describe important similarities and differences between the articles. • use details from each article to illustrate the similarities and differences you describe. • restate your opinion and draw a conclusion based on your analysis. • use correct grammar, usage, punctuation, and spelling.

On Your Own: Integrating Ideas

- "Fake news" is a problem as old as news itself. To read about famous examples of fake news—some of them more outrageous than others—visit the following site: http://hoaxes.org/archive/display/category/newspapers_and_magazines.

- With the rise of fake news has come the rise of websites that try to debunk fake news. Two sites are broadly respected: FactCheck.org and PolitiFact.com. Glenn Kessler also mentions Snopes.com and RealorSatire.com. Check out one or all of those sites; chances are good you will be using them in the future.

- In Washington, D.C., the Newseum is a museum devoted to the history of journalism. Many of its exhibits appear on its website, newseum.org. There you can learn why accurate news is vital to the "experiment" Thomas Jefferson wrote about at the beginning of this chapter.

> **REFLECT**
>
> Is the news important in your life? Will it become more important to you as you age? Why or why not?

On Your Own: Integrating Ideas: Invite students to work in pairs as they explore the suggested websites and ask them to share what they discover with the whole group.

Chapter 8 (continued)

Assessment

Connect to Testing: This Connect to Testing section focuses on making inferences, analyzing text structure and purpose, and identifying point of view.

Encourage students to work in pairs to choose the correct answers to the questions and then to compare their answers with those of another pair of students. If there is disagreement, encourage the groups to try to reach a consensus as they discuss the reasons for their choices.

Answers to Connect to Testing Questions:

1. **Part A:** C. The key word is *evaluate*. Although Choices A, B, and D may be true in part, Choice C addresses the author's main idea—that readers need to be highly critical.
   Part B: B. and C. These steps directly support ways that readers evaluate what they read. (DoK 2)

2. D. This structure is reflected in the title, the introduction, and the headings throughout the passage. (DoK 2)

Connect to Testing

In this chapter, you made inferences, analyzed text structure, and determined the author's point of view and purpose. The following questions are examples of how these skills may be tested on standardized tests.

1. **Part A:** What is the central idea of "The Fact Checker's Guide"?
   A. People should read more news articles from reliable sources.
   B. People should understand the consequences of spreading fake news stories.
   C. People should evaluate news stories using the methods the author describes.
   D. People should realize that members of all political parties spread fake news stories.

   Part B: Select two sentences from the passage that best support the answer in Part A.
   A. *Anyone active on social media has probably done this at least once: shared something based on the headline without actually reading the link.*
   B. *So the first thing you can do to combat the rise of "fake news" is to actually read articles before sharing them.*
   C. *And when you read them, pay attention to the following signs that the article may be fake.*
   D. *There are fake news stories generated by both left-leaning and right-leaning websites, and the same rules apply to both.*
   E. *There's ABC News, the television network, with the Web address of abcnews.go.com.*
   F. *If it seems too fantastic, it probably is.*

2. How does the author structure the passage to develop the central idea?
   A. by identifying the most common types of fake news stories
   B. by explaining how fake news stories mislead people
   C. by ordering fake news stories from least to most believable
   D. by describing ways to determine whether a story is fake news

ELL Support: Using Connect to Testing and Assessments See the *Connections* ELL Teacher Resource (p. 22) for ideas on adapting this section for ELLs.

3. Read the sentence below. It has a misplaced modifier.

> Eric told us he had read a fake news story in the morning after lunch.

Choose the answer that best corrects the misplaced modifier in the sentence.

A. After lunch, Eric told us he had read a fake news in the morning.

B. Eric told us he had read a fake news story after lunch in the morning.

C. In the morning after lunch, Eric told us he had read a fake news story.

D. Eric told us, in the morning, he had read a fake news story after lunch.

4. **Part A:** What is the author's main purpose in writing the passage?

A. to slow the spread of fake news

B. to show how fake news is a growing problem

C. to explain that all political parties spread fake news

D. to identify the sources of fake news

Part B: Which sentence from the passage best supports the answer in Part A?

A. *Anyone active on social media has probably done this at least once: shared something based on the headline without actually reading the link.*

B. *So the first thing you can do to combat the rise of "fake news" is to actually read articles before sharing them.*

C. *There are fake news stories generated by both left-leaning and right-leaning websites, and the same rules apply to both.*

D. *There's ABC News, the television network, with the Web address of abcnews.go.com.*

5. In the passage, the author refers to a website named Snopes. Which sentence from the passage most clearly shows the author's actual point of view about Snopes?

A. *About midway through the article on the protest, the founder of Snopes.com—which debunks fake news on the Internet—is suddenly "quoted," saying he approves of the article.*

B. *It also goes on to describe Snopes as "a website known for its biased opinions and inaccurate information they write about stories on the internet."*

C. *It's like a weird inside joke, and in the readers' minds it should raise immediate red flags.*

D. *Our friends at Snopes have also compiled a Field Guide to Fake News Sites, allowing you to check whether the article comes from a fraudster.*

3. A. (DoK 1)

4. **Part A:** A. The essay is persuasive. The author is trying to convince the audience to do something (in fact, eight things). By convincing readers to take these steps, the author hopes to stop the spread of fake news.
Part B: B. The author is seeking action from the readers by telling them "the first thing you can do . . . ." (DoK 3)

5. D. Point of view is revealed clearly by the phrase "our friends at Snopes," and the general tone of the sentence is one of approval. (DoK 2)

Remediation: Connect to Testing Questions 3 and 5 will be especially difficult for struggling readers. Read each question aloud and have students take turns reading the answer choices. As a group, discuss whether each choice is correct or incorrect until the group reaches consensus about the correct answer.

Chapter 9

Evaluating Reasons and Evidence

Debunk It! How to Stay Sane in a World of Misinformation
by John Grant

Introduction

Chapter Goals: Have students read through the goals and mark any words that are unfamiliar. Discuss the meanings of any academic vocabulary within the goals that students marked as unfamiliar. Consider posting the Chapter Goals.

Preview Academic Vocabulary: Read and discuss the meanings of the academic vocabulary.

claim: *the writer's or speaker's opinion which he/she is attempting to prove is true.* The attorney made the <u>claim</u> that his client had been framed.

clause: *a group of words with a subject and a verb; clauses can be independent (can stand alone) or dependent (cannot stand alone).* All sentences contain at least one <u>clause</u>, and many sentences, like this one, contain more.

complex sentence: *a sentence with one independent clause and at least one dependent clause.* If you join two sentences with a subordinating conjunction, you'll create a <u>complex sentence</u>. Example: When I eat spaghetti, I use a fork and a spoon.

compound sentence: *a sentence with two or more independent clauses.* If you join two complete sentences with a coordinating conjunction, you'll create a <u>compound sentence</u>. Example: I like pizza, but I adore spaghetti.

compound–complex sentence: *a sentence with two or more independent clauses and at least one dependent clause.* A <u>compound-complex sentence</u> combines at least three ideas into one sentence. Example: I like pizza, but I adore spaghetti, which I eat with a fork and a spoon.

Evaluating Reasons and Evidence

Preview Concepts

The following poster was made in 1936 by the United States government. It tells readers how to detect a fake doctor called a "cancer quack."

BEWARE
THE CANCER QUACK

A REPUTABLE
PHYSICIAN DOES
NOT
PROMISE A CURE
DEMAND ADVANCE
PAYMENT · ADVERTISE

U.S. PUBLIC HEALTH SERVICE
IN COOPERATION WITH THE AMERICAN SOCIETY FOR THE CONTROL OF CANCER

According to the poster, what is evidence that a doctor is a "cancer quack"?

Why is evidence important when you make an important decision?

> **CHAPTER GOALS**
>
> In this chapter you will:
>
> • examine the interactions between ideas, people, and events.
>
> • analyze how sections of a text work together.
>
> • evaluate the reasons and evidence supporting a claim.
>
> • analyze different types of sentences.

> **PREVIEW ACADEMIC VOCABULARY**
>
> claim
>
> clause
>
> complex sentence
>
> compound sentence
>
> compound–complex sentence
>
> dependent clause
>
> evidence
>
> independent clause
>
> reason
>
> simple sentence

ELL Support: Academic Vocabulary See <u>Teaching Vocabulary in the ELL Teacher Resource (p. 18)</u> for ideas to use for teaching vocabulary throughout *Connections.*

Preview Concepts Remind students that *fake* means "false, untrue, not real." Explain that a "cancer quack" is a fake cancer doctor. As necessary, use sketches or images to teach concepts such as doctor/physician and cancer. Also, use pantomime to teach the following concepts: promise a cure, demand advance payment, and advertise. Have students work in multilevel pairs or groups to answer the questions about the poster using the following sentence frames:

• The evidence that shows a doctor is a "cancer quack" is . . . .

• Evidence is important when you make a decision because . . . .

Making Connections

Read the following excerpt from a government website.

MAKING CONNECTIONS

As you read the excerpt in this chapter, you'll identify how the author supports a claim.

Homeopathy, also known as homeopathic medicine, is an alternative medical system that was developed in Germany more than 200 years ago. . . .

Supporters of homeopathy point to two unconventional theories: "like cures like"—the notion that a disease can be cured by a substance that produces similar symptoms in healthy people; and "law of minimum dose"—the notion that the lower the dose of the medication, the greater its effectiveness. . . .

Most rigorous clinical trials and systematic analyses of the research on homeopathy have concluded that there is little evidence to support homeopathy as an effective treatment for any specific condition.

—National Center for Complementary and Integrative Health

The excerpt uses the phrases "rigorous clinical trials" and "systematic analyses." Using either a dictionary or your own knowledge, define each word.

Word	What Does It Mean?
rigorous	
clinical	
systematic	
analyses	

What is the purpose of performing "rigorous clinical trials" and "systematic analyses" on medical treatments? Use the word "evidence" in your response.

ELL Support: Making Connections Explain to students that homeopathy is natural medicine. Homeopaths believe that giving less medicine works better. They also believe that it is best to give medicine that is the same as the problem. As you do so, show pictures of homeopathic medicines from various websites. Have students work in multilevel pairs or groups to read the passage and define the words using an ELL print or online dictionary.

Rephrase the question under the chart as follows: *Why do people do rigorous clinical trials, or tough scientific tests, and systematic analyses, or organized studies?*

Provide a sentence frame such as the following for students to answer in their multilevel pairs or groups:

- People do rigorous clinical tests and systematic analyses because they want to . . . .

dependent clause: *a clause that depends on another clause and cannot stand alone as it is.* This <u>dependent clause</u> in your essay is a sentence fragment that should be corrected. Example: which I eat with a fork and a spoon

evidence: *facts, examples, data, expert opinions, and anecdotes that serve to support an author's claims and reasons in an argument.* Unfortunately for the defendant, the attorney did not provide enough <u>evidence</u> for the jury to set him free.

independent clause: *a clause that can stand alone as a complete sentence.* A sentence is an <u>independent clause</u>. Example: I like pizza.

reason: *a statement or kind of evidence that tells or shows why a claim is true.* If you can't give me a convincing <u>reason</u> to vote against the new law, then I plan to vote for it.

simple sentence: *a sentence that contains one independent clause.* One way to improve your writing is to combine <u>simple sentences</u> into longer ones. Examples: I like pizza. I adore spaghetti.

⌖ Gr7Ch9Vocabulary.pptx

Preview Concepts: Ask students to list synonyms for the word *quack* as it is used on the poster. Lists may include *fake, fraud, cheat, imposter, phony, sham, con, pretender,* or *poseur.* Explain that *quack* is used primarily to describe dishonest or ignorant doctors.

Making Connections:

Possible Answers to Chart:

rigorous: strict, accurate, precise
clinical: observing direct experience of a patient
systematic: methodical; using a planned thoroughness, regularity, or oversight
analyses: detailed examinations of a complex subject
Sample answer: The purpose is to gather evidence that proves that the medical treatments work effectively.

Tech-Connect Suggestion: The full report about homeopathy is here: http://1.usa.gov/1JVrtNf. Interested students will be able to find other websites that defend the integrity of this approach such as https://abchomeopathy.com.

Lesson Support

First Read: Analyzing Interactions of Ideas, People, and Events

Before Reading: Read the introduction and objective. Use a historical example to demonstrate a relationship between ideas, actions, and events.

- In the 1770s, a common idea in the American colonies was that the British government could not tax its colonies unless the colonists could elect representatives to serve in the British parliament.

- This idea, summed up as "no taxation without representation," led some Americans to take actions directly challenging British authority, such as the Boston Tea Party.

- Similar ideas and actions eventually culminated in events such as the American Revolutionary War and, ultimately, American independence.

Model how to annotate the first paragraph. In lieu of students reading and annotating the text independently, you may read the passage aloud using a think-aloud to model how to ask questions and annotate the text.

Preview Vocabulary: Preview unfamiliar vocabulary to aid comprehension. Ask students to circle unfamiliar words as they complete the first read. Then guide students to determine the words' meanings using the context. Encourage students to support their responses with evidence and confirm their initial definitions with a dictionary. Words that students might find difficult include:

infectious: *capable of spreading rapidly to others, as in a disease. Measles used to be a deadly* <u>infectious</u> *disease, but today it is mostly controlled by vaccines.*

intimately: *marked by close, personal connection. During their weekly sleepovers, the two girls* <u>intimately</u> *shared their secrets and dreams.*

brainchild: *a product of one person's creative efforts and imagination. The modern smartphone is generally considered the* <u>brainchild</u> *of Steve Jobs.*

First Read: Analyzing Interactions of Ideas, People, and Events

John Grant is a writer of fiction and nonfiction. In *Debunk It! How to Stay Sane in a World of Misinformation*, Grant argues against "woo." "Woo" consists of ideas that seem science-like but aren't supported by scientific evidence.

Objective: As you read, pay attention to how ideas can influence people's actions and lead to events. Underline ideas that seem to directly affect people. Then draw an arrow connecting the idea to the people it affects.

Record any questions you have in the My Thoughts column.

—— First Read

---- Second Read

excerpt
Debunk It!
How to Stay Sane in a World of Misinformation
by John Grant

	My Thoughts

1   What's often difficult for us to realize is quite how recent of a science medicine is. For example, while the idea that some diseases are infectious seems obvious to us, it wasn't as obvious to our ancestors: One reason <u>epidemics spread so swiftly</u>

5   <u>through ancient Rome was that the Roman doctors often prescribed sick people a trip (or a series of trips) to the public baths—where, of course, they mixed intimately with everyone else.</u> Again, the notion that illness—especially mental illness— was a consequence of people being invaded by demons lasted

10   for many centuries (and can still be found in some communities today). . . .

Medicine is a relatively new science.

The word *homeopathy* refers to a form of medicine in which you try to treat a symptom by applying something that would cause the *same* symptom. It was the brainchild

15   of a German physician called Christian Friedrich Samuel Hahnemann, who was active in the late eighteenth century and the first part of the nineteenth. He saw that the failure rate of contemporary medicine was astonishingly high and

178   Chapter 9 • Unit 2   ©Perfection Learning® • No Reproduction Permitted

---

ELL Support: First Read Before students read the passage, review the definition of *homeopathy*. Also, explain that the author used the made-up word *woo* as a name for all crazy ideas that are not scientific. Have students read the text in multilevel pairs or small groups, pausing at the end of each paragraph to summarize by using a <u>Main Ideas and Supporting Details graphic organizer from the ELL Teacher Resource (p. 61)</u>. Also, encourage students to take notes and draw sketches in the margins around the article so they can be sure they understand the topic of each paragraph.

concluded this was because physicians misunderstood what

20 symptoms were. They thought symptoms were a product
of the illness, whereas Hahnemann suggested they were
manifestations of the body *coping with* the disease. In many
instances he was absolutely correct. If you have a fever, for
example, that's because your body's immune system is fighting

25 the infection.

So Hahnemann's big idea was that the way to cure illness
was not to counter the symptoms but to help them. Instead
of applying something that would have the opposite effect
to the symptom (throwing iced water over someone with a

30 fever, for example), he suggested using medicines that would
have the same effect as the symptom. However, Hahnemann
was conscious that increasing a symptom could be dangerous
in itself, so he said the dosages in his medicines should be very
small.

35 Extremely small.

Um, smaller even than that.

Hahnemann decreed that his medicines should be diluted
several times, the mixture being given a **prescribed** number
of shakes between each dilution. The overall result is that most

40 homeopathic medicines are so dilute that there's *not a single*
molecule of the supposed active ingredient left in the dose. In
some cases the dose could be the size of all the world's oceans
and there *still* wouldn't be a relevant molecule in it.

Even if somehow you managed to beat the impossible odds

45 and be so lucky as to have that single molecule of the active
ingredient in your dose, what effect can a single molecule have

---

manifestations: signs
prescribed: recommended
molecule: a piece of matter made of two or more atoms

My Thoughts

The father of homeopahty believed in using extremely small doses of medicines that would amplify a patient's symptoms.

The father of homeopathy suggested medicine be extremely diluted—so diluted that it wouldn't be effective.

---

contemporary: *modern; current; happening in the present time.* Contemporary transportation in big cities includes automobiles, buses, trains, bicycles, motor scooters, taxis, and of course, walking.

decreed: *commanded, ordered, or directed with authority.* Since his daughter was born on a Tuesday, the king decreed that every Tuesday would be a holiday.

dilution: *the act of making a liquid thinner and less concentrated, usually by adding water.* The medicine tasted so horrible that dilution with fruit juice was the only way to swallow it.

relevant: *having significance or bearing on the subject at hand.* The detail about the bank robbery is fascinating, but it is not relevant to your essay about volcanoes.

phenomenon: *an observable fact or event.* The phenomenon of the northern lights has fascinated humans for centuries. *flimsy: lacking strength or substance.* When the earthquake hit, all the flimsy, poorly constructed buildings crashed to the ground.

flimsy: *lacking strength or substance.* When the earthquake hit, all the flimsy, poorly constructed buildings crashed to the ground.

After Reading: Use the following questions to check comprehension.

Text-Based Discussion Questions

1. What factors influenced Hahnemann to develop homeopathic cures? *He saw that many cures in the late 1700s didn't work.* What other reasons might have caused the ineffectiveness of cures in the late 1700s? What reasons might cause people to seek out homeopathic cures today? *Answers will vary.*

2. How did Hahnemann's view of symptoms differ from traditional medical treatments? *Hahnemann believed that illnesses should be treated by increasing the symptoms instead of trying to lessen the symptoms.*

3. Why did Hahnemann prescribe such small doses of his treatments? *Because homeopathic treatments are meant to increase the symptoms of a disease, Hahnemann realized that if a symptom is too strong, it could be counterproductive or even dangerous.*

 Gr7Ch9Read1.pptx

Chapter 9 *(continued)*

Lesson Support

Debunking: Debunking is the act of exposing the falsehood or sham of a myth, belief, or idea. The word was first used by an American novelist, William Woodward (1874–1950), who used it to mean "to take the bunk out of things." *Bunk* had become a slang word for "nonsense," ever since a certain U.S. representative used it to refer to a long, dull, nonsensical speech directed to his constituents in Buncombe County, NC.

About the Author: The award-winning author of more than seventy books, John Grant (b. 1949) writes nonfiction, science fiction, and fantasy. He is also famous as an editor for numerous U.K. publishing houses. For example, he has coedited *The Encyclopedia of Fantasy* and wrote three editions of *The Encyclopedia of Walt Disney's Animated Characters,* both considered definitive editions in their fields. Today, this expatriate Scot lives in New Jersey with his wife. When asked by an interviewer if he recalls his first story, he answered, "Yes . . . I was seven. It was called 'The Ghost of Horror Mansion.' " He sometimes writes under his real name, Paul Barnett, as well as under several pseudonyms, including Eve Devereux. This book is targeted at younger readers. Find his website at www.johngrantpaulbarnett.com

---

on your body? Just in the same way that a single molecule of **strychnine** can't do you any harm, a single molecule of ★ medicine can't do you any good.

50   Of course, Hahnemann couldn't have been aware of this as a problem, since no one knew about molecules at the time. Modern fans of homeopathy, however, obviously *are* aware of the dilution **conundrum**. They've therefore proposed the idea that the active agent, even though completely absent because

55   of the dilution, might have "imprinted" itself upon the water in such a way that its one-time presence is still felt. For this to ★ be the case would require some revision of the known laws of physics. That, some homeopaths maintain, is the fault of physics, not the fault of homeopathy!

60   Other homeopaths propose that the supposed "memory" the water has of the active ingredient could be due to **quantum entanglement**. Alas, although quantum entanglement is a genuine phenomenon, it's a flimsy one: Even under laboratory conditions it's extraordinarily difficult ★

65   to make an entanglement last longer than a tiny fraction of a second. There's no chance at all that entanglements could survive the multiple shakings involved in a homeopathic dilution. Besides, how would changing the state of a few **subatomic** particles turn water into a medicine?

70   There's a more fundamental problem with the "water's memory" claim. Any water we drink has had a long history—a history lasting billions of years. During that time it has been recycled in all sorts of ways, and has held all manner of other

---

strychnine: a deadly poison
conundrum: problem
quantum entanglement: the theory that two or more particles smaller than atoms affect each other (are "entangled") no matter how far apart they are
subatomic: smaller than atoms

My Thoughts

Remediation: First Read Students may be confused by Grant's use of quotation marks in lines 70 and following. Explain that these are called *scare quotes* (or *shudder* or *sneer quotes*) and that they are used to express irony. They imply skepticism or disagreement along with the idea that the word is being misused. Students may be familiar with the hand gesture known as "air quotes" or "finger quotes," which mimics the appearance of quotation marks and is popular with comedians.

substances **in solution**, any one of which could have left

75 an "imprint." Why should water retain the "memory" of a

homeopathic molecule but not that of *everything else* with ★

which it has been in contact—including all the gazillions of

poops that have floated in it?

The notion of "water's memory" takes homeopathy over

80 the conceptual border into the realm of outright woo—

especially when we read of some homeopaths claiming they

can email the "imprint" to their patients, who can supply their

own water! Even if you look just at basic homeopathy, though,

of the kind that Hahnemann invented, the dilutions mean

85 that all you get when you buy a homeopathic medicine is very

expensive water.

On the plus side, it's pretty hard to do yourself any damage

with a homeopathic overdose.

---

in solution: dissolved in water
woo: to seek support or favor

My Thoughts

_____

_____

_____

_____

Modern fans of

homeopathy offer

illogical explanations

of how diluted

medicines work.

_____

_____

_____

FIRST RESPONSE: KEY IDEAS AND DETAILS

Based on your first reading, can an idea have powerful effects?
Explain your thinking. Record your first response in your journal.

Focus on Analyzing Interactions of Ideas, People, and Events

Roughly the first half of the passage from *Debunk It!* is a
history text. Typically, history texts describe the ways in which
people, events, and ideas interact with each other. Through close
reading, you can analyze these interactions.

Reread this section of the text. Then answer the questions that
follow.

What's often difficult for us to realize is quite how recent of a

science medicine is. For example, while the idea that some diseases

are infectious seems obvious to us, it wasn't as obvious to our

ancestors: One reason epidemics spread so swiftly through ancient

continued on next page

TECH-CONNECT

Post your response
on your class web
page as instructed by
your teacher. Read
two other students'
responses and
comment positively
on them.

Tech-Connect Suggestion: Students may
enjoy exploring episodes of *MythBusters*, a
science program on the Discovery Channel
in which two special effects technicians
use modern technology to test—and often
debunk—the validity of popular urban
legends. Episodes can be found at
www.discovery.com.

FIRST RESPONSE: KEY IDEAS AND DETAILS

After students write responses in their
journals, ask them to list several examples
of ideas that they believe had "powerful
effects." Here are a few possibilities: the
idea that Earth was round not flat; the
idea that the Earth moves around the
sun; the idea that humans could go to
the moon; the idea of cell phones, the
Internet, or that people can fly.

**Focus on Analyzing Interactions of
Ideas, People, and Events:** To help
students understand the interplay between
ideas, people, and events, display these
three terms. Draw a line under them. Then
ask students to return to the text and
find examples for each category. Then ask
students to indicate how each idea affected
people or events. Draw arrows to indicate
cause and effect.

ELL Support: First Response—Key Ideas and Details Rephrase
the question to *Did Dr. Hahnemann's ideas about homeopathy have
powerful results?*

Have students work in multilevel pairs or small groups to answer the
question orally, using the following sentence frame:

- Yes/No, Dr. Hahnemann's ideas about homeopathy had/didn't
  have powerful results because . . . .

Chapter 9 (continued)

Lesson Support

Possible Answers to Questions and Chart:

See answers on Student Book insert page to the right.

 Gr7Ch9Read1.pptx

Rome was that the Roman doctors often prescribed sick people a trip (or a series of trips) to the public baths—where, of course, they mixed intimately with everyone else.

What idea about curing illness did Roman doctors seem to have?

> They seemed to think it was related to being dirty or needing the therapeutic benefits of taking a bath.

What did Roman doctors often tell sick people to do?

> to bathe in the public baths

What event did the Roman doctors' idea about curing illness help to cause?

> epidemics

Use your answers from above to complete the diagram below.

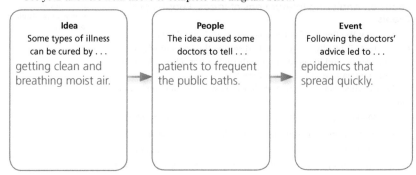

Idea	**People**	**Event**
Some types of illness can be cured by . . . getting clean and breathing moist air.	The idea caused some doctors to tell . . . patients to frequent the public baths.	Following the doctors' advice led to . . . epidemics that spread quickly.

Remediation: First Read At some point during the chapter, discuss the concept of irony. It is ironic that doctors and their advice could actually make people sicker. It is ironic because it is the opposite of what logic would dictate or what people might expect.

Your work on the previous page illustrates something important. An idea (how to treat disease) can influence people (doctors and their patients) and lead to an event (an epidemic). People tend to underestimate the force of ideas in history, but ideas are just as important as people and events in the history of our world.

(Speak and Listen Share your answers with a partner. Talk about how a Roman doctor's treatment for an illness could not just cause an epidemic but also make it worse.

CONNECT TO ESSENTIAL QUESTION

One definition of "science" is that it is a way to discover trustworthy evidence about the world. How could science discover trustworthy evidence about homeopathy?

Second Read: Analyzing Structure and Purpose

The excerpt is roughly composed of four major sections, each with a different purpose.

- First section: paragraph 1 (lines 1–11)
- Second section: paragraphs 2 and 3 (lines 12–34)
- Third section: paragraphs 4–7 (lines 35–49)
- Fourth section: paragraphs 8–12 (lines 50–88)

Objective: Read the text a second time. In the My Thoughts column, next to each section described above, write one sentence that sums up the central idea of the section.

Focus on Analyzing Structure and Purpose

As discussed, the first half of the excerpt from *Debunk It!* is a history text. Grant uses that history as part of a larger argument he is making. Specifically, Grant is arguing that a practice called *homeopathy* does not actually treat illness, despite what its believers say. We'll evaluate part of Grant's argument later. Right now, let's consider the author's structure of this excerpt as it relates to his purpose.

Because the excerpt is from a book, it doesn't have the structure of an argument your teacher might have you write. Specifically, the excerpt doesn't have

- an introduction with a claim.
- a body with reasons and evidence supporting the claim.
- a conclusion restating the claim.

That said, the excerpt does have a structure, and each part of that structure serves at least one purpose. One way to analyze the structure of a passage is to ask these questions:

- Why is this section here?
- What does this section accomplish (do)?

REFLECT

Have you or someone you know tried a homeopathic treatment? After reading this passage, has your opinion of homeopathy changed? Why or why not?

continued on next page

ELL Support: Second Read Remind students that they can use their Main Idea and Details graphic organizers to summarize each paragraph. Also, they can consult their notes and sketches around the article completed during the first read. Provide the following sentence frames for multilevel pairs or groups to use in their discussions of the article's structure:

- The Roman doctors treated illnesses by . . . .
- When they did this, sick people . . . .
- This example shows that . . . .

(Speak and Listen: Student discussions may veer into the next logical question: *Could this happen today? Could a doctor's treatment make an illness worse not better? Is part of John Grant's purpose to inspire this question?*

Tech-Connect Suggestion: Steer students to photographs of the Roman public baths in Bath, England, such as the one at https://commons.wikimedia.org/wiki/File:Baños_Romanos,_Bath,_Inglaterra,_2014-08-12,_DD_26.JPG. Ask them to imagine dozens of sick people in these pools of water at the same time.

Second Read: Analyzing Structure and Purpose

Before Reading: Remind students that during a second read they are asking the question *How?* Here, they are analyzing how the writer structures a text to achieve his purpose.

After Reading: Use the following questions to check comprehension.

Text-Based Discussion Questions

1. Why does Grant open the excerpt with examples of how early people misunderstood medical treatments? *By explaining ways that people misunderstood treatments, he is priming his audience to accept the idea that homeopathic medicine, which was originally invented in the late 1700s, is also based on faulty and incorrect ideas.*

2. The final line of the text says, "On the plus side, it's pretty hard to do yourself any damage with a homeopathic overdose." Are there any dangers to using homeopathic medicines? Base your inferences on the text. *Answers will vary. Students may note that some medical problems can't be treated by homeopathic means. For example, appendicitis requires surgery.*

3. What is the effect of the two clipped phrases in lines 35 and 36? *They are a dramatic and entertaining way to emphasize his key point that the dosages are far too tiny to be effective. They also bring a conversational tone to the text.*

Focus on Analyzing Text Structure: Caution students: although there are historical details in this text, it is not structured chronologically. The sections are connected by ideas, not a sequence of events.

Chapter 9 *(continued)*

Lesson Support

Sample Answers to Chart

See answers on Student Book insert page to the right.

 Gr7Ch9Read2.pptx

▼ **Write:** Sample answer: *Grant does not trust homeopathy or its defenders. I think this tone helps his argument, which warns readers not to trust "doctors" who claim that homeopathy is effective. He debunks its principles by stating that Hahnemann knew nothing "about molecules at the time." He calls the theories "flimsy" and shocks readers with the suggestion that if they were true, then the "gazillions of poops" that have been in water would "imprint" it too. Finally, he calls the theory "outright woo."*

Complete the chart below.
- Under "Central Idea of Section," explain what the section is about.
- Under "Possible Purpose of Section," make a claim about the author's purpose for the section. Use words such as *inform, tell, define, convince,* and so on.

Part of the chart has been completed for you.

Major Section	Central Idea of Section	Possible Purpose of Section
Paragraph 1 (lines 1–11)	Before modern medicine, people's ideas about the causes and cures of diseases were often wrong.	to show that modern medical science has overcome incorrect ideas
Paragraphs 2 and 3 (lines 12–34)	Two centuries ago, a doctor wondered if using small doses of medicine to make symptoms stronger could cure a disease.	to define homeopathy and explain Hahnemann's theories of treatment
Paragraphs 4–7 (lines 35–49)	Most homeopathic medicines don't even have a molecule of actual medicine.	to inform readers about how weak a homeopathic dose is
Paragraphs 8–12 (lines 50–88)	Modern homeopaths suggest that medicines "imprint" themselves on water or that the molecules become entangled at the subatomic level.	to convince readers that the claims of homeopaths are not supported by science

▼ **Write** An author's tone is his or her attitude toward the topic. What is Grant's tone toward homeopathy and its defenders? Do you feel his tone helps or hurts his argument? In your reading response journal, write a paragraph in which you make a claim about Grant's tone. Use details from the passage to support your claim.

ELL Support: Write Explain that tone is the way an author shows his/her opinion or feelings about a subject. List some descriptors for tone on the board: serious, humorous, negative, angry. Use facial expression and tone of voice to demonstrate each. Have students work in multilevel pairs or small groups to write about the author's tone. Provide the following sentence frames:

- When Grant thinks of homeopathy, he thinks . . . .
- Grant's tone toward homeopathy is . . . .
- One example that shows this tone is . . . .
- Another example of this tone is . . . .

Third Read: Evaluating Reasons and Evidence

The excerpt from *Debunk It!* claims that homeopathy does not treat illness. But how well does Grant support his claim?

Objective: As you read the excerpt a third time, draw a star next to any evidence (facts, examples, quotations) that Grant uses to support his argument against homeopathy.

Focus on Evaluating Reasons and Evidence

To evaluate, or judge, an argument, you need to examine how well its claim is supported with reasons and evidence. A *claim* is an idea an author wants readers to agree with. Reasons explain why readers should agree with a claim. Evidence is real-world information intended to show readers that the author's claim and reasons are accurate.

Here is a simple example of an argument:

Claim: All students in the United States should get a two-year college degree. [This is what the author wants the reader to agree with.]

Reason: On average, people with two-year college degrees make more money than people with a high school diploma. [This explains why readers should agree with the claim.]

Evidence: According to the U.S. Department of Labor, the average pay for a person with a high-school degree is $678. In comparison, a person with a two-year degree makes $798 a week. That's an extra $120 per week, or $6,240 per year. [This shows readers the reasoning is based on facts, not just the author's beliefs.]

To evaluate an argument, it helps to break it into its parts. Reread the following section of *Debunk It!* Then use the chart on the next page to identify and analyze the claim, reason, and evidence.

> Hahnemann decreed that his medicines should be diluted several times, the mixture being given a prescribed number of shakes between each dilution. The overall result is that most homeopathic medicines are so dilute that there's not a single molecule of the supposed active ingredient left in the dose. In some cases the dose could be the size of all the world's oceans and there still wouldn't be a relevant molecule in it.

continued on next page

Remediation: Third Read Consider comparing the structure of this text to a building with four stories or floors. Each floor rests upon the floor beneath it to create a whole building. They each contribute to the final product and the overall purpose in an interdependent structure. To reinforce the simile, you may want to flip the four rows of the chart upside down.

ELL Support: Third Read Before students reread the article, model the process of identifying claims, reasons, and evidence. Reread the first paragraph and use a think-aloud as you identify the claim, the first reason, and the first piece of evidence. Say: *Grant's claim is that scientific medicine is new. His reason is that doctors didn't know about infection in ancient Rome. His evidence is that Roman doctors told sick patients to go to the public baths. There they made others sick. So sickness spread.*

Third Read: Evaluating Reasons and Evidence

Before Reading: Review the introduction and the objective with students. If helpful, before students begin their third read, revisit the definitions and examples of the terms *claim*, *evidence*, and *reason* on pages 176 and 177 of this teacher's edition. That way, students will have those definitions fresh in their minds before they start locating and annotating examples of evidence in the passage.

Point out that the purpose of this read is to evaluate, or judge, the strength of Grant's argument against homeopathy.

Suggest to students that evaluating an argument does not mean "Do you agree with it?" It means, "Did the author do a good job making the case (i.e., supporting the claim)?" Readers may evaluate an argument positively but still disagree with its claims and conclusions.

After Reading: Use the following questions to check comprehension.

Text-Based Discussion Questions

1. How does the author support the claim that Roman doctors were misguided? *He supports it with two examples: their recommendation of the public baths and their blaming invading demons who cause illnesses.*

2. According to Grant, what prompted Hahnemann to develop his theories? *The high "failure rate of contemporary medicine" led him to conclude that physicians misunderstood symptoms and their meaning.*

3. Why do you think Grant debunks Hahnemann's theory? *He debunks it to prove a larger point: all treatments must be based on science and evidence.*

 Gr7Ch9Read3.pptx

Lesson Support

Focus on Evaluating Reasons and Evidence: Suggest that students can easily modify this chart to evaluate any text that supports a claim with reasons and evidence. You might even challenge them to apply it to a letter to the editor in their local newspapers.

Possible Answers to Chart:

Reason: Because of the dilution process, not enough medicine remains in the final product to affect a human body.

Evidence 1: No, the section does not provide data from scientific studies.

Evidence 2: No, the section does not provide quotations from experts.

Evidence 3: Yes. There is a description that compares the dosage to something "the size of the world's oceans" without a single useful molecule in it. There is an example stating that one molecule of a deadly poison cannot hurt a human body, so how could one molecule of a medicine help it?

Even if somehow you managed to beat the impossible odds and be so lucky as to have that single molecule of the active ingredient in your dose, what effect can a single molecule have on your body? Just in the same way that a single molecule of strychnine can't do you any harm, a single molecule of medicine can't do you any good.

Claim	
What is the central claim of the argument of *Debunk It*?	Homeopathy does not treat illness.
Reason	
What reason does this section give to support the claim?	
Evidence	
Data from scientific studies	
Quotations from experts	
Descriptions or examples that help the reader understand what Grant is saying	

Do you think Grant offers enough evidence in this section to support his claim about homeopathy? Could he offer more or better evidence, and if so, what? Explain your reasoning below.

(Speak and Listen According to Grant, homeopaths claim water can "remember" being in contact with molecules it no longer holds. By answering the homeopaths' ideas, Grant is addressing counterclaims, or claims opposed to his. With a partner, discuss why a writer might want to address counterclaims in an argument.

Language: Complex Sentences with Subordinating Conjunctions and Relative Pronouns

In chapter 3, you learned the four types of sentences: simple, compound, complex, and compound-complex. Here is a quick review of the four types:

Simple: A simple sentence has only one independent clause. An independent clause can stand on its own as a complete thought. In the following examples, independent clauses are underlined.

> Example: We keep animals in zoos or as pets for many reasons.

Compound: A compound sentence has at least **two** independent clauses. The clauses are joined by a comma and coordinating conjunction (*and, but, for, nor, or, yet*) or by a semicolon.

> Example: An adult chimpanzee is about five times stronger than an adult human, and Lucy got into everything.

Complex: A complex sentence has at least one independent clause and at least one dependent clause. A dependent clause contains a subject and verb but does not express a complete thought. It can't stand on its own. In the following examples, dependent clauses are in (parentheses).

> Example: We also keep animals in captivity (because we enjoy seeing them and spending time with them.)

continued on next page

(Speak and Listen:** Remind students that counterclaims are in opposition to the author's claims. In this case, the claim is that homeopathy is bunk (nonsense). The counterclaim is that water holds memories of molecules it no longer contains. He debunks this idea with the graphic example of "gazillions of poops."

Explain to students that when evaluating an argument, they should ask the following: *Is the writer fairly and accurately representing the opposing viewpoint?* Sometimes a writer will try to misrepresent the ideas he/she disagrees with by presenting a distorted or exaggerated description of them. Ask students: *Do you think the author fairly represents the ideas of modern homeopathy? Does he use examples or quotations from prominent practitioners? Does he misrepresent homeopaths by sharing the theories of a small group as opposed to the vast majority?*

More advanced students may want to consider if the author is guilty of the straw man fallacy, or substituting a person's actual position or argument with a distorted, exaggerated, or misrepresented version of the position of the argument. In this fallacy, a writer presents a weak version of the opposing viewpoint so that he can easily knock it down. (Like it's easy to knock down a man of straw.) Students could conduct research to confirm that Grant is fairly representing modern homeopaths.

Language: Complex Sentences with Subordinating Conjunctions and Relative Pronouns: Suggest that understanding these four sentence types is a precursor to being able to vary sentences effectively during the revision stage of the writing process.

 Gr7Ch9Language.pptx

ELL Support: Speak and Listen Explain that "addressing a counterclaim" means to explain a different opinion and why it is incorrect. One counterclaim that Grant includes is that homeopaths believe that water has memory of molecules it has touched. Ask students to explain the fact that Grant uses to show this counterclaim is wrong. (*He says that if this were true, then water would remember all the molecules it has ever touched.*) Ask students why Grant would use a counterclaim. (*He wants to show what homeopaths believe. Then he can tell what is wrong with those belief or opinions.*) Have students work in multilevel pairs or small groups and use these sentence frames to further discuss counterclaims:

- Grant tells that water remembers molecules it has touched. Grant tells that this counterclaim is wrong because . . . .

- Grant uses a counterclaim to . . . .

- All writers use counterclaims to . . . .

Chapter 9 (continued)

Lesson Support

Compound-Complex: A compound-complex sentence has at least two independent clauses and at least one dependent clause.

> Example: The whales may also float near the top of the pool for long periods; as a result, they may end up with a sunburn or a flopped-over dorsal fin, (which is a common sight on captive male killer whales.)

Well-written complex sentences clearly explain the relationship between the ideas in a sentence. In a complex sentence, a less important idea in a dependent clause is combined with a more important idea in an independent clause. Dependent clauses are often joined to independent clauses by subordinating conjunctions and relative pronouns.

Here are some commonly used subordinating conjunctions:

after	although	as	because
before	even if	if	once
since	so that	than	though
unless	until	when	while

The relative pronouns are

that	which	whichever	who
whoever	whom	whomever	

Read the following examples of sentences with subordinating clauses. The clauses are <u>underlined</u>, and the subordinating conjunctions and relative pronouns are **bold**.

> **After** <u>I took three doses of the medicine,</u> my fever disappeared .
>
> We will go to the beach **when** <u>you feel better.</u>
>
> My five-year-old brother has much more energy **than** <u>I have.</u>
>
> **Because** <u>I was tired after playing soccer,</u> I went to bed instead of going to the party.
>
> The favorite student, **who** <u>is new to our class,</u> is the one who answered all of the questions.

Notice that the subordinating conjunction or relative pronoun shows the relationship between the ideas by answering the questions: *When? Why? Which one?* and *To what extent?* Use a comma after a dependent clause at the beginning of a sentence. Also use a comma (or a pair of commas) to set off dependent clauses that are not essential to the meaning of the sentence.

Rewrite the sentence pairs on the next page as single complex sentences using the subordinating conjunction or relative pronoun shown in parentheses.

ELL Support: Language Explain that a compound sentence is a sentence made up of two complete sentences. Write the example: The girl runs, and the boy jumps. Have students identify the two complete sentences: *(The girl runs. The boy jumps.)*

Explain that a complex sentence is a sentence made up of a complete sentence and a phrase. Use the example: Because she is on the team, the girl runs. Have students identify the complete sentence *(the girl runs)* and the phrase *(Because she is on the team)*. Explain that this phrase can't be a sentence because it is not a complete thought.

Explain that a compound-complex sentence has at least two complete sentences and at least one phrase. For example, Because they are on the team, the girl runs, and the boy jumps. Have students identify the two complete sentences. *(the girl runs, the boy jumps)* and the phrase *(Because they are on the team)*.

Explain that subordinating conjunctions are linking words that

1. John Snow was practicing medicine in the 1850s. Doctors thought "foul air" caused the deadly disease cholera. (when)

2. Snow didn't know what caused the disease. He wanted to find out. (although)

3. He studied maps of London's water system. His study of the maps revealed to him the patterns of illness. (which)

4. Many people drank from wells contaminated by sewage. These same people became sick with cholera. (who)

5. Foul air had nothing to do with cholera. Snow discovered this. (that)

Answers to Exercises:

1. When John Snow was practicing medicine in the 1850s, doctors thought "foul air" caused the deadly disease cholera.

2. Although Snow didn't know what caused the disease, he wanted to find out.

3. He studied maps of London's water system, which revealed to him the patterns of illness.

4. Many people who drank from wells contaminated by sewage became sick.

5. Snow discovered that foul air had nothing to do with cholera.

Tech-Connect Suggestion: Some students may be interested in diagramming sentences as a way to visualize these various structures. Tree diagrams such as Reed-Kellogg diagrams will demonstrate and analyze different sentence patterns. You can download a free app that makes practicing diagramming fun at http://diagramming-sentences.software.informer.com.

---

connect phrases to sentences. Give examples: *when, where, who.*

Have students work in multilevel pairs or groups to complete the exercises. Then review their answers together as a class, identifying the compound and complex sentences and the subordinating conjunctions.

Remediation: Language Have students analyze a piece of their own writing for sentence types. First, have them label their sentences as A = simple; B = compound; C = complex; and D = compound-complex. Then have them tally the totals. If they depend heavily on one type, suggest that they can make their writing more interesting by combining sentences in various ways. Another option is to do this as a class using a sample of student writing.

Chapter 9 *(continued)*

Assessment

Project-Based Assessments

Digital Presentation: At each step in the process, check students' progress, giving students due dates for them to submit and for you to approve their choice of topic, their sources, and the first draft of their presentation. Here is an example of how to break down this assignment:

- Conduct online research. Turn in topic for digital presentation and get teacher approval. Due date:

- Turn in list of three sources. Due date:

- Turn in bulleted list of information for presentation (see page 190). Due date:

- Turn in first draft of presentation. Due date:

- Present final digital presentation to class. Due date:

Project-Based Assessments

Digital Presentation

Conduct research and create a digital presentation about treating a common illness. First, search online using terms such as *common illness*. Develop a list of common illnesses and choose one to research.

Next, find three reliable sources of information. Websites that end in *.edu*, *.gov*, or *.org* usually have reliable information. Check the site's About tab to find out if it is maintained by a reputable source, such as a hospital or a medical school.

Gather the following information for your presentation:

- name of the illness

- what causes the illness

- description of its symptoms

- treatment(s) of the illness

- how long it takes to get over the illness

- three sources used for the project: name of article, website, and date

Finally, create an interesting and well-organized computer presentation. Each slide should have both an image and text. Read the rubric carefully so you know what is expected of you from the beginning. Practice your commentary with the presentation before presenting to the class. If working with a partner(s), decide in advance who will share which slides.

> **TECH-CONNECT**
>
> Download your presentation to a flash drive so that you can bring it to school. Be sure to open your files before your presentation, especially when using a computer that isn't your own.

	Use the following guidelines for your presentation.
To receive the highest score (4.0), the presentation must meet all of these criteria.	Your presentation • uses images and text in a professional, appealing way. • demonstrates understanding of the cause and symptoms of the illness. • describes the treatment(s) and duration of the illness. • demonstrates confidence, eye contact, and proper volume. • uses correct grammar, usage, punctuation, and spelling.

ELL Support: Project-Based Assessments Have students work in multilevel pairs or small groups to complete the chosen project. Help students find linguistically accommodated websites so that they can understand the language. Once student pairs or groups have conducted research, provide them with examples of a digital presentation and/or brochures to help them understand the requirements. Students can use the following sentence frames in either project:

- . . . is a common illness.

- . . . is caused by . . . .

- Its symptoms are . . . .

- To treat . . . people . . . .

Brochure

Create a trifold brochure about an illness and its treatment using a word processing or design program. Follow the steps given for the digital presentation on page 74 to choose an illness and its treatment and then gather information. Design your brochure so that readers will be able to understand the illness and its treatment. Use pictures to reinforce the writing. Include your list of three sources on the back of the brochure.

Use the following guidelines for your brochure.	
To receive the highest score (4.0), the brochure must meet all of these criteria.	Your brochure • looks professional and is visually appealing. • demonstrates an understanding of the illness through details. • includes pictures that support the text. • demonstrates that you clearly understand the illness and its treatment. • uses correct grammar, usage, punctuation, and spelling.

On Your Own: Integrating Ideas

1. Doctors give children vaccines to protect them from deadly diseases such as polio and measles. Lately, however, some people have begun questioning the safety of vaccines. Watch the episode of *Frontline*, an award-winning investigative show on PBS, that discusses this controversy: www.pbs.org/video/2365449467/.

2. People sell fake medicine because they can make a lot of money. That's why it's important to investigate any medicine or treatment by consulting reliable sources, including the Food and Drug Administration's website: www.fda.gov.

3. Is quackery dead, or is it still going strong? Spend time researching whether any famous people on television or the Internet are considered "quacks" by the mainstream medical community. Quackwatch.org is a site dedicated to exposing scientifically doubtful or phony health treatments.

> **CONNECT TO ESSENTIAL QUESTION**
>
> Doctors are authority figures. In general, we are taught to trust authority figures. When is it right to question what an authority figure tells us? Is that an easy thing to do?

Brochure: This project is an extension of the Digital Presentation project and involves similar research.

Tech-Connect Suggestion: Steer students to a list of the 205 Most Common Illnesses at http://www.ranker.com/list/list-of-common-diseases-most-common-illnesses/diseases-and-medications-info. Note that they are listed in (roughly) alphabetical order and not by frequency of occurrence.

On Your Own: Integrating Ideas: Activity 3: Students could research the topic further by finding websites in support of and in opposition to vaccinations and developing a list of arguments for both sides.

• It takes . . . to heal from . . . .

• Sources:

When students complete their projects, they should revise and edit them using the <u>Informational Writing Revision Checklist (ELL Teacher Resource, p. 69)</u> and the <u>Proofreading Checklist (ELL Teacher Resource, p. 71)</u>.

Chapter 9 (continued)

Assessment

Connect to Testing: This Connect to Testing section focuses on analyzing how ideas, people, and events interact and analyzing an argument.

Encourage students to work in pairs to choose the correct answers to the questions and then to compare their answers with those of another pair of students. If there is disagreement, encourage the groups to try to reach a consensus as they discuss the reasons for their choices.

Answers to Connect to Testing Questions:

1. **Part A:** B. The key phrase here is "influence the thinking of modern homeopaths." Choice A is true but it didn't impact modern homeopaths. Choice C is not true; this is suggested by modern homeopaths, not Hahnemann. Choice D is also not true because Hahnemann didn't know about molecules.
Part B: A., C., D. Choice B is giving background about Hahnemann. Choices E and F are modern theories not influenced by Hahnemann. (DoK 2)

(continued)

Connect to Testing

In this chapter, you examined how ideas, people, and events interact; considered the functions of sections of a nonfiction text; and evaluated the reasons and evidence provided in an argument. When you take assessments, you will be tested over these skills and your ability to support your ideas by using textual evidence.

1. **Part A:** How did Samuel Hahnemann influence the thinking of modern homeopaths?

   A. He argued that symptoms were produced by illnesses.

   B. He suggested that making symptoms stronger could help cure an illness.

   C. He believed that water could remember being exposed to samples of a chemical.

   D. He pointed out that any homeopathic treatment needed to have very few molecules.

   Part B: Which two details from the passage best support the answer to Part A?

   A. *The word* homeopathy *refers to a form of medicine in which you try to treat a symptom by applying something that would cause the same symptom.*

   B. *He saw that the failure rate of contemporary medicine was astonishingly high and concluded this was because physicians misunderstood what symptoms were.*

   C. *So Hahnemann's big idea was that the way to cure illness was not to counter the symptoms but to help them.*

   D. *The overall result is that most homeopathic medicines are so dilute that there's not a single molecule of the supposed active ingredient left in the dose.*

   E. *They've therefore proposed the idea that the active agent, even though completely absent because of the dilution, might have "imprinted" itself upon the water in such a way that its one-time presence is still felt.*

   F. *Other homeopaths propose that the supposed "memory" the water has of the active ingredient could be due to quantum entanglement.*

ELL Support: Using Connect to Testing and Assessments See the *Connections* ELL Teacher Resource (p. 22) for ideas on adapting this section for ELLs.

2. Read this sentence and answer the question that follows.

> John Snow founded epidemiology. He is famous among scientists. Epidemiology has saved many lives.

Which is the best way to combine the sentences into a compound–complex sentence?

A. John Snow founded epidemiology, he is famous among scientists, and epidemiology has saved many lives.

B. John Snow, who is famous among scientists, founded epidemiology and saved many lives.

C. John Snow founded epidemiology, which has saved many lives, and he is famous among scientists.

D. John Snow saved many lives by founding epidemiology, so he is famous among scientists.

3. **Part A:** How does paragraph 6 (lines 37–43) contribute to the structure of the passage?

A. It describes how small a molecule is.

B. It explains why a homeopathic dose is mostly water.

C. It captures the reader's interest by summarizing the dilution process.

D. It presents the reason for why Hahnemann decided homeopathy didn't work.

Part B: Which detail from paragraph 6 best supports the answer to Part A?

A. *Hahnemann decreed that his medicines should be diluted several times.* . . .

B. *. . . the mixture being given a prescribed number of shakes between each dilution.*

C. *. . . there's not a single molecule of the supposed active ingredient.* . . .

D. *. . . the dose could be the size of all the world's oceans.* . . .

4. **Part A:** Which of the following is a claim of *Debunk It!* by John Grant?

A. Hahnemann's original idea was reasonable.

B. Hahnemann's fellow doctors thought he was a quack.

C. Hahnemann misled patients on the true causes of disease.

D. Hahnemann misunderstood how molecules interact with each other.

continued on next page

2. C. (DoK 1)

3. **Part A:** B. (DoK 2)

Part B: C. The phrase "not a single molecule" directly supports the concept "mostly water." (DoK 2)

4. **Part A:** D. (DoK 1)

(continued)

Chapter 9 *(continued)*

Assessment

Answers to Connect to Testing Questions:

4. **Part B:** C. (DoK 2)

5. **D.** This sentence supports the idea that "imprinting" is unreasonable by asking a logical question. The other choices help define imprinting and make observations about it, but they do not address the judgment that the theory is flawed. (DoK 2)

Part B: Which detail from the passage best supports the answer to Part A?

A. . . . *this was because physicians misunderstood what symptoms were.*

B. *If you have a fever . . . that's because your body's immune system is fighting the infection.*

C. . . . *a single molecule of medicine can't do you any good.*

D. . . . *might have "imprinted" itself upon the water in such a way that its one-time presence is still felt.*

5. Which of the following details gives a reason for why the homeopathic idea of "imprinting" is flawed?

A. . . . *a single molecule of medicine can't do you any good.*

B. . . . *might have "imprinted" itself upon the water in such a way that its one-time presence is still felt.*

C. . . . *the supposed "memory" the water has of the active ingredient could be due to quantum entanglement.*

D. *Why should water retain the "memory" of a homeopathic molecule but not that of everything else with which it has been in contact. . . .*

Remediation: Connect to Testing Focus attention on questions 1 and 3, which present less reading load yet are good examples of questions about reasons and evidence and the functions of sections of a nonfiction text. Read each question aloud and have students take turns reading the answer choices. As a group, discuss whether each choice is correct or incorrect until the group reaches consensus about the correct answer.

Chapter 10

Analyzing Point of View

Preview Concepts

Think of a time when you changed your mind about something. The "something" could a song, a type of food, or a television show. Or it could be more important: a friendship, a subject in school, or what is best in life.

What did you originally think?

What do you think now?

What caused you to change your mind? Be specific.

CHAPTER GOALS

In this chapter you will:

- cite evidence to support an idea.
- examine how story elements interact.
- analyze the development of a character's point of view.
- make your language precise and concise.

PREVIEW ACADEMIC VOCABULARY

concision

evidence

point of view

precision

Analyzing Point of View

The Giver
by Lois Lowry

Introduction

Chapter Goals: Have students read through the goals and mark any words that are unfamiliar. Discuss the meanings of any academic vocabulary within the goals that students marked as unfamiliar. Consider posting the Chapter Goals.

Preview Academic Vocabulary: Read and discuss the meanings of the academic vocabulary.

> **concision:** *the act of writing as clearly and briefly as possible.* If you learn and practice <u>concision</u>, you can reduce your twenty-page draft to a ten-page story that you can submit to the contest.

> **evidence:** *facts, examples, data, expert opinions, and anecdotes that serve to support an author's claims and reasons in an argument.* The thief was given his freedom because there was not enough <u>evidence</u> to convict him.

> **point of view:** *the perspective, position, or outlook from which a story is told.* The story was told from first-person <u>point of view</u>; the narrator told her story of the tornado and its aftereffects.

> **precision:** *the act of writing specifically, exactly, and accurately.* A writer who values <u>precision</u> keeps a dictionary or thesaurus close at hand.

Gr7Ch10Vocabulary.pptx

Preview Concepts: Give students the opportunity to share their experiences in a whole-class discussion, but encourage them to practice *precision* and *concision* as they keep their recollections brief.

ELL Support: Academic Vocabulary See <u>Teaching Vocabulary in the ELL Teacher Resource (p. 18)</u> for ideas to use for teaching vocabulary throughout *Connections*.

ELL Support: Preview Concepts Be sure students understand that *originally* means "at first" or "before." Model how to answer the questions so that students understand what is expected of them. Then have students work in multilevel pairs or groups and use the following sentence frames to write their own answers:

- I used to think . . . .
- Now I think . . . .
- I changed my mind because . . . .

Chapter 10 (continued)

Introduction

Making Connections:

> **Sample Answer:**
>
> The society has evolved to eliminate individual choice; it seems that everything in it is predictable and "determinate." The man that they describe is "loose," and so the two people are worried. He is "a variable" that can't be predicted, and this is "contrary to science." They call him "the indeterminate particle," which means that he is random and unpredictable. This society is frightening because free choice and individuality are what make us human. These characters seem more like robots than humans.

Tech-Connect Suggestion: Students may be surprised to learn that this excerpt is from a novella written in 1953. The man being described in this excerpt is Thomas Cole, a man from 1913, who arrives in Reinhart and Sherikov's world due to an accident with a time machine that was being used for research. The entire novel, with its original illustrations, is at Project Gutenberg at http://www.gutenberg.org/files/32154.

Making Connections

It is good practice to preview a text before you read it. Consider the text features, the genre (type of writing), and the structure of the text. This will help you make predictions about the central ideas and the style. For example, you are about to read an excerpt from a science fiction story. Because you've read this genre before, you might predict that the story will include futuristic technology and settings that include outer space and other planets. As you read, correct and confirm your predictions to enhance your comprehension. Try this with the texts you will be reading in this chapter.

In the excerpt below, a man from the 20th century travels two hundred years into the future. Earth is now united in one society. Two members of this society, Reinhart and Sherikov, discuss what the appearance of this man means.

> Reinhart considered. "But it worries me, a man like that out in the open. Loose. A man who can't be predicted. It goes against science. We've been making statistical reports on society for two centuries. We have immense files of data. The machines are able to predict what each person and group will do at a given time, in a given situation. But this man is beyond all prediction. He's a variable. It's contrary to science."
>
> "The indeterminate particle."
>
> "What's that?"
>
> "The particle that moves in such a way that we can't predict what position it will occupy at a given second. Random. The random particle."
>
> "Exactly. It's—it's *unnatural*."
>
> Sherikov laughed sarcastically. "Don't worry about it, Commissioner. The man will be captured and things will return to their natural state. You'll be able to predict people again, like laboratory rats in a maze."
>
> —"The Variable Man" by Philip K. Dick

What can you infer about the society that Reinhart and Sherikov describe? Use details from the text to support your response.

MAKING CONNECTIONS

You will be reading an excerpt in this chapter about a future society. Pay attention to how the main character feels when he is thinking about the idea of "family."

ELL Support: Make Connections Explain to students that this story is about the future. Write *year 2200* on the board so students understand. Sketch the main characters in a comic book format to help students understand the story. Say: *Two future men are talking about a man from our time (year 20XX). They don't like this man because he is unpredictable. They don't know what he will do. In 2200, they can predict everyone's behavior. But they can't predict this man's behavior.* Then read the excerpt aloud slowly, pointing to your sketches and speech bubbles.

Rephrase the question for students: *What is the future society like?* Have students work in multilevel pairs or small groups to respond to the question. Students can draw pictures that represent their inferences.

In this science fiction novel, a boy named Jonas lives in a future society where emotions are limited and everyone is assigned a job at age twelve. Jonas has just been named the Receiver, which means he is able to absorb memories from an adult called the Giver. In this scene, Jonas has just experienced The Giver's memory of a childhood birthday party.

Objective: As you read, keep this question in mind: How much direct experience has Jonas had with older people? Underline any sentences that show Jonas's experience with older people. Record any questions you have in the My Thoughts column.

——— First Read
---- Second Read
——— Third Read

excerpt
The Giver
by Lois Lowry

My Thoughts

1   Jonas opened his eyes and lay contentedly on the bed still

luxuriating in the warm and comforting memory. It had all

been there, all the things he had learned to treasure.

Event

"What did you perceive?" The Giver asked.

5   "Warmth," Jonas replied, "and happiness. And—let me

think. *Family*. That it was a celebration of some sort, a holiday.

And something else—I can't quite get the word for it."

Emotion

Event

"It will come to you."

"Who were the old people? Why were they there?" It

10   had puzzled Jonas, seeing them in the room. The Old of the

community did not ever leave their special place, the House of

the Old, where they were so well cared for and respected.

"They were called Grandparents."

"Grand parents?"

15   "Grandparents. It meant parents-of-the-parents, long ago."

"Back and back and back?" Jonas began to laugh. "So

actually, there could be parents-of-the-parents-of-the-parents-

of-the parents?"

Remediation: First Read Since most of this excerpt is dialogue, have a volunteer read the part of Jonas as you read the part of The Giver. Have another volunteer read the sentences that are not dialogue.

ELL Support: First Read If possible, have students view this scene from the film before they read. Then have students read the text in multilevel pairs, pausing at the end of each paragraph to summarize the events on a Story Map graphic organizer from the ELL Teacher Resource (p. 52). Also, encourage students to draw sketches in the margins around the story or on a separate piece of paper as in a graphic novel, so they can be sure they understand the story. Model doing so by taking notes and drawing sketches for the first paragraph.

Before Reading: Read the introductory paragraph to establish background and context. Ask students to define the term *science fiction* and to make predictions about the text based on what they know about this genre.

As a pre-reading activity, invite students to share memories of childhood birthday parties, especially sensory details *(birthday cakes, blowing out candles, making wishes, party games, gifts, singing "Happy Birthday to You")*. Make a list of details that are mentioned more than once. Explain that this is the type of memory that The Giver shares with Jonas.

Finally, read the objective together and then ask students to read the text on their own.

Preview Vocabulary: Preview unfamiliar vocabulary to aid comprehension. Ask students to circle unfamiliar words as they complete the first read of a text. After the first read, guide students to determine the words' meanings using the context. Encourage students to support their responses with evidence. Have students confirm their initial definitions with a dictionary. Words that students might find difficult include:

contentedly: *in a way that expresses satisfaction or happiness.* After the Thanksgiving feast, everyone sank contentedly into the couch, watched football, and waited for dessert.

luxuriating: *indulging oneself in an extremely pleasant experience.* After her six children left for school, Mona found herself luxuriating in all the peace and quiet.

wisp: *a thin, threadlike fragment of something.* A wisp of steam rose from the teapot and reminded me of my grandmother's kitchen.

faltered: *spoke brokenly and unevenly; wavered in speech.* When it was her turn to answer, the child faltered, completely unable to collect her thoughts.

reassuring: *encouraging; restoring confidence.* The mayor was always reassuring the citizens that the roads and bridges did not need repair . . . but he was wrong.

Chapter **10** *(continued)*

Lesson Support

Text-Based Discussion Questions

1. How are families different in the society where Jonas lives? *Jonas doesn't know what grandparents are. Also, when adults get too old to "contribute to the society," they aren't a part of their children's lives any longer. They go to live with the other Childless Adults. Families aren't close because when parents are no longer needed by their children, they stop having a relationship.*

2. What can you infer about the character of The Giver? *He is kind and patient. He is old.*

3. What does Jonas's society value? What does it condemn? *It values safety and security. It values useful people. It doesn't value relationships, love, or risk.*

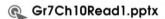 Gr7Ch10Read1.pptx

---

		My Thoughts

The Giver laughed, too. "That's right. It's a little like
20 looking in a mirror."

Jonas frowned. "But my parents must have had parents! I never thought about it before. <u>Who are my parents-of-the-parents?</u> *Where* are they?"

"You could go look in the Hall of Open Records. You'd
25 find the names. But think, son. If you apply for children, then who will be their parents-of-the-parents? Who will be their grandparents?"

"My mother and father, of course."

"And where will they be?"

30 Jonas thought. "Oh," he said slowly. "When I finish my training and become a full adult, I'll be given my own dwelling. And then when Lily does, a few years later, she'll get *her* own dwelling, and maybe a spouse, and children if she applies for them, and then Mother and Father—"

35 "That's right."

"As long as they're still working and contributing to the community, they'll go and live with the other Childless Adults. And they won't be part of my life anymore.

"And after that, when the time comes, they'll go to the
40 House of the Old," Jonas went on. He was thinking aloud. "And they'll be well cared for, and respected, and when they're released, there will be a celebration."

"Which you won't attend," The Giver pointed out.

"No, of course not, because I won't even know about it. By
45 then I'll be so busy with my own life. And Lily will, too. So our children, if we have them, won't know who their parents-of-parents are, either.

"It seems to work pretty well that way, doesn't it? The way
we do it in our community?" Jonas asked. "I just didn't realize
50 there was any other way, until I received that memory."

"It works," The Giver agreed.

Jonas hesitated. "I certainly liked the memory, though.
I can see why it's your favorite. I couldn't quite get the word
for the whole feeling of it, the feeling that was so strong in
55 the room."

"Love," The Giver told him.

Jonas repeated it. "Love." It was a word and concept new
to him.

They were both silent for a minute. Then Jonas said, "Giver?"
60 "Yes?"

"I feel very foolish saying this. Very, very foolish."

"No need. Nothing is foolish here. Trust the memories and
how they make you feel."

"Well," Jonas said, looking at the floor, "I know you don't
65 have the memory anymore, because you gave it to me, so
maybe you won't understand this—"

"I will. I am left with a vague wisp of that one; and I have
many other memories of families, and holidays, and happiness.
Of love."

70 Jonas blurted out what he was feeling. "I was thinking
that . . . well, I can see that it wasn't a very practical way to
live, with the Old right there in the same place, where maybe
they wouldn't be well taken care of, the way they are now,
and that we have a better-arranged way of doing things. But
75 anyway, I was thinking, I mean feeling, actually, that it was
kind of nice, then. And that I wish we could be that way, and
that you could be my grandparent. The family in the memory

My Thoughts
Event
Emotion

©Perfection Learning® • No Reproduction Permitted

Chapter 10 • Unit 2   **199**

About the Author: Born in Honolulu in 1937, Lois Lowry admits that she was a "solitary child who lived in the world of books and my own vivid imagination." Her father was an Army dentist, so the family lived all over the world. At a young age, Lowry married a naval officer and continued the same kind of life, having four children of her own. It wasn't until her children were older that she went to graduate school and began to write professionally. Lowry has written more than 30 children's books and has won two Newbery Medals (one for *The Giver*) and the international Hans Christian Andersen Award. She is known for writing about difficult topics: racism, illness, murder, death, and the Holocaust among them. *The Giver* is the first book in a quartet that ended with *Son* in 2012. Today, Lowry is a grandmother, and she continues to write and speak to audiences who love her work. For more information go to her website: www.loislowry.com.

Tech-Connect Suggestion: The film adaptation of *The Giver* was released in 2014. Jeff Bridges plays the title character and Brenton Thwaites, the role of Jonas. It is 97 minutes long.

Lesson Support

Dystopian Literature: At first, *The Giver* appears to describe a society that is *utopian*, a place where everything is perfect and peaceful. However, it soon becomes clear that the novel is *dystopian*, that is, it reveals a "bad" society that is contrary to what the author believes in. Dystopian novels usually serve as a warning to readers: either shape up or this could happen to us! *Gulliver's Travels* (1726) was the first dystopian novel. Among the most famous are *Brave New World* by Aldous Huxley (1932), *Nineteen Eighty-Four* by George Orwell (1949), *Player Piano* by Kurt Vonnegut (1952), *Fahrenheit 451* by Ray Bradbury (1953), *The Stand* by Stephen King (1978), and *The Handmaid's Tale* by Margaret Atwood (1985). Other modern dystopian novels for young adults are *The Last Star* by Rick Yancey (2016), *The Selection* by Keira Cass (2012), and *The Hunger Games* series by Suzanne Collins (2008).

FIRST RESPONSE: KEY IDEAS AND DETAILS

Focus on Citing Evidence: The word *evidence* derives from the Latin *evidentia*, which means "proof" from the stem *evidens*, which means "obvious and apparent." This suggests that evidence not only supports or proves a claim but also connects clearly to the claim and is easy to recognize.

 Gr7Ch10Read1.pptx

---

seemed a little more—" He faltered, not able to find the word he wanted.

80   "A little more complete," The Giver suggested.

   Jonas nodded. "I liked the feeling of love," he confessed.

   He glanced nervously at the speaker on the wall, reassuring himself that no one was listening. "I wish we still had that," he whispered. "Of course," he added quickly, "I do understand

85 that it wouldn't work very well. And that it's much better to be organized the way we are now. I can see that it was a *dangerous* way to live."

   "What do you mean?"

   Jonas hesitated. He wasn't certain, really, what he had

90 meant. He could feel that there was *risk* involved, though he wasn't sure how. "Well," he said finally, grasping for an explanation, "they had *fire* right there in that room. There was a fire burning in the fireplace. And there were candles on a table. I can certainly see why those things were outlawed.

95   "Still," he said slowly, almost to himself, "I did like the light they made. And the warmth."

FIRST RESPONSE: KEY IDEAS AND DETAILS

Based on your first reading of this text, how much direct experience has Jonas had with older people? Write your answer in your journal.

Focus on Citing Evidence

When you write about a topic, it helps to imagine three things about your readers:

- They are smart enough to understand what you're writing about.
- They don't know the topic as well as you do.
- Your readers can only understand what you're telling them if you give them enough details from the text.

My Thoughts

_____

Emotion

_____
_____
_____
_____
_____
_____

Emotion

_____
_____
_____
_____
_____
_____

TECH-CONNECT

Post your answer to the First Response question to your class web page or another site as per your teacher's instructions.

Remediation: First Read If students have difficulty understanding evidence, remind them that a good lawyer would never stand in front of a jury and simply declare, "That person is guilty!" A good lawyer (like a good writer) must supply the jury with evidence: facts, examples, anecdotes, testimony from witnesses and experts, data, photographs, diagrams—all relevant *proof* that the defendant committed the crime.

The details your readers need to understand your ideas is *evidence*. Evidence develops your ideas and makes them clear for your readers.

When you gather evidence, it's important to clarify why the evidence matters. Why is a certain detail important? What does it show or suggest? In the chart below, the third column is for explaining what the evidence shows.

Complete the following chart by filling in the second and third columns. The shaded cells have been completed for you.

Moment in Excerpt	Textual Evidence	What It Suggests About Jonas's Experience with Older People
When Jonas first thinks about the dream	*"Who were the old people? Why were they there?"*	Jonas doesn't understand why older people would be at a party. Maybe he's never seen old people at a celebration before.
When Jonas first thinks about the House of Old	*The Old of the community did not ever leave their special place, the House of the Old, where they were so well cared for and respected*	The old people never leave the House of Old, so maybe Jonas has never . . . seen any old people in his community at all.
When Jonas learns what grandparents are	*"But my parents must have had parents! I never thought about it before. Who are my parents-of-the-parents? Where are they?"*	If he hasn't met his own grandparents, it's likely he hasn't met any old people at all. Older people are not involved in the central life of the society.
When Jonas thinks the old way wasn't a "practical way to live."	*"I can see that it wasn't a very practical way to live, with the Old right there in the same place . . ."*	He has never lived with old people before or even heard of old people living in families before.

☾**Speak and Listen** Share your chart with a partner. Use the following questions to help you evaluate one another's charts:

1. Are direct quotes from the text included?

2. Do the quotes provide evidence of Jonas's experience with older people?

3. Do your partner's explanations of what the evidence shows seem reasonable? Why or why not?

Add or change the information in your chart based upon your partner's evaluation.

☾**Speak and Listen:** Suggest that here, *reasonable* means "logical, making sense, or appropriate." This does not mean that students must agree with each other's explanations, only that they "make sense."

ELL Support: Speak and Listen Have students work in multilevel pairs or small groups to first discuss their charts using the following modified questions and sentence frames:

- Are there quotes in your chart? Yes/No, there are/are not quotes in my chart.

- Do the quotes give evidence about Jonas's experience with older people? Yes/No, the quotes do/do not give evidence about Jonas's experience with older people.

- Are your explanations of the evidence reasonable (make sense)? Yes/No, my explanations are/are not reasonable because . . . .

Lesson Support

▼ **Write:** Remind students that they may need to explain what is happening in the excerpt for someone who has not read the book.

Remind students that textual evidence includes both direct quotations and paraphrases or summaries of a text. If needed, model how to write sentences with both types of evidence:

- Jonas has never seen older people before because he says, [direct quotation].

- In the excerpt [summary of part of the text], which reveals that older adults do not take an active part in their children's and grandchildren's lives.

Second Read: Analyzing the Interaction of Story Elements

Before Reading: Remind students that during a second read they should focus on answering the question *How*? A useful question might be, *How do the interaction of story elements begin a change in Jonas?*

Review what students have learned about analyzing a character through evidence such as a character's words, thoughts, feelings, and actions. As students read and annotate, encourage them to consider what the evidence reveals about Jonas.

After Reading: Use the following questions to check comprehension.

Text-Based Discussion Questions

1. What lines from the text hint at the fact that everything is not perfect in Jonas's society? *Jonas has never experienced love before. He doesn't know his grandparents and will be separated from his parents once he no longer needs them. Members have to "apply" for spouses.*

2. What conflicts does Jonas experience in the excerpt? *He struggles with feeling the warmth and love in the memories, which aren't available to people in his society. He's been taught these things are dangerous.*

3. Why would Jonas's society not want its members to have memories of the past? *So that people won't want to go back to the way things were. So they won't miss the love and relationships.*

▼ **Write** Now write a paragraph about how much direct experience Jonas has had with older people. Make sure that even someone who hasn't read the book will know what you're talking about.

On a separate sheet of paper:

- Write a sentence claiming how much direct experience Jonas has had with older people.

- Then support that statement with at least three pieces of evidence you gathered in the table. Use phrases such as *for example* or *for instance* to introduce your evidence.

- Finally, write at least one sentence summing up what the evidence shows. Use a sentence such as the following:

     This evidence suggests that Jonas . . . .
     The evidence proves that Jonas . . . .

Second Read: Analyzing the Interaction of Story Elements

The excerpt from *The Giver* isn't action-packed, but something important is happening to Jonas. Analyzing the details can help you figure out what's going on.

Objective: Reread the excerpt from *The Giver*. Write "Event" next to the main event that sparks the conversation between The Giver and Jonas. Then write "Emotion" next to any emotional response the conversation brings out in Jonas.

Focus on Analyzing the Interaction of Story Elements

Stories are made of parts—events, characters, settings, and so on—and all of them affect each other. Sometimes the effects are obvious, as when a tornado (event) takes a girl and her dog (characters) from their Kansas farm (setting) to the Land of Oz (setting).

Other times, as with the excerpt from *The Giver*, the effects are not as dramatic. This is when close reading—taking the time to examine the parts of a story and how they interact—is useful.

1. According to the introduction before the story, what is the overall (main) setting of *The Giver*?

ELL Support: Write Have students work in multilevel pairs or small groups to write their response, using the following sentence frames. These can also be found in the ELL Teacher Resource as a student handout (p. 36).

- In this book, a boy named Jonas . . . .

- Jonas thinks that older people are . . . .

- Jonas is surprised to learn that . . . .

- In Jonas's world, older people are . . . .

- I know this because . . . .

Second Read Make sure students understand the literary elements: event (thing that happens), emotion (feeling), setting (time and place of a story), characters (people or animals in the story). Model identifying an event and an emotion in the first few paragraphs of the story. Have students work in multilevel pairs or small groups to

2. Who are the characters in the excerpt?

3. What event starts the conversation between the characters?

4. What feelings does Jonas have during his conversation with The Giver? Write down the line numbers where you see evidence of these feelings.

5. Overall, how do the event and the conversation affect Jonas's feelings about his overall setting?

Focus on Analyzing the Interaction of Story Elements:

Sample Answers to Questions:

1. A future society in which emotions are limited and everyone has a job starting at age 12. People take an active part in the society as long as they are useful. Relationships are not valued.

2. Jonas and The Giver

3. The memory of a party that Jonas receives from The Giver

4. At different points throughout the conversation, Jonas feels happy (lines 5–6), confused/puzzled (lines 10–15), foolish (line 61), nervous (line 83), and uncertain (lines 89–96).

5. He appreciates that his society is safe, but he likes the light and warmth of how society used to be, so he might be thinking something in his society is missing.

 Gr7Ch10Read2.pptx

reread the story and answer the questions. If necessary, help students to identify the setting time and place, the characters, and the different instances of dialogue or conversation.

Remediation: Second Read Remind students that setting includes both time (year, season, time of day) and place (geographical location and inside or outside). Characters can be major (Jonas and The Giver) or minor (Lily). Events happen in a series, usually in chronological order and are collectively called *plot*. Most plots can be represented as distinct events on a timeline.

Lesson Support

Third Read: Analyzing Points of View

Before Reading: Review the introduction with students. Augment the definition of "third-person point of view" by explaining that a third-person narrator can be limited (inside the story, as in *The Giver*) or omniscient (completely outside the story, seeing things that happen simultaneously or that one character could never "see").

Then, make sure students understand that in this read they will look for evidence of the other meaning of "point of view"—a character's attitude toward people, ideas, and events.

After Reading: Use the following questions to check comprehension.

Text-Based Discussion Questions

1. What does the comparison of grandparents to looking in a mirror (line 19) show us about The Giver? *It shows that he is older and self-aware of his appearance.*

2. Based on his responses to Jonas's questions (lines 51 and following), what can you infer about The Giver's attitude toward the society? *The Giver admits that the society "works," but he describes the old society as "a little more complete." He encourages Jonas to think about love and its risks. From these details, we can infer that The Giver believes the society is wrong to remove love and emotions from people's lives.*

3. When Jonas thinks about the risks he feels in the memory of the party, he isn't sure what is risky or dangerous, so he settles on the fire and candles as examples. How might the feeling of risk and danger be related to Jonas's feeling of love? *Love is dangerous because you risk being hurt or rejected by people. Jonas sort of feels this but can't put it into words. One way the society protects its members is to remove love.*

Focus on Analyzing Points of View:

> **Sample Answers to Charts and Questions:**
>
> See answers on Student Book insert page to the right.

Third Read: Analyzing Points of View

The questions you answered after the second read examined how the conversation with The Giver affected Jonas's emotions. But what about Jonas's point of view?

In fiction, the phrase *point of view* has at least two meanings. Point of view can refer to the narrator's position in relation to the story being told.

- First-person point of view: This is when the narrator is a character within the story. In Chapter 6, *Catch Me If You Can* is told from a first-person point of view.

- Third-person point of view: This is when the narrator is standing outside of the events of the story. *The Giver* is told from a third-person point of view.

But point of view has a second meaning. It can refer to a character's or a narrator's attitude toward people, ideas, and events. Characters' words, thoughts, feelings, and actions are evidence of their point of view.

Objective: Read the excerpt from *The Giver* a third time. Pay attention to Jonas's point of view toward the idea of "family." Draw a box around any evidence that shows Jonas's point of view.

Focus on Analyzing Points of View

Just as a person's point of view about something can develop and change over time, so can the point of view of a narrator or character.

In the chart below, identify one positive and one negative feeling Jonas has about the family he saw in the memory. Then write down evidence from the text showing that feeling.

Point of view toward the family in the memory	Positive feeling: feelings of warmth, love, and completeness	Evidence from text: *"I liked the feeling of love," he confessed.* *"I did like the light they made. And the warmth."*
	Negative feeling: danger, risk, uncertainty	Evidence from text: *"they had fire right there in that room."* *"I can certainly see why those things were outlawed."* *He could feel that there was risk involved.*

Remediation: Third Read A character's point of view may be difficult for struggling readers to discern. One way to support understanding is to ask students to write or speak using that character's voice. In other words, answer these questions as if you were Jonas (or The Giver): *What do you think about how society organizes families? Why do you think this way?*

ELL Support: Third Read Guide students to reread the text and complete the chart by reading lines aloud and asking questions: *What is Jonas feeling? What words show you this feeling?* Provide the following sentence frames for multilevel pairs or groups to use as they answer the questions that follow the chart:

- Before, Jonas's point of view about how families are organized was . . . . Before, he had . . . point(s) of view.

- Now, Jonas's point of view about how families are organized is . . . . Now, he has . . . point(s) of view.

Now think about Jonas's point of view about how society organizes families. In the chart below, identify one positive and one negative feeling Jonas has. Then write down evidence from the text showing that feeling.

	Positive feeling: satisfaction, comfort, security	Evidence from text: *"It seems to work pretty well that way, doesn't it? The way we do it in our community?"* *"it's much better to be organized the way we are now."*
Point of view toward how society organizes families	Negative feeling: skepticism, doubt, uncertainty, longing	Evidence from text: *"I was thinking, I mean feeling, actually, that it was kind of nice, then."* *". . . I wish we could be that way . . ."* *"I liked the feeling of love."*

Before Jonas received the memory, what do you think his point of view was toward how his society organizes families? Do you think he had more than one point of view at that time?

continued on next page

Possible Answers to Questions:

Before receiving the memory, Jonas thought his society's organization of families was practical and effective. No, he didn't have more than one point of view yet.

(continued)

 Gr7Ch10Read3.pptx

Chapter 10 (continued)

Lesson Support

Possible Answers to Questions:

Now that Jonas has the memory, his point of view is more doubtful and uncertain. Now, he is experiencing conflicting points of view. He feels unsure and confused.

Speak and Listen: Sample answer: *The Giver views the way his society organizes families as wrong. The society believes family is for having children but not for experiencing emotional satisfaction and love. The Giver values the old ways more. He misses experiencing the emotions of love and warmth and happiness. He says, "Trust the memories and how they make you feel."*

Write: Remind students that when they quote directly from a text (and they should), they must use quotation marks, correct punctuation (commas and end punctuation inside the closing quotation marks), and line numbers cited in parentheses.

Language: Expressing Ideas Precisely and Concisely: Invite one volunteer to read the "Vague" sentence in each pair and another to read the "Precise" one. Suggest that it is always easier to recognize wordiness or vagueness in someone else's writing than it is to recognize it in our own, a validation for peer review.

 Gr7Ch10Language.pptx

---

Now that Jonas has the memory, what is his point of view about how his society organizes families? Does he have just one point of view?

Speak and Listen With a partner, talk about the character known as The Giver. How do you think The Giver views the way his society organizes families? Why do you think so? During your conversation, point to specific evidence from the text.

Write Based on your conversation with your partner, write a paragraph in your reading journal about The Giver's point of view regarding families in his society. Use evidence from the text in your paragraph.

Language: Expressing Ideas Precisely and Concisely

When you write and then revise your first draft, you look for ways to improve the precision and concision of your ideas.

Precision means using words that are specific or exact. You can improve your writing's precision by replacing vague words and phrases with more specific ones.

> **Vague:** *The Giver* has themes about many things.
> **Precise:** *The Giver* develops themes of love, family, and sacrifice in society.

Concision means describing things clearly and briefly, without extra words. You can improve your writing's concision in three ways:

- Replace phrases with single words that mean the same thing.

> **Wordy:** In order to find *The Giver*, I had a need to visit the public library.
> **Concise:** To find *The Giver*, I needed to visit the public library.

ELL Support: Speak and Listen and Write Have students work in multilevel pairs or small groups to first discuss the questions then write answers.

- The Giver thinks that families in the past were . . . .
- The Giver thinks that families today are . . . .
- The Giver wishes that . . . .
- I know this because he . . . .

• Delete phrases that don't add meaning.

> **Wordy:** In the book called *The Giver*, Jonas is chosen by other people to get the memories of a Giver.
>
> **Concise:** In *The Giver*, Jonas is chosen to get the memories of a Giver.

• Avoid repeating words or ideas.

> **Wordy:** *The Giver* is set in a dystopia, and its bad society is one in which most members of a community of people feel few emotions.
>
> **Concise:** *The Giver* is set in a dystopia in which most members of a community feel few emotions.

So when you revise, focus on making your writing more precise and concise. Your ideas will be clearer, and your readers will have a better experience.

Revise each sentence below as described.

1. Replace phrases with single words.

My report is entirely focused on *The Giver*, a book that a number of people find controversial.

2. Delete phrases that add no meaning.

The Giver was written by the author named Lois Lowry and published in the year 1993.

continued on next page

Sample Revisions:

1. My report is about *The Giver*, a book that some people find controversial.

2. *The Giver* was written by Lois Lowry and published in 1993.

(continued)

ELL Support: Language Students will find it challenging to identify phrases that are too wordy or unnecessary. Identify these phrases for them. Then provide the following in a word bank for students to use to replace the phrases: *a children's book author, some people, receives The Giver's memories about when old and young people used to live together, published in 1993, written by Lois, Jonas visits The Giver, about, which is awarded each.*

Chapter **10** *(continued)*

Sample Revisions:

3. The book won the famous Newbery Medal, which is awarded each year to a children's book author.

4. In *The Giver*, Jonas visits The Giver to learn memories, and he receives The Giver's memories about when the old and the young lived together.

---

3. Avoid repetition.

The book won the famous Newbery Medal, which is a famed medal awarded each and every year to the author who writes a book for children.

> **REFLECT**
>
> Was there ever a time when you began questioning something about your society that you had never questioned before? What brought about that questioning? What happened as a result?

4. Replace vague words.

In *The Giver,* this one character goes to another character to learn memories, and he finds out about old people.

Remediation: Project-Based Assessments The Roundtable Discussion assumes that students have some prior knowledge of dystopian literature and/or films. If they do not, suggest that they write the Personal Essay.

Project-Based Assessments

Personal Essay

The Giver describes a society in which citizens have little freedom to make decisions. Your society is different. As you age, you'll make many decisions that will affect you, your loved ones, and your society.

Write a one-page personal essay in which you answer these questions:

- In your life, what do you think will be the single most important decision you ever make?
- Why will this decision be so important? Who will be affected?
- Is there just one good choice in the decision? And is there only one good outcome? Or are the decision and its possible outcomes more complicated than just "good" and "bad"?

TECH-CONNECT

Listening to your writing can reveal awkward sentences. Use your computer or cell phone to make a recording as you read your paper aloud. Listen to your recording and use it to revise your writing.

Use the following guidelines for your personal essay.	
To receive the highest score (4.0), your essay must meet all of these criteria.	Your essay should • clearly state what you think will be the most important decision you make. • explain why that decision will be so important and who will be affected. • discuss whether the choices and outcomes involved in this decision are simple or complicated. • maintain a formal style. • contain correct grammar, spelling, and punctuation.

Roundtable Discussion

A utopia is a perfect society in which human beings are free to become their best selves. A dystopia is the opposite: a flawed, bad society in which citizens are dehumanized and treated unfairly, often by a powerful government or corporation.

Books and movies about dystopias are popular. *The Giver* is one example. Others include *The Hunger Games, Divergent,* and *The Ear, the Eye, and the Arm.* The final book and movie of the Harry Potter series show the magical world becoming dystopian. A dystopia even appears in the animated movie *The Lion King* when Scar takes over the hunting grounds.

Participate in a roundtable discussion on the following questions.

> Why might people enjoy reading or watching movies about dystopias? What is the appeal?

continued on next page

Project-Based Assessments

Personal Essay: This speculative essay does not require the use of text-based evidence, so it will be accessible to all students who can imagine their futures. You may want to approve their choice of topics to avoid any that might be controversial, inappropriate, or impossible to analyze. You may want to ask: *What decisions did/ will Jonas face in his life? (choice of spouse, whether to have children) Are any of these decisions ones that you think you will face someday?*

ELL Support: Personal Essay Have students work in multilevel pairs or small groups to write a one-page personal essay with illustrations. Beginning and intermediate students can respond with labeled pictures that show their decision and its impact as a flowchart, timeline, or comic strip. (See graphic organizers in the ELL Teacher Resource, p. 49.) Provide the following sentence frames:

- The most important decision I will make is . . . .
- This decision is so important because . . . .
- The people who will be affected by this decision are . . . .
- There is/is not just one choice in this decision because . . . .
- There is/is not just one good outcome in this decision because . . . .

Provide the Informational Writing Revision Checklist (p. 69) and the Proofreading Checklist (p. 71) from the ELL Teacher Resource.

Chapter **10** (continued)

Assessment

Roundtable Discussion: Another option is to organize students into groups of 4 or 5 with one student appointed as discussion leader. Limit each person's response in each round to 2 or 3 minutes. Have the discussion leader also serve as timekeeper. Encourage all participants to refer not only to *The Giver* but also to other dystopian books, stories, or films.

In a roundtable discussion, all members of the group are equal and everyone participates. Arrange your seats in a circle so that everyone can see each other. The teacher or a discussion leader may sit in the middle. Come to the discussion with an open mind. You will be evaluated on the following:

Expectations for Discussion	
Listening	**Speaking**
Listen respectfully.	Speak at least once.
Look at the speaker.	Give reasons or examples.
Take notes on what the speaker is saying.	Ask questions.
Write down follow-up questions.	Explain and offer reasons to support your idea.
Reflect on what others say and be open to changing your mind based on new evidence.	Use appropriate tone of voice and language for an open exchange of ideas.
	Invite comments.

Instructions for a Roundtable Discussion

1. The discussion leader (teacher or student) begins by asking the following questions:

> Why might people enjoy reading or watching movies about dystopias? What is the appeal?

2. Allow each member the chance to reply to the questions.

3. Take notes on comments you disagree with or you have questions about. Record what is said and who said it.

4. Go around the circle again, and allow everyone to ask a follow-up question. Questions should be directed to the person who made the original comment. Try phrasing your questions in this way:

   - Explain what you mean by . . . .
   - Who agrees/disagrees with (name of participant)? Why?

5. Close the discussion by having everyone respond to the following questions:

> Do you think authors and filmmakers want their stories about dystopias to have important real-world effects? If so, what might they be?

ELL Support: Roundtable Discussion Explain that a dystopia is an imaginary place where people are unhappy or afraid, often because the government treats people badly. Pronounce the word and have students repeat it after you. Provide the following sentence frames for students to use during the discussion:

- I think people read stories and watch movies about dystopias because . . . .
- I think people like dystopias because . . . .

Allow time for students to practice their sentences with you or in multilevel pairs before beginning the discussion. Explain that students should monitor (check) their understanding during the discussion, and if they need help understanding or participating, they should raise their hand and you will assist them with paraphrases or sentence frames.

Use the following guidelines for the roundtable discussion.	
To receive the highest score (4.0), the discussion must meet all of these criteria.	During the discussion, you should • listen carefully when others speak; make notes about what they said. • offer thoughtful feedback and encourage everyone to participate. • share reasonable opinions and support your opinion with examples. • speak to the question or point at hand in a clear, concise manner.

On Your Own: Integrating Ideas

1. Read *The Giver* if you haven't already read it. It is clear why it won the Newbery Medal. (Even if you have read it before, it might be worth reading again.)

2. *The Giver* was made into a 2014 movie starring Jeff Bridges and Meryl Streep. Many critics didn't like it. They thought the movie wasn't as thought-provoking as the book. If you read the book, watch the movie to see whether you agree with the critics. While watching, you can also practice analyzing how a movie communicates its content—through its choices of lighting, sound, music, color, camera angles, and so on.

3. If dystopian literature appeals to you, find some books mentioned earlier in this chapter. Two more advanced books, *1984* and *Animal Farm*, both by George Orwell, also depict dystopian societies.

> **CONNECT TO ESSENTIAL QUESTION**
>
> The Essential Question is "Can we trust what we see, hear, and read?" How do you think Jonas would answer this question after getting The Giver's memory?

ELL Support: On Your Own: Integrating Ideas The Giver has been translated into many languages. Consider giving ELLs the opportunity to read in their first language or to read the English version side by side with a version in their first language.

Assessment

Connect to Testing: This Connect to Testing section focuses on making inferences, identifying point of view, and analyzing how elements of a story interact.

Answers to Connect to Testing Questions:

1. **Part A:** A. Choice B is incorrect because Jonas has been named The Receiver as his special job. Choices C and D are incorrect because Jonas knows his parents who raised him. (DoK 2)

   Part B: D. The speaker on the wall and the comment about it is evidence that some conversations are listened to. (DoK 2)

2. A. The other choices change the meaning of the sentence. Choice A simply makes it more precise and concise. (DoK 1)

(continued)

Connect to Testing

In this chapter, you cited textual evidence to support your ideas, analyzed how elements of a story interact, and examined how an author develops the characters' points of view. You also practiced editing sentences for precision and concision. When you take assessments, you will be tested on such skills.

1. Part A: Based on the passage, which statement about *The Giver* is most likely true?

   A. Some people in the society are monitored.

   B. All young people receive the memories of old people.

   C. Children do not know who their original parents are.

   D. Parents do not get to watch their children grow up.

   Part B: Which sentence from the passage best supports the answer to Part A?

   A. *Jonas opened his eyes and lay contentedly on the bed still luxuriating in the warm and comforting memory.*

   B. *"Who are my parents-of-the-parents?"*

   C. *"I liked the feeling of love," he confessed.*

   D. *He glanced nervously at the speaker on the wall, reassuring himself that no one was listening.*

2. Read the sentence below.

   > Among other reasons, *The Giver* is a controversial book for the reason that it brings up controversial questions about older people and how society treats them.

   Which of the following best revises the sentence without changing its meaning?

   A. One reason *The Giver* is controversial is because it questions how society should treat older people.

   B. One reason why *The Giver* brings up controversial issues is to ask questions about older people.

   C. *The Giver* is a book that brings up many issues, including one that older people should not ask questions about.

   D. *The Giver* is controversial for one reason: it makes older people ask questions about society.

Remediation: Connect to Testing Focus on questions 1 and 3, which present less reading load and test the skills of making inferences and finding evidence. Read each question aloud and have students take turns reading the answer choices. As a group, discuss whether each choice is correct or incorrect until the group reaches consensus about the correct answer.

3. In the excerpt from *The Giver*, how does the character of The Giver most affect the resolution of this part of the story?

   A. by convincing Jonas to begin looking for his grandparents

   B. by helping Jonas to understand what love feels like

   C. by forcing Jonas to confront how horrible his society is

   D. by causing Jonas to realize how well their community works

4. **Part A:** In *The Giver*, how does the memory that Jonas receives most directly affect him?

   A. It leads him to miss his own grandparents.

   B. It leads him to recall his own birthday party.

   C. It frightens him into thinking people are listening.

   D. It makes him want to experience a loving family.

   Part B: Which evidence from *The Giver* supports the answer to Part A?

   A. *"So our children, if we have them, won't know who their parents-of-parents are, either."*

   B. *"I wish we still had that,"* he whispered.

   C. *He glanced nervously at the speaker on the wall, reassuring himself that no one was listening.*

   D. *"I can see that it was a dangerous way to live."*

5. **Part A:** What does the conversation between The Giver and Jonas mainly reveal about their points of view?

   A. It conveys how different their experiences of family have been.

   B. It expresses their shared, growing dislike of the community.

   C. It shows how little they know about each other's thoughts about family.

   D. It illustrates that they agree their community is better than others.

   Part B: Which two choices best support the answer in Part A? Choose one choice for each character.

   A. *"And—let me think. Family. That it was a celebration of some sort, a holiday. And something else—I can't quite get the word for it."* (Jonas)

   B. *"You could go look in the Hall of Open Records."* (The Giver)

   C. *"When I finish my training and become a full adult, I'll be given my own dwelling."* (Jonas)

   D. *"It seems to work pretty well that way, doesn't it? The way we do it in our community?"* (Jonas)

   E. *"It works,"* The Giver agreed. (The Giver)

   F. *"I am left with a vague wisp of that one; and I have many other memories of families, and holidays, and happiness. Of love."* (The Giver)

3. B. The Giver is a very gentle character in this excerpt. He does not convince Jonas to seek his grandparents (although he does mention that the Hall of Open Records contains this information). He does not force him to think anything. He causes Jonas to question how well his community works, not to realize how well it works. (DoK 2)

4. **Part A:** D.

   Part B: B. The word *that* in this quotation refers to "the feeling of love" in line 81. (DoK 2)

5. **Part A:** A. The Giver experienced a traditional family that loved each other, celebrated birthdays, and included members of all ages spending time together.

   Part B: A. and F. Choice A reveals Jonas's ignorance of holiday celebrations and love. Choice F reveals The Giver's memories of them. (DoK 2)

ELL Support: Connect to Testing and Assessments See the *Connections* ELL Teacher Resource (p. 22) for ideas on adapting this section for ELLs.

Unit 2 Writing

Writing an Informative Text

Introduction

Preview Academic Vocabulary:

central idea statement: *a sentence that contains the key idea of a piece of writing.* If you write your <u>central idea statement</u> before you do your research, you will probably change it before you draft.

domain-specific vocabulary: *words that are typically used only in a specific field of study.* Examples include *cell membrane* (biology), *linking verb* (English), and *software* (computers).

outline: *a plan for a longer written work, usually written in phrases, that shows each part and section.* The author's <u>outline</u> for her proposed history of the Mississippi River was ten pages long!

sources: *print or digital texts or graphics that provide information for a writing project.* It is appropriate to use NASA and data from the International Space Station as <u>sources</u> for your report, but it is not appropriate to use a blog by a student who wants to be an astronaut.

transitions: *words and phrases that show the connections among ideas and details.* The story would be easier to understand if the writer used <u>transitions</u> to show how much time passes between events.

 G7U2WritingInformative

Writing an Informative Text

Scientific knowledge is in perpetual evolution; it finds itself changed from one day to the next.
—**Jean Piaget**

"Question everything," Guy Harrison writes. "Debunk it!" says John Grant. In this unit, you read about whether you can trust the evidence of your senses. Scientists have the job of testing whether ideas are accurate because even when those ideas are trustworthy, they can be proven false as people learn more. And in the last few centuries, science has overturned ideas that people held for thousands of years.

In this chapter, you will write an informative text in which you describe how a long-held belief about the natural world was proven false by modern science.

> **CONNECT TO ESSENTIAL QUESTION**
>
> Is science a way to test every idea? Or are there limits to what science can test?

WRITING PROMPT

Why does the sun rise? What is fire? Where do mountains come from? Over the centuries, humans developed ideas to explain such natural occurrences. Some of those ideas were reasonable and based on evidence, but they turned out to be wrong anyway.

In an informative text, describe one of those long-held ideas that science eventually proved wrong. Explain how science disproved that idea, and describe the idea that replaced it. Develop your descriptions and explanations with facts, details, and examples.

Because you will be writing about scientific ideas, you will likely use some domain-specific vocabulary. This means you will have to provide some definitions for your readers. And you will likely need at least one graphic, such as a photo or diagram, to illustrate the ideas you discuss. Your informative text should be two pages, typed, double-spaced, and in a standard 12-point Times New Roman font.

Prepare to Write

Read the prompt carefully. Underline key words that explain the requirements of the task. Break it down based on purpose, audience, content, and additional requirements by filling in the chart on the next page.

ELL Support: Academic Vocabulary See <u>Teaching Vocabulary in the ELL Teacher Resource (p. 18)</u> for ideas to use for teaching vocabulary throughout *Connections.*

Purpose	to explain
Audience	classmates, teacher
Content Requirements	
Additional Requirements	

▼ The Writing Process

Brainstorm

The history of science is full of reasonable ideas, which were later overturned by modern discoveries, observations, and experiments. The chart below shows just a few of them. Don't avoid a topic just because you don't recognize a word or phrase like *phlogiston* or *luminiferous*. You're doing research, which means you'll eventually find out what it means. (A good dictionary will also tell you what each *part* of the word means, which will help you even more.)

Choose one idea below that catches your eye and get started.

Famous Ideas That Modern Science Proved Incorrect	
Physical Science	**Astronomy**
• Heavy objects fall faster than lighter ones. • The four basic elements are earth, air, fire, and water. • Objects burn if they contain a material called *phlogiston*. • Dalton's theory of the indivisible atom (Atoms cannot be destroyed.)	• The geocentric universe (Stars and planets rotate around Earth.) • The heliocentric universe (Stars and planets rotate around the Sun.) • The luminiferous ether • The steady-state universe • The nature of comets and shooting stars
Life Science	**Earth Science**
• Fossils and the history of life • Spontaneous generation • The four humors (bodily fluids that determine personality) • The miasma theory of disease ("Bad air" causes illness.) • The blank slate theory of the human mind (The brain has no rules for learning at birth.) • Lamarck's theory of evolution (Any changes to a creature are passed on.)	• The age of Earth • Neptunism (All rocks were formed from waters of an ancient ocean.) • Plutonism (All rocks were formed by volcanic activity.) • The expanding and shrinking Earth • The formation and shapes of the continents

continued on next page

Prepare to Write: Content requirements include the following: *long-held idea that was proven wrong, how it was disproved by science, describe the idea that replaced it, domain-specific vocabulary, at least one graphic, two pages*

▼ The Writing Process

Brainstorm: If students find or have another idea for a topic, encourage them to pursue it. However, require students to get your approval before they begin. This will ensure the topic's appropriateness and accessibility and make sure there is sufficient and reliable research to support it. Decide on the number of sources required, perhaps three for a paper of this length, and communicate this to the students.

ELL Support: Brainstorm Have students work in multilevel pairs or small groups on this project. Beginning and intermediate students can draw and label pictures to explain the original scientific theories and the new ones. Explain to all students that they can choose a new theory if they cannot find or understand the information about the one they have chosen. Provide the following sentence frames for students to discuss and write about their chosen theory:

- This idea interests me because . . . .

- I know that . . . .

Writing (continued)

Find Sources: Many students will rely on online sources, if available to them. Remind them of the following cautions, however:

- Wikipedia can be unreliable because anyone can contribute to a post. However, students can use it as a basis for further research. Other online encyclopedias are closely researched and edited by a staff of writers, including Encyclopedia Britannica (www.britannica.com) and infoplease. com.

- If the website ends in *.gov, .org,* or *.edu,* it is likely to be more credible than those ending in *.com.*

- Encourage students to look for sites that write on scientific topics. Good sources include www.sciencemag. org, www.scientificamerican. com, and sciencenews.org. Some science publications also have sites for students, such as www. scienceforstudents.org.

- If the information was written more than ten years ago, it should be considered unreliable.

Remind students that reliable sources have been reviewed by the author's peers and more than one person agrees on their accuracy.

Model how to investigate the reliability of a source by displaying a website and reading the About/About Us tab. For example, share two sites with differing political views: www.theamericanconservative.com and www.motherjones.com.

The following web page is a great source for explaining the difference among scholarly journals, news magazines, and popular magazines: http://guides.ucf.edu/scholarlyjournalsvsmagazines.

Which idea on the previous page seems most interesting to you?

Why is this idea interesting to you?

What, if anything, do you know about this idea already?

What, if anything, do you know about the idea that replaced it?

Find Sources

Find sources and gather evidence to develop your text. Find two or three sources on your chosen topic. The first source should be an encyclopedia such as *World Book, Collier's, Encyclopedia Britannica,* or some other credible and respected reference. This will give you some solid facts about your topic.

Always evaluate your sources to make sure they are credible, or are written by experts who have studied the topic extensively. Identify any bias or logical fallacies, such as loaded language and overgeneralization, which writers use instead of solid facts and evidence. (See page 148 for more about fallacies.)

Record information about your sources (including the encyclopedia) in the chart below. Include the title of the article or book, the author's name, the website name, the publisher, and the date of publication.

Title of Source	Name of Journal or Website	Author Name	Publisher	Date of Publication
1:				
2:				
3:				

Gather Information

Take notes on your sources. As you record information, always write down the source the information came from.

When researching a topic, having questions in mind before you read will guide your reading and help your note-taking. Jot down the answers as you find them in the text.

Some questions related to the prompt are listed on the next page. When you find information that answers one or more of these questions, record it in your response journal or in a computer file.

Gather Information: If students have listed their sources in a chart such as the one on page 217, they can simply reference their sources by source number—and page number—as they take notes.

ELL Support: Find Sources and Gather Information Students should work in their multilevel pairs or groups to read linguistically accommodated material about the theory they have chosen. Public libraries often provide access to online databases where students can find encyclopedia or children's magazine articles that will be appropriate for their level. Newsela.com (which has nonfiction articles at various reading levels) may also have some articles on their scientific theories. As students read, encourage them to take notes on the Taking Notes graphic organizer from the ELL Teacher Resource (p. 54). Encourage students to draw sketches in the graphic organizer so they understand and remember the details.

Writing *(continued)*

Questions About the Old and New Ideas: Students will find these questions helpful to guide their research. The goal is that eventually students can develop these types of questions on their own before they begin researching a topic. Remind students that their questions will probably change as they research and gain more knowledge about their topic.

Questions About the Old Idea:

- What is the old idea normally called?

- When was the old idea generally believed, or for how long?

- What aspect of the natural world did the old idea explain?

- What are the details of that explanation? For example, if the old idea explained why the Sun moves across the sky, then what was the explanation for that apparent movement?

- Are any famous people associated with the old idea? If so, who? When and where did those people live?

- Why were people convinced by the old idea? Did it seem to make sense, given what people saw and experienced? Or were there other reasons people believed it?

- Did the old idea have weaknesses, or things it couldn't explain well? If the old idea did have such holes, how did supporters of the idea respond to them?

Questions About the New Idea:

- What is the new idea normally called?

- When did the new idea begin to be accepted? Is it fully accepted, or do some people still not believe it is accurate?

- Did the new idea emerge in a short amount of time (say, less than five years), or did it take a long time to develop and be accepted?

- Are any famous people associated with the new idea? If so, who? When and where did those people live?

- What caused the old idea to be overturned? Was it new discoveries, a famous experiment, or an improved piece of equipment like a microscope or a telescope?

- How is the new idea better than the old idea? For example, does the new idea explain events or new evidence that the old idea could not?

If other useful questions occur to you, write them in the space below.

Write a Central Idea Statement:
Require students to turn in their central idea statements so that you can check their progress and ensure that they have a strong central idea statement. Make sure students have a good understanding of both ideas and their relationship before they begin to organize and draft.

Write a Central Idea Statement

Once you have sufficient information about your topic, draft a central idea statement that will appear in your introduction. Your central idea statement explains to readers what your text will inform them about.

Study the following sentence frames. They show possible ways to draft your central idea statement.

- For many years, scientists accepted [name of old idea], but in more recent times, that idea was replaced with [name of new idea].

- Long ago, people thought [description of old idea], but now we know that [description of new idea].

- It might seem obvious today that [description of new idea], but in fact, people used to believe [name of old idea].

Now, write your central idea statement below. This is just a draft. It may change as you develop and revise your text.

My central idea statement:

Writing (continued)

Organize Ideas: Students may want to explore published informative essays to observe strategies to introduce topics in creative ways that will hook readers and pull them in (the way a hook catches a fish). For example, in their student books, they might refer to "The Fact Checker's Guide for Detecting Fake News" on page 159 for ideas. They can also refer to these texts to observe how professional authors write strong conclusions. Make sure they are aware when texts are excerpts; if they are, they should not consider the first and last sentences to be introductions or conclusions, respectively.

Organize Ideas

You have researched, taken notes, and drafted a central idea statement. Before you begin writing, plan the order of information in your text.

Your text should have an introduction, a body, and a conclusion. You already have a draft of your central idea, which will give you some focus. Study the following sample outline.

I. Introduction

  A. Introduce the topic and capture your readers' interest. For example:
- If you're writing about phlogiston, you could ask readers if they've ever wondered what fire is and where it comes from.
- If you're writing about fossils, you could have readers imagine that they're climbing a mountain and come across fossils of ancient shark teeth.

  B. Briefly state what both the old and the new ideas explain. For example, both might explain why the sun moves, how old the Earth is, why people get sick, and so on.

  C. Provide your central idea statement.

II. Body

  A. Present the old idea.
1. Who developed the old idea (if known)
2. Where and when it was developed (if known)
3. How the old idea explained something about the natural world

  B. Explain what happened to the old idea.
1. Problems with the old idea
2. New evidence or discoveries the old idea could not explain

  C. Present the new idea
1. Who developed the new idea
2. Where and when it was developed
3. How the new idea explains something about the natural world
4. What the new idea does or explains better than the old idea

III. Conclusion

  A. Summarize your main points and restate your central idea statement.

ELL Support: Organize Ideas Work with students to model using the outline to plan an essay on one of the scientific theories students have not chosen. Reproduce the class outline on chart paper or project it for students to consult as they develop their own. Have students continue working in their multilevel pairs or small groups to plan and organize their essays. Consider reducing the length of the response to two body paragraphs for advanced-intermediate students and remind beginning and intermediate students that they can use labeled visuals to communicate their ideas.

B. Leave a final thought. For example:
  - Did the change force humanity to think of itself differently? If so, how?
  - Did the change lead to a new treatment of disease and thus save lives?

Provide Graphics

Because you are writing about scientific ideas, your readers will probably find it helpful to have one or more graphics. For example:

- If you're writing about the geocentric theory of the universe, you can include a diagram of what it looks like, with labels for Earth, the sun, the planets, and so on.

- If you're writing about one of Galileo's experiments regarding the motion of heavy and light objects, you can include images of that experiment. Again, include labels explaining exactly what the images are showing.

- If you're writing about the formation of the continents, your readers would benefit from seeing a map of Pangaea and another map of how Earth currently looks.

Graphics in an informational text should look professional and convey important information clearly. Make sure the graphics you include add information to the text. Provide captions for the graphics, or refer directly to them in your text.

First Draft

Use your outline and any graphics to write a draft of your research paper. Here are some hints:

- Refer to your notes while drafting.
- Write quickly. You will revise and proofread later.
- Write on every other line or double-space if working on a computer. This will make it easier to make revisions.
- If you take a break and then return to writing, reread what you have written before continuing. This will help you resume the flow of thought.

continued on next page

REFLECT

Consider using headers in your paper to help your reader follow your ideas. A good header is a word or phrase that accurately summarizes the content of the section that follows it.

Provide Graphics: Remind students that graphics might include relevant photographs, diagrams, illustrations, graphs, maps, timelines, or even audio or visual clips. Explain that they must credit the source of any graphics they use. Students who need a greater challenge can create their own bar graph, timeline, or diagram in a word processing program or by using an online site such as www.canva.com.

First Draft: You may also want to ask students to prepare an alphabetical list (by authors' last names) of their sources (also called a bibliography) using either APA or MLA style. You may want to introduce your students to online citation makers. These include www.bibme.com and www.easybib.com. Google Docs also provides bibliography templates for students and will require students to understand how to write a Works Cited/Bibliography page on their own.

Take a moment to reinforce the note about plagiarism in the Reflect sidebar to make sure students understand its importance. Remind them that they must provide citations for any information that is not general knowledge. Many schools now subscribe to plagiarism checkers such as Turnitin.com or SafeAssign. A good free option is PlagiarismChecker.com.

ELL Support: First Draft Model writing the introduction and two body paragraphs to the class essay using the outline you created on page 220. Have students continue to work in their multilevel pairs or small groups to draft their essays. Advanced students will do the bulk of the composing, but intermediate and beginning students should be involved as visual creators and possibly even scribes.

Writing *(continued)*

Lesson Support

Revision: Explain that the term *revise* literally means to "look at again" with new, fresh eyes. It is best if those "new eyes" belong to someone other than the writer, which is why peer reviewing is so helpful to writers, even professional ones.

First Peer Review: You may want to model this peer-review strategy before you organize students into groups by asking for a volunteer and working through steps 2–7 with you as the peer reviewer.

- Don't copy and paste directly from other works. This is called plagiarism, and it is cheating. If you do quote directly from another work, place that text within quotation marks.
- If you are quoting a source, make sure to cite the source in your draft.
- Mark this Draft #1.

Revision

Having other students and your teacher read your text can be hugely helpful. Listen to their questions and comments on your writing. Following their advice can help improve your writing.

Three ways to revise your paper are shown.

First Peer Review

This review will help you judge whether your ideas are clear and flow logically. With a group of two to three people, complete the following steps:

> **Steps for Peer Review**
>
> 1. Select a timekeeper. Each writer gets 10 minutes. Stick to the time.
> 2. One person begins by reading aloud his or her introduction while other members listen.
> 3. Pause. The same writer reads the introduction aloud a second time.
> 4. The writer asks, "Does the introduction make you want to know more?" Each member responds as the writer takes notes.
> 5. The writer reads the entire paper, pauses, and then reads it again.
> 6. As the writer reads, members take notes.
> 7. The writer asks, "What questions do you have about my paper? Do you understand the old and new ideas? Is anything unclear about either?" The writer jots down replies.
> 8. Repeat steps 1–7 with the next writer.

Use Transitions

Transitional words and phrases help your readers to follow the relationship between your ideas. As you revise, find ways to improve your transitions both between and within paragraphs.

©Perfection Learning® • No Reproduction Permitted

ELL Support: Revision Provide the following sentence frames for students to use to give feedback to their peers. With a volunteer, model how to use the sentence frames to review and revise the class essay. Have students work in new multilevel pairs or small groups to review their drafts. Highlight the questions in exercises 4 and 7 above and tell students to use them as they read and revise their draft.

- (Yes/No), your introduction (does/does not) make me want to read more. Can you . . . ?

- I don't understand . . . . Can you . . . ?

Connections • © Perfection Learning®

Transitions for Showing Relationships		
Show a Sequence	Show a Contrast	Show Cause and Effect
then	but	so
next	however	then
finally	although	because
first, second, third	in contrast	therefore
before, after, later	on the other hand	as a result

Revise your draft based on your peers' questions and comments. Mark this paper Draft #2.

Second Peer Review

With a partner, trade texts and use the following checklist to evaluate:

Think big. Look at the draft as a whole.

- Is everything covered that is required by the prompt?
- Is the flow between paragraphs smooth or choppy?
- Is the tone consistent throughout?

Think medium. Look at the draft paragraph by paragraph.

- Does the introduction hook readers and make them want to read more?
- Does each paragraph develop the central idea with definitions of domain-specific words, concrete details, and relevant examples?
- Are the right kind of graphics included? Do the graphics clearly support the content of the text?
- Should headings be added between paragraphs? Will they help the readers better understand what each paragraph is about?

Think small. Look at the draft sentence by sentence.

- Which sentences are long and confusing? short and choppy?
- Are any sentences unclear?
- Are there errors in spelling, grammar, or usage?

ELL Support: Second and Final Peer Review Provide the Informational Writing Revision Checklist from the ELL Teacher Resource (p. 69) for students to use as they review each other's drafts. With a volunteer, model using the checklists to review, revise, and edit the class essay. Have students work in new multilevel pairs or small groups to review, revise, and edit their drafts.

Writing *(continued)*

Final Peer Review: Remind writers that it is always easier to spot errors in grammar, usage, and punctuation in someone else's draft. That's why proofreading for each other is such good practice.

Final Text: Consider combining all of your students' informational reports into a class anthology for posterity. Let the group choose a Table of Contents and a fitting title that reflects the theme of this unit, such as *Scientific "Truths": Then and Now, Why We Should Not Believe Everything We Think We "Know,"* or *Science is Not Always Right.*

Final Peer Review

Ask another student to read your paper and evaluate it using the rubric below.

Use the following guidelines for your informative text.	
To receive the highest score (4.0), your informative text must meet all of these criteria.	Your text should • contain a central idea statement that explains what the text is about. • be organized into an interesting introduction, body, and conclusion. • develop the central idea statement with facts and examples. • be organized logically and include good transitions. • demonstrate a clear and interesting style of writing; include a variety of sentence types. • contain correct grammar, usage, punctuation, and spelling.

Proofread

As you prepare a final draft, make sure you have included standard grammar and punctuation. Proofread carefully for omitted words and punctuation marks. If you used a word processing program, run spell-check, but be aware of its limitations. Proofread again to find the kinds of errors the computer can't catch.

Final Text

Share your completed text with audiences beyond your classroom. Read it to your family and friends. Upload your finished digital copy to your class website. If you have a school or personal blog, share your text with your readers.

Practice Performance Task

A performance task tests your ability to understand selections of literature or informational text and then demonstrate your knowledge in writing. The task may begin with several multiple-choice or short-answer questions on key vocabulary and the central ideas of the passage(s). The task ends with a writing assignment.

Complete the following performance task based upon selections from Unit 2. You will read three sources and answer questions. Finally, you will complete a longer writing task.

Source #1

Read the following excerpt from *Think: Why You Should Question Everything* by Guy Harrison from Chapter 7 of this unit.

> On one hand, it makes sense for us to see some patterns of things that
> aren't really there in order to be very good at seeing real ones that matter.
> On the other hand, we need to be aware of this phenomenon because it
> can lead to a confident belief in things that are not real or true. . . . Good
> skeptics understand how the brain often creates false patterns, so we
> know to be very cautious when considering claims of UFO sightings, for
> example, or anything else that is unusual. It only makes sense to be <u>skeptical</u>
> and ask for additional evidence when people claim to have seen or heard
> extraordinary things. Maybe they did, maybe they didn't. Given what we
> now know about the brain, however, are you going to believe someone who
> tells you she saw a flying saucer or Bigfoot last week? She doesn't have to be
> lying to be wrong. Anyone with perfect vision can see poorly.

1. Which of the following best states the central idea of the paragraph?
   A. A skill that helps us can also harm us.
   B. A confident belief is usually mistaken.
   C. Questioning what others tell us is wise.
   D. Our brains make patterns to help us survive.

2. **Part A:** What is the meaning of *skeptical* as it is used in this paragraph?
   A. convinced
   B. doubtful
   C. cheating
   D. curious

continued on next page

Practice Performance Task

The purpose of this section is to prepare students for the types of performance tasks they will be completing on standardized testing. The task requires students to synthesize knowledge gained and skills developed throughout the unit. If used as test prep, review with students the process of answering multiple-choice questions, including eliminating answers that are clearly incorrect.

This performance task could be used as an assessment over Unit 2, instead of the Unit 2 assessment on pages 460–468. It could be completed entirely during two class periods by having students complete questions 1–9 and the planning stage of the writing task during one class period and complete the comparison/contrast essay during the second class period. Another option is to assign the writing to be completed at home.

Answers to Practice Performance Task:

1. C. Choice A is too broad and the text does not support Choice B. Choice D may be true, but the author warns about "false patterns" that lead to false confidences. (DoK 2)

2. **Part A:** B. The author encourages doubt and to "ask for additional evidence." (DoK 1)

(continued)

ELL Support: Practice Performance Task Have students work in multilevel pairs or small groups to read and answer the questions. Then have students work in the same multilevel pairs or small groups to write a response to the performance task prompt on p. 229. Adjust the length of student responses as necessary. Instead of an essay, students can write a paragraph or complete a graphic organizer such as the <u>Compare and Contrast graphic organizer found in the ELL Teacher Resource (p. 53).</u> As necessary, demonstrate using the graphic organizer by comparing and contrasting dogs and cats. Provide the <u>Informational Writing Revision Checklist from the ELL Teacher Resource (p. 69)</u> for students to use to finalize their written response.

Assessment *(continued)*

Lesson Support

Answers to Practice Performance Task:

2. **Part B:** D. (DoK 2)

3. D. Students who choose this answer understand the relationship of the "false patterns" to false conclusions, such as "I just saw a flying saucer." (DoK 2)

4. **Part A:** A. Choice B is a supporting detail, not a central idea. Although the author cites social media in the first sentence, he does not blame all of fake news on it so Choice C is also incorrect. Choice D is also a supporting detail that explains the main idea. (DoK 2)

(continued)

Part B: Which phrase from the paragraph supports the answer in Part A?

A. *see some patterns of things*

B. *lead to a confident belief*

C. *understand how the brain creates*

D. *we know to be very cautious*

3. According to the paragraph, why might people claim to see a flying saucer?

A. They might be trying to deceive others.

B. They might have poor vision.

C. They might want to get attention.

D. They might be seeing false patterns.

Continue the performance task by reading a second source and answering questions.

Source #2

Read the following excerpt from "The Fact Checker's Guide for Detecting Fake News" by Glenn Kessler from Chapter 8 of this unit.

Anyone active on social media has probably done this at least once: shared something based on the headline without actually reading the link.

Let's face it, you've probably done this many times. According to a study released in June by computer scientists at Columbia University and the French National Institute, 59 percent of links shared on social media have never actually been clicked.

So the first thing you can do to combat the rise of "fake news" is to actually read articles before sharing them. And when you read them, pay attention to the following signs that the article may be fake. There are fake news stories generated by both left-leaning and right-leaning websites, and the same rules apply to both.

4. **Part A:** What is the central idea of this excerpt?

A. There are ways to fight the spread of fake news.

B. Fake news is spread by left- and right-leaning sources.

C. Social media are to blame for the spread of fake news.

D. Computer scientists are studying the spread of fake news.

Part B: Which sentence from the excerpt supports the answer to Part A?

A. *Anyone active on social media has probably done this at least once: shared something based on the headline without actually reading the link.*

B. *According to a study released in June by computer scientists at Columbia University and the French National Institute, 59 percent of links shared on social media have never actually been clicked.*

C. *So the first thing you can do to combat the rise of "fake news" is to actually read articles before sharing them.*

D. *And when you read them, pay attention to the following signs that the article may be fake.*

5. Which of these best describes the relationship between the first two paragraphs of the excerpt?

A. The first paragraph describes why a reader would share fake news; the second paragraph describes fake news.

B. The first paragraph makes an assumption about the reader's actions; the second paragraph links that action to larger social trends.

C. The first paragraph states that most people on social media share news stories; the second paragraph explains that nearly all those stories are fake.

D. The first paragraph explains how society has changed because of social media; the second paragraph describes ways to fight against that change.

6. Read this sentence from the first paragraph of the excerpt.

> Let's face it, you've probably done this many times.

What tone does the sentence convey?

A. annoyed

B. cheerful

C. friendly

D. pleading

Continue the performance task by reading a third source and answering questions.

Source #3

Read the following excerpt from *Debunk It!* by John Grant from Chapter 9 of this unit.

> There's a more fundamental problem with the "water's memory" claim.
>
> Any water we drink has had a long history—a history lasting billions of years.
>
> During that time it has been recycled in all sorts of ways, and has held all

continued on next page

Answers to Practice Performance Task:

4. **Part B:** C. This is one strategy to "combat the rise of 'fake news,'" according to the author. (DoK 2)

5. B. The phrase "has probably done this at least once" makes this assumption about readers; the second paragraph offers proof that the assumption is true by explaining a study done at two reputable institutions. (DoK 2)

6. C. The author conveys no sense of annoyance nor is he pleading. Choice B is too positive. The tone of this sentence is casual, like friendly conversation. (DoK 3)

(continued)

Assessment *(continued)*

Answers to Practice Performance Task:

7. A. The author chooses to end his debunking argument with a light, humorous observation. (DoK 2)

8. **Part A:** B. The comparison to the effect of "gazillions of poops," mocks, or laughs at, the idea that water retains the qualities of a single homeopathic molecule. (DoK 2)

(continued)

---

manner of other substances in solution, any one of which could have left an "imprint." Why should water retain the "memory" of a homeopathic molecule but not that of *everything else* with which it has been in contact—including all the gazillions of poops that have floated in it?

The notion of "water's memory" takes homeopathy over the conceptual border into the realm of outright woo—especially when we read of some homeopaths claiming they can email the "imprint" to their patients, who can supply their own water! Even if you look just at basic homeopathy, though, of the kind that Hahnemann invented, the dilutions mean that all you get when you buy a homeopathic medicine is very expensive water.

On the plus side, it's pretty hard to do yourself any damage with a homeopathic overdose.

7. The following sentence appears at the end of *Debunk It!*

On the plus side, it's pretty hard to do yourself any damage with a homeopathic overdose.

Why does the author most likely include this sentence at the end of the excerpt?

A. to leave the reader with a final, funny thought

B. to warn the reader not to take too much medicine

C. to convince the reader that homeopathy is not effective

D. to encourage the reader to distrust homeopathic medicine

8. **Part A:** What is the author's tone when writing about the idea that water has a memory for molecules it touched?

A. angry

B. mocking

C. cautious

D. reasonable

Part B: Which detail from the passage best supports the answer to Part A?

A. *There's a more fundamental problem with the "water's memory" claim.*

B. *Why should water retain the "memory" of a homeopathic molecule but not . . . all the gazillions of poops that have floated in it?*

C. *The notion of "water's memory" takes homeopathy over the conceptual border into the realm of outright woo. . . .*

D. *. . . the dilutions mean that all you get when you buy a homeopathic medicine is very expensive water.*

9. What is the main claim in this excerpt?

A. People who sell homeopathic remedies are deliberately misleading others.

B. Water has been recycled many times over billions of years.

C. The idea that water remembers only certain molecules makes no sense.

D. Hahnemann's homeopathic medicines worked better than today's do.

Your Assignment

WRITING PROMPT

You have just read excerpts from three texts in Unit 2. Choose two of those passages. Find the full version of each text in its chapter. Using those full versions, write an explanatory essay comparing and contrasting the authors' purposes for writing their texts and how they addressed the Essential Question "Can you trust what you see, hear, and read?" Explain how the organization of information in each text helps the authors achieve their purposes. Cite textual evidence from each text to support your analysis.

Read the prompt carefully. Underline words that indicate ideas that should be included in your essay. Create a graphic organizer similar to the following to help you plan your ideas.

Passage One	Passage Two
Author's purpose:	Author's purpose:
Evidence of author's purpose:	Evidence of author's purpose:
Description of organization:	Description of organization:

continued on next page

Answers to Practice Performance Task:

8. **Part B**: B. (DoK 2)

9. C. The word *deliberately* makes choice A incorrect; the author does not accuse anyone of this. Choice B may be true, but it is not the main claim in the text. Choice D is the opposite of what the author claims because he debunks Hahnemann's theories. (DoK 2)

Your Assignment

Remind students that Venn diagrams are also useful graphic organizers to plan comparison/contrast essays.

 Gr7U2PerformanceTask.pptx

Assessment *(continued)*

Essential Question Connection: Revisit the Essential Question: *Can you trust what you see, hear, and read?* You may want to have students write a response essay to this question based on the selections they've read and the discussions they've had throughout the unit. Ask students to include whether their thoughts surrounding this question have changed, and if so, how have they changed and why. Encourage them to refer to the selections and their impact in helping them form their answer to the questions.

Passage One	Passage Two
Evidence of organization:	Evidence of organization:

Your Assignment (continued)

Develop an outline to organize your ideas before you begin writing. Study the explanation below to understand how your writing will be evaluated.

Your compare and contrast essay will be scored using the following criteria:

Reading Comprehension:
- How well did you understand the texts?
- Does your writing reflect your understanding of the sources?

Writing Expression:
- Does your writing address the requirements of the prompt?
- Does your essay compare and contrast each author's purpose for writing?
- Does your essay compare and contrast how the organization of each passage supports that purpose?
- Does your essay include references or quotations from both sources?
- Is your essay well organized with ideas that fit together logically?
- Does the writing style contain precise, accurate language and content appropriate to the purpose, task, and audience?

Writing Conventions:
- Does your writing follow the rules of standard English with few errors in grammar, usage, and spelling?
- When you are done writing, evaluate your essay using the list above. Revise your writing as needed.

Unit 3

Essential Question
How is technology shaping society?

Not a day goes by that you do not use some type of technology. If you are reading these words in a book, you can thank the fifteenth-century invention of the printing press. If you used a subway, bus, car, or even bicycle to get to school, you can thank not just the ancient inventor of the wheel and axle but also all of the men and women who built on that simple machine. When you eat today, that food almost certainly originated in farms and factories fed by fertilizers and fossil fuels, both of which are produced by technology.

It's easy to describe relationships between individual people and technology. Less obvious, though, is how such technologies shape entire societies. The printing press, for example, led to newspapers and books. This, in turn, led to large populations sharing a common language and set of experiences. According to historians, such sharing helped produce nations—entire societies of people calling themselves German or English or French, for example. The printing press literally helped produce a type of society that hadn't existed before.

In this unit, you will explore the ways in which technology shapes modern society. You will read nonfiction texts about how digital communication affects young people and how the rise of robots influences the job market. You will read a poem on how industrial technology bent the physical world to human whims and a story of how digital technology could subject humans to the power of corporations. Finally, you will write a story regarding an interaction between a character, a technology, and the society that produced both.

> **GOALS**
> - To analyze the interactions of people, ideas, and events
> - To examine the effect of repetition on meaning in a poem
> - To compare differing presentations of a topic
> - To determine the theme of a poem
> - To analyze competing interpretations of evidence
> - To write a fictional story regarding technology and society

---

ELL Support: Preview Unit 3 Essential Question See the *Connections* ELL Teacher Resource (p. 33) for ideas for introducing the unit essential question.

Unit 3

Essential Question: How is technology shaping society?

Introduction

Goals: Have students read through the goals and mark any words that are unfamiliar. Discuss the meanings of any academic vocabulary within the goals that students marked as unfamiliar. Consider posting the Unit Goals.

Introduction Suggestions

1. Play clips from films centering on technology and society:

   - *Avatar* (2009) Set on the planet Pandora, *Avatar* pits the Na'vi inhabitants against Earth invaders intent on stealing the planet's resources.

   - *A.I.* (2001) This film raises the question of whether humans might somehow become less human than androids.

   - Other suggestions include *WALL-E* (2008), *Jurassic Park* (1993), *Minority Report* (2002), *Interstellar* (2014), *The Social Network* (2010).

2. As a class, develop a list of groundbreaking technologies that transformed society. Have students link items by category, including <u>Communications</u> (printing press, telegraph, telephone, cell phones, Internet, etc.) and <u>Transportation</u> (steam engine, locomotive, internal combustion engine, automobile, airplane, jet engine, etc.).

3. Have students write a response to one of the following quotations:

   - "Humanity is acquiring all the right technology for all the wrong reasons." —R. Buckminster Fuller, American architect and inventor

   - "The real danger is not that computers will begin to think like men, but that men will begin to think like computers." —Sydney Harris, journalist and author

   - "Any sufficiently advanced technology is equivalent to magic." —Arthur C. Clarke, British writer and inventor

 Gr7Unit3Opener.pptx

Chapter 11

Analyzing Interactions of People, Ideas, and Events

Smarter Than You Think
by Clive Thompson

Introduction

Chapter Goals: Have students read through the goals and mark any words that are unfamiliar. Discuss the meanings of any academic vocabulary within the goals that students marked as unfamiliar. Consider posting the Chapter Goals.

Preview Academic Vocabulary: Read and discuss the meanings of the academic vocabulary.

> **point of view:** *opinion or perspective on a topic.* The author shared his point of view on learning techniques, giving his readers a clear picture of his opinion on the matter.

> **purpose:** *goal or reason for writing.* The author's purpose was to convince his readers that building wind turbines would be beneficial for the community.

 **Gr7Ch11Vocabulary.pptx**

Preview Concepts: Introduce the questions on page 232 and note their purpose: to elicit students' ideas about how their classroom works. As they answer the questions, encourage them to consider the use of technology, noting its current role in the classroom, as well as how it might be used in the future to improve learning.

Chapter 11

Analyzing Interactions of People, Ideas, and Events

Preview Concepts

In this chapter, you will be reading a passage about the idea of "the classroom"—specifically, how classrooms are organized, and how well that organization helps them achieve their purposes.

1. What, in your opinion, is the main purpose of your classroom?

2. Describe one thing your classroom does right in achieving that purpose.

3. Describe one thing your classroom could do better in achieving that purpose. Be fair and constructive in your response. Then share your answers with a partner.

> **CHAPTER GOALS**
>
> In this chapter you will
> - analyze the interactions between individuals, events, and ideas.
> - analyze how text structure helps readers understand an idea.
> - determine an author's purpose in writing a text.
> - practice using dashes in sentences.
>
> **PREVIEW ACADEMIC VOCABULARY**
>
> point of view
>
> purpose

ELL Support: Academic Vocabulary See Teaching Vocabulary in the ELL Teacher Resource (p. 18) for ideas to use for teaching vocabulary throughout *Connections*.

ELL Support: Preview Concepts Be sure students understand that *purpose* means "the reason for doing something," *achieve* means "to gain or do well," and *constructive* means "helpful." As a class, discuss possible purposes for the classroom. List ideas on the board. Then have students work in multilevel pairs or groups and use the following sentence frames to answer the questions:

- The main purpose of our classroom is to . . . .
- One thing our classroom does to achieve this purpose is . . . .
- One thing our classroom must do better to achieve this purpose is . . . .

Making Connections

Read the following quotations about education. You'll respond to one of them.

> Do not train a child to learn by force or harshness; but direct them to it by what amuses their minds, so that you may be better able to discover with accuracy the peculiar bent of the genius of each.
>
> — Plato (428–438 B.C.E.), Greek philosopher

> Plants are shaped by cultivation and men by education. . . . We are born weak, we need strength; we are born totally unprovided, we need aid; we are born stupid, we need judgment. Everything we do not have at our birth and which we need when we are grown is given us by education.
>
> — Jean Jacques Rousseau (1712–1778), French philosopher

> Let us think of education as the means of developing our greatest abilities, because in each of us there is a private hope and dream which, fulfilled, can be translated into benefit for everyone and greater strength for our nation.
>
> — John F. Kennedy (1917–1963), thirty-fifth President of the United States

Of the quotations above, which one made the strongest impression on you? Explain why it made the strongest impression.

> **MAKING CONNECTIONS**
>
> As you read the passage in this chapter, you'll analyze how interactions between people, events, and ideas over the last 30 years have led to a quiet revolution in how math is taught in a fifth-grade classroom.

Sample Answers to Questions on page 232:

1. The main purpose of my classroom is to provide a space that allows my fellow classmates and me to learn.

2. I think that sitting at a larger desk with other students helps me learn, because it allows me to learn from my fellow students.

3. I think that if we had access to laptops in class that my classmates and I could learn better. Sometimes it is hard for me to take notes as quickly as I need to, and a laptop would allow me to take notes faster and keep better track of them.

Making Connections: Preview the quotations on page 233, noting that they focus on the general concept of education's role in society. Encourage students to respond to one of the quotations using their personal experience and opinions to elaborate on its meaning. Have volunteers share their responses with the class, making sure students hear at least one response to each quotation.

Sample Response to Question, page 233:

Plato's quote made the strongest impression on me. I think that everyone learns differently—at different paces and in different ways. Different people are interested in different subjects. I think schools that provide rigid structures for learning do not support students in the way that Plato mentions.

ELL Support: Make Connections Have students work in multilevel pairs or groups (or work together as a class) to read and paraphrase each quotation on p. 233. Once students understand the content of each quote, have them draw sketches so they will remember the content. Rephrase the question as *Which quote do you like best? Why?* Provide the following sentence frames for students to use as they respond to the question in their multilevel pairs or groups:

- The quote that made the strongest impression on me is the one by . . . . This quote impressed me because . . . .

  OR

- The quote I like best is the one by . . . . I like this one best because . . . .

Chapter 11 (continued)

First Read: Analyzing Interactions of People, Ideas, and Events

Before Reading: Read the introductory paragraph on page 234 to establish background and context. Ask students to define the term *digital technology*. Activate background knowledge by asking students to consider types of digital technology used in their classrooms, past or present.

Read the objective, and then have students read the passage on their own.

Preview Vocabulary: Preview unfamiliar vocabulary to aid comprehension or ask students to circle unfamiliar words as they complete the first read of a text. After the first read, guide students to determine the words' meanings using the context. Encourage students to support their responses with evidence. Have students confirm their initial definitions with a dictionary. Words that students might find difficult include:

festooned: *decorated.* Anna walked into the party, fascinated by the multicolor balloons and ribbons that <u>festooned</u> the walls and ceilings.

dynamics: *how people or things behave and react to each other in a situation.* Amalia hated going to science class because she felt that the <u>dynamics</u> in the classroom did not help her learn.

subsidize: *support financially.* The state's government did not <u>subsidize</u> music classes in its elementary schools.

aggressive: *marked by forceful energy and action.* Liliana was determined to find the perfect summer program and spent all of her free time doing an <u>aggressive</u> search on the Internet.

augmented: *add on to; supplement.* Carmen was falling behind in physics class, so her parents <u>augmented</u> her studies by hiring a private tutor.

 Gr7Ch11Vocabulary.pptx

First Read: Analyzing Interactions of People, Ideas, and Events

The author Clive Thompson studies how digital technology affects modern society. The following excerpt is from his book *Smarter Than You Think*, which was published in 2013. Because digital technology changes so quickly, some of the ideas that were new then might seem normal to you now.

Objective: As you read, look for and circle the names of people when they first appear. Record any questions you have in the My Thoughts column.

—— First Read
---- Second Read
—— Third Read

excerpt
Smarter Than You Think
by Clive Thompson

My Thoughts

1   (Matthew) shouldn't be doing work remotely this advanced. He's ten years old, and this is only the fifth grade. Matthew is a student at Santa Rita Elementary, a public school in Los Altos, California, where his sun-drenched classroom is festooned with

5   a giant paper X-wing fighter, student paintings of trees, and racks of kids' books. Normally grade five math is simpler fare— basic fractions, decimals, and percentages. You don't reach **inverse trig** until high school.

But Matthew's class isn't typical. For the last year, they've

10   been using the Khan Academy, a free online site filled with thousands of instructional videos that cover subjects in math, science, and economics. The videos are lo-fi, even crude: about five to fifteen minutes long, they consist of a voice-over by Khan describing a mathematical concept or explaining how

15   to solve a problem while hand-scribbled formulas appear on-screen. The site also includes software that generates practice problems, then rewards hard work with badges—for answering a "streak" of questions right, say.

---
inverse trig: a type of math that studies angle measures in right triangles

Remediation: First Read The concepts and vocabulary in this passage may be challenging for struggling students. Form groups of four and instruct students to take turns reading the passage aloud in sections as follows: paragraphs 1–3, paragraphs 4–5, paragraphs 6–8, paragraphs 9–11. Have them stop after each section to summarize main ideas, work through confusing concepts, and decipher unfamiliar words.

ELL Support: First Read Have students read the text in multilevel pairs or small groups, pausing at the end of each paragraph to summarize ideas on a <u>Main Ideas and Supporting Details graphic organizer from the ELL Teacher Resource (p. 51)</u>. Also, encourage students to take notes and draw sketches in the margins around the article to help them understand the key idea of each paragraph. When students finish reading, have them sketch an image of the classroom described in the article *(students each working on a computer or tablet; teacher circulating and helping)*.

. . .

20   How did these elementary school kids zoom ahead to high-school-level material?

    In part because the site lets them learn at their own pace—allowing their teacher, (Kami Thordarson) to offer much more customized instruction. The problem with traditional classroom

25 dynamics, Thordarson tells me, is that they don't easily account for the way kids learn at different rates. When she stands up at the chalkboard lecturing on a subject, there's a predictable pattern that takes hold: one quarter of the kids quickly fall behind, so they tune out. Another quarter already know the

30 material, so they tune out. At best, "you're teaching to this middle group of students," Thordarson sighs.

What works better? Personalized, one-on-one tutoring. Back in 1984, the educational scholar Benjamin Bloom compared students taught in regular classrooms—one

35 teacher lecturing to the assembled class—to students who got months of one-on-one attention or instruction in small groups. These tutored students did far better; two **standard deviations** better, in fact. To get a sense of how much of an improvement that is, think of it this way: If you took a

40 regular-classroom kid who was performing in the middle of the pack and gave her one-on-one instruction for a few months, she'd leap to the **ninety-eighth percentile**. This became known as the "Two Sigma" phenomenon, and in the decades since, public-school teachers have struggled to give

45 students more one-on-one time. This isn't easy, given that the average class in the United States has roughly twenty-five children. (Worse, after years of slightly falling, that number is

standard deviations: a number that expresses how much a subgroup differs from the average found in a large group
ninety-eighth percentile: doing better than ninety-eight percent of her peers

My Thoughts

Main idea: Khan
Academy videos help
fifth graders do
advanced math.

After Reading: Use the following questions to check comprehension.

Text-Based Discussion Questions

1. Based on the context, what does Kami Thordarson mean by the phrase "traditional classroom dynamics"? Why does she believe traditional methods are problematic? *"Traditional classroom dynamics" include the teacher standing in front of a class to give a lecture (lines 24–27). These methods are problematic because they don't account for the fact that students learn at different rates (line 25–26). So about half the class "tunes out," either because they are confused or because they already know the material (lines 28–29).*

2. According to the article, what teaching method works best, and why? Why don't schools use this method? *Line 32 states that it is better to use "personalized, one-on-one tutoring." This method is more effective because it tailors the teaching to what each individual student needs in order to advance. Schools don't use this method because classes are too big and teachers don't have enough time to spend on individual tutoring (lines 44–50).*

 Gr7Ch11Read1.pptx

ELL Support: First Read Show students a Khan Academy video on a math concept that they have studied before. Before students watch, explain that this is the kind of video the students in the article are watching in their math class. Ask students to answer the following questions using a think, pair, share strategy:

- Did you like the video? Why or why not?
- Have you used Khan Academy (or other math) videos before?
- Do you like them? Why or why not?
- Are they helpful? Why or why not?
- Would you like a math class with all videos? Why or why not?

Chapter 11 (continued)

Lesson Support

About the Author: Clive Thompson is a Canadian journalist best known for his writing about technology and its impact on society. Thompson was born in 1968 in Toronto, Canada. As a child, Thompson became interested in computers and gaming systems. However, his parents did not want to buy a computer for the family out of fear that it would take up all of young Thompson's time. Instead, Thompson began reading about computer programming and using computers at the library.

Thompson decided that he wanted to be a journalist and studied English at the University of Toronto. After graduating in the early 1990s, Thompson began working as a freelance writer for various publications. At this time, the Internet was just beginning to become popular. Thompson moved to New York and began to write articles about the Internet's effects on politics, shopping, and more.

Thompson continues to write pieces about technology and its effect on society. He has written articles for publications such as *The New York Times Magazine*, *Smithsonian*, and *Wired*.

Tech-Connect Suggestion: Using polleverywhere.com, ask students to cast their vote for Most Revolutionary Technology—the technology that has most transformed society. Use the real-time chart feature to display the results.

---

now rising again, due to budget cuts.) Until the government decides it's willing to subsidize smaller classes, how can

50 teachers get more personal time?

One way is by using new-media tools to **invert** the logic of instruction. Instead of delivering all her math lessons to the entire class, Thordarson has them watch Khan videos and work on the online problems. This way, the students who quickly "get

55 it" can blast ahead—and Thordarson can focus more of her class time on helping the students who need coaching. Other teachers are even more aggressive about inverting their classes: They assign videos to be watched at home, then have the students do the homework in class, flipping their instruction inside out.

60 This makes curious psychological sense. A video can often be a better way to deliver a lecture-style lesson, because students can pause and rewind when they get confused—impossible with a live classroom lesson. In contrast, homework is better done in a classroom, because that's when you're likely to need to ask the

65 teacher for extra help. (Or to ask another student: Thordarson and her colleagues noticed students helping one another, sharing what they'd learned, and tutoring each other.)

"Kids get to work in their place where they're most comfortable," says Thordarson as we wander around her class.

70 "They're allowed to jump ahead. It gives kids who are above grade level a chance to just soar! And for kids who struggle, it gives them a chance to work through some of those issues without everybody watching."

Still, as Thordarson quickly points out, the Khan Academy

75 isn't enough on its own. You can't just plunk kids in front of laptops and say, "Go. The point isn't to replace teachers.

---

invert: turn upside-down

236   Chapter 11 • Unit 3   ©Perfection Learning® • No Reproduction Permitted

---

My Thoughts

Main idea: Students who get personalized, one-on-one instruction do much better than those taught in a large group.

Main idea: Using teaching videos frees up class time for individual homework help for students and allows advanced students to learn at their own pace.

It's to help them reshape their classes in new ways—and spend more time directly guiding students. You can't even

80   say it makes the teacher's job easier. If anything, it has made Thordarson's job more challenging; there's more noise, more kids talking, and she's constantly darting around the room to help out. One U.S. federal study found that students learned best in classrooms with precisely this sort of "blended"

85   learning—traditional teachers augmented with online instruction. But the increase in learning wasn't because of any magic in the medium. It's just that online tools helped students and teachers spend more time on the material.

Judging by Thordarson's success, though, it works. She's seen particularly strong improvements at the low end: Only three

90   percent of her students were classified as average or lower in end-of-year tests, down from thirteen percent at midyear—and other math teachers at Santa Rita have seen similar results. The kids who need help have been getting more of it; the kids who want to push ahead are pushing ridiculously far.

95   "It's like having thirty math tutors in my room," Thordarson says.

FIRST RESPONSE: KEY IDEAS AND DETAILS

Based on your first reading of this text, what idea is leading to the changes in classrooms such as Kami Thordarson's? Record your first response in your journal.

Focus on Analyzing Interactions of People, Ideas, and Events

The excerpt from *Smarter Than You Think* is about change—specifically, a change in how teachers and students in an elementary classroom use their time. This change arose through an interaction of people, ideas, and events. Let's look at these interactions more closely.

My Thoughts

Main Idea: Online tools free Thordarson to spend more time on the material, resulting in fewer students earning average or low scores on tests.

TECH-CONNECT

Post your First Response answer on your class webpage. Compare your answers to those posted by other students.

CONNECT TO ESSENTIAL QUESTION

How has a recent technology shaped your math classroom? (Or has one?)

Focus on Analyzing Interactions of People, Ideas, and Events:

Introduce the questions on pages 238–239 and note their purpose: to help students review how the article explains the factors that led to positive change in Thordarson's classroom. Remind students to refer to any text annotations as they answer the questions independently.

Chapter 11 (continued)

Lesson Support

Answers to Questions:

1. Matthew, a student; Kami Thordarson, a math teacher; Benjamin Bloom, an educational scholar

2. Thordarson's classroom time is used for one-on-one instruction with the students who need extra help. Less time is spent on general instruction and demonstration of problem solving. Instead, students watch online videos that offer instruction and practice. This way students can learn at their own pace.

3. Personalized, one-on-one tutoring works better than whole-class instruction.

4. Benjamin Bloom, an educational scholar, compared students who were taught by listening to a teacher lecture to a class and those who received one-on-one tutoring. The latter students improved so dramatically that schools began trying to provide students with more one-on-one time with teachers and tutors.

(continued)

1. Who are the people named in the passage? What are their roles or jobs?

2. How is classroom time used in Kami Thordarson's math classroom? According to the passage, how does that use of time differ from time use in most classrooms?

3. The way time is used in Kami Thordarson's classroom is partly based on an idea. What is that idea?

4. What event in the 1980s made that idea well known? Who was involved in that event?

5. What technology has been important in changing Thordarson's classroom? How has that technology interacted with the idea you discussed in the previous question?

CONNECT TO ESSENTIAL QUESTION

During your years of schooling, what new technology has come into your classroom? Has it been useful, or does it have more drawbacks than benefits?

Speak and Listen Share your answers with a partner. Did you both identify the same idea behind the use of time in Thordarson's classroom? Do you have a similar description of the event in the 1980s that made the idea well known? Use the terms *people*, *ideas*, and *events* in your discussion.

Write Using the answers to your questions and your partner discussion, write a paragraph explaining how Benjamin Bloom's actions in 1984 led to an idea that has influenced the lives of Kami Thordarson and her students. Use the terms *idea* and *event* at least once in your response.

Second Read: Analyzing Text Structure

The central idea of the excerpt is this: Using technology to increase one-on-one teaching leads to better student performance. The author develops this central idea in sections, with each section doing a specific job. What are these sections?

- First section: Paragraphs 1–3 (lines 1–20)
- Second section: Paragraphs 4–5 (lines 21–49)
- Third section: Paragraphs 6–8 (lines 50–72)
- Fourth section: Paragraphs 9–11 (lines 73–95)

How does each section help develop the central idea so the reader understands it? To determine this, identify the main idea of each section.

Objective: Draw lines dividing the sections from each other. Then read the passage aloud with a partner, taking turns reading every other section. When you get to the end of each section, discuss with your partner what you think the main idea of the section is. Write the main idea of the section in the "My Thoughts" column.

5. Video technology has led to several improvements. A recorded lecture is often better than a live lecture because students can pause and rewind to reinforce new concepts. Thordarson has been freed up to spend more one-on-one time with the low-performing students who need help to improve their performance. And being able to work on homework in class allows students to help each other—and even jump ahead.

Speak and Listen: As students share their answers with a partner, encourage them to discuss their personal responses to the article. How do the ideas in the passage relate to the ideas discussed about how their classroom is organized? Do they think Bloom's ideas are relevant? Would they rather watch lectures on video and use class time for homework and personal tutoring?

Write: As students write their paragraphs, suggest that they address the following question: *Which factors—people, ideas, and/or events—make implementing Bloom's ideas possible, difficult, or impossible?*

Second Read: Analyzing Text Structure

Before Reading: Remind students that during a Second Read, they are analyzing how an author communicates his or her main ideas by asking the question *How?* In this case, students are analyzing how the structure of the text helps the author develop his central idea.

Read aloud the introductory section. Point out that, even though the text does not have subheads to introduce each of the four sections, the text has sections nonetheless.

Make sure students understand the procedure for the Second Read described on page 239. As they discuss the main idea of each section, encourage them to note the methods the author uses to convey this idea.

 Gr7Ch11Read2.pptx

Chapter 11 (continued)

Lesson Support

After Reading: Use the following questions to check comprehension.

Text-Based Discussion Questions

1. In lines 51–59, what does it mean to "invert the logic of instruction"? *This means switching up the traditional way of doing things. Instead of delivering a lecture, the teacher assigns students to watch a video at home. Class time is used for "homework" so that the teacher can monitor individual understanding.*

2. What did a federal study say about why using technology helped improve students' learning? *The study showed that having students learn from videos at home gave teachers more class time to use for individual help. As a result teachers and students could spend more time on the material (lines 82–87).*

Focus on Analyzing Text Structure: Remind students that good nonfiction writers organize information according to what will best convey their ideas. After considering WHAT they want to say, they decide HOW they will say it, choosing the most appropriate structures. Although a nonfiction text often contains an overall structure, its paragraphs and sentences may feature other structures, depending on the purpose of each part. Note that analyzing text structure can help students understand how a part—a sentence, a paragraph, or a section—contributes to the development of an author's ideas. If necessary, review common text structures, including cause and effect, compare and contrast, chronology, description, problem/solution, categorization, and question and answer.

Introduce the chart on page 240 and point out the headings. Review the entries for the first row, noting the main idea and purpose. Then ask students how this section is structured. Make sure students understand that the author draws in the reader and introduces the topic by using description. Have students complete the rest of the chart independently.

Answers to Chart:

See answers on Student Book insert page to the right.

Focus on Analyzing Text Structure

Any text is made of parts: sentences, paragraphs, sections, and so on. Skilled authors know how to make those parts work together to develop a central idea. Clive Thompson is a skilled author. Each section of this excerpt has a purpose.

As sections develop a central idea, they also help you, the reader. When thinking about the purpose of a section, ask yourself: How does this section help me? What is it trying to do for me? For example, does the section:

- raise the reader's interest?
- clearly introduce an idea for the reader?
- help the reader understand through details or examples?
- make a claim about why the idea and its effects are important?

Through structure, a skilled author both develops an idea *and* guides the reader through it.

Finish the chart below. Part of the chart has already been completed for you.

- Under "Main Idea of Section," state what the section is about.
- Under "Possible Purpose(s) of Section," make a claim about the purpose of the section for readers. Use words such as "inform," "explain," "point out," and so on.

Major Section	Main Idea of Section	Possible Purpose(s) of Section
Paragraphs 1–3 (lines 1–21)	A classroom is using technology to help fifth-grade students learn how to do tenth-grade math.	to inform readers of something incredible and get them wondering how it happened
Paragraphs 4–5 (lines 22–50)	Classroom time is organized to provide one-on-one tutoring, which research shows gets better results.	to explain the problems of a traditional classroom and how personalized one-on-one instruction is a good solution
Paragraphs 6–8 (lines 51–73)	Video teaching outside the classroom is beneficial for both advanced and struggling students.	to offer reasons why using teaching videos is a better way to teach all students
Paragraphs 9–11 (lines 74–96)	Technology doesn't make the teacher irrelevant. "Blended" classrooms are successful because teachers have more time to spend on the material.	to clarify the role of the teacher in a "blended" classroom

©Perfection Learning® • No Reproduction Permitted

ELL Support: Second Read Model rereading the first and second section of the article and identifying the main idea and purpose of the sections. Then model completing the first two rows of the chart. Then have students work in multilevel pairs or small groups to reread the article. Remind students that they can use their Main Idea and Details graphic organizers (p. 51) they completed during the first read. They can review the main idea of each paragraph, put these main ideas together, and determine the central idea of each section. Be sure students understand that they can use the information above the chart to complete the Purpose row. For example, the purpose of the section can be one of the following: to raise/get the reader's interest, to introduce an idea, to help the reader understand through details and examples, to make a claim or give an opinion about an idea.

Third Read Before students reread the article and identify the point of view and purpose, remind students that *point of view* means "the

Connections • © Perfection Learning®

Speak and Listen Share your answers from the chart in a class discussion. Use hand signals to indicate when you want to talk.

- Thumbs up means you want to share something new.
- A peace sign means you have something to add to the last person's statement.

Finish by discussing these questions:
- Why do you think Clive Thompson used eleven paragraphs to develop his central idea?
- Could he have just stated it, given several sentences of evidence, and left it at that?
- What are the pros and cons of both approaches?

Write Although the activity divided the passage into four sections, it's also true that each paragraph plays a unique role in developing the central idea. In your response journal, write the central idea. Then write eleven bullet points stating the purpose of each paragraph. Share your answers with a partner.

Third Read: Analyzing Point of View and Purpose

In nonfiction, an author's point of view is the attitude or opinion the author has toward the topic he or she is writing about. An author's purpose is the reason the author is writing a text—what the author hopes the text will accomplish.

Objective: Read the text a third time. Draw boxes around at least five words or phrases that suggest the author's point of view toward the topic.

Focus on Analyzing Point of View and Purpose

An author's point of view and purpose are different, but related. For example, an author with negative feelings about a topic writes to get readers to share those feelings. In other words, one of the author's purposes is to get readers to develop negative feelings too.

The relationship between point of view and purpose is most obvious in argumentative texts. Such texts are written with strong points of view that authors hope readers will accept.

continued on next page

Speak and Listen: Encourage students to refer to specific lines of text during the discussion, paying attention to how the author links different ideas. Ask which sections were particularly interesting and have students analyze why these parts stood out. Encourage students to look for text structures, including posing questions, linking causes and effects, etc., and note whether these helped to clarify ideas.

Write: Remind students to refer to their completed charts and any text markings as they write their analysis.

Third Read: Analyzing Point of View and Purpose

Before Reading: Have students pair up to discuss the introduction and objective.

Make sure students understand the purpose of the Third Read. Then, remind students of the different purposes for writing, including persuading, entertaining, or informing.

Ask students whether one purpose tends to express a point of view more clearly than others. Most students will probably say that persuasive texts express their points of view most openly. Suggest that an author's point of view is sometimes clear, but other times a point of view must be inferred.

After Reading: Use the following questions to check comprehension.

Text-Based Discussion Questions

1. What types of evidence does the author present to support the idea that "blended" learning (lines 82–84) works? Give examples to support your response. *The author presents several types of evidence, including anecdotes (lines 1–18); quotes from Thordarson (lines 30–31, 68–69, 95); Bloom's expert opinion (lines 32–36); research data (lines 37–42, 82–84, 89–92); and examples from the classroom throughout the article.*

2. What do you think Thordarson means in line 95 when she says, "It's like having thirty math tutors in my room"? Explain your response. *When she cites the number 30, she probably is referring to her average class size. She is saying that every student acts like a tutor to the other members in the class because everyone has more class time to work together on practice problems.*

opinion, thoughts, and feelings of an author about a topic," and *purpose* means "the reason the author is writing." Reread the first paragraph and use a think aloud to model identifying the point of view and purpose. Say: *In the first paragraph, I can tell the author's point of view on this new math class is positive. I can tell this because in the last sentence he gives his opinion. This opinion shows that he is impressed by the math class. He can't believe that ten-year-olds are doing high school math. The purpose of this paragraph is to get the readers interested and impressed by this math class too.* Have students work in multilevel pairs or small groups to identify point of view and purpose throughout the article. Provide the following sentence frames for students to use to respond to the questions in discussion and in writing:

- Thompson's point of view on . . . is . . . . I know because . . . .
- Thompson wants . . . to happen in the real world. I know because . . . .

Lesson Support

Focus on Analyzing Point of View and Purpose: Tell students to refer to ideas they marked in the text during this read as they answer the questions on page 242. Then have students share their answers with the class. Ask volunteers to play "devil's advocate" by adopting a point of view that is different from Thompson's. Can they poke holes in his opinion? Broaden the discussion by asking students:

- Do you think the methods applied in Thordarson's classroom should be adopted more broadly across the country?

- Is there enough evidence about the success of these methods?

- What obstacles might arise to the implementation of "blended" learning?

Answers to Questions:

1. Thompson views using videos in math classrooms as beneficial to the students' educations. Videos allow students who may struggle with traditional lectures the opportunity to rewind and review tough concepts—giving them a better opportunity to succeed. These videos also allow advanced students to continue to learn at their own pace and push ahead if they want.

2. Thompson's purpose is to educate his readers about the benefits of one-on-one instructions in classrooms and to explain how video lectures are one way to make this possible. Thompson might want more classrooms to adopt the style of education being used in Thordarson's class.

 Gr7Ch11Read3.pptx

---

Explanatory texts present information on a topic without necessarily taking a strong position. However, explanatory texts are also written with a definite point of view and purpose. The excerpt from *Smarter Than You Think* is such an explanatory text. There's a definite a point of view and purpose, but it's not as clearly or powerfully stated as an argumentative text would be.

1. In the space below, describe Clive Thompson's point of view on using videos in math classrooms. Use the words and phrases you boxed as evidence to support your answer.

2. In the space below, describe Thompson's purpose in writing the text. Say more than just "to explain" or "to convince." Describe what you think Thompson might want to happen in the real world because of his writing.

Language: Using Dashes

Clive Thompson uses dashes skillfully and in several ways.

- To introduce a list:

> Normally grade five math is simpler fare—basic fractions, decimals, and percentages.

- To set off a parenthetical element:

> Back in 1984, the educational scholar Benjamin Bloom compared students taught in regular classrooms—one teacher lecturing to the assembled class—to students who got months of one-on-one attention or instruction in small groups.

- To emphasize set-off text:

> A video can often be a better way to deliver a lecture-style lesson, because students can pause and rewind when they get confused—impossible with a live classroom lesson.

- To indicate a change in thought:

> This way, the students who quickly "get it" can blast ahead—and Thordarson can focus more of her class time on helping the students who need coaching.

Read the following sentences. Then rewrite each so it uses at least one dash.

1. If you need help with math, and many students do, you can visit online tutors.

2. Students can work with online tutors on many platforms, such as desktop computers, laptops, and phones.

Language: Using Dashes: Use the chart under the ELL activity on this page to help students understand when to use a hyphen, an en dash, and an em dash.

Answers to Questions:

1. If you need help with math—and many students do—you can visit online tutors.

2. Students can work with online tutors on many platforms—desktop computers, laptops, and phones.

(continued)

 Gr7Ch11Language.pptx

ELL Support: Language Review the examples of using dashes on p. 243. Make sure students understand that the dash in question is an *em* dash, which is not the same as a hyphen or an *en* dash. Point out the difference between these marks using this chart.

Punctuation	Use	Example
hyphen -	in phone numbers	555-123-4567
en dash –	to show a range of numbers or dates	1998–2001
em dash —	to set off or point out extra information, to indicate a change in thought	She rose from her chair—without excusing herself—and left the dinner table.

Lesson Support

3. You can work with tutors at most times of day—giving you more flexibility.

4. Some of the best universities host MOOCs—Massive Open Online Courses—which let you watch college-level math lectures.

5. You get to watch the world's best teachers teaching some of the world's trickiest math—for free!

Assessment

Project-Based Assessments

Letter to the Principal: Encourage students to think about their audience as they write their letters. Challenge them to think about how writing for their principal changes their word choice and content. If students have trouble with this, have them write their letter for their friends first and then edit it for their principal.

Encourage students to show their math teachers the article and ask their opinions about the methods used in Thordarson's classroom. They may wish to include this information in their letters.

---

3. You can work with tutors at most times of day. This is giving you more flexibility.

4. Some of the best universities host MOOCs, which is short for Massive Open Online Courses, and which let you watch college-level math lectures.

5. You get to watch the world's best teachers teaching some of the world's trickiest math, and you get to do so for free!

Project-Based Assessments

Letter to the Principal

Imagine your school is thinking about changing your math class to be exactly like Kami Thordarson's. It would rely heavily on videos, working with your peers, and one-on-one tutoring. Do you like that idea? Or do you want your math class to remain as it is?

For this project, you will write a letter to your principal that politely expresses your opinion about the possible change to your math class. Fairly and accurately describe how your math class currently runs. Then explain if and how it should change. Provide at least two reasons to support your explanation.

ELL Support: Project-Based Assessments—Letter to the Principal Have students work in multilevel pairs or groups to write a letter. Provide the following letter and sentence frames or use the Letter Format Template in the ELL Teacher Resource (p. 55). When students complete their letter, provide the revising and editing checklists, so they can polish their writing before delivering their letter to the principal.

Date

Dear Principal,

We just read an article about . . . by Clive Thompson.

Mr. Thompson shows that . . . .

I think we should . . . . We should do this because . . . .

Sincerely,

Write a formal letter, not an email. Use business letter format in a block style and include the following: date, recipient's address, salutation, body, closing, and signature. Visit Purdue Online Writing Lab to view an example: owl.english.purdue.edu. In the search box, type business letter.

Use the following guidelines for your letter to the principal.	
To receive the highest score (4.0), the letter must meet all of these criteria.	Your letter to the principal • expresses your opinion about the possible change. • fairly and accurately describes your current math class. • explains why one type of classroom is better than the other. • gives at least two reasons supporting your explanation. • is in business letter format with a header, salutation, body, and closing. • uses correct grammar, usage, mechanics, and spelling.

Write a Narrative

Imagine it is the year 2099. You are in your favorite class. It could be art, math, science, even some future subject that hasn't been invented yet—whatever you like best. Your teacher announces, "Students, our school just got an exciting new technology that will make your learning experience in this class even better." What could it be? A shrinking ray? A time machine? A device that lets you talk to animals, plants, or minerals? Because it's the year 2099, that technology could be pretty wild.

Write a narrative (a story) about the day in 2099 that your favorite class gets this new technology. Your narrative must:

- describe the "exciting new technology" your teacher mentioned.

- show the new technology in action.

- present at least one outcome of using the technology.

- paint a picture of the setting (your futuristic classroom, for instance).

- depict characters (yourself, your teacher, and anyone else important to the story).

- use realistic dialogue, which can also have futuristic slang.

> **TECH-CONNECT**
> Share your story on your class website. Read other students' stories as well.

continued on next page

Write a Narrative: Writers of science fiction and fantasy often talk about "world building"—the use of specific details about every facet of life in an imagined setting. Most of these details exist in the background as the story focuses on plot and characters. Details about an imaginary time or place can reflect local customs, architecture, fashion, occupations, social problems, language—everything that brings a world to life. Before students write, encourage them to use their imaginations to construct the world of 2099. Suggest that they consider the daily habits of their own lives by asking, "What could these things be like in my 2099 world?" Encourage them to write bullet points, freewrite, and/or sketch as they brainstorm. Remind students that writers usually make many more notes than they end up using. Nevertheless, engaging in this process allows them to pick and choose which details to include. It can even help spark new plot ideas.

ELL Support: Project-Based Assessments—Write a Narrative ELLs will benefit from using a Story Map graphic organizer from the ELL Teacher Resource (p. 52) to develop their 2099 narratives. In addition to filling out traditional story elements such as characters, problem, events, and resolution, have them zoom in on the setting. Provide a separate sheet with prompts to help them flesh out setting details:

- Fashion: clothes, hair, makeup

- Transportation: travel to work and school

- Architecture: family homes, schools, other buildings

- Class Structure: rich and poor, educated and uneducated, etc.

- Language: slang, different languages

- Culture: crafts, music, art, drama

(continued)

Writers, take note: Although Clive Thompson is positive about using new technologies in the classroom, your story does not have to be so upbeat. What if the new technology seems great at first but has unintended, bad consequences? What if something goes drastically wrong? What if it accidentally ruins your favorite subject—or does something even worse? This is your story to tell, and not all stories end happily.

Use the following guidelines for your narrative.	
To receive the highest score (4.0), the narrative must meet all of these criteria.	Your narrative • describes the new technology, how it works, and at least one outcome from using it. • includes a setting, characters, and dialogue. • uses correct grammar, usage, mechanics, and spelling.

On Your Own: Integrating Ideas

1. Clive Thompson mentions that Kami Thordarson's classroom uses something called "Khan Academy." Guess what? It's still around, and it's bigger and better than ever. You can visit it at khanacademy.org. Search for the type of math you have the hardest time understanding. Preview the videos and see if they help you better understand the topic.

2. Does your school mostly use textbooks? Has it switched (or will it soon switch) to using tablets? An ongoing debate exists regarding the pros and cons of each. You can learn about different points in the debate at tablets-textbooks.procon.org. Where do you stand after reading about it?

3. Your school organizes people, space, and time in specific and purposeful ways: Students are divided into grades, for example, and teachers into departments. The space may be defined by classrooms, hallways, gymnasiums, the library, and so on. Each day comprises class periods, lunch schedules, passing time, and more.

   Whether you're in a private school, a public school, a home school, or in some other model, the way you learn resulted from interactions of people, ideas, and events. So, where did your model of schooling come from? Who or what is responsible for it? What are its goals? And is it really the best way for humans to learn? Conduct research to answer these questions. Start by interviewing your teacher.

ELL Support: Project-Based Assessments—Write a Narrative Have students work in multilevel pairs or groups to complete the narrative. Beginning and intermediate students can tell their story through a graphic novel or comic strip format, using images, labels, and speech and thought bubbles to convey details. When students complete their narrative, provide the Narrative Writing Revision Checklist (p. 68) so they can improve their writing.

Connect to Testing

In this chapter, you analyzed how people, ideas, and events interact; how the structure of a text develops ideas and guides readers; and how an author conveys point of view. You'll be tested over such reading skills during assessments. Answer the question below before reading the Explanation.

1. Read the following sentence from the passage.

    How did these elementary school kids zoom ahead to high-school-level material?

What role does this sentence play in developing the central idea of the text?

A. It poses a rhetorical question that has no answer but prompts readers to think.

B. It introduces an explanation of how the students are performing so well.

C. It leads to a description of how digital technology has affected one student.

D. It begins a comparison between past and present ways of learning math skills.

EXPLANATION

continued on next page

Chapter 11 *(continued)*

Assessment

Answers to Connect to Testing Questions:

2. D. Choice A provides a general point of view on a specific student's achievements. Choice B describes Thordarson's practices but doesn't offer a point of view or opinion about them. Choice C describes Thordarson's point of view but not necessarily the author's. The best choice is D because it offers a judgment of Thordarson's teaching. (DoK 2)

3. **Part A:** B.

   Part B: D. The best Choice is B supported by Choice D in Part B. While there is some support that the teacher's job is more stressful (Choice A), it does not appear to be stressful for the students. The text does not support Choices C and D. (DoK 1)

4. A. Dashes should be used to set off the phrase "often underfunded." (DoK 1)

---

2. Which sentence from the passage best expresses the author's point of view concerning how Kami Thordarson runs her math classroom?

   A. *Matthew shouldn't be doing work remotely this advanced.*

   B. *Instead of delivering all her math lessons to the entire class, Thordarson has them watch Khan videos and work on the online problems.*

   C. *Still, as Thordarson quickly points out, the Khan Academy isn't enough on its own.*

   D. *Judging by Thordarson's success, though, it works.*

3. **Part A:** According to the passage, what word best describes the learning and teaching in the new classroom structure?

   A. stressful

   B. lively

   C. confusing

   D. impersonal

   Part B: Which sentence from the passage best supports the answer to Part A?

   A. *When she stands up at the chalkboard lecturing on a subject, there's a predictable pattern that takes hold: one quarter of the kids quickly fall behind, so they tune out.*

   B. *Instead of delivering all her math lessons to the entire class, Thordarson has them watch Khan videos and work on the online problems.*

   C. *In contrast, homework is better done in a classroom, because that's when you're likely to need to ask the teacher for extra help.*

   D. *If anything, it has made Thordarson's job more challenging; there's more noise, more kids talking, and she's constantly darting around the room to help out.*

4. Read the following sentences.

   > Public education is often underfunded. It needs more economic support.

   Which of the following correctly revises the sentences into a single sentence?

   A. Public education—often underfunded—needs more economic support.

   B. Public education—often underfunded, needs more economic support.

   C. Public education, often underfunded—needs more public support.

   D. Public education—often underfunded, needs more—public support.

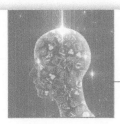

Chapter 12

Analyzing Repetition and Structure in Poetry

Preview Concepts

At this point in your life, you have probably read many nonfiction texts about machines. In your science books, you've read about simple machines such as the wedge, inclined plane, or pulley, for example. Perhaps you have read a history article about the Wright brothers and their invention of the airplane. And you have likely read or watched a science fiction movie or novel that involved machines.

But what about poetry? Are machines an appropriate subject for poetry? Why or why not?

Share your answers with a partner. Summarize your conclusions from your discussion.

CHAPTER GOALS

In this chapter you will

- determine a poem's central idea.
- analyze the repetition of sounds in a poem.
- examine how a poem's structure contributes to its meaning.
- learn about allusions to myths, the Bible, and literature.

PREVIEW ACADEMIC VOCABULARY

alliteration

allusion

anaphora

central idea

stanza

syntax

Analyzing Repetition and Structure in Poetry

The Secret of the Machines
by Rudyard Kipling

Introduction

Chapter Goals: Have students read through the goals and mark any words that are unfamiliar. Discuss the meanings of any academic vocabulary within the goals that students marked as unfamiliar. Consider posting the Chapter Goals.

Preview Academic Vocabulary: Read and discuss the meanings of the academic vocabulary.

alliteration: *the use of words that begin with the same beginning sound.* Esperanza used <u>alliteration</u> to name all of her childhood stuffed animals—including Elvis the Elegant Elephant.

allusion: *in a text, a reference to another work of literature, art, or history.* Example: Juan is a real Romeo. He is always pining over a girl he can't date. The author frequently used <u>allusions</u> in her writings, making Nicholas certain that she had read many classic books.

anaphora: *repetition of a word or phrase at the beginning of multiple sentences that follow after each other.* Example: Churchill wrote: "We shall fight in France, we shall fight on the seas and oceans, we shall fight with growing confidence and growing strength." Leland noted the author's use of <u>anaphora</u>; he thought that this repetition of words helped to create a consistent rhythm to the poem.

central idea: *a unifying theme or idea in a text.* Rafaela thought the author did a good job of conveying the <u>central idea</u> that people always long for what they cannot have.

(continued)

ELL Support: Academic Vocabulary See <u>Teaching Vocabulary in the ELL Teacher Resource (p. 18)</u> for ideas to use for teaching vocabulary throughout *Connections*.

ELL Support: Preview Concepts Use gestures, simple explanations, and images to help students understand the meaning of the following words: *wedge, inclined plane, pulley, Wright brothers, airplane, machines, poetry.* Rephrase the questions as follows: *Can people write poetry about machines? Why or why not?*

Have students work in multilevel pairs or groups and use the following sentence frames to answer the questions:

- People can/cannot write poetry about machines because . . . .

- My partner thinks people can/cannot write poetry about machines because . . . .

- I agree/don't agree with my partner because . . . .

Chapter 12 (continued)

Introduction

stanza: *a division of a poem consisting of a series of lines arranged together in a usually recurring pattern of meter and rhyme.* The second <u>stanza</u> of the poem describes the author's feeling about a fire that consumes his house.

syntax: *the way in which words are put together to form phrases and sentences.* Yoda's <u>syntax</u> gives his character a unique way of speaking. Try you must!

🔍 Gr7Ch12Vocabulary.pptx

Preview Concepts: Lead a class discussion on the questions on page 249. Ask students what associations come to mind when they hear the word *machine*. Write students' responses on the board and then ask for examples of specific machines. Finally, ask whether machines are an appropriate subject for poetry. Encourage students to suggest what types of poems could be written about a machine, including odes, limericks, haiku, rhyming verse, free verse, etc. What might be some themes related to machines or technology?

Making Connections: Introduce the poem "All Watched Over by Machines of Loving Grace" by Richard Brautigan on page 250, noting that it was written in 1967. Then read the poem aloud. Ask students to respond to the poem, encouraging them to note their honest first reactions. After discussing these responses, ask students what idea is expressed in the poem. Consider the following discussion prompts:

- What wish does the speaker express about computers?

- At the time the poem was written, microprocessors had not yet been invented, and no one used personal computers. Does this knowledge change your opinion about what the poem is about?

- What tone comes across in the poem?

- What do people think about computers in today's society? How do they affect people's lives—in both positive and negative ways?

- What do you think the speaker means by "a cybernetic ecology / where we are free of our labors"? In the 21st century, do computers help free us from labor?

Making Connections

Listen as your teacher reads aloud the following poem. As you listen, think about what the central idea of the poem could be.

All Watched Over by Machines of Loving Grace
by Richard Brautigan

I like to think (and
the sooner the better!)
of a cybernetic meadow
where mammals and computers
live together in mutually
programming harmony
like pure water
touching clear sky.

I like to think
(right now, please!)
of a cybernetic forest
filled with pines and electronics
where deer stroll peacefully
past computers
as if they were flowers
with spinning blossoms.

I like to think
(it has to be!)
of a cybernetic ecology
where we are free of our labors
and joined back to nature,
returned to our mammal
brothers and sisters,
and all watched over
by machines of loving grace.

A central idea of this poem is that plants, animals, and computers should be combined to create a paradise. In each stanza, underline one line that develops this central idea.

The first two stanzas speak of mammals and machines living side-by-side. With a partner, talk about how the third stanza is different. Refer to details in that stanza to support your ideas. Record your observations in your response journal and be prepared to discuss.

_____
cybernetic: computerized

> **MAKING CONNECTIONS**
>
> As you read the poem in this chapter, try to determine its central idea and how the lines develop it.

ELL Support: Making Connections After you read the poem aloud once, have students work in multilevel pairs or groups (or as a class with you) to reread the poem stanza by stanza, drawing sketches of what the poet describes. It is not necessary that students understand every single word, but they should have an image and a sense of what each stanza conveys. However, explain that *cybernetic* has to do with computers.

First Read: Determining a Central Idea

Rudyard Kipling published "The Secret of the Machines" in 1911. Many of the machines he describes had existed for only a few years. Nonetheless, machines had already changed the world profoundly.

Objective: Based on the title, the poem is likely about a hidden or forgotten truth about machines. As you read the poem, underline lines that seem to reveal what the secret is.

—— First Read
‑‑‑‑ Second Read
—— Third Read

The Secret of the Machines
by Rudyard Kipling

My Thoughts

1   We were taken from the **ore-bed and the mine**, ★

We were melted in the furnace and the pit—

We were cast and wrought and hammered to design,

We were cut and filed and tooled and gauged to fit.

5   Some water, coal, and oil is all we ask,

And a thousandth of an inch to give us play:

And now, if you will set us to our task,

We will serve you four and twenty hours a day!

This introduced the machine's background and desire to serve humans

We can pull and haul and push and lift and drive, ★

10   We can print and plough and weave and heat and light,

We can run and race and swim and fly and dive,

We can see and hear and count and read and write!

The purpose of this section is to show all the humanlike things machines can do.

Would you call a friend from half across the world?

If you'll let us have his name and town and state,

15   You shall see and hear your crackling question hurled

Across the arch of heaven while you wait.

Has he answered? Does he need you at his side?

You can start this very evening if you choose,

And take the Western Ocean in the stride

20   Of **seventy thousand horses and some screws!**

The purpose of this section is to show how machines allows for communication between people who are far apart.

ore-bed and the mine: where metals are found
seventy thousand horses and some screws: the horsepower of a passenger ship's propellers

ELL Support: First Read Have students read the poem in multilevel pairs or small groups, pausing after every 5 lines to summarize ideas using a Main Ideas and Supporting Details graphic organizer from the ELL Teacher Resource (p. 51). Encourage students to take notes and draw sketches in the margins around the poem so they can be sure they understand the topic of each section.

Remediation: First Read Suggest that struggling students read the poem in four sections: lines 1–12, lines 13–24, lines 25–36, and lines 37–50. After each section, have them pause to summarize what they read in the My Thoughts column. Encourage them to also jot down questions or things they find confusing. Students should then read the poem again, underlining lines that suggest something about the "secret" of the machines.

First Read: Determining a Central Idea

Before Reading: Before reading the introduction and objective, point out the title of the First Read: Determining a Central Idea.

Ask students what types of texts they think of when they hear the term *central idea*. Students will likely mention informational or persuasive texts. Suggest that some poems can also have a central idea. In this case, the central idea might be an answer to this question: What is the secret of the machines?

Review the introductory paragraph and objective with students, making sure they understand the task involved with the First Read.

As an alternative to students reading the poem silently, you might read the poem aloud to the class as they listen along. Or ask three or more volunteers to read the poem aloud at the same time, thus mimicking the collective speaker (the "we") of the machines in the poem.

Preview Vocabulary: Preview unfamiliar vocabulary to aid comprehension. Ask students to circle unfamiliar words as they complete the first read of a text. After the first read, guide students to determine the words' meanings using the context. Encourage students to support their responses with evidence. Have students confirm their initial definitions with a dictionary. Words that students might find difficult include:

cast: *to shape something by pouring it into a mold while molten.* The artist used the mold of a cat to <u>cast</u> the metal hood ornament.

wrought: *worked into shape in a careful or decorative way.* Ruby <u>wrought</u> her project carefully and for many hours.

gauged: *calculated or measured.* Ramon <u>gauged</u> the distance between the two snowbanks before making his leap across the frozen pond.

quay: *a long structure where boats can be tied up.* Francis steered the boat cautiously toward the <u>quay</u>, where he would dock it until the morning.

Chapter 12 (continued)

Lesson Support

After Reading: Use the following questions to check comprehension.

Text-Based Discussion Questions

1. Who is the speaker of the poem? Explain your response with details from the poem. *The speaker is the machines themselves. Several things make this clear. First is the use of the pronouns we and us. The speakers—the machines— also refer to what they are made of: "We were taken from the ore-bed and the mine . . . ." (line 1). The speaker refers to how they were made in lines 2–4. And throughout the poem, the speaker refers to the machines' uses. For example, "We can pull and haul and push and lift and drive" (line 9).*

2. What perspective on machines is presented in lines 1–36? *The machines seem powerful and capable of amazing feats from plowing, planting, and reaping, to transporting everything from people to water to words.*

3. What new idea about machines is presented in lines 37–44? *These lines introduce the idea that machines cannot think or correct the mistakes of their operators. "We are not built to comprehend a lie, . . . If you make a slip in handling us you die!" (lines 38, 40).*

About the Author: Rudyard Kipling was an English writer best known for his poems and stories set in India. Kipling was born in 1865 in Bombay, India, during British imperial rule. At the age of five, Kipling went to England to attend school. After he finished his education, Kipling returned to India in 1882. He began working as a serious writer—trying his hand at journalism, poetry, and fiction. He published his book *Plain Tales from the Hills* in 1888, which was very popular in England. This inspired Kipling to move to London in 1889.

After marrying Caroline Balestier in 1892, the pair moved to Vermont in the United States, where Kipling *The Jungle Book* (1894). Kipling began writing children's stories and poems, many of which were inspired by his own children. In 1907, Kipling was awarded the Nobel Prize for Literature, becoming the first British author to receive this honor. Kipling eventually moved back to England. He died there in 1936.

252   Grade 7 • Chapter 12

The **boat-express** is waiting your command!
You will find the *Mauretania* at the quay,
Till her captain turns the lever 'neath his hand,
And the monstrous nine-decked city goes to sea.

25 Do you wish to make the mountains bare their head
    And lay their new-cut forests at your feet?
Do you want to turn a river in its bed,
    Or plant a barren wilderness with wheat?
Shall we pipe aloft and bring you water down
30   From the never-failing **cisterns** of the snows,
To work the mills and **tramways** in your town,
    And irrigate your orchards as it flows?

    It is easy! Give us dynamite and drills!
    Watch the iron-shouldered rocks lie down and quake
35   As the thirsty desert-level floods and fills,
    And the valley we have dammed becomes a lake.

But remember, please, the Law by which we live,
    We are not built to comprehend a lie,
We can neither love nor pity nor forgive.
40   If you make a slip in handling us you die!
We are greater than the Peoples or the Kings— ★
    Be humble, as you crawl beneath our rods!—
Our touch can alter all created things,
    We are everything on earth—except The Gods!

boat-express: a train that takes passengers to their ships
cisterns: water tanks
tramways: electric trains used in public transportation

My Thoughts

The purpose of this section is to describe a technologically advanced ship.

The purpose of this section is to describe how machines can alter nature.

The purpose of this stanza is to show the power of the machines to change nature.

The purpose of this stanza is to convince the reader that machines are not like humans. They don't have feelings or morals.

252   Chapter 12 • Unit 3   ©Perfection Learning® • No Reproduction Permitted

45 *Though our smoke may hide the Heavens from your*
    eyes,

    It will vanish and the stars will shine again

    Because, for all our power and weight and size

50 *We are nothing more than children of your brain!*

> My Thoughts
>
> The purpose of this stanza is to conclude the poem by making the reader understand the limitations of machines.

FIRST RESPONSE: KEY IDEAS AND DETAILS

In your response journal, write a single sentence to sum up what "The Secret of the Machines" is about.

> **REFLECT**
>
> Read the last stanza again. What lesson or message do those lines present to the reader?

Focus on Determining a Central Idea

We are used to finding central ideas in informational texts and even stories. But poems also have central ideas. As with all genres, a poem's central idea is what it says about its subject, including what the subject does. The subject of a poem can be anything from the poet's own life to the universe itself. We can state the central idea of a poem in the form of a sentence about the subject. For example, the central idea of "All Watched Over by Machines of Loving Grace" might look like this:

> The speaker looks forward to a time when technology and nature are joined together to meet all human needs.

Complete the chart below to determine the central idea of "The Secret of the Machines." Describe how each machine helps society, according to Kipling. Then write lines from the poem supporting your description.

Machine	How the Machine Helps Society	Supporting Lines
The telephone (lines 13–19)	It allows people to contact others halfway across the world almost instantly.	"You shall see and hear your crackling question hurled / Across the arch of heaven while you wait."

continued on next page

Focus on Determining a Central Idea:

Deepen students' understanding about how the central idea of a poem differs from its theme with an anecdote like the following:

Suppose you go to a movie with a friend. When you get home, your little sister asks, "What was the movie about?" You might say something like, "Well, a teenager gets stranded in the forest for a whole week and has to try to survive." Then your mom asks, "So did you learn anything?" And you reply, "Yes. Sometimes, danger can reveal a person's true capabilities."

Ask students which answer exemplifies a theme and which exemplifies a central idea. Have students discuss what is different about the two answers and develop a definition of the term *central idea*.

> **Answers to Chart:**
>
> See answers on Student Book insert page to the left.

 Gr7Ch12Read1.pptx

Chapter 12 (continued)

Lesson Support

Sample Answer to Question, page 254:

The central idea of "The Secret of the Machines" is that even though machines are so powerful they can transform the world, they are still the tools of their human creators.

Machine	How the Machine Helps Society	Supporting Lines
The passenger ship (lines 20–24)	It can move many people across oceans quickly.	*You can start this very evening if you choose, / And take the Western Ocean in the stride* *And the monstrous nine-decked city goes to sea.*
Dams and water pipelines (lines 25–32)	They can make crops grow in a desert, power a town, and water orchards.	*Shall we pipe aloft and bring you water down* *as the thirsty desert-level floods and fills,* *to work the mills and tramways in your town,*
Dynamite and drills (lines 33–36)	They can reshape landscapes, feeding water into fields, cities, and power generators.	*Do you want to turn a river in its bed* *Watch the iron-shouldered rocks lie down and quake / As the thirsty desert-level floods and fills, / And the valley we have dammed becomes a lake?*

Refer to the sentences and supporting lines in the chart you just completed and ask yourself: What single important idea could all of these lines be developing?

Sometimes, you have to draft a few ideas until you find what you believe is the right one. In the space below, write three different sentences in which you "try out" different possible central ideas.

ELL Support: First Read English language learners may benefit from hearing the poem read aloud while following along with the text in the book. Several versions are available on YouTube. Search for *Rise of the Machines Rudyard Kipling*. One version of the poem on YouTube features a virtual movie created from a still picture of Rudyard Kipling and a recording of Kipling reading the poem. See http: youtu.be/vcO2Kq3e9tw

Viewing this digital recreation of Kipling may spark some conversations about whether viewing this type of video technology is engaging or unsettling.

With a partner, share the central idea sentence you believe is the most accurate. Talk to your partner about why that central idea is likely the best one. Refer to details from the poem in your answer.

CONNECT TO
ESSENTIAL QUESTION

"The Secret of the Machines" describes how humans use machines to transform nature. How can transforming nature also transform human society?

Second Read: Examining the Impact of Repeated Sounds

Many poems rhyme, or use similar sounding words at the ends of lines. But poems can use sound repetition in many other ways. Consider this short poem:

> I love the springtime blooms in pink and white.
> I love the summer surge of humid heat.
> I love the autumn leaves in colors bright.
> I love the winter snow, a linen sheet.

This poem uses a few kinds of repetition.

- It repeats sounds at the start of nearby words—for example, "summer surge" and "humid heat." This type of repetition is called *alliteration*.

- It repeats phrases at the beginning of lines—in this case, "I love the . . . ." This type of repetition is called *anaphora*.

- It uses meter, or repeats patterns of stressed and unstressed syllables. In the poem, each line has 10 syllables grouped into 5 feet made up of one unstressed and one stressed syllable. Note that some lines open with two unstressed syllables.

Some sections of "The Secret of the Machines" use similar sound patterns.

Objective: Your teacher will read aloud "The Secret of the Machines." Listen for the types of repetition described above. Draw a star next to any stanza that seems rich with such repetition.

Focus on Examining the Impact of Repeated Sounds

As mentioned, sections of "The Secret of the Machines" uses the sound devices described above. Consider the sounds of the second stanza (lines 9–12):

> We can pull and haul and push and lift and drive,
> We can print and plough and weave and heat and light,
> We can run and race and swim and fly and dive,
> We can see and hear and count and read and write!

Why does Kipling use so many different types of repetition in

continued on next page

ELL Support: Speak and Listen Have students work in multilevel pairs or small groups and use these sentence frames to discuss the poem:

I think the central idea of the poem is . . . .

This detail in line . . . suggests that . . . .

I think your central idea is . . . because . . . .

Which details in the poem support the idea that . . . ?

ELL Support: Second Read Read the poem aloud again. Then model rereading the first 5 lines of the poem to identify the repetitive elements, including the number of beats, the words at the beginning of the line, and the sounds (rhyme) at the end of the lines. Have students work in multilevel pairs or groups to identify the repetitive elements in stanza 2.

(Speak and Listen: Suggest that before students share their central ideas with a partner, they jot down at least three supporting details.

Second Read: Examining the Impact of Repeated Sounds

Before Reading: Have students pair up to read the introductory section and the objective. Then, as a class, make certain students understand the task involved in this Second Read: listening for and drawing stars to indicate sound repetition, including alliteration, anaphora, and meter.

Remind students that for a Second Read, they should ask the question *How*? In this case, a useful "how" question to consider is, *How does the use of repeated sounds help the poem communicate its message?*

Read the poem aloud or ask one or more volunteers to read it.

After Reading: Use the following questions to check comprehension.

Text-Based Discussion Questions

1. In lines 1–4, what role does the poet's use of anaphora play in the overall poem? *The repeated use of the phrase "We were" helps introduce the speaker of the poem—the machines.*

2. In lines 13–32, how does the use of sound show the machines' pride at being able to respond to people's needs? *The poet has the speaker ask questions about what a person might need: "Would you call a friend from half across the world?" (line 13); "Do you want to turn a river in its bed? / Or plant a barren wilderness with wheat?" (lines 27–28). These questions use sound in two ways. First is the repetition of the pattern "Do you?/Would you?" Second is the way the pitch varies in questions, rising at the end.*

Focus on Examining the Impact of Repeated Sounds: Introduce the chart on page 256 and review the headings. Ask a volunteer to read the second stanza aloud. Then work through the first sound pattern (alliteration) with the class before instructing students to complete the chart independently.

 Gr7Ch12Read2.pptx

Chapter **12** *(continued)*

Lesson Support

Sample Response to Question:

The second stanza describes the tasks machines can do and creates the regular, rhythmic sound of a mechanical process.

Answers to Chart:

See answers on Student Book insert page to the right.

Speak and Listen: Have students share their completed charts in small groups. Before students get in their groups, make sure they understand that the discussion should focus on why the poet may have chosen these particular sound repetitions. In other words, what do these sounds tell the reader about the poem's meaning? Encourage students to jot down notes about important points that arise during the discussion.

Write: Have students write the answer to the question on page 256 independently. To guide their response, encourage students to refer to their charts, their notes from group discussions, and any text annotations.

---

this stanza? What impact does such repetition have on the poem's meaning?

In the space below, describe what the second stanza is about.

Describe three different sound patterns, including rhyme and meter, that are found in this stanza. Give one example of each.

Sound Pattern in Stanza	Example from Stanza
	print and plough (line 10) *run and race* (line 11) *read and write* (line 12)
anaphora (repeated words at the beginnings of lines)	*We can* repeats four times (lines 9–12)
repeated patterns within consecutive lines	Each line is 11 syllables. Each line is a list of 5 one-syllable verbs separated by the word *and*.

Speak and Listen Form groups of three or four. Have one partner read the second stanza aloud. Then discuss how the repetition of sounds you described above might help express what the stanza is all about.

Write Based on the results of your discussion, write a paragraph that analyzes how the repetition of sounds in the second stanza helps express its main idea. Give at least two quotes from the poem in your response.

TECH-CONNECT

Share a digital copy of your response. Read two other students' responses. Give one positive comment and one suggestion to each. Be polite and specific in your feedback.

ELL Support: Speak and Listen and Write Have students work in multilevel pairs or small groups and use these sentence frames to discuss and write about stanza 2. These can also be found as a student handout in the ELL Teacher Resource (p. 28).

- (Sentence 1) In the poem's second stanza, the poet describes . . . .

- (Sentence 2) To express this idea, the poet uses sound repetition in several ways.

- (Sentences 3–4) First, the poet . . . (type of sound repetition; example from poem; effect of this detail).

- (Sentences 5–6) Second, the poet . . . (type of sound repetition; example from poem; effect of this detail).

- (Sentences 7–8) Third, the poet . . . (type of sound repetition; example from poem; effect of this detail).

Third Read: Analyzing How Structure Helps Develop an Idea

Objective: Read "The Secret of the Machines" a third time. After each stanza, write one sentence in the "My Thoughts" column stating the purpose of the stanza. You will write eight sentences. Consider how the visual arrangement of the lines and their indentations communicate meaning.

Focus on Analyzing How Structure Helps Develop an Idea

In informational texts, paragraphs are typically used to develop the central idea with examples, facts, definitions, and so on. Literary texts, especially poetry, have a broader range of structures to develop ideas. That said, "The Secret of the Machines" is organized much like an informational text.

How are the stanzas in "The Secret of the Machines" like paragraphs? Why are the lines of some stanzas staggered and others are lined up together on the right?

In the chart below, collect your sentences stating the purpose of each stanza. You may edit or replace your sentences to make them more accurate.

Stanza	What the stanza is mainly about
1 (lines 1–8)	Through various processes, machines were created by humans to serve human needs.
2 (lines 9–12)	Machines are capable of performing many tasks once done by humans and/or animals.

continued on next page

Remediation: First Read Before reading aloud "The Secret of the Machines" to the class, group struggling students with those who are more advanced to prepare for the second reading. Have them alternate reading sections of the poem aloud. While listening, students should mark examples of the sound repetitions you shared with the whole class. After reading the poem, have students point out the details they marked, explaining their effect on the reader. As they share, encourage students to mark any details they missed.

ELL Support: Third Read Have students work in multilevel pairs or small groups to reread the poem and state the main idea of each stanza. Model doing so with the first stanza. Paraphrase the sample main idea from the chart as follows: *Machines were made by humans to help humans do many things.*

Third Read: Analyzing How Structure Helps Develop an Idea

Before Reading: Review with students the objective to ensure they understand the task involved in the Third Read. For this final read, assign parts to students and conduct a Readers Theater-style reading by having individual students read lines 1–8 and then having the entire class or a small group of students read the stanza that is indented and in block style (lines 9–12). Continue in the same way for the other stanzas.

After Reading: Use the following questions to check comprehension.

Text-Based Discussion Questions

1. In the beginning of the poem, the speaker uses the passive voice with examples that include: "We were taken . . . / We were melted . . ." (lines 1–2); "We were cut and filed and tooled and gauged to fit" (line 4). How does the passive voice help establish the relationship between humans and machines expressed in the poem? *The passive voice draws the reader's attention to what is being acted upon— the machines. It also shows that humans directed the action (the machines' creation).*

2. How does the speaker's voice change in the second stanza, and how does this change affect the reader's understanding of the machines? *The speaker now uses the active voice, for example: "We can pull and haul and push and lift and drive" (line 9). This shows that once they have been created, the machines are the "doers," capable of many different actions.*

Focus on Analyzing How Structure Helps Develop an Idea:
Ask students to consider what the structure of the stanzas in this poem have in common with paragraphs in an informational text. Have them write their answers on page 257 and then ask volunteers to share their responses with the class. Make sure students understand that despite this specific similarity—each stanza is based on a main idea—poetry stanzas are quite different from informational paragraphs.

Introduce the chart on page 257. Have students refer to what they wrote in the My Thoughts column to complete the chart independently

 Gr7Ch12Read3.pptx

Lesson Support

Answers to Chart:

See answers on Student Book insert page to the right.

(**Speak and Listen:** Remind students that new ideas developed during their partner discussion may prompt them to revise their charts. Suggest that before revising they remember that the same idea may be phrased in several ways. If students find their idea statements about a given stanza agree, the wording doesn't have to be identical.

Stanza	What the stanza is mainly about
3 (lines 13–20)	Machines can bridge long distances, transporting both ideas and humans swiftly across the world.
4 (lines 21–24)	An enormous ocean liner transports passengers across the sea in luxury.
5 (lines 25–32)	Machines give humans power over nature, enabling them to move mountains, direct rivers, and more.
6 (lines 33–36)	Tools such as dynamite and drills allow humans to transform their environment.
7 (lines 37–44)	Although machines are powerful, they cannot think or alter their behavior, so humans must use them with care. They don't have human emotions.
8 (lines 45–50)	Machines may have awesome powers, but they are human creations.

(**Speak and Listen** Discuss your answers to the chart with a partner. If you decide to change your answers based on your discussion, use a different color pen or pencil to cross out or add information.

Write Based on your chart and your conversation, write a paragraph explaining how "The Secret of the Machines" uses stanzas to develop its central idea. Begin with a sentence restating the central idea. Then write at least three sentences telling how stanzas develop that central idea.

Language: Interpreting Figures of Speech

Figures of speech convey feelings and ideas beyond the simple meanings of words and are used in literary and informational text. One type of figure of speech is allusion.

An *allusion* is a reference to characters, settings, or events from myths, the Bible, or literature. Allusions bring with them ideas and feelings, but only if a reader is familiar with the source.

The tables below list some common mythological, Biblical, and literary allusions and their meanings.

Allusions to Greek Myths	
Allusion	**Description**
Achilles' heel	The warrior Achilles cannot be harmed except on one of his heels. He is killed by an injury to that heel.
Gordian knot	The leader Alexander, faced with a knot that cannot be untied, draws his sword and cuts it in half.
Hercules	A strong and courageous Greek god uses his enormous strength to accomplish great feats.
Prometheus	A Titan takes fire from the gods and gives it to humanity, who live and thrive because of it. The gods punish Prometheus by chaining him to a mountain and having an eagle attack him each day.

Allusions to the Bible	
Allusion	**Description**
the garden of Eden	The garden of Eden is a perfect land where the first humans live, with rivers and fruit trees providing water and food. The people must leave Eden after they disobey God.
Job	Job is a wealthy man who experiences great misfortune and tragedy. Despite his suffering, Job patiently believes in the justice and goodness of God.

continued on next page

Write: Point out that students do not have to explain how all eight stanzas develop the poem's central idea. Rather, the task is to explain how the structure of the poem helps illustrate the central idea, using details from some of the stanzas to support their analysis.

Language: Interpreting Figures of Speech: Remind students that although these allusions may be unfamiliar, students probably read, see, and use allusions all the time. Students are probably more familiar with allusions to popular culture and memes. Examples:

- Geometry is my kryptonite. It totally brings down my grade point average. (Allusion to Superman comic.)

- That team's appearance in the national tournament is a real Cinderella story. (Allusion to fairy tale.)

Ask students to share some allusions. Note that writers use allusions to "shorthand" an idea by substituting it with something that represents that idea. For example, instead of writing, "I worked the entire weekend—even skipping a party—trying to finish my essay," you might write, "I made a real Herculean effort."

 Gr7Ch12Language.pptx

ELL Support: Write Have students work in multilevel pairs or small groups and use these sentence frames to first discuss and then write about the structure of the poem. These can also be found as a student handout in the ELL Teacher Resource (p. 37)

- (Sentence 1) The poem "The Secret of the Machines" by Rudyard Kipling is about . . . .

- (Sentence 2) To express this idea, the poet structures the poem by . . . .

- (Sentences 3–4) Each stanza contains . . . (number of lines or syllables; idea).

- (Sentences 5–6) In the _____ stanza, for example, . . . (type of sound repetition; example from poem; effect of this detail).

- (Sentences 7–10) Another example is . . . .

Chapter 12 *(continued)*

Lesson Support

Sample Answers to Questions:

1. My brother Mike was greedy with his candy, refusing to share it with anyone.

2. Despite my brother's greedy behavior, I dealt with him patiently and kindly.

(continued)

Allusions to the Bible	
Allusion	**Description**
Leviathan	Leviathan is an enormous, fire-breathing sea monster larger than any sea creature.
the good Samaritan	A man generously helps a stranger who has been beaten and robbed, when others have ignored the stranger.

Allusions from Famous Literature	
Allusion	**Description**
albatross	In the poem "The Rime of the Ancient Mariner," a sailor kills an albatross (a large seabird), bringing a curse on the ship and its crew. The crew then hangs the albatross around the sailor's neck as punishment.
Frankenstein's monster	In *Frankenstein; or, the Modern Prometheus*, scientist Victor Frankenstein builds a creature from the bodies of dead people. The creature escapes Frankenstein's control and goes on to harm others.
Jekyll and Hyde	In *The Strange Case of Doctor Jekyll and Mister Hyde*, a kind, decent scientist (Jekyll) takes a formula that transforms him into a cruel, cunning villain (Hyde).
Scrooge	In *A Christmas Carol*, Ebenezer Scrooge is a bitter and greedy person who learns to share his wealth and treat others kindly.

Each sentence below contains an allusion. Rewrite the sentence so it no longer uses the allusion but keeps its meaning.

1. My brother Mike was being a real Scrooge about sharing his candy.

2. For my part, I responded to my brother's greediness better than even Job could.

ELL Support: Language Show pictures of each allusion and have students sketch similar pictures next to each allusion in their books. If appropriate, model how to use an Internet search engine to research allusions. Have students work in multilevel pairs or groups to complete the items. Beginning and intermediate students can draw and label sketches to convey the meaning of each item.

3. But my irritation toward him was practically of Leviathan-like proportions.

4. When it came to getting Mike to share his candy, however, I knew his Achilles' heel.

5. I pretended to cry. Mike couldn't stand it when anyone cried—he always had to be the good Samaritan.

6. Most of the time I don't use such dirty tricks, but I'll admit it: I have a bit of a Jekyll and Hyde personality.

REFLECT

Reread "All Watched Over by Machines of Loving Grace." What allusion is present throughout this poem?

Project-Based Assessments

Poem About Modern Technology

Kipling's "The Secret of the Machines" was first published in 1911. Since then, many more machines and technologies have transformed our world. The chart below lists some of these technologies in categories.

continued on next page

Sample Answers to Questions:

3. However, my irritation toward my brother still raged on inside me.

4. When it came to getting Mike to share his candy, however, I knew his greatest weakness.

5. I pretended to cry. Mike couldn't stand it when anyone cried—he always felt compelled to help people in need.

6. Most of the time I don't use such dirty tricks, but I'll admit it—even I have a dark side.

Assessment

Project-Based Assessments

Poem About Modern Technology: Remind students that their poems should express a central idea about the specific machines they have chosen. Before they begin drafting, encourage students to freewrite about the machines, bringing up whatever ideas and details come to mind. Remind them not to censor themselves or correct mistakes as they freewrite, noting that often first thoughts are those with the most power. After freewriting, students can go through their work, circling the most interesting material. They can then consider how they will structure their poem and begin to draft.

Chapter **12** *(continued)*

Assessment

Digital Presentation: These free digital presentation tools are among those recommended for use by students:

- Prezi—a cloud-based program that allows students to adapt templates, adding text, images, and video to create their own slideshows. Go to prezi.com.

- Kizoa—an online program that provides tools for creating slideshows, videos, and animated collages. Go to www.kizoa.com.

Transportation	Communication	Computer-Related	Other
electric car	the Internet	calculator	artificial limb, organ
helicopter	portable music player	digital camera	lasers
jet airplane	radio	personal computer	radar
rocket	satellite	robotics	space probes
self-driving car	smartphone	video game console	space station
submarine	television	voice recognition	X-ray machine

Write a poem similar to "The Secret of the Machines," using a first-person speaker with the perspective of a machine. Include at least three machines in your poem. Your poem should have a minimum of three stanzas, with at least four lines per stanza and a clear rhyme scheme. Use alliteration in one line. Use anaphora in two consecutive lines.

	Use the following guidelines for your poem.
To receive the highest score (4.0), your poem must meet all of these criteria.	**Your poem** • is about three or more machines. • is written from a machine's first-person perspective. • has a minimum of three stanzas, with at least four lines per stanza and a clear rhyme scheme. • uses alliteration in one line and anaphora in two consecutive lines.

Digital Presentation

Conduct research and create a digital presentation about the history of one of the technologies listed in the table above.

Remember to use only reliable sources for your information. Websites that end in *.edu*, *.gov*, or *.org* usually have more reliable information than sites with many contributors such as Wikipedia. When it comes to the history of technology, some of the best sources include large public universities, science museums, history museums, and government organizations.

TECH-CONNECT

Save your presentation to a flash drive so you can bring it to school. Be sure to open your file before your presentation to make sure it will work on the school computer.

ELL Support: Project-Based Assessments—Digital Presentation Have students work in multilevel pairs or groups to create a digital presentation. Encourage them to narrow their focus so that they are researching a specific technology. Writing captions for pictures and images will help reinforce what they have learned in this chapter and further develop their English language skills. And the visual work involved in researching and selecting images will help complement their verbal skills.

Gather the following information for your presentation:

- the primary inventor or inventors of the technology
- important dates related to the technology, including when it was invented, when it became popular or commonly used, and when it was replaced by a newer technology
- significant changes to the technology over time, for example, how computers became smaller, or when private companies began launching rockets
- at least one important effect the technology has had on human society
- three sources used for the project: name of article, website, and date

Finally, create an interesting and well-organized computer presentation. Each slide should have both an image and text. Read the rubric carefully so you know what is expected of you from the beginning. Practice your presentation. If working with a partner, decide in advance who will share which slides.

Use the following guidelines for your presentation.	
To receive the highest score (4.0), the presentation must meet all of these criteria.	Your presentation • uses images and text in a professional, appealing way. • clearly identifies the invention and names its inventor(s). • explains important ways the invention has changed over time. • describes at least one important effect the technology has had on modern society. • demonstrates confidence, eye contact, and proper volume. • uses correct grammar, usage, punctuation, and spelling.

On Your Own: Integrating Ideas

1. Some fans of Rudyard Kipling's poetry have made "The Secret of the Machines" the basis of YouTube videos. One such video uses a recording of Kipling reading his poem and pairs it with a photo of the poet. Just go to YouTube and type in "The Secret of the Machines." If you watch two or more videos, think about why the producers of the videos might have made the choices they did.

2. Compare the two poems about machines in this chapter. (See pages 250 and 251-253.) Analyze the effect of rhyme scheme, meter, and graphical elements (punctuation, capitalization, line arrangement).

> **CONNECT TO ESSENTIAL QUESTION**
>
> In the year 600, the planet held about 200 million people. By 1800, that number had grown to 1 billion people. Now, Earth holds 7.5 billion people. What part has technology played in this change?

continued on next page

Assessment

On Your Own: Integrating Ideas:

Activity 3: Students who are more advanced may appreciate reading more works by Rudyard Kipling. Encourage them to note similarities among his various works.

Tech Connect Suggestion: After students write in their response journals about the Reflect prompt, have them share their answers on Poll Everywhere. Ask volunteers to make a graph that displays students' opinions about which technology is most important.

3. "The Secret of the Machines" is written from a first-person point of view of the machines that humans have built. Of course, machines don't yet think in the ways that human beings do. But many people who study technology believe that machines will one day become as smart as humans—and probably smarter. But what happens then? Are we, as a society, ready for it? The philosopher Sam Harris thinks a lot about these issues, and he is more than a little concerned. You can watch him give a fascinating 15-minute talk on this issue. Go to TED.com, search for "Sam Harris," and watch his talk "Can we build AI without losing control over it?"

4. Rudyard Kipling wrote about more than machines, of course. He was the author of *Just-So Stories* and *The Jungle Book*, and he won the Nobel Prize for Literature in 1907. His most famous poem is probably "If—." As with "The Secret of the Machines," it features anaphora and alliteration. It also has a clear theme. You can find and download any of his work for free at Project Gutenberg. Just go to Gutenberg.org and search for Rudyard Kipling.

> **REFLECT**
>
> Think about the list of technologies presented in the Project-Based Assessments on page 262. Which technology is most important to you personally? Why?

Rudyard Kipling

264   Chapter 12 • Unit 3

Connect to Testing

In this chapter, you identified a central idea, considered the effects of repetition, analyzed how structure affects meaning, and learned about several common allusions. When you take assessments, you will be tested over such skills and your ability to support your ideas by using textual evidence. Here is an example of this type of question. Try to answer the question before reading the Explanation.

1. Read the following stanza from "The Secret of the Machines."

> *Though our smoke may hide the Heavens from your eyes,*
> *It will vanish and the stars will shine again*
> *Because, for all our power and weight and size*
> *We are nothing more than children of your brain!*

What is the main idea of this stanza?

A. Machines will eventually take over the world and control humanity.

B. Machines are powerful, but without humans they would not exist.

C. Machines will one day be able to produce their own "children."

D. Machines dirty the air, which humans are working to clean up.

EXPLANATION

continued on next page

Connect to Testing: This Connect to Testing section focuses on determining a poem's central idea; analyzing the repetition of sounds in a poem; examining how a poem's structure contributes to its meaning; and learning about allusions.

Encourage students to work in pairs to choose the correct answers to the questions and then to compare their answers with those of another pair of students. If there is disagreement, encourage the groups to try to reach a consensus as they discuss the reasons for their choices.

Answers to Connect to Testing Questions:

1. B. (DoK 2)

(continued)

ELL Support: Connect to Testing and Assessments See the Connections ELL Teacher Resource (p. 22) for ideas on adapting this section for ELLs.

Chapter 12 *(continued)*

Assessment

Answer to Connect to Testing Questions:

2. A. The allusion in this sentence is the reference to the albatross. This refers to a the poem "The Rhyme of the Ancient Mariner" in which an albatross is a bad omen, a harbinger of disaster. Choice A most closely fits the meaning of the allusion. (DoK 1)

3. D. The use of the repetition emphasizes the role of machines and what they can do. The use of "we" emphasizes that all machines are speaking. Choice B is saying the opposite of this. It is incorrect. Choice D is not supported by the text. There is some support for Choice A because of the use of the passive voice. The machines are being acted upon, but ultimately Choice D is the best answer. (DoK 2)

4. **Part A:** A. Stanza 3 describes how machines can help someone call a friend or travel across the ocean. Stanza 4 describes an ocean liner that can accomplish this task. (DoK 2)

   Part B: C. Stanza 5 describes ways of altering natural landscapes to benefit humans. Stanza 6 describes how inventions and machines can help humans do this. (DoK 3)

   (continued)

---

2. The following sentence contains an allusion.

   > For some people, carrying a smartphone feels like lugging around an albatross.

   Which of these best restates the meaning of the sentence?

   A. For some people, carrying a smartphone is a burden.

   B. For some people, carrying a smartphone is birdlike.

   C. For some people, carrying a smartphone is useful.

   D. For some people, carrying a smartphone is heavy.

3. Read the first four lines of "The Secret of the Machines."

   > We were taken from the ore-bed and the mine,
   >   We were melted in the furnace and the pit—
   > We were cast and wrought and hammered to design,
   >   We were cut and filed and tooled and gauged to fit.

   What is the impact of the repetition of "we were" at the beginning of each line?

   A. It reminds readers that only humans can produce machines.

   B. It stresses that each machine was created in a different way.

   C. It makes readers believe that the machines are coming to life.

   D. It emphasizes that all the machines share similar beginnings.

4. **Part A:** Which of these best describes the relationship between stanza 3 and stanza 4 (lines 13–24)?

   A. Stanza 3 describes a task; stanza 4 describes how a machine can do that task.

   B. Stanza 3 describes a region of the world; stanza 4 describes a city far from that region.

   C. Stanza 3 describes a person; stanza 4 describes how a machine can replace that person.

   D. Stanza 3 describes a type of communication; stanza 4 describes how that communication works.

   Part B: Which two stanzas have a relationship that most closely resembles the relationship between stanzas 3 and 4?

   A. stanzas 1 and 8

   B. stanzas 2 and 6

   C. stanzas 5 and 6

   D. stanzas 6 and 7

5. Part A: What is the central idea of "The Secret of the Machines"?

A. Machines can destroy as much as they build.

B. Humans are using machines to produce a paradise.

C. Humans have made machines that can transform the world.

D. Machines view themselves as slaves that do dangerous jobs.

Part B: Which line from the poem best restates its central idea?

A. *And now, if you will set us to our task,* (line 7)

B. *Do you wish to make the mountains bare their head* (line 25)

C. *We are not built to comprehend a lie* (line 38)

D. *Our touch can alter all created things* (line 43)

5. **Part A:** A. Choice B is not supported by the poem. Choice C is true according to the poem, but this is a key idea and not the overall central idea of the entire poem. Choice D is incorrect because the machines speaking in the poem emphasize that they are "greater than the Peoples or the Kings." This is the opposite of the idea that machines are slaves. Choice A is the best answer. (DoK 2)

Part B: D. Choice D emphasizes the idea that machines can be used to destroy just as much as they can be used to build. (DoK 2)

Chapter 13

Comparing Presentations of a Topic

Robots will eliminate 6% of all US jobs by 2021, report says
by Olivia Solon

Introduction

Chapter Goals: Have students read through the goals and mark any words that are unfamiliar. Discuss the meanings of any academic vocabulary within the goals that students marked as unfamiliar. Consider posting the Chapter Goals.

Preview Academic Vocabulary: Read and discuss the meanings of the academic vocabulary.

> **central idea:** *a unifying theme or idea in a text.* Jocelyn liked *The Wizard of Oz* for its central idea—there's no place like home.

> **connotation:** *the positive or negative association suggested by a word.* Kareem did not enjoy being called "aloof" because of its negative connotations.

> **denotation:** *the literal meaning of a word, as listed in a dictionary.* Iman did not know the meaning of "voluminous" and went to look for its denotation in the dictionary.

> **media:** *communication tools or outlets, such as television, radio, or newspapers.* Malcolm did not like the way his favorite actor was often presented in the media.

 Gr7Ch13Vocabulary.pptx

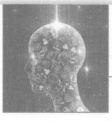

Chapter 13

Comparing Presentations of a Topic

Preview Concepts

Robots occupy an important place in our popular culture. They show up in movies, television shows, books, comic books, and so on. And our feelings about robots aren't consistent. Sometimes we love them, and sometimes we don't.

1. What is a common positive idea in popular culture about the relationship between robots and humans?

2. What is a common negative idea in popular culture about the relationship between robots and humans?

Robots aren't just the stuff of science fiction, of course. They've been part of the real world for the last century, and they're only getting more important. In this chapter, you'll be considering some of the real-world consequences of the rise of robots in human lives.

CHAPTER GOALS

In this chapter you will

- examine the central ideas in articles.
- compare and contrast a text with a video based on that text.
- analyze how authors writing about the same topic shape their presentations of information.
- consider the connotations and denotations of words.

PREVIEW ACADEMIC VOCABULARY

central idea

connotation

denotation

media

ELL Support: Academic Vocabulary See <u>Teaching Vocabulary in the ELL Teacher Resource (p. 18)</u> for ideas to use for teaching vocabulary throughout *Connections*.

Preview Concepts Display images of robots both real and imaginary (from movies). Rephrase the questions as follows: *Why do people like robots? Why do people dislike robots?* Have students work in multilevel pairs or groups and use the following sentence frame to answer the questions.

- People like/dislike robots because . . . .

Making Connections

Read the following excerpt from the 1920 play *R.U.R.* (*Rossum's Universal Robots*) by Czech playwright Karel Čapek. The word *robot* comes from a Czech word meaning "forced labor" and first appeared in the play. In this excerpt, a woman named Helena Glory meets with two executives of a robot manufacturing company.

MAKING CONNECTIONS

As you read the articles in this chapter, pay attention to how they develop their central ideas.

Helena: Why do you make them?

Busman: Hahaha, that's a good one! Why do we make robots!

Fabry: So that they can work for us, Miss Glory. One robot can take the place of two and a half workers. The human body is very imperfect; one day it had to be replaced with a machine that would work better.

Busman: People cost too much.

Fabry: They were very unproductive. They weren't good enough for modern technology. And besides, . . . besides . . . this is wonderful progress that . . . I beg your pardon.

Helena: What?

Fabry: Please forgive me, but to give birth to a machine is wonderful progress. It's more convenient and it's quicker, and everything that's quicker means progress. Nature had no notion of the modern rate of work. From a technical point of view, the whole of childhood is quite pointless. Simply a waste of time.

1. What central idea is presented in this part of the play?

2. Does the idea in the play seem relevant today? Why or why not?

Preview Concepts: Ask students to name examples of how robots are used today. Discuss what different types of robots have in common. Then have students consider whether or not each type of robot has benefited people—and if so, how?

Answers to Questions, page 268:

1. Robots help humans do important tasks. Robots can help humans do important calculations or household chores.

2. Robots could one day take over the world. Robots could outsmart humans and rebel against them.

Making Connections: Before students read the excerpt from *R.U.R.,* note that the play was written in 1920. Although Leonardo da Vinci sketched plans for a humanoid robot in around 1495, human-like robotic devices had not been invented when Karel Capek wrote his play. During the 1700s, inventors began developing automatons—mechanical toys like a duck that bent its neck and flapped its wings. Robotic devices first developed in industry—beginning in 1913 with Ford's moving conveyor belt, which boosted assembly line production. It wasn't until 1954 that an autonomous, programmable robotic arm appeared, signaling the advent of modern robots. Ask students why, given these facts, Capek may have written about robots, a term meaning "forced labor"?

Answers to Questions:

1. The central idea is that robots and machines are much more productive than human beings.

2. The play seems relevant today because it deals with robots and machines taking over jobs that humans normally do. This is something that happens in real life. Because machines can work faster and cost less than human labor, many people are losing their jobs.

ELL Support: Making Connections Before you read the play aloud, display a map to make sure that students understand that the Czech Republic is a country in Europe and Czech is a language.

Read the play aloud with two advanced students, each person taking a role. If possible, have lab coats or safety goggles (or display pictures of them) to show that Busman and Fabry are scientists. Have students work in multilevel pairs or groups and use the following sentence frames to answer the questions.

- The central idea of this part of the play is . . . .

- This idea seems/does not seem relevant (important) today because . . . .

Chapter 13 (continued)

First Read: Analyzing the Development of Central Ideas

Before Reading: Read the introductory remarks on page 270 and confirm that students understand the objective.

Preview Vocabulary: Preview unfamiliar vocabulary to aid comprehension. Have students note any unfamiliar words as they complete the first read. Guide students to determine such words' meanings using the context. Encourage students to support their responses with evidence. Have students confirm their definitions with a dictionary. Difficult words might include:

virtual: *a digital version of something real.* Kylie is thankful that she has grown up in the age of virtual assistants like Siri—she never has to type anything into Google.

complex: *consisting of many different and connecting parts.* Siddarth knew that he could not leave all of his studying for the night before the exam because the concepts were too complex.

disruptive: *causing trouble and preventing something from continuing as usual.* Marco could not concentrate on what he was reading with his young siblings running around; their giggles were disruptive.

logistics: *the careful organization of a complicated activity or operation.* Linda had to repeat the plans for the party so that her brother could understand all of the logistics.

concierges: *people who are employed to handle personal tasks such as arranging reservations and running errands.* The concierges at the hotel were quite helpful and provided us with restaurant recommendations around the city.

portends: *to give warning of, or predict.* Yang thinks that her brother's move portends a change in her family's future.

correlation: *a relationship or connection between two or more things.* Magda's research showed a correlation between school start time and academic performance.

First Read: Analyzing the Development of Central Ideas

One long-term trend in the world of work is automation, or the replacement of human workers with machines. Over the decades, robots have replaced humans in jobs that required repetitive or easily programmable actions. But what happens as machines grow more sophisticated? What other jobs could they take? And how should societies help workers prepare for that future?

Objective: The passage below has two important ideas regarding automation. The first important idea appears in the first half of the passage; the second one appears in the second half. Underline each idea. Then draw boxes around two sentences with details related to each idea. Record any questions you have in the My Thoughts column.

—— First Read
---- Second Read
—— Third Read

excerpt
Robots will eliminate 6% of all US jobs by 2021, report says
by Olivia Solon, *The Guardian*

My Thoughts

1   By 2021, robots will have eliminated 6% of all jobs in the US, starting with customer service representatives and eventually truck and taxi drivers. That's just one cheery takeaway from a report released by market research company

5   Forrester this week.

These robots, or intelligent agents, represent a set of AI-powered systems that can understand human behavior and make decisions on our behalf. Current technologies in this field include virtual assistants like Alexa, Cortana, Siri and Google

10 Now as well as chatbots and automated robotic systems. For now, they are quite simple, but over the next five years they will become much better at making decisions on our behalf in more complex scenarios, which will enable mass adoption of breakthroughs like self-driving cars.

15 These robots can be helpful for companies looking to cut costs, but not so good if you're an employee working in a simple-to-automate field.

ELL Support: First Read Be sure students understand that *automation* means "using robots or machines to do jobs." Have students read the article in multilevel pairs or small groups, pausing after each paragraph to summarize ideas using a Main Ideas and Supporting Details graphic organizer from the ELL Teacher Resource (p. 51). Also, encourage students to take notes and draw sketches in the margins around the article so they can be sure they understand the topic of each section.

Remediation: First Read Pair struggling students with those who are more advanced to work through the first read and mark the text. Have them alternate reading aloud the following sections: lines 1–14, lines 15–30, lines 31–53, and lines 54–68. Have them briefly discuss marking the text for important ideas and details.

"By 2021 a disruptive tidal wave will begin. Solutions powered by AI/cognitive technology will displace jobs, with the biggest impact felt in transportation, logistics, customer service and consumer services," said Forrester's Brian Hopkins in the report.

The Inevitable Robot Uprising has already started, with at least 45% of US online adults saying they use at least one of the aforementioned digital concierges. Intelligent agents can access calendars, email accounts, browsing history, playlists, purchases and media viewing history to create a detailed view of any given individual. With this knowledge, virtual agents can provide highly customized assistance, which is valuable to shops or banks trying to deliver better customer service.

Forrester paints a picture of the not-too-distant future.

"The doorbell rings, and it's the delivery of a new pair of running shoes, in the right style, color and size, just as you needed to replace your old ones. And here's the kicker: you didn't order them. Your intelligent agent did."

In the transportation industry, Uber, Google and Tesla are working on driverless cars, while similar technology is creeping its way into trucking to replace expensive human drivers.

It's easy to get dazzled by such innovations, but what happens to the 6%? The call center staff, the taxi drivers and the truckers. There may be new jobs created to oversee and maintain these automated systems, but they will require an entirely different skillset.

"Six percent is huge. In an economy that's really not creating regular full-time jobs, the ability of people to easily find new employment is going to diminish. So we will have people wanting to work and struggling to find jobs because

My Thoughts

_____
_____
_____
_____
_____
_____
_____
_____
_____
_____
_____
_____
_____
_____
_____
_____
_____
_____
_____
_____
_____
_____
_____
_____
_____
_____
_____
_____
_____
_____
_____

After Reading: Use the following questions to check comprehension.

Text-Based Discussion Questions

1. Reread the scenario described in lines 32–35. What might be positive and negative about such a development? *Sample answer: Artificial intelligence that anticipates people's needs would be convenient and would save time. But some people enjoy shopping for themselves. Shopping by AI could put some brick-and-mortar stores out of business, which means fewer retail jobs.*

2. Why does automation result in "people wanting to work and struggling to find jobs" (line 47)? What might be one way to solve this problem? *People who lose their jobs to robots can't always find work in other areas. Some people could be trained for new jobs that will rise with the increase in robots and other technology.*

☞ **Gr7Ch13Read1.pptx**

About the Author: Olivia Solon is a freelance journalist best known for her articles on technology and digital culture. Solon began her journalism career covering topics on media and marketing for business. She then went on to specialize in science, technology, and media. Solon has written for *Wired* and *The Guardian,* among other publications. She also frequently comments on issues related to technology for the BBC and Sky News.

Chapter 13 (continued)

Lesson Support

Focus on Analyzing the Development of Central Ideas: Have students share with the class the two important ideas they marked during this read. Then introduce the diagram on page 273. Have students complete it independently and then share what they wrote with the class.

---

the same trends are beginning to occur in other historically richer job creation areas like banking, retail and healthcare,"

50 said Andy Stern, the former president of the Service Employees International Union.

"It's an early warning sign and I think it just portends a massive wind of change in the future."

55 Studies have shown that higher rates of unemployment are linked to less volunteerism and higher crime. Taxi drivers around the world have already reacted with violent protest to the arrival of ride-hailing app Uber. Imagine how people react when Uber eliminates drivers from its fleet.

"There is a lot of correlation between unemployment and 60 drug use," said Stern. "Clearly over time, particularly in urban settings, the lack of employment is tinder for lighting a fire of social unrest."

The challenge posed by automation is not being taken seriously enough at a policy level, Stern added. "Politicians 65 would rather talk about getting a college degree and technical skill training, things that are probably five to 10 years too late. We don't really have a plan and we don't appreciate how quickly the future is arriving."

My Thoughts

The conclusion of this article is much more negative. It predicts higher unemployment leading to social unrest.

FIRST RESPONSE: KEY IDEAS AND DETAILS

According to the passage, how could widespread unemployment affect society? Record your answer in your response journal.

Focus on Analyzing the Development of Central Ideas

In nonfiction, a central idea is an idea that an author wants readers to understand fully. Some nonfiction texts, like the article you just read, have two or more central ideas.

The central idea in the first half of the article is this: by 2021, robots will eliminate 6% of jobs.

TECH-CONNECT

As directed by your teacher, send a question you had about the article to Poll Everywhere or post it on your class website.

What do you think is the central idea in the second half of the passage?

CONNECT TO
ESSENTIAL QUESTION

The article focuses on the negative effects of automation. Are there positive effects to society that the article does not describe?

Authors develop, or say more about, a central idea with information such as details, examples, quotations, and so on. By developing a central idea, the author gives readers a fuller understanding of the idea and its importance.

The diagram below restates the first central idea of the passage and one of its supporting details. Complete the diagram with two other supporting details.

REFLECT

You might have heard the expressions "the bare bones of an idea" and "fleshing out an idea." How are those expressions related to the development of a central idea?

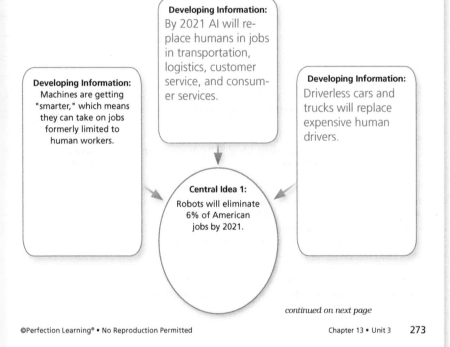

Developing Information:
By 2021 AI will replace humans in jobs in transportation, logistics, customer service, and consumer services.

Developing Information:
Machines are getting "smarter," which means they can take on jobs formerly limited to human workers.

Developing Information:
Driverless cars and trucks will replace expensive human drivers.

Central Idea 1:
Robots will eliminate 6% of American jobs by 2021.

continued on next page

Answer to Question, page 273:

Some experts are concerned that societies are not preparing their workers for these changes.

Answers to Diagram:

See answers on Student Book insert page to the left.

ELL Support: Focus on Analyzing the Development of Central Ideas and Write Model rereading the first few paragraphs and identifying the central idea and key details. Remind students they can use their graphic organizers they completed during the first read. Have students work in multilevel pairs or small groups to complete both central idea diagrams. Then students can remain in their pairs or groups to write the summary paragraph, using these sentence frames:

• The second central idea of this passage is . . . .

• For example, ... Also, ... Finally, ...

Chapter 13 (continued)

Lesson Support

Answers to Diagram:

See answers on Student Book insert page to the right.

▼**Write:** By completing the second diagram, students have already created much of the material for their paragraphs. Remind students to flesh out their paragraphs with transitional words and phrases that describe how these elements fit together.

▌Second Read: Comparing Media Portrayals of a Topic

Before Reading: Point out that students will now read another article about robots. Then they will watch a video version of the article.

Review the objective with students. Make sure they understand the concept of *mood* with this definition:

> **mood:** *the feelings or atmosphere created by an author through his or her choice of words, details, and diction.*

Tell students that, although readers usually talk about *mood* in relation to fiction or poetry, most types of texts, including videos, display or present moods.

Before showing the video, briefly discuss how the experience of watching a video might be different from reading a text on the same subject. Discussion prompts might include:

- What additional features might be included in a video?
- How do these features help convey information?
- What are the advantages and disadvantages of each medium (text vs. video)?

Have students make a prediction about the mood of the video and write their answer in the shaded bracket on page 276. Preview the questions in the chart on pages 276–277. Then show the video at https://www.newsy.com/stories/robots-could-take-6-percent-of-us-jobs-by-2021/ or go to Newsy.com and search for the article's title. Encourage students to take notes as they watch and jot down the time stamps where they occur.

🖱 **Gr7Ch13Read2.pptx**

Work with a partner to fill out the following diagram. When you're finished, the diagram should identify the second central idea of the passage and three pieces of information that help develop that central idea.

Developing Information: Unemployment is related to increased crime and drug abuse.

Developing Information: The robot revolution will lead to fewer jobs in certain fields.

Developing Information: Policy makers (politicians) do not understand how soon the changes will occur.

Central Idea 2: Some experts worry that societies are unprepared for automation.

▼**Write** Use the information in the diagram above to write a paragraph summarizing the second central idea of the passage.

▌Second Read: Comparing Media Portrayals of a Topic

Broadcasting, print publishing, and the Internet are forms of media. When you read a book or magazine article, you're reading print media. When you read an article or watch a video on a website, you're consuming media on the Internet.

Some websites provide both text and video versions of the same topic. Compared with texts, videos have many more features, including human presenters, images and motion, music, text graphics, and so on. As a result, the experience of reading a text and watching a video version on the same subject is quite different.

TECH-CONNECT

Post your paragraph on your class webpage. Compare your paragraph to those posted by other students.

ELL Support: Second Read Before students read, explain that *media* means "ways information is communicated to the public, including radio, television, newspapers, magazines, Internet, etc." Also, explain that *mood* is "the feeling a reader gets from a text." Display words and descriptions that describe mood from the student book: *alarming* (feeling danger), *amusing* (funny), *reassuring* (calming), and *exciting* (interesting). Have students read the article in multilevel pairs or small groups, pausing after each paragraph to summarize ideas using a Main Ideas and Supporting Details graphic organizer from the ELL Teacher Resource (p. 51).

Objective: First, read the article that follows. As you read, circle any words or phrases that show the author's personality or express a mood. After you read the text, you will watch a video version of this article.

Robots Are Slowly Taking Over the Job Market
by Lindsey Pulse, Newsy.com

My Thoughts

1 Robots are taking over the work world, but that doesn't mean machines will take everyone's jobs—for now.

A study by Forrester Research found 6 percent of all U.S. jobs will be replaced by robots by 2021—starting with those in
5 customer service.

Forrester found that eventually, robots will take over most craftsmen and factory jobs. They'll also come for taxi and truck drivers. Uber is already at the forefront of that innovation.

And while these robots can be good for companies looking
10 to cut costs and increase efficiency, where does that leave employees who get the boot?

The argument for a more automated workforce is that it will create new jobs in robot creation and robot management. But that argument can really only apply to those capable
15 of becoming engineers. Not everyone can create artificial intelligence software.

And there's not a lot anyone can do to stop artificial intelligence from seeping into the work world.

McDonald's has been using self-service ordering kiosks in
20 various locations since last year. Other food chains followed suit.

And right now, most robots are pretty basic. They can take commands, like Amazon's Alexa or Apple's Siri. But over the next several years, those robots will learn how to do even more.

That includes the ability to predict human behavior and
25 figure out complex scenarios.

Preview Vocabulary: Preview unfamiliar vocabulary to aid comprehension or have students note any unfamiliar words as they complete the first read of a text. After the first read, guide students to determine the words' meanings using the context. Encourage students to support their responses with evidence. Have students confirm their initial definitions with a dictionary. Words that students might find difficult include:

innovation: *a new method, idea, or product.* Ramon was thankful for technological <u>innovation</u> every time he unlocked his smartphone.

kiosks: *a small structure used to sell merchandise or services.* Andris rushed to one of the <u>kiosks</u> in the airport to check in and print his boarding pass.

scenarios: *a description of possible actions or events in the future.* Katy tried to imagine different <u>scenarios</u> of what life would be like at college.

Chapter 13 (continued)

Lesson Support

After Reading/Viewing: Use the following questions to check comprehension.

Text-Based Discussion Questions

1. What is similar and different about how the text and the video express tone? *The text of the article expresses a critical, anxious tone through word choice and sentence structure. For example, she uses dashes to set off concerns: "but that doesn't mean machines will take everyone's jobs—for now" (lines 1–2). She also asks a question to pose a problem: "where does that leave employees who get the boot?" (lines 10–11). In the video, the presenter expresses tone through varying the pitch in her voice, which comes across as upbeat. The music adds to this tone.*

2. How does the text convey the idea that the use of artificial intelligence in the workplace is inevitable? How does the video reinforce this idea? *The text gives examples about what is already happening: "McDonald's has been using self-service kiosks in various locations since last year" (lines 19–20). The video presents images that show automation of jobs that used to be held by humans.*

Answers to Chart:

See answers on Student Book insert page to the right.

 Gr7Ch13Read2.pptx

For now, it appears jobs that require physical interaction, like management, are in the clear, along with jobs that can be unpredictable, like construction work—but for how long, we can't really say.

Before you watch the video version of the article, make a prediction: What mood will the video have? Will it portray the topic in a way that alarms, amuses, reassures, or excites? Or will there be no apparent mood at all? Explain your prediction.

Review the questions in the chart. As you watch the video, record notes in the chart on how the video presents information. **Note:** Search using the title of the article. The video is found on the Newsy.com site. The video is less than two minutes long. Watch it at least three times to gather enough information to complete the chart.

Video Version of "Robots Are Slowly Taking Over the Job Market"
During Viewing
Presenter: What is the presenter's tone? How does she want to make you feel?
The presenter's tone is serious. She wants me to feel informed but concerned about how robots will affect the future of jobs.
Music: Is there music? Describe what it sounds like. Is it intended to affect your reception of the information? If so, how?
There is music. It sounds mysterious. I think this is supposed to make me feel unsure about the future.

ELL Support: Second Read After playing the video several times, model answering the first question in the chart. Then have students work in multilevel pairs or small groups to complete the rest of the chart. Rephrase the questions as necessary, especially those about music: *Is there music? Describe what it sounds like. How does the music make you feel? How does this relate to the information in the video?* When they are done, show the video again. Doing so will help them monitor their comprehension of the video.

Video Version of "Robots Are Slowly Taking Over the Job Market"
Text Graphics: Are there text graphics? What do they say? What purposes do they seem to have? Are they helpful?
There are text graphics. They provide information and statistics related to what the presenter is talking about. They are helpful in learning facts about the topic.
Other Images: What people or things does the video show? What do they add to the presentation of the information?
The video shows different types of robots that are being used and developed. They provide a visual that helps me understand the concept.
After Viewing
Overall Impressions: What did you think of the video clip? What emotions did you experience? Was the tone of the video a good match for the information presented? Why or why not?
The video clip made me nervous for the future. I think that the tone of the video was a good match for the information presented. It did not alarm me, but it made me feel informed.

Focus on Comparing Media Portrayals of a Topic

When watching the video at Newsy.com, you probably noticed that the text of the article is found under the video. This digital text has different features from the print version found in this book. It includes links to the Forrester Research study cited in the article. It also provides links to other articles on the same topic. You can click on the buttons under SHARE to share the article's URL on social media or send it to yourself via email. How could you use these features if you were conducting a research report on this topic?

Use this chart on the following page to gather information to help you compare and contrast the article and the video. The first row has been completed for you.

continued on next page

Focus on Comparing Media Portrayals of a Topic: Before showing the class the video, briefly discuss how the experience of watching a video might be different from reading a text on the same subject. Discussion prompts might include:

- What additional features might be included in a video?
- How do these features help convey information?
- What are the advantages and disadvantages of each medium (text vs. video)?

Have students make a prediction about the mood of the video and write their answer in the shaded bracket on page 276. Preview the questions in the chart on pages 276–277. Then show the video at http://www.newsy.com/stories/robots-could-take-6-percent-of-us-jobs-by-2021/ or go to Newsy.com and search for the article's title. Encourage students to take notes as they watch and jot down the time stamps where they occur.

Chapter 13 (continued)

Lesson Support

Answers to Chart:

See answers on Student Book insert page to the right.

(Speak and Listen: Remind students to refer to their charts and text markings during the discussion. If possible, provide groups with a tablet or laptop so they can reference the video.

▼Write: Encourage students to support their response with examples. After describing specific examples, remind them to cite lines of text or time stamps that pinpoint video details.

Third Read: Analyzing Presentations of the Same Topic

Before Reading: Preview the chart on pages 279–280 with students. Then have them read both articles with the task in mind and fill in the chart.

After Reading: Use the following questions to check comprehension.

Text-Based Discussion Questions

1. What similar criticism of government and business do both articles present? *Both articles state that leaders are not preparing society to adjust to the increase in automation—and that people will suffer as a result. "The challenge posed by automation is not being taken seriously enough at a policy level, Stern added" (Guardian article, lines 63–64). "But that argument can really only apply to those capable of becoming engineers" (Newsy.com article, lines 14–15).*

2. Compare and contrast the articles' points of view on artificial intelligence (AI). *Both articles list examples of AI systems. They both note that AIs are currently simple and predict that will change. The Guardian article notes that "they will become much better at making decisions on our behalf in more complex scenarios" (lines 11–13). Newsy.com agrees, predicting AIs will soon have "the ability to predict human behavior and figure out complex scenarios" (lines 24–25). The Guardian*

(continued)

Question	Article	Video
What is the central idea of each version?	Robots are taking over more and different types of jobs.	Robots are taking over more and different types of jobs.
Do you get a sense for the personality of the author (article) or the speaker (video)? If so, describe that personality.	The author's point of view comes out in phrases such as "[will] come for taxi and truck drivers" and "will get the boot." It's informal and negative.	The presenter is friendly, talkative, straightforward; much more personality comes through in her voice and demeanor.
Describe the tone with which the subject matter is portrayed.	slightly negative but conversational. The tone is more pessimistic than the other article.	informational and serious

(Speak and Listen Although the article and the video present the same information, their portrayals of the subject matter are clearly quite different. With a group of three or four classmates, share your charts and discuss how the article and the video differ.

▼Write Based on your discussion with your classmates, write a paragraph that describes what you think is the most important difference between the article and the video's portrayal of the subject. Refer specifically to the video's use of music, text graphics, and imagery in your answer. Complete your paragraph by explaining one likely reason the producers made the video so different from the article.

REFLECT

Which portrayal was more informative? Which portrayal was more entertaining? If you were doing research for an essay about robots and society, which would you find more useful?

Third Read: Analyzing Presentations of the Same Topic

The two articles you read present much of the same information, but they differ in their presentation of that information. But in what ways do they differ?

Objective: Read the two articles again. (You do not need to watch the video again.) As you read, circle any supporting details that are similar. In the "My Thoughts" column, jot down your observations about how the conclusions of each article are different.

TECH-CONNECT

Post your paragraph on your class website. Read other students' responses and comment positively on two or more of them.

ELL Support: Speak and Listen and Write Have students work in multilevel pairs or small groups and use these sentence frames to discuss and then write about the article and video. These can also be found as a student handout in the ELL Teacher Resource (p. 37)

- (Sentence 1) Today, I read . . . and then watched . . . .
- (Sentence 2) The most important difference between the article and the video is . . . .
- (Sentence 3) Although both contained the same content, the (article or video) was more . . . than the (article or video).
- (Sentence 4) There are several reasons that . . . .
- (Sentences 5–7) For example, (describe specific detail and its effect).
- (Sentence 8) The producers probably made the video so different from the article to . . . .

Focus on Analyzing Presentations of the Same Topic

The two articles in this chapter are similar, but there are some important differences in the conclusions they reach about robots and the job market. Complete the chart below to compare and contrast the articles.

Question	"Robots Will Eliminate 6% of All U.S. Jobs"	"Robots Are Slowly Taking Over the Job Market"
On what report are both articles based?	a report by the marketing research company Forrester	a report by the marketing research company Forrester
Identify statistics (numbers) that appear in both articles.	By 2021, 6% of jobs in the U.S. will have been replaced.	By 2021, 6% of jobs in the U.S. will have been replaced.
Identify the kinds of jobs the articles say will disappear.	customer service representatives truck and taxi drivers	crafts and factory workers taxi and truck drivers customer service
What examples of artificial intelligence does each article give?	Intelligent agents like Alexa, Cortana, Siri, Google Now	McDonald's, Alexa, Siri
Who does each article quote? What are their names and jobs?	Brian Hopkins, who helped write the Forrester report; Andy Stern, former president of the Service Employees International Union (SEIU)	No people are quoted.

continued on next page

goes further, however, providing an example of what may result of this development, noting it "will enable mass adoption of breakthroughs like self-driving cars" (lines 13–14).

Focus on Analyzing Presentations of the Same Topic: Introduce the chart on pages 279–280, noting that it will help students compare the texts of the two articles about robots they have read in this chapter. Have students revisit the articles as they complete the chart independently.

Answers to Chart:

See answers on Student Book insert page to the left.

 Gr7Ch13Read3.pptx

ELL Support: Third Read Model rereading the first few paragraphs of each article and filling out the first row of the chart. Then have students work in multilevel pairs or small groups to reread the articles and complete the chart.

Remediation: Third Read To facilitate completing the comparison chart, form a small group of 3 to 4 students, including both struggling students and those who are more advanced. To help students focus, suggest that they revisit the articles one at a time, completing column 2 before going on to complete column 3.

Chapter 13 (continued)

Lesson Support

Answers to Chart:

See answers on Student Book insert page to the right.

☾**Speak and Listen:** Encourage students to compare both the ideas in the article and the types of details (examples, anecdotes, statistics, quotations) provided as support.

Question	"Robots Will Eliminate 6% of All U.S. Jobs"	"Robots Are Slowly Taking Over the Job Market"
What does each article claim about whether society is ready for the change?	Andy Stern suggests that our society is not ready for the change.	There is no claim.
What idea does each article want the reader to take from it?	Society might not be prepared for the disruption caused by the automation of jobs. This could be bad—not just for individuals—but dangerous for society as a whole.	Some jobs, including mine, might be safe for a while, but not for long.

☾**Speak and Listen** Form a small group and discuss the important differences between the two articles. Consider these questions:

- Are the articles similar or different in how they interpret the facts?
- Does one article go further in its interpretation of the facts than the other?

> **REFLECT**
>
> Which article made you ponder your own future more? Why?

Language: Subject and Verb Agreement

In the present tense, subjects and verbs must agree with each other in number. Plural subjects take plural verbs, and singular subjects require singular verbs. Following this rule becomes more difficult when the subject and verb are separated or when the sentence has multiple subjects.

Two or more subjects in a clause form a compound subject. Depending on how the subjects are related, a compound subject may take a singular or a plural verb. Consider the following sentences with compound subjects.

- <u>Alexa, Cortana, Siri, and Google Now</u> are virtual assistants.
- If <u>Alexa or Siri</u> hears its name, it listens for a command.

In the first sentence, the subjects are joined by the word *and*, making the compound subject plural. In the second sentence, the subjects are joined by *or*, showing a choice between the subjects. They are not acting together, so the compound subject is singular. Remember, in a complex sentence like this one, the subject and verb in the dependent clause must agree and the subject and

©Perfection Learning® • No Reproduction Permitted

ELL Support: Speak and Listen Have students work in multilevel pairs or small groups and use these sentence frames to compare the two articles:

- The articles are similar/different in how they interpret (think about) the facts.
- For example, article 1 says . . . . Also/But article 2 says . . . .
- Article . . . interprets/does not interpret the facts better than article . . . . For example, article . . . says . . . . Also/But, article . . . says . . . .

verb in the independent clause must agree. Study the following sentence.

- Virtual assistants like Alexa, Cortana, Siri, or Google Now are quite simple, but over the next five years they will become much better.

In this sentence, the subject is *virtual assistants*, which is plural. The names may appear to be a compound subject, but the names are the objects in the prepositional phrase. The word *like* is used as a preposition.

In the following sentences, underline the subject and circle the correct verb.

1. The car full of teenagers (pulse / pulses) with loud music even though two police cars (follow, follows) behind.

2. Jeremy, the oldest of six kids, (love / loves) to babysit.

3. Shelly, Mika, and I (wants / want) to see the school play.

4. Jobs that require physical interaction, like management, (is / are) in the clear.

5. A robot or a computer program like a self-service ordering kiosk (replaces / replace) several human workers.

Project-Based Assessments

Op-Ed

An op-ed is a written opinion published by a newspaper or magazine that typically appears opposite the editorial page. It has a named author and focuses on an issue of importance.

Research the following question. Then write an op-ed for your local newspaper.

- What is the proper role of government, if any, in helping large groups of workers replaced by robots?

Follow these steps to help you.

1. Read two op-eds from a local newspaper. Study how an op-ed is written. How does it start? How does the opinion develop? What reasons and information does it give?
2. Research. Find three reliable sources on how governments have assisted workers who lost their jobs to robots.
3. Take careful notes and put the ideas into your own words.
4. Once you've done research, state your opinion on the question above.
5. Write your op-ed. It should be between 200 and 300 words.

> **CONNECT TO ESSENTIAL QUESTION**
>
> On balance, is the human world improved or hurt by the spread of robots?

continued on next page

Language: Subject and Verb Agreement: Remind students that the subject of a sentence is never in a prepositional phrase. As they complete the exercises on page 281, they can cross out any phrases that come between the subject and verb.

Answers to Exercises:

1. pulses
2. loves
3. want
4. are
5. replaces

Gr7Ch13Language.pptx

Project-Based Assessments

Op-Ed: A good place to begin research about government's role in helping displaced workers is "Artificial Intelligence, Automation, and the Economy," a policy report published by the office of President Barack Obama on December 20, 2016. Suggest that students refer to the Policy Responses section that begins on page 26 of the report. The report can be found at https://obamawhitehouse.archives.gov/sites/whitehouse.gov/files/documents/Artificial-Intelligence-Automation-Economy.PDF.

ELL Support: Language Together with volunteers, identify and circle the subject of each sentence. Explain how to conjugate verbs for single and plural subjects. Then have students work in multilevel pairs or groups to complete the items. Review the answers as a class, emphasizing the subject and verbs.

Assessment

Job Fair Pamphlet: Make sure students understand that the focus of the pamphlet is the job. They need not include personal material about why the job interests them or why it would be a good fit for them.

It may be helpful to show students what a job pamphlet might look like. Some examples include:

- "Become a Veterinarian and Make a Difference," published by the Association of American Veterinary Medical Colleges (AAVMAC): http://www.aavmc.org/data/images/career%20brochure%20-%20web.pdf

- "Careers in Biology," published by the American Institute of Biological Sciences: https://www.aibs.org/careers/resources/career_brochure.pdf

- "Launching a Career as a Court Reporter," published by the Court Reporters Board of California: http://www.courtreportersboard.ca.gov/formspubs/student_career.pdf

---

6. Ask two people to read your op-ed and give you feedback. Revise your op-ed based on their suggestions.
7. Check your writing for mistakes in grammar usage, punctuation, transitions, and spelling.

Use the following guidelines for your op-ed.	
To receive the highest score (4.0), the op-ed must meet all of these criteria.	Your op-ed • includes a clearly stated opinion. • acknowledges an opposing opinion/counterargument. • demonstrates the appropriate structure and length of an op-ed. • uses evidence to support your opinion. • uses correct grammar, punctuation, and spelling.

Job Fair Pamphlet

The second article states, "Not everyone can create artificial intelligence software." That's probably true. But not everyone *wants* that job. What is your dream job? What education or training would you need in order to get it?

Research a job you are interested in. Then use a word processing program to create a trifold, double-sided pamphlet to present information about the job. Imagine you are making the pamphlet for a job fair, which is an event where people come to learn about jobs.

Research the Job

1. Brainstorm jobs. Investigate what really interests you. Would you like to be an astronaut, a politician, a movie star, or a professional athlete? For this activity, the sky is the limit.
2. Visit the U.S. Bureau of Labor Statistics' online Occupational Outlook Handbook (OOH) at bls.gov/ooh/.
3. Spend time exploring the OOH Page. You can search for jobs by data such as pay, education level, and growth rate. You can also browse through "Occupation Groups" such as "Arts and Design" or "Entertainment and Sports." Use the features of these digital texts including links and pop-up explanations to enhance your understanding of what you are reading.
4. Once you've settled on an interesting job, record as much information as you can gather about it from the OOH website.

Make the Pamphlet

1. Find the trifold template in your word processing program and choose a style.
2. Your brochure will open in a new file. Save and name the

ELL Support: Project-Based Assessments Have students work in multilevel pairs or groups to write the op-ed or create a pamphlet. Together with students, brainstorm sentence frames that they can use for each project. For the pamphlet project, beginning and intermediate students may draw images with labels to represent their ideal job. Provide the Proofreading Checklist from the ELL Teacher Resource (p. 71) for students to finalize their op-eds or pamphlets.

file. Locate the front page of the brochure and add a title and a picture. (Pictures can be downloaded from the Internet.)

3. Design the inside and back of the brochure and include the following information:
   - the name of the job
   - a brief description of what people in the job typically do
   - the minimum amount of training or education required to get started in the job, e.g., high-school diploma, two-year degree, apprenticeship, four-year degree, graduate degree, or more
   - the average starting salary
   - the future prospects for the job, e.g., whether robots will likely displace human workers
   - at least two visual aids to support your text, such as photos of people performing the job or graphs showing trends over time

Use the following guidelines for your job fair pamphlet.	
To receive the highest score (4.0), the pamphlet must meet all of these criteria.	Your pamphlet • contains the name and description of the job. • includes the minimum education required to get started. • displays the average beginning salary. • discusses the future prospects for the job. • includes at least two visuals that support an understanding of the job. • is well organized, neat, and professional. • uses correct grammar, punctuation, and spelling.

On Your Own: Integrating Ideas

1. As mentioned at the beginning of this chapter, the word *robot* was first used in the 1920 play *R.U.R.* (*Rossum's Universal Robots*) by Karel Čapek. You can find a public domain recording of the play at Archive.org.

2. Robots are the subject of many famous science-fiction stories, but the writer Isaac Asimov wrote many of the most celebrated, beginning with his short story collection *I, Robot* (1950), which is still in print and can probably be found in your school library. Asimov imagined that advanced robots would be programmed to obey three laws that would protect people from harm. Select and read some of Asimov's stories or read another text about intelligent robots.

> **REFLECT**
>
> As you get older, how can you respond to the problem of automation in the workplace? Are there things you can do to make sure you have a good chance of keeping a job?

On Your Own: Integrating Ideas:

Activity 2: Students may also be interested in contemporary science fiction featuring robots and themes about humans and technology. The following books are recommended for middle school students:

- *MILA 2.0* (2013) by Debra Driza is a thriller about a teenage android who develops human emotions. With her scientist creator, she flees from government agents who want to use her as a secret weapon. *MILA 2.0* is the first installment of a trilogy, followed by *Renegade* (2014) and *Redemption* (2015).

- *Revolution 19* (2012) by Gregg Rosenblum is set fourteen years after military robots turn against their creators and take over the world, forcing human survivors to live under their control. It centers on three siblings seeking to rescue their parents, who have been captured by robot raiders. *Revolution 19* is the first book in a trilogy that includes *Fugitive X* (2013) and *City 1* (2015).

- *Rat Runners* (2015) by Oisín McGann is set in a future London controlled by mega-corporation WatchWorld. The plot features a group of teenage orphans who band together to survive in a city patrolled by half-human/half-robot sentinels called SafeGuards.

Remediation: Project-Based Assessments Some students may need further guidance. Break the projects into smaller chunks with assignments that are due every few days. These mini-assignments can serve as check-ins for monitoring students' progress and providing targeted guidance.

Chapter 13 *(continued)*

Assessment

Connect to Testing: This Connect to Testing section focuses on analyzing the development of central ideas, comparing media portrayals of a topic, analyzing presentations of the same topic, and understanding denotation and connotation.

Encourage students to work in pairs to choose the correct answers to the questions and then to compare their answers with those of another pair of students. If there is disagreement, encourage the groups to try to reach a consensus as they discuss the reasons for their choices.

Answers to Connect to Testing Questions:

1. **Part A:** C. Choice C is the best choice because it best reflects the central idea of the second part of the article: that society is not prepared for the changes that will come with more jobs being performed by AI. (DoK 2)

   Part B: D. Choice D supports the idea that society is unprepared for the future. (DoK 2)

2. Answers will vary. The images of robotics and AI help students visualize the technology and better understand the types of tasks that machines can possibly do in the future. The images of Alexa and people using Siri provide more details about the kinds of tasks these AI "assistants" can already do. The allusion to Michelangelo's *Creation of Adam* makes a statement about how humans are playing God by creating artificial intelligence. This implies a warning about the relationship between humans and their created robots. (DoK 3)

(continued)

Connect to Testing

In this chapter, you analyzed the development of central ideas, compared media portrayals of a topic, and analyzed presentations of the same topic. When you take assessments, you will be tested over these skills.

1. **Part A:** Which sentence from "Robots will eliminate 6% of all US jobs by 2021" best summarizes one of that article's two central ideas?

   A. *These robots, or intelligent agents, represent a set of AI-powered systems that can understand human behavior and make decisions on our behalf.*

   B. *Intelligent agents can access calendars, email accounts, browsing history, playlists, purchases and media viewing history to create a detailed view of any given individual.*

   C. *"It's an early warning sign and I think it just portends a massive wind of change in the future."*

   D. *Imagine how people react when Uber eliminates drivers from its fleet.*

   Part B: Which sentence offers details that develop the central idea in Part A?

   A. *These robots can be helpful for companies looking to cut costs, but not so good if you're an employee working in a simple-to-automate field.*

   B. *Current technologies in this field include virtual assistants like Alexa, Cortana, Siri and Google Now as well as chatbots and automated robotic systems.*

   C. *In the transportation industry, Uber, Google and Tesla are working on driverless cars, while similar technology is creeping its way into trucking to replace expensive human drivers.*

   D. *We don't really have a plan and we don't appreciate how quickly the future is arriving.*

2. How is the experience of watching the video of "Robots Are Slowly Taking Over the Job Market" different from reading the article? Refer to specific ways the video helps you understand the concepts in the article.

ELL Support: Connect to Testing and Assessments See the ELL Teacher Resource (p. 22) for ideas on adapting this section for ELLs.

3. Read the sentences below. Choose the sentence where the subject and verb do **not** agree.

A. Artificial intelligence, or AI, is an area of computer science.

B. Two of the activities computers with artificial intelligence is designed for include speech recognition and problem solving.

C. Robotics, or the design and operation of robots, is also a field related to artificial intelligence.

D. Industrial robots used in manufacturing are just one type of robot.

4. **Part A:** What central idea can be found in **both** articles about robots?

A. Robots will replace a significant number of workers at their jobs.

B. Widespread unemployment will lead to crime and social unrest.

C. Forrester Research released a report with disturbing findings.

D. Robots will become able to do more sophisticated jobs over time.

Part B: Select one sentence from each article to support the answer to Part A.

A. *By 2021, robots will have eliminated 6% of all jobs in the US, starting with customer service representatives and eventually truck and taxi drivers.* (article 1)

B. *For now, they are quite simple, but over the next five years they will become much better at making decisions on our behalf in more complex scenarios, which will enable mass adoption of breakthroughs like self-driving cars.* (article 1)

C. *Studies have shown that higher rates of unemployment are linked to less volunteerism and higher crime.* (article 1)

D. *A study by Forrester Research found 6 percent of all U.S. jobs will be replaced by robots by 2021—starting with those in customer service.* (article 2)

E. *But over the next several years, those robots will learn how to do even more.* (article 2)

F. *For now, it appears jobs that require physical interaction, like management, are in the clear, along with jobs that can be unpredictable, like construction work—but for how long, we can't really say.* (article 2)

5. Which of these describes an important difference between the two articles about robots?

A. *The Guardian* article explains how society should respond to automation.

B. *The Guardian* article draws a connection between unemployment and crime.

C. The Newsy article discusses how robots are changing customer service jobs.

D. The Newsy article describes how robots are growing more sophisticated with time.

3. B. The subject *Two* requires a plural verb. The verb should be *are* not *is*. (DoK 1)

4. **Part A:** A. Both articles quote the same study by Forrester Research. Choice B is a supporting detail found only in the first article. Although Choice C mentions the study, it doesn't include the central idea of the study. Choice D is also mentioned in both articles, but it is a supporting detail not a central idea.

   Part B: A., D. Both of these choices summarize the Forrester Research report. (DoK 3)

5. B. Choice A is not explored in either article, although the first article describes the negative consequences of humans being put out of work by AI. Choices C and D are incorrect because both articles mention these facts. Thus, the best answer is Choice B because *The Guardian* article makes this connection. (DoK 3)

Chapter 14

Determining Theme

Feed
by M. T. Anderson

Introduction

Chapter Goals: Have students read through the goals and mark any words that are unfamiliar. Discuss the meanings of any academic vocabulary within the goals that students marked as unfamiliar. Consider posting the Chapter Goals.

Preview Academic Vocabulary: Read and discuss the meanings of the academic vocabulary.

> **point of view:** *opinion or perspective on a topic.* I did not agree with my father's <u>point of view</u>, but I know that it's okay to have different opinions.

> **theme:** *the central idea of a work of literature.* Ruby's favorite book communicated a <u>theme</u> about friendship: You discover who your true friends really are when you fall on hard times.

🖱️ **Gr7Ch14Vocabulary.pptx**

Preview Concepts: Point out the questions on page 286 and have students answer them independently. Ask volunteers to share their answers with the class. Briefly discuss the following points:

- What kinds of activities have been transformed by the Internet?

- What activities do you think may be transformed by technology in the future?

- Should people be concerned about any technological transformations? If so, what kinds—and why?

Chapter 14

Determining Theme

Preview Concepts
It is hard for young people to remember a time without the Internet, websites, and social media such as Facebook or Instagram. You have probably never known life without such technology. And like all technologies, it can be good or bad for individuals and society.

1. Describe one way in which the technology of the Internet has led to a more interesting world.

2. Now describe one way in which the Internet might actually be harmful to people who use it a lot.

CHAPTER GOALS

In this chapter you will

- determine the theme of a story.
- analyze the interaction of story elements.
- observe how an author develops the points of view of different characters.
- use context clues to understand the meanings of words.

PREVIEW ACADEMIC VOCABULARY

point of view

theme

ELL Support: Academic Vocabulary See <u>Teaching Vocabulary in the ELL Teacher Resource (p. 18)</u> for ideas to use for teaching vocabulary throughout *Connections*.

Preview Concepts Use images, gestures, and simple definitions to help students understand the following words: *Internet, websites, social media, technology, individuals, society.*

Have students work in multilevel pairs or groups and use the following sentence frames to answer the questions:

- The Internet has made the world more interesting by . . . .

- The Internet can be harmful (bad) for people who use it a lot because . . . .

Making Connections

Read the following sentences.

Extreme boredom provides its own antidote.
—François de La Rochefoucauld, a 17th-century French author

If life . . . were possessed of any positive intrinsic value, there would be no such thing as boredom at all: mere existence would satisfy us in itself, and we should want for nothing.
—Arthur Schopenhauer, a 19th-century German philosopher

Isn't "not to be bored" one of the principal goals of life?
—Gustave Flaubert, a 19th-century French author

A well-stocked mind is safe from boredom.
—from *Childhood's End* by Arthur C. Clarke

The quotations above show that some great minds have thought about boredom's importance, meaning, and solutions. Choose one of the sentences above. Restate in your own words what the sentence means. Then state whether you agree with the author's point of view, and explain why.

> **MAKING CONNECTIONS**
>
> As you read the excerpt from the novel in this chapter, think about how the narrator's struggles with boredom help to develop the theme.

---

1. The Internet makes the world more interesting because it is easier to find out what is happening around the world. You can also become friends with people you will never meet in person. There is a wealth of information at your fingertips. If you have a question, you can get an instant answer. Also, you can learn about all kinds of topics, including watching videos about how to solve a math problem and how to fix your bike.

2. The Internet can be harmful to people who use it a lot because they might stop interacting with real people or with people who are different from them. It's easier online to only be friends with people who agree with you.

Making Connections: Point out the quotations about boredom on page 287 and have students complete the activity. Encourage them to consider how they and others they know handle boredom and how technology might affect their ability to deal with boredom. Remind students to keep these ideas in mind as they read the excerpt from *Feed*.

Answers to Question:

Sample Answer: Extreme boredom provides its own antidote.

If you are bored enough, you will find ways to entertain yourself—therefore curing your boredom. I agree with this point of view, because sometimes one has to be bored in order to find creative ways to cure boredom.

ELL Support: Make Connections First, use gestures and pantomime to confirm that students understand what *boredom* means. Have students work in multilevel pairs or groups (or work together as a class) to read and paraphrase each quotation on p. 287. Once students understand the content of each quotation, they can choose one to write about. Provide sentence frames such as the following for students to respond to the prompt in their multilevel pairs or groups:

- The quote by . . . means . . . .

- I agree/don't agree with this quote because . . . .

Lesson Support

First Read: Comparing Points of View

Before Reading: Read the first paragraph on page 288 and activate background knowledge about the genre by asking students to share common elements of science-fiction texts. Have them make predictions about this text based on the genre and the headers throughout.

Read the header: Comparing Points of View. Inform students that, in this case, "point of view" isn't referring to whether the story is being told by a first- or third-person narrator. Instead, "comparing points of view" means understanding two or more characters' attitudes toward someone or something in the story.

Point out the excerpt from *Feed* on page 288 and read aloud the objective. Explain that during this read they should note how the main character, Titus, feels about feednet and whether others in the story might feel differently. Have students read the text on their own.

Preview Vocabulary: Preview unfamiliar vocabulary to aid comprehension or ask students to circle unfamiliar words as they complete the first read of a text. After the first read, guide students to determine the words' meanings using the context. Encourage students to support their responses with evidence. Have students confirm their initial definitions with a dictionary. Words that students might find difficult include:

decrypt: *to decode or decipher.* Marleigh had to use a pen and paper to <u>decrypt</u> the message in the jumbled letters.

naysayer: *a person who always says no.* Keegan thought her father was such a <u>naysayer</u>—he never let her do anything fun.

First Read: Comparing Points of View

Before reading a text, you should preview the headers and the genre and make predictions about the text. This excerpt is from the science-fiction novel *Feed*. A teenager named Titus lives in a future world where everyone has the Internet connected wirelessly into their brains. As the story begins, Titus and his friends take a trip to the Moon, where Titus meets a girl named Violet. A strange event at a dance club knocks the friends out, and when they wake up, they find themselves disconnected from the feed.

Objective: Preview the section headers and make predictions about the main character's point of view. As you read, identify characters who feel differently than Titus does about feednet and write "might feel differently" in the margin. As you read, make predictions about what will happen next based on other science-fiction novels you have read.

—— First Read
- - - - Second Read
—— Third Read

from
Feed
by M. T. Anderson

My Thoughts

1   **Awake**

The first thing I felt was no credit.

I tried to touch my credit, but there was nothing there.

It felt like I was in a little room.

5   My body—I was in a bed, on top of my arm, which was

asleep, but I didn't know where. I couldn't find the Lunar GPS

to tell me.

FS

Someone had left a message in my head, which I found,

and then kept finding everywhere I went, which said that

10   there was no transmission signal, that I was currently

disconnected from feednet. I tried to chat Link and then Marty,

FS

but nothing, there was no transmission signal, I was currently

disconnected from feednet, of course, and I was starting to get

scared, so I tried to chat my parents, I tried to chat them on

15   Earth, but there was no transmission etc., I was currently etc.

So I opened my eyes.

288   Chapter 14 • Unit 3   ©Perfection Learning® • No Reproduction Permitted

---

ELL Support: First Read Use sketches and gestures to make sure students understand that the characters in this story were connected to the Internet (or "feed") in their brains, but now they are not. Have students read the story in multilevel pairs or small groups, pausing after each paragraph to summarize the details on a <u>Story Map graphic organizer from the ELL Teacher Resource (p. 52)</u>. Also, encourage students to take notes and draw sketches in the margins around the story so they can be sure they understand what is happening in each section.

College Try

"Nothing," she said.

I had gotten up and was sitting on a chair beside her. We

20 were in a hospital. We took up a ward.

Link was still asleep. Nurses went by.

I said, "I can't see anything. Through the feed."

. . . .

We'd been up for fifteen or twenty minutes. Everything in

25 my head was quiet. . . .

"What do we do?" she asked.

I didn't know.

Boring

There was nothing there but the walls. We looked at them,

30 and at each other. We looked really squelch. Our hair and

stuff. We had remote relays attached to us to watch our blood

and our brains.

There were five walls, because the room was irregular. One

of them had a picture of a boat on it. The boat was on a pond

35 or maybe lake. I couldn't find anything interesting about that

picture at all. There was nothing that was about to happen or

had just happened.

I couldn't figure out even the littlest reason to paint a

picture like that.

40 ### Still Boring

Our parents had been notified while we were asleep. Only

Loga hadn't been touched by the hacker. She hadn't let him

touch her, because he looked really creepy to her, so she stood

way far away. There were also others, people we'd never met,

45 who had been touched, and they were in the wards, too. He

had touched thirteen people in all.

My Thoughts

After Reading: Use the following questions to check comprehension.

Text-Based Discussion Questions

1. Name two details in lines 1–15 that help the reader understand what "feednet" is. Explain why these details are clues to the term's meaning. *In lines 1–2, Titus notes, "The first thing I felt was no credit. I tried to touch my credit, but there was nothing there." By credit, Titus probably means money. He is "feeling" it in his head, which probably means feednet is installed in his brain and manages his money. In line 8, Titus notes, "Someone had left a message in my head." So feednet seems to operate in a person's brain, connecting people to sites and programs, much like the Internet.*

2. How does the loss of feednet affect Titus in lines 18–39? *He seems unnerved by sensing only his immediate surroundings. "I said, 'I can't see anything. Through the feed'" (line 22). As Titus and his friend look around the room, they seem a bit stunned. "There was nothing there but the walls. We looked at them, and at each other" (lines 29–30).*

Gr7Ch14Read1.pptx

About the Author: M. T. Anderson is an author of children's books, best known for his young adult novels. Anderson grew up near Boston, Massachusetts. He attended Harvard University, Cambridge University, and Syracuse. While in school, Anderson studied English literature and creative writing. Many of Anderson's odd jobs—including burger chef and radio DJ—inspired his writings.

Anderson mainly writes literature for children, penning both picture books and young adult novels. He is best known for challenging his young readers with sophisticated topics and language. One of his most popular novels is *Feed*, a satire set in a dystopian future. *Feed* was a National Book Award finalist and won the *L.A. Times* Book Award in 2003 for Young Adult fiction.

Some of Anderson's other notable publications include *The Pox Party*, *The Astonishing Life of Octavian Nothing*, and *The Game of Sunken Places*.

Please note: The language used in this excerpt has been edited. If students choose to read the entire book, explain that it does contain adult language.

Lesson Support

Background on Cyberpunk:

M. T. Anderson's *Feed* is an example of cyberpunk, a subgenre of science fiction. Often set in the distant future, cyberpunk authors imagine societies in which science and technology have become extremely advanced. These futuristic worlds often include forms of biotechnology that merge elements of technology with the human brain or other body parts. In cyberpunk, these high-tech advancements intertwine with larger problems in society as a whole. These include alienation, corporate domination, and extreme poverty. Often, the future is painted as dystopian.

The genre began taking shape in the 1960s and 1970s at a time when authors were experimenting with other forms of literature and storytelling. One of the earliest inspirations for the cyberpunk movement was Phillip K. Dick's *Do Androids Dream of Electric Sheep?* (1968). This was later turned into the movie *Blade Runner* (1982). A year later, writer Bruce Bethke published a short story that coined the term "cyberpunk." It was not until William Gibson published his 1984 novel *Neuromancer* that the genre finally took off.

Readers of all ages continue to enjoy cyberpunk. Besides *Feed*, cyberpunk novels that interest middle grade readers include *Ready Player One* by *Ernest Cline* (2011), *Shipbreaker* by Paolo Bacigalupi (2009), and *iBoy* by Kevin Brooks (2010).

	My Thoughts

There was a police officer there, waiting in a chair. He told us that we would be off-line for a while, until they could see what had been done and check for viruses, and decrypt the
50 feed history to get information to use against the guy in court. They said that they had identified him, and that he was a hacker and a naysayer of the worst kind.

FS

might feel differently

We were frightened, and kept touching our heads. Suddenly, our heads felt real empty. At least in the hospital
55 they had better gravity than the hotel.

Missing the Feed

I missed the feed.

I don't know when they first had feeds. Like maybe, fifty or a hundred years ago. Before that, they had to use their hands
60 and their eyes. Computers were all outside the body. They carried them around outside of them, in their hands, like if you carried your lungs in a briefcase and opened it to breathe.

People were really excited when they first came out with feeds. It was all *da da da, this big educational thing, da da*
65 *da, your child will have the advantage, encyclopedias at their fingertips, closer than their fingertips, etc.* That's one of the great things about the feed—that you can be supersmart without ever working. Everyone is supersmart now. You can look things up automatic, like science and history, like
70 if you want to know which battles of the Civil War George Washington fought in and [stuff].

FS

It's more now, it's not so much about the educational stuff but more regarding the fact that everything that goes on, goes on on the feed. All of the feedcasts and the instant news,
75 that's on there, so there's all the entertainment I was missing without a feed, like the girls were all missing their favorite

feedcast, this show called *Oh? Wow! Thing!*, which has all
these kids like us who do stuff but get all pouty, which is what
the girls go crazy for, the poutiness.

80   But the braggest thing about the feed, the thing that
made it really big, is that it knows everything you want and
hope for, sometimes before you even know what those things
are. It can tell you how to get them, and help you make buying
decisions that are hard. Everything we think and feel is taken

85 in by the corporations, mainly by data ones like Feedlink and
OnFeed and American Feedware, and they make a special
profile, one that's keyed just to you, and then they give it to
their branch companies, or other companies buy them, and
they can get to know what it is we need, so all you have to do

90 is want something and there's a chance it will be yours.

        Of course, everyone is like, *da da da, evil corporations, oh
they're so bad*, we all say that, and we all know they control
everything. I mean, it's not great, because who knows what
evil [things] they're up to. Everyone feels bad about that.

95 But they're the only way to get all this stuff, and it's no good
getting [mad] about it, because they're still going to control
everything whether you like it or not. Plus, they keep like
everyone in the world employed, so it's not like we could do
without them. And it's really great to know everything about

100 everything whenever we want, to have it just like, in our brain,
just sitting there.

        In fact, the thing that made me [mad] was when they
couldn't help me at all, so I was just lying there, and couldn't
play any of the games on the feed, and couldn't chat anyone,

105 and I couldn't do a . . . thing except look at that stupid boat
painting, which was even worse, because now I saw that there

My Thoughts

FS

might feel differently

FS

Lesson Support

FIRST RESPONSE: KEY IDEAS AND DETAILS

Focus on Comparing Points of View:
Point out the questions on pages 292–293 and have students answer them independently. Remind them to refer to their text annotations as they respond. Ask volunteers to share their responses with the class. Following a brief discussion, ask students to respond to the Reflect prompt on page 292.

> **Answers to Questions, page 292:**
>
> He misses it and wants it back. His feelings are mixed because it is run by corporations, but corporations are the only source of everything.
>
> It is all he talks and thinks about. He seems lost without feednet. For example: "Suddenly, our heads felt real empty" (line 54). "I missed the feed" (line 56).

🖰 Gr7Ch14Read1.pptx

🕮 **Speak and Listen:** Suggest that students also consider what the hacker has accomplished through this action. Who are the naysayers of technology in the world today?

---

was no one on the boat, which was even more stupid, and was kind of how I felt, that the sails were up, and the rudder was, well, whatever rudders are, but there was no one on board to
110 look at the horizon.

FIRST RESPONSE: KEY IDEAS AND DETAILS
Based on your first reading, how does Titus feel about feednet? Correct or confirm the predictions you made before reading the text. Record your first response in your journal.

Focus on Comparing Points of View

A character's *point of view* is the set of thoughts and feelings he or she has about something. The text offers ample evidence about how Titus feels about feednet because he is the narrator and spends most of his time talking about himself and how he feels.

How does Titus feel about feednet?

How do you know Titus feels this way? What are some words, phrases, or sentences in the text that support your claim about his point of view?

🕮 **Speak and Listen** The hacker might have a different point of view about feednet. The excerpt isn't clear on the hacker's motivations, but there is one possible clue. In line 52, Titus says the police called him "a hacker and a naysayer of the worst kind." A naysayer is someone who says "no." But what could the hacker be saying "no" to?

With a partner, talk about the possible motivations of the

> **My Thoughts**

> **CONNECT TO ESSENTIAL QUESTION**
>
> Does *Feed* depict a society in which technology has brought wonderful things? Or has technology brought about something terrible? Could it be both?

> **REFLECT**
>
> Would you want to live in a society in which you were constantly connected to a feed of information and products? Do you already?

ELL Support: Speak and Listen Explain that the word *hacker* has several shades of meaning. In this context, it refers to someone who gets around security measures to break into a computer, program, or file. Usually, the "hack" is committed to stealing money, secrets, or other documents or to damaging files or causing other harm.

Write Have students work in multilevel pairs or small groups and use these sentence frames to write about the hacker's and Titus's points of view on the feed.

- The hacker's point of view of the feed would be . . . .
- Titus's point of view of the feed is . . . .
- Their points of view are different because . . . .

hacker, that "naysayer of the worst sort." What could he be saying "no" to? How might it be related to feednet?

▼Write Based on your discussion, write a prediction in your response journal. If you were to continue reading *Feed*, what do you think the hacker's point of view about the feed would be? How would it differ from Titus's opinion? Use what you know about science-fiction dystopian novels to inform your predictions.

TECH-CONNECT

Conduct an Internet search to find a quote about corporations and consumerism. Choose a favorite and tweet it to your teacher or classmates as per your teacher's instructions, or post it to a pin board or class website.

Second Read: Analyzing the Effects of Setting

Feed is set roughly 100 years in the future. As with most science-fiction stories, the setting strongly shapes the behaviors of the characters and the plot events.

Objective: Read the text a second time. Write the abbreviation "FS" for "Future Setting" next to any character behavior or plot event that is possible only because of the future setting.

Focus on Analyzing the Effects of Setting

You can describe two settings in *Feed*: The larger setting (the type of reality the characters live in) and the local setting (where the character Titus is currently narrating events from).

1. What is the larger setting of *Feed*?

2. What major event in the story makes sense only because of the larger setting of *Feed*?

3. How does living in the larger setting seem to have shaped Titus's personality?

continued on next page

ELL Support: Second Read Before students reread the story, explain that the *setting* is "the time and place of the story." There is a larger story, which is the community or society that the story takes place in, and then there is the local setting, which is the place that this scene takes place in. Ask volunteers to respond to these questions to help their peers: *What is the world like in this story? What is the larger setting? (The world is a futuristic place in which the Internet is connected to people's brains.) Where is Titus in this scene? What is the local setting? (Titus is in the hospital without a computer in his brain.)* Have students reread the article in multilevel pairs or small groups, pausing after each paragraph to identify details that show the future and local setting.

▼Write: After students write their predictions, have them share them with the class. Conduct an informal poll. Are students in agreement about the hacker's point of view? Categorize their opinions and take a vote.

Second Read: Analyzing the Effects of Setting

Before Reading: Set a purpose for reading by explaining that the focus of the second read will be analyzing how setting can affect characters and events.

Ask students to list settings of science fiction books and movies they know. Briefly discuss what role setting plays in science fiction works. Is setting more important in this genre, and if so—how?

Finally, read the introductory paragraph and objective with students, making sure they understand the task of the Second Read. For this read, you may ask students to read with a partner.

After Reading: Use the following questions to check comprehension.

Text-Based Discussion Questions

1. In lines 60–62, Titus describes how in the past, computers were separate from the body. "They carried them around outside of them, in their hands, like if you carried your lungs in a briefcase and opened it to breathe." What do these lines suggest about Titus's world? *They suggest that the virtual world is as much a part of human experience as breathing. It seems that everything that happens in "the feed" is so essential to people who are an extension of their own minds and bodies.*

2. Lines 68–71 read, "You can look things up automatic, like science and history, like if you want to know which battles of the Civil War George Washington fought in . . ." What does this sentence suggest about the feed's supposed educational advantages? *It shows that the feed has made humans less intelligent because they don't feel the need to retain basic facts about history. Titus doesn't even know which war Washington fought.*

Focus on Analyzing the Effects of Setting: Have students respond to the questions on pages 293–294 and then share them with a partner or small group.

Chapter 14 (continued)

Lesson Support

Answers to Questions:

1. Hundreds of years in the future, where humans engage regularly in spaceflight and are linked to something called "feednet," an advanced communications platform on which people can talk, play games, and make purchases.

2. The fact that a hacker could disrupt Titus and his friends' connection to feednet makes sense only because *Feed* is set in the future.

3. Because Titus lives in a future with feednet and because he seems to have been hooked up to feednet for a long time, he seems to lack a deep inner life. Without the constant stimulation and gratification provided by the feed, he doesn't know how to move past feeling bored and empty.

4. a hospital on the Moon

5. Titus and his friends are recovering after being attacked by a hacker who severed them from feednet. Titus spends his time thinking about how bored he is, how much he misses the feed, and how annoyed he is by the painting of a boat on the wall.

6. ithout constant stimulation from the feed, his inner monologue becomes more reflective. He thinks about what life was like when the feed was invented, reflects on how the feed knows what he wants, and mulls over the role of corporations in his world. He also spends more time thinking about the painting on the wall.

Gr7Ch14Read2.pptx

Speak and Listen: The first mention of the boat appears in lines 33–39, and the second mention of the boat appears in lines 105–110.

Write: As students think about Titus's explicit reactions to the picture, they should also consider what the boat painting might represent in the story. What do Titus's reactions to the picture suggest about his overall situation?

---

4. The larger setting of *Feed* sets the stage for what happens in the local setting. What is the local setting of the excerpt from *Feed*?

5. Why is Titus in the local setting? What does he do and think while there?

6. Does being in the local setting without contact with feednet have an effect of Titus? If so, what?

Speak and Listen With a partner, read aloud the two times that Titus describes the picture of the boat. Then discuss this question:
- Has Titus changed between his first and second descriptions of the picture? If so, how?

Write Based on your discussion, write a paragraph describing how Titus either did or did not change during the excerpt. Support your response with details from the text.

ELL Support: Speak and Listen and Write: Have students work in multilevel pairs or small groups and use these sentence frames to discuss and then write about whether Titus has changed.

- Titus has/has not changed from the first description of the picture to the second.
- In the first description of the picture, Titus is . . . .
- Also,/But in the second description of the picture, Titus is . . . .

Third Read: Determining Theme

Titus, the main character in this excerpt from *Feed*, has a fairly clear point of view about feednet. But does everyone feel as Titus does about feednet?

Objective: As you read the text a third time, think about what message the author might be trying to express. Underline any sentences that seem to suggest such a message.

Focus on Determining Theme

Before identifying the theme of a story, you need to be clear on what a theme *is* and what it *isn't*. First, let's define some concepts people commonly mistake for theme.

A topic is not a theme. Topics are ideas such as liars and their lies, as in *Catch Me If You Can*, and individualism within societies, as in *The Giver*. Themes comment on a topic, but a topic is not a theme.

What is the topic of *Feed*?

A summary is not a theme. Summaries tell readers the main characters and events in a story. Understanding what happens in a story is only one step in determining the theme.

The author's purpose is not a theme. Authors may write to entertain, inform, or teach, but theme is separate from purpose.

Identify the author's main purpose in writing *Feed*.

A moral is not a theme. Morals appear in fables and folktales. They are obvious and often stated at the very end of the story. Themes, in contrast, are not stated. You need to analyze the elements of the story to determine the theme.

continued on next page

ELL Support: Third Read Before students reread the story, review all the material on theme on pp. 295–296. Paraphrase and use gestures and images to convey the information on these pages. To help students understand fables and folktales, read or watch a video of "The Tortoise and the Hare" or "The Boy Who Cried Wolf" so students know what they are. There are animated versions of these stories on YouTube. Once students understand theme, have them reread the story in multilevel pairs or small groups, taking notes on the theme. Then these groups can work together to complete the chart on p. 297.

Third Read: Determining Theme

Before Reading: Before students read the excerpt a third time, review the definition of *theme* by comparing it to other elements outlined on pages 295–296. To deepen students' understanding, apply these literary terms to a story that is familiar to the whole class, asking students to describe its topic, summarize the plot, consider character growth, and work out its theme. Then have students read the excerpt from *Feed* a third time, underlining details that hint at its message.

After Reading: Use the following questions to check comprehension.

Text-Based Discussion Questions

1. Reread lines 72–79. Based on this description, what do you think makes feednet different from today's Internet? Explain your response with details from the story. *Titus's description of what's on feednet makes it seem a lot like the Internet. He mentions "feedcasts . . . instant news . . . entertainment." He even describes a show called Oh? Wow! Thing! that seems like a reality show. It seems like the only difference between feednet and the Internet is that feednet is actually part of a person's brain. Titus and his friends have instant access all the time, without having to find an external connection.*

2. What do you think of the feednet profile feature Titus describes in lines 80–90? Explain your response. *Sample Answer: This seems dangerous to me. It might be convenient to have your individual needs catered to, giving you access to products you are genuinely interested in. But it gives corporations way too much control. Businesses have instant access to targeted customers and can convince people to buy things they don't need.*

Answers to Questions:

Topic: Technology

Main purpose: to show the reader what could happen in the future if we rely too much on technology

 Gr7Ch14Read3.pptx

Chapter 14 *(continued)*

Lesson Support

Answers to Question:

"The Tortoise and the Hare"—slow and steady wins the race.

"The Boy Who Cried Wolf"—When a person lies too often, they won't be believed when they tell the truth.

You probably know the fable "The Tortoise and the Hare" or the folktale "The Boy Who Cried Wolf." Identify the moral of *one* of these stories.

CONNECT TO ESSENTIAL QUESTION

Although *Feed* is set in the future, do its ideas about technology and society seem relevant today?

A conflict or problem is not a theme. The central conflict or problem that the main character tries to overcome is extremely important to the theme, but it is not the same as the theme.

At this point, you're asking yourself: "Well, what is theme, anyway? How can I figure it out?"

Theme is the author's message. It is a truth or insight about life that the author wants to convey. A story's theme is not as obvious as a moral, because you have to analyze the story to figure it out. So how can you determine a story's theme?

- **First, decide what the central conflict is.** What central problem or obstacle is the main character trying to overcome? How does the conflict resolve? In success or failure?

- **Second, summarize the plot.** Write a short description of the beginning events, the characters, conflict, and how the conflict resolves.

- **Third, think about how the main character grows or changes throughout the story.** The theme is often revealed through changes in the main character over the course of the story. Consider what lessons the character learned or how his or her thinking about life changed. In some stories, theme arises based on a lesson the character failed to learn.

- **Fourth, look for repeated ideas or images throughout the work.** Ideas are usually statements a character or narrator explicitly states. Images are often objects or events that happen to a character.

After you follow these steps, you'll likely have gathered enough information to figure out the theme. Remember, all of the above must be supported by evidence from the text.

TECH-CONNECT

Post your sentence describing the theme of *Feed* on your class website. It will form the basis of an all-class discussion.

Fill in the chart to help you determine the theme of the excerpt from *Feed*. Some sentence starters are included for you.

Steps to Finding Theme	Your Response
Describe the central conflict. What main problem or obstacle is the character trying to overcome?	Titus wants to be reconnected to the feed. Titus's main problem is that he has been disconnected from the feed. Titus feels bored and left out.
Summarize the plot. Write a short description of the beginning and what happens before the resolution.	*Feed* is the story of a society in the future where everything is shared through the feed. Titus has been disconnected from the feed by a hacker, and tries to function in society off-line.
What repeated ideas or images are there?	Everything that you could ever want, or want to know, is on the feed. The feed knows what you want before you even know that you want it. It meets your every need.
Does the main character, Titus, change or grow during the story? If so, how? If not, why not? [Hint: Think about the image you identified above.]	Not really. Titus does not know how to be in the world disconnected from the feed, and he does not learn how by the end of the passage.
Review your responses above. Then finish the following sentence. The theme of this excerpt from *Feed* is. . . .	that technology can be dangerous if you rely on it too much.

Answers to Theme Chart:

See answers on Student Book insert page to the left.

Chapter **14** *(continued)*

Lesson Support

Speak and Listen: Remind students to phrase their themes as universal statements that can be applied to anyone's life.

Language: Using Context Clues: Note that slang phrases are types of idioms—figures of speech that mean something other than the literal definitions of their component words. While many idioms are commonly accepted in a particular language, slang is usually specific to a particular group or context. It is used in informal situations, usually in conversation.

> **Answers to Chart:**
>
> See answers on Student Book insert page to the right.

 Gr7Ch14Language.pptx

Speak and Listen Share your answers from the chart in a class discussion.

Discuss this question:
- What is the theme of this excerpt from *Feed*?

Refer to words, phrases, and sentences from the text in your class discussion. Use hand signals to indicate when you want to talk. Thumbs up means you want to share something new.

Language: Using Context Clues

Roughly 100 years ago, if you were walking down the street of a city, you might hear people saying things such as:
- "He's the bee's knees." (He's an extraordinary person.)
- "That's the cat's meow." (That's really great.)
- "Don't take any wooden nickels." (Don't do anything stupid.)

These days, the only place you might hear these phrases are in movies, television shows, or plays set in the 1920s. Such slang, or informal speech, is no longer part of everyday life.

So, if the past has its own slang, what about the future? M. T. Anderson, the author of *Feed*, came up with slang terms that, while unfamiliar, a reader can use context clues to figure out.

In the table below, use the context clues to write a definition of the underlined slang term.

Sentences	Definition of Slang Term
There was nothing there but the walls. We looked at them, and at each other. We looked really squelch. Our hair and stuff. We had remote relays attached to us to watch our blood and our brains.	squelch: weird
But the braggest thing about the feed, the thing that made it really big, is that it knows everything you want and hope for, sometimes before you even know what those things are.	braggest: greatest

©Perfection Learning® • No Reproduction Permitted

TECH-CONNECT

Send a private email to your teacher telling him or her how the class discussion went. Be polite and specific. Describe one thing that went well. Give one recommendation for how to make the next all-class discussion better.

ELL Support: Language Use a think aloud to model using context clues to determine the meaning of *squelch*. Say: *First, I read the whole context—all the sentences around the word. Then I decide if the word is positive* (smile) *or negative* (frown). *Then I try to replace the word with a word I know. I can use a general word like* bad *or a more specific word like* messy *or* strange. Have students work in multilevel pairs or groups to use context clues to define *braggest* and any other words in the story they had trouble understanding. Have students share their words and definitions with the class.

Connections • © Perfection Learning®

Project-Based Assessments

Response Essay

Although *Feed* is set in the future, much of what Titus talks about easily applies to the present day. Read the excerpt below from *Feed.*

> Everything we think and feel is taken in by the corporations. . . . Of course, everyone is like, *da da da, evil corporations, oh they're so bad,* we all say that, and we all know they control everything. I mean, it's not great, because who knows what evil [things] they're up to. Everyone feels bad about that. But they're the only way to get all this stuff, and it's no good getting [mad] about it, because they're still going to control everything whether you like it or not. Plus, they keep like everyone in the world employed, so it's not like we could do without them. And it's really great to know everything about everything whenever we want, to have it just like, in our brain, just sitting there.

Write a one-page response to Titus's ideas about the role of corporations in our lives. First, accurately summarize Titus's ideas. Then explain whether you agree or disagree with his ideas. Support your ideas with examples from your life and the lives of your friends and family. Organize your essay clearly, using a good introduction, body, and conclusion.

	Use the following guidelines for your response essay.
To receive the highest score (4.0), the essay must meet all of these criteria.	**Your essay should** • accurately summarize Titus's ideas about the role of corporations in our lives. • explain your own position on Titus's ideas. • be supported with examples from your life and the lives of your friends and family. • end with a satisfying conclusion. • maintain a formal style. • contain correct grammar, spelling, and punctuation.

continued on next page

Project-Based Assessments

Response Essay: To broaden students' thinking about this topic, encourage them to review the quotes on corporations and consumerism collected during the Tech-Connect activity on page 293.

Chapter **14** (continued)

Assessment

Write a Book Chapter: Make sure students understand that although their book chapters should be based on the events in the excerpt, they can feel free to use their imaginations to further develop the setting, characters, and the hacker's motivation—as long as any new details do not contradict what they have read. Encourage students to freewrite about the character of the hacker, developing a detailed character sketch. Some strategies include describing the character in detail, writing physical descriptions, personal likes and dislikes, and other details. Explain that some writers also explore a character by writing a first-person diary entry.

If possible, set aside time for students to read aloud their chapters to the class.

Write a Book Chapter

The motivations of the hacker in *Feed* remain mysterious. All we know about him is from the following excerpt.

> Our parents had been notified while we were asleep. Only Loga hadn't been touched by the hacker. She hadn't let him touch her, because he looked really creepy to her, so she stood way far away. There were also others, people we'd never met, who had been touched, and they were in the wards, too. He had touched thirteen people in all.
>
> There was a police officer there, waiting in a chair. He told us that we would be off-line for a while, until they could see what had been done and check for viruses, and decrypt the feed history to get information to use against the guy in court. They said that they had identified him, and that he was a hacker and a naysayer of the worst kind.

Write a chapter for *Feed* written from the point of view of the hacker. Your chapter must
- be based on the events described in the excerpt above.
- describe the dance club setting where the events take place.
- make clear the hacker's motivations for separating Titus and others from the feed.
- have a clear ending.

Use the rubric below to guide your writing.

	Use the following guidelines for your book chapter.
To receive the highest score (4.0), the book chapter must meet all of these criteria.	Your chapter • is based on the events of the excerpt from *Feed*. • is written from the hacker's point of view. • clearly shows the hacker's motivations. • uses narrative techniques, such as dialogue and description, to develop experiences, events, and characters. • uses descriptive details and sensory language to convey experiences and events. • provides a conclusion that follows from the events narrated. • contains correct grammar, spelling, and punctuation.

TECH-CONNECT

Listening to your writing can reveal awkward sentences or clunky dialogue. Use your computer or cell phone to make a recording as you read your chapter aloud. Listen to your recording and use it to revise your writing.

ELL Support: Project-Based Assessments Have students work in multilevel pairs or groups to write the response essay and/or book chapter. Together with students, brainstorm sentence frames that they can use for each project. Also, provide an outline or story map graphic organizer for students to use when organizing their ideas. For the book chapter project, beginning and intermediate students may create a graphic novel chapter with words, phrases, and sentences (depending on their language level) in descriptions as well as speech and thought bubbles. Provide the Proofreading Checklist from the ELL Teacher Resource (p. 71) for students to finalize their projects.

On Your Own: Integrating Ideas

1. Sherry Turkle, a professor at the Massachusetts Institute of Technology (MIT), has spent most of her career considering how modern communications technologies affect our personal relationships. Her presentation "Connected, but alone?" discusses how modern communication technologies can actually isolate us from each other: https://www.ted.com/talks/sherry_turkle_alone_together.

2. In *Feed*, people are controlled not through being deprived of goods and services but by having all their needs and pleasures met. The book *Brave New World* by Aldous Huxley, published in 1932, explores similar themes, and it is a classic of dystopian literature. Search for it in your school or public library.

3. What do doctors mean when they talk about "Internet addiction disorder"? Is it a true addiction, as some people are addicted to drugs and alcohol? Or should it be called something else? Do some research on the Internet to answer these questions.

> **REFLECT**
>
> Have you ever been bored while on the web or the Internet? If so, how was that possible, given everything that's available on it?

On Your Own: Integrating Ideas:

Activity 2: Students may benefit from watching the 1998 film based on the book *Brave New World*.

Assessment

Connect to Testing: This Connect to Testing section focuses on determining the theme of a story, examining the interaction of setting on characters and events, and analyzing point of view. If necessary, review how to answer two-part, evidence-based questions.

Encourage students to work in pairs to choose the correct answers to the questions and then to compare their answers with those of another pair of students. If there is disagreement, encourage the groups to try to reach a consensus as they discuss the reasons for their choices.

Answers to Connect to Testing Questions:

1. **Part A:** C. Choice A is incorrect because the struggle does not yet result in the maturation of the main character. Choice B is not supported by the text. Choice D is hinted at by the hacker's action, but this is not the central idea supported by the characters and the conflict. (DoK 2)
   Part B: E., F. These choices emphasize how humans rely on the feed to meet their needs and how the main character feels when he is unconnected from it. (DoK 2)

2. D. The best answer is Choice D because it is supported by many details from the text including the fact that the feednet is direcly plugged into people's brains. (DoK 2)
   (continued)

Connect to Testing

In this chapter, you determined the theme of a story, examined the interaction of the setting on characters and events, and analyzed point of view. When you take assessments, you will be tested over your ability to analyze texts in these ways and support your analysis with textual evidence.

1. **Part A:** Which of the following is the main theme statement represented by this excerpt of *Feed*?

   A. Only through struggle can young people grow into adults.

   B. Making art is a way to strengthen the mind and improve the heart.

   C. Constant technological stimulation can dull our ability to amuse ourselves.

   D. The history of human society is one of progress, but some people will always resist it.

   Part B: Which sentences from *Feed* best support the answer to Part A? Select **two** choices.

   A. *I couldn't figure out even the littlest reason to paint a picture like that.*

   B. *They said that they had identified him, and that he was a hacker and a naysayer of the worst kind.*

   C. *They carried them around outside of them, in their hands, like if you carried your lungs in a briefcase and opened it to breathe.*

   D. *That's one of the great things about the feed—that you can be supersmart without ever working.*

   E. *But the braggest thing about the feed, the thing that made it really big, is that it knows everything you want and hope for, sometimes before you even know what those things are.*

   F. *In fact, the thing that made me [mad] was when they couldn't help me at all, so I was just lying there, and couldn't play any of the games on the feed, and couldn't chat anyone, and I couldn't do a . . . thing. . . .*

2. According to the excerpt from *Feed*, how has the invention of feednet most affected human society in the future?

   A. It has improved medical treatments.

   B. It has made a few people amazingly wealthy.

   C. It has caused people to resist new technologies.

   D. It has bound people and technology more closely.

ELL Support: Connect to Testing and Assessments See the ELL Teacher Resource (p. 22) for ideas on adapting this section for ELLs.

3. **Part A:** Read these sentences from the beginning of the excerpt from *Feed*.

   The first thing I felt was no <u>credit</u>.

   I tried to touch my <u>credit</u>, but there was nothing there.

   Which word has the closest meaning to the word *credit* as it is used in these sentences?

   A. belief

   B. contact

   C. mind

   D. debt

   Part B: Which detail from *Feed* best supports the answer to Part A?

   A. *My body—I was in a bed, on top of my arm, which was asleep, ...*

   B. *Someone had left a message in my head, which I found, ...*

   C. *I tried to chat Link and then Marty, but nothing, there was no transmission signal, ...*

   D. *So I opened my eyes.*

4. **Part A:** Which of the following best describes Titus's point of view regarding the corporations that make profiles for feednet?

   A. He finds it frightening that he has no choice in whether to use their technology.

   B. He believes that corporations do more good than harm in his world.

   C. He assumes corporations do bad things, but believes no alternatives exist.

   D. He welcomes the idea that corporations help people learn more about their own wants.

   Part B: Which of the sentences from *Feed* best supports the answer to Part A?

   A. *We were frightened, and kept touching our heads.*

   B. *But the braggest thing about the feed, the thing that made it really big, is that it knows everything you want and hope for, sometimes before you even know what those things are.*

   C. *Of course, everyone is like, da da da, evil corporations, oh they're so bad, we all say that, and we all know they control everything.*

   D. *But they're the only way to get all this stuff, and it's no good getting [mad] about it, because they're still going to control everything whether you like it or not.*

5. How does Titus mostly respond to being disconnected from feednet over time?

   A. He is mostly bored.

   B. He is mostly angry.

   C. He is mostly frightened.

   D. He is mostly lonely.

3. **Part A:** B. Based on the context, credit is what allows Titus to connect to the feed. The word *contact* is closest to the meaning in this context. (DoK 1)
   Part B: C. (DoK 2)

4. **Part A:** C. Based on the lines about corporations, Titus feels frustrated but resigned to the fact that corporations have much control over the feednet. (DoK 3)
   Part B: D. (DoK 2)

5. A. This answer is supported by Titus's conversation with the girl in the hospital. "What do we do?" she asked. I didn't know. Titus's response to the picture of the boat also supports the fact that he is overwhelmingly bored. (DoK 1)

Chapter 15

Analyzing Different Interpretations of Evidence

It's 'digital heroin': How screens turn kids into psychotic junkies
by Dr. Nicholas Kardaras, *New York Post*

Why calling screen time 'digital heroin' is digital garbage
by Rachel Becker, *The Verge*

Introduction

Chapter Goals: Have students read through the goals and mark any words that are unfamiliar. Discuss the meanings of any academic vocabulary within the goals that students marked as unfamiliar. Consider posting the Chapter Goals.

Preview Academic Vocabulary: Read and discuss the meanings of the academic vocabulary.

point of view: *opinion or perspective on a topic.* The author held the point of view that violence in video games was dangerous to young minds.

purpose: *goal or reason for writing.* The author's purpose was to provide an entertaining review of the new superhero movie.

⟲ **Gr7Ch15Vocabulary.pptx**

Preview Concepts: Introduce the questions on page 304 and have students respond to them independently. Have students share their responses with the class. Point out any common threads in students' experiences. For example, if adults disapproved of a movie, website, or video game, was it because of the technology itself, or the content?

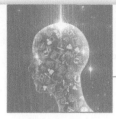

Chapter 15

Analyzing Different Interpretations of Evidence

Preview Concepts

This unit is about how technology affects society. Here is a question adults ask all the time about you and your classmates:

- How are new communication technologies affecting our kids?

1. Think of a time when an adult was worried about your watching a video, visiting a website, or playing a video game. Why did the adult have that point of view about the video, site, or game? Did he or she give any reasons or evidence to support that point of view?

2. Did you agree with that adult's point of view? Did you agree with the reasons or evidence offered?

Making Connections

When trying to convince a reader, writers sometimes make logical fallacies. A logical fallacy is committed when a writer relies on emotion and incorrect thinking to convince the audience that his or her point of view is correct. Two examples of logical fallacies are loaded language and sweeping generalizations.

CHAPTER GOALS

In this chapter you will

- cite textual evidence to support an analysis of a text.
- determine an author's point of view and purpose.
- examine how authors writing on the same topic can interpret the same evidence differently.
- correct misplaced modifiers.

PREVIEW ACADEMIC VOCABULARY

point of view

purpose

ELL Support: Academic Vocabulary See Teaching Vocabulary in the ELL Teacher Resource (p. 18) for ideas to use for teaching vocabulary throughout *Connections*.

Preview Concepts Use images, gestures, and simple definitions to help students understand the following words: *point of view, video game, website, video.* Have students work in multilevel pairs or groups and use the following sentence frames to answer the questions:

- The adult thought the video/game/site was . . . .

- The adult did/did not give reasons and evidence to support his/her point of view. For example, ...

- I did/did not agree with the adult's point of view. I did/did not agree with the adult's reasons and evidence.

Loaded Language: Words that have strong positive or negative connotations: *dangerous influence, innocent children*

Overgeneralization: Concluding that what is true in one case (or for one person) is true for all other situations (or people): *My mom is a really bad driver. All women are worse drivers than men.*

Below are excerpts from two letters from the 1950s that citizens wrote to their senators about the dangers of comic books. Read them and then answer the questions that follow.

My dear Senator Hendrickson,

I believe that the [Parent–Teacher Associations] all over the country could unite to have these comics banned, many cities have done this and as Dr. [Wertham] says, we have laws that prohibit selling poison, why can't we prohibit these people from selling poison to our children's minds?

—Eugenia Y. Genovar, November 24, 1953

Dear Sir,

I have been reading comic books for seven to nine years. Every kind of book that was written. I have never robbed a bank or things like that. My personal opinion is I think reading crime books makes a young or old person not want to commit a crime, because in every story the old saying "Crime don't pay" is carried out. The person or persons committing the crime are always caught. The fear of this stops crime and stops juvenile delinquency. . . .

—Robert Merdian, June 22, 1954

What is each writer's point of view about whether comic books cause young people to commit crimes? Identify any loaded language or overgeneralizations in the letters.

> **MAKING CONNECTIONS**
>
> In this chapter, you'll explore how authors on different sides of an issue shape their arguments.

Sample Answers to Questions, page 304:

1. My mom did not want me to play a video game at my friend's house because there was a lot of fighting in it. She told me that she did not want me to see so much violence.

2. I did not agree with my mom's point of view. I know that the violence in a video game is just fake and watching fake violence doesn't make we want to do violent things.

Making Connections: Have students respond to the letters on page 305. Suggested prompts:

- Were you surprised to discover that people worried about how comic books affected young people during the 1950s?

- What do these letters suggest about similar worries today?

- Are today's movies, TV shows, websites, and video games more influential than 1950s comic books?

Answers to Question, page 305:

Eugenia's point of view is that comic books influence young people to commit more crimes. Robert's point of view is that comic books actually help stop young people from wanting to commit crimes. Eugenia's purpose for writing is to unite Parent-Teacher Associations to ban comic books. Robert's purpose for writing is to share a young person's point of view that comic books can actually have a positive influence.

ELL Support: Make Connections Display pictures of crime comic books to help students understand what *crime* and *comic books* are. Have students work in multilevel pairs or groups (or work together as a class) to read and paraphrase each letter. Provide sentence frames for students to respond to the questions in their multilevel pairs or groups:

- Eugenia's point of view of crime comic books that they . . . .

- She is writing because she wants . . . .

- Robert's point of view of crime comic books is that they . . . .

- He is writing because he wants . . . .

Chapter 15 (continued)

Lesson Support

First Read: Finding Supporting Evidence

Before Reading: Introduce the *New York Post* article on page 306, noting that it is the first of two argumentative/persuasive articles they will read in this chapter. Remind students that persuasive arguments present ample evidence in support of claims. Ask students to name various types of evidence, including facts, research data, examples, anecdotes, expert opinion, personal experience, etc. Make sure students understand the types of evidence they will be marking during the first read. This complex text may present a challenge for some readers. Scaffold the reading by using a think-aloud to read and annotate the first few paragraphs. Then have students read the rest of the article on their own.

Preview Vocabulary: Preview unfamiliar vocabulary to aid comprehension or ask students to circle unfamiliar words during the first read. Guide students to determine the words' meanings using the context and support their responses with evidence. Have students confirm their initial definitions with a dictionary. Difficult words include:

intuitively: *showing an ability to know or understand things without proof or evidence; based on feelings.* Caroline intuitively knew something was wrong the moment she walked through the door.

apathetic: *having or showing little to no feeling or emotion.* Sitting silently on the couch looking bored, Gordon was apathetic about the party-planning process.

agitated: *troubled, nervous, or worried.* Mirabella looked agitated, biting her lip as she waited for the plane to take off.

psychotic: *having a mental disorder that makes a sufferer lose contact with reality.* Jaime was psychotic, hearing voices and seeing things that were not there.

axiom: *a statement that everyone believes to be true.* The math teacher wrote the axiom on the board for the students to copy down: "Things that are equal to the same things are also equal to one another."

 Gr7Ch15Vocabulary.pptx

First Read: Finding Supporting Evidence

Dr. Nicholas Kardaras is an expert on addiction, a condition in which a person becomes dependent on a chemical such as a drug. Addiction can drive people's behavior and cause them to suffer without the chemical. In the following editorial, Kardaras argues that screen technologies are as addictive as cocaine or heroin, two dangerous illegal drugs. It is a controversial claim, as you will see later in the chapter.

Objective: As you read, underline two sentences with evidence based on personal experiences—either the author's or those of other people. Write PE (for "personal experience") next to each sentence. Then, draw a box around two sentences with evidence based on scientific research. Write SR (for "scientific research") next to those sentences. Record any questions you have in the My Thoughts column.

—— First Read
---- Second Read
—— Third Read

excerpt

It's 'digital heroin': How screens turn kids into psychotic junkies

by Dr. Nicholas Kardaras, in the *New York Post*, August 27, 2016

My Thoughts

1   Many parents intuitively understand that **ubiquitous** glowing screens are having a negative effect on kids. We see the aggressive temper tantrums when the devices are taken away and the wandering attention spans when children are

5   not perpetually stimulated by their hyper-arousing devices. *PE*

Worse, we see children who become bored, apathetic, uninteresting and uninterested when not plugged in. *PE*

But it's even worse than we think.

We now know that those iPads, smartphones and Xboxes

10   are a form of digital drug. Recent brain imaging research is showing that they affect the brain's frontal cortex—which *SR* *BE*

controls **executive functioning**, including impulse control— in exactly the same way that cocaine does. . . .

ubiquitous: found everywhere
executive functioning: decision-making

©Perfection Learning® • No Reproduction Permitted

ELL Support: First Read Explain that *personal experience* is "something that happens to a person" and *scientific research* means "studies done to answer a question." Also, use images, symbols, and words to explain that the doctor writing the article argues that technology (screens) = drugs for addiction. Have students read the article in multilevel pairs or small groups, pausing after each paragraph to summarize the ideas on a Main Ideas and Supporting Details graphic organizer from the ELL Teacher Resource (p. 51). Also, encourage students to take notes and draw sketches in the margins around the article, so they can be sure they understand the topic of each section.

This addictive effect is why Dr. Peter Whybrow, director
15 of neuroscience at UCLA, calls screens "electronic cocaine"
and Chinese researchers call them "digital heroin." In fact,
Dr. Andrew Doan, the head of addiction research for the
Pentagon and the US Navy—who has been researching video
game addiction—calls video games and screen technologies
20 "digital pharmakeia" (Greek for drug).

That's right—your kid's brain on *Minecraft* looks like a
brain on drugs. No wonder we have a hard time peeling kids
from their screens and find our little ones agitated when their
screen time is interrupted. In addition, hundreds of clinical
25 studies show that screens increase depression, anxiety and
aggression and can even lead to psychotic-like features where
the video gamer loses touch with reality.

In my clinical work with over 1,000 teens over the past 15
years, I have found the old axiom of "An ounce of prevention
30 is worth a pound of cure" to be especially true when it comes
to tech addiction. Once a kid has crossed the line into true tech
addiction, treatment can be very difficult. Indeed, I have
found it easier to treat heroin and crystal meth addicts than
lost-in-the-matrix video gamers or Facebook-dependent
35 social media addicts.

According to a 2013 Policy Statement by the American
Academy of Pediatrics, 8- to 10-year-olds spend 8 hours a day
with various digital media while teenagers spend 11 hours
in front of screens. One in three kids are using tablets or
40 smartphones before they can talk. Meanwhile, the handbook
of "Internet Addiction" by Dr. Kimberly Young states that 18
percent of college-age internet users in the US suffer from
tech addiction.

My Thoughts

POV
BE
PE
SR
BE

PE

BE

SR

After Reading: Use the following
questions to check comprehension.

Text-Based Discussion Questions

1. What is the main idea of the first
    paragraph (lines 1–7)? What supporting
    evidence does the author present in this
    paragraph? *The main idea is that screen
    time is having a devastating effect
    on kids. The author does not provide
    supporting evidence in this paragraph—
    only generalizations based on personal
    experiences like "We see the aggressive
    temper tantrums when the devices are
    taken away" (lines 2–4) and "we see
    children who become bored, apathetic,
    uninteresting and uninterested when
    not plugged in" (lines 6–7).*

2. What is the author's argument in the
    second and third paragraphs? What
    evidence does the author provide to
    support this argument? *The author
    argues that today's technology is a
    type of drug that causes an addictive
    effect similar to that of narcotics. He
    cites "Recent brain imaging research"
    that compares the frontal cortex of
    technology users with that of drug
    addicts (lines 10–13). The author also
    mentions two addiction experts who
    agree with his argument (lines 14–20).*

Gr7Ch15Read1.pptx

About the Author: Dr. Nicholas Kardaras
is an author and speaker known for his
specialty in the areas of mental health
and addiction. After experiencing
addiction firsthand, Kardaras continued
his education—receiving a master's degree
in social work and a PhD in psychology.
Kardaras has devoted his professional life to
teaching, speaking, and educating the public
on adolescent addiction, and in particular,
addiction to screens and technology. In
2016, Kardaras published a book, *Glow
Kids*, on the dangers of screen addiction
in developing minds. Kardaras is also a
frequent contributor to *Psychology Today*.

Remediation: First Read The article's high-interest topic and
controversial argument may motivate struggling students to
persevere through the scientific concepts and difficult vocabulary.
Encourage students to move past unfamiliar words on the first read.
They can then go back and write down unfamiliar words to look up
later. You may also want to review challenging vocabulary with these
students before they read.

Encourage students to monitor their reading and to stop and reread
if they find their comprehension breaking down. Tell them to keep
reading ahead and to find information they understand and connect
it back to what they don't yet understand.

Chapter 15 (continued)

Lesson Support

FIRST RESPONSE:
KEY IDEAS AND DETAILS

Tech-Connect Suggestion: Conduct a poll on Poll Everywhere about whether students agree with the author's argument, disagree, or need to know more before offering an opinion. Use the real-time chart feature to display the results as they are compiled.

Focus on Finding Supporting Evidence:
Introduce the chart on page 309, making sure students understand the headers. Remind students to refer to the evidence they marked in the text as they complete the chart.

 Gr7Ch15Read1.pptx

---

45 Once a person crosses over the line into full-blown addiction—drug, digital or otherwise—they need to **detox** before any other kind of therapy can have any chance of being effective. With tech, that means a full digital detox—no computers, no smartphones, no tablets. The extreme digital detox even eliminates television. The prescribed amount of

50 time is four to six weeks; that's the amount of time that is usually required for a hyper-aroused nervous system to reset itself. But that's no easy task in our current tech-filled society where screens are ubiquitous. A person can live without drugs or alcohol; with tech addiction, digital temptations

55 are everywhere.

---

detox: let the body rid itself of a harmful substance

My Thoughts

FIRST RESPONSE: KEY IDEAS AND DETAILS
Based on your first reading of this text, what do you think of Kardaras's argument? How well does it match with your personal experience? Record your first response in your journal.

TECH-CONNECT

Post your First Response answers on your class webpage. Compare your answers to those posted by other students.

Focus on Finding Supporting Evidence

Kardaras's claim is explicit: video screen addiction is a real problem among young people, and it can be as difficult to treat as heroin addiction. He supports this claim with evidence of two kinds: evidence based on personal experience and evidence based on scientific research.

The chart on the next page divides the evidence into personal experience and scientific research. The shaded cells are completed for you and list the researchers and those who had the personal experience. Complete the unshaded cells to explain what the research said and describe the experiences.

Claim: Video screen addiction is a real problem among young people, and it can be as difficult to treat as heroin addiction.			
Personal Experience		Scientific Research	
Who had the experience?	What was the experience?	Who did the research?	What did that research say?
parents	They see the tantrums children throw when they take away screens.	Dr. Kimberly Young	In the U.S., 18% of college-age Internet users suffer from technology addiction.
Dr. Nicholas Kardaras	He has found it easier to treat users of heroin and crystal meth than some video gamers and social media addicts.	Brain-imaging researchers	They show that iPads, smartphones, and Xboxes affect the brain in the same way cocaine does.

Speak and Listen With a partner, discuss the evidence that Kardaras presents to support his claim that video game addiction is a serious problem. What evidence is most convincing? What is least convincing?

Write Based on the results of your conversation, write a paragraph in which you explain which piece of evidence you found least convincing. Give one reason you found the evidence unconvincing. If necessary, use these sentence frames to get started.

- The evidence I found least convincing is . . .
- I believe this evidence is least convincing because . . .

CONNECT TO ESSENTIAL QUESTION

About 200 years ago, some thinkers actually made the same claims about reading stories and novels that Kardaras is making about digital screens. What does this tell you about how people sometimes receive new technologies?

Second Read: Determining Point of View and Purpose

When reading any text, it's important to distinguish between an author's point of view and his or her purpose for writing.

- An author's point of view is the attitude (opinions and feelings) the author has toward the topic he or she is writing about.

continued on next page

ELL Support: Speak and Listen Have students work in multilevel pairs or small groups to discuss and write about the questions, using these prompts and sentence frames:

- What evidence do you think is best/worst? Why?
- The best (most convincing) evidence is . . . .
- This evidence is the best (most convincing) because . . . .
- The worst (least convincing) evidence is . . . .
- This evidence is the worst (least convincing) because . . . .

Answers to Chart:

See answers on Student Book insert page to the left.

Speak and Listen: Encourage students to consider whether or not further evidence would help support Kardaras' argument. Where might they find relevant evidence? Do they think any experts might be opposed to his point of view? Where might they go to find out?

Write: Students may also want to note what evidence might help persuade them to agree with Kardaras' argument.

Second Read: Determining Point of View and Purpose

Before Reading: Make sure students understand the difference between an author's point of view and an author's purpose for writing. Review the objective on page 310 before students read the article a second time. An alternative option for this second read is to focus in on lines 9–27. Read them aloud with the class and discuss the author's point of view and purpose. As a class, identify the claims and evidence. Then have them read the entire article and complete the Focus on activities on pages 310–311.

After Reading: Use the following questions to check comprehension.

Text-Based Discussion Questions

1. Lines 21–22 read, "That's right—your kid's brain on *Minecraft* looks like a brain on drugs." What is the effect of this sentence on the reader? What do you think Kardaras' purpose was in writing it? *This sentence is pretty dramatic, making me feel like maybe technology is more damaging than I thought. Kardaras probably wrote it for this purpose—to shock people into taking his ideas seriously.*

2. According to Kardaras, what is one difference between treating drug addiction and treating digital addiction? Do you agree with Kardaras' comparison? *Kardaras believes it's harder to kick a digital addiction because our society runs on technology, making screens tough to avoid. "A person can live without drugs or alcohol; with tech addiction, digital temptations are everywhere" (lines 53–55).*

Chapter 15 (continued)

Lesson Support

Focus on Determining Point of View and Purpose: Have students preview the activity on pages 310–311 and ask any questions before completing it independently. Remind students to refer to what they marked in the text as they write their responses.

Samples Answers to Questions:

1. The topic of Kardaras' article is technology addiction. Kardaras' point of view is that too much screen time can be addictive. "Recent brain imaging research is showing that they affect the brain's frontal cortex—which controls executive functioning, including impulse control—in exactly the same way that cocaine does. . . ."

2. Kardaras' primary audience is parents. I think Kardaras wants to alarm his readers so that they take necessary actions to prevent screen addiction in their children.

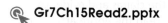 **Gr7Ch15Read2.pptx**

- An author's purpose is why the author is writing the text—what the author hopes the text will accomplish. Part of determining an author's purpose is looking at both what the author says and the language the author uses to say it.

Objective: Read the text a second time.

- Underline one sentence that provides evidence of the author's point of view. Write the abbreviation POV by that sentence.
- Circle two phrases that seem intended to have a powerful emotional effect on the audience.

> **REFLECT**
>
> Do you think anyone might disagree with Kardaras's argument? Why might someone disagree with it?

Focus on Determining Point of View and Purpose

Kardaras's point of view about the topic is not subtle. It might be one you have encountered from adults or even your peers.

1. In the space below, state both the topic and Kardaras's point of view about it. As evidence of his point of view, quote the sentence you underlined.

Kardaras's purpose in writing this editorial is only slightly less obvious than his point of view. When determining an author's purpose, focus on not just what the text says but how it says it. And Kardaras has a pretty powerful way with words. Just look at some of what he says:

- *But it's even worse than we think.*
- *a form of digital drug*
- *"electronic cocaine"*
- *"digital heroin"*
- *psychotic-like features*
- *your kid's brain on* Minecraft *looks like a brain on drugs*

©Perfection Learning® • No Reproduction Permitted

ELL Support: Second Read Review the definitions for *point of view* and *purpose*. Then model rereading and identifying the author's point of view and purpose in the first few paragraphs. Have students reread the article in multilevel pairs or small groups, pausing after each paragraph to identify details that show the author's point of view or purpose.

Speak and Listen and Write Have students work in multilevel pairs or small groups to discuss and then write about the point of view and purpose of the article. These sentence frames can also be found as a student handout in the ELL Teacher Resource (p. 38).

- (Sentence 1) In his article Dr. Nicholas Kardaras writes about . . . .
- (Sentence 2) In his argument he expresses the point of view that . . . .
- (Sentence 3) To support his ideas, Kardaras notes that . . . .

Connections • © Perfection Learning®

Kardaras uses loaded language to stir up a strong response in the reader. These emotional words are meant to persuade the audience to agree with the author. However, sometimes loaded words can be manipulative and indicate bias on the part of the author.

2. In the space below, answer these questions:
- Who is Kardaras's primary audience?
- Based on his word choice, what effect do you think Kardaras intended this editorial to have on his audience?

(Speak and Listen With a partner, discuss how Kardaras's word choice could affect what his audience thinks of him, not of the topic. Give reasons to support your ideas.

Write Write a paragraph in which you explain both Kardaras's point of view and his purpose in writing the editorial. Focus on how he uses emotionally powerful words and phrases to try to achieve that purpose.

Third Read: Analyzing Interpretations of Evidence

Kardaras made a powerful claim, and powerful claims tend to earn strong responses. Three days after his editorial appeared in the *New York Post*, the following response was published on *The Verge*, a website devoted to news about technology, science, art, and culture. The writer, Rachel Becker, is a trained scientist who has reported for several reputable science magazines and websites.

Objective: Read the excerpt that begins on the next page from Becker's editorial. Then go back to Kardaras's editorial and read it a third time. This time, look for any evidence that both Kardaras and Becker both cite in their editorials and write "BE" (for "Both Editorials") next to the evidence in both excerpts.

(Speak and Listen: As students discuss Kardaras' word choices, have them consider their own initial reactions to his ideas. Ask: *What did you think of the author after first reading the article?*

Write: Make sure students consider which particular emotions are evoked by each powerful word.

Third Read: Analyzing Interpretations of Evidence

Before Reading: Explain that Kardaras' article prompted a lot of feedback. One critical response, by the writer Rachel Becker, followed three days later on the website *The Verge*.

Point out that in arguing against Kardaras' point of view, Becker cited some of the same evidence. Briefly discuss how the same evidence can support opposing opinions. Explain that Becker's editorial is a rebuttal— an opinion written to contradict another author's point of view. In writing a rebuttal, an author often examines evidence to see if there are flaws in its interpretation.

Point out that one way of misusing evidence is called "cherrypicking." This involves selecting only the details that support an opinion while leaving out other details that may cause readers to question an argument.

After students read Becker's article, ask them to reread Kardaras' article and look for examples of evidence used by both authors. Remind them to mark this evidence in both excerpts.

- (Sentence 4) The author's purpose in writing this article is . . . .
- (Sentence 5) To accomplish this purpose, he tries to get readers to . . . .
- (Sentences 6–9) To make sure that readers _____, the author uses powerful words, such as . . . .

    This affects readers by making them feel . . . .

    The author also writes ". . . . " (direct quotation)

    These words are effective because . . . .

Lesson Support

Preview Vocabulary: Preview unfamiliar vocabulary to aid comprehension or ask students to circle unfamiliar words as they complete the first read of a text. After the first read, guide students to determine the words' meanings using the context. Encourage students to support their responses with evidence. Have students confirm their initial definitions with a dictionary. Words that students might find difficult include:

psychotherapist: *a person who treats mental and emotional disorders with counseling.* Julian always felt better after talking with his <u>psychotherapist</u>.

scaremongering: *spreading alarming news in order to make people feel worried or afraid.* Rocky's <u>scaremongering</u> about ghosts had its desired effect, making people who believed his stories afraid to rent the house.

manipulation: *controlling someone or something to one's own advantage.* By crying and throwing a tantrum, Aiko used <u>manipulation</u> to get her parents to let her stay up later.

predominant: *being most frequent or common.* Padma's favorite color was blue, so she made it the <u>predominant</u> color in her painting.

analogizing: *explaining one thing by comparing it to another.* To help his students understand the concept of DNA, Mr. Hoffman considered <u>analogizing</u> it to a twisted ladder.

discipline: *an area, or branch of knowledge.* The university's <u>disciplines</u> of study included sociology and psychology.

catatonia: *a condition where changes in muscle tone or activity are seen; often associated with mental disorders.* The patient displayed classic signs of <u>catatonia</u>, sitting unmoving for hours on end.

predispose: *to have a tendency toward something.* Some people think being born in Hawaii will <u>predispose</u> you to love surfing.

---

excerpt
Why calling screen time 'digital heroin' is digital garbage
by Rachel Becker, *The Verge*, August 30, 2016

My Thoughts

1   The supposed danger of digital media made headlines over the weekend when psychotherapist Nicholas Kardaras published a story in the *New York Post* called "It's 'digital heroin': How screens turn kids into psychotic junkies." In
5   the op-ed, Kardaras claims that "iPads, smartphones and Xboxes are a form of digital drug." He stokes fears about the potential for addiction and the ubiquity of technology by referencing "hundreds of clinical studies" that show "screens increase depression, anxiety and aggression." We've seen
10   this form of scaremongering before. People are frequently uneasy with new technology, after all. The problem is, screens and computers aren't actually all that new. There's already a whole generation—millennials—who grew up with computers. They appear, mostly, to be fine . . . If computers
15   were "digital drugs," wouldn't we have already seen warning signs? . . .

   This style of manipulation is most obvious in Kardaras' use of statistics: "According to a 2013 Policy Statement by the American Academy of Pediatrics, 8- to 10-year-olds spend
20   8 hours a day with various digital media while teenagers spend 11 hours in front of screens," he writes. His article takes general aim at screens, but specifically stokes fears about video games and the internet. . . . He makes no mention of television, which remains the predominant form of media for
25   children and teens, according to a 2013 policy statement from the American Academy of Pediatrics. . . .

BE

BE

ELL Support: First Read Before students read the new article, explain that this new writer (Becker) is writing against the other writer (Kardaras) that they just read. Becker disagrees with Kardaras. She quotes him and tells why he is wrong. Have students read the new article in multilevel pairs or small groups, pausing after each paragraph to summarize ideas on a <u>Main Ideas and Supporting Details graphic organizer from the ELL Teacher Resource (p. 51).</u>

Kardaras' op-ed goes on to warn that exposure to screens can cause "addiction," and he quotes researchers analogizing screen time to heroin and cocaine. "That's right—your kid's

30 brain on *Minecraft* looks like a brain on drugs," he writes. This is, strictly speaking, true—at least, from a neuroimaging standpoint. This is a **hoary old trope** in science writing, and it's apparently loosely based on **fMRI**, which is hardly the most accurate discipline. The brain's reward center, the ventral

35 striatum, is what makes you feel good when you eat, . . . take cocaine, or play video games.

Yale psychiatrists Robert Leeman and Marc Potenza write in a 2013 review paper that there are neurobiological and genetic parallels between substance abuse and problematic

40 behaviors, like excessive . . . internet use. But because these are things pretty much everyone engages in, it's hard to draw a line between one person's activity and another person's addiction.

Kardaras' loose talk on addiction is what makes his

45 argument so tough to believe. About 1.6 percent of Americans use heroin, but a quarter of them wind up addicted, according to an estimate from the National Institutes of Drug Addiction. Something like 16 percent of cocaine users become dependent on the drug within 10 years of trying it for the first time, say

50 scientists in the journal *Neuropsychopharmacology*. Digital devices, as well as video games, are far more widespread than either of these drugs. If they were, in fact, comparable, we should be seeing a lot more people displaying "catatonia," with their iPads dropped dramatically beside them.

| My Thoughts |
| BE |
| BE |

hoary old trope: frequently used idea
fMRI: functional magnetic resonance imaging, a way of scanning the brain and measuring its activity

After Reading: Use the following questions to check comprehension.

Text-Based Discussion Questions

1. What is the main idea in Becker's first paragraph (lines 1–16)? *Becker's main idea is that Kardaras' article "stokes fears about the potential for addiction" by making generalizations to alarm people based on questionable evidence.*

2. In lines 23–24, Becker writes, "He makes no mention of television, which remains the predominant form of media for children and teens." Why do you think Kardaras did not mention television? *Sample answer: He probably left out television because it is an older technology that people are less alarmed about. And including statistics about television may have weakened his argument. For example, saying that teens spend about 11 hours a day in front of screens may seem less worrisome when you realize much of that time is spent watching TV.*

⌕ **Gr7Ch15Read3.pptx**

About the Author: Rachel Becker is a science journalist best known for her work as a staff science reporter for *The Verge*. Becker began her career in the field of archaeology and neuroimmunology (the study of the brain and the immune system). Becker has worked all over the world at dig sites and labs. She went to school at Stanford and Harvard University before going on to study science writing at MIT. Since focusing her writing on science, Becker has published articles in publications such as *Smithsonian*, *National Geographic News*, and *Slate*. Becker continues to write about many areas of science for *The Verge*.

Remediation: First Read Struggling students may benefit from reading Becker's editorial aloud with a partner and working together to find examples of evidence used by both authors.

Chapter **15** *(continued)*

Lesson Support

Focus on Analyzing Interpretations of Evidence: Point out the activities on pages 314–316 and clarify any questions students may have. Have students complete the activities independently and be prepared to discuss their responses with the class.

As you discuss the questions on pages 314–315, use follow-up questions to help students more deeply analyze the text. Question 1: Follow up by asking whose personal experience seems more valid and why: parents or Karadaras's own experience with addicts?

As you read each of the examples of the use of the pronoun *we*, discuss who the authors are including in *we*? Parents? The scientific community? The informed public/readers? How would you as a reader respond differently if the author used the pronoun *I*?

Answers to Questions:

1. Possible response: He reports his own experience as a psychotherapist treating thousands of kids; he also describes the experiences of parents who have seen how their kids respond to screens.

(continued)

---

55 The tech-as-addiction metaphor is sloppy, though it might not be wrong. The problem is we don't have a good handle on what qualifies as tech addiction—if it exists at all, how common it is, and what kind of environmental and **physiological** conditions predispose someone to it.

---
physiological: relating to the way in which a living organism functions

Focus on Analyzing Interpretations of Evidence

Becker's editorial is a rebuttal to Kardaras's editorial. *Rebut* means "to contradict." One way Becker rebuts Kardaras's claim is to suggest that the evidence might be flawed and that his interpretation of it may be misleading.

1. Remember that Kardaras provides two kinds of evidence: personal experience and research. Whose personal experience does Kardaras cite as evidence?

Both Kardaras and Becker use the readers' personal experience as evidence. Did you notice how often each uses the word *we*?
- Kardaras: "We see the aggressive temper tantrums when the devices are taken away . . ."
- Kardaras: "No wonder we have a hard time peeling kids from their screens . . ."
- Becker: "We've seen this form of scaremongering before."
- Becker: "If computers were 'digital drugs,' wouldn't we have already seen warning signs?"

Using *we* suggests that the readers share the same experience and already know (and agree with) what the author is saying. Kardaras is saying that his fellow parents have observed these troubling behaviors. Becker, on the other hand, says that readers have evidence that disproves Kardaras's claim.

REFLECT

The editorials discuss screen use among children and teenagers. But what about adults and their screen use? Should we be concerned about them, as well?

ELL Support: Focus on Analyzing Interpretations of Evidence Remind students that *personal experience* is "what people do and what happens to people." Have students work in multilevel pairs or small groups to discuss and write about the questions, using these prompts and sentence frames:
- Who does Kardaras/Becker mean by "we"?
- Kardaras means . . . when he writes "we."
- Becker means . . . when she writes "we."
- Is your personal experience the same as Kardaras' or Becker's?
- Why doesn't Becker use parents' personal experiences?
- She . . . .
- Whose personal experience is best (most convincing)? Why?

2. How do you feel about the authors calling on your personal experience as evidence? Do you agree that what they have seen is the same as what you have seen?

3. Becker does not mention the other type of personal experience that Kardaras uses in his editorial. Speculate: Why do you think she didn't mention that evidence?

4. In your opinion, whose use of personal experience as evidence is more convincing for their claim: Kardaras's or Becker's? Why do you think so?

Becker also analyzes Kardaras's evidence—specifically, whether the evidence means what he says its means. Different authors can look at the same evidence and reach different conclusions. Authors always say what *they* believe the evidence means.

Consider Kardaras's use of brain imaging research. Kardaras says that iPads, smartphones, and Xboxes affect the brain's frontal cortex in exactly the same way that cocaine does. That sounds scary, right? But look at what Becker says about Kardaras's use of that research:

> This is, strictly speaking, true—at least from a neuroimaging standpoint. This is a hoary old trope in science writing, and it's apparently loosely based on fMRI, which is hardly the most accurate discipline. The brain's reward center . . . is what makes you feel good when you eat, . . . take cocaine, or play video games.

continued on next page

Answers to Questions:

2. Responses will vary.

3. Possible response: She probably can't refute it. Specifically, she can't say that parents haven't had the experience of aggressive or distracted children. She also can't contradict Kardaras' personal experience as a psychotherapist treating what he calls screen addiction.

4. Possible response: Kardaras' use of personal experience is more convincing. He points to specific shared experiences of a group of people. Even if the readers don't have children, they might be disposed to believe it, knowing that kids and teenagers can be difficult to separate from their screens. And Kardaras' appeal to his own professional experience, as someone who has treated many people with not just screen addiction but also drug addiction, lends a lot of weight to that evidence.

 Gr7Ch15Read3.pptx

• Becker's/Kardaras' personal experience is best (most convincing) because . . . .

Lesson Support

Answers to Chart:

Row 2

Source and Evidence: Screens increase depression, anxiety, aggression, and psychotic-like behavior.

What Kardaras says the evidence means: That screens are dangerous because they lead to antisocial and self-destructive behavior.

Row 3

Source and Evidence: *8- to 10-year olds spend 8 hours a day with digital media; teenagers spend 11 hours per day in front of screens; one in three kids use tablets or smartphones before they can talk* (lines 36–40).

What Kardaras says the evidence means: That excessive screen use is a big part of the problem and cause of all the addiction problems.

What Becker says about the evidence: A 2013 Policy Statement says that television, not video games and the Internet, are the main form of media for children and teens. She says Kardaras doesn't mention that fact because he is deliberately stoking fears about video games and the Internet.

If you read it closely, Becker says Kardaras's use of evidence is weak in two ways:

- The research isn't "the most accurate." This means that evidence comparing cocaine use and screen use might not be trustworthy or true.

- And, even if the evidence is accurate, it doesn't necessarily mean using screens is as harmful as using cocaine. According to Becker, eating food also affects the brain's "reward center." So, maybe playing video games is more like eating food than it is like doing drugs.

In other words, Becker suggests the brain imaging research is flawed and that Kardaras is choosing the scariest evidence to make his case.

The last two rows of the chart below will help you continue to examine Becker's interpretation. The blue-shaded cells have been completed for you. Complete the sentence starters in the other cells.

TECH-CONNECT

Use an online polling site to compare which editorial your classmates agree with more: Kardaras's or Becker's. Post your results on your class website.

Source and Evidence	What Kardaras says the evidence means	What Becker says about the evidence
Source: Brain imaging research **Evidence:** iPads, smartphones, and Xboxes affect the frontal cortex the same way cocaine does	Digital screens are as harmful and addictive as cocaine.	• The research method might be flawed, leading to bad evidence. • He ignores the fact that safer pleasures, like eating, also affect the brain's reward center. Video games might be more like food than drugs.
Source: Hundreds of clinical studies **Evidence:** Screens increase See answers in shaded sidebar to the left.	That screens	• She calls it "scaremongering." • She says that Kardaras and others are just uneasy with new technology. • She says that a generation of computer users "appear, mostly, to be fine."
Source: 2013 Policy Statement by the American Academy of Pediatrics **Evidence:**	That excessive screen use	The same 2013 Policy Statement

Speak and Listen At the end of her editorial, Becker writes, "The tech-as-addiction metaphor is sloppy, though it might not be wrong."

- Why do you think she says this?
- Why admit that Kardaras might be right?

Discuss these questions with a partner.

> **CONNECT TO ESSENTIAL QUESTION**
>
> What do you think is the most important *positive* effect of all these screens in our lives? What about the most important *negative* effect?

Language: Comma Usage

Commas are used to create a break between elements in a sentence. They set off introductory words and transitions from the main clause and separate clauses in a sentence.

Commas After Introductory Words and Phrases

Study the sentence below from "It's 'digital heroin.'"

> In fact, Dr. Andrew Doan, the head of addiction research for the Pentagon and the US Navy, calls video games and screen technologies "digital pharmakeia."

In this sentence, the phrase *in fact* is used as an introduction to the clause that follows. (Remember, a clause is a complete thought with a subject and verb.) Introductory words and phrases require a comma to set them off from the rest of the sentence.

How do you know when a word or phrase is introductory? An introductory element is not necessary to understand the rest of the sentence. If the phrase *in fact* were removed from the example, the sentence would still function and make sense.

Introductory phrases often double as transitions—words that show a connection between a sentence and the one before it. Phrases like *in fact*, *for example*, and *in addition* connect ideas, but they are not strictly necessary for understanding the sentence. Take a look at another example:

> In addition, hundreds of clinical studies show that screens increase depression, anxiety and aggression . . .

Again, the phrase *in addition* could be removed from the sentence without disrupting its meaning. It shows the relationship between this sentence and the previous sentence and introduces the main clause.

Commas That Separate Clauses in a Sentence

A compound sentence consists of two independent clauses connected with a conjunction (such as *and*, *but*, and *or*). A comma is placed after the first clause and before the conjunction.

continued on next page

Speak and Listen: Before students discuss the bullet points, have them consider what Becker means when she says the tech-as-addiction metaphor "might not be wrong."

Language: Comma Usage: Help students distinguish between conjunctions that join independent clauses and phrases by displaying the following sentences:

- I spend a little more than an hour a day on my computer or cell phone, but my brother spends four to five hours a day online. (*Comma needed between two independent clauses.*)

- I spend time online working on homework and using social media. (*No comma needed between two phrases.*)

- It's easy to lose track of time when you are doing online research and when you are checking Twitter and Instagram at the same time. (*No comma needed between two phrases.*)

- Many parents limit their children's screen time, and some even install browsers that will lock a user out after a certain amount of time has passed. (*Comma needed between two independent clauses.*)

 Gr7Ch15Language.pptx

ELL Support: Language Explain that commas are used after words or phrases that aren't needed in a sentence. Emphasize this by writing the examples on the board and crossing out or erasing the introductory phrase and showing that the phrase is still correct by placing a star next to it. Use symbols and text to explain that a comma plus (+) a connecting word (*but, or, and*) = a period (.) In other words, a comma plus a conjunction can take the place of a period.

Have students work in multilevel pairs or groups to complete the items, adding or subtracting commas from each sentence. Review and explain correct responses with the class.

Chapter 15 *(continued)*

Lesson Support

Answers to Questions:

1. On the other hand, video gaming has its benefits.

2. I enjoy using my smartphone, but I try not to overuse it.

3. Although there are drawbacks to screen use, people are unlikely to unplug altogether.

4. You can try to set limits for yourself, or you can use apps that monitor your use.

(continued)

Study the example sentence below. Each independent clause is underlined.

> About 1.6 percent of Americans use heroin, but a quarter of them wind up addicted . . .

The following sentences contain comma errors. Rewrite each one, and place the comma correctly.

1. On the other hand video gaming has its benefits.

2. I enjoy using my smartphone but, I try not to overuse it.

3. Although, there are drawbacks to screen use people are unlikely to unplug altogether.

4. You can try to set limits for yourself or you can use apps that monitor your use.

5. Of course people lived full lives for thousands of years, before digital devices existed.

6. As Rachel Becker says the majority of digital users, are not showing the troubling signs of addiction.

Project-Based Assessments

Develop a Public Service Announcement

A public service announcement (PSA) is a short audio or video advertisement intended to alert the public about a social problem and to suggest a solution. Kardaras's editorial about "digital heroin" is not a PSA, but he clearly wants to alert the public to a problem. (In the full article, he suggests steps parents should take, but that section does not appear in the excerpt.) Imagine that Kardaras's message were turned into an audio PSA, one that describes the problem and recommends a solution. What would it sound like?

For this project, you will create a 30-second audio PSA to raise awareness of "digital heroin" and what you can do to fight the problem.

Follow these steps to create your own audio PSA:

1. Visit the website psacentral.org/campaigns to find PSAs from the past and present. Find topics that interest you and watch the PSAs about them. This will help you think about how to develop your PSA and how your voice should sound.

continued on next page

5. Of course, people lived full lives for thousands of years before digital devices existed.

6. As Rachel Becker says, the majority of digital users are not showing the troubling signs of addiction.

Assessment

Project-Based Assessments

Develop a Public Service Announcement: As students listen to sample PSAs, suggest that they pay particular attention to the opening words. Encourage them to consider which PSAs grabbed their interest right away, analyzing the types of openers that were most effective. Encourage them to apply this analysis to writing their own PSA openers.

ELL Support: Project-Based Assessment—Public Service Announcement Have students work in multilevel pairs or groups to write and perform the PSA. Together with students, brainstorm sentence frames that they can use for their PSAs:

- You should . . . . You should not . . . .
- It is important . . . . Remember . . . .

Beginning and intermediate students may create a visual PSA or poster with words, phrases, and sentences, depending on their language level.

Chapter 15 *(continued)*

Assessment

Roundtable Discussion: You may want to ask students to conduct their own research before the discussion. Instruct them to find another article that contains evidence in support of Kardaras' or Becker's central claims. Students should print out their articles, highlight evidence that pertains to the discussion, and refer to the evidence during the discussion.

Encourage students to use accountable talk during the discussion, modeling how to build on what others have said. If necessary, post sentence frame examples:

- I agree/disagree with _____ because _____.

- Some evidence that builds on/contradicts what _____ claims is . . . .

- I'm not sure I understand what _____ means? Can you explain . . . .

After completing the roundtable discussion, consider having volunteers write a brief summary of the discussion to distribute to the class. Summary points might include:

- How many students agreed with the opinion of each author at the beginning of the discussion?

- What were the major reasons for supporting each opinion?

- What were the major arguments against each opinion?

- Did the discussion change students' opinions? Did the discussion change your own opinion?

2. Write a 30-second announcement that is 85 to 100 words in length. Practice reading your announcement until it sounds professional and is within the time limit. Read clearly and with the appropriate feeling. Should you sound serious, sad, anxious, or friendly? The tone of your voice needs to match the tone of your words.

3. Record the announcement on a smartphone voice memo app or on a computer using recording software. Your announcement must be between 28 and 32 seconds in length.

4. If you have access to audio editing software, you could add music or sound effects to increase the effectiveness of your PSA.

5. Before submitting your PSA as your teacher directs, play it for another student or an adult. Ask for feedback using the rubric below as a guide. Change your PSA based on this feedback.

6. Submit your digital recording and text electronically to your teacher or present it to the class as instructed.

Use the following guidelines for your public service announcement.	
To receive the highest score (4.0), the public service announcement must meet all of these criteria.	Your announcement • clearly and creatively explains the problem using facts and/or personal examples. • offers a reasonable solution to the problem that people can follow easily. • is digitally recorded and is 30 seconds in length. • sounds professional, with clear speech and good vocal variety to communicate ideas.

Roundtable Discussion

Participate in a roundtable discussion on the following questions:

> What do you think about the central claim that Kardaras and Becker's editorials debate—that screens are "digital heroin"?
>
> What experiences or observations about screens make you think this way?

In a roundtable discussion, all students are equal and everyone participates. Arrange your seats in a circle. Your teacher or a discussion leader may sit in the middle. Come to the discussion with an open mind. You will be evaluated on the following:

Expectations for Discussion	
Listening	**Speaking**
Listen respectfully	Speak at least once
Look at the speaker	Give reasons or examples
Take notes on what the speaker is saying	Ask questions
Write down follow-up questions	Explain and justify (offer reasons to support your idea)
	Invite comment

ELL Support: Project-Based Assessments—Roundtable Discussion: Provide the following sentence frames for students to use in the discussion:

- I think/don't think that screens are digital heroin because I have observed (seen) . . . .

- I think/don't think that screens are digital heroin because I have experienced (felt/done) . . . .

Allow time for students to practice their sentences with you or in multileveled pairs before beginning the discussion. Explain that students should monitor (check on) themselves during the discussion, and if they need help understanding or participating, they can raise their hand and you can assist them with paraphrases or sentence frames.

Instructions for a Roundtable Discussion

1. The discussion leader (teacher or student) begins by asking the following questions:

> What do you think about the central claim that Kardaras and Becker's editorials debate—that screens are "digital heroin"?
>
> What experiences or observations about screens make you think this way?

2. Allow each member the chance to reply to the questions.

3. Take notes on comments you disagree with or you have questions about. Record what was said and who said it.

4. Go around the circle again and allow everyone to ask a follow-up question. Questions should be directed to the person who made the original comment. Try phrasing your questions in this way:
   - Explain what you mean by . . .
   - Who agrees/disagrees with (name of participant)? Why?

5. Close the discussion by having everyone respond to the following questions:

> Did your opinion change during the roundtable discussion? Why or why not?

Use the following guidelines for the roundtable discussion.	
To receive the highest score (4.0), the discussion must meet all of these criteria.	During the discussion, you should • listen carefully when others speak; make notes about what they said. • offer thoughtful feedback and encourage everyone to participate. • share reasonable opinions and support your opinion with examples. • speak to the question or point at hand in a clear, concise manner.

On Your Own: Integrating Ideas

1. Kardaras's main concern about screens is that they are addictive. But perhaps a more common concern is whether playing violent video games can encourage violent behavior. The website ProCon.org is one place to start looking into this topic. Visit videogames.procon.org and see what the evidence is.

2. To learn more about the history and impact of video games, check out this site from the Public Broadcasting System: www.pbs.org/kcts/videogamerevolution. A companion program, *The Video Game Revolution*, might be available in your school media center or at your public library.

3. Read the Slate.com article "The Caped Crusader: Fredric Wertham and the Campaign Against Comic Books" by Jeet Heer. Consider how concerns about video games are similar to and different from the "great comic-book scare."

On Your Own: Integrating Ideas:

Activity 2: Steer English language learners—and others who might benefit from extra visual/verbal reinforcement—to watch this program.

Activity 3: Encourage students who read this article to consider how it relates to the Connect to Essential Question sidebar on page 309.

Remediation: Project-Based Assessments—Roundtable Discussion Taking part in the roundtable discussion should aid students' comprehension of the concepts and vocabulary in this chapter. Pair students with more advanced students to develop notes that contain questions and evidence that they can refer to during the discussion.

Chapter **15** *(continued)*

Assessment

Connect to Testing: This Connect to Testing section focuses on citing evidence to support an analysis, determining an author's point of view and purpose, examining how authors on different sides of an issue interpret the same evidence, and correcting misplaced modifiers.

Encourage students to work in pairs to choose the correct answers to the questions and then to compare their answers with those of another pair of students. If there is disagreement, encourage the groups to try to reach a consensus as they discuss the reasons for their choices.

Answers to Connect to Testing Questions:

1. D. The question is asking for the strongest evidence in support of the claim. Choice A is a statement about parents' personal experience. It is not the strongest evidence. Choice B is a restatement of the central claim. Choice C explains other researchers who support Kardaras' central claim, which is evidence from expert testimony. However, the strongest evidence is Choice D because it cites hundreds of clinical studies that deal with mental health issues. (DoK 2)

2. Even though Mrs. Rodriquez wanted to limit her son's screen time, she knew he needed his phone in case of an emergency and he couldn't do his homework without his laptop. (DoK 1)

3. A., E. (DoK 3)

(continued)

Connect to Testing

In this chapter, you cited evidence to support an analysis, determined an author's point of view and purpose, and examined how authors on different sides of an issue interpret the same evidence. When you take assessments, you will be tested over your ability to use these skills.

1. One central idea from Kardaras's editorial is that excessive screen time harms the mental health of children. Which sentence from the editorial provides the strongest evidence to support this claim?

   A. *Many parents intuitively understand that ubiquitous glowing screens are having a negative effect on kids.*

   B. *We now know that those iPads, smartphones and Xboxes are a form of digital drug.*

   C. *This addictive effect is why Dr. Peter Whybrow, director of neuroscience at UCLA, calls screens "electronic cocaine" and Chinese researchers call them "digital heroin."*

   D. *In addition, hundreds of clinical studies show that screens increase depression, anxiety and aggression and can even lead to psychotic-like features where the video gamer loses touch with reality.*

2. Rewrite the following sentence correcting comma errors.

   Even though, Mrs. Rodriquez wanted to limit her son's screen time she knew he needed his phone in case of an emergency and he couldn't do his homework without his laptop.

3. What two sources of evidence does Nicholas Kardaras mention in his editorial "Digital Heroin" that Rachel Becker in "Digital Garbage" does not?

   A. the personal experience of parents

   B. brain imaging research

   C. a 2013 Policy Statement by the American Academy of Pediatrics

   D. hundreds of clinical studies

   E. his clinical work with more than 1,000 teenagers

   F. research by the National Institutes of Drug Addiction

ELL Support: Connect to Testing and Assessments See the ELL Teacher Resource (p. 22) for ideas on adapting this section for ELLs.

4. **Part A:** Which sentence from "Digital Heroin" most clearly states Nicholas Kardaras's point of view about digital screens?

   A. *But it's even worse than we think.*

   B. *We now know that those iPads, smartphones and Xboxes are a form of digital drug.*

   C. *Once a kid has crossed the line into true tech addiction, treatment can be very difficult.*

   D. *A person can live without drugs or alcohol; with tech addiction, digital temptations are everywhere.*

   Part B: Which sentence from "Digital Garbage" most clearly shows Rachel Becker distinguishing her position from Kardaras's position?

   A. *In the op-ed, Kardaras claims that "iPads, smartphones and Xboxes are a form of digital drug."*

   B. *People are frequently uneasy with new technology, after all.*

   C. *Kardaras' op-ed goes on to warn that exposure to screens can cause "addiction," and he quotes researchers analogizing screen time to heroin and cocaine.*

   D. *Kardaras' loose talk on addiction is what makes his argument so tough to believe.*

5. **Part A:** Which source do Kardaras and Becker both cite?

   A. Dr. Peter Whybrow

   B. Chinese researchers

   C. American Academy of Pediatrics

   D. Dr. Kimberly Young

   Part B: How does Becker criticize Kardaras's use of evidence from the source cited in Part A?

   A. She claims that Kardaras is not considering all the facts from that source.

   B. She claims the source that produced the evidence is biased.

   C. She claims that the research producing that evidence is flawed.

   D. She claims the evidence actually proves the opposite of what Kardaras claims.

4. **Part A:** B. Choice D is a fact and not representative of a point of view or opinion. Choice C is also a fact. Choice A is a point of view but it is very vague. Choice B is the best answer because it states the author's point of view. (DoK 2)

   Part B: D. Choices A and C are restatements of Kardaras' claims. Choice B is a fact that both authors would agree with. Choice D offers Becker's point of view on Karadaras' position. (DoK 3)

5. **Part A:** C. (DoK 3)

   Part B: A. In her article, Becker accuses Karadaras of cherry-picking evidence from the study to support his claims and ignoring the fact that children and teens spend most of their screen time watching television. (DoK 2)

Unit 3 Writing

Writing a Fictional Narrative

Introduction

Preview Academic Vocabulary:
Read and discuss the meanings of the academic vocabulary.

dialogue: *conversation between characters in a story.* From the <u>dialogue</u> between the two characters, I could infer that they were close friends.

narrative: *nonfiction or fictional writing that tells a story.* The <u>narrative</u> of the scientist's life jumped back and forth in time.

pacing: *the rate at which the events in a story progress.* The <u>pacing</u> of the action in the story was fast at first and then slowed down in the middle, causing me to lose interest in the story.

resolution: *in a story, the end of the conflict.* In the story's <u>resolution</u>, the hero defeated the villain.

 Gr7U3WritingNarrative.pptx

Writing a Fictional Narrative

Technology can be our best friend, and technology can also be the biggest party pooper of our lives.
—**Steven Spielberg**

The real danger is not that computers will begin to think like men, but that men will begin to think like computers.
—**Sydney Harris**

The nonfiction selections in this chapter dealt with problems and solutions—specifically, how technologies can solve problems while at the same time creating others. And in *Feed*, the fiction selection in the chapter, Titus struggles with fear, loneliness, and boredom after being disconnected from feednet.

A variety of fiction stories feature technology. Some involve characters who face more dramatic problems—artificial intelligence taking over society, for example, or scientists rushing to cure a plague or blow up an asteroid. In still other stories, the problem with technology may be less serious. Maybe the main character bickers with a lazy robot that doesn't want to do its job. Or perhaps the story is about the robot itself, putting up with human foolishness. And some stories about technology root themselves in the real world, exploring what happens when robots put people out of work or when teenagers post something regrettable to social media.

In this chapter, you will write a fictional narrative in which a character confronts some problem related to technology.

> **WRITING PROMPT**
>
> Write a story in which the main character confronts a problem related to a technology. Your narrative:
>
> - must have a vivid setting, a main character, and a clearly depicted problem.
>
> - should show the character confronting and trying to solve the problem.
>
> - must depict how the problem is resolved (with or without success) and the logical outcomes from that resolution.
>
> Your narrative should also make use of thoughtful description, realistic dialogue, and careful pacing. The final product will be two to three typed pages, double-spaced, using a standard-sized font.

ELL Support: Academic Vocabulary See <u>Teaching Vocabulary in the ELL Teacher Resource (p. 18)</u> to use for teaching vocabulary throughout *Connections*.

Prepare to Write

Read the prompt closely. Underline key words that explain what you must do. Break it down based on purpose, audience, content, and additional requirements by filling in the chart below.

Purpose	to write a fictional story about a character confronting a problem relating to technology
Audience	classmates, teacher, social media users
Content Requirements	• main character • clear problem that drives the plot • vivid setting • clear resolution and outcome
Additional Requirements	two to three typed pages, double-spaced, standard-sized font

▼ The Writing Process

Brainstorm

To get started with your story, read through the chart below. It lists possible problems, settings, technologies, main characters, and people or things that might oppose the main character. Circle options that look interesting.

Note: You are not limited to the ideas in this chart. If you are interested in ideas that do not appear here, write those ideas in the margins.

> **CONNECT TO ESSENTIAL QUESTION**
>
> What is more interesting to you: exploring how a technology affects an entire society, or exploring the relationship between an individual and a technology?

Common Problems
• A character has a technology that can change society and must decide how to use it.
• A character has a technology that can change society and is hunted by others who want it for their own purposes.
• A character encounters a technology (possibly but not necessarily intelligent) that threatens society.
• A character who fears the effect of a new technology and fights to stop its spread.
• A society dependent on a technology approaches disaster when the device breaks or gets stolen.
• A society adopts a technology that seems wonderful at first but hides a terrible secret.

Settings	
• the past, present, or future	• a large, real-world city
• a planet, space station, or spaceship	• an undiscovered civilization
• another dimension	• a local, real-world place: your home, school, mall, library, hospital, etc.
• your hometown or city	

continued on next page

Prepare to Write: Read and analyze the prompt as a class. Introduce the chart on page 325. Explain that Content Requirements refers to the story elements their narrative should contain. Explain that the purpose of the chart is to closely analyze the prompt. They will have opportunities to flesh out the plot, characters, and setting as they brainstorm their narratives.

> **Sample Answer to Chart:**
>
> See answers on Student Book insert page to the left.

▼ The Writing Process

Brainstorm: Introduce the charts on pages 325–326, noting that they contain ideas about settings, characters, technologies, and possible conflicts that might arise in their narratives. Explain that the chart summarizes common conflicts often featured in science fiction novels. Students will need to flesh these out with their own original ideas. Explain that students can select points from the charts or simply use the notes to jump-start other ideas.

ELL Support: The Writing Process Review with students the problems, settings, technologies, and characters, using sketches and simple explanations to make sure students understand each choice. Students can sketch symbols and write words next to each list so they will remember each item.

Have students work in multilevel pairs or small groups to discuss and create their story. Beginning and intermediate students can draw and label pictures to represent their ideas for their problems, settings, technologies, and characters. For their final product, they can create a graphic novel with labels, descriptions, and speech and thought bubbles.

Writing *(continued)*

Generate Ideas: Introduce the brainstorming prompts on pages 326–328. Explain to students the purpose of these prompts: to get them thinking "on the page," prodding their imaginations into action. Remind students not to worry about correct grammar or spelling at this point. The most important thing is to put their brains in gear, writing freely. Encourage students to use whatever writing tool they find most comfortable—handwriting or typing.

The Problem: Conflict is the center of any story. Often, determining a problem can give rise to ideas for the rest of the story. However, students may prefer to start elsewhere. If creating a futuristic setting is what sparks the imagination, encourage students to begin there. The setting itself may contribute to the conflict the main character faces.

Technologies
• **Technology of the mind:** reading, controlling, or manipulating other minds
• **Technology of transportation:** time travel, space travel, teleportation (instantly moving from one place to another)
• **Technology of the body:** mental connection to the Internet, devices that enhance physical abilities (strength, intelligence) or any of the five senses, invisibility
• **Technology of transformation:** nanites (microscopic machines that can destroy or build any type of matter), artificial viruses, weapons of all sorts
• **Technology that comes to life:** anything from toasters to elevators to artificial satellites

Main Characters	People or Things Opposing the Main Character
• you, a friend, or a relative	• the technology itself
• someone modeled after a famous person you admire	• a large corporation
• a mysterious outsider	• a powerful government or agency
• an intelligent machine	• individuals seeking profit
• a scientist who has lost control of the technology	• a person or group against the technology
• a person nobody would expect	• a person or group seeking to ruin the world
	• a person or group seeking to change the world in ways that benefit only themselves

Generate Ideas

To help you generate ideas, try the following creative prewriting activities. **Note:** As you write your story, you might find your ideas changing. This is fine; go where the story takes you.

The Problem

Which problem in the chart on pages 325–326 appeals to you most? (If none appeal, write your own.)

Why does the problem appeal to you? What about it is interesting? Be specific.

The Setting

What setting in the chart appeals to you most? Why? (If none appeal, explain one of your own.)

In the space below, brainstorm the setting. What kind of world produces the problem you wrote about above? What sorts of things would your main character see, hear, and feel?

The Technology

Which technology in the chart appeals to you most? (If none appeal, develop and explain your own.)

What does the technology look like? Write notes about its size, weight, shape, color, and any other features worth description. Be as specific as you can: Instead of saying "large," say "the size of a minivan." Instead of saying "red and shiny," say "gleaming like polished copper." You can also draw a picture of the technology.

The Setting: Remind students who want to set their narratives in the future or in an unknown world to explore what various aspects of that society might look like.

It may be helpful to identify settings of popular science fiction books and/or movies. Then students could build on these familiar settings.

Suggest that they imagine as many details as possible to create a fully developed setting. As they draft their stories, they can describe the most important details needed to move the plot along and make their story interesting.

Remediation: Generate Ideas Meet with a group of struggling students to help them identify the problem, setting, technology, and other elements of their story. Model how to use these elements to plan their own stories.

Writing *(continued)*

The Main Character: Make sure students consider whether they want to write in first or third person. Remind them that a first-person narration reads like a diary entry, allowing the narrator to directly convey thoughts and feelings. While this may appeal to some students, others may want to step back as they tell their story, writing in the third person to provide a broader point of view.

The Main Character

Who in the chart on pages 325–326 will be the main character? (If none appeal, come up with your own.)

From what point of view will you write: first or third person?

Describe your character. Young or old? Male or female? Is the character joking and confident, quiet and thoughtful, or angry and brave? Be specific.

People or Things Against the Main Character

Who or what in the chart on pages 325–326 will oppose the main character? (If none appeal, come up with your own.)

Describe the person, group, or thing opposing the main character. What does this person, group, or thing want, and why?

Organize Ideas

Fiction writers often use story maps to plan their details. A story map helps them ensure that the story elements work together well.

Your Story Map	
Setting:	Main Character:
Problem:	

Beginning (introduces the main character, the setting, and the problem):

Middle (builds the story as the character tries to deal with the problem):

End (wraps up the story and tells how the problem is resolved):

First Draft

Use your story map to write a draft of your fictional narrative.
Here are some hints:
- Refer to your notes while drafting.
- Write quickly. You will revise and proofread later.

continued on next page

Organize Ideas: Encourage students to sit back and review their brainstorming notes before filling out their story maps. Have them circle details that stand out and consider what they can include in a two- to three-page story. Explain that they need not include every detail on the story map. They should, however, jot down the most important elements they want to include.

First Draft: Remind students to refer to their brainstorming notes and story maps as they write their drafts. Encourage them to resist the urge to edit as they go. Most writers usually include more details in a first draft than what eventually ends up in a story. It is best, however, to wait until the revising stage to decide whether a given detail, line of dialogue, scene, or character is key to the story.

Remediation: Organize Ideas Require students to turn in their story maps for your review. You may need to help them focus their ideas or flesh them out. Regular checks on their progress will keep struggling students on track and encourage them to write an engaging narrative.

Writing *(continued)*

Revision: Before students begin the review and revision process, remind them that the heart of good writing is revision. Point out that professional writers expect to spend more time revising than they do writing a first draft. Encourage students to view the first draft as an exploration in which they discover what is most appealing about their stories. Revising will help students build on the best elements and pinpoint details that either do not contribute to the heart of the story or stand in its way.

In commenting on a first draft, remind students not to focus on tinkering with sentences or fine-tuning grammar. Instead, they should focus on the major story elements:

- Is there a solid, uncomplicated plot?
- Is the major character well defined?
- Are the setting and technology interesting?
- Is there a clear resolution and outcome?

At this time, review the Reflect sidebar notes on pages 331 and 332. Remind students to refer to these tips as they review other students' narratives and reflect on their own.

Draft 1: Group Peer Review: Before the first peer review, have students read their story aloud to themselves and make revisions. Then have them read the Steps for Peer Review on page 330. Make sure students understand the process. If many students are new to this activity, you may want to conduct a fishbowl review.

- Write on every other line, or double-space if working on a computer. This will make it easier to make revisions.
- If you take a break and then return to drafting, reread what you have written before continuing. This will help you resume the flow of thought.
- Mark this version of your narrative Draft 1.

Revision

Have others (other students, your teacher, or your relatives) read your narrative. Listen carefully to their questions and comments. Applying their advice can help refine your writing. You can put your narrative through the three types of review that follow.

Draft 1: Group Peer Review

This review will evaluate whether your story is engaging and its sequence of events is logical. In a group of two to three people, complete the following steps:

Steps for Peer Review

1. Select a timekeeper. Each writer gets 15 minutes. Respect the time limit.
2. One writer begins by reading aloud the first two sentences of the story while other people listen.
3. Pause. The same writer reads the first two sentences aloud a second time.
4. The writer asks, "Does the beginning of my narrative make you want to know more?" As each member responds, the writer takes notes on the draft.
5. The writer reads aloud the entire story once. As the writer reads, members take notes.
6. The writer asks, "What questions do you have about the events of the story? Is there anything you'd like to see better developed or described?" The writer jots down replies.
7. The members hand over their notes to the writer.
8. Repeat Steps 1–7 with the next member, who becomes the writer.

As soon as possible after the group peer review, revise your draft based on your peers' questions and comments. Mark this paper Draft 2.

©Perfection Learning® • No Reproduction Permitted

ELL Support: Group Peer Review Have students work in multilevel pairs or small groups to review their drafts. Highlight the questions in Steps 4 and 6 in the Peer Review for students to use as they read their draft. Provide the following sentence frames for students to use to give feedback to their peers:

- Yes/No, your introduction does/does not make me want to read more. Can you . . . . ?
- I don't understand . . . . Can you . . . . ?

Remediation: Group Peer Review Organize mixed groups of struggling students and more advanced writers for the first peer review. Remind students to note positive comments first before mentioning areas that need improvement. Have students use their peers' comments to help them write their second drafts.

Connections • © Perfection Learning®

Draft 2: Markup Review

For Draft 2, you will conduct a markup review to improve your word choice and sentence variety.

Tools needed: colored pencils

Step 1: With a green colored pencil, bracket [ ] the first word of each sentence. Make a list of these words on a separate sheet of paper. Identify their parts of speech.
Evaluate: Are a variety of words used? Which word(s) appear most?
Action: Reduce the number of identical first words by half. Try starting sentences with descriptive phrases or clauses.

Step 2: Underline each sentence in the paper with alternating blue and orange colored pencils. Sentence 1—orange, sentence 2—blue, sentence 3—orange, and so on.
Evaluate: Do the sentence lengths vary? Are most sentences the same length? Are any too long and wordy?
Action: Add variety by combining short sentences or breaking up long ones. Strive for a balance of long and short sentences.

Step 3: Circle all the *being* verbs with red pencil. Use this list to help you.

> **am, is, was, were, be, being, been**

Evaluate: Are *being* verbs overused? Can they be replaced with any action verbs?
Action: Reduce the number of *being* verbs by half.

Step 4: Choose a black pencil and draw a box around "dead" words. Refer to the following list of overused words below.

> **a lot, also, awesome, awful, cool, fun, funny, get, good, got, great, have to, like, really, very**

Evaluate: Can dead words be replaced with more specific ones? Use a thesaurus to find more interesting substitutes.
Action: Reduce the number of dead words by half.

When you finish the steps above, mark the version Draft 3.

REFLECT

A good narrative opens by pulling the reader into the action. Try the following:

- Begin with dialogue. Example: "I always knew this mind-reading technology would embarrass me!" said Xorn, furious.
- Begin at the most suspenseful part, then describe events leading up to the crisis. Example: As the nanites melted her shoes, Rania's mind flashed back to her mom's warning.
- Begin in the middle of the action. Example: After five minutes of matching wits with the elevator, I began to realize how outclassed I was.

Draft 2: Markup Review: Have students review the steps for a markup review on page 331 and make sure students understand the process. Consider reviewing the difference between the active and passive voice, noting that using active voice can make stories more compelling.

ELL Support: Markup Review Together with students, brainstorm replacement words for forms of the verb *be, a lot, awesome, awful*, and the other words in the boxes on page 331. Demonstrate using a thesaurus to brainstorm ideas. Then model revising a student's draft step by step. Use a different student's draft for each step. Have students work in multilevel pairs or small groups to complete each step after you model it.

Assessment (continued)

Lesson Support

Draft 3: Individual Peer Review: Have students refer to the rubric as they read another person's narrative. For each bullet point in the rubric, the reviewer should write a description of how the writing does or does not meet the criteria described. If needed, provide sentence starters: The narrative introduces . . . . characters. The main characters are . . . . and they are . . . .

Proofread: As students proofread their narratives, have them note any questions about grammar or punctuation and ask for clarifications. Point out that writers often miss errors in their own writing. Encourage them to ask another student to lend a fresh eye to the proofreading process.

Final Narrative: Have students use the suggestions on page 332 to share their final essays. Encourage students to consider their intended audience when deciding how and where to publish their work.

Draft 3: Individual Peer Review

Ask one student to read Draft 3 and rate it using the rubric below.

	Use the following guidelines for your fictional narrative.
To receive the highest score (4.0), the narrative must meet all of these criteria.	The narrative should • introduce a narrator and one or more characters. • establish a setting and context for the story. • organize an event sequence that unfolds logically. • use techniques such as dialogue, pacing, and description. • use precise words and phrases, details, and sensory language to capture action and convey events. • provide a conclusion that follows from the events. • use correct grammar, usage, punctuation, and spelling.

Proofread

As you prepare a final draft, make sure you have used standard grammar and punctuation. Proofread carefully for omitted words and punctuation marks. If you used a word processing program, run spell check, but be aware of its limitations. Proofread again to detect the kinds of errors the computer can't catch.

Final Narrative

Share your completed narrative with audiences beyond your classroom. Read it to your family and friends. Upload your finished digital copy to your class website. If you have a school or personal blog, share it with your readers.

> **REFLECT**
>
> Good pacing means the story flows at the right rate. It doesn't drag or move too quickly. Use description to slow down the pace. Use dialogue or describe action to pick up the pace. Try reading your narrative aloud to judge whether the action is happening too quickly or too slowly.

ELL Support: Individual Peer Review Have students work in new multilevel pairs or small groups to review their drafts. Before they begin, read through the Narrative Writing Revision Checklist from the ELL Teacher Resource (p. 68). Use student narratives to model how to revise and proofread for elements listed in the checklist.

Practice Performance Task

A performance task evaluates your ability to comprehend selections of literature or informational text and then demonstrate your knowledge in writing. The task may begin with several multiple-choice or short-answer questions on key vocabulary and the central ideas of the passage(s). The task culminates with a writing assignment.

Complete the following performance task based on selections from Unit 3. You will read three sources and answer questions. Finally, you will complete a longer writing task.

Source #1

Read the following excerpt from *Smarter Thank You Think by* Clive Thompson from Chapter 11 of this unit.

> One way [teachers can get more one-on-one time with students] is by using new-media tools to invert the logic of instruction. Instead of delivering all her math lessons to the entire class, Thordarson has them watch Khan videos and work on the online problems. This way, the students who quickly "get it" can blast ahead—and Thordarson can focus more of her class time on helping the students who need coaching. Other teachers are even more aggressive about inverting their classes: They assign videos to be watched at home, then have the students do the homework in class, flipping their instruction inside out.
>
> This makes curious psychological sense. A video can often be a better way to deliver a lecture-style lesson, because students can pause and rewind when they get confused—impossible with a live classroom lesson. In contrast, homework is better done in a classroom, because that's when you're likely to need to ask the teacher for extra help. (Or to ask another student: Thordarson and her colleagues noticed students helping one another, sharing what they'd learned, and tutoring each other.)
>
> "Kids get to work in their place where they're most comfortable," says Thordarson as we wander around her class. "They're allowed to jump ahead. It gives kids who are above grade level a chance to just soar! And for kids who struggle, it gives them a chance to work through some of those issues without everybody watching."

Practice Performance Task

The purpose of this section is to prepare students for the types of performance tasks they will be completing on standardized testing. The task requires students to synthesize knowledge gained and skills developed throughout the unit. If used as test prep, review with students the process of answering multiple-choice questions, including eliminating answers that are clearly incorrect.

This performance task could be used as an assessment over Unit 3, instead of the Unit 3 assessment on pages 469–476. It could be completed over two class periods by having students answer questions 1–8 and complete the planning stage of the writing task during one class period and writing the essay during the second class period. Another alternative is to assign the writing to be completed at home.

ELL Support: Practice Performance Task Have students work in multilevel pairs or small groups to read and answer questions. Then have students work in the same multilevel pairs or small groups to write in response to the performance task prompt. Adjust the length of student responses as necessary. Students can write a paragraph or complete a graphic organizer. Provide an outline or the Claim, Reasons, and Evidence graphic organizer from the ELL Teacher Resource (p. 60) for students to use as their response or to prepare for their response. Provide the Argumentative Writing Revision Checklist from the ELL Teacher Resource (p. 70) for students to use to finalize their written response.

Assessment *(continued)*

Answers to Practice Performance Task:

1. D. From the context, the phrase means to flip the normal way instruction is done. The choice that is closest to this in meaning is Choice D. (DoK 2)

2. **Part A:** B. According to the text, Thordarson has students watch videos so that she can "focus more of her class time on helping students who need coaching." Coaching is similar to tutoring, Choice B. (DoK 2)

   Part B: B. (DoK 2)

3. **Part A:** B. The article presents examples of advanced students who can "blast ahead" and students who need more coaching. Choice B is the best choice. (DoK 2)

   (continued)

---

1. Read the sentence below.

   > One way [teachers can get more one-on-one time with students] is by using new-media tools to invert the logic of instruction.

   What is the meaning of the phrase <u>invert the logic of instruction?</u>
   A. help students enjoy class more than they normally would
   B. make the teacher work harder outside class than during class
   C. let the struggling students do what they want during class
   D. change which tasks are done during and outside class

2. **Part A:** How has technology changed how Tami Thordarson runs her classroom?
   A. She shows videos during her lectures.
   B. She tutors more during class time.
   C. She works directly with advanced students.
   D. She assigns more homework.

   Part B: Which of the following **best** supports the answer to Part A?
   A. *Instead of delivering all her math lessons to the entire class, Thordarson has them watch Khan videos and work on the online problems.*
   B. *This way, the students who quickly "get it" can blast ahead—and Thordarson can focus more of her class time on helping the students who need coaching.*
   C. *(Or to ask another student: Thordarson and her colleagues noticed students helping one another, sharing what they'd learned, and tutoring each other.)*
   D. *"Kids get to work in their place where they're most comfortable," says Thordarson as we wander around her class.*

3. **Part A:** What is the author's point of view regarding the use of videos in the classroom?
   A. Few students benefit from their use.
   B. Most students benefit from their use.
   C. Struggling students benefit from their use.
   D. High-performing students benefit from their use.

Part B: Which of the following best supports the answer to Part A? Select two choices.

A. *One way [teachers can get more one-on-one time with students] is by using new-media tools to invert the logic of instruction.*

B. *Instead of delivering all her math lessons to the entire class, Thordarson has them watch Khan videos and work on the online problems.*

C. *Other teachers are even more aggressive about inverting their classes: They assign videos to be watched at home, then have the students do the homework in class, flipping their instruction inside out.*

D. *A video can often be a better way to deliver a lecture-style lesson, because students can pause and rewind when they get confused—impossible with a live classroom lesson.*

E. *"It gives kids who are above grade level a chance to just soar!"*

F. *"And for kids who struggle, it gives them a chance to work through some of those issues without everybody watching."*

Continue the performance task by reading a second source and answering questions.

Source #2

Read the following excerpt from "Robots will eliminate 6% of all US jobs by 2021, report says," by Olivia Solon from Chapter 13.

By 2021, robots will have eliminated 6% of all jobs in the US, starting with customer service representatives and eventually truck and taxi drivers. That's just one cheery takeaway from a report released by market research company Forrester this week. . . .

"Six percent is huge. In an economy that's really not creating regular full-time jobs, the ability of people to easily find new employment is going to diminish. So we will have people wanting to work and struggling to find jobs because the same trends are beginning to occur in other historically richer job creation areas like banking, retail and healthcare," said Andy Stern, the former president of the Service Employees International Union. "It's an early warning sign and I think it just portends a massive wind of change in the future."

Studies have shown that higher rates of unemployment are linked to less volunteerism and higher crime. Taxi drivers around the world have already

continued on next page

Part B: E., F. Choices E and F are the best answers because they explain how both struggling and advanced students can succeed through a flipped classroom environment. Choices A, B, and C focus on how instruction in a flipped classroom is set up. Choice D hints at the fact that "confused" students can stop a video and replay it to clarify concepts, but it is not the strongest evidence for the answer to Part A. (DoK 2)

(continued)

Assessment *(continued)*

Answers to Practice Performance Task:

4. D. The word *relationship* means a "connection" or "correlation." Choice D uses the word *correlation*. (DoK 2)

5. C., F. Choices A, B, and D are not mentioned in the article. Choice E is mentioned but it is a supporting detail about the types of jobs that will be taken over by robots. Choices C and F are both central ideas. (DoK 2)

(continued)

---

reacted with violent protest to the arrival of ride-hailing app Uber. Imagine how people react when Uber eliminates drivers from its fleet.

"There is a lot of correlation between unemployment and drug use," said Stern. "Clearly over time, particularly in urban settings, the lack of employment is tinder for lighting a fire of social unrest."

4. Which sentence uses a word that means the same as *relationship*?

   A. *That's just one cheery takeaway from a report released by market research company Forrester this week. . . .*

   B. *In an economy that's really not creating regular full-time jobs, the ability of people to easily find new employment is going to diminish.*

   C. *Imagine how people react when Uber eliminates drivers from its fleet.*

   D. *"There is a lot of correlation between unemployment and drug use," said Stern.*

5. What are two central ideas of the article? Select two choices.

   A. Society will create more full-time jobs.

   B. Protests can have dangerous outcomes.

   C. Unemployment and crime are connected.

   D. Automation will lead to more leisure time.

   E. The jobs of truck and taxi drivers are at risk.

   F. Automation will cause more unemployment.

Continue the performance task by reading a third source and answering questions.

Source #3

Read the following excerpt from *Feed* by M. T. Anderson from Chapter 14.

But the braggest thing about the feed, the thing that made it really big, is that it knows everything you want and hope for, sometimes before you even know what those things are. It can tell you how to get them, and help you make buying decisions that are hard. Everything we think and feel is taken in by the corporations, mainly by data ones like Feedlink and OnFeed and American Feedware, and they make a special profile, one that's keyed just to you, and then they give it to their branch companies, or other companies buy them, and they can get to know what it is we need, so all you have to do is want something and there's a chance it will be yours.

Of course, everyone is like, *da da da, evil corporations, oh they're so bad*, we all say that, and we all know they control everything. I mean, it's not great, because who knows what evil [things] they're up to. Everyone feels bad about that. But they're the only way to get all this stuff, and it's no good getting [mad] about it, because they're still going to control everything whether you like it or not. Plus, they keep like everyone in the world employed, so it's not like we could do without them. And it's really great to know everything about everything whenever we want, to have it just like, in our brain, just sitting there.

6. What is the central idea of this excerpt from *Feed*?
   A. The feed corporations don't care about society.
   B. Corporations have both positive and negative effects on society.
   C. People should be making the decisions that are now being made by corporations.
   D. Most people don't fully understand how corporations affect society.

7. Read the following sentence from *Feed*.

   Of course, everyone is like, *da da da, evil corporations, oh they're so bad*, we all say that, and we all know they control everything.

   What impact does this sentence have on the paragraph in which it appears?
   A. It shows Titus totally agrees with the arguments against corporations.
   B. It shows Titus wants corporations to play less of a role in society.
   C. It shows Titus thinks corporations are making human beings less free.
   D. It shows Titus doesn't take the arguments against corporations too seriously.

8. How does the author develop Titus's mixed point of view about the feed? Choose two answers.
   A. Titus briefly admits problems with corporations.
   B. Titus totally agrees with the claims that corporations are mostly bad.
   C. Titus argues that corporations are essential to his life.
   D. Titus openly mocks the idea that corporations are evil.

6. B. Choice A is incorrect because Titus explains both the good and bad things about corporations. Choice C is true, but it isn't the central idea of the excerpt. Choice D is unsupported because Titus clearly understands how corporations manipulate people's wants to their own ends. The best answer is Choice B. (DoK 2)

7. D. In this sentence, Titus is admitting that many people argue against the impact of corporations. He is switching from praising them to admitting that they can be controlling. Choice D is the best answer. (DoK 3)

8. A., C. Choice A is correct because Titus says that corporations are "not great, because who knows what evil [things] they are up to." Choice B is incorrect because Titus mentions the problems briefly and then dismisses them. Choice C is true because Titus says "they keep everyone in the world employed, so it's not like we can live without them." Choice D is also incorrect. (DoK 2)

Assessment (continued)

Your Assignment:

Suggest that students read the prompt several times, underlining key words and phrases that explain the focus of the essay. Encourage students to develop an original claim that must include evidence from three texts from the unit and can also include their own knowledge, experience, and opinions.

Suggest that students create a graphic organizer to organize their ideas before they write the essay. Remind students to keep their claim in mind as they revisit the selections so they can target the most relevant evidence. Noting evidence in the graphic organizer will help them locate these details as they draft their essays. Require students to include direct quotations and line numbers in their essay if you so desire.

Suggest that students review the qualifications on page 338 before writing their essays.

 Gr7U3PerformanceTask.pptx

Your Assignment

> ### WRITING PROMPT
>
> Technology has both positive and negative effects on society. Your assignment is to write an essay in which you argue whether technology is shaping modern society in ways that are *mostly* positive or *mostly* negative. Use textual evidence from three sources within the chapters in the unit to support your claim. (You can use sources other than those provided in this Performance Task.)
>
> Before you begin writing, revisit all the works you studied in Unit 3, keeping the purpose of this writing task in mind. Decide which three selections best lend themselves to your argumentative essay.

Read the prompt carefully. Underline words that indicate ideas that should be included in your essay. Before you begin writing, create a list of sources and the evidence they provide supporting your claim to help you organize your ideas. Be sure to identify the source of each idea.

Your writing will be evaluated on the following qualifications. Read these before you begin writing. Then use them to evaluate your finished essay.

Reading Comprehension:
- How well did you understand the texts?
- Does your writing reflect your understanding of the sources?

Writing Expression:
- Does your argumentative essay address the requirements of the prompt?
- Does your essay make a claim based upon an opinion?
- Is your claim supported with reasons and evidence?
- Is your essay clearly organized with ideas that fit together to create a well-constructed argument?
- Does the writing style contain precise, accurate language and content appropriate to the purpose, task, and audience?

Writing Conventions:
- Does your writing follow the rules of standard English for grammar, usage, and spelling?

Remediation: Practice Performance Task Help struggling students by reviewing their claims and evidence before they begin writing.

Unit 4

Essential Question
What does history tell us about ourselves?

When you study history or read and learn about decisions that were made by those who came before you, what does it mean to you? Is history just a set of facts and figures to be memorized? Is history just a series of events that took place a long time ago? How is history relevant to you and your life?

When our country was no more than thirteen colonies and facing the decision of whether to remain under Great Britain's rule or gather troops to fight for independence, the patriot Patrick Henry pointed to England's history with the colonies. Over and over, King George had abused the rights of the colonists. In a passionate speech, Henry stated: "I have but one lamp by which my feet are guided; and that is the lamp of experience. I know of no way of judging of the future but by the past." In this same way, you base decisions in your own life on the lessons of the past.

History can also teach you how to stand up for what you believe in. The Revolutionary War, for instance, would not have taken place if a group of colonists hadn't decided to rebel against unfair treatment by Great Britain. Similarly, the Civil Rights Movement would never have taken place in the United States if citizens hadn't stood up for equal rights.

In this unit you will consider the question: What does history teach us about ourselves? You will explore several works of historical fiction and compare nonfiction texts on similar topics. You will read about real and imagined historical figures who endured injustice and war and how these events affected them and their families. You will also research and write about a person from history and identify elements in his or her story that inspires you.

> **GOALS**
> - To understand how the setting shapes conflict and characters in literature.
> - To compare a fictional account of historical events with a nonfiction account.
> - To determine the theme of a passage and analyze how it is developed through setting and conflict.
> - To compare how an author develops characters' points of view.
> - To analyze how authors use figurative language, sensory language, dramatic irony, and dramatic techniques to create meaning.
> - To analyze how the format and structure of a play communicate theme.
> - To write a research paper on the impact of a historical figure.

©Perfection Learning® • No Reproduction Permitted

339

ELL Support: Introduction to Essential Question See the <u>ELL Teacher Resource (p. 33)</u> for ideas for introducing the unit essential question.

Unit 4

Essential Question: What does history tell us about ourselves?

Introduction

Goals: Have students read through the goals and mark any words that are unfamiliar. Discuss the meanings of any academic vocabulary within the goals that students marked as unfamiliar. Consider posting the Unit Goals.

Introduction Suggestions

Use one or more of the following activities to introduce the unit:

- Invite students to recount a story about a family member, friend, or acquaintance who fought in World War II, Vietnam, Desert Storm, or the wars in Iraq.

- Ask students what they know about the history of their city or state. How old is it? At what time was the area first settled? When did their family first arrive?

- Encourage students to tell what information they can learn about a place from the following everyday clues such as place names, buildings (new and old), roads, cemeteries, and monuments.

- Ask: *What can photographs tell us about history?*

- Ask: *What written resources help us to learn about history? What kind of information does each resource provide?* Discuss the difference between primary sources, like firsthand accounts, and secondary sources, like history books.

Tech-Connect: If students aren't already using the Library of Congress for social studies projects, this unit provides many opportunities for them to take advantage of the library's vast online collection. They can watch a video that highlights the Library's online collections and offers techniques to help students better navigate the Library's website at https://youtu.be/ieRI9CaVdMw.

 Gr7U4Opener.pptx

Chapter **16**

Discovering How Story Elements Shape Literature

The Lions of Little Rock
by Kristin Levine

Introduction

Chapter Goals: Have students read through the goals and mark any words that are unfamiliar. Discuss the meanings of any academic vocabulary within the goals that students marked as unfamiliar. Consider posting the Chapter Goals.

Preview Academic Vocabulary: Read and discuss the meanings of the academic vocabulary.

> **conflict:** *the problem, struggle, or obstacle faced by a character or characters.* The conflict of "To Build a Fire" is man against nature.

> **historical fiction:** *a genre of fiction that takes place in the past and conveys information about real events, places, and/or people.* The Street of a Thousand Blossoms is historical fiction that begins near the start of World War II.

> **nonfiction:** *a genre of writing that tells about real people, places, and/or events, rather than made-up ones.* Three-Eight Charlie is exciting nonfiction about the first flight around the world by a woman.

> **point of view:** *the perspective, position, or outlook from which a story is told.* The first-person point of view of The Kite Runner helps the reader understand the perspective of the narrator.

> **setting:** *the time and place where events occur.* The setting of Stephen Crane's The Red Badge of Courage is the Civil War.

 Gr7Ch16Vocabulary.pptx

Chapter **16**

Discovering How Story Elements Shape Literature

Preview Concepts

How does the setting of a story affect the characters and the plot?

Think about the following popular books. How does the setting of the story—the time and place where the action takes place—affect the characters and the conflict? Could the plot have occurred anywhere or does the setting directly shape the events and the conflict?

Work with a partner to complete the chart below and analyze how setting affects other story elements. The first row has been completed for you. Fill in the rest of the chart. In the final two rows, add stories or books you have read recently.

Book/Story	Setting	How does the setting affect the characters and the conflict?
Little Women	A family living in a small town in New England in the years before and after the Civil War, approximately 1861–1876	Because of the Civil War, the girls' father is away. As a result, they struggle to earn a living without him and they worry about his safety. Their lives are influenced by the uncertainty of war.
Harry Potter books		
The Hunger Games books		

ELL Support: Academic Vocabulary See Teaching Vocabulary in the ELL Teacher Resource (p. 18) for ideas to use for teaching vocabulary throughout *Connections.* .

ELL Support: Preview Concepts Once you have reviewed all the academic vocabulary, especially words like *conflict, setting,* and *characters,* have students complete the chart in multilevel pairs or small groups. Suggest that students choose books or movies with which they are familiar, not necessarily the ones in the chart.

Making Connections

The following is from the short story by Edgar Allan Poe. This excerpt shares details of the torture chamber in which the narrator finds himself. As you read, underline words and phrases that describe characteristics of the setting.

PREVIEW ACADEMIC VOCABULARY

conflict

historical fiction

nonfiction

point of view

setting

All this I saw indistinctly and by much effort: for my personal condition had been greatly changed during slumber. I now lay upon my back, and at full length, on a species of low framework of wood. To this I was securely bound by a long strap . . . . It passed in many convolutions about my limbs and body, leaving at liberty only my head, and my left arm to such extent that I could, by dint of much exertion, supply myself with food from an earthen dish which lay by my side on the floor. . . .

A slight noise attracted my notice, and, looking to the floor, I saw several enormous rats traversing it. They had issued from the well, which lay just within view to my right. Even then, while I gazed, they came up in troops, hurriedly, with ravenous eyes, allured by the scent of the meat. From this it required much effort and attention to scare them away.

— "The Pit and the Pendulum" by Edgar Allan Poe

What is the effect of the setting on the conflict the narrator faces? Will this setting be to his advantage or disadvantage? Explain.

MAKING CONNECTIONS

In this chapter you will analyze how the setting of a story impacts the characters and conflict.

Preview Concepts: Encourage students to ask themselves these questions, as they analyze the setting:

- *Does the setting bring about events or situations?*
  Which events or situations does the setting affect?

- *Does the setting influence the way these events happen?*
  How does it influence these events?

- *Could this same story (and same events) occur at a different time or place?*

Making Connections

Words That Describe Setting Answers:

Words that describe the setting: *lay upon my back, on a species of low framework of wood, bound by a long strap, food from an earthen dish which lay by my side on the floor, enormous rats traversing it, well . . . to my right.*
The effect of the setting is that it creates the conflict the narrator is facing. The setting is to his disadvantage because he is tied up and there are rats on the floor of the room.

ELL Support: Making Connections Search Google Images for appropriate pictures of "The Pit and the Pendulum." Then read the excerpt slowly, pointing to different aspects of the setting that Poe mentions. When you finish reading, point to and label parts of the setting students can use in their responses *(framework of wood, long strap, food from an earthen dish, enormous rats, well)*. Have students work in multilevel pairs or groups to discuss and then to answer the questions, using the following sentence frames:

- The setting is dangerous because there is/are . . . .

- The narrator has problems with . . . .

Lesson Support

📖 First Read: Analyzing How Setting Affects Conflict

Before Reading: Read the paragraph introducing the First Read. Ask students to identify the words that describe the story setting. (*segregated Little Rock, Arkansas, in the late 1950s*) Then ask a volunteer to reread the sentence that explains the conflict. *(The girls' friendship is tested when it is revealed that Liz has been passing for, or pretending to be, white.)* Make sure students understand that "segregated" involves imposing the separation of one racial group from the rest of society with separate schools, housing, neighborhoods, public facilities, transportation, parks, etc.

Read the objective, making sure that students understand that setting isn't just a matter of place but also of the time in which characters live and events occur.

Remind students that during the first read of the close reading process, they should focus on the central ideas of the text.

Preview Vocabulary: Preview unfamiliar vocabulary to aid comprehension or ask students to circle unfamiliar words as they complete the first read of the text. After the first read, guide students to determine the words' meanings using the context. Encourage students to support their responses with evidence. Have students confirm their initial definitions with a dictionary. Words that students might find difficult include:

integration: *the act of including members of all races equally in schools, housing, public facilities, parks, etc.* The City Council voted to end segregation and to facilitate the <u>integration</u> of all public facilities.

avowed: *declared; acknowledged; maintained.* The minister <u>avowed</u> a deep interest in promoting equality in every aspect of society.

official: *authorized; allowed.* The <u>official</u> purpose of the meeting was to support our candidate, but we all knew that the real goal was to finance his campaign.

harassed: *hassled; attacked.* When the bully <u>harassed</u> the new girl, our teacher sent him to the principal.

📖 First Read: Analyzing How Setting Affects Conflict

This passage is from *The Lions of Little Rock,* a novel about Marlee and Liz who live in segregated Little Rock, Arkansas, in the late 1950s. The girls' friendship is tested when it is revealed that Liz has been passing for, or pretending to be, white.

Objective: As you read the first passage, underline words and phrases that explain the setting of the story.

—— First Read
---- Second Read
—— Third Read

from
The Lions of Little Rock
by Kristin Levine
Chapter 15: "Talking to Daddy"

My Thoughts

1   I woke up the next morning in a good mood. The presentation was over, and I'd done my part. Everything was as it should be. Except my teeth felt fuzzy, like I hadn't brushed them before bed. But I *always* brushed them before bed, even

5   when . . . then I remembered.

I went into the kitchen and made myself a bowl of oatmeal. Daddy was reading the paper. There was an article about the election the weekend before on the front page:
Little Rock votes against integration 19,470 to 7,561.

10 *Schools to be closed indefinitely.*

Daddy slammed down the paper, making me jump. "Sorry," he said. But he scowled as he said it, and I realized then, certain as could be, that when asked if Negroes and whites should go to school together, he had voted yes. "Are

15 you ready to go, Marlee?"

I nodded, even though I'd only had two spoonfuls of my oatmeal.

It was quiet in the car. Daddy gripped the steering wheel like he was driving in a snowstorm. Not that it snowed much

20 in Little Rock, but I'd seen a movie where there was one once,

ELL Support: First Read Display images and give simple explanations to help students gain background knowledge about segregation (keeping black and white people separate—different schools, different restaurants), the Little Rock Nine (nine black high school students who went to an all-white high school), integration (the opposite of segregation, mixing people together, letting people of all colors go anywhere), and the Ku Klux Klan (a racist group that uses violence against black people). Have students read the story in multilevel pairs or small groups, pausing after each page to summarize the key events and details on the <u>Story Map from the ELL Teacher Resource (p. 52)</u>. Also, encourage students to take notes and draw sketches in the margins around the story so they can be sure they understand the topic of each section.

and the actor clutched the steering wheel so tight, his knuckles
turned white.

My Thoughts

"Daddy?" I asked.

"What?"

25 "Can you find her for me? Maybe get her phone
number?"

Daddy shook his head. "Marlee, you need to leave that girl
alone."

"But she's my best friend."

30 "She *was* your friend. Now she's someone else."

No, she wasn't. Liz was funny and outspoken and clever,
and I didn't see how all that had changed, just because people
were now calling her colored. But Daddy and I usually got
along so well. I trusted him. "I don't know," I said finally.

35 "I want to hear her side of the story first."

"Marlee, you can't still be friends with Liz."

"Why not?"

"**Segregationists** don't take kindly to Negroes who try to
pass as white. Liz and her family are in real danger. The farther

40 away you stay from them, the better."

"You're worried about me?" I asked.

"Yes, I am," said Daddy. "Why do you think I drive you to
school every day?"

I shrugged.

45 Daddy ran a hand through his hair. "Do you remember
when I invited that colored minister, Pastor George, to come
speak at our church?"

I nodded.

---

segregationists: people who believed that white people and black people should be kept separate,
in schools, restaurants, buses and other public locations

---

escorted: *ushered; led.* The police <u>escorted</u>
the students from the building to safety.

solicit: *seek; ask for.* The mayor plans
to <u>solicit</u> support from all parties in the
disagreement.

racists: *prejudiced people; bigots.* The
<u>racists</u> made biased comments toward
everyone with dark skin.

The following words are found in the
timeline on pages 350–354.

redress: *amends; correction for wrong
done.* The Legal <u>Redress</u> Committee seeks
to challenge and correct discriminatory
practices.

After Reading: Use the following
questions to check comprehension.

Text-Based Discussion Questions

1. Why did Daddy want Marlee to stay
   away from Liz? *People know that Liz is
   Black and tried to pass as White. Daddy
   is afraid that Marlee could be in danger
   if she continues to be seen with Liz.*

2. What did Marlee learn about her
   neighbor, Mr. Haroldson, and Sally's
   mother, Mrs. McDaniels? *Both were
   KKK sympathizers, who would support
   segregation and discrimination.*

3. Why did the town vote against opening
   the schools? *The majority in town
   opposed integration. Rather than
   integrating, they decided to close
   the schools.*

 Gr7Ch16Read1.pptx

Remediation: First Read If students struggle with the selection,
call on volunteers to summarize the beginning, middle, and end of
the selection.

Chapter 16 (continued)

Lesson Support

Background Information: Jim Crow is a term referring to state-sanctioned discrimination in the South. The Jim Crow era began after the withdrawal of federal troops protecting Southern Blacks following the Civil War. Jim Crow laws allowed the segregation of schools, transportation, housing, prisons, hospitals, and public facilities such as restrooms, parks, and swimming pools. Signs reading "Whites Only" or "Colored" were posted on phone booths, toilets, drinking fountains, etc. The local, state, and national governments authorized Jim Crow and helped to promote Jim Crow laws. Discrimination and bigotry were not relegated to the South. Numerous Supreme Court decisions supported Jim Crow laws, though they were repeatedly challenged and eventually found unconstitutional in the decades after World War II.

Tech-Connect Suggestion: For an overview of Jim Crow and the legacy of slavery, direct students to www.pbs.org/wnet/jimcrow/.

"The next day there was a note tucked in with our paper.

50 It said, *You let your youngest walk to school tomorrow, she won't make it*. And it was signed, *KKK*."

"The Ku Klux Klan is in Little Rock?"

Daddy nodded.

"Who's in it?"

55 "Hard to tell, since it's a secret organization. However, the Capital Citizens' Council, or CCC, is not a secret club. Their avowed purpose is to support segregation in Little Rock. It seems reasonable to assume that some of their members are Klan **sympathizers**, at the very least."

60 "Do we know any CCC members?" I asked.

"Mr. Haroldson, from next door."

He was a nice old man who sometimes gave me penny candy. At least, I'd always thought he was nice.

"And Mrs. McDaniels, Sally's mother, is a member of the

65 Mothers' League."

"What's that?" I asked.

"A women's group, associated with the CCC, that formed last year to oppose integration at Central."

This was a lot to take in. "Isn't everyone allowed to have

70 their own opinion?"

"Of course," said Daddy. "But the reason there were police all over David's graduation last May was not because people have different opinions. The FBI was there to protect Ernest Green because they were worried that someone was going to

75 try to kill him."

I had never really thought about why we'd gotten so few tickets to David's graduation that Granny hadn't even

---

sympathizers: people who agree with and uphold the views of a particular group or individual

My Thoughts

been able to go. Apparently, there was a lot I hadn't thought about.

80   "But you still support integration, right?"

"I do," said Daddy. "And I still talk to Pastor George. He's Betty Jean's husband, you know."

I hadn't known. How could I? "Why haven't you ever told me any of this?"

85   "These are issues for grown-ups to deal with, not children."

"The Little Rock Nine weren't much older than me."

Daddy sighed, but he didn't answer.

"I thought things settled down at Central once they called the soldiers in."

90   "Somewhat," said Daddy. "At least that was the official story. But things were not ever pleasant for them there. Minnijean Brown got expelled."

She was the colored girl who'd dumped a bowl of soup on the boys who were picking on her. That was something Liz

95   would do.

"If they were still being harassed, why didn't they complain?"

Daddy shrugged. "Maybe they did and nothing was done. Maybe they thought if they showed any weakness, it would only get worse. In any case, last year the pictures from Central told the

100   whole world Little Rock is filled with hate. And now the town's gone and voted against opening the schools. We are not *just* a town of racists, but those of us who believe in integration . . ." He shook his head. "We can't seem to find our voice."

Daddy was so upset, for a minute I thought he was going

105   to cry. That scared me as bad as anything he'd said. I knew what it was like to have trouble finding your voice, so I reached over and patted his arm. He didn't look at me.

My Thoughts

R

©Perfection Learning® • No Reproduction Permitted

About the Author: Kristin Levine says she has kept a diary since she was eight years old. After high school she lived in Vienna, Austria, for a year, where she worked as an *au pair.* After college, she became a teacher, then a writer. Today she's a novelist; her works include *The Best Bad Luck I Ever Had* and *The Paper Cowboy.*

Chapter **16** *(continued)*

Lesson Support

FIRST RESPONSE:
KEY IDEAS AND DETAILS

Marlee and her father have a close relationship. When they begin talking about the trouble at school, Marlee mentions that she and her father got along well and that she trusted him. When he seems about to cry over the upsetting vote against integration, she pats his arm in sympathy.

Focus on Analyzing How Setting Affects Conflict: Remind students that outward conflicts often lead to inner conflicts. Suppose they see a bully picking on another student. This is an outward conflict (person vs. person), but they must decide what to do about it. Do they step in? Are they afraid to get involved? This is inner conflict or self vs. fear, shame, etc.

 Gr7Ch16Read1.pptx

---

"I mean it, Marlee. I don't want to scare you too much—I'll keep you safe—but I do want you to be careful. Which means
110 you stay away from Liz."

I nodded to show him I understood what he was saying.

But I didn't promise that I would.

My Thoughts

R

FIRST RESPONSE: KEY IDEAS AND DETAILS
Based on your first read of the passage, describe the relationship between Marlee and her father in your response journal. Support your description using evidence from the text.

TECH-CONNECT

Post your description to your class website. View two of your classmates' descriptions and comment positively on them.

Focus On Analyzing How Setting Affects Conflict

The setting of a story includes the time and place where events take place. The story's setting often influences the conflicts in the story. Then the conflicts influence the choices the characters make. As you know, there are many different types of conflict. Here are just a few:

- person vs. person—a character struggles against another character
- person vs. nature—a character struggles against forces in nature, often fighting for his or her life
- person vs. self—a character struggles with a quality within his or her own personality. Examples include fear, anger, hatred, worry, or insecurity.
- person vs. society—a character struggles against the rules of society or the laws of the government.

In the graphic organizer on the next page, describe the setting by filling in the top three boxes. Then think about how the setting reveals conflict between groups in the city of Little Rock and also the personal conflicts that Marlee faces.

Time	Place	Situation
the late 1950s	Little Rock, Arkansas	Little Rock has closed their public schools in opposition to integration. Marlee has just learned that her friend Liz has been passing as White and her dad tells Marlee she can't see Liz again.

Conflicts/Type of conflict
See answers in sidebar to the right.

(**Speak and Listen** Discuss your answers to the chart above with a partner. Consider the following question:
- How are the time and place responsible for the conflict in the story?

▼ **Write** Write two or three paragraphs explaining how the setting of the story affects the conflicts in the story. Use evidence from the story to support your response, including paraphrasing the text and directly quoting it.

Second Read: Analyzing How Point of View Affects a Story

This passage is written from first person point of view, meaning that one of the characters is telling the story. The narrator is Marlee. Marlee's version of events is influenced by who she is—a young white girl. The reader is seeing the events and interactions from Marlee's perspective—which is different from other characters' perspectives.

Objective: Read the passage again or listen as your teacher reads the passage aloud. Think about Marlee's reactions to what her father tells her, and write R next to Marlee's responses.

ELL Support: Speak and Listen and Write Have students work in multilevel pairs or small groups to discuss and write about the questions, using these sentence frames. These can also be found as a student handout in the ELL Teacher Resource (p. 39).

- Marlee's daddy struggles with . . . .
- An example of this conflict is . . . .
- Marlee struggles with . . . .
- An example of this conflict is . . . .
- Marlee and her father struggle with . . . .
- An example of this conflict is . . . .

Answers to Analyzing How Setting Affects Conflict chart:

See answers in Student Book insert page to the left.

Conflicts/Type of conflict Answers:
—Marlee struggles with her father (person vs. person), who forbids her from continuing her friendship with Liz.
—Marlee struggles with herself (person against self). She values her friendship with Liz and wants to hear Liz's side of the story, but her father says to stay away from Liz.
—Marlee and her father struggle with the bigotry of their city and their friends and neighbors (person against society).

▼ **Write:** Suggest that students turn each example of conflict into a paragraph looking to the story for specific evidence to support each one.

Second Read: Analyzing How Point of View Affects a Story

Before Reading: Point out some reasons that writers choose the first-person point of view. This point of view allows the reader to experience what the character is seeing, feeling, and thinking. It involves the reader in the narrator's feelings and helps the reader understand the narrator's actions and reactions. However, the first-person point of view is limited to what the narrator chooses to report.

After Reading: Use the following questions to check comprehension.

Text-Based Discussion Questions
1. In the opening, Marlee says her teeth feel "fuzzy." What is the reason? *The fuzziness of her teeth reflect her worry and confusion about what happened with Liz and the school.*

2. In the car, Marlee says her father "gripped the steering wheel like he was driving in a snowstorm." What did she mean? *He gripped the steering wheel tightly because he was upset and worried.*

3. Why is Marlee's father upset and worried? *He is upset about the city's vote to close down the school in order to avoid integration. He is worried about what might happen in his city and the city schools, and especially whether his daughter will be safe.*

Lesson Support

Focus on Analyzing How Point of View Affects a Story: Discuss with students the fact that Marlee's father understands the potential danger of Marlee's relationship with Liz. He knows that race relations in the South have a long and difficult history, stemming from slavery and the Civil War. He understands that in the late 1950s, the United States is going through a troublesome transition toward greater racial equality and the end of Jim Crow laws. He realizes that such changes do not happen smoothly, and that people likely will be hurt in the process. Marlee, by comparison, is still somewhat innocent about bigotry and discrimination. She cares about her friend and doesn't recognize the significant implications of interracial friendship during that time. She seems to be much more colorblind than the rest of society, or even her father.

> **Answers to Focus on Analyzing How Point of View Affects a Story:**
>
> See answers in Student Book insert page to the right.

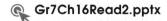 **Gr7Ch16Read2.pptx**

Focus on Analyzing How Point of View Affects a Story

Consider this example.

> A car and a truck enter a busy intersection. The person driving the red car makes a left turn and is hit by the blue pickup. The person driving the red car says he was in the middle of the intersection waiting to make a left turn, which he did when the light turned yellow. The person driving the pickup says she entered the intersection with the sun in her eyes, and the red car turned right in front of her.

The story changes, then, depending on who tells it. The two versions of the events are told from different points of view.

In the same way, your opinion as a reader is shaped by Marlee's opinions about the events going on around her. If Marlee's dad were telling the story, you as a reader would get an entirely different perspective.

In the graphic organizer below, several sentences from the passage are provided in the left column. In the right column, explain what they reveal about Marlee's point of view of the conflicts taking place in Little Rock. In the third column, explain what the lines indicate about Daddy's point of view.

Lines from Passage	Marlee's Point of View	Daddy's Point of View
"She was your friend. Now she's someone else." *No, she wasn't. Liz was funny and outspoken and clever, and I didn't see how all that had changed, just because people were now calling her colored. But Daddy and I usually got along so well. I trusted him. "I don't know," I said finally. "I want to hear her side of the story first."*	She wants to continue her friendship with Liz. She doesn't understand why her dad won't let her see Liz.	Marlee's friendship with Liz is dangerous to his daughter. He values her safety more than the experience of friendship.

ELL Support: Second Read Review the definitions for *point of view* and *narrator*. Draw a sketch of the sample story, so students understand the different perspectives. Then model rereading and identifying the narrator's point of view and responses in the first few paragraphs. Have students reread the story in multilevel pairs or small groups, pausing to identify details that show the narrator's point of view or reactions.

Lines from Passage	Marlee's Point of View	Daddy's Point of View
This was a lot to take in. "Isn't everyone allowed to have their own opinion?" "Of course," said Daddy. "But the reason there were police all over David's graduation last May was not because people have different opinions. The FBI was there to protect Ernest Green because they were worried that someone was going to try to kill him." *I had never really thought about why we'd gotten so few tickets to David's graduation that Granny hadn't even been able to go. Apparently, there was a lot I hadn't thought about.*	Marlee is willing to shrug off the community conflict as a difference of opinion. She doesn't understand how deep the conflict between races goes. She is young and her parents have protected her from the conflicts in the community.	Daddy recognizes that the conflict might easily lead to violence and even death.
Daddy was so upset, for a minute I thought he was going to cry. That scared me as bad as anything he'd said. I knew what it was like to have trouble finding your voice, so I reached over and patted his arm. He didn't look at me. "I mean it, Marlee. I don't want to scare you too much—I'll keep you safe—but I do want you to be careful. Which means you stay away from Liz." *I nodded to show him I understood what he was saying.* *But I didn't promise that I would.*	Marlee is afraid of her father's emotions. Seeing a parent out of control is strange for many kids. Marlee is uncertain how to react so she tries to comfort him. However, she isn't ready to obey Daddy unconditionally.	Daddy is angered by the racism in his community but he is also focused on his concern for Marlee's safety.

▼ Write Use the chart to help you analyze how the author develops the points of view of Marlee and Daddy in the story. Focus on how they each view Liz and the events going on in Little Rock. Use your notes from the chart you completed to write a few paragraphs. On the next page are some sentence starters to help you get started.

continued on next page

▼Write: Encourage students to distinguish the basic difference between the two points of view: Marlee thinks her friendship with Liz is most important. Her father thinks Marlee's safety is paramount. Point out that their opening sentence can be very simple: i.e., Marlee's and Daddy's points of view are different.

ELL Support: Write Have students work in multilevel pairs or small groups to discuss and then write about the point of view of the story using these sentence frames. These can also be found as a student handout in the ELL Teacher Resource (p. 39).

- Marlee and Daddy have different points of view.
- Marlee sees Liz as . . . .
- For instance, Marlee says . . . .
- From Daddy's point of view, Liz is . . . .
- For instance, Daddy says . . . .

Chapter 16 *(continued)*

Lesson Support

✎ **Speak and Listen:** Offer a few sentence starters for this activity:

Compliments:

- You made a good point about . . . .
- Your best idea is . . . .

Improvements:

- I didn't understand . . . .

📖 **Third Read: Comparing and Contrasting Historical Fiction and Nonfiction**

Before Reading: Briefly review with students the differences between historical fiction and nonfiction. Historical fiction takes as its subject real characters, settings, and events but presents them within a narrative frame. An author of historical fiction might invent characters, settings, and especially dialogue, but the author intends readers to accept such elements as realistic, i.e., as plausible within the surrounding historical context.

Historical nonfiction, in contrast, typically aims to describe people, settings, and events as they "really were." Although historical nonfiction can present events as if they were part of a story (e.g., unfolding through conflicts between people and ideas, having a climax and resolution) nothing in historical nonfiction is invented.

Read the introduction and objective, making sure students understand the purpose of the Third Read. Have students read the excerpt from *The Lions of Little Rock* again on their own. Then read the excerpt on pages 350–354.

- Marlee's and Daddy's points of view are . . . .
- Marlee sees Liz as . . . . For instance, ...
- From Daddy's point of view, Liz is . . . .
- Marlee wants . . . . because she says . . . .
- Daddy is worried about . . . . He says . . . .

✎ **Speak and Listen** With a small group of students, take turns reading your paragraphs aloud. Each group member should offer a compliment and a suggestion for improvement. Listen and record these comments. Edit your paragraphs based on your classmates' suggestions.

📖 **Third Read: Comparing and Contrasting Historical Fiction and Nonfiction**

Reread the passage from the novel a third time. Then read the following historical timeline of the Little Rock Nine.

Objective: As you read, underline historical details that refer to people and events discussed by the characters in the *The Lions of Little Rock*.

Little Rock Central High School
National Historic Site
Crisis Timeline
from www.nps.gov

		My Thoughts
1	**May 17, 1954**	
	The United States Supreme Court rules racial segregation in public schools is unconstitutional in *Brown v. Board of Education of Topeka*. Five days later, the Little Rock School	
5	Board issues a policy statement saying it will comply with the Supreme Court's decision. In May 1955, The Supreme Court further defines the standard of implementation for **integration** as being "with all **deliberate** speed," in *Brown II* and charges the federal courts with establishing guidelines for compliance.	

---

integration: combining of black and white citizens, in this case, in schools
deliberate: carefully and considerate of the consequences

ELL Support: Third Read Before students read the new article, explain that this is a timeline that lists dates and explains what happened on that date. Have students read the new article in multilevel pairs or small groups, pausing after each paragraph to summarize ideas on a <u>Main Ideas and Supporting Details graphic organizer from the ELL Teacher Resource (p. 51)</u>. Also, encourage students to take notes and draw sketches in the margins around the story so they can be sure they understand the event on each date.

10 **August 23, 1954**

Under the direction of Pine Bluff attorney Wiley Branton, chairman of the state's **NAACP** Legal Redress Committee, the NAACP **petitions** the Little Rock School Board for immediate integration.

15 **May 24, 1955**

The Little Rock School Board adopts the Blossom Plan of gradual integration beginning with the high school level (starting in September 1957) and the lower grades during the next six years.

February 8, 1956

20 Federal Judge John E. Miller dismisses the NAACP suit (*Aaron v. Cooper*), declaring that the Little Rock School Board has acted in "utmost good faith" in setting up its plan of gradual integration. In April, the Eighth Circuit Court of Appeals upholds Judge Miller's dismissal.

25 **August 27, 1957**

The segregationist Mother's League of Central High School holds its first public meeting. They seek a temporary court order to stop school integration. Two days later, the courts approve the order on the grounds that integration could 30 lead to violence. Federal Judge Ronald Davies reverses the court order and tells the School Board to proceed with its desegregation plan.

September 2, 1957 – (Labor Day)

Governor Orval Faubus orders the Arkansas National 35 Guard to prohibit African American students from entering Central High School and announces his plans in a televised speech.

My Thoughts

_____
_____
_____
_____
_____
_____
_____
_____
_____
_____
_____
_____
_____
_____
_____
_____
_____
_____
_____
_____
_____
_____
_____
_____
_____
_____
_____
_____
_____
_____

NAACP: National Association for the Advancement of Colored People, a group that works for the human rights of African Americans

After Reading: Use the following questions to check comprehension.

Text-Based Discussion Questions

1. Where is the information on the timeline from? *The Little Rock Central High School National Historic Site*

2. Why is the timeline called a "Crisis Timeline"? *It describes a time of crisis [great difficulty or trauma] at the Little Rock Central High School.*

3. Why does the timeline begin with May 17, 1954? *On that day, the Supreme Court ruled that segregation in public schools is illegal; this decision triggered the timeline events which followed.*

 Gr7Ch16Read3.pptx

Remediation: Third Read If students find the timeline difficult, have a volunteer read each segment aloud and summarize what happened on that date.

Lesson Support

Background Information: To help students understand the timeline, explain that it explains the conflict between the federal (national) government and the state government of Arkansas. State and local leaders including Governor Orval Faubus and the Mothers' League did not want to follow the order of the Supreme Court and President Eisenhower. In many ways, the federal government often tries to give states freedom to make their own laws. For example, the U.S. sets the voting age at 18 and the drinking age at 21, but states can set their own laws about the age when a teenager can drive a car. However, in issues of human rights, the federal government often overrules state and local laws. Can students think of other federal laws that overruled state laws?

September 3, 1957

40   The Mother's League holds a "sunrise service" at Central High attended by members of the Citizen's Council, parents and students. On September 20, Federal Judge Ronald Davies rules that Governor Faubus has not used the troops to preserve law and order and orders them removed. Faubus removes the Guardsmen and the Little Rock Police

45   Department moves in.

September 23, 1957

    An angry mob of over 1,000 whites gathers in front of Central High School, while nine African American students are escorted inside. The Little Rock police remove the nine

50   children for their safety. President Eisenhower calls the rioting "disgraceful" and orders federal troops into Little Rock.

September 24, 1957

    One thousand, two hundred members of the 101st Airborne Division, the "Screaming Eagles" of Fort

55   Campbell, Kentucky, roll into Little Rock. These federal troops take over and the Arkansas National Guard must follow their lead.

September 25, 1957

    Under troop escort, the "Little Rock Nine" are escorted

60   back into Central High School for their first full day of classes.

May 25, 1958

    Senior Ernest Green becomes the first African American student to graduate from Central High School.

June 3, 1958

65   Highlighting numerous discipline problems during the school year, the school board asks the court for permission to delay the desegregation plan in *Cooper v. Aaron*.

My Thoughts

June 21, 1958

Judge Harry Lemley grants the delay of integration until
70 January 1961. The judge states that while the African American

students have a constitutional right to attend white schools,

the "time has not come for them to enjoy [that right.]"

September 12, 1958

The United States Supreme Court rules that Little Rock
75 must continue with its desegregation plan. The School Board

orders the high schools to open on September 15. Governor

Faubus orders four Little Rock high schools closed as of 8:00

a.m., September 15, 1958, until the public could vote on

integration.

80 **September 16, 1958**

The Women's Emergency Committee to Open Our Schools

(WEC) forms and begins to solicit support for reopening the

schools.

September 27, 1958

85 <u>Citizens vote 19,470 to 7,561 against integration and the</u>

<u>schools remain closed.</u>

May 5, 1959

Segregationist members of the school board vote not

to rehire 44 teachers and administrators they say supported
90 integration.

May 8, 1959

The WEC and local businessmen form Stop This Outrageous

Purge (STOP) and work to get voter signatures to remove the

three segregationist board members. Segregationists form the
95 Committee to Retain Our Segregated Schools (CROSS).

May 25, 1959

Through the efforts of STOP, three segregationists are voted

off the school board and three moderate members are retained.

My Thoughts

Chapter 16 *(continued)*

Lesson Support

Focus on Comparing and Contrasting Historical Fiction and Nonfiction:

Review the characteristics of historical fiction. Historical fiction contains details about real people, places, or events, but the details are imaginary. Ask students to tell what parts of the story are fictional. *(The characters, the relationship between Marlee and Liz, and the conversation between Marlee and her father are made up.)* What part is based on fact? *(The setting is Little Rock in the late 1950s. The situation, the conflict over impending integration, the facts about the Little Rock Nine, and the groups opposing and promoting integration are also based on fact.)* Then review the characteristics of nonfiction: Nonfiction is based on facts; it is true; no part of nonfiction writing is imaginary.

Answers to Chart:

2. September 23, 1957—An angry mob of over 1,000 people gathers in front of Central High School while nine African-American students are escorted inside. The Little Rock police remove the nine children for their safety. President Eisenhower calls the rioting "disgraceful" and orders federal troops into Little Rock.

For the rest of the answers, see the chart on Student Book insert page to the right.

 Gr7Ch16Read3.pptx

August 12, 1959

Little Rock public high schools reopen, nearly a month

100 early. Segregationists rally at the State Capitol where Faubus

advises them that it is a "dark" day, but they should not give

up the struggle. They then march to Central High School where

the police and fire departments break up the mob. Twenty-one

people are arrested.

My Thoughts
_____
_____
_____
_____
_____

Focus on Comparing and Contrasting Historical Fiction and Nonfiction

Study the chart below. The first column lists a fact from the nonfiction timeline and the second column explains how that fact is treated in the historical fiction novel excerpt. Complete the chart with facts from the timeline and corresponding textual evidence from the novel excerpt. For the second column, paraphrase or quote directly from the novel excerpt.

Little Rock Central High School National Historic Site Crisis Timeline	The Lions of Little Rock (historical fiction)
1. *September 25 - Under troop escort, the "Little Rock Nine" are escorted back into Central High School for their first full day of classes.*	Marlee states, "I thought things settled down at Central once they called the soldiers in."
2. Answers for this section can be found in the sidebar to the left.	*"In any case, last year the pictures from Central told the whole world Little Rock is filled with hate."*
3. *June 3, 1958—Highlighting numerous discipline problems during the school year, the school board asks the court for permission to delay the desegregation plan in Cooper v. Aaron.*	*"But things were not ever pleasant for them there. Minnijean Brown got expelled."* She was the colored girl who'd dumped a bowl of soup on the boys who were picking on her.
4. *September 27, 1958 Citizens vote 19,470 to 7,561 against integration and the schools remain closed.*	*"And now the town's gone and voted against opening the schools. We are not just a town of racists, but those of us who believe in integration . . ."*

Connections • © Perfection Learning®

Fiction and nonfiction texts approach their subjects differently. Nonfiction texts:

- are primarily intended to supply information, so writers focus on accurately explaining facts.
- capture the big picture of a historical event by explaining actions taken by leaders and how their actions cause other events.
- often rely on print features, such as headers, graphics, and charts to communicate key ideas.

Historical fiction texts:

- take a narrower focus.
- usually describes events, both real and imaginary, by focusing on the lives of characters.
- feature interactions between characters to provide a glimpse into the motivations and emotions experienced by people involved in history.
- engage the imagination and entertains the reader, while often providing historically accurate information.

Speak and Listen Work with a partner to fill in the following Venn diagram, comparing the two texts. Consider the purpose, focus, format, writing style, and the point of view contained in each text.

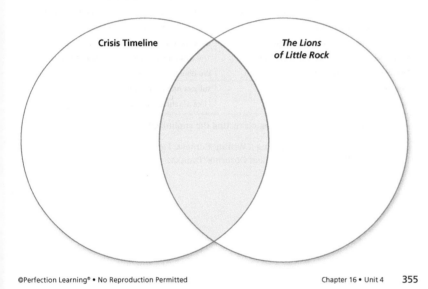

Crisis Timeline

The Lions of Little Rock

Speak and Listen: Before students fill out the Venn diagram, suggest that they get five index cards and write each of the following topics on cards: *purpose, focus, format, writing style,* and *point of view*. On one side they can write about the nonfiction timeline, on the other side about *The Lions of Little Rock* (historical fiction).

ELL Support: Speak and Listen Have students work in multilevel pairs or small groups to discuss and complete the diagram.

Chapter 16 (continued)

Lesson Support

▼ **Write:** Have students use their diagram and index cards to develop a paragraph.

Language: Capitalization: In their response journals, have students record the capitalization rules that give them the most trouble. When they are proofreading their writing assignments, have them refer to this page in their journal. Instruct them to add other grammar rules they miss most often on their writing assignments.

Possible answers:

1. A few years ago, after winning a writing contest, I got to visit the state capitol and meet Governor Tanaka.

(continued)

 Gr7Ch16Language.pptx

▼ **Write** Work with your partner to write a summary of your comparison of the two texts. Present your summary to the class.

Language: Capitalization

The excerpt from *The Lions of Little Rock* shows off a variety of uses for capital letters—in personal titles such as Pastor George, names such as the Mothers' League, and place names such as Little Rock. Capital letters begin a sentence, a proper noun, and each major word in a title. These rules are simple enough to remember. The tricky rules often concern when not to capitalize words. Common nouns and seasons are generally lowercase, but what about job titles or directional words?

The chart below contains some tips about when—and when not—to capitalize.

Capitalize . . .	Do not capitalize . . .
the first word in a quotation of a complete sentence.	the first word in a quotation of an incomplete sentence.
He asked, "When will we get there?"	She explained they would "get there when we get there."
nouns that form part of a name.	nouns that are not part of a name.
We visited the Gateway Arch last summer.	We walked under the arch, staring up in awe.
I rode with Aunt Ana and Uncle Miguel.	I enjoy spending time with my aunt and uncle.
We also saw Badlands National Park.	There are 59 national parks in this country.
titles for specific individuals.	titles that do not name individuals.
In 1797, President Washington stepped down.	At the time, the president had no term limit.
I had an appointment with Doctor Li.	She has been my doctor for years.
directions that refer to specific regions.	directions that do not refer to regions.
My father got a job in Northern California.	The window faced east, revealing the sunrise.
Elizabeth rarely sees her family in the South.	We bike the trail on the western edge of town.
course titles.	subject names that are not titles.
Are you taking Algebra this year?	I like algebra, but I prefer geometry.

Rewrite the following sentences, correcting the capitalization.

1. A few years ago, after winning a Writing Contest, I got to visit the State Capitol and meet Governor Tanaka.

©Perfection Learning® • No Reproduction Permitted

ELL Support: Language Review each of the examples in the chart, explaining that each item in the first column is a name of someone or something. Each item in the second column is not a specific person or place. It is not a name. Have students work in multilevel pairs or groups to complete the items. Review and explain correct responses as a class.

Connections • © Perfection Learning®

2. To find the Public Library, head northwest on baker street until you reach the Town Square and then look for the Statue of Ben Franklin.

3. Janelle always had trouble with Geography, but when she took professor Martinez's class, global studies, she found Geography easier to understand.

4. Despite the terrible review he read in the Newspaper, Ahmed called the movie "One heck of a ride!"

Project-Based Assessments

Historical Background

Write an explanation of the process of integration in the schools in Little Rock, Arkansas. Your report should provide background information that would help readers of the novel *The Lions of Little Rock* to understand the events, leaders, and community groups involved in the excerpt you read in this chapter.

continued on next page

2. To find the public library, head northwest on Baker Street until you reach the town square and then look for the statue of Ben Franklin.

3. Janelle always had trouble with geography, but when she took Professor Martinez's class, Global Studies, she found it easier to understand.

4. Despite the terrible review he read in the newspaper, Ahmed called the movie "one heck of a ride!"

Tech-Connect Suggestion: Students might be interested in learning more about the U.S. Supreme Court decision in *Brown v. Board of Education* (1954), as well as Topeka's civil rights story. For more information, go to www.nps.gov/brvb/index.htm.

Assessment

Project-Based Assessments

Historical Background: Students might find it helpful to check out the timeline on the National Park Service website: www.nps.gov/chsc/learn/historyculture/stories.htm.

ELL Support: Project-Based Assessments Have students work in multilevel pairs or groups to write the historical background and/or the historical fiction. Together with students, brainstorm sentence frames that they can use for their projects. Beginning and intermediate students may create visual representations for either project, such as an illustrated timeline or a graphic novel, labeling with words, phrases, or sentences according to their level. Provide the Informational Writing Revision Checklist (p. 69) or the Narrative Writing Revision Checklist (p. 68) from the ELL Teacher Resource for students to finalize their projects.

Project-Based Assessments—Historical Background Instead of completing the entire project, have students complete one part of the project alone or with a partner. They could reread the excerpt from the novel and take notes about the people, places, and events mentioned. Then they could write down three to five questions that aren't answered by the excerpts from this chapter.

Chapter 16 (continued)

Assessment

Historical Fiction: Students could work with partners to fine-tune their dialogue. After both students finish a draft of dialogue, they might then take turns reading their work together.

Here are some steps to help you.

1. Begin by rereading the excerpt from the novel. Take notes about the people, places, and events mentioned. Write questions you have that aren't answered by the excerpts.
2. Conduct research to find answers to your questions. As much as possible, use primary sources for your research.
   - A *primary source* is an eyewitness account of historical events. Examples include journals, biographies, government documents, and newspaper articles from the time period.
   - Primary sources tend to be more accurate because they were written by people who witnessed the events. For example, a good primary source is *The New York Times* from September 25, 1957, which can be found online at nytimes.com.
   - Government websites, academic websites, and established periodicals are also good sources for historical research.
   - Keep records of all of your sources.
3. Use notes from your research to write a one to two page historical companion to the book *The Lions of Little Rock*. Present your information in a way that is appealing to your audience—seventh-graders reading the book. Include text features such as headers, bullet points, quotations, and photos to support your written text. Use a word processing or design program to make your project visually appealing.
4. Include a list of sources used in your research. Follow your teacher's instructions for formatting these sources.

	Use the following guidelines for your historical background report.
To receive the highest score, the report must meet all of these criteria.	**Your report** • presents accurate background information related to the events, groups, and people mentioned in *The Lions of Little Rock*. • includes two or more primary sources as well as other reliable sources. • includes text features (photos, headers, bullet points) that support the writing. • is appropriate for a seventh-grade audience. • is visually appealing. • uses correct grammar, word usage, spelling, and punctuation.

Historical Fiction

Write an imaginary conversation between two people involved in the events surrounding the integration of Central High in Little Rock. Your characters might be real people, such as one of the Little Rock Nine. Or they might be imaginary characters based on real people, such as students or teachers at Central High School. Use the dialogue from *The Lions of Little Rock* as a model for your writing.

Here are some suggestions to help you:

1. Conduct research on the Little Rock Nine and the events that took place in September 1957. Use reliable sources, including primary sources when possible, and keep a record of your source information. (See an explanation of primary sources under the Historical Background project.)

2. Think about possible conversations you might write about. Suggestions include, but aren't limited to
   - one of the Little Rock Nine and his or her parent the night before the first day of school
   - two of the Little Rock Nine as they approach the school or at school during the first day
   - two students attending Central High on September 25

3. In your dialogue, communicate how the characters feel about the events and how they respond to the conflict. Are they brave, worried, anxious, or angry? Your writing should be entertaining as well as historically accurate.

4. Include a list of works used in your research. Follow your teacher's instructions for the formatting of sources.

Use the following guidelines for your historical fiction conversation.	
To receive the highest score, the historical ficiton must meet all of these criteria.	Your historical fiction conversation • presents an imaginary conversation related to the events, groups, and people mentioned in *The Lions of Little Rock*. • accurately represents historical events mentioned. • includes dialogue between two characters involved in the events. • communicates the feelings and motivations of the characters. • uses correct grammar, word usage, and punctuation.

On Your Own: Integrating Ideas

1. Read the entire book *The Lions of Little Rock* by Kristin Levine. Visit the author's website to learn more about the book.
2. Read *Warriors Don't Cry* by Melba Pattillo Beals, one of the Little Rock Nine who became a journalist. The book explains her first year at the school and her determination in the face of abuse.
3. Research oral histories about the Civil Rights movement in Little Rock during the 1960s. Visit the Library of Congress website to watch videos of those involved in Civil Rights and the integration of schools.

On Your Own: Integrating Ideas:
Activities 1 and 2: Encourage students who read *The Lions of Little Rock* or *Warriors Don't Cry* to write and share a review with the class or they could post it online and invite classmates to comment on it.

Assessment

Connect to Testing: This Connect to Testing section focuses on analyzing setting and point of view and comparing historical fiction and nonfiction.

Encourage students to work in pairs to choose the correct answers to the questions and then to compare their answers with those of another pair of students. If there is disagreement, encourage the groups to try to reach a consensus as they discuss the reasons for their choices.

Answers to Connect to Testing Questions:

1. **Part A:** A.

   Part B: D. Based on Marlee's conversation with his daughter, he is more concerned about protecting his family than taking a stand for Civil Rights (Choice B). There is no evidence for Choice D. We can infer that he is less trusting of other people currently, but it is not as clear as the correct answer, Choice A. (DoK 2)

2. A. Choices B, C could possibly be true because Marlee's father is older and has more knowledge about current events. Choice D is an opinion and thus not the best answer. Choice A is the best answer because Marlee's father has a strong opinion that is implied in the conversation. Because she is young, Marlee's opinions are not as strong, and thus she presents a less biased point of view. (DoK 3)

3. **Part A:** B.

   Part B: A. The excerpt mentions that the vote against integration happened the weekend before, and the timeline shows exactly when this occurred: September 27, 1958; Citizens vote 19,470 to 7,561 against integration and the schools remain closed. (DoK 3)

   (continued)

Connect to Testing

Tests may require you to answer questions about setting, point of view, or the differences and similarities between a historical fiction excerpt and a nonfiction text on the same subject. Here are some examples of these types of questions.

1. **Part A:** How does the setting of *The Lions of Little Rock* affect Marlee's father's state of mind?

   A. It makes him want to protect his family.

   B. It makes him want to get involved in the Civil Right movement.

   C. It makes him less trusting of other people.

   D. It makes him curious about what will happen next locally.

   Part B: Which of the following provides the strongest evidence for the answer to Part A?

   A. *"She was your friend. Now she's someone else."*

   B. *A women's group, associated with the CCC, that formed last year to oppose integration at Central.*

   C. *This was a lot to take in. "Isn't everyone allowed to have their own opinion?"*

   D. *"I mean it, Marlee. I don't want to scare you too much—I'll keep you safe—but I do want you to be careful."*

2. How would *The Lions of Little Rock* most likely be different if it were told from Marlee's father's point of view?

   A. It would involve a more biased opinion.

   B. It would include more historical analysis.

   C. It would be more informative about civil rights.

   D. It would be boring.

3. **Part A:** According to the timeline, Marlee's conversation with her dad takes place in

   A. September 1957.

   B. September 1958.

   C. May 1959.

   D. August 1959.

Remediation: Connect to Testing Review responses with students. With questions 4 and 5, model for them how to use the text to answer each question.

Part B: Which of the following provides the strongest evidence for the answer to Part A?

A. *There was an article about the election the weekend before on the front page: Little Rock votes against integration 19,470 to 7,561. Schools to be closed indefinitely.*

B. *"But the reason there were police all over David's graduation last May was not because people have different opinions. The FBI was there to protect Ernest Green because they were worried that someone was going to try to kill him."*

C. *"I thought things settled down at Central once they called the soldiers in."*

D. *In any case, last year the pictures from Central told the whole world Little Rock is filled with hate.*

4. Read the following entry from the timeline.

> May 25, 1958
>
> Senior Ernest Green becomes the first African American student to graduate from Central High School.

How does the conversation between Marlee and her father further develop the facts in this entry of the timeline? In your answer refer to specific details from the excerpt.

continued on next page

---

4. Daddy mentions that the FBI was at the graduation to protect Ernest Green, because they were worried that somebody might try to kill him. It implies that Green faced much opposition during his senior year at Central High School. (DoK 3)

(continued)

ELL Support: Connect to Testing and Assessments See the ELL Teacher Resource (p. 22) for ideas on adapting this section for ELLs.

Assessment

Answers to Connect to Testing Questions:

5. Marlee struggles with trying to understand the bigotry of her city and some of their family friends, neighbors, and acquaintances. She accepts everyone—regardless of race—but she has had long-standing relationships with some of the town's bigots and is having trouble making sense of the racism of these people. She also struggles with her father, who forbids her from continuing to see her best friend, Liz, a Black girl who has been passing as White, because he fears that relationship may endanger Marlee. Marlee cannot accept his perspective. (DoK 2)

5. How does the setting influence the conflict between Marlee and society and Marlee and her father? In your answer, explain the conflicts and how specific elements of the setting cause the conflicts. Support your conclusions with evidence from the text.

Chapter 17

Learning About History Through Fiction

Preview Concepts

We make inferences every day in all kinds of situations. Read the following situation and make inferences based on what you read in the text and your own experience.

> Crack! Thunder struck and rain poured. Max stared blankly out the window, trying to contain his emotions that raged like the weather. He was beginning to lose it. Dropping the kite from his hand, Max broke out into sobs. His mother comforted him, "It's okay. We'll just find something else to do." She began to unpack the food from a basket on the counter and offered him a sandwich. Max snapped, "I don't wanna sand-mich!" Boom! A flash lit up the living room. Max screamed and covered his ears.

Inferences about Max:

Evidence from text:

Inferences about the situation:

Evidence from text:

CHAPTER GOALS

In this chapter you will

- use evidence to make inferences about text.
- analyze an author's use of literary devices and language.
- compare a fictional account of a historical event with a nonfictional account.
- demonstrate knowledge of standard spelling.

PREVIEW ACADEMIC VOCABULARY

figurative language

inferences

metaphor

repetition

sensory language

textual evidence

ELL Support: Academic Vocabulary See <u>Teaching Vocabulary in the ELL Teacher Resource (p. 18)</u> for ideas to use for teaching vocabulary throughout *Connections.*

ELL Support: Preview Concepts Use simple definitions to explain *inferences* (good guesses made from details), *situation* (the facts and events that affect someone in a time and place), and *experience* (what someone has done in their life). Have students work in multilevel pairs or groups to read the passage, pausing to illustrate it as they read. As a class, sketch the situation on the board and use the following prompts for discussion and writing:

- What inference can you make about Max? What is Max feeling? Why?

- What inference can you make about the situation? What is the weather? What were Max and his mother going to do? Why can't they do it?

Chapter 17

Learning About History Through Fiction

The Drummer Boy of Shiloh
by Ray Bradbury

Introduction

Chapter Goals: Have students read through the goals and mark any words that are unfamiliar. Discuss the meanings of any academic vocabulary within the goals that students marked as unfamiliar. Consider posting the Chapter Goals.

Preview Academic Vocabulary: Read and discuss the meanings of the academic vocabulary.

figurative language: *language that goes beyond the literal, appealing to the senses through the use of comparison, exaggeration, imagery, and other devices.* The author's use of <u>figurative language</u> helps to bring his characters to life.

inference: *a conclusion that is based on background knowledge and evidence in a text.* Based on her short story, I drew an <u>inference</u> that the author had firsthand knowledge of Japan.

metaphor: *a comparison of two unalike things that does not use a word of comparison (i.e., like or as).* The poem contains many celestial <u>metaphors</u> to describe the girl's beauty, such as, "She is a bright star."

repetition: *using the same or similar sounds, words, or ideas multiple times.* Repetition helps an audience remember great speeches. For example: "I have a dream."

sensory language: *language that appeals to the senses.* I could picture and even smell the roses because of the <u>sensory language</u> in the poem.

(continued)

textual evidence: *support for an inference about a text.* We found <u>textual evidence</u> in the passage to support our idea that the boy was brave.

 Gr7Ch17Vocabulary.pptx

Chapter 17 (continued)

Introduction

Preview Concepts: Make sure students understand that making inferences involves formulating reasonable guesses based on clues or evidence in the text as well as their own experience. They can confirm their inferences as they read and/or research. Sometimes they will have to revise an inference.

> **Answers to page 363:**
>
> Inferences about Max: *Max is very young.*
> Evidence from text: *His reaction to the the fact that he can't fly his kite, his sobs, his mother's reaction to his crying, and Max's language.*
> Inferences about the situation: *Max had been expecting to go on a picnic; the rain interfered with his plans.*
> Evidence from text: *Max's disappointment and general reaction; his mother's suggestion in the hopes of comforting Max, that they will find something else to do; the basket that was packed and ready.*

Making Connections:

> **Answers to Questions:**
>
> *Students may say they know Sherlock Holmes is a detective known for his great skill.*
> *He is enthusiastic about science. He is surprisingly observant and strong.*

Making Connections

Read the following excerpt.

> This was a lofty chamber, lined and littered with countless bottles. Broad, low tables were scattered about, which bristled with retorts, test-tubes, and little Bunsen lamps, with their blue flickering flames. There was only one student in the room, who was bending over a distant table absorbed in his work. At the sound of our steps he glanced round and sprang to his feet with a cry of pleasure.
>
> "I've found it! I've found it," he shouted to my companion, running towards us with a test-tube in his hand. "I have found a re-agent which is precipitated by hemoglobin, and by nothing else." Had he discovered a gold mine, greater delight could not have shone upon his features.
>
> "Dr. Watson, Mr. Sherlock Holmes," said Stamford, introducing us.
>
> "How are you?" he said cordially, gripping my hand with a strength for which I should hardly have given him credit. "You have been in Afghanistan, I perceive."
>
> "How on earth did you know that?" I asked in astonishment.
>
> "Never mind," said he, chuckling to himself.
>
> —*A Study in Scarlet*, by Arthur Conan Doyle

What did you already know about the character of Sherlock Holmes before reading this excerpt?

What inference might you make about Sherlock Holmes, based on the way he acts in this excerpt? Underline details in the text that support your response.

> **MAKING CONNECTIONS**
>
> In this chapter you will make inferences based on evidence from a text.

ELL Support: Make Connections Display pictures of Sherlock Holmes and Dr. Watson. Then read the excerpt with volunteers reading the roles of Sherlock, Dr. Watson, and Stamford as you read the narration. Guide volunteers to act out the scene as they read. As a class, sketch a picture of what is happening in the scene. Have students work in multilevel pairs or groups to discuss and then write about the questions, using the following prompts and sentence frames:

Q: Who is Sherlock Holmes? What is his job? What is he like as a person?

A: Sherlock Holmes is . . . . He is . . . .

Q: Who is Dr. Watson? What is his job? What is he like as a person?

A: Dr. Watson is . . . . He is . . . .

This story was written by Ray Bradbury, an author best known for writing science fiction. What inferences can you make about the characters, setting, and situation based on the text?

Objective: As you read, make inferences about the setting and the boys' feelings. Write two inferences in the My Thoughts column. Underline lines in the text that support your inferences.

—— First Read

---- Second Read

—— Third Read

excerpt
The Drummer Boy of Shiloh
by Ray Bradbury

My Thoughts

1   In the April night, more than once, blossoms fell from the orchard trees and lit with rustling taps on the drumskin. At midnight a peach stone left miraculously on a branch through winter flicked by a bird fell swift and unseen struck once like

5   panic, which jerked the boy upright. In silence he listened to his own heart ruffle away away—at last gone from his ears and back in his chest again.

The boy is scared.

After that he turned the drum on its side, where its great ★ lunar face peered at him whenever he opened his eyes.

10   His face, alert or at rest, was solemn. It was a solemn time and a solemn night for a boy just turned fourteen in the peach orchard near Owl Creek not far from the church at **Shiloh**. . . .

The drummer boy is sad and thinking about the seriousness of war.

The boy turned on his side. A moth brushed his face, but it was a peach blossom. A peach blossom flicked him, but it was

15   a moth. Nothing stayed put. Nothing had a name. Nothing was as it once was.

If he stayed very still, when the dawn came up and the soldiers put on their bravery with their caps, perhaps they ★ might go away, the war with them, and not notice him living

He wants to disappear.

20   small here, no more than a toy himself.

Shiloh: a small town in southwest Tennessee

Q: What does Sherlock do in this scene? What does this show about him?

A: Sherlock . . . . This shows that he is . . . .

First Read Provide ELLs with background knowledge about the Civil War so that they can make inferences about the situation. Use a map to explain that in the Civil War, the Northern part of the United States fought against the Southern part. Sometimes family members fought against each other—cousins against cousins or even brothers against brothers. Use pictures to explain that boys played drums to help the soldiers march together. Explain that a general is in charge of the army. Have students read the excerpt in multilevel pairs or groups, pausing at the end of each page to take notes using a Story Map graphic organizer from the ELL Resource (p. 52). Encourage students to also take notes and draw sketches in the margins around the story so they can be sure they understand and remember the main events.

Before Reading: Activate background knowledge by asking students what they know about the Civil War (1861–1865) and why it is also called the War Between the States. *(The Northern states battled the Southern states over the issue of slavery and states' rights.)* Point out that the Battle of Shiloh (April 6–7, 1862), fought in Tennessee, was one of the bloodiest clashes of the Civil War.

Read with students the introductory paragraph and the objective, making sure they understand the purpose of the First Read. As a class, review the definition of *inference*: a conclusion that is based on background knowledge and evidence in a text. Then have a volunteer read the first paragraph, and ask students what clues, or evidence in the text, convey the idea that everything is not right on this April night. Ask students to continue to read the excerpt on their own.

Preview Vocabulary: Preview unfamiliar vocabulary to aid comprehension or ask students to circle unfamiliar words as they complete the first read of a text. After the first read, guide students to determine the words' meanings using the context. Encourage students to support their responses with evidence. Have students confirm their initial definitions with a dictionary. Words that students might find difficult include:

lunar: *relating to the moon; moonlike. The rocket circled the moon before making a* lunar *landing.*

solemn: *serious.* The girl made a solemn promise to stay with her little brother at the park.

assume: *suppose; take for granted.* The seventh grade math teacher assumes her students all know the multiplication tables.

legitimate: *lawful; valid.* The sixteen-year-old was proud to earn a legitimate driver's license.

innocents: *ones who are free of guilt or sin, especially because of lack of knowledge.* Those innocents, not even school age yet, should not have to face such hardship.

Chapter **17** (continued)

Lesson Support

After Reading: Use the following questions to check comprehension.

Text-Based Discussion Questions

1. Why does the boy think, "Nothing was as it once was"? *He knows that his life is forever changed by his joining the army.*

2. What words describe the general? *kind, understanding, thoughtful, experienced, worldly-wise*

3. Why does the boy answer with silence when the general asks, "Run off from home or join legitimate, boy?" *Because he ran from home to join the army, and he won't lie and say he joined legitimately.*

4. Why did the general cry? *He knows that the battle of Shiloh and the war, as well, are going to be terrible.*

 Gr7Ch17Read1.pptx

---

"Well, by thunder now," said a voice. The boy shut his eyes to hide inside himself, but it was too late. Someone, walking by in the night, stood over him. "Well," said the voice quietly, "here's a soldier crying *before* the fight. Good. Get it over.
25 Won't be time once it all starts."

And the voice was about to move on when the boy, startled, touched the drum at his elbow. The man above, hearing this, stopped. The boy could feel his eyes, sense him slowly bending near. A hand must have come down out of the
30 night, for there was a little *rat-tat* as the fingernails brushed and the man's breath fanned the boy's face.

"Why, it's the drummer boy, isn't it?"

The boy nodded, not knowing if his nod was seen. "Sir, is that you?" he said.

35 "I assume it is." The man's knees cracked as he bent still closer. He smelled as all fathers should smell, of salt-sweat, tobacco, horse and boot leather, and the earth he walked upon. He had many eyes. No, not eyes, brass buttons that watched the boy.

He could only be, and was, the general. "What's your
40 name, boy?" he asked.

"Joby, sir," whispered the boy, starting to sit up.

"All right, Joby, don't stir." A hand pressed his chest gently, and the boy relaxed. "How long you been with us, Joby?"

"Three weeks, sir."

45 "Run off from home or join legitimate, boy?"

Silence.

"Fool question," said the general. "Do you shave yet, boy? Even more of a fool. There's your cheek, fell right off the tree ★ overhead. And the others here, not much older. Raw, raw, the
50 lot of you. You ready for tomorrow or the next day, Joby?"

My Thoughts

"I think so, sir."

"You want to cry some more, go on ahead. I did the same last night."

"You, sir?"

55 "It's the truth. Thinking of everything ahead. Both sides figuring the other side will just give up, and soon, and the war done in weeks and us all home. Well, that's not how it's going to be. And maybe that's why I cried."

"Yes, sir," said Joby.

60 The general must have taken out a cigar now, for the dark was suddenly filled with the Indian smell of tobacco unlighted yet, but chewed as the man thought what next to say.

"It's going to be a crazy time," said the general. "Counting both sides, there's a hundred thousand men—give or take

65 a few thousand—out there tonight, not one as can spit a sparrow off a tree, or knows a horse clod from a **Minie ball**. Stand up, bare the breast, ask to be a target, thank them and sit down, that's us, that's them. We should turn tail and train four months, they should do the same. But here we are,

70 taken with spring fever and thinking it **bloodlust,** taking our **sulphur** with cannons instead of with molasses, as it should be—going to be a hero, going to live forever. And I can see all them over there nodding agreement, save the other way around. It's wrong, boy, it's wrong as a head put on

75 **hindside** front and a man marching backward through life. Sometime this week more innocents will get shot out of pure **Cherokee** enthusiasm than ever got shot before. Owl Creek

---

Minie ball: a kind of bullet used during the Civil War
bloodlust: desire for bloodshed
sulphur: a chemical given as a medicine
hindside: the backside or backwards
Cherokee: a Native American tribe

My Thoughts
_____
_____
_____
_____
_____
_____
_____
_____
_____
_____
_____
_____
_____
_____
_____
_____
_____
_____
_____
_____
_____
_____
_____
_____
_____

About the Author: The remarkable Ray Bradbury (1920–2012) created an impressive collection of work that spanned eight genres, including nearly 50 books and hundreds of short stories. His efforts won him fame and many awards, such as the 2004 National Medal of Arts, an Emmy award (for a teleplay) and an Academy Award nomination (for a screenplay). The Ray Bradbury Theater TV series, based on his work, ran for 65 episodes, from 1985 to 1992. In an essay Bradbury wrote, "In my later years I have looked in the mirror each day and found a happy person staring back. Occasionally I wonder why I can be so happy. The answer is that every day of my life I've worked only for myself and for the joy that comes from writing and creating. The image in my mirror is not optimistic, but the result of optimal behavior."

Chapter **17** *(continued)*

Lesson Support

The Civil War in Literature: The Civil War (1861–1865) has been a topic of interest for American writers of fiction and nonfiction for the past 150 years. Tens of thousands of books have been written on the topic. Gettysburg College, near the site of the war's most famous battle, published a list of the top two hundred Civil War nonfiction books in 2016. Many fiction writers have used the war as the setting for a book. *Red Badge of Courage* and *Gone with the Wind* are among the most celebrated Civil War novels, neither written by a soldier. "An Occurrence at Owl Creek Bridge," by Ambrose Bierce, a Civil War soldier, is probably the most famous short story about that period.

FIRST RESPONSE: KEY IDEAS AND DETAILS

Before students write in their journals, you may want to point out that Ray Bradbury uses the general to characterize the battle and foreshadow what it will be like.

The general suggests that it will be a bloodbath, pointing out that 100,000 unprepared men will be fighting. He adds that the idea of a quick war is wrong; many boys will die.

---

was full of boys splashing around in the noonday sun just a few hours ago. I fear it will be full of boys again, just floating,

80   at sundown tomorrow, not caring where the current takes them."

My Thoughts

_____

_____

_____

_____

The reconstructed Shiloh Church, Shiloh, Tennessee

FIRST RESPONSE: KEY IDEAS AND DETAILS

How does the author portray the battle that will soon take place? What lines foreshadow the coming battle? Write your answer in your response journal. Be ready to defend your analysis using evidence from the passage and also be ready to explain the evidence if needed.

Focus on Making Inferences

Consider what you can infer about the characters and the setting in the excerpt from "The Drummer Boy of Shiloh." Use the graphic organizer on the next page to identify inferences and specific sentences and details that support your inferences. The first row has been completed for you.

ELL Support: Focus on Making Inferences Have students work in multilevel pairs or groups to discuss and then write about their inferences, using these prompts and sentence frames:

Q: Did the boy join the army legally (legitimately)? Or did he run away from home? How do you know?

A: The boy . . . .

Q: How does the general feel about the battle? Why? What does he think about the abilities of the soldiers on both sides?

A: The general feels . . . . He feels this way because . . . . He thinks the soldiers on both sides are . . . .

Q: Why are the soldiers fighting? How do they feel or what do they think about fighting? What does the general say about this? Are the soldiers ready for war? What does the general think will happen?

A: The general says that the soldiers are fighting because . . . . They

Inferences about the boy	Evidence
1. The boy is scared about the battle that will take place the next day.	*His face, alert or at rest, was solemn. (line 10)* *perhaps they might go away, the war with them, and not notice him living small here (lines 18–19)*
2. The boy ran away from home to join the army.	*"Run off from home or join legitimate, boy?"* *Silence. (lines 45–46)*

Inference about the general	Evidence
1. The general takes his responsibilities seriously.	*"You want to cry some more, go on ahead. I did the same last night."* (lines 52–53)
2. The general is wise and understands war.	*"Both sides figuring the other side will just give up, and soon, and the war done in weeks and us all home. Well, that's not how it's going to be. And maybe that's why I cried."* (lInes 55–58)

Inferences about the battle	Evidence
1. The general believes that both sides are fighting because they are obsessed with noble ideas about war. They are going into battle unprepared.	*"But here we are taken with spring fever and thinking it bloodlust . . . going to be a hero, going to live forever."* (lines 69–72) *"We should turn tail and train four months"* (lines 68–69)
2. Many boys will die.	*"Owl Creek was full of boys splashing around . . . I fear it will be full of boys again, just floating, at sundown tomorrow, not caring where the current takes them."* (lines 77–81)

▼Write The Battle of Shiloh was fought on April 6–7 in 1862. Based on the passage, make inferences about the situation and actual outcome of the battle based on the excerpt from "The Drummer Boy of Shiloh." Explain which words or details led you to make your inferences.

TECH-CONNECT
Conduct online research to check your inferences about the Battle of Shiloh.

Answers to Focus on Making Inferences:

See answers on Student Book insert page to the left.

 Gr7Ch17Read1.pptx

▼**Write:** Students can refer to their charts, especially the last two rows, as they make inferences about the situation and actual outcome of the battle.

---

think fighting is . . . . The soldiers are/are not ready for war. The general thinks that in the battle . . . .

Write Have students work in multilevel pairs or groups and focus on the general and what the reader learns from him instead of making predictions about the battle. Suggest that they read what the general says at the end of the passage, starting with "It's the truth." Then they can use these sentence frames. These can also be found as a student handout in the ELL Teacher Resource (p. 39).

- The general knows . . . . The general says . . . .
- The general also says . . . .
- This shows . . . .
- This also shows . . . .
- The reader can infer that . . . .

Chapter 17 (continued)

Second Read: Analyzing an Author's Use of Language

Before Reading: In addition to reading the introductory remarks and objective, have students read the text (including the definitions) before the chart on page 370. Before rereading the entire excerpt, with the class reread the final paragraph on page 365 and analyze the literary devices together. Then have students read the entire excerpt on their own.

After Reading: Use the following questions to check comprehension.

Text-Based Discussion Questions:

1. How would you summarize the plot of the passage? *A Civil War drummer boy wakes up frightened and crying. Just then, a general walks by, stops, and talks with the boy. The general speaks about his fears, the war, and the terrible battle ahead.*

2. Why does the author refer to the drummer boy as "the boy" and to the general as "the general" without naming either one? *He is suggesting that they are like other generals and other young soldier boys in their fears and worries about war.*

3. Is the following description effective: "Owl Creek was full of boys splashing around in the noonday sun just a few hours ago. I fear it will be full of boys again, just floating, at sundown tomorrow, not caring where the current takes them"? *Yes, it puts a visual picture in the reader's mind by contrasting the living and the dead.*

Focus on Analyzing an Author's Use of Language: You may want to point out that Bradbury's use of figurative language serves to emphasize the horrors of war.

> **Answers to Focus on Analyzing an Author's Use of Language:**
>
> See answers on Student Book insert page to the right.

Speak and Listen: Tell students their opinion should be supported with examples of language that is effective or not effective in communicating emotions.

Second Read: Analyzing an Author's Use of Language

As you read the text again, pay attention to how the use of language reveals the author's voice and style.

Objective: Underline examples of language that create a picture in your mind. Place a star by examples of figurative language that compare objects in the story to other objects.

> **REFLECT**
>
> What is your favorite line from the excerpt? Why?

Focus on Analyzing an Author's Use of Language

Bradbury chooses his words carefully. He wants the reader to experience what it's like to be a fourteen-year-old waiting to fight in his first battle. Here are some of the literary devices Bradbury uses.

sensory language: language that appeals to the senses, helps the reader see, feel, and smell the scene being described

metaphor: comparison of two unalike things

repetition: repeating a word or phrase for emphasis

foreshadowing: when a writer gives an advance hint of what is to come later in the story

Complete the chart below with examples from the excerpt.

Literary Device		Word or Phrase	Effect on Reader
sensory language	1.	*his own heart ruffle away, away—at last gone from his ears and back in his chest again.*	1. helps the reader feel the fast beating of the boy's heart and his anxiety.
	2.	*a little rat-tat as the fingernails brushed and the man's breath fanned the boy's face*	2. communicates a gentle mood and creates a feeling of intimacy between boy and general.
metaphor	1.	*its great lunar face peered at him whenever he opened his eyes.*	Recognition of how young, small, afraid and vulnerable he feels.
	2.	*. . . not notice him living small here, no more than a toy himself.*	
repetition	1.	*His face, alert or at rest, was solemn. It was a solemn time and a solemn night for a boy just turned fourteen . . .*	1. Sense of the seriousness of the situation is heightened.
	2.	*Nothing stayed put. Nothing had a name. Nothing was as it once was.*	2. Sense of the world being out of order, upset, and confusing
foreshadowing	1.	*Sometime this week more innocents will get shot out of pure Cherokee enthusiasm . . .*	This solemn image creates a sense of fear and foreboding.
	2.	*I fear it will be full of boys again, just floating, at sundown tomorrow, not caring where the current takes them.*	

Speak and Listen Share your answers to the chart with a partner. Then discuss the following questions:

- What emotions do you feel as you read the passage?
- Is his language effective at communicating these emotions? Why or why not?

ELL Support: Second Read Review the definitions of *sensory language, metaphor,* and *repetition*. Then model rereading the story and identifying one of each device, explaining its effect on the reader. Record your responses on the board so students can use them as a guide. Have students reread the story in multilevel pairs or small groups, pausing to identify Bradbury's use of language. Review the chart on p. 370 as a class before students discuss the answers in their multilevel pairs or groups, using the following sentence frames:

- When I read the passage, I feel . . . .
- I think the author wants me to feel . . . .
- The author's language does/does not give these emotions to the reader because . . . .

Third Read: Analyzing a Fictional Account of a Historical Event

Reread the excerpt from "The Drummer Boy of Shiloh" a third time. Then read the excerpt below. It is a nonfiction article about drummer boys during times of war.

Objective: Underline ideas that provide information that helps you better understand details from the short story.

excerpt
Drummer Boys
by Stephen Currie

		My Thoughts

1   Throughout much of American history, drummer boys made a small but important contribution to American military units. These children, <u>some as young as nine years old</u>, courageously faced the enemy with little more than <u>a drum and a pair of</u>
5 <u>sticks.</u> A few became the first to fall in the line of duty.

    Early American armies were largely volunteer affairs. Few formal age restrictions existed, and youngsters <u>who lied about their age were often enlisted with little scrutiny.</u> <u>Those who were clearly underage sometimes became drummers.</u> A typical
10 drummer boy was between twelve and sixteen years old, although a few even younger boys managed to enlist.

    Drummers served in all our early conflicts—the Revolutionary War, frontier battles, the War of 1812, the Mexican War, and the <u>Civil War.</u> These young soldiers
15 played a vital role, as they served as the <u>primary means of</u> <u>communication between officers and men.</u> The drum and **fife** called troops to arms, signaled changes in strategy, and provided the **cadence** for marching. . . .

    By the Civil War, drumbeats had become more
20 sophisticated. Drummer boys sounded the daily calls and

---
fife: small flute-like instrument
cadence: a beat or rhythm used to keep soldiers in step when marching

---

ELL Support: Third Read Have students read the new article in multilevel pairs or small groups, pausing after each paragraph to summarize ideas on a <u>Main Ideas and Supporting Details graphic organizer from the ELL Teacher Resource (p. 51).</u> Also, encourage students to take notes and draw sketches in the margins around the article to aid comprehension and to help them remember the topic of each paragraph. Once they have read the article, have students work in their multilevel pairs or groups to complete the chart on p. 373.

Reflect: Have students submit their favorite lines to Poll Everywhere and display answers as a word cloud or as an open-ended response. Or you can create a multiple-choice question with lines from the text and compile the results for students to see which one is most popular.

Tech-Connect Suggestion: Students can read about the Battle of Shiloh at https://www.nps.gov/shil/learn/historyculture/shiloh-history.htm.

 Gr7Ch17Read2.pptx

Third Read: Analyzing a Fictional Account of a Historical Event

Before Reading: Have students pair up to discuss the introductory paragraph and objective. Then remind the class to keep in mind the purpose, focus, format, writing style, and point of view of the fiction and nonfiction selections as they compare them. If needed, review the differences between historical fiction and nonfiction described on page 350 of this Teacher's Edition.

Preview Vocabulary: Preview unfamiliar vocabulary to aid comprehension.

    restrictions: *limits; controls.* The army places <u>restrictions</u> on where the soldiers may travel in the war zone.

    scrutiny: *inspection.* The government ordered <u>scrutiny</u> of all passengers entering the country from the war zone.

    infantry: *foot soldiers.* The <u>infantry</u> took a stand on the hillside and fought valiantly.

After Reading: Use the following questions to check comprehension.

Text-Based Discussion Questions

1. Why did the military allow children to join as drummers? *There were few age restrictions; by tradition, they had always allowed boys to serve as drummers; they had a need for their help.*

2. What jobs did the drummer boys perform beyond drumming? *They did chores, cared for the wounded, sharpened surgical instruments, and buried the dead.*

3. Why did Congress prohibit youths from serving, in 1864? *War had become even more deadly. People's ideas about the appropriateness of children being exposed to war had changed.*

provided beats for marching drills. A well-trained **regiment** could maneuver expertly without spoken commands, with only the drumbeats transmitting the orders.

25   The boys also performed a number of less colorful duties. <u>Most helped with camp chores such as carrying water, and one even served as a barber</u>, while another peddled sweets to the soldiers. After a battle, the youngsters faced more serious tasks. They helped remove and care for the wounded, sharpen the surgeon's instruments, and bury the dead.

30   Several heroic or tragic tales involving drummer boys emerged from the Civil War. Most of these were romantic works of fiction. One famous ballad, for example, <u>claimed to tell the mournful end of "The Drummer Boy of Shiloh."</u> Historic research indicates that no such individual existed. . . .

35   The new weapons of the Civil War helped end the days of children soldiers. War had become a more professional and deadly business. An act of Congress passed in March 1864 prohibited the enlistment of anyone under age sixteen. The echo of young drumbeats faded as **bugles**, telegraphs, and,

40 later, radios guided the infantry into battle.

    The drummer boys played a crucial role in our early American armies. They joined up for the excitement of soldiering and aged quickly in the harsh realities of war. They risked, and sometimes lost, their lives for the cause of freedom

45 at an age when most children now think only of school or play. Today <u>we can look with pride on the drummer boys' bravery when the United States, like the boys themselves, was a youngster filled with dreams of glory.</u>

---

regiment: a military unit

bugles: a valveless brass instrument similar to a trumpet

My Thoughts

Focus on Analyzing a Fictional Account of a Historical Event

Writers of historical fiction who base their stories on actual events usually alter or adapt them to fit their purposes. The goal of historical fiction is to entertain. So the author often takes liberty with characters and events to make the story more engaging.

Fill in the following graphic organizer, contrasting the way details are represented in the first and the second passages. Use direct quotations from the texts or paraphrase the information. Include line numbers for reference.

Idea	The Drummer Boy of Shiloh by Ray Bradbury	Drummer Boys by Stephen Currie
Age of drummers	Not stated directly, but can be inferred from the text that he is younger than 13: "Fool question," said the general. "Do you shave yet, boy? Even more of a fool."	*some as young as nine years old (line 3) usually 12 to 16 years old but some lied about their age (lines 7–11)*
Duties in and after battle	Not stated directly: Text only says that he is a drummer boy.	*sounded daily calls and provided beats for marching drills. (lines 20–21) helped with camp chores such as carrying water, and one even served as a barber, while another peddled sweets to the soldiers. helped remove and care for the wounded, sharpen the surgeon's instruments, and bury the dead. (lines 25 and following)*
The person known as "The Drummer Boy of Shiloh"	Not discussed directly, but the title is "The Drummer Boy of Shiloh," and a drummer boy is the main character.	*Historic research indicates that no such individual existed. (line 34)*
Drummer boys' responses to fighting in a war	*perhaps they might go away, the war with them, and not notice him living small here, no more than a toy himself. "here's a soldier crying before the fight."*	*They joined up for the excitement of soldiering and aged quickly in the harsh realities of war. (lines 42–43)*

Focus on Analyzing a Fictional Account of a Historical Event:

Answers to Focus on Analyzing a Fictional Account of a Historical Event:

See answers on Student Book insert page to the left.

 Gr7Ch17Read3.pptx

Chapter **17** *(continued)*

Lesson Support

Speak and Listen: Reread the last sentence of the excerpt on page 372. Ask: *Do you agree with the idea that we should "look with pride on the drummer boys' bravery when the United States . . . was a youngster filled with dreams of glory"? Why or why not?* Students might consider the following issues in their argument:

- the effects of war on drummer boys;
- the feelings of the drummer boys;
- the efforts of the drummer boys;
- the need for drummer boys.

Write: Students can use the topics and details from the comparison chart as the basis for outlining and developing their paragraphs.

Language: Spelling Rules: Have students write each spelling rule or commonly confused word group in their response journals, focusing on those that are most difficult for them.

 **Gr7Ch17Language.pptx**

Speak and Listen Review your answers to the chart with a partner. Then discuss the following question:

- Should the fact that children were allowed to serve as drummer boys in wars be celebrated or condemned?

Support your opinion with evidence from the texts.

Write Write several paragraphs analyzing how the short story represents, or does not represent, the facts presented in "Drummer Boys" by Stephen Currie.

Language: Spelling

It is important to use correct spelling when writing assignments for school or when writing emails and other communication with community leaders and business people. Informal spelling and abbreviations are fine to use when texting with family and friends. However, in most other situations, including correspondence about job opportunities, you should use correct spelling and complete words and phrases.

Basic Spelling Rules

1. Most of the time, you should place *i* before *e* in words, except after *c*.
   Examples: *re̲ceipt, dece̲ive, fri̲end, belie̲ve*
2. When forming the plural of a word, most of the time you simply add *s*.
   Examples: *dogs, tractors, pears, rocks*
3. If a word ends in *-s, -x, -z, -ch,* or *-sh,* add *-es* to make it plural.
   Examples: *coa̲ches, wis̲hes, gras̲ses, box̲es*
4. If a noun ends in *y*, change the *y* to an *i* and add *-es* to make the plural.
   Examples: *fly/flies, factory/factories, story/stories, baby/babies*

Also remember that spell-check is a helpful tool, but it is not a substitute for carefully proofing your writing. Spell-check doesn't catch mistakes in words that are often confused such as *their, there,* and *they're* or *your* and *you're.* Read the following commonly confused words.

Commonly Confused Words

whose—possessive for "of who"	*who's*—contraction for "who is"
Whose book is this?	Who's going to the game?

ELL Support: Speak and Listen Have students work in multilevel pairs or small groups to discuss the drummer boys, using these sentence frames and prompts:

- Should boys be drummer boys? Why or why not?
- Yes/No, boys should/should not be drummer boys because . . . .

Write Have students work in multilevel pairs or small groups to write about the two texts, using these sentence frames. These can also be found as a student handout in the ELL Teacher Resource (p. 39).

- One fact from the article is . . . .
- And the short story shows . . . .
- Another fact from the article is . . . .
- And the short story shows . . . .

your—possessive for "of you" Your bike is in the yard.	you're—contraction for "you are" You're going to be late for school.
their—possessive form of "they" Their shoes were by the front door.	there—in that place The baseball is over there.
they're—contraction for "they are" They're going to be home soon.	
passed—past tense of "to pass" I passed the vegetables to my mom.	past—at a previous time The past month has been very rainy.
its—possessive form of "it" The dog buried its bone by the tree.	it's—contraction for "it is" It's never too late to try.

Read the sentences below. Circle any misspelled or incorrect words, and rewrite the sentence correctly in the space provided.

1. I can't beleive that they're team won the game.

2. The two deputys had not seen are stolen cars.

> **REFLECT**
>
> What words do you often confuse? Add them to the list of Commonly Confused Words.

3. I saw so many churchs that day and recieved so many complements on my camera that I was exhausted.

continued on next page

Language: Spelling Create a chart or word wall of the rules and examples. Encourage students to create flash cards of words they have trouble spelling. Have students work in multilevel pairs or groups to complete the items. Review and explain correct responses as a class.

Answers to Sentences:

1. believe, their
2. deputies, our
3. churches, received, compliments

Chapter 17 (continued)

Assessment

Answers to Sentences:

4. read, your, won

5. advice, coaches, wait, meet, stopped

Project-Based Assessments

Response Essay: Make sure students understand the idea of a romantic work of fiction: "romantic" does not refer to romance or love. A romantic work tends to be idealized and overly positive, not showing the gritty, harsh realities of life. In other words, students need to consider whether the story presents the difficult parts of the drummer boy's experience or an optimistic view. Is it realistic or idealized, true to life or romantic?

---

4. When I red you're writing, it was easy to see why you one first place in the essay contest.

5. The advise of the coachs was to weight and continue the meat after the rain stoped.

Project-Based Assessments

Response Essay

The writer of "Drummer Boys" claims "Most of the tales involving drummer boys were romantic works of fiction." Is Bradbury's account an example of one of these "romantic works of fiction" or is it a realistic portrayal of the people and battles involved? Provide evidence from the text to support your point of view.

Write a thesis statement that makes a claim about whether Bradbury's story portrays war as a romantic adventure. Then use direct quotations from the text as evidence to support your claim.

Use the following guidelines for your response essay.	
To receive the highest score, the essay must meet all of these criteria.	Your response essay • makes a claim about whether Bradbury's portrayal of war is romantic or realistic. • provides strong evidence from the text, including direct quotations. • demonstrates an understanding of the ideas found in both texts in the chapter. • uses correct grammar, word usage, punctuation, and spelling.

ELL Support: Project-Based Assessments Have students work in multilevel pairs or groups to write the response and/or argumentative essays. Students can write a paragraph or several paragraphs, depending on their language abilities. Provide the following sentence frames. When students finish their drafts, provide the Informational Writing Revision Checklist (p. 69) and Argumentative Writing Revision Checklist (p. 70) from the ELL Teacher Resource for students to finalize their essays.

- Is the story of the drummer boy true to life?
- I think the story . . . .
- The story shows the drummer boy . . . .
- The story also shows . . . .

Argumentative Essay

The writer of "Drummer Boys" claims "One famous ballad, for example, claimed to tell the mournful end of "The Drummer Boy of Shiloh." Historic research indicates that no such individual existed. . . ." Research to find facts that support or disprove the idea that the drummer boy of Shiloh was a fictional character.

As much as possible, use primary sources such as journals, letters, and newspaper articles from the time period or from eyewitnesses. Also use secondary sources about the Civil War from reliable Internet sources. Keep a thorough record of all sources you consult during your research.

Based on your research, make a claim about whether the drummer boy of Shiloh was a real person. Support your answer with evidence. Follow your teacher's instructions for citing your sources and creating a Works Cited page.

Use the following guidelines for your argumentative essay.	
To receive the highest score, the essay must meet all of these criteria.	Your argumentative essay • makes a claim about the reality of the drummer boy of Shiloh. • supports the claim with evidence from primary and secondary sources. • is based on relevant and sufficient evidence. • is clearly organized and easy to follow. • uses correct grammar, word usage, punctuation, and spelling.

On Your Own: Integrating Ideas

1. Read the rest of *The Drummer Boy of Shiloh*. How does this excerpt affect your understanding of the entire short story?
2. Watch a documentary about either the Revolutionary War or the Civil War. Ken Burns' *The Civil War* is an award-winning account of the conflict. Episode Two: A Very Bloody Affair (1862) covers the Battle of Shiloh.
3. Find online recordings of Revolutionary War or Civil War marches. As you listen, try to hear the cadence of the drums.

Argumentative Essay: Remind students that a convincing argumentative essay should offer evidence, facts, reasons, and other support for their opinion about the drummer boy of Shiloh. It should also account for counterclaims by articulating the opposing opinion and then providing arguments against it.

On Your Own: Integrating Ideas:

Activity 2: Students might be interested in learning that 40 million Americans viewed *The Civil War,* when it first aired on PBS in September 1990. It was restored in 2015. The nine-part, award-winning series contains 16,000 historical photographs, as well as paintings, interviews, letters, and other first-person accounts. Among its distinguished voice actors are Morgan Freeman, Jeremy Irons, Julie Harris, and Sam Waterston. Student volunteers could review different parts of the series and report back to their classmates.

Chapter **17** *(continued)*

Assessment

Connect to Testing: This Connect to Testing section focuses on making inferences, analyzing literary devices, and comparing historical fiction and nonfiction.

Encourage students to work in pairs to choose the correct answers to the questions and then to compare their answers with those of another pair of students. If there is disagreement, encourage the groups to try to reach a consensus as they discuss the reasons for their choices.

Answers to Connect to Testing Questions:

1. **Part A:** B. Choice A is incorrect because the passage indicates that he is crying. Choice C and D are incorrect because he has only been with the regiment for three weeks and no battles are mentioned. Choice C incorrectly understates the boy's emotions about battle. The text supports B.

   Part B: B. Only Choice B reflects any of his fear and anxiety. (DoK 2)

2. Part A: B. Choice A is incorrect because the general's words indicate a knowledge of what war is like. Choice B is supported by the general's references to other battles and his seeming knowledge of what the drummer boys are going through. Choice C might be true of some generals, but it's not specifically supported by the general's words in this passage. Choice D is not specifically stated or implied here; on the contrary, he expresses reluctance about the fighting ahead. (DoK 2)

   (continued)

Connect to Testing

In this chapter you practiced making inferences, analyzing literary devices, and comparing and contrasting historical fiction and historical nonfiction. You will be tested on these skills on reading tests. Answer these questions to help you practice these skills.

1. **Part A:** Which of the following is the best inference about Joby based on the information in the excerpt from "The Drummer Boy of Shiloh"?

   A. He is highly confident and ready for the task ahead of him.

   B. He is somewhat nervous and afraid.

   C. He does not like the idea of heading into battle.

   D. He has fought in several other battles before the current one.

   Part B: Which of the following provides the best evidence for the answer to Part A?

   A. *After that he turned the drum on its side, where its great lunar face peered at him whenever he opened his eyes.*

   B. *"Well," said the voice quietly, "here's a soldier crying before the fight. Good. Get it over. Won't be time once it all starts."*

   C. *"All right, Joby, don't stir." A hand pressed his chest gently, and the boy relaxed. "How long you been with us, Joby?"*
      "Three weeks, sir."

   D. *"Raw, raw, the lot of you. You ready for tomorrow or the next day, Joby?"*
      "I think so, sir."

2. **Part A:** What can you infer about the general's experience, based on the evidence in the excerpt from "The Drummer Boy of Shiloh"?

   A. He is relatively new in the armed forces.

   B. He has been through many battles.

   C. He loves being in the midst of battle.

   D. He would like to lead more soldiers than he does.

ELL Support: Connect to Testing and Assessments See the ELL Teacher Resource (p. 22) for ideas on adapting this section for ELLs.

Remediation: Connect to Testing Work with struggling students on question 2 to find the correct answer (B) and to identify lines that show the general understanding of the real motivations behind fighting and his knowledge of the horror ahead.

Part B: Provide two examples of evidence from the text that supports the answer to Part A.

3. What is one piece of information included in both *The Drummer Boy of Shiloh* and *Drummer Boys*?

A. Drummer boys could be quite young.

B. Drummer boys transmitted messages.

C. Drummer boys sometimes did chores in camps.

D. Drummer boys often helped wounded soldiers.

4. Which of the following could you infer about drummer boys, based on the information in *Drummer Boys*?

A. They were generally ambitious but were not always able to survive war.

B. They were clever and resourceful.

C. They were brave, sometimes surprisingly so.

D. They were able to walk long distances without feeling tired.

Read the following excerpt then answer the question that follows:

> The man's knees cracked as he bent still closer. He smelled as all fathers should smell, of salt-sweat, tobacco, horse and boot leather, and the earth he walked upon. He had many eyes. No, not eyes, brass buttons that watched the boy.

5. Part A: The author's description of the general indicates that he is a(n)

A. ruthless fighter who loves violence.

B. godlike figure who is worshiped by his men.

C. nurturing person who understands his soldiers.

D. old man who is tired of war.

Part B: Provide evidence from the excerpt above to support the answer to Part A.

Part B: Possible answers might include lines that indicate the general understands the real motivations behind fighting and in which he predicts the horrible outcome of the upcoming battle. "Both sides figuring the other side will just give up, and soon, and the war done in weeks and us all home. . . . Well, that's not how it's going to be. We should turn tail and train four months, they should do the same. But here we are, taken with spring fever and thinking it bloodlust, taking our sulphur with cannons instead of with molasses, as it should be—going to be a hero, going to live forever." (DoK 2)

3. A. Only Choice A is supported clearly by both passages. The other information is contained exclusively in "Drummer Boys." (DoK 3)

4. C. Choices A and D are incorrect because the passage doesn't refer to these traits directly and they cannot be inferred from the information provided. Choice B can be inferred from the many duties that they must fulfill, but not all drummer boys were "clever." Answer C is the better choice, given that bravery is demonstrated by the facts about drummer boys in the passage and that bravery is also mentioned directly in the last paragraph. (DoK 2)

5. **Part A:** C. The excerpt does not support any of the other choices; the general does not come across as ruthless, godlike, or tired.

   Part B: The strongest evidence is that he "smelled as all fathers should smell . . . ." This indicates that the general is like a good parent who cares about his children. Also, he doesn't shame the boy for his tears but makes the boy feel better by telling him that he too was crying about the upcoming battle. (DoK 2)

Chapter 18

Analyzing the Structure of a Story

Our Jacko
by Michael Morpurgo

Introduction

Chapter Goals: Have students read through the goals and mark any words that are unfamiliar. Discuss the meanings of any academic vocabulary within the goals that students marked as unfamiliar. Consider posting the Chapter Goals.

Preview Academic Vocabulary: Read and discuss the meanings of the academic vocabulary.

connotation: *the positive or negative association suggested by a word.* The word *courageous* has a positive <u>connotation</u>, while the connotation of *foolhardy* is negative.

figurative language: *language that goes beyond the literal, appealing to the senses through the use of comparison, exaggeration, imagery, and other devices.* <u>Figurative language</u> highlights the gloominess of the story's setting.

mood: *the feeling that a work of literature creates in a reader.* The <u>mood</u> of that Edgar Allan Poe story is eerie and frightening.

theme: *the central meaning or universal truth of a literary text, developed through the characters and their conflicts.* The main <u>theme</u> of this novel is *You have the power to create a happy future for yourself.*

 Gr7Ch18Vocabulary.pptx

---

Chapter 18

Analyzing the Structure of a Story

Preview Concepts

With a partner, share what you know about World War I from classes, books, and other sources.

This picture is a reenactment of a World War I battle. What can you infer about the conditions of the war based on this photo?

ELL Support: Academic Vocabulary See <u>Teaching Vocabulary in the ELL Teacher Resource (p. 18)</u> for ideas to use for teaching vocabulary throughout *Connections*.

Preview Concepts Use the photo on p. 380 to help students gain background information for the text in this chapter. Explain that the soldier in the picture is dressed like a soldier from World War I. Use gestures to explain gas masks. Show pictures of trench warfare from history.com: https://tinyurl.com/ya8ebu95. Videos of WW1 reenactments are also available on this site. Preview these to make sure content is appropriate for your students.

Explain the following vocabulary: *infer* (make a good guess from details) and *conditions* (the way something is). Have students work in multilevel pairs or small groups to answer the questions. Provide the following sentence frames to support students:

• World War I was fought in the years 19. . . .

Making Connections

Read the following excerpt from the poem "Dulce et Decorum Est" by Wilfred Owen, a British soldier who fought in World War I. The title refers to a Latin phrase "It is sweet and fitting to die for one's country."

> Bent double, like old beggars under sacks,
> Knock-kneed, coughing like hags, we cursed through sludge,
> Till on the haunting flares we turned our backs,
> And towards our distant rest began to trudge.
> Men marched asleep. Many had lost their boots,
> But limped on, blood-shod. All went lame; all blind;
> Drunk with fatigue; deaf even to the hoots
> Of gas-shells dropping softly behind.
>
> Gas! GAS! Quick, boys!—An ecstasy of fumbling
> Fitting the clumsy helmets just in time,
> But someone still was yelling out and stumbling
> And flound'ring like a man in fire or lime.—
> Dim through the misty panes and thick green light,
> As under a green sea, I saw him drowning.

Which words and phrases best describe what it is like to be a soldier in World War I? Which words best communicate the author's unique voice?

> **MAKING CONNECTIONS**
>
> In this chapter you will read a story about a soldier who fought in World War I.

The second stanza of the poem describes a gas attack. How does the picture on page 380 help you understand what is happening in this stanza?

Preview Concepts: The photograph shows the soldiers facing a poison-gas attack. It suggests that the situation is frightening and dangerous. The gear looks uncomfortable.

Making Connections:

> **Answers to Making Connections Questions:**
>
> *All went lame; all blind; / Drunk with fatigue;* Students may select different words and phrases from the poem. The picture shows how cumbersome the protective gear was, suggesting the great danger of the situation.

- The war was fought between the countries of . . . .
  The war was . . . .

- I infer that . . . .

ELL Support: Making Connections Have students work in multilevel pairs or groups to read the poem. Instruct them to take notes and draw sketches so they understand and remember the images and details. Students should also work in their multilevel pairs or groups to discuss and write responses to the questions.

Lesson Support

First Read: Analyzing Parallel Stories

Before Reading: Make sure students understand the meaning of *artifact* (an object or item that is produced by the skill of human beings, especially an item of historical interest). Encourage them to give examples, such as pottery, tools, weapons, ornaments, clothing, pictures, or documents. Invite them to predict what the artifact in the story might be and to give their reasons.

Preview Vocabulary: Preview unfamiliar vocabulary to aid comprehension or ask students to circle unfamiliar words as they complete the first read of a text. After the first read, guide students to determine the words' meanings using the context. Encourage students to support their responses with evidence. Have students confirm their initial definitions with a dictionary. Words that students might find difficult include:

intense: *forceful. The argument was so* <u>*intense*</u>*, I feared it would turn violent.*

adamant: *unwavering; firm.* My parents were <u>adamant</u> that I could not attend the late-night party.

irreplaceable: *impossible to replace, or find a substitute for.* My stolen watch, a gift from my father, is <u>irreplaceable</u>.

After Reading: Use the following questions to check comprehension.

Text-Based Discussion Questions

1. What two family artifacts did the narrator and his mother find? *They found the journal and photograph of a family member who died in World War I. The excerpt later mentions a tin hat and shell case.*

2. What experiences did Jacko recall in his letter to Ellie? *He recalled walks along the river with his family.*

3. Why was the family discussion so intense? *Everyone had strong feelings about the journal and whether the narrator should take it to school.*

4. What do you learn about Jacko from the first page of his journal? *He was a lieutenant, an actor, and an Englishman.*

First Read: Analyzing Parallel Stories

This story is about an artifact from World War I and the importance that artifact has for a family.

Objective: Think about how the author tells the story of Jacko from World War I at the same time as he describes the story of Jacko's family and the journal.

---- Second Read

excerpt
Our Jacko
by Michael Morpurgo

	My Thoughts

1   Hidden away under more Christmas decorations, my mother had found a large brown envelope. She gave it to my father. He opened it and took something out.

    "It's here," he said. "The notebook." He turned to the first

5 page and read out loud: "*This book belongs to Lt. Jack Morris, actor, Shakespeare Memorial Theatre, Stratford-upon-Avon.* That's Our Jacko! It's got a title: *In my mind's eye. Thoughts of home, some poems I know and love.*" He turned the notebook over and looked at the back." It says, *To whoever may find*

10 *this, please return it to the theater in Stratford, where I work; or to Ellie, my dear wife, and to Tom, our little son, at Mead Cottage, Charlecote Road, Hampton Lucy. I should be forever grateful. Lt. Jack. Morris, Sherwood Foresters. Ypres, Belgium.* It's his writing, Our Jacko's handwriting, from a hundred years

15 ago," my father said, in a whisper almost.

    At that moment, something fell out of the notebook and onto the table. I picked it up. It was a photograph. A young man in uniform stood there, hand resting on a table beside him, stiff and stern, looking at me out of his black-and-white

20 world. Looking me straight in the eye, knowing—I could see it—that he was going to die, that he was telling me so, too. He looked more like a boy dressing up than a soldier.

Remediation: First Read The parallel stories may make this text challenging for some students. If needed, read the text aloud to the class, stopping periodically to allow students to explain the main point of each section. After the first read, call on volunteers to summarize first Jacko's story and then the narrator's story.

ELL Support: First Read Have students read the excerpt in multilevel pairs or groups, pausing at the end of each page to take notes on the main events and details using a <u>Story Map graphic organizer from the ELL Teacher Resource (p. 52)</u>. Encourage students to take notes and draw sketches in the margins around the story so they can be sure they understand and remember the main events and details. You may also want to read the excerpt aloud as a class, asking for volunteers to read as different characters. Have these volunteers act out the frame story and the story that Jacko tells.

"Here," my father went on, handing the notebook to Otto, "you read it. It's in pencil. I can't read it too well."

25   Otto began to read in a hushed voice. We all listened.

"June 18, 1915

Dearest Ellie,

I hope one day, when all this is over, to come home and bring this little notebook with me. Should it come home
30   *without me, then you will know forever how much you and little Tom are in my thoughts; you, and the walks we went on down the river, and the poems we loved to read together. I will write nothing of this place or of the war. It is a nightmare that one day I shall wake from and then forget. And if I don't*
35   *wake, then you shall never know. I don't want you ever to know.*

I want only to write of the good times, to see them and you again in my mind's eye; to read them again and again, to remind me that there is goodness and beauty and love in this
40   *world, to remind me of you and of our Tom."*

Otto paused for a moment, and then read on:

"Our first walk together:

In my mind's eye . . . I am walking down through the meadows along the river beyond Half Moon Spinney, where
45   *I walked when I was a boy, where I walked with you, Ellie, where one day you and Tom and I will walk together, and I will pick a buttercup and hold it under his chin to see if he likes butter or pick a dandelion clock and puff on it to tell the time.*

It is best as it is now in the early morning, the cows
50   *wandering legless through the mist. I am alone with them and with birdsong. I am walking where Will Shakespeare walked, where he fished, where he dreamed the dreams of*

My Thoughts

Gr7Ch18Read1.pptx

About the Author: Michael Morpurgo (1943–) was born in England during World War II. As a young man, he joined the army, married, had kids, and taught school. While teaching, he started writing stories for his students. Then he and his wife moved and started a farm in Wales. Morpurgo continued writing. In time, he wrote 130 books, including *War Horse, Why the Whales Came,* and *Kensuke's Kingdom. War Horse* was adapted into a play and, later, a movie directed by Steven Spielberg.

Chapter 18 (continued)

Lesson Support

Tech-Connect Suggestion: The National World War I Museum and Memorial website offers online exhibits, a collection database—with photographs, letters, and many items brought back from the war—as well as an interactive World War I timeline. Students can explore many fascinating links from the website at www.theworldwar.org/.

	My Thoughts

his plays and his poems, along the bank where he sat and wrote, maybe. A kingfisher flew for him, too, and it flew for
55 *us once—do you remember, Ellie? As it flies for me now, in my mind's eye. Straight like an arrow on fire out of the mist. And a heron lifts off, unhurried. Heron, kingfisher, they were both taught to fish as I was, by their fathers—and mothers—and I shall teach Tom, when I come home. The river flows slow now,*
60 *in gentle eddies, unhurried. She's taking her time. The aspen trees are quivering in the breeze. The whole world along the river trembles with life."*

No one spoke, not for a long time. Otto was turning the pages of the notebook. . . .

65 I had been looking at the photo of Our Jacko all the time Otto was reading. It was as if I could hear his voice in every word. I turned the photo over. On the back was written: *Jack Morris, my husband, father of Tom, son, actor, soldier. Our Jacko. Born: September 23, 1892, Stratford. Killed: October 20,*
70 *1915, Ypres. He may have no known grave, but he rests in our hearts forever.*

We then had the most intense family discussion I can ever remember, about whether I should or should not take it to school for the exhibit. My father said I could take in the tin
75 hat and the shell case, but that the rest was private and too precious. I argued that no one had thought the notebook precious when it had been stuffed away in an old envelope for years.

It surprised me how adamant my father was about it—but I
80 was even more surprised when Otto piped up in my defense.

"The photo and the notebook may be precious and unique and irreplaceable," he said, "but they tell Our Jacko's story. Everyone should know his story."

World War I helmet

FIRST RESPONSE: KEY IDEAS AND DETAILS

Why does the author tell this story? Write an answer in your response journal. Be sure to use details to support your response, and be ready to defend or explain your answer with the help of those details.

TECH-CONNECT

Post your ideas about the author's purpose to the class website. Include some details that helped you to infer the author's purpose.

Focus on Analyzing Parallel Stories

The excerpt from "Our Jacko" begins with a story about Jacko's ancestors. Then it flashes back to Jacko's experiences during World War I. The author structures the narrative so two parallel stories are being told at the same time. This technique is sometimes called a story-within-a-story. Use the following graphic organizer to analyze the two stories.

Story Element	Jacko	Jacko's Ancestors
Setting	June 18, 1915; Ypres, Belgium	Christmas 2015, (Possibly in England)
Characters	Jacko; his wife, Ellie; their son, Tom	Mother, Father, Otto, narrator
Conflict	World War I; Jacko is also fighting with himself and the horrors of war and the awful things he must do to survive in a war.	Jacko's family is conflicted about whether Jacko's story should be shared with the school.

FIRST RESPONSE: KEY IDEAS AND DETAILS

Point out that often readers must look for clues in writing to determine the author's purpose. Suggest that students begin with the main topic of "Our Jacko" (*World War I*). Encourage them to tell what point the author is making about World War I. (*The war caused great personal loss with effects that were felt across generations.*)

Possible response to author's purpose: The author's purpose was to show the great loss that comes with war and the profound, long-term effect war has on families.

Focus on Analyzing Parallel Stories

Answers to Focus on Analyzing Parallel Stories:

See answers on Student Book insert page to the left.

 Gr7Ch18Read1.pptx

Lesson Support

Speak and Listen: Jocko's candid description of his own conflict causes the conflict among his ancestors about how much of Jocko's story should be shared.

Write: Students can refer to the summary of their Speak and Listen activity when they write their paragraph. Remind them to start with a topic sentence and to provide several supporting details.

Second Read: Exploring Theme

Before Reading: Confirm that students understand the objective. Remind them that the theme of the selection is not the topic. Ask: *What is the topic of "Our Jacko"?* (war / World War I) The theme is a truth about war. It is the meaning of the story. Tell them that the topic can help them figure out the theme, by asking a question such as *What is the story saying about the topic/war?*

After Reading: Use the following questions to check comprehension.

Text-Based Discussion Questions

1. Jacko wrote: *"I will write nothing of this place or of the war."* Why will he write nothing of the place or the war? *Both are too terrible, too horrifying. He doesn't want his wife to be exposed to the horror.*

2. Why does Jacko write about his walks with Ellie and Tom? *The walks take him away from the horror of war to a happier time and place.*

3. What evidence does the story provide to show that the war had a deep effect on Jacko's ancestors? *The journal had been saved for a hundred years. The narrator's family had an intense discussion about whether it should leave the house for the school exhibit. The father was adamant about keeping it at home.*

Focus on Exploring Theme: As necessary, revisit the difference between topic and theme.

🖱 **Gr7Ch18Read2.pptx**

Speak and Listen With a partner, discuss the following question:
- How are the two conflicts in the story related?

Summarize your discussion in the space below.

Write Write a paragraph in which you explain the relationship between the two stories in the excerpt from "Our Jacko."

Second Read: Exploring Theme

Read the story again or listen as your teacher or your classmates read it.

Objective: Underline details and sentences that reveal the theme of the story.

Focus on Exploring Theme

Review the concept of theme by studying the following chart.

What is theme?
Theme
• is the central idea of a story, poem, or other piece of writing.
• can be stated as a sentence that expresses a general, universal truth explored by the author.
• is usually inferred rather than directly stated.
• is supported by the characters, conflict, and resolution.
Theme is NOT
• the topic. Examples: love, friendship, war.
• a summary of what happens.
• the purpose.
• the moral.
• the conflict or problem.

Use the graphic organizer on the following page to help you analyze the theme of this story. Identify details about the characters and the conflict in the text. Then record the theme of the story.

ELL Support: Speak and Listen and Write Have students work in multilevel pairs or small groups to discuss and write about the conflicts, using these sentence frames:

- The conflict told in Jacko's letters is . . . .
- The conflict in the narrator's story is . . . .
- Both stories are connected by . . . .

| Characters: | Jacko: a sensitive, talented, artistic man |
| | Narrator: inquisitive, observant, sensitive |

| Conflict: | War (people against people); conflict among family members about sharing Jacko's diary |

| Theme: | War causes terrible loss that touches families across generations. |

Write Write a short paragraph in which you explain and defend your decision about the theme of the passage. Refer to details from the passage that you used to determine the theme.

CONNECT TO ESSENTIAL QUESTION

Why would someone want to prevent historical facts and personal experiences from being shared?

Third Read: Analyzing Figurative Language

In this story, the writer creates the voice (or perspective) of the narrator Jacko by using figurative language. This in turn contributes to the mood of the story.

Objective: As you read the passage a third time, focus on the section that begins "Our first walk together: . . ." in which Jack describes walking by the river with his wife. Think about the author's use of language in this section of the passage.

Focus on Analyzing Figurative Language

Writers use many kinds of figurative language to make their writing come alive.

- **Simile:** Compares two seemingly different things using *like* or *as*: *as fast as the speed of light, bursting on the scene like a tsunami.*

- **Metaphor:** Says that one thing *is* another: *my love for this city is a firmly rooted tree; the general was a cheetah on the prowl.*

- **Personification:** Gives human qualities to nonhuman things: *The leaves danced in the fall breeze. The trees spread their arms and waved away the birds.*

REFLECT

How do you think Jacko would feel about his journal being put on display?

continued on next page

ELL Support: Write Have students work in multilevel pairs or small groups to discuss and then write about the theme. Provide the following sentence frames to support students. These can also be found as a student handout in the ELL Teacher Resource (p. 40).

- The theme of the passage is . . . .
- One story detail that supports this theme is . . . .
- Another story detail that supports this theme is . . . .

Remediation: Third Read Review the theme chart on p. 386 with students. Then work with them to determine the story theme by asking, *What is the topic of the passage? (war) What is the author saying about war? That is the theme of the story. (War causes terrible loss that touches families across generations.)*

Answers to Focus on Exploring Theme:

See answers on Student Book insert page to the left.

Write: Have students exchange their paragraphs with another student. Then instruct them to identify the theme and underline evidence from the text that the writer uses to support his conclusion about the theme. If the editing students can't do this, he/she should offer suggestions to improve the paragraph.

Reflect: Jacko was an actor, and his profession gives a clue about how he might respond to other people seeing his journal: He was used to performing and was likely comfortable being in front of an audience.

Tech-Connect Suggestion: Students can find a detailed explanation of theme at https://youtu.be/CFToXJehlhA.

Third Read: Analyzing Figurative Language

Before Reading: Explain that *voice* is the author's style or the qualities that make his or her writing unique and communicate his/her (or the character's) personality. For this read students will focus on how the writer creates a unique voice for the character of Jacko. Encourage students to think about how Jacko's voice is different from the narrator's voice. To confirm their understanding, read lines 42–63 together as a class. Discuss examples of language that communicate Jacko's character. Encourage students to indicate why specific words or phrases reveal his voice.

After Reading: Use the following questions to check comprehension.

Text-Based Discussion Questions

1. In what way is the "story within a story" like a flashback? *It gives information about a past event that is connected to the story's present time.*

2. What connections does the "story within a story" have to the story's present time? *The family is connected to Jacko, who is a relative of the narrator, likely a great-great-great grandfather. Jacko's journal provides information about his life and death.*

(continued)

Lesson Support

3. What is revealed about the narrator and his family from their discovery of Jacko's journal? *The story reveals that the narrator has a close-knit family. They discuss what is going on. They are curious and interested in their family history.*

Focus on Analyzing Figurative Language: Remind students that they already learned about sensory language— language that appeals to the senses and helps the readers to see, feel, hear and smell a scene. Similarly, figurative language— similes, metaphors, and personification— breathes life into characters, setting, and events and enables the reader to connect to the ideas and emotions of the story.

Answers to Focus on Analyzing Figurative Language

Possible responses:

See answers on Student Book insert page to the right.

⊕ Gr7Ch18Read3.pptx

Speak and Listen: Remind students that the mood is the atmosphere, or feeling, of the writing. The mood can be positive, for example: cheerful, light-hearted, optimistic, or playful. Or the mood can be negative, for example: pensive, haunting, painful, or pessimistic.
(The mood of "Jacko" is pensive, haunting, and nostalgic.)

Write: Encourage students to begin with a simple topic sentence about the mood of the passage. (i.e., The mood of the passage is _____.) Then they can use their examples of figurative language to support this statement.

Reflect: If the mood of the journal had been pessimistic and painful, they would have been less likely to share it.

Authors generally use figurative language to create the emotional mood of their writing. Mood is the feeling that a work of literature creates in the reader. Some words create strong emotional impressions. The emotional impression of a word or phrase is also called *connotation*.

Fill in the following graphic organizer, identifying three examples of figurative language from "Our Jacko," what they mean, and what effect they achieve through their connotation.

Figurative Language	Meaning	Emotional Effect
Straight like an arrow on fire out of the mist.	The kingfisher moves quickly and mysteriously.	It makes me feel the majesty and beauty of nature.
Heron, kingfisher, they were both taught to fish as I was, by their fathers—and mothers— and I shall teach Tom, when I come home.	He feels a connection with the birds; they are all teachers/students.	It makes me sad, knowing he didn't survive.
The river flows slow now, in gentle eddies, unhurried. She's taking her time. The aspen trees are quivering in the breeze. The whole world along the river trembles with life.	The world is full of life and motion	It makes me feel how interconnected the world is and sad about war.

Speak and Listen With a partner, review your answers to the graphic organizer. Based on your answers, what is the mood of the story?

Write Write a paragraph describing how the figurative language in the passage creates an overall mood. Use your examples from the organizer above as support for your conclusions.

> **REFLECT**
>
> If the emotional effect of the writing in the journal had been different, would the family have been more likely to share the journal?

ELL Support: Third Read Before students reread, use sketches and gestures to make sure they understand the words in the sample similes, metaphors, and personifications. Have students read the excerpt in multilevel pairs or small groups, pausing after each paragraph to sketch images of the figurative language. Once students have reread the excerpts, have students work in their multilevel pairs or groups to complete the chart. Provide this sentence frame for students to use in completing the third column of the chart:

- I feel . . . .
- This language makes me feel . . . .

Write Have students work in multilevel pairs or small groups to discuss and write about figurative language, using these sentence frames:

- The mood of the story is . . . . (The mood of the story is tender and thoughtful.)

Language: Word Meanings

Writers have one main tool to help them communicate their ideas to readers—words. Words may be used in a number of ways, some more subtle or imaginative than others. The chart below contains some tips about word relationships and nuances of meaning. Understanding the uses of language will make you a better reader and writer.

Word Relationships	
Two words that mean the same thing are called *synonyms*.	*wild* and *feral*
	tired and *weary*
Two words that have opposite meanings are called *antonyms*.	*dim* and *bright*
	polite and *rude*
An analogy uses a comparison to communicate a relationship or to explain complex ideas.	*I am to this town what Hadrian was to his wall: a builder.*

Nuanced Meanings
Words have a *denotation* (dictionary definition) and a *connotation* (positive or negative association). Writers choose words with connotations that fit their point of view and influence the reader. Consider the difference between a *cheap trinket* and an *inexpensive figurine*. Which phrase paints the object in a more positive light?
Which of the following words communicates a greater degree of anger?
His racist comments <u>bothered</u> me.
His racist comments <u>infuriated</u> me.
Choose words that fit the nuanced meaning you want to communicate.

Read the sentences below, all of which contain examples of figurative language. Answer the questions after each sentence.

1. After wandering around for several hours, we came to the movie theater, only to find that it was completely empty. Rewrite the sentence with an antonym for *empty*?

What different impression does the sentence give?

Language: Word Meanings: Make sure students understand the difference between denotation (dictionary definition) and connotation. Ask them what denotation *sleepy* and *exhausted* share. *(Both mean "tired.")* Encourage them to explain the difference in connotation. (Sleepy *has the connotation of slightly tired or drowsy, whereas* exhausted *connotes extreme fatigue.)* Use additional examples as needed: *chef/cook; clever/sneaky; smile/smirk.*

Encourage students to use online tools to help them choose the best words for their writing. Display a word entry on merriam-webster.com. Demonstrate how to use the Thesaurus tab to find synonyms and antonyms. Also show students where they can scroll down within the dictionary tab and find synonyms, antonyms, related words, and near antonyms.

Answers to Language Exercises:

1. packed; full

   With an antonym, the sentence would suggest that it might be difficult to get a seat.

 Gr7Ch18Language.pptx

- An example of figurative language that shows this is . . . .
- Another example of figurative language that shows this is . . . .

ELL Support: Language Word webs are a useful way to visually illustrate word connections. Challenge students to create extensive word webs, starting with the vocabulary in the Language lesson. Also, support students with understanding connotations by reminding students that *connotation* means "the positive or negative feeling you get from a word." Provide ELL online or print dictionaries so students can look up the meanings of *bothered* and *infuriated* to decide which is stronger and angrier. Have students work in multilevel pairs or groups to complete the numbered exercises. Review and explain correct responses as a class.

Chapter **18** *(continued)*

Assessment

Answers to Language Exercises:

2. *Disobedient* has a negative connotation that the child is behaving badly; *disciplined* carries the negative connotation of a punishment. However, *disciplined* has a more positive connotation than *punished*.

   The lively child was encouraged by the teacher.

3. The analogy means that Longbottom isn't very intelligent by comparing how much gold the Weasleys have with the amount of brains Longbottom has. The Weasleys are poor, thus, Longbottom is being insulted.

Project-Based Assessments

Letter: Students might begin by brainstorming first-person responses to the following questions: *What do you feel about Jacko's brave death? What do you feel about finding his journal? What do you feel about learning details of his life? What do you find most poignant, interesting, and/or surprising that you learned about him? What three questions would you like to ask him? Why are you interested in finding out that information? What would you like to tell him about yourself? What would you like to tell him about contemporary life?*

2. The <u>disobedient</u> child was <u>disciplined</u> by the teacher. What are the connotations or nuanced meanings of the underlined words in the sentence?

Rewrite the sentence, replacing the underlined words to give the sentence a different connotation.

3. Explain the following analogy from J. K. Rowling: "Longbottom, if brains were gold, you'd be poorer than Weasley, and that's saying something."

Project-Based Assessments

Letter

Write a letter from the narrator of the story to Jacko. The letter should describe the narrator's feelings about Jacko's bravery, as well as his happiness to have Jacko's notebook. Include questions that the narrator might want to ask Jacko. The letter could tell something about life in the present day, as well.

Begin by conducting research on WWI so that you can ask appropriate questions in your letter. When searching for information to add to your letter, use search terms such as *World War I* and *Ypres*. You can also search for other details from Jacko's story, such as *Stratford-upon-Avon*.

Next, write a letter that has at least three paragraphs, each exploring a different topic or question.

As you edit your letter, review the rubric on the next page so that you will know what is expected of you.

ELL Support: Project-Based Assessments—Letter Have students work in multilevel pairs or groups to write the letter. Provide a <u>Letter Format Template from the ELL Teacher Resource (p. 55)</u>. As a class, brainstorm sentence frames for the letter such as the following:

- My name is . . . . I am . . . .
- I found your notebook in . . . .
- I felt . . . when I read your notebook.

Use the following guidelines for your letter.	
To receive the highest score, the letter must meet all of these criteria.	Your letter • contains examples and details that show that you understand the characters in the original story. • includes questions to Jacko about the war and his experiences. • is logically organized and formatted as a letter. • uses correct grammar, word usage, punctuation, and spelling.

Oral Presentation

Imagine you are the narrator of the story and must give a presentation about Jacko and World War I in class. Write a presentation that explains who the notebook belonged to, why the notebook was returned to the narrator's family, and what the notebook means to the narrator. Base your presentation on the story and fill in missing details as needed.

When developing the presentation, stay focused on the subject. Your goal is to teach fellow students about World War I as well as describing the notebook and the life events associated with it.

Include visual aids, such as pictures of soldiers and artillery. Make sure your pictures are appropriate and not overly graphic.

Practice your presentation so that you can speak confidently. Use note cards as needed, but make eye contact with your audience.

Use the following guidelines for your presentation.	
To receive the highest score, the letter must meet all of these criteria.	Your presentation • contains examples and details that show that you understand the original story and where the narrator fits in it. • includes visual aids that help your audience understand your subject. • is presented in a professional manner that demonstrates adequate preparation. • uses correct grammar, word usage, punctuation, and spelling.

On Your Own: Integrating Ideas

1. Read a first person account by a soldier who served in World War I, preferably at Ypres. What do you learn from this account that the story doesn't necessarily tell you?
2. Find other letters written by World War I soldiers to their families. What do these letters tell you about the war?
3. Read poetry written by soldiers who fought in WWI. A good resource is warpoetry.co.uk. Share your favorite with your classmates.

Oral Presentation: Encourage students to create a simple chart or outline with a section for each part of their presentation:

- Section 1: who the notebook belonged to
- Section 2: why the notebook was returned to the narrator's family
- Section 3: what the notebook means to the narrator

Under each section they should identify whether information that can be found in the story; whether it requires research about World War I; whether it depends on their own ideas/imagination. They can use this as a preliminary outline for developing their presentation.

On Your Own: Integrating Ideas:

Activity 1 and 2: At the Library of Congress World War I: Stories from the Veterans History Project, students can find letters and other firsthand accounts.

Remediation: On Your Own: Integrating Ideas Have students work with a partner to find and analyze a letter from the Library of Congress.

ELL Support: Project-Based Assessments—Oral Presentation Have students work in multilevel pairs or groups to write, practice, and perform the oral presentation. Each member of the group can participate in aspects of the project as their language skills allow. For example, beginning and intermediate students can create and label the visuals while advanced students write and deliver the oral presentation. When students finish their drafts, provide the Informational Writing Revision Checklist from the ELL Teacher Resource (p. 69) for students to finalize their presentations. Allow time for students to practice their oral presentations in multilevel pairs or groups before delivering them to the class.

Assessment

Connect to Testing: This Connect to Testing section focuses on making inferences, identifying theme, and analyzing the interaction of multiple story lines.

Encourage students to work in pairs to choose the correct answers to the questions and then to compare their answers with those of another pair of students. If there is disagreement, encourage the groups to try to reach a consensus as they discuss the reasons for their choices.

Answers to Connect to Testing Questions:

1. **Part A:** B. The passage does not support the idea that the narrator's father is possessive (Choice A); selfish (Choice C); or negative about the assignment. (Choice D). Only Choice B makes sense given information in the passage.

    Part B: A, E. Choices B, C, and D do not refer to the father, but instead to other characters: Jacko (B), the narrator (C), and the entire family (D). Only A and E reference the father and support the answer in Part A. (DoK 2)

2. A. The story is about the connection of the past to the present, and a central theme relates to this topic. While family love is a topic of the story, the story does not suggest that love rises above all earthly conflicts (Choice B). Jacko is loyal to his country, but the story does not suggest that loyalty is the greatest virtue (Choice C). Jacko appears to be courageous, but the story does not focus on his courage (Choice D). (DoK 2)

3. **Part A:** D.

    Part B: B., C. In these lines, Jacko focuses on the people he loves. (DoK 2)

    (continued)

Connect to Testing

Questions on reading tests may ask you to analyze the structure of a story, identify theme, and analyze the effects of figurative language. Often a second part of the question will test your ability to find textual evidence that supports the correct inference. Answer the following questions.

1. **Part A:** Based on the passage, what would you most likely infer about the narrator's father?

    A. He is possessive of his personal items.

    B. He respects and honors Jacko.

    C. He prefers to get his own way in family conflicts.

    D. He doesn't like the narrator's school assignment.

    Part B: Which of the following lines from the excerpt best supports the answer to Part A? Choose two.

    A. *It's his writing, Our Jacko's handwriting, from a hundred years ago," my father said, in a whisper almost.*

    B. *I will write nothing of this place or of the war. It is a nightmare that one day I shall wake from and then forget.*

    C. *It was as if I could hear his voice in every word. I turned the photo over. On the back was written:* Jack Morris, my husband, father of Tom, son, actor, soldier.

    D. *We then had the most intense family discussion I can ever remember, about what I should or should not take it to school for the exhibit.*

    E. *My father said I could take in the tin hat and the shell case, but that the rest was private and too precious.*

2. Which of the following best describes the theme of the story?

    A. Stories from the past should be shared with future generations.

    B. Love rises above all earthly conflicts.

    C. Loyalty to one's country is the greatest virtue.

    D. At times one must have courage when courage seems impossible.

3. **Part A:** Jacko's journal is used as a

    A. record of wartime events.

    B. notebook to keep his poems and writings in.

    C. list of things he wanted to do when he got home.

    D. way to focus on the people he loved.

Remediation: Connect to Testing Students might find it helpful to read the questions and responses with a partner before answering.

Part B: Which of the following lines from the excerpt best support the answer to Part A? Choose two.

A. *I hope one day, when all this is over, to come home and bring this little notebook with me.*

B. *you will know forever how much you and little Tom are in my thoughts; you, and the walks we went on down the river, and the poems we loved to read together.*

C. *I want only to write of the good times, to see them and you again in my mind's eye . . .*

D. *It is best as it is now in the early morning, the cows wandering legless through the mist . . .*

E. *The aspen trees are quivering in the breeze. The whole world along the river trembles with life.*

4. Describe the relationship between the two stories in the excerpt. How does one story affect the other? Refer to details from the text to support your answer.

4. The two stories share a connection to Jacko, who is a relative of the narrator, likely a great-great-great grandparent, and the author of a recently discovered journal from World War I. His journal provides information about Jacko's life and death. The discovery leads to an intense family discussion/interaction about whether the details of Jacko's journal are too private to be shared with others. Jocko's conflict about sharing the horrors of war with his family becomes wrapped up in the conflict of his ancestors. How much should they share? When is something too private or too difficult? Ultimately, the family decides that openness is the best way to honor their ancestor. (DoK 2)

ELL Support: Connect to Testing and Assessments See the ELL Teacher Resource (p.22) for ideas on adapting this section for ELLs.

Chapter 19

Analyzing an Author's Portrayal of War

Fallen Angels
by Walter Dean Myers

Introduction

Chapter Goals: Have students read through the goals and mark any words that are unfamiliar. Discuss the meanings of any academic vocabulary within the goals that students marked as unfamiliar. Consider posting the Chapter Goals.

Preview Academic Vocabulary: Read and discuss the meanings of the academic vocabulary.

appositive phrase: *a group of words that renames or gives more information about a noun; often includes a noun and any modifiers.* In the following sentence, the words "my friend from middle school" form an <u>appositive phrase</u>: Litauo, my friend from middle school, moved to New York City.

dramatic irony: *a situation in which the audience or reader knows something that the character(s) don't know.* <u>Dramatic irony</u> in the play creates suspense over whether the main character will discover the ambush that could end his life.

point of view: *the perspective, position, or outlook from which a story is told.* The novel's omniscient <u>point of view</u> gives the thoughts of all the characters.

prepositional phrase: *a group of words that begins with a preposition and ends with an object.* "Down the sidewalk" and "across the school yard" are <u>prepositional phrases</u>.

verbal phrase: *a group of words that includes a verb form but acts as another part of speech. Verbal phrases include gerund phrases, participial phrases, and infinitive phrases.* Being good comes easy for me. *Being good* is a <u>verbal phrase</u>.

Chapter 19

Analyzing an Author's Portrayal of War

Preview Concepts

Irony is a literary term that has to do with a difference between expectations and reality. One type of irony is dramatic irony. Dramatic irony is a difference between what the reader or audience knows and what one or more of the characters know. Dramatic irony can add suspense or humor to a story.

Suppose you are watching a sit-com in which Jack and Maggie are sitting in Maggie's apartment. They kiss. Suddenly there is a knock on the door. It's Emma, Jack's girlfriend! Jack hides in the bathroom. Emma comes in. Upset, she tells Maggie that she thinks Jack is cheating on her. Maggie reassures Emma that Jack is faithful. Emma then goes into detail about what a great friend Maggie is as Maggie tries to come up with supportive answers.

With a partner, discuss how this is an example of dramatic irony. What does the audience know that Emma doesn't know?

What emotions does this create in the viewer?

Can you think of any other examples of dramatic irony from books, memes, or movies?

ELL Support: Academic Vocabulary See <u>Teaching Vocabulary in the ELL Teacher Resource (p. 18)</u> for ideas to use for teaching vocabulary throughout *Connections*.

Preview Concepts Draw a series of sketches similar to a comic strip to illustrate the ironic scene described here. Use gestures and speech bubbles to explain what is happening and words like *audience* and *viewers* (pointing to the students and pantomiming watching or viewing something). Have students work in multilevel pairs or small groups to answer the questions using the following sentence frames:

• The audience knows that . . . .

• The viewer feels . . . .

• Another example of dramatic irony is when . . . .

Making Connections

Read the following excerpt from Lyndon Baines Johnson's speech about the Vietnam War from April 7, 1965.

> Why are we in South Vietnam?
>
> We are there because we have a promise to keep. Since 1954 every American president has offered support to the people of South Vietnam. We have helped to build, and we have helped to defend. Thus, over many years, we have made a national pledge to help South Vietnam defend its independence.
>
> And I intend to keep that promise.
>
> To dishonor that pledge, to abandon this small and brave nation to its enemies, and to the terror that must follow, would be an unforgivable wrong.

With a partner, discuss the following questions.

1. How does Johnson answer the question about why America is fighting in Vietnam?

2. What do you know about the Vietnam War based on what you've seen and read?

> **MAKING CONNECTIONS**
>
> In this chapter you will read a story about African American soldiers in the Vietnam War and analyze their points of view of the war.

 Gr7Ch19Vocabulary.pptx

Preview Concepts: Offer students some examples of dramatic irony, and then ask volunteers for additional suggestions.
Examples:

During the movie *Titanic*, the audience is aware that the ship will hit an iceberg and sink, but the passengers have no idea.

In *Romeo and Juliet*, the audience knows Juliet has taken a sleeping potion, but Romeo thinks she is dead.

In *The Truman Show*, the audience knows that Truman is "the show," on view for everyone, but Truman only learns this fact over time.

In many horror movies, the audience knows that a killer is in the house (or room or car), but a character, who is clueless, enters anyway.

Making Connections:

> **Possible Answers to Questions:**
>
> 1. Johnson said that America had made a promise to defend South Vietnam's independence, a promise the country must keep.
>
> 2. Answers may vary, but students may be aware that the United States, after many protests and great disagreement, did leave South Vietnam, ending United States support in that civil war.

ELL Support: Making Connections Provide background knowledge about the Vietnam War. Students should understand that the war was long (1954–1975). Many people in the U.S. didn't like the war because many Americans died. Then have students work in multilevel pairs or groups to read the excerpt, pausing to take notes on a Main Ideas and Supporting Details graphic organizer from the ELL Teacher Resource (p. 51). Students should also work in their multilevel pairs or groups to discuss and write responses to the questions, using these sentence frames:

- America was fighting in Vietnam because . . . .
- I know that the Vietnam War was . . . .

Chapter 19 *(continued)*

Lesson Support

First Read: Analyzing the Impact of Setting on Conflict

Before Reading: Activate background knowledge by inviting students to discuss what they know about the impact of war on young men going into battle for the first time. Remind them about the Ray Bradbury short story, "The Drummer Boy of Shiloh." How would a soldier likely feel before and after a conflict? *(Before: fear, anticipation, worry. After: shock, relief, worry about the next battle.)*

Instruct students to read the introduction and objective with a partner or to listen as you read the introduction and objective aloud. Use a think-aloud strategy to model how to find and underline details about the setting. Remind students that during the first read of the close reading process, they should focus on the key ideas or answering the question *What is this text mainly about?*

Preview Vocabulary: Preview unfamiliar vocabulary to aid comprehension. Ask students to circle unfamiliar words as they complete the first read of a text. After the first read, guide students to determine the words' meanings using the context. Encourage students to support their responses with evidence. Have students confirm their initial definitions with a dictionary. Words that students might find difficult include:

truce: *cease fire. The soldiers stopped fighting, as soon as leaders from both sides agreed to a* truce.

gung ho: *enthusiastic, combative.* Although the new soldiers seemed gung ho at first, their eager attitude quickly changed.

quota: *the part due from (or to) a particular person or group.* The new salesperson just made her quota for the month, selling five cars.

orientation: *training.* During the orientation, the nurse's aides took patients' temperatures.

First Read: Analyzing the Impact of Setting on Conflict

The Vietnam War was a long, drawn-out conflict that started in 1954 and ended in 1975. The United States was slowly drawn into the war between communist North Vietnam and anti-Communists in South Vietnam.

This story describes fighting in 1968 Vietnam, from the point of view of Richie Perry, an African American teen. Unable to afford college, Perry enlists in the army and is sent to Vietnam where he befriends Peewee, another African American teen.

Objective: As you read, identify details about the setting. Think about how the author reveals details about what it is like to fight in Vietnam.

—— First Read

---- Second Read

—— Third Read

excerpt
Fallen Angels
by Walter Dean Myers

	My Thoughts

1   Saturday. My ninth day in country. The army paper *Stars and Stripes* was full of the truce talks in Paris, but the <u>war</u> was still going on. In the distance F-100's streaked across the sky. I saw a lot of planes, mostly jets and helicopters, and all ours. I didn't

5   see any enemy planes. I didn't even know If they had any. . . .

I was less nervous than I was when I first got in country. <u>We were in Nam to stop the North Vietnamese from taking over South Vietnam.</u> I didn't feel really gung ho or anything, but I was ready to do my part.

Perry: Not excited

10   One of the new guys who came in was from **Fort Dix**. He looked like one of the characters from an **Archie Andrews comic**, but he was <u>so scared</u> it wasn't funny. He told us his name was Jenkins.

"What's it like so far?" he asked Peewee.

Jenkins: Afraid

15   "Ain't nothing to it," Peewee said.

"You been here long?" Jenkins asked.

Fort Dix: an Army training base in New Jersey
Archie Andrews comic: a popular comic strip during the 1950s and 1960s

396   Chapter 19 • Unit 4   ©Perfection Learning® • No Reproduction Permitted

---

ELL Support: First Read Explain that Peewee is teasing Jenkins—"pulling his leg." Students might not be familiar with this idiomatic expression that the narrator uses at the end of the conversation between Peewee and Jenkins. Focus on the start of their conversation, underscoring the fact that the narrator says Peewee is lying.

Have students read the excerpt in multilevel pairs or groups, pausing at the end of each page to take notes on the main events and details using a story map and/or creating a graphic organizer version of the story. Encourage students to also take notes and draw sketches in the margins around the story so they can understand and remember the main events and details. You may also want to read the excerpt aloud as a class, with volunteers each taking a role and acting out the story.

396   Grade 7 • Chapter 19   Connections • © Perfection Learning®

"Eight months," Peewee lied. "I got to kill eight more Cong before I get my quota. Then I can go home."

20 "How many you kill so far?"

"A hundred and thirty-two," Peewee said. "I weigh a hundred and forty. Whatever you weigh, that's how many you got to kill to leave early."

"I never heard of that," Jenkins said.

25 "That ain't for regular rotation," Peewee went on. "That's just so you can leave early."

"Oh." Jenkins took it all in.

"Air force guys can get their quota in one or two days," Peewee said.

30 "What did you do, machine gun most of them?" Jenkins' eyes were wide.

"No, man," Peewee shook his head. "They issue you so many bullets per week, see? But each one you turn back in you get a quarter for. So mostly I sneak up on the suckers and cut their

35 throats. That way I save my bullets. Way I figure, by the time I get back to the World I have me enough to buy a little Chevy."

"None of that is true," Jenkins said. He was pissed at Peewee for pulling his leg.

The sergeant came in and picked three guys for guard

40 duty. The ranger volunteered again, and they got Jenkins and one other guy. Jenkins was shaking when he left the **hooch**.

"Don't forget to save your bullets!" Peewee called out to him.

That night the mosquitoes ate us up. I had bites all over my body. Back home I thought mosquitoes never bit black people.

45 Not as much as they bit white people, anyway. Maybe Vietnamese mosquitoes just bit blacks and whites and didn't bite Asians.

My Thoughts

Peewee: teases new kid to cover his fear

humor

Jenkins: Naive about war

humor

---

hooch: small huts used to house soldiers

©Perfection Learning® • No Reproduction Permitted   Chapter 19 • Unit 4   397

After Reading: Use the following questions to check comprehension.

Text-Based Discussion Questions

1. The narrator says, "I didn't feel really gung ho or anything, but I was ready to do my part." What did he mean? *Even though he wasn't enthusiastic about fighting, he would support his country and do his job.*

2. What did the lieutenant warn the men about during the orientation? *He warned them about the enemy, malaria, the black market, and drugs.*

3. Why did the narrator and Peewee get silent at the end, when they were waiting for the plane? *They were scared.*

Gr7Ch19Read1.pptx

© Perfection Learning® • Connections   Grade 7 • Chapter 19   397

Lesson Support

About the Author: Walter Dean Myers (1937–2012) got teased as a kid because of a speech impediment. He found comfort in books. Myers's mother died when he was little, and he was raised by a family in Harlem. A high school English teacher advised him to write—no matter what. He joined the army and struggled to survive and write. Then he discovered James Baldwin, the African American writer whose work inspired Myers to write about his own life. Myers was the author of many books—including *Jazz, Lockdown, Monster,* and *Master Juba*—and the recipient of many awards.

We finally got the orientation lecture. This young-looking lieutenant showed us a slide of a map of Nam. Then he showed us where we were.

50 "You are not in Disneyland," he said. "The little people you see running around over here are not **Mouseketeers**. Some of them are friendly, and some of them have a strong desire to kill you. If you remember that, and manage to kill them before they kill you, then you have a good chance of getting through

55 your year of service here.

"Take your pills. Once a week for **malaria**, twice a week if you're too stupid to remember the day you last took them. . . .

"Stay away from the **black market**. Anything you buy that's worth a damn will be taken away from you, or you'll

60 lose it.

"Stay away from dope. There's only two kinds of people in Nam. People who are alert twenty-four hours a day, and people who are dead.

"If you see anything else they got over here that we don't

65 have at home, stay away from it. What these people use on a daily basis will kill you as fast as an RPG."

"What's an RPG?" a guy in the front asked.

"That's a rocket-propelled grenade. Stay away from them, too. If you have any more questions, ask your unit commanders

70 when you reach them. Good luck."

When we got outside, the mosquitoes got us. The lieutenant hadn't even mentioned them, but we had been given a supply of insect **repellent**.

Mouseketeers: actors on a television show centered around the famous cartoon character Mickey Mouse, popular in the 1950s and 1960s
malaria: a disease transmitted by the bite of a mosquito
black market: illegal trading of goods that are not allowed to be bought and sold
repellent: bug spray

My Thoughts

Lieutenant: War is a job. It's about survival.

Orders. Me, Peewee, Jenkins, and another guy were
75 assigned to the 196th. We were going to Chu Lai. I
remembered that was where Judy Duncan was assigned.

"What's that like?" Jenkins asked the sergeant in
headquarters.

"That's First Corps," the sergeant said. "All you do up there
80 is look around for charlie, and when you see him you call the
marines. Light stuff."

"Charlie?" Jenkins looked toward me and Peewee.

"Charlie is the bad guy over here." The sergeant put his
arm around Jenkins' shoulders. He was obviously enjoying
85 himself. "Sometimes we call him charlie, sometimes we call him
Victor Charlie, sometimes we call him Vietcong. That is, unless
he sends us his business card with his full name and address
on it."

We packed our gear and lined up outside, waiting for the
90 truck to the airport. We were going to Chu Lai in a C-47. I
thought guys from other hooches were going, but there were
only the four of us.

"I bet I kill me a Cong before you get one," Peewee said.

"You can have them all," I said. . . .

95 Peewee didn't say much after that and neither did I. I was
scared. My mouth was going dry, and I could see that Peewee
was scared, too. Jenkins was crying. It made me feel a little
better to see him crying like that.

"Load 'em up!"

100 Me and Peewee got on the trucks between boxes of
peanut butter, and started to the airport and to wherever the
hell Chu Lai was.

My Thoughts

Sergeant: Uses humor
to downplay the
seriousness of war
humor

All are afraid.

Lesson Support

FIRST RESPONSE: KEY IDEAS AND DETAILS

Ask a volunteer to read the second paragraph of the selection and identify the sentence that gives the narrator's initial view of the war. *(I didn't feel really gung ho or anything, but I was ready to do my part.)* Point out that they can infer from other evidence that the narrator's feelings are more complex than his initial explanation suggests. Ask: *What does the narrator say about the danger and discomfort that soldiers faced? How does he convey this information?*

Focus on Analyzing the Impact of Setting on Conflict:
Call on a volunteer to read the paragraph that introduces *Fallen Angels* and explains the story setting. Ask whether the Vietnam War is an internal or external conflict. *(External: people versus people)* Encourage them to look for internal conflicts and additional external conflicts that develop because of the setting.

Answers to Focus on Analyzing the Impact of Setting on Conflict:

1. The setting is a frightening place of death, destruction, and discomfort, with mysterious but dangerous enemy soldiers.

2. The setting is dangerous with treacherous enemies who will kill you if you don't kill them; with dangerous diseases, and vicious insects; with a black market that sells dangerous items, especially drugs that can dull your senses and make you more vulnerable to the enemy.

3. person vs. person—American soldiers vs. enemy soldiers
   soldiers vs. drug dealers and black marketeers

(continued)

🖱 **Gr7Ch19Read1.pptx**

FIRST RESPONSE: KEY IDEAS AND DETAILS

Write a sentence that describes the narrator Perry's point of view of the war. Write your answer in your response journal. Include evidence from the passage that supports your inference.

TECH-CONNECT

Post your answer to the First Response question to your class website. Read two of your classmate's answers and comment positively on them.

Focus on Analyzing the Impact of Setting on Conflict

For many novels, especially historical fiction, the setting directly impacts the conflict faced by the characters. In this excerpt, the author doesn't go into great detail about the setting. The reader must infer what war-torn Vietnam is like based on what characters say and do.

1. What can you infer about the setting from the narrator's thoughts and feelings?

2. What can you infer about the setting from the orientation lecture given by the lieutenant?

3. Based on what you learn about the setting, describe the conflicts that result. Use the following types of conflict to help you.
   person vs. person—

©Perfection Learning® • No Reproduction Permitted

ELL Support: First Response and Focusing on Analyzing the Impact of Setting on Conflict Before students respond to the questions, review definitions of *point of view, evidence, inference, setting,* and *conflict.* Have students work in multilevel pairs or small groups to discuss and write about point of view, setting, and conflict, using these prompts and sentence frames for the exercises on pp. 400–401.

First Response: Perry's point of view of the war is . . . .
For example, he . . . . Also, he . . . .

1. What is the setting like? How do Perry's thoughts and feelings show the setting?

A: The setting is . . . . For example, Perry says, " . . . ."
Also, Perry feels . . . .

2. How does the lieutenant's speech show the setting?

person vs. nature—

person vs. self—

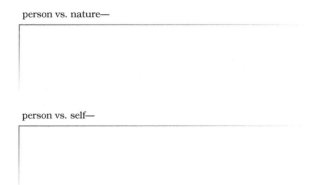

Write Summarize what it is like to fight in the Vietnam War based on the excerpt. Explain how the setting results in multiple conflicts.

Second Read: Making Inferences About Characters

With your class or a small group of students, read the text aloud assigning the parts of Perry (the narrator), Peewee, Jenkins, the lieutenant, and the sergeant.

Objective: As you read the passage, make inferences about how each character views the war and how it affects his interactions with other characters. Write your inferences in the My Thoughts sidebar. Underline evidence that supports your inferences.

Focus on Making Inferences About Characters

This excerpt reveals much about the main characters, Perry, Peewee, Jenkins, the lieutenant, and the sergeant, and their points of view of the Vietnam War.

Myers keeps his description of the characters to a minimum. Instead, he allows the readers to understand what the characters are like based on how they interact with each other. Fill in the following chart to help you analyze the characters in the story. For Perry, Peewee, and Jenkins, fill in **three** examples of what each says/does and **three** explanations of what each is like. For the lieutenant and sergeant, fill in **one** example and **one** explanation.

continued on next page

A: The lieutenant says, ". . . ." This shows that the setting is . . . .

3. The characters have conflicts with other characters. For example, ...

The characters have conflicts with nature. For example, ...

The characters have conflicts with themselves. For example, ...

ELL Support: Write Have students work in multilevel pairs or small groups to write about setting. Provide the following sentence frames to support students:

- The setting of the story is . . . .
- Because of the setting, the characters struggle with . . . .
- One conflict is . . . .
- Another type of conflict is . . . .
- An example of this conflict is . . . .

person vs. nature—soldiers vs. malaria
soldiers vs. vicious mosquitoes

person vs. self—soldiers vs. their own fear
soldiers vs. their own bad decisions

Write: Encourage students to use their answers to the Focus questions as an outline to answer the Write question.

Second Read: Making Inferences About Characters

Before Reading: Read aloud the introduction and objective with students, making certain they understand the activity. If necessary, remind students that an *inference* is a conclusion that is based on background knowledge and evidence.

Assign the following parts: Perry (the narrator), Peewee, Jenkins, the lieutenant, and the sergeant. While reading and/or listening, have students annotate the text by inferring how each character views the war.

After Reading: Use the following questions to check comprehension.

Text-Based Discussion Questions

1. How is the narrator's reaction to fighting the war different from Peewee's? How is it similar? *The narrator doesn't joke about the war as Peewee does; however, like Peewee, he doesn't express his fear directly.*

2. How does Jenkins' reaction to fighting the war differ from Peewee's? *Jenkins shows his fear directly, unlike Peewee.*

3. What is the purpose of the lieutenant's orientation? *The purpose is to prepare new soldiers and enhance their chances of survival.*

Focus on Making Inferences About Characters: After completing the inference charts, lead a discussion about stock characters that writers often use. A stock character is often a stereotype. Writers use these characters because they don't take much time to develop. The reader can easily identify the role the character will play in the action. Examples include the crazy criminal mastermind and the dumb henchman, the nerd, and the innocent. Ask: Is Jenkins a stock character in this excerpt? Is he the typical innocent? Have students make predictions about what will happen to Jenkins.

Lesson Support

Answers to Focus on Making Inferences About Characters:

See answers to the second and third columns in Student Book insert page to the right.

Answers to fourth column: What is his point of view of the war?

Perry: 1. He accepts the war and his duty to fight.
2. He understands that discomfort is a fact of war, and he's just trying to get through it all.
3. He recognizes that war is terrible.

Peewee: 1. Peewee is afraid of fighting but in order to distract himself from his fear, he picks on Jenkins who is naive and has no emotional resources to hide his fear.
2. He makes a challenge but in reality he is very scared. It's a coping mechanism.
3. He doesn't want to think about how terrible the war is and how awful it is to have to fight.

Jenkins: 1.–3. Jenkins is terrified of the war. He has little experience and no emotional ability to even pretend that he is brave.

The lieutenant: 1. He knows that war is about outsmarting or outfighting the enemy, and he wants to prepare the men for it. He has no illusions about what war is like, but it's a job for him.

The sergeant: 1. He seems hardened toward the war. He talks about "Charlie" as if he's been fighting for years. He understands the ins and outs of war.

 Gr7Ch19Read2.pptx

Character	What he says/does How he interacts with other characters	What is he like?	What is his point of view of the war?
Perry	1. "I was less nervous than I was when I first got in country. . . . I didn't feel really gung ho or anything, but I was ready to do my part." 2. *That night the mosquitoes ate us up. I had bites all over my body.* 3. *Peewee didn't say much after that and neither did I. I was scared.*	1. He is unsure but willing to fight. 2. He is matter-of-fact and resigned about the discomfort he must face. 3. He is honest and observant.	See answers in shaded box to the left.
Peewee	1. *"A hundred and thirty-two," Peewee said. "I weigh a hundred and forty. Whatever you weigh, that's how many you got to kill to leave early."* 2. *"I bet I kill me a Cong before you get one," Peewee said.* 3. *Peewee didn't say much after that and neither did I.*	1. He directs his humor toward enlistees who are greener than he is. 2. He makes a bold challenge in order to show his bravery. 3. He feels fear as much as the next soldier but it doesn't always come out directly.	
Jenkins	1. *"What did you do, machine gun most of them?" Jenkins' eyes were wide.* 2. *Jenkins was shaking when he left the hooch.* 3. *Jenkins was crying.*	1. He is naive and unfamiliar with war. He is gullible. 2. He fears that he will die and he recognizes that war is about death and dying. 3. He is too innocent to even try to cover-up his fear.	

ELL Support: Speak and Listen Have students work in multilevel pairs or small groups to discuss and complete the chart. Encourage students to draw pictures with labels in the third column to communicate what the characters are feeling. Explain vocabulary words, including *honest* (tells the truth), *teasing* (laughing at someone, making jokes about someone), *bragging* (saying you are great), *brave* (not scared), *innocent* (knows very little, believes others easily), and *afraid* (scared).

When students complete the chart, have them discuss it in new multilevel pairs or small groups. Provide the following sentence frames for the discussion:

- . . . changes from the beginning of the story. At first he is . . . . By the end he is . . . .
- This change shows that . . . is . . . .

Character	What he says/does How he interacts with other characters	What is he like?	What is his point of view of the war?
the lieutenant	1. *"Some of them are friendly, and some of them have a strong desire to kill you. If you remember that, and manage to kill them before they kill you, then you have a good chance of getting through your year of service here."*	1. He is using fear to try to get the men to take the danger seriously and perhaps save the lives of the new enlistees.	
the sergeant	1. *"Charlie is the bad guy over here." The sergeant put his arm around Jenkins' shoulders. He was obviously enjoying himself.*	He seems smug in his knowledge of the war and is condescending toward the new soldiers. He jokes about charlie sending his business card.	

(Speak and Listen Share your answers to the chart with a partner. Discuss the following questions:

- Do any of the characters change from the beginning to the end of the excerpt? Why?

- What does this change reveal about the characters?

Third Read: Analyzing Author's Use of Humor

Read the excerpt a third time.

Objective: Think about how the author uses humor in a situation that is usually not humorous. Label examples with the word **humor**.

Focus on Analyzing Author's Use of Humor

The interaction between the characters in the excerpt results in some humorous moments. Identify three humorous interactions between the characters on the next page.

continued on next page

ELL Support: Third Read Before students reread, make sure they understand that humor is something that is funny (pantomime laughing). Students may have trouble identifying the nuances that make this excerpt humorous. Instruct students to look for places where people are teasing or making fun of others. If necessary, read those parts aloud with volunteers, acting out the laughing, pointing at, and shame that is associated with those scenes. Have students reread the excerpt in multilevel pairs or small groups, pausing after each page to ask if anyone is using humor or teasing someone.

(Speak and Listen: Suggest that students reread the last few paragraphs of the selection before deciding whether the characters change. Ask them to consider whether the characters change or the situation changes.

Third Read: Analyzing Author's Use of Humor

Before Reading: Read the introductory remarks and confirm that students understand the objective. Ask students to consider why the author might be using humor in a story set in a war.

After Reading: Use the following questions to check comprehension.

Text-Based Discussion Questions

1. At the beginning of the passage, the narrator says, "My ninth day in country." What is the impact of this information? *It helps the reader understand that the narrator has only been in Vietnam for a few weeks.*

2. In what ways do each of the three characters all show their fear at the end of the passage? How do their reactions show their personality? *Peewee and the narrator become silent; the narrator admits he's afraid; and Jenkins is crying.*

3. How does the way the narrator and the other characters talk reveal the setting? *The characters use slang:* gung ho, back to the World, Nam, dope. *They make references to the black market and Archie comics. These specific references make the writing realistic and help the reader understand what it was like to be a young person in 1968 fighting in the Vietnam War.*

Focus on Analyzing Author's Use of Humor: Point out that humor is sometimes used to make a serious point. Ask students what point the author might be making with humor in *Fallen Angels. (Possible answer: War is absurd.)*

Tech-Connect Suggestion: The Vietnam Veterans Memorial in Washington, D.C., honors servicemen and women who fought and died in the Vietnam War. The website gives extensive information about soldiers memorialized on the wall, a photo gallery, women on the wall, Medal of Honor recipients, and an extensive links page, among other topics. Students can find the website at http://thewall-usa.com/.

Lesson Support

Answers to Focus on Analyzing Author's Use of Humor:

1. "What did you do, machine gun most of them?" Jenkins' eyes were wide.

   "No, man," Peewee shook his head. "They issue you so many bullets per week, see? But each one you turn back in you get a quarter for. So mostly I sneak up on the suckers and cut their throats. That way I save my bullets. Way I figure, by the time I get back to the World I have me enough to buy a little Chevy."

   "None of that is true," Jenkins said. He was pissed at Peewee for pulling his leg.

2. "Charlie?" Jenkins looked toward me and Peewee.

   "Charlie is the bad guy over here." The sergeant put his arm around Jenkins' shoulders. He was obviously enjoying himself. "Sometimes we call him charlie, sometimes we call him Victor Charlie, sometimes we call him Vietcong. That is, unless he sends us his business card with his full name and address on it."

3. The narrator is bitten by mosquitoes. He wonders if Vietnamese mosquitoes "just bit blacks and whites and didn't bite Asians."

4. Peewee feeds Jenkins information that the reader knows is untrue, that he's making fun of Jenkins' gullibility, but Jenkins is unaware. In the following excerpt, the dramatic irony is that Peewee has only been there for about eight days, not eight months; the reader knows this, but Jenkins does not.

   "What's it like so far?" he asked Peewee.

   "Ain't nothing to it," Peewee said.

   "You been here long?" Jenkins asked.

   "Eight months," Peewee lied.

   (continued)

Examples of humor:

1.

2.

3.

4. *Dramatic irony* is a literary device in which the reader knows something that one or more of the characters don't know. Are any of the examples of humor above examples of dramatic irony? Explain what you know that one of the characters doesn't know.

ELL Support: Third Read Once students have reread the excerpt, have students work in their multilevel pairs or groups to take notes and answer the questions about dramatic irony using the following prompts and sentence frames:

Q: How long has Peewee been in Vietnam? How long does he pretend he's been there?

- The audience knows that Peewee has been in Vietnam for . . . . Jenkins thinks Peewee has been in Vietnam for . . . .

- I think the soldiers' treatment of Jenkins is . . . . I feel this way because . . . .

- Peewee and the sergeant tease Jenkins because . . . . This shows that they are . . . .

5. Most of the humor is at the expense of Jenkins. How do you as a reader feel about the other soldiers' treatment of Jenkins?

6. Why do you think Jenkins is the target of humor? What does it reveal about Peewee and the sergeant?

(Speak and Listen With a partner discuss what effect the addition of humor has on the readers' experience of the passage. Also consider what the use of humor reveals about the personalities of the characters. Summarize your explanation in your response journal. Share your summary with the rest of the class.

Language: Using Phrases Effectively

To communicate effectively and specifically, writers use phrases and clauses. Study the following explanations and examples of commonly used phrases.

> A *phrase* is a group of related words that do not contain a subject and a verb.
>
> Here are several different types of phrases.
>
> **prepositional phrases:** begin with a preposition and end with an object
>
> Examples: in the end, up the stairs, after the storm
>
> **appositive phrases:** renames or gives more information about a noun, often includes a noun and any modifiers.
>
> Examples: Natalia, the girl standing over there, is my sister.
>
> Somalia, a country on the coast of east Africa, is experiencing a severe famine.
>
> **verbal phrases:** look like verbs but act like adjectives or nouns. Gerund and participial phrases can end in –*ing* or –*ed*; infinitive phrases begin with *to*.
>
> Examples: KJ's goal is to become a doctor. (Infinitive phrase)

continued on next page

5. Answers will vary, but students may say that they felt sympathy for Jenkins and worried about his vulnerability.

6. In part, Jenkins is the target because he's inexperienced and naive. In part, he is the target because Peewee is scared himself. The sergeant uses Jenkins as pure entertainment.

Gr7Ch19Read3.pptx

(Speak and Listen: You might want to break down these questions by asking students whether they found the "humor" funny, serious, or sad. Encourage them to think about the reason for their response to the humor. Also ask them what the humor shows about how each character feels about being in Vietnam.

ELL Support: Speak and Listen Have students work in multilevel pairs or small groups to discuss humor. Use these sentence frames:

- The humor in the story made me feel . . . .
- The humor shows that Peewee/the Sergeant/Jenkins/Perry is . . . because . . . .

Chapter 19 *(continued)*

Lesson Support

Language: Using Phrases Effectively:

Sample responses:

1. Talking on the phone can be fun.

2. On the very top floor of the building, the elevator suddenly stopped working.

3. I love to binge-watch, *This Is Us,* my favorite television show.

4. Covered in mud and soaking wet, our dog ran into the house.

 Gr7Ch19Language.pptx

---

Working around the clock, the firefighters finally put out the fire. (Participial phrase)

In my free time I enjoy playing video games. (Gerund phrase)

Punctuation with phrases: Commas are often used to set off phrases.

Use a single comma with an introductory verbal phrase or with prepositional phrases of four or more words at the beginning of a sentence.

Examples: By the end of the war, he was sick of fighting.

Swimming with all her might, she finally reached the shore.

Use a pair of commas to set off phrases that fall in the middle of a sentence.

Examples: The pond, frozen over since early December, is now safe for ice-skating.

My teacher, a fine pianist, spent the summer traveling with a jazz band.

Incorrect use of commas: Do not set off phrases used as the subject of a sentence.

Incorrect: To eat dinner together, was her plan.

Incorrect: Swimming in the lake, is my favorite summer activity.

Write sentences using the following phrases correctly. Add commas as needed.

1. Use the phrase *talking on the phone* as the subject of a sentence.

2. Write a sentence with a prepositional phrase at the beginning of the sentence.

3. Use the phrase *my favorite television show* as an appositive.

ELL Support: Language The language structures in these phrases are quite complex. To help students learn the names of the different kinds of phrases, create a grammar wall with the names of the phrases and the examples. Ask students to work in multilevel pairs to give another example for each type of phrase on the grammar wall. Place these new examples (correcting as necessary) on the grammar wall. Then summarize the comma rules by explaining that if the phrase is a subject (who or what is doing the action), then no comma is used. Have students work in multilevel pairs or groups to complete the items. Review and explain correct responses as a class.

4. Use the phrase *covered in mud and soaking wet* at the beginning of a sentence.

Project-Based Assessments

Diary

Imagine what a diary by one of the soldiers depicted in the passage would be like. Would it be Jenkins' diary, full of fear and concern? Or would it be the tough sergeant's diary, a record of goals achieved and milestones met? Write a diary entry as you imagine one of the soldiers writing it, using details from the passage and from your own research as needed. For example, you might read some other accounts of the Vietnam War written by young people who fought.

When you're writing the diary entry, capture the character's style of writing based on what you infer about his personality from the excerpt. Although you want the writing to be realistic, follow your teacher's guidelines for appropriateness.

Use the following guidelines for your diary.	
To receive the highest score, the letter must meet all of these criteria.	**Your diary** • presents information in a way that grabs the reader's attention. • is faithful to character's voice and personality as based on the excerpt. • follows the style and format of a diary. • uses correct grammar, word usage, punctuation, and spelling.

Personal Interview

Interview a family member or friend who fought in the Vietnam War or another war or conflict.

Before you interview the person, prepare 7 to 10 questions to guide the conversation. As the discussion progresses, ask other questions as you think of them. Use an app and your phone to record the conversation or take good notes so you can remember the details later when you write.

continued on next page

Assessment

Project-Based Assessments:

Diary: If students select Jenkins or Peewee, they might consider writing about their flight on the C-47 to Chu Lai to join the 196th. If they choose the lieutenant or sergeant, they might consider writing about their impressions of the new soldiers and what they hoped to accomplish.

Personal Interview: Invite students to work with a partner or in a small group to brainstorm some interview questions. Point out that their interviews will vary even if they start with similar questions, because their interviewees will all be different. Also, they should go with the flow during their interview, following up on their initial questions with comments and new questions.

Instead of writing down the interview, students can edit their recorded conversation using a recording app or recording software such as GarageBand. Have students post their final interviews to the class website or share it during class.

Tech-Connect Suggestion: Storycorp.org contains resources for conducting good interviews. The storycorp app can be used to write questions, record conversations, and upload interviews to the Library of Congress and StoryCorps.me.

ELL Support: Project-Based Assessments—Diary Have students work in multilevel pairs or groups to write the diary. Provide the Letter Format Template from the ELL Teacher Resource (p. 55). Show pictures of soldiers in Vietnam to provide ideas for writing. As a class, brainstorm sentence frames for the diary such as the following:

Dear Diary,

I am writing to you from . . . . It is the year . . . . I have been here . . . .

Vietnam is . . . . For example, ... Also, ...

We are going to . . . . We will . . . there.

I feel . . . because . . . .

When students finish their drafts, provide the Narrative Writing Revision Checklist ELL Teacher Resource (p. 68) for students to finalize their diary entries.

Chapter 19 (continued)

Assessment

On Your Own: Integrating Ideas:

Activity 1: Volunteers might read and review one of Myers's war novels for their classmates. Students might also be interested in Tim O'Brien's celebrated "linked" short stories, *The Things They Carried,* based on his experiences in Vietnam.

Alternative activity: In the movie *Forrest Gump,* the main character is deployed to Vietnam. Students might enjoy watching the movie, which contains absurdist humor, and comparing its war-related sequences with *Fallen Angels.*

After your interview, write a summary of the interview. Begin by introducing the interviewee. Next, include the questions you asked the interviewee and his or her responses. However, do not merely copy down the person's words. Paraphrase the responses to your questions and also use direct quotations—especially when what the interviewee said represents his or her personality or is unique. Edit out information that isn't to the point.

Use the following guidelines for your interview.	
To receive the highest score, the interview must meet all of these criteria.	Your interview • includes 7 to 10 questions. • summarizes the interviewee's answers. • includes good direct quotations and paraphrases of answers. • uses correct grammar, word usage, punctuation, and spelling.

On Your Own: Integrating Ideas

1. Read the rest of the book *Fallen Angels* by Walter Dean Myers. Check out Myers' website for information about his companion books on war, including *Invasion* (WWII) and *Sunrise Over Fallujah* (Iraq War).
2. Research the Vietnam War from a Vietnamese perspective. In the story, the sergeant says some of the locals are friendly. Is this based on fact? What were the attitudes of the local residents in Vietnamese villages toward U.S. soldiers?
3. Consider how "The Drummer Boy of Shiloh" and *Fallen Angels* deal with the effects of war on young people. Use evidence from both stories to infer similar themes. Share these themes in a online post or in a class discussion.
4. With a small group, discuss the following quotation from Walter Dean Myers:

   "Memories of wars fade away, even from those who fought in them. In interviewing WWII vets for *Invasion,* I could see how often films, newspaper accounts, and documentaries influence the recollection of actual events. Heroes are created decades after the events, and stories are retold to fit the mood of the country. The human elements are often lost because they don't fit the shifting momentums of the times. Books like *Fallen Angels* help to counter this trend."

ELL Support: Project-Based Assessments—Personal Interview Have students work in multilevel pairs or groups to write and practice questions for the personal interview. Students who are interviewing someone in their first language should work in monolingual pairs or small groups to write and practice interview questions.

Before students conduct their interviews, provide phrases such as the following to allow students to monitor their understanding and seek clarification: *Pardon? Can you repeat that? I don't understand.*

Also, recommend that students record their interviews with their phones or another recording device so they can more easily summarize their interviews.

Connect to Testing

In this chapter you practiced analyzing setting and conflict, inferring characterization, and analyzing the author's use of humor. For these skills, questions on reading tests may look like the following.

1. Read the following paragraph.

> I was less nervous than I was when I first got in country. We were in Nam to stop the North Vietnamese from taking over South Vietnam. I didn't feel really gung ho or anything, but I was ready to do my part.
>
> One of the new guys who came in was from Fort Dix. He looked like one of the characters from an Archie Andrews comic, but he was so scared it wasn't funny. He told us his name was Jenkins.

Part A: How does Jenkins' point of view differ from the narrator's point of view?

A. Jenkins is shy, while the narrator wants to get to work.

B. Jenkins is very timid, while the narrator is more confident.

C. Jenkins is suspicious, while the narrator is more trusting.

D. Jenkins is concerned about combat, while the narrator is excited about it.

Part B: Which of the following provide the strongest evidence for the answer to Part A? Choose three.

A. *I was less nervous than I was when I first got in country.*

B. *We were in Nam to stop the North Vietnamese from taking over South Vietnam.*

C. *I didn't feel really gung ho or anything, but I was ready to do my part.*

D. *He looked like one of the characters from an Archie Andrews comic*

E. *but he was so scared it wasn't funny.*

F. *He told us his name was Jenkins.*

Read the following excerpt from the lieutenant's orientation speech.

> "You are not in Disneyland," he said. "The little people you see running around over here are not Mouseketeers."

2. The lieutenant says this to the new recruits in order to

A. encourage them that Vietnam is an innocent, harmless place for recreation.

B. make fun of the Vietnamese and their culture.

C. give them confidence that they are fighting an important war.

D. warn them that war is not a thrilling adventure.

continued on next page

Connect to Testing: This Connect to Testing section focuses on analyzing setting and conflict, making inferences about characters, and analyzing the use of humor.

Encourage students to work in pairs to choose the correct answers to the questions and then to compare their answers with those of another pair of students. If there is disagreement, encourage the groups to try to reach a consensus as they discuss the reasons for their choices.

Answers to Connect to Testing Questions:

1. **Part A:** B. The text does not support the idea that the narrator wants or looks forward to combat (Choices A, D) or that he is trusting (C). Only Choice B accurately reflects the text, which shows Jenkins's fear and timidity and the narrator's relative confidence.

   Part B: A, C, E (DoK 2)

2. D. The point of the lieutenant's words is to stress that they are not on vacation playing at war games. (DoK 2)

(continued)

Chapter 19 (continued)

Assessment

Answers to Connect to Testing Questions:

3. **Part A:** C.

   Part B: The sergeant has been in Vietnam longer, so he has more experience fighting. He explains to Jenkins and the others what can be expected in the area to which they are being shipped. He also explains who "Charlie" is. Conversely, the narrator has only been in Vietnam for nine days at the beginning of the excerpt. (DoK 2)

4. Examples include Peewee's lies to Jenkins about how many men he has killed and if he kills as many men as the number of pounds he weighs, he can leave early. Another example is the sergeant's comment about the Vietcong sending them his business card with his name and address on it. Humor shows how the soldiers try to make light of a serious situation and to cope with their fear and worry. It's unexpected but realistic due to the subject matter. It also shows how they try to pick on weaker, frightened soldiers, perhaps because they are feeling the same way though not showing it, or perhaps to make themselves feel better or stronger. (DoK 2)

3. **Part A:** How does the sergeant's point of view differ from the narrator's point of view?

   A. The sergeant is bored by his job, while the narrator is new to it.

   B. The sergeant is nervous about the upcoming battle, while the narrator is unconcerned.

   C. The sergeant is tough and worldly, while the narrator is more naïve.

   D. The sergeant distrusts the soldiers, while the narrator has respect for them.

   Part B: Provide evidence from the text to support the answer to Part A.

4. Explain two places where Myers uses humor in his writing. Is humor expected or unexpected? Why does Myers include humor? Write a paragraph in which you answer these questions.

©Perfection Learning® • No Reproduction Permitted

Remediation: Connect to Testing Have students work with a partner to read each question and eliminate incorrect answers.

Connections • © Perfection Learning®

Chapter 20

Analyzing the Format of a Play

Preview Concepts

Read the following excerpt. Then answer the questions to help you understand the purpose of unique features of this text.

(AT RISE: *Elizabeth stands at downstage center. If lighting is used, she stands in a spotlight. She's in her 20s and shows great determination, intelligence, and impatience. She speaks directly to the audience.*)

ELIZABETH: I'm not sure exactly when I decided to become a doctor. I only know it happened. Even before I could put it into words!

Maybe it was when I walked with my father around the town. I saw raggedy children with their runny noses, fever blisters, and open sores. . . .

(WOMAN 1, WOMAN 2, MAN 1, *and* MAN 2 *enter stage right and left, pointing at* ELIZABETH.)

WOMAN 1: Have you heard? *She* wants to be a doctor!

WOMAN 2: But she's a woman!

MAN 1: Women can't be doctors!

ELIZABETH: (*Confronting them*) Why?

WOMAN 1: (*Using a mocking tone*) Why?

WOMAN 2: (*Using a mocking tone*) Why?

MAN 1: (*Using a mocking tone*) Why?

MAN 2: Why? Because women aren't fit to be doctors!

1. Based on the structure of the excerpt, what type of literature is this?

> **CHAPTER GOALS**
>
> In this chapter you will
> - analyze the theme of a play.
> - analyze how the format and structure of a play help to communicate theme.
> - identify dramatic techniques used in a scene.
> - analyze the purpose of a scene within a longer play.

> **PREVIEW ACADEMIC VOCABULARY**
>
> aside
> chorus
> conflict
> dialogue
> domain-specific words
> monologue
> multiple-meaning words
> narrator
> theme

ELL Support: Academic Vocabulary See Teaching Vocabulary in the ELL Teacher Resource (p. 18) for ideas to use for teaching vocabulary throughout *Connections*.

Preview Concepts Together with volunteers, read and act out the excerpt, noting how the volunteers do what is in parentheses. Name and label these as stage directions and the volunteers as actors. Beginning and intermediate students can pair up and act out the roles with short lines. Guide volunteers to use an exaggeratedly mocking tone so the other students understand what mocking means.

Chapter 20

Analyzing the Format of a Play

Elizabeth Blackwell
by Cynthia Mercati

Introduction

Chapter Goals: Have students read through the goals and mark any words that are unfamiliar. Discuss the meanings of any academic vocabulary within the goals that students marked as unfamiliar. Consider posting the Chapter Goals.

Preview Academic Vocabulary: Read and discuss the meanings of the academic vocabulary.

aside: *in a play, an actor's remarks that are not supposed to be heard by others present.* Antony's aside in the first act reveals his evil intention.

chorus: *in a play, actors who act or speak as a group.* The chorus warns the audience of difficulties the main character will face.

dialogue: *conversation between characters.* The play's dialogue is lively, especially the arguments between the characters Lee and Jim.

domain-specific words: *words with a particular meaning in an area of study or a content area.* Nucleus, chloroplast, and mitochondria are examples of domain-specific words from biology.

monologue: *in a play, a speech given by one actor to express inner thoughts or feelings.* Jean's first monologue reveals her love of travel.

multiple-meaning words: *words that have different meanings in different contexts.* Cell is a multiple-meaning word with numerous different meanings.

Chapter **20** *(continued)*

Introduction

narrator: *in a play, one or more actors who speak directly to the audience to tell a story or give information about a scene.* At the end of the play, the <u>narrator</u> explains what happens to the characters in the future.

theme: *the central meaning or universal truth of a literary text, developed through the characters and their conflicts.* The main <u>theme</u> of this novel is *You have the power to create a happy future for yourself.*

🖱 **Gr7Ch20Vocabulary.pptx**

Preview Concepts: Discuss with students elements of a play that make the genre different from a novel or short story. Point out that plays often begin with a cast of characters which includes a very brief description of each character. The cast is followed by the setting, which describes the scene (where the play takes place) and time (when the play takes place). A character's name in capital letters shows who is speaking; the dialogue follows. Stage directions are in parentheses, indicating how the character is reacting, interacting, and/or moving. Ask students to tell what we learn from the first stage directions, AT RISE, when the curtain rises. (*We learn where Elizabeth is standing and, briefly, what she is like.*) Who would be included in a cast of characters of this opening? (*Elizabeth, Woman 1, Woman 2, Man 1, Man 2*)

1. It is a play.

2. The parentheses give stage directions.

3. Those words show that the characters' reactions are disrespectful.

4. The setting is at least 100 years ago, before women were encouraged to become doctors.

Making Connections: Ask students what the opening they just read shows about the prejudice that Elizabeth Blackwell faced. *(She faced extreme prejudice because she was a woman.)* What does the fact that she graduated first in her class show about her character? *(She was very determined, hardworking and strong-willed.)*

2. Why are some lines in parentheses?

3. Why are the lines (*Using a mocking tone*) especially important for understanding the interaction between the characters?

4. What can you infer about the setting? Support your inference with evidence.

Discuss your answers to the questions above with a partner.

Making Connections

Read the following entry about Elizabeth Blackwell from an online biographical encyclopedia:

> Elizabeth Blackwell was born on February 3, 1821, in Bristol, England. As a girl, she moved with her family to the United States, where she first worked as a teacher. Despite widespread opposition, she later decided to attend medical college and graduated first in her class, thus also becoming the first woman to receive her M.D. in the United States. She created a medical school for women in the late 1860s, eventually returning to England and setting up a private practice. Blackwell died on May 31, 1910, in Hastings.

> **MAKING CONNECTIONS**
>
> In this chapter you will read and analyze the theme and format of a play about the life of Elizabeth Blackwell.

ELL Support: Preview Concepts Have multilevel pairs or small groups answer the questions using the following sentence frames:

1. This is a . . . .

2. The words in parentheses tell the actors . . . .

3. The words *[Using a mocking tone]* are important because they tell . . . .

4. I infer that the story happens in . . . because . . . .

Make Connections If necessary, display maps of England and the United States to show the places referred to in the paragraph. Have students work in multilevel pairs or groups to read the paragraph, pausing to underline important events. Encourage students to draw sketches so they can understand and remember the details.

First Read: Determining Theme

This is an excerpt from a play about the life of Elizabeth Blackwell (1821–1910), who was the first woman in the United States to earn a medical degree. As you read, remember that it is meant to be experienced as a performance on stage. Pay attention to special features like stage directions. Visualize the action as if you were watching the play onstage.

Objective: As you read, underline repeated ideas that help you understand the theme of this scene.

—— First Read

---- Second Read

Elizabeth Blackwell
by Cynthia Mercati

My Thoughts

1 **ELIZABETH:** Father was a very unusual man! He believed completely in the equality of people. A very strange idea for the time!

MR. BLACKWELL: (*Stepping forward and speaking to the*
5 *audience*) All human beings—black, white, men, women, rich, and poor—should have the same rights!

(*AUNT BARBARA steps forward to speak to her brother. She's a very proper and prissy lady like the other aunts.*)

AUNT BARBARA: You couldn't mean that women should   The aunts are against
10 have the same rights as men!   equality.

THREE AUNTS: Indeed he couldn't!

MR. BLACKWELL: I certainly do! That's why I've decided to hire a **governess** for my daughters!

(*MRS. BLACKWELL steps forward. She's quieter than her*
15 *husband and daughter.*)

MRS. BLACKWELL: But, husband dear, our house is already bursting at the seams! How will we fit in one more person?!

MR. BLACKWELL: We'll just have to try! The governess will teach our girls the same subjects the boys are learning in public
20 school.

governess: a woman who takes responsibility for the care and sometimes the education of children in wealthy households

---

ELL Support: First Read Together with volunteers, read and act out the excerpt as students follow along. Beginning and intermediate students can pair up to take on the roles with short lines. Encourage volunteers to pantomime what is in parentheses. Pause at the end of each page to allow time for all students to take notes on the main events and details using a Story Map graphic organizer from the ELL Teacher Resource (p. 52). Students may also create a graphic novel version of the play using the Graphic Novel graphic organizer from the ELL Teacher Resource (p. 56) or an online comic strip generator such as www.storyboardthat.com/storyboard-creator. Encourage students to also take notes and draw sketches in the margins around the story so they can be sure they understand and remember the main events and details.

First Read: Determining Theme

Before Reading: Read the introductory paragraph on page 413 and ask students to preview the text. How do they know it is a play? What text features will help them understand what is happening. Remind students to visual what is happening as they read.

Then read the objective. Explain that theme is often revealed through repeated ideas in a text. When they annotate any text, they should mark repeated ideas and terms. Finally, remind students that the first read of a text focuses on the key ideas in the passage by asking the question *What is this text about?* Have students read the text on their own.

Preview Vocabulary: Preview unfamiliar vocabulary or ask students to circle unfamiliar words as they complete the first read. Guide students to determine the words' meanings using the context. Encourage students to support their responses with evidence. Have students confirm their definitions with a dictionary. Difficult words might include:

equality: *the sameness in value; equal value.* Because of her belief in the equality of all people, she treated everyone fairly.

prissy: *overly prim or precise; caring too much about dressing and behaving properly.* Her prissy refusal to get her hands dirty during the camping trip made her unpopular with the rest of the group.

determination: *strength; willpower.* His determination to get ahead at work led to great success.

balderdash: *nonsense.* His ideas about talking bats are pure balderdash!

conviction: *certainty; passion.* When she believes in a plan, she carries it out with conviction.

criticism: *disapproval.* Although his father's criticism hurt, the boy knew his parent was right.

 Gr7Ch20Vocabulary.pptx

Chapter 20 *(continued)*

Lesson Support

After Reading: Use the following questions to check comprehension.

Text-Based Discussion Questions

1. Why does Mr. Blackwell plan to hire a governess? *He wants a teacher for his daughters, so they can have the same educational and professional opportunities as his sons.*

2. What does his plan suggest about that time period, the early to mid-1800s? *Women had limited educational opportunities.*

3. What words best describe Mr. Blackwell? *open-minded, progressive, fair.*

4. What do Woman 1, Woman 2, Man 1, and Man 2 represent? *They stand for people who oppose equality for women and fair wages for workers and who support slavery and child labor.*

 Gr7Ch20Read1.pptx

Background Information: Students may not understand how limited women's rights were during Elizabeth Blackwell's day (1821–1910). For starters, women did not gain the right to vote until 1920, ten years after Blackwell's death. The first state to give married women some control over their property and earnings was New York in 1848; the last one gave these rights in 1900. Minimum wage laws were extended to women in 1937 and 1938. Women gained additional wage and employment protections under the Equal Pay Act (1963) and Title VII of the Civil Rights Act (1964). In 1972, Title IX prohibited sex discrimination in education programs receiving federal support. Students can find more detailed information about the legal history of women's rights at http://www.nwhp.org/resources/womens-rights-movement/detailed-timeline/.

MRS. BLACKWELL: *(With mild protest)* But, husband dear. What will they do with such knowledge?

MR. BLACKWELL: They'll do all sorts of interesting things. Just like their brothers! *(He beckons to ANNA to stand next to*
25 *him.)* Anna, what do you want to be when you grow up?

ANNA: A writer!

MR. BLACKWELL: Excellent!

(ANNA returns upstage. MR. BLACKWELL indicates for MARIAN to join him.)

30 Marian, what do you want to be?

MARIAN: A composer of music.

MR. BLACKWELL: Wonderful!

(MARIAN returns upstage. MR. BLACKWELL turns to ELIZABETH.) Elizabeth?

35 *(ELIZABETH steps forward. She is a very young girl now.)*

MRS. BLACKWELL: Husband! Elizabeth is far too young to have any idea what she wants to be.

(MRS. BLACKWELL and everyone except ELIZABETH and MR. BLACKWELL exit stage left as ELIZABETH answers.)

40 **ELIZABETH:** I know I want to be something great, Papa!

MR. BLACKWELL: I believe you will, Elizabeth! There's a special determination about you. A special spark.

ELIZABETH: *(With a dreamy enthusiasm)* I can see myself on a big, white horse, leading a charge into battle! Or painting
45 a famous picture! Or . . . or . . . making a big, important speech while thousands of people cheer!

MAN 1: *(Entering stage left)* As if women could say anything important!

MAN 2: *(Entering stage right)* As if women could do
50 anything important!

My Thoughts

414   Chapter 20 • Unit 4   ©Perfection Learning® • No Reproduction Permitted

---

Remediation: First Read To make sure students are following the play format, read the opening excerpt aloud with students and ask simple questions: Who will speak next? What do these words in parentheses mean?

(MR. BLACKWELL puts his hands on ELIZABETH's shoulders.)

MR. BLACKWELL: *(Speaking seriously)* Never forget, child. The greatest thing in life is to find a cause you believe in and fight for it!

55   **ELIZABETH:** *(To the audience)* Father works for all kinds of causes.

    WOMAN 1 and WOMAN 2: *(Entering stage left and stage right)* I'll say he does!

    (MR. BLACKWELL speaks to the audience as if giving a
60 *speech. The WOMEN and MEN become very angry.)*

    MR. BLACKWELL: I work to end slavery!

    MAN 1: Slave trade is my business. How dare you try to stop it!

    MR. BLACKWELL: I work to end child labor! It's criminal
65 that children five and six years old are made to work 14 hours a day in coal mines and factories.

    MAN 2: I can save all kinds of money using those children in my mine. I don't have to pay them half of what I pay adults!

    MR. BLACKWELL: Everyone is entitled to earn a decent
70 living!

    WOMAN 1: Stop your **jabbering** about decent wages. You'll take away some of the profits from my husband's cloth factory.

    MR. BLACKWELL: Good!

    WOMAN 2: Mr. Blackwell also wants to make our hospitals
75 cleaner and better run!

    MAN 2: And he wants to raise our taxes to do it!

    ELIZABETH: *(Proudly)* <u>My father believes that women should be free and equal citizens.</u> They should not be considered just the property of their husbands!

---

jabbering: to talk rapidly or unintelligibly

My Thoughts

The Men & Women represent those who oppose Mr. Blackwell's ideas about human rights.

©Perfection Learning® • No Reproduction Permitted

About the Author: Students might have seen one of Cynthia Mercati's plays, which have been produced in all fifty states and viewed by thousands of young people. The award-winning playwright is also a professional actress who sometimes performs in her own plays. Her works include *Cinderella, or, It's Okay to Be Different; Long Live Rock and Roll;* and *The Baseball Show.*

Chapter 20 *(continued)*

Lesson Support

FIRST RESPONSE: KEY IDEAS AND DETAILS

Review different types of conflict in literature: person vs. person; person vs. self; person vs. society; person vs. nature. Point out that the play contains several kinds of conflict. Encourage them to provide evidence to support their conclusion about the central conflict in the play. Help students understand what is meant by the term "society" in the conflict person vs. society.

---

80 **MAN 1 and MAN 2:** Balderdash!

MAN 1: Mr. Blackwell, you are a **crackpot**!

ELIZABETH: How dare you say such things about my father! He's a very great man!

MAN 2: He's crazy as a loon!

85 *(Marching determinedly to MAN 2, ELIZABETH gives him a kick in the leg.)*

ELIZABETH: You take that back!

(Quickly, MR. BLACKWELL restrains his daughter.)

MR. BLACKWELL: It's all right, Elizabeth. When you

90 have new and different ideas, you're likely to take a lot of punishment! *(with conviction)* But the important thing is not to let the criticism bother you. <u>Just keep on working for what you believe.</u>

(MR. BLACKWELL exits stage right. The people on stage

95 *speak to ELIZABETH quickly and firmly. They take a step closer to her with every word. They soon surround her.)*

MAN 1: You better forget what he said, Elizabeth Blackwell! The world doesn't work that way!

MAN 2: Not for women!

100 **ELIZABETH:** *(Crossing down stage center, she folds her arms and looks forward.)* I'm not listening to you!

MR. BLACKWELL: *(Peeking out stage right to give this one line)* That's the spirit, Elizabeth!

---

crackpot: an irrational and unreliable person, likely to say absurd things

---

FIRST RESPONSE: KEY IDEAS AND DETAILS

What is the central conflict of this scene from the play? Write your response in your response journal.

My Thoughts

TECH-CONNECT

Share your response on your class website or tweet your answer to your teacher.

ELL Support: First Response and Focus on Determining Theme Before students respond to the questions, review definitions for *conflict, characters,* and *theme.* Also, be sure students understand that *prejudice* means "believing people of a different race, sex, or religion are less important or worse than you are." Have students work in multilevel pairs or small groups to discuss and write about conflict and theme, using these prompts and sentence frames:

- The main conflict (problem) in the story is that . . . .
- The characters have conflicts with each other. For example, ...
- The characters have conflicts with the world. For example, ...
- The characters have conflicts with themselves. For example, ...

Focus on Determining Theme

Determining the theme of a play is similar to determining the theme of a story or novel. Earlier in this chapter you analyzed the theme of a short story. Use the same steps to analyze the theme of this scene from a play. Use the following graphic organizer to record important details about the characters, conflict, and repeated ideas. Finally, determine the theme of the play and write it in the final row.

Characters:	Elizabeth wants to become a doctor; must stand up to prejudice/sexism.
	Mr. Blackwell stands up to many forms of injustice.
	Mrs. Blackwell doesn't understand the need to promote her daughters' education/careers.
	Woman 1 and Woman 2 and Man 1 and Aunts represent society's ideas about human rights.
	Elizabeth's sisters are creative, smart, and motivated.
Conflict:	People against people (Mr. Blackwell and his wife about how to educate Elizabeth and their other children.)
	People against society (Mr. Blackwell against prejudice; Elizabeth against sexism)
	Person against self (Mrs. Blackwell and the aunts can't imagine a world without sexism.)
Repeated Ideas:	People face many forms of prejudice.
	Girls face sexism.
Theme:	Some brave/determined people try to reach their dreams, despite prejudice.

Write Write a paragraph that explains the theme of the excerpt. Support your conclusions with details about the characters, conflict, and repeated ideas from the text.

Speak and Listen Read a partner's paragraph explaining the theme of the scene. Does your partner's theme meet the following characteristics? If not, offer specific suggestions for improvement.

continued on next page

Focus on Determining Theme:

Remind students that the theme is the central meaning of a literary text, developed through the characters and their conflicts. Invite volunteers to identify the theme of the short opening of the play (from Preview Concepts). *(Possible responses: Prejudice may hinder opportunities; prejudice may stop people from reaching their dreams; people should aim for their dreams, despite prejudice.)*

Answers to Focus on Determining Theme:

See answers on Student Book insert page to the left.

 Gr7Ch20Read1.pptx

Write: Point out that supporting the theme will not necessarily require using all of the information in the graphic organizer. Instruct students to choose the strongest evidence for their theme.

Speak and Listen: Remind students to offer at least one positive comment and only gentle criticism.

ELL Support: Write Have students work in multilevel pairs or small groups to write about theme. Provide the following theme statement sentence frames. These can also be found as a student handout in the ELL Teacher Resource (p. 40).

- A theme of the passage is . . . .
- One story detail that supports this theme is . . . .
- Another story detail that supports this theme is . . . .

Chapter 20 (continued)

Lesson Support

Second Read: Analyzing the Unique Format of a Play:

Before Reading: Before the class reads the scene, discuss the different characters and what they know/imagine about each one. What are their approximate ages? What character traits do they display? Are they stereotypes or developed characters? Encourage them to use this information along with the stage directions as they attempt to match the sound of their voice to the age and personality of a character.

After Reading: Use the following questions to check comprehension.

Text-Based Discussion Questions

1. In what way does Mr. Blackwell's attitude toward women differ from the aunts' attitude? *Mr. Blackwell believes that women should have the same rights as men; the aunts do not.*

2. How does Mr. Blackwell differ in his beliefs from the group of men in the play? *He supports equality for all people; he opposes slavery and child labor; the group of men does not.*

3. What can you infer about Mr. Blackwell based on how different he is from the groups in the play? *You can infer that Mr. Blackwell was an extremely unusual man—a great man, Elizabeth says— for having such progressive attitudes, especially at that time.*

Focus on Analyzing the Unique Format of a Play:
Discuss these answers to the questions under Objective: in the student book. *(The different groups represent types of people in society. The men and women stand for people who oppose equality for women and decent wages; and who support slavery and child labor. The aunts stand for women who have a traditional view of their role and who believe women are not deserving of the same rights as men.)*

 Gr7Ch20Read2.pptx

A theme
- is the central idea of a story, poem, or other piece of writing.
- is stated as a sentence that expresses a general, universal truth explored by the author.
- is supported by the characters, conflict, and repeated ideas.

Second Read: Analyzing the Unique Format of a Play

This time read the play as a class. Assign the following parts to members of the class.

| Elizabeth | Mr. Blackwell | Aunt Barbara | Aunt 2 | Man 1 | Woman 1 |
| Aunt 3 | Mrs. Blackwell | Anna | Marian | Man 2 | Woman 2 |

Perform the play. Follow the stage directions that indicate where to move on stage and when to enter and exit. Read the parts with expression, paying attention to the directions that explain characterization. Try to match the sound of your voice to the age and personality of the character.

Objective: What is the purpose of the groups of aunts, of men, and of women? Why does the playwright include them? Write your observations in the My Thoughts Column.

Focus on Analyzing the Unique Format of a Play

Watching a play is a different experience from reading a book. Although this play is based on a real person, the author's goal is not to communicate with accuracy all of the factual details of Blackwell's life. Instead, she creatively portrays elements of Elizabeth's relationship with her father.

Drama uses a unique form and structure in which to communicate ideas. Think of a play as a relationship between the actors on stage and the audience.

Invisible Fourth Wall

Often the actors perform a story as if no one is watching. It's as if the action on stage is taking place in a room with four walls. The fourth wall that separates the actors on stage from the audience is invisible. The audience can see everything happening on stage, but the actors are unaware that the audience is there. There is no interaction between the audience and the actors on stage.

ELL Support: Second Read Assign parts to new volunteers and then reread and act out the excerpt as students follow along. Beginning and intermediate students can pair up to take on the roles with short lines. Guide the new volunteers to pantomime what is in parentheses. Pause at the end of each page to allow time for all students to take any new notes on the main events and details on their story map and/ or their graphic novel version of the play.

Aside

Some plays include a narrator who speaks to the audience about what is happening on stage. The narrator may just be someone who talks about the events. Or the narrator may be one of the characters who interacts with other characters and then steps out of the action to talk to the audience. Many times, no other characters hear what the character/narrator is saying. When a narrator or a character breaks out of the story to talk directly to the audience, it is called an *aside*. It is also called *breaking the fourth wall*.

Chorus

When a group of actors speaks together commenting on a character's actions or motivations, it is called a *chorus*. Use of a chorus of actors dates back to ancient Greek theater when a group of actors in masks would provide narration and explain transitions between scenes. Today, playwrights use a chorus creatively. Sometimes the chorus speaks in unison; other times individual members speak. This adds variety and interest to the scene.

Here are some common dramatic techniques used in plays.

- **narrator**—one or more actors speak directly to the audience to tell a story or give information about a scene. A character may be the narrator or a performer who is not involved in the action may be the narrator.

- **dialogue**—conversation between characters in a play

- **monologue**—a character speaks his thoughts aloud to another character or the audience

- **aside**—a short remark made by a character to the audience. No other characters hear this comment.

- **chorus**—group of actors that speak together in a play.

Think about the techniques the playwright uses to emphasize the theme of the work. Identify these techniques using the graphic organizer here and on the next page.

Element in the Play	Example from the Play (Include line numbers)	What effect does this have? Why does the playwright use this dramatic technique?
Elizabeth—narrates the play and steps into the action to play herself	Elizabeth describes her father (lines 1–3) Elizabeth takes to her father (lines 40 and following)	It makes the play more personal to hear the narrator speak from experience and then step into the action. It draws the audience into the action.

continued on next page

Lesson Support

Possible Answers to Chart:

See answers on Student Book insert page to the right.

Possible Answers to Questions:

1. The men (Man 1 and 2) (lines 47–50) suggest that women are less valuable than men. In lines 62 and following the men and women act as an audience who is against changes in working conditions for children, minimum wages, and raising taxes to support hospitals. In lines 97–99, the men discourage Elizabeth from listening to her father's advice.

2. All of the lines of the men (Man 1 and 2) and women (Woman 1 and 2) are negative. They are in opposition of promoting the rights of groups of people, including women, African Americans, and children.

(continued)

Element in the Play	Example from the Play (Include line numbers)	What effect does this have? Why does the playwright use this dramatic technique?
Use of a chorus—aunts, man 1 & 2, and woman 1 & 2	**MAN 1:** Slave trade is my business. How dare you try to stop it! (lines 62 and following)	The chorus represents the attitudes of society toward human rights, including the rights of women, children, and African Americans. It shows how difficult it was to hold unique beliefs.
Elizabeth—speaks directly to the audience	**ELIZABETH:** (To the audience) Father works for all kinds of causes. (line 55)	This creates a personal connection between the narrator and the audience. The playwright uses this comment to transition to information about Mr. Blackwell and his causes.
Dialogue between characters	Conversation between Mr. and Mrs. Blackwell in lines 16–20.	It reveals characterization and conflict in a very engaging and interesting way.

1. Where does the chorus of the men and women speak together or say similar things? Cite line numbers.

2. What ideas do all of the lines of the men and women have in common?

Remediation: Speak and Listen Have students work with a partner to complete the chart. Students might participate further in the activity by taking notes in their journals.

3. What can you infer about the purpose of the chorus in this scene?

3. The choruses are meant to represent the attitudes of people in society who don't want equality and human rights.

Speak and Listen With a small group, share your answers to the chart and the questions above. Then discuss the following questions:

- In what ways is reading/watching a play different from reading a biography of Elizabeth Blackwell?

- Which do you prefer? Why?

TECH-CONNECT

To help you answer the questions in the Speak and Listen activity, have each group member find a different biography of Elizabeth Blackwell from an online source. Focus on information about Blackwell's father and her early upbringing. Have each member read aloud from a different biography.

Third Read: Analyzing the Purpose of a Scene

Read the text a third time with a small group of classmates. Assign each group member parts to read.

Objective: Based on the theme of this scene, what purpose does this part play in the entire scope of Elizabeth Blackwell's life story?

Focus on Analyzing the Purpose of a Scene

This scene captures just a small part of the entire one-act play about Elizabeth Blackwell. As you know, Elizabeth Blackwell goes on to become the first woman to graduate from medical school in the United States. She was a pioneer in promoting women's advancement in the medical field in the United States and in the United Kingdom. Her entire life was spent proving that women are intelligent and capable of pursing any career opportunity they desire.

Read the flow chart on the next page. Then write a summary of the scene in the empty box in the flow chart to show how the scene fits into the story of Elizabeth Blackwell's life.

continued on next page

ELL Support: Speak and Listen Have students work in multilevel pairs or small groups to discuss the difference between watching and reading plays, using these sentence frames:

- Watching a play is different from reading a play because . . . .

- I like watching/reading plays because . . . .

Third Read: Analyzing the Purpose of a Scene

Before Reading: Although we learn a great deal about Elizabeth's father in this scene, the focus remains on Elizabeth Blackwell, the first American woman to become a doctor. Ask: *What do we learn about Elizabeth from this scene? (How she came to get an education and to consider a career as a doctor.) Why is her father important? (He had a strong, positive effect on her; he made her believe in herself and in her determination to succeed.)* For this read, students will think about how this scene fits into the overall story of Blackwell's life.

After Reading: Use the following questions to check comprehension.

Text-Based Discussion Questions

1. How did Elizabeth's attitude about women's rights differ from her mother's attitude? *Elizabeth seems to support her father's attitude that women should have the same rights as men and are worthy of a good education. Her mother, by contrast, held a traditional view that women should not have the same rights as men and had no need for a good education.*

2. Why did Elizabeth think her father was a great man? *She admired his support for important causes and his belief in the equality of all people.*

3. What effect did Mr. Blackwell have on Elizabeth? *He influenced her belief in the equality of all people, and specifically women. His encouragement and high expectations made Elizabeth believe in her ability to achieve high goals.*

Focus on Analyzing the Purpose of a Scene: Discuss these answers to the questions under Objective: in the student book on page 421. *(The purpose of the scene is to show the influence of Elizabeth's father on her confidence in herself and her ability to achieve her dreams; and on her belief in the equality of women, their right to an education, and their capacity for achievement.)*

 Gr7Ch20Read3.pptx

Chapter **20** *(continued)*

Lesson Support

Answers to Focus on Analyzing the Purpose of a Scene:

Possible responses:

See answers on Student Book insert page to the right.

▼ **Write:** Clarify that the focus of this writing exercise is not to write a summary but instead to explain how the scene from the chapter fits into Elizabeth's overall life. The question to address is *Why did the author include this scene in a play about Elizabeth Blackwell?*

Language: Determining Word Meaning: Have partners work together to identify the content area to which each of the following domain-specific words belong. Point out that they are all multiple-meaning words.
face (math), *depression* (history), *migration* (history or science), *atmosphere* (science), *cell* (science), *area* (math), *resource* (history), *product* (math), *energy* (science). Discuss different meanings of the words, if time permits.

 **Gr7Ch20Language.pptx**

Life of Elizabeth Blackwell

> Summary: Elizabeth Blackwell's father was a reformer and human rights activist. He encouraged his daughter's dreams and hired a governess to make sure they received a quality education. He opposed slavery and child labor. He encouraged Elizabeth to ignore what society said about the abilities of women and to never give up working for what she believed. He had a great impact on Elizabeth's life.

↓

> Elizabeth's father dies and she becomes a teacher to support the family.

↓

> Reverend Dickson, a former doctor, encourages her to pursue medicine as a career.

↓

> In 1947, Elizabeth is accepted into Geneva Medical College.

↓

> On January 23, 1849, Elizabeth Blackwell becomes the first woman to earn a medical degree in the United States.

↓

> Elizabeth dedicates her life to fighting prejudice against women studying and practicing medicine.

▼ **Write** Write a few paragraphs in which you explain how the scene you read in this chapter is important in a play about Elizabeth's life. What is its purpose and how does it fit with the overall theme?

Language: Determining Word Meaning

In this chapter you learned words and terms that are specific to reading and performing plays. Words that have a particular meaning within an area of study or a content area are called *domain-specific*. For example, you learn vocabulary words related to science, math, or the study of literature. What terms can you name that are domain-specific for each of these subjects?

Many domain-specific words are multiple-meaning words. This means that the same word may have one meaning in one context and another meaning in another context. Sometimes these meanings are quite different. Sometimes you can determine the meaning of a domain-specific word from the context. At other times you will need to look up the word in a dictionary.

The chart beginning on the next page provides some examples of domain-specific words with their differing meanings.

ELL Support: Write Have students work in multilevel pairs or small groups to write a summary and explain the purpose of the scene. Provide the following sentence frames to support students. These can also be found as a student handout in the <u>ELL Teacher Resource (p. 40)</u>.

- Elizabeth Blackwell's father was . . . .
- He believed . . . . He gave his daughters . . . . He was against . . . . Elizabeth learned . . . from her father. She was . . . .
- This scene shows how Mr. Blackwell . . . . This scene helps develop the theme . . . . It develops this theme by . . . .

Word	Means . . .	And also means . . .
strike	a labor stoppage growing out of protest of management	attack (military); hit forcefully; get a perfect score (bowling)
meter	the rhythm in a line of poetry	a machine that measures things; a unit of measurement in the metric system
grain	a crop such as wheat, which yields flour	a tiny particle of something; the natural shape within a cross-section of a log

Read the following sentences. Under each sentence, write the meaning of the boldfaced word. Use a dictionary to confirm or refine the definition you infer from the context. Then write another meaning of the word, using the dictionary as needed.

1. The professor showed me a machine that measured **waves** of electricity.
Definition:

Another Meaning:

2. When the blood tests came back, Susan learned that she did not have enough **iron** in her diet.
Definition:

Another meaning:

continued on next page

ELL Support: Language Have students work in multilevel pairs or groups to complete the items. Provide online or print ELL dictionaries and encourage students to use them throughout the activity. Also, encourage students to illustrate the multiple meanings of each word whenever possible. Review and explain correct responses as a class.

Lesson Support

Possible Answers to Questions:

3. Definition: capacity for holding information

   Another meaning: recall

4. Definition: a kind of bait

   Another meaning: to attract

5. Definition: scenery

   Another meaning: a collection

3. I was impressed, initially, with the size of the tiny computer's **memory**; it held a lot of information.

   Definition:

   Another meaning:

4. The sign of an experienced fisherman is that he knows how to pick a good **lure**.

   Definition:

   Another meaning:

5. Many people consider the most complex part of a stage production to be the building of the **set**.

   Definition:

   Another meaning:

Project-Based Assessments

Dramatic Scene

Work with a small group to write a scene that dramatizes a historical event from a famous person's life. Write a one- to two-page script that includes a narrator, dialogue, and an aside. For a greater challenge, include a chorus of actors. Then perform the scene for the class.

Here are some steps to help you:

1. Choose a historical event or person you find interesting or that you are currently studying in social studies or science.
2. Identify a meaningful event in the person's life and research the details. Note the main characters involved in the event.
3. Rewrite the facts into a script. Your script should include the following elements:
   - a narrator who introduces the scene and provides background. This may be one of the characters who steps in and out of the action.
   - dialogue between characters
   - an aside in which a character speaks directly to the audience
   - stage directions that explain where the characters should move, to whom they are speaking, and how the lines should be read.
4. Use the excerpt from this chapter as a guide for formatting your script, including writing the name of the character speaking in all caps followed by a colon and placing stage directions in parentheses or brackets.
5. Practice your scene following the stage directions you've written. Keep props and costumes simple, using a hat, glasses, or a cane instead of dressing in full costume.
6. Perform your scene for the class. Use appropriate speaking voices. Have your script in hand, but avoid being tied to it.

Use the following guidelines for your scene.	
To receive the highest score, the dramatic scene must meet all of these criteria.	Your dramatic scene • portrays a historical event or important event in the life of a historical figure. • is based on researched facts but presents the facts in a creative way. • includes a narrator, dialogue, stage directions, and an aside. • is presented in a professional manner. • is typed and formatted like a play. • includes the participation of all group members. • uses correct grammar, word usage, spelling, and punctuation.

Project-Based Assessments

Dramatic Scene: Ask students to vote on an historical event or person. Additional subjects they might consider: Theodore Roosevelt, Eleanor Roosevelt, Sequoyah, Lewis and Clark expedition, Martin Luther King Jr. After they choose a subject, suggest that students break down the project into small segments, such as preliminary research, choosing a scene, additional research, outlining the scene, sharing sections of the scene, and writing dialogue.

ELL Support: Project-Based Assessments Have students work in multilevel groups to write the dramatic scene and/or documentary. Encourage students to use the encyclopedia entry from p. 412 for ideas (and even language they can borrow) for their project. Beginning and intermediate students can contribute to the group by illustrating the scenes, which will help with stage directions and/or can be used in the documentary.

When students finish their drafts, provide the Narrative Writing Revision Checklist from the ELL Teacher Resource (p. 68) for students to finalize their projects.

Chapter **20** *(continued)*

Assessment

Documentary: Students could begin their research at the online version of an exhibit titled, Elizabeth Blackwell, America's First Female M.D., held at the National Library of Medicine, the National Institutes of Health, on January 23–September 4, 1999. It can be found at https://www.nlm.nih.gov/exhibition/blackwell/.

Students can use a storyboard to write their documentary. Explain how to create a simple two-column chart in Word. In the left-hand column, students should record the visual image that will be shown on the screen (Header: What do you see?) This could be as simple as describing the image (i.e., a picture of Elizabeth Blackwell's childhood home) or it could be a thumbnail image from an online source. The right-hand column should contain the narration for the documentary. (Header: What do you hear?) Students can also make suggestions for background music.

On Your Own: Integrating Ideas:

Activity 3: A good resource is Susan Casey's *Women Invent: Two Centuries of Discoveries That Have Shaped Our World* (Chicago Review Press, 1997).

Alternative Activity: Students might enjoy reviewing the movie or reading the book *Hidden Figures* by Margot Lee Shetterly about the brilliant African American women who worked at NASA as mathematicians during the American-Russian space race.

Documentary

A documentary is a movie, television, or radio program that provides a factual record or report. Documentaries use text, images, and music to convey facts about a person's life. Write a script for a 3- to 5-minute documentary film about Blackwell's life. (Or choose another person who fought for human rights according to your teacher's guidelines.)

Although the goal of your documentary is to present facts, it should be as captivating to the viewer as a well-written piece of fiction. Think about how you can creatively communicate the events of Blackwell's life.

	Use the following guidelines for your documentary script.
To receive the highest score, the script must meet all of these criteria.	Your script • raises interesting questions about its subject. • presents provocative ideas about the time in which it takes place. • offers information in an entertaining and inviting manner. • uses correct grammar, word usage, spelling, and punctuation.

On Your Own: Integrating Ideas

1. Read several articles about 19th century medicine. Which of the advancements made since then have turned out to be the most significant?
2. Read about other women pioneers in medicine, such as Florence Nightingale, Elizabeth Anderson, Maria Montessori, Virginia Apgar, and Antonia Novello.
3. Research current female innovators in science, medicine, or technology. What do these women have in common with Elizabeth Blackwell?

ELL Support: Connect to Testing and Assessments See the ELL Teacher Resource (p. 22) for ideas on adapting this section for ELLs.

Connect to Testing

In this chapter you practiced the skills of determining theme, analyzing structure, and identifying the author's purpose. You will be tested on these skills on reading tests. Answer the following questions to help you practice these skills.

Read the following excerpt from the play and then answer the questions that follow.

> **ELIZABETH:** *(With a dreamy enthusiasm)* I can see myself on a big, white horse, leading a charge into battle! Or painting a famous picture! Or . . . or . . . making a big, important speech while thousands of people cheer!
>
> **MAN 1:** *(Entering stage left)* As if women could say anything important!
>
> **MAN 2:** *(Entering stage right)* As if women could do anything important!

1. Which of the following best describes the central conflict of the scene in the excerpt above?

   A. business owners vs. employees

   B. women's desire for rights vs. men's ideas about women

   C. Elizabeth's dreams vs. society's expectations of women

   D. Mr. Blackwell's plans for his daughters' education vs. Mrs. Blackwell's plans

2. Write a paragraph describing the theme of the scene in this chapter. Refer to details in the text to support your answer.

Connect to Testing: This Connect to Testing section focuses on determining theme, analyzing characters, and identifying the purpose of a scene.

Encourage students to work in pairs to choose the correct answers to the questions and then to compare their answers with those of another pair of students. If there is disagreement, encourage the groups to try to reach a consensus as they discuss the reasons for their choices.

Answers to Connect to Testing Questions:

1. C. The excerpt shows Elizabeth's dreams to accomplish something great versus traditional social expectations which kept women as housewives who were not educated. (DoK 2)

2. Responses to theme may vary, as will details of support; possible themes: Women must overcome society's expectations in order to pursue their dreams. Because of the support of her radical father, Elizabeth Blackwell was able to overcome society's views of women's abilities and become the first American woman to become a doctor. (DoK 2)

(continued)

Chapter **20** *(continued)*

Assessment

Answers to Connect to Testing Questions:

3. **Part A:** C.

    Part B: D. Choice D supports Choice C because Mrs. Blackwell is mildly concerned that educating their daughters will go to waste because women at that time didn't need an education to be a mother and a homemaker. (DoK 2)

4. **Part A:** D.

    Part B: Choices B, E, and G all describe Mr. Blackwell's encouragement of Elizabeth's goals and dreams. Some students may also argue for Choice C because this is evidence of Elizabeth's hopes and dreams. Accept C at your discretion. (DoK 3)

3. **Part A:** In the passage, Mrs. Blackwell's character could best be described as

    A. terrified but aware of the need for women's rights.

    B. enraged at the injustice confronting her daughter.

    C. skeptical that her daughter will benefit from an education.

    D. angry that her husband was paying too much attention to her daughter.

    Part B: Which of the following provides the strongest evidence for the answer to Part A?

    A. (MRS. BLACKWELL steps forward. She's quieter than her husband and daughter.)

    B. **MRS. BLACKWELL:** *But, husband dear, our house is already bursting at the seams! How will we fit in one more person?!*

    C. **MR. BLACKWELL:** *We'll just have to try! The governess will teach our girls the same subjects the boys are learning in public school.*

    D. **MRS. BLACKWELL:** (With mild protest) *But, husband dear. What will they do with such knowledge?*

4. **Part A:** The purpose of the scene in the chapter is to

    A. provide a factual description of an event from Elizabeth's childhood.

    B. establish the setting of America in the 1800s.

    C. describe the poor working conditions people faced in the 1800s.

    D. explain the influence of Mr. Blackwell on his daughter's character.

    Part B: Which of the following provides the strongest evidence for the answer to Part A? Choose all that apply.

    A. **MRS. BLACKWELL:** *Husband! Elizabeth is far too young to have any idea what she wants to be.*

    B. **MR. BLACKWELL:** *I believe you will, Elizabeth! There's a special determination about you. A special spark.*

    C. **ELIZABETH:** (With a dreamy enthusiasm) *I can see myself on a big, white horse, leading a charge into battle! Or painting a famous picture! Or . . . or . . . making a big, important speech while thousands of people cheer!*

    D. **MAN 1:** (Entering stage left) *As if women could say anything important!*

    E. **MR. BLACKWELL:** (Speaking seriously) *Never forget, child. The greatest thing in life is to find a cause you believe in and fight for it!*

    F. **ELIZABETH:** *You take that back!*

    G. **MR. BLACKWELL:** *It's all right, Elizabeth. When you have new and different ideas, you're likely to take a lot of punishment! (with conviction) But the important thing is not to let the criticism bother you. Just keep on working for what you believe.*

Remediation: Connect to Testing Invite students to read the questions and responses with a partner before answering.

Writing a Research Paper

Those who cannot remember the past are
condemned to repeat it.
—George Santayana

Study the past if you would define the future.
—Confucius

In this unit, you read a mixture of nonfiction and fiction on historical subjects ranging from the civil war to civil rights. In this chapter, you'll research and write about a historical figure to explore the qualities that led that person to advance a cause, right a wrong, or lead a nation.

WRITING PROMPT

Think of a person from history that you find intriguing. It may be a charismatic leader, someone who was the first to achieve something, an inventor, or an average person who spoke out against injustice. Research and write a biographical sketch of that person that captures both the actions and the character of the person. While the paper should include basic biographical facts, the central focus should be on an event or action that made history. In your conclusion, identify a lesson you learned by studying this person's life. Find five good sources to use for your research. Your final paper should be two to three typed pages and double-spaced. Use Times New Roman 12 point font.

Look over the prompt. Underline key words that explain the requirements of the task. Then fill in the following graphic organizer to identify what you must do.

Purpose	
Audience	
Content Requirements	
Additional Requirements	

Writing a Research Paper

Introduction

Preview Academic Vocabulary: Read and discuss the meanings of the academic vocabulary.

copyright: *the legal right to produce or sell a book.* The author owns the <u>copyright</u> to his new novel.

reliability: *trustworthiness.* Our teacher questioned the <u>reliability</u> of one of my sources that came from a political website.

thesis statement: *the central idea of a paper.* Tom had to revise his <u>thesis statement</u> so it covered the last section.

paraphrase: *to state the meaning of a text in one's own words.* After reading the long paragraph, Jenny had to <u>paraphrase</u> it.

plagiarizing: *taking someone else's work as one's own.* <u>Plagiarizing</u> another writer is considered just cause for a failing grade.

Writing Prompt: Ask students to identify the key requirements of their research paper: (1) Research and write a biographical sketch that sums up both the actions and the character of a historical figure. (2) Emphasize an event or action involving that figure that made history. (3) Identify a lesson they learned from their investigation of this person. They should also fill in the chart with the details.

Make sure they understand the number of sources required (at least 5); the length of the paper (2–3 typed pages, double-spaced, using Times New Roman 12-point font). You may also want to remind them to use one-inch margins.

 Gr7U4WritingResearch.pptx

ELL Support: Academic Vocabulary See <u>Teaching Vocabulary in the ELL Teacher Resource (p. 18)</u> for ideas to use for teaching vocabulary throughout *Connections*.

Writing *(continued)*

Brainstorm: Point out to students that a research paper is time consuming, so it's important to find a historical figure that will keep their interest. If they like the subject, their audience is likely to enjoy it as well. Offer some possible suggestions:

- Lewis, Clark, Sacagawea (amazing explorers of the American West)
- Jerrie Mock (the first woman to fly around the world)
- Rachel Carson (the great environmentalist)
- Louis Leakey, Mary Leakey (pioneer anthropologists)
- Frederick Douglass (escaped slave, who became a leading abolitionist)
- Sonia Sotomayor (associate justice of the Supreme Court)

The Writing Process

Brainstorm

First, gather some general ideas about people from history that you find interesting. Use the following questions to direct your thinking. Jot down notes in the margins.

1. Think about people you have studied in your history classes. Which people did you find intriguing and want to know more about?
2. What movies have you seen lately that made you want to learn more about a person who made history?
3. What historical fiction books have you read? Did any of the events or people make you want to learn more about them on the Internet to see if the movie was historically accurate?
4. To get more ideas, Google a topic that interests you. For example, *women scientists* or *who invented the computer*.

From your notes, create a list. Narrow down the topics to two or three. Then conduct some initial research online to make sure you can find five sources on the person. If you can't find enough sources, choose a different person.

Gather Ideas

Create an organizer similar to the one shown. Write the name of the person you have chosen to research in the center circle. Then note what event they were involved in or what action they took that made them worthy of study. In the circles surrounding the center circle, write details about the person and the event that you currently know about.

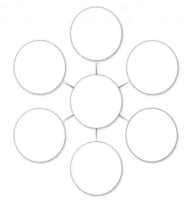

ELL Support: Writing Prompt Have students work in multilevel pairs or small groups on this project, including all the activities. Paraphrase the prompt: *Think of a person from history that you are interested in. The person may be a leader or a person who did something important, like making something new or helping others. Read about this person. Write about the person's life. Write about what he or she did that was important. Tell what you learned about life from this person.*

After completing the graphic organizer, you'll have a better idea of what questions need to be answered about your topic. Write the *who, what, when, where, why,* and *how* about your subject and event below. Then write one question you have about each of these points. If your answer is "I don't know," that's okay. That's the point of the exercise.

Who? _____

One question I would like to answer:

What? _____

One question I would like to answer:

When? _____

One question I would like to answer:

Where? _____

One question I would like to answer:

continued on next page

Gather Ideas: Once students have an idea of the questions they hope to answer, they can begin researching. As they learn more about their subject, they are likely to branch out in unexpected directions. Surprises can make research more interesting and exciting for them and for their audience.

ELL Support: Gather Ideas You may also adapt the research requirements of the project as follows:

1. Find two reliable sources.
2. Put each source on a note card.
3. Use these sources to answer the six questions on pages 431–432.

Writing (continued)

Conduct Research: Point out the importance of keeping accurate notes about their sources. They may need this information for their bibliography/works cited page and for in-text citations. They should also carefully check the reliability of any source they plan to use; an unreliable source would call into question the information they are using.

Why? _____

One question I would like to answer:

How? _____

One question I would like to answer:

Conduct Research

Use the questions you generated to guide your research. Many sources can be found online, but not all sources are equal in quality and reliability.

Evaluate sources carefully to make sure the author or creator is reliable. Websites that end in .gov (published by the government) or .edu (sponsored by a college or other educational facility) are generally trustworthy. The following questions will help you evaluate the quality of your sources:

1. Who wrote it? Is the author an expert on the topic? Was the writer an eyewitness to the events described? Sources written by someone who witnessed or was involved in the events are called primary sources. Sources written by someone who was not directly involved in the events are referred to as secondary sources. Reading primary sources such as letters, diaries, and biographies can offer new perspectives on historical figures and challenge your assumptions about events of the past.

2. What is the purpose? Websites that are trying to sell a product or make money may misrepresent information to persuade viewers. Books or magazines published by political institutions may only present one side of an issue or contain bias.

3. When was it written? Sometimes new information is discovered that impacts what we know about history. Check for the copyright year or year of publication. More recent information is usually better than something written 25 years ago, unless it is a primary source.

ELL Support: Second Read Students should work in their multilevel pairs or groups to read linguistically accommodated resources about the historical figure they have chosen. As students read, encourage them to take notes on a Biography graphic organizer from the ELL Teacher Resource (p. 57). Encourage students to draw sketches in the graphic organizer so they can be sure they understand and remember the details.

Take Notes

As you read your sources, take notes on key ideas you want to include in your paper. Notes can be recorded in a word processing file, a note-taking program, or on paper note cards.

When taking notes, either:

- write the information in your own words—paraphrase what the source says, or
- quote the source word for word. Be sure to put the quoted information in quotation marks.

This will help you avoid plagiarizing, or taking someone else's work as your own, when you write your paper. When writing about a person, include quotations to share important things the person said or wrote. However, using too many direct quotations can make your writing choppy.

Always include source information under the note—author's name, title of the article or book, website name, publisher, and date of publication. At the top write a short description of the information.

Sample note for direct quotation

Lost Opportunities for Girls' Education ————————— Description

"A lost opportunity for education not only hurts the girls forced into early marriage, but has far-reaching and long-lasting repercussions for their children and communities." —— Quotation

—Agnes Odhiambo, women's rights in Africa researcher

Odhiambo, Agnes. "Why Keeping Girls in School Can Help South Sudan" www.hrw.org.HumanRightsWatch. 10 Oct 2014. Page 95. —— Source Information

Organize Ideas

Your paper should open with an introduction that includes a thesis statement or a main idea statement. This sentence should include the name of the historical figure and the impact he or she had on the world. For example, if you were writing about Elizabeth Blackwell, your thesis statement might be *Elizabeth Blackwell was the first woman to graduate from medical school, proving that women could be effective doctors.*

Before you begin writing, make a plan for your paper. Think about how to logically organize your ideas. When writing about the life of a person, chronological order makes sense. Provide background information, facts about main accomplishments, and impact on history. Use the order of the graphic organizer on the next page to help you organize your notes into a logical order.

Take Notes: Depending on the source, note-taking can take several forms: (1) direct quotes; (2) paraphrasing; (3) summarizing (a condensed review). Stress the importance of avoiding plagiarism when paraphrasing.

Make students aware of the fact that online programs allow teachers to easily check for plagiarism. These include www.plagiarismchecker.com and www.plagtracker.com.

If you desire, require students to include in-text citations for all information that is not common knowledge. A good source for teaching about citing text is the OWL Purdue Online Writing Lab: (https://owl.english.purdue.edu/owl/). Search for *in-text citations.* Instruction is provided for both MLA and APA styles.

You may also require students to include a Works Cited or bibliography page with their report. Many online sources explain how to compile such pages. To teach students how to compile a page on their own, use the Purdue Online Writing Lab at https://owl.english.purdue.edu/owl/. Another option is to use online bibliography page makers such as easybib.com or bibme.org.

Organize Ideas: To develop a thesis statement, students should try answering this question: *Why is your historical figure important to the world?* The answer could be tweaked as a thesis statement. Have students work with a partner to strengthen their thesis statements by replacing vague words with clear, specific language. Then have them turn them in for your approval before they begin to develop their outlines.

As students develop outlines, they might jot down reminders about where to insert specific research notes.

Remind students to use good transitional phrases that are appropriate for writing that is written in chronological order. Ask students to share appropriate words and phrases as you make a list on the board. Possibilities include: *first, next, afterward, later, in (date), when,* and *before.*

Writing *(continued)*

First Draft: Direct students' attention to the second bullet: *Write quickly. You will revise and proofread later*. Remind them of the importance of letting their thoughts and ideas flow, rather than getting distracted by grammar, punctuation, or spelling. Revision and proofreading should take place at a later stage, when they have finalized their research, note-taking, organization, and ideas.

To help students understand when to use in-text citations and how to write good sentences that acknowledge sources, display a chart in class with examples such as the following:

- Lisa Brown, a professor at Yale University, notes, "..." (Brown 3).

- Ken Burns' documentary shows that Jackie Robinson's dogged determination to play major league baseball changed the sport forever.

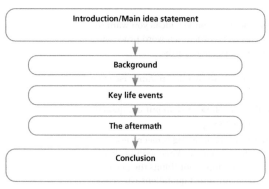

Organize the notes you've taken and put them in order according to the topics on the graphic organizer. You may find that you don't have enough information for some of the main ideas. Conduct more research so that you have strong facts and details about each point.

First Draft

Use your outline to write a first draft of your paper. Here are some tips for drafting:

- Refer to the order in the graphic organizer.

- Write quickly. You will revise and proofread later.

- Write on every other line or double-space if working on a computer. This will make it easier to make revisions.

- If you take a break and then return to drafting, reread what you have written before continuing. This will help you resume the flow of thought.

- Mark this paper Draft #1.

- Make sure to include your citations in your draft.

As you write your paper, include the sources from your notes. These in-text citations usually record the author's last name and a page number: (Odhiambo 95). Formats vary, so follow your teacher's instructions carefully. Including citations in your draft will save time later. Also, compile a list of all the sources used in your research and follow your teacher's instructions for formatting.

Revision

When you complete your first draft, show it to others. Here are three ways to revise your paper.

> **REFLECT**
>
> As you write, keep an eye out for problems. Each sentence in your paper should flow clearly into the next. If your ideas aren't making sense to you, they will not make sense to your readers either.

ELL Support: First Draft Have students continue to work in their multilevel pairs or small groups to draft their biographies. Provide the following sentence frames to guide students:

_____ was an important person because . . . . He/she lived from . . . to . . . . During this time, people needed . . . . They also needed . . . . _____ worked hard to . . . . Also, he/she . . . . From_____'s life and work, I learned that people . . . . I also learned that I . . . .

First Peer Review

This review will evaluate whether your ideas are interesting and whether they flow together in a logical order. With a group of two to three people, complete the following steps.

Steps for Peer Review

1. Select a timekeeper. Each writer gets ten minutes. Stick to the time.
2. One person begins by reading aloud his or her introduction while other members listen.
3. Pause. The same writer reads the introduction aloud a second time.
4. Writer asks, "Does the introduction of my research paper make you want to know more? Does it clearly explain what my paper is about?" Each member responds, as the writer takes notes on his or her draft.
5. Writer reads the entire paper, pauses, and then reads it again.
6. As writer reads, members take notes.
7. Writer asks, "What questions do you have about the person I wrote about? What else do you want to know about him or her?" Writer jots down replies.
8. Repeat Steps 1–7 with the next writer.

As soon as you've finished the peer review, look over the feedback you received. Revise, or edit, the paper now, changing it according to these comments. Mark this Draft #2.

Second Peer Review

Second Review: Teacher/Parent Review

Ask an adult or older sibling to read your paper and evaluate it using the following rubric.

Thesis statement
Is my main idea clearly stated in the introduction?

Content
Is there enough information given about the person and their contribution to history?
What information or ideas are missing?
Do any points need to be more developed?

Organization of Ideas
Are the main points logically organized?
Are good transitions used between paragraphs? between ideas?

Conclusion
Does my conclusion reinforce the thesis statement?
Does it bring the paper to a satisfying close?

Grammar, Usage, Punctuation, and Spelling
Are there any mistakes in grammar, usage, punctuation, and spelling?

When you finish, label this Draft 3.

First Peer Review: Encourage students to keep an open mind to feedback from their peers. It's hard to be objective about our own writing, especially when we've put in a lot of time and effort. Students should think about this review as an opportunity to hear about any issues that require change. A first draft is not supposed to be written in stone. Feedback offers a chance for students to improve their work—and get a better grade!

Second Peer Review: Students should keep in mind that, as they critique other students' work, they are learning about how to write a better paper. In a way, they are functioning as editors—and everybody needs a good editor.

To prevent student editors from simply answering the questions in the Second Peer Review with a simple yes or no, require students to add a "because" statement to each answer. For example: *Yes, because the order follows in chronological order* or *No, the conclusion isn't satisfying because it introduces new information.*

ELL Support: Revision Before students revise and edit, read through the Informational Writing Revision Checklist (p. 69). Then model how to revise writing by displaying a student biography and explaining how to revise the text for each item on the checklist, such as checking the topic sentence. Display another student biography to demonstrate how to revise for the second item on the checklist.

First Peer Review Have students work in several new groups of multilevel pairs or small groups to review their drafts. Allow time between each review for students to work in their original multilevel pairs or groups to revise or edit their work.

Writing (continued)

Lesson Support

Final Peer Review: Remind students of the importance of offering positive feedback, congratulating fellow students for strong points in their work, and offering only gentle advice about changes.

Final Essay: Encourage students to publish their research report online using Google Docs or your class or school website. Require students to include hyperlinks to their online sources.

Final Peer Review

Ask a classmate to read your paper. Have him or her give it a rating using the rubric below.

Use the following guidelines for your research paper.	
To receive the highest score, the narrative must meet all of these criteria.	Your research paper should • discuss a historical figure and his or her involvement in an important historical event. • include engaging description of the life and personality of the person and the events surrounding his or her contributions to history. • be logically organized and include good transitions. • have a clear and interesting writing style that includes a variety of sentence types. • cite sources to avoid plagiarism and include a list of all sources consulted for the paper. • use correct grammar, word usage, punctuation, and spelling.

Proofread

Proofreading is important. Before you turn in your paper, check for mistakes in punctuation and grammar. Make sure, as well, that you didn't leave any words out of sentences. Check for mistakes that your spell check program won't find, such as using *there* instead of *their* and other easily confused words.

Final Essay

Share your completed essay with audiences beyond your classroom. Read it to your family and friends. Upload your finished digital copy to your class website. Find an appropriate website and ask the editors to publish it. If you have a school or personal blog, share it with your readers.

Practice Performance Task

A performance task determines how well you understand literary and informational texts. The task may start with multiple-choice or short answer questions. These questions usually cover the main ideas of the passages and also important vocabulary. The questions prepare you to complete a writing assignment.

Complete the following performance task based on selections from this unit.

Source #1

Read the following excerpt from *The Lions of Little Rock*.

"I thought things settled down at Central once they called the soldiers in."

"Somewhat," said Daddy. "At least that was the official story. But things were not ever pleasant for them there. Minnijean Brown got expelled."

She was the colored girl who'd dumped a bowl of soup on the boys who were picking on her. That was something Liz would do.

"If they were still being harassed, why didn't they complain?"

Daddy shrugged. "Maybe they did and nothing was done. Maybe they thought if they showed any weakness, it would only get worse. In any case, last year the pictures from Central told the whole world Little Rock is filled with hate. And now the town's gone and voted against opening the schools. We are not just a town of racists, but those of us who believe in integration . . ." He shook his head. "We can't seem to find our voice."

Daddy was so upset, for a minute I thought he was going to cry. That scared me as bad as anything he'd said.

continued on next page

Unit 4 Assessment

Practice Performance Task

The purpose of this section is to prepare students for the types of performance tasks they will be completing on standardized testing. The task requires students to synthesize knowledge gained and skills developed throughout the unit. If used as test prep, review with students the process of answering multiple-choice questions, including eliminating answers that are clearly incorrect.

This performance task could be used as an assessment over Unit 4, instead of the Unit 4 Assessment on pages 477–485. It could be completed entirely during class time. Alternatively, the task may be completed over two class periods by having students complete questions 1–6 and the planning stage of the writing task during one class period and writing the essay during the second class period. Another alternative is to assign the writing to be completed at home.

ELL Support: Practice Performance Task Have students work in multilevel pairs or small groups to read and answer questions. Then have students work in the same multilevel pairs or small groups to write in response to the performance task prompt. Adjust the length of student responses as necessary. Students can write a paragraph or complete the graphic organizer. Provide the Informational Writing Revision Checklist from the ELL Teacher Resource (p. 69) for students to use to finalize their written response from pp. 440–442.

Assessment *(continued)*

Lesson Support

Answers to Practice Performance Task:

1. Possible response: Marlee would support integration. Her friend Liz is African American and she doesn't feel that she should stay away from her because she is different. (DoK 2)

2. A. (DoK 2)

3. D. (DoK 2)

(continued)

I knew what it was like to have trouble finding your voice, so I reached over and patted his arm. He didn't look at me.

"I mean it, Marlee. I don't want to scare you too much—I'll keep you safe—but I do want you to be careful. Which means you stay away from Liz."

I nodded to show him I understood what he was saying.

But I didn't promise that I would.

1. What is most likely Marlee's point of view about integration?

2. What could you infer about Marlee's father's opinion of his community?
   A. He is ashamed that the community has voted against integration.
   B. He is neutral about his community's decision.
   C. He wishes he lived in another community.
   D. He wants integration to happen at a slower pace.

3. What is the connotation of the phrase *find our voice* in the passage?
   A. It suggests that no one is sufficiently interested in integration.
   B. It suggests that people in favor of integration aren't effectively organized.
   C. It suggests that integration is too difficult to achieve in the United States.
   D. It suggests that integration advocates haven't been able to communicate well.

Source #2

Continue the performance task by reading this passage and answering the questions that follow.

MR. BLACKWELL: Everyone is <u>entitled</u> to earn a decent living!

WOMAN 1: Stop your jabbering about decent wages. You'll take away some of the profits from my husband's cloth factory.

MR. BLACKWELL: Good!

WOMAN 2: Mr. Blackwell also wants to make our hospitals cleaner and better run!

MAN 2: And he wants to raise our taxes to do it!

ELIZABETH: *(Proudly)* My father believes that women should be free and equal citizens. They should not be considered just the property of their husbands!

MAN 1 and MAN 2: Balderdash!

MAN 1: Mr. Blackwell, you are a crackpot!

ELIZABETH: How dare you say such things about my father! He's a very great man!

MAN 2: He's crazy as a loon!

(Marching determinedly to MAN 2, ELIZABETH gives him a kick in the leg.)

ELIZABETH: You take that back!

4. Write a short summary of this passage.

---

4. Possible response: Mr. Blackwell supports human rights like fair wages and good hospitals. By contrast, the Men and Women support oppressive views. Elizabeth proudly proclaims her father's support of women's rights and his greatness. The Men and Women claim he is crazy. (DoK 2)

(continued)

continued on next page

Assessment *(continued)*

Answers to Practice Performance Task:

5. A. This is supported by Elizabeth's statement about women being free and equal citizens. Although she says her father believes this, it can be inferred that she shares this viewpoint because she says it with pride. (DoK 2)

6. B. From the context, Mr. Blackwell believes that everyone has a right to earn a living. Although Choice D is close in meaning, it is not the same. Everyone has a right to earn a living, but not everyone is guaranteed a living. (DoK 2)

Your Assignment: Make sure students have a clear understanding of the writing prompt by asking these questions:

- What is the basic objective of the comparison essay? (*to compare the main female character from Lions of Little Rock and from "Elizabeth Blackwell"*)

- What is the basis for the comparison? (*both were females who clashed with family members and their community*)

- What areas should students compare? (*conflicts and relationships with fathers*)

- How should students support their ideas? (*with evidence from the text*)

- Post the rubric you will use to evaluate student writing.

5. What could you infer about Elizabeth's feelings about men and women being paid equally?

   A. She most likely feels it is important that everyone be paid equally.

   B. She most likely feels wage amounts have to be decided by managers.

   C. She most likely feels that factory workers need to be paid more.

   D. She most likely feels that she needs to consider the effects of wage equality further.

6. Based on the context, the word *entitled* most nearly means

   A. to provide the means to

   B. to give a right to

   C. to give a title to

   D. to guarantee

Your Assignment

> **WRITING PROMPT**
>
> Use *The Lions of Little Rock* and the play "Elizabeth Blackwell" as your two sources. Compare them as portraits of strong female characters who face opposition from family and their communities. Return to each source as needed. As you write your comparison, support your main idea with details from the passages.

Before you begin your comparative essay, fill in the graphic organizer on the next page to organize your thoughts. Consider the main characters, the conflicts they are facing, and their relationship with their fathers based upon the excerpts you read. Return to the texts to find evidence to support the similarities in the texts.

	Lions of Little Rock	Elizabeth Blackwell
Similarity 1/ Evidence		
Similarity 2/ Evidence		
Similarity 3/ Evidence		

Explanation

Read the prompt carefully before you begin writing. Underline key words that explain what you are required to do. Study the rubric on the next page before you being writing.

Use the information from the graphic organizer to write your essay. Before you begin, sketch out an outline on a sheet of paper. Explain the evidence carefully and thoroughly. Arrange your ideas so they flow together logically.

Assessment *(continued)*

Lesson Support

Essential Question Connection: Revisit the Essential Question: *What does history tell us about ourselves?* You may want to have students write a response essay to this question based on the selections they've read and the discussions they've had throughout the unit. Ask students to include whether their thoughts surrounding this question have changed, and if so, how have they changed and why. Encourage them to refer to the selections and their impact in helping them form their answer to the questions.

 Gr7U4PerformanceTask.pptx

Rubric

Your response will be scored using the following criteria:

Reading Comprehension
- How well did you understand the texts?
- Did your writing reflect your understanding of the sources?

Writing Expression
- Does your writing address the requirements of the prompt?
- Does your comparison reflect the content of both sources?
- Is your comparison well organized with reasons that flow logically?
- Does the writing style contain precise, accurate language and content?
- Is your writing appropriate for the purpose, task, and audience?

Writing Conventions
- Does your writing follow the rules of standard English with few errors in grammar, word usage, and spelling?

When you are finished writing, evaluate your essay using the rubric above. Revise your writing as needed.

Acknowledgments

Pages 10–12, Decety J and Cowell J (2016) OUR BRAINS ARE WIRED FOR MORALITY: EVOLUTION, DEVELOPMENT, AND NEUROSCIENCE. Front Young Minds. 4:3. doi: 10.3389/frym.2016.00003.

Pages 48–51, ZOO COMPLICATED: ARE CAPTIVE ANIMALS HAPPY? by Kathryn Hulick from Muse magazine, © by Carus Publishing Company. Reproduced with permission. All Cricket Media material is copyrighted by Carus Publishing Company, d/b/a Cricket Media, and/or various authors and illustrators. Any commercial use or distribution of material without permission is strictly prohibited. Please visit http://www.cricketmedia.com/info/licensing2 for licensing and http://www.cricketmedia.com for subscriptions.

Pages 83–85, "Why I am a Vegetarian" by Matthieu Ricard from A PLEA FROM THE ANIMALS. Copyright 2014 by Matthieu Ricard. Previously published in French as "Plaidoyer pour les Animaux: Vers une Bienveillance pour Tous." English copyright 2016, from A Plea for the Animals: The Moral, Philosophical, and Evolutionary Imperative to Treat All Beings with Compassion. Published by Shambhala Publications. Used by permission.

Pages 89–91, VEGETARIANISM by Judy Krizmanic from Muse magazine, © by Carus Publishing Company. Reproduced with permission. All Cricket Media material is copyrighted by Carus Publishing Company, d/b/a Cricket Media, and/or various authors and illustrators. Any commercial use or distribution of material without permission is strictly prohibited. Please visit http://www.cricketmedia.com/info/licensing2 for licensing and http://www.cricketmedia.com for subscriptions.

Pages 120–123, Excerpt(s) from CATCH ME IF YOU CAN: THE TRUE STORY OF A REAL FAKE by Frank W. Abagnale, copyright © 1980 by Frank W. Abagnale. Used by permission of Broadway Books, an imprint of the Crown Publishing Group, a division of Penguin Random House LLC. All rights reserved.

Pages 140–143, Reprinted from Guy P. Harrison, THINK: WHY YOU SHOULD QUESTION EVERYTHING (Amherst, NY: Prometheus Books, 2013), pp. 61–64. Copyright © 2013 by Guy P. Harrison. All rights reserved. Used with permission of the publisher; www.prometheusbooks.com.

Pages 159–162, THE FACT CHECKER'S GUIDE FOR DETECTING FAKE NEWS. From The Washington Post, November 22, 2016, © 2016 The Washington Post. All rights reserved. Used by permission and protected by the copyright laws of the United States. The printing, copying, redistribution, or retransmission of this content without express written permission is prohibited.

Pages 178–181, DEBUNK IT! HOW TO STAY SANE IN A WORLD OF MISINFORMATION

Pages 197–200, Excerpt from THE GIVER by Lois Lowry. Copyright © 1993 by Lois Lowry. Reprinted by permission of Houghton Mifflin Harcourt Publishing Company. All rights reserved.

Pages 234–237, Excerpt(s) from SMARTER THAN YOU THINK: HOW TECHNOLOGY IS CHANGING OUR MINDS FOR THE BETTER by Clive Thompson, copyright © 2013 by Clive Thompson. Used by permission of Penguin Press, an imprint of Penguin Publishing Group, a division of Penguin Random House LLC. All rights reserved.

Pages 251–253, "All Watched Over by Machines of Loving Grace" from THE PILL VERSUS THE SPRINGHILL MINE DISASTER by Richard Brautigan. Copyright © 1968 by Richard Brautigan. Reprinted by permission of Houghton Mifflin Harcourt Publishing Company. All rights reserved.

Pages 270–272, ROBOTS WILL ELIMINATE 6% OF ALL U.S. JOBS BY 2021, REPORT SAYS" by Olivia Solon. Copyright Guardian News & Media Ltd. 2017

Pages 275–276, ROBOTS ARE SLOWLY TAKING OVER THE JOB MARKET

Pages 288–292. FEED. Copyright © 2002 M.T. Anderson. Reproduced by permission of the publisher, Candlewick Press, Somerville, MA.

Pages 306–308, "It's 'digital heroin': How screens turn kids into psychotic junkies" by Dr. Nicholas Kardaras was originally published in the *New York Post* on August 27, 2016. Reprinted with permission from the author.

Pages 312–314, WHY CALLING SCREEN TIME 'DIGITAL HEROIN' IS DIGITAL GARBAGE by Rachel Becker, originally published on The Verge on August 30, 2016. Copyright Vox Media, Inc. Used by permission.

Pages 342–346, "Talking to Daddy" from THE LIONS OF LITTLE ROCK by Kristin Levine, copyright © 2012 by Kristin Levine. Used by permission of G. P. Putnam's Sons Books for Young Readers, an imprint of Penguin Young Readers Group, a division of Penguin Random House LLC. All rights reserved.

Pages 350–354, THE HISTORY BEHIND THE LITTLE ROCK NINE from the Arkansas Department of Parks & Tourism at arkansas.com. Used by permission.

Pages 365–368, THE DRUMMER BOY OF SHILOH by Ray Bradbury. Reprinted by permission of Don Congdon Associates, Inc. Copyright © 1960 by the Curtis Publishing Company, renewed 1988 by Ray Bradbury.

Pages 371–372, DRUMMER BOYS by Stephen Currie from Cobblestone magazine, © by Carus Publishing Company. Reproduced with permission. All Cricket Media material is copyrighted by Carus Publishing Company, d/b/a Cricket Media, and/or various authors and illustrators. Any commercial use or distribution of material without permission is strictly prohibited. Please visit http://www.cricketmedia.com/info/licensing2 for licensing and http://www.cricketmedia.com for subscriptions.

Pages 382–384, "Our Jacko" by Michael Morpurgo from THE GREAT WAR: STORIES INSPIRED BY ITEMS FROM THE FIRST WORLD WAR. Reprinted by permission of Candlewick Press. All rights reserved.

Pages 396–399, From FALLEN ANGELS by Walter Dean Myers. Copyright © 1988 by Walter Dean Myers. Reprinted by permission of Scholastic Inc. (Digital rights) Reprinted by permission of DeFiore and Company, on behalf of the Estate of Walter M. Myers. Copyright © 1988 by Walter Dean Myers.

Photo Credits: iStock: pp. 379 (middle), 384; Library of Congress: p. 176 (middle), NPS Photo: p. 367; Thinkstock.com: all other photos

Using Technology in the Classroom

Cell Phones

Depending upon the policies at your school, consider using hand-held technology to gauge student understanding of a concept, to capture notes and ideas for later use, or to communicate with teachers or fellow classmates. Because smartphones are essentially mini-computers, their uses are practically unlimited. Students can also download free apps to use during classroom activities. Even students with cell phones that aren't smart phones can text and use Twitter to submit answers and communicate with teachers.

Tips for Using Cell Phones in the Classroom

Establish and clearly communicate rules. This use of technology will be more manageable if students are required to keep their phones off and out of sight unless they have been instructed to use them. Communicate and enforce clear consequences for misusing phones. A manageable option is to plan to use cell phones only for introductory activities during the first ten minutes of class and/or for formative assessment during the final ten minutes of class. This gives students clear boundaries for cell phone use.

Work with school administration: Schools have varying policies about cell phone usage. Communicate your plans and goals with your administrator and technology personnel. Work with them to establish boundaries for technology use and to ensure all students have equal access to technology.

Start simple: Don't try to incorporate too much technology at once. Choose two ideas (e.g., cell phones and Google Docs) and use them exclusively for a semester. Consider integrating a skill that most students can already do, such as texting answers to a classroom poll or using a cell phone camera to illustrate a story. Starting small, with technology you know and love, is better for both you and your students.

Provide options: Not all students will have a phone, but they may have other mobile devices with the ability to email, text, or access the Internet. If possible, provide school-owned technology to students who don't own a device. Another option is to provide optional assignments for students without access to any technology.

Have a practice day: Early in the course, spend a class period explaining and practicing the technology you plan to implement during the course. This will help you work out any problems before using the technology in an actual lesson.

Suggested Tech-Connect Content

PollEverywhere.com Use this free site to generate polls in the form of multiple-choice or free-form text response questions. Display the poll for the class using a projector. Stude44nts submit their responses by texting, tweeting, or using a web browser. Responses are instantly compiled and can be displayed on a graph, in a list, or as a collage, among other options. Teachers can ask students to sign their answers for accountability. Use Poll Everywhere to solicit student reactions to the first reading of a text or to gauge student understanding of concepts and for formative assessment.

Using Technology in the Classroom (continued)

Edmodo.com Edmodo is a secure, social learning platform for teachers, students, schools, and districts. It provides a safe and easy way for classes to connect and collaborate, share content, and access homework, grades, and school notices. Teachers can post quizzes, polls, and assignments, which students can take and turn in online. The site keeps track of who has completed assignments. Assignments can be locked to prevent late work from being turned in. Students can post questions about assignments and ask and respond to comments and questions from other classmates. Public domain texts can be posted on Edmodo, and then students can post comments or respond to classmates' comments. Multiple classes within a school or across the district can all respond to the same text. (Copyrighted material should not be posted.)

Twitter.com Ask students to ask questions and respond to questions by sending a text to a Twitter account. Both students and teachers must have accounts. Students' accounts should include their name or initials so that the teacher can recognize them and give them a participation grade. Create a hashtag (#) for your class, topic, or assignment. (It's a good idea to check your hashtag first on hashtags.org to make sure it isn't already in use.) After you register your hashtag, you can begin tweeting your followers. Students type their responses. By adding @ and your hashtag, they can send their reply directly to you. Students can also search hashtags (#) for topics to find what others have to say about a subject.

Google Docs This is a platform to share online documents, work on them in real time with your students or colleagues, and store your documents and your files. Teachers can post assignments and track grades using word processing programs and spreadsheets. Students can create and turn in their own writing assignments. This site is great for group projects because multiple students can work on an assignment at the same time. Classmates can edit each other's writing, share files, or upload images and videos from multiple locations. Recently, Google Apps for Education added Google Classroom, which allows teachers to create assignments within Google Apps and students to turn in assignments from Google Docs. Other features include real-time feedback on student work, commenting, homework collection, and organization.

Google Maps and Google Earth Online maps can be used to provide background information for reading assignments. Students can view pictures of Little Rock Central High School and the Tennessee countryside where the Battle of Shiloh was fought. Photos allow students to experience the places about which they are reading.

Teacher:	**Class:**	**Text:**

Classroom Demographics: Briefly describe the students in the class and any special needs or adaptations.

Overall Chapter Objectives: What are the key standards for the chapter?

First Read: Key Ideas and Details

Students should have the opportunity to struggle with the text within a predetermined time limit. Keep the purpose simple. Key questions: What does the text say? What are the main ideas?

Purpose for Reading:

Standard(s) Covered:

First Response:

Text-Based Discussion Questions:

Writing or Speaking/Listening Activity:

Second Read: Key Ideas and Details OR Craft and Structure

Students should read the text with support (teacher-led, audio recording, or partner read). How does the writer create meaning? How is the text structured?

How will students read the text the second time:

Standard(s) Covered:

Text-Based Discussion Questions:

Mini-Lesson: (What concepts do students need to understand in order to master the standard?)

Writing or Speaking/Listening Activity:

Third Read: Craft and Structure OR Integration of Knowledge and Ideas

Is there another text or other artistic medium on the same subject with which students can make connections? In a nonfiction text, is the reasoning valid and the evidence relevant and sufficient?

Standard(s) Covered:

Text-Based Discussion Questions:

Mini-Lesson: *(What concepts do students need to understand in order to master the standard?)*

Writing or Speaking/Listening Activity:

Technology Integration: *How can technology enhance or contribute to the reading experience with collaborative learning, online research, or demonstration of skill?*

Language Mini-lesson:

Assess: *How will learning be assessed? Project-based or written assessment?*

Formative assessment:

End of chapter assessment:

Accommodations: *How will you differentiate the lesson for ELL/ESE students?*

Writing Rubric

Name _____ Date _____

	Please use the following guidelines for your writing.
Score 4.0	Writing exceeds expectations and goes beyond what was taught. • Writing has a clear central idea included in a well-developed introduction. • Body is organized clearly with good transitional words and phrases. • Ideas fit together logically to create a cohesive whole. • Conclusion brings the writing to a satisfying close. • Writing maintains a formal style. • Writing is free from grammar, spelling, and punctuation errors.
Score 3.0	Writing meets expectations and reflects what was taught. • Writing has a main idea included in an introduction. • Body is organized clearly and uses mostly effective transitional words and phrases. • Ideas fit together somewhat cohesively. • Conclusion brings the writing to a mostly satisfying close. • Writing mostly maintains a formal style. • Writing has few grammar, spelling, and punctuation errors.
Score 2.0	Writing somewhat meets expectations and reflects what was taught. • Writing has a main idea but it is not clearly communicated. Introduction is not well organized. • Body is not organized clearly and uses few transitional words and phrases. • Ideas do not always fit together to create a cohesive whole. • Conclusion does not bring the writing to an effective close. • Writing does not maintain a formal style. • Writing has some grammar, spelling, and punctuation errors.
Score 1.0	Writing does not meet expectations or reflect what was taught. • Writing does not have a main idea. Introduction is not well organized or is missing entirely. • Body is not organized clearly and uses no transitional words and phrases. • Ideas do not fit together to create a cohesive whole. • Conclusion does not bring the writing to an effective close or is missing entirely. • Writing uses informal words, language, and style. • Writing includes many grammar, spelling, and punctuation errors.
Score 0.0	Even with help, no understanding or skill is demonstrated, or the writing project was not attempted.

Project Rubric

Name _____ Date _____

	Please use the following guidelines for your project.
Score 4.0	Presentation exceeds expectations and goes beyond what was taught. • Project incorporates appropriate technology and meets all the requirements for content, style, and length. • Project is professional. Presentation is effective, and the audience is carefully considered. • All elements of the project were completed on time. • Text is free from typographical and grammatical errors.
Score 3.0	Presentation meets expectations and reflects what was taught. • Project incorporates technology and meets all the requirements for content, style, and length. • Project is mostly professional with minor elements that could be more polished; presentation is effective and the audience is considered. • All elements of the project were completed on time. • Text is mostly free from typographical and grammatical errors.
Score 2.0	Presentation somewhat meets expectations and reflects what was taught. • Project doesn't incorporate correct technology, or technology is used ineffectively. • Project does not meet all of the requirements for content, style, and length. • Project lacks professionalism; presentation is somewhat effective, but the audience isn't considered. • Some elements of the project were not completed on time. • Text contains some typographical and grammatical errors.
Score 1.0	Presentation does not meet expectations or reflect what was taught. • Project doesn't incorporate correct technology, or technology is used ineffectively. • Project meets few of the requirements for content, style, and length. • Project lacks professionalism; presentation was ineffective, and the audience wasn't considered. • Many elements of the project were not completed on time. • Text contains many typographical and grammatical errors.
Score 0.0	Even with help, no understanding or skill is demonstrated, or project was not attempted.

Unit 1 Summative Assessment

Name _____ Date _____

Vocabulary

Directions: Circle the letter of the word that best completes the sentence.

1. Children _____ in a supportive school.
   - A. approve
   - B. command
   - C. flourish
   - D. sprint

2. Because the girl was angry at her brother, she insulted him _____.
   - A. spitefully
   - B. wearily
   - C. truthfully
   - D. clumsily

3. Her greatest _____ is her kindness to everyone.
   - A. regret
   - B. perfection
   - C. nuisance
   - D. virtue

4. When the man slipped on a banana peel, the boys _____ unkindly.
   - A. tittered
   - B. organized
   - C. recommenced
   - D. reassured

5. The dog seemed _____ after a week lost in the woods without food.
   - A. confident
   - B. frail
   - C. vigorous
   - D. unfaithful

6. The soldiers escaped _____ by digging a tunnel under the prison.
   - A. ambush
   - B. captivity
   - C. survival
   - D. heartbreak

7. The football field was _____ after the home team won the championship.
   - A. indignant
   - B. motionless
   - C. ordinary
   - D. chaotic

8. He has not had a bite of meat since becoming a _____.
   - A. psychotherapist
   - B. representative
   - C. vegetarian
   - D. professional

9. The injured woman walked _____ after her accident.
   - A. willingly
   - B. automatically
   - C. bashfully
   - D. feebly

10. Scientists are counting every _____ of bird in this state.
    - A. arrival
    - B. species
    - C. boundary
    - D. observation

11. The salesman waited at the _____ for someone to answer the door.
    - A. locker
    - B. radiator
    - C. threshold
    - D. balcony

12. The entire community thanked her for her _____ actions.
    - A. altruistic
    - B. enjoyable
    - C. superstitious
    - D. dependable

13. The soldiers threatened to _____ the spy.
    - A. appeal
    - B. resolve
    - C. execute
    - D. embarrass

14. The whole city was ruined during the _____.
    - A. inspection
    - B. interview
    - C. construction
    - D. genocide

15. His bad temper is a serious _____.
    - A. impression
    - B. vice
    - C. injury
    - D. disagreement

Directions: Read the following excerpt from a short story. Mark the text as you read, and then answer the questions that follow.

Departure

by Sherwood Anderson

Young George Willard got out of bed at four in the morning. It was April and the young tree leaves were just coming out of their buds. The trees along the residence streets in Winesburg are maple and the seeds are winged. When the wind blows they whirl crazily about, filling the air and making a carpet underfoot.

George came downstairs into the hotel office carrying a brown leather bag. His trunk was packed for departure. Since two o'clock he had been awake thinking of the journey he was about to take and wondering what he would find at the end of his journey. . . .

The westbound train leaves Winesburg at seven forty-five in the morning. Tom Little is conductor. His train runs from Cleveland to where it connects with a great trunk line railroad with terminals in Chicago and New York. Tom has what in railroad circles is called an "easy run." Every evening he returns to his family. In the fall and spring he spends his Sundays fishing in Lake Erie. He has a round red face and small blue eyes. He knows the people in the towns along his railroad better than a city man knows the people who live in his apartment building.

George came down the little incline from the New Willard House at seven o'clock. Tom Willard carried his bag. The son had become taller than the father.

On the station platform everyone shook the young man's hand. More than a dozen people waited about. Then they talked of their own affairs. Even Will Henderson, who was lazy and often slept until nine, had got out of bed. George was embarrassed. Gertrude Wilmot, a tall thin woman of fifty who worked in the Winesburg post office, came along the station platform. She had never before paid any attention to George. Now she stopped and put out her hand. In two words she voiced what everyone felt. "Good luck," she said sharply and then turning went on her way.

When the train came into the station George felt relieved. He scampered hurriedly aboard. Helen White came running along Main Street hoping to have a parting word with him, but he had found a seat and did not see her. When the train started Tom Little punched his ticket, grinned and, although he knew George well and knew on what adventure he was just setting out, made no comment. Tom had seen a thousand George Willards go out of their towns to the city. It was a commonplace enough incident with him. In the smoking car there was a man who had just invited Tom to go on a fishing trip to Sandusky Bay. He wanted to accept the invitation and talk over details.

George glanced up and down the car to be sure no one was looking, then took out his pocket-book and counted his money. His mind was occupied with a desire not to appear green. Almost the last words his father had said to him concerned the matter of his behavior when he got to the city. "Be a sharp one," Tom Willard had said. "Keep your eyes on your money. Be awake. That's the ticket. Don't let anyone think you're a greenhorn."

After George counted his money he looked out of the window and was surprised to see that the train was still in Winesburg.

The young man, going out of his town to meet the adventure of life, began to think but he did not think of anything very big or dramatic. Things like his mother's death, his departure from Winesburg, the uncertainty of his future life in the city, the serious and larger aspects of his life did not come into his mind.

He thought of little things—Turk Smollet wheeling boards through the main street of his town in the morning, a tall woman, beautifully gowned, who had once stayed overnight at his father's hotel, Butch Wheeler the lamp lighter of Winesburg hurrying through the streets on a summer evening and holding a torch in his hand, Helen White standing by a window in the Winesburg post office and putting a stamp on an envelope.

The young man's mind was carried away by his growing passion for dreams. One looking at him would not have thought him particularly sharp. With the recollection of little things occupying his mind he closed his eyes and leaned back in the car seat. He stayed that way for a long time and when he aroused himself and again looked out of the car window the town of Winesburg had disappeared and his life there had become but a background on which to paint the dreams of his manhood.

16. Part A: Which statement best expresses a theme of the story?
    A. Young people should try to escape from their dull small towns.
    B. Young people do not appreciate the good things in their lives.
    C. Young people from small towns do not know how hard city life can get.
    D. Young people must follow their dreams so they can become adults.

Part B: Give two pieces of evidence from the story to support the answer to Part A. Explain how the evidence supports your answer.

17. Part A: Why does George hurriedly board the train as soon as it arrives?

    A. He is embarrassed that his father is carrying his bag.

    B. He is uncomfortable with the attention being paid to him.

    C. He hopes that nobody will think he is inexperienced.

    D. He wants to show everybody that he is ready to move on.

    Part B: Which sentences from the story best support the answer to Part A? **Choose two.**

    A. *On the station platform everyone shook the young man's hand. More than a dozen people waited about.*

    B. *When the train came into the station George felt relieved.*

    C. *His mind was occupied with a desire not to appear green.*

    D. *After George counted his money he looked out of the window and was surprised to see that the train was still in Winesburg.*

    E. *The young man's mind was carried away by his growing passion for dreams.*

18. What do the people of Winesburg think of George? Do different characters have different points of view? Write a paragraph explaining how the people of Winesburg see George, citing textual evidence for support. (6 points)

19. What does the story suggest about small-town values? How do those values compare with city values and morals? Think about George's interaction with Winesburg residents and his father's advice. Write a paragraph explaining what you learn about small-town values from the story. (6 points)

20. The story ends with a metaphor about George and the start of his adult life. What does the figurative language in the story's final sentence mean, and what does it say about George and his departure from Winesburg? Write a short essay on a separate sheet of paper, using evidence from the story to support your analysis. (12 points)

Reading Informational Text

Directions: Read the following article from a government anti-bullying blog. Mark the text as you read. Then answer the questions that follow.

Why Do We Hurt Each Other?

by Emily P., high school senior, Bayfield, Colorado,
with Maureen Perkins, Health Resources and Services Administration

In a small town like Bayfield, Colorado, no one thinks anything bad happens; especially not bullying. People think, "How can bullying be a problem here?" It is a problem—a big one. Bullying happens everywhere—whether in a small town or big city. I started a bullying prevention project because I wanted to raise awareness among my fellow students that bullying is a problem and help them understand the huge impact that bullying can have on their peers. I wanted people to realize how damaging bullying is.

I wasn't physically bullied. I was harassed and taunted because of a false rumor being spread about me. None of the bullying I ever experienced was physical; however, I can guarantee that it hurt just as much, if not more.

Because of the pain I suffered, I wanted other students at my high school to realize that it is a big problem. In order to really reach the students, I would have to get them involved, and I thought that the best way to do that was with a school-wide assembly.

I had students take two surveys, one before the assembly, and the other after the assembly. The first [of the] two surveys gathered basic information about what the students think happens in their school. The first survey asked students the following questions:

- Do you think bullying is a problem?
- Have you shared or liked anything mean on social media?
- What mean things have you heard or said in school?

The second survey asked for bullying experiences and stories kids could share anonymously.

During the assembly I had students come up to the stage and read aloud the hurtful comments that had been said and heard in the school. I also had students share some of the anonymous stories from other students about their personal experiences. Many of the students said that hearing these comments and stories helped them really grasp the intensity of hurtful words and the impact that those words could leave on people.

After the assembly I had the students participate in a follow-up survey to collect students' opinions, what they learned from the assembly and how they will bring that knowledge to the community. This follow-up survey was very important to me. I wanted to make sure [the assembly] was truly helpful to the students and that it highlighted how much bullying is a problem and why [bullying] needs to be stopped. The students' participation in the assembly drew more attention to the issue and had a great impact on my peers.

I know that an assembly like this is just the first step to dealing with bullying at my school, but it was an important step to take—to begin to raise awareness and voice students' concerns about bullying. I plan to continue working on this project and hope to impact many other schools. As a part of our **Friends of Rachel** chapter, the high school students went down to the elementary school to help teach the kids about the effects of bullying and why it is so damaging. We hope that by bringing this message to younger age groups, we can prevent this problem and help to decrease the bullying problem in Bayfield. I am also working on bringing my assembly presentation to our middle school.

I think that raising awareness about bullying can help students realize what they are doing is wrong, and take steps to one day stop bullying completely. I want this message to be spread around and impact as many people as possible. Bullying is the most damaging and unnecessary thing in this world and is something that could definitely be removed from society.

Friends of Rachel: an anti-bullying organization

21. Part A: What was the authors' overall purpose for writing this passage?

    A. to explain how she is trying to stop bullying in her school

    B. to give information to readers about different forms of bullying

    C. to describe for readers the bullying experience that caused her so much pain

    D. to convince readers that bullying other students is harmful and wrong

Part B: Give two pieces of evidence from the story to support the answer to Part A. Explain how the evidence supports the answer.

22. Write a summary of the article in one paragraph. Explain the central ideas of the article in your summary. (6 points)

Directions: Read this paragraph from the text. Then answer the question that follows.

I had students take two surveys, one before the assembly, and the other after the assembly. The first [of the] two surveys gathered basic information about what the students think happens in their school. The first survey asked students the following questions:

- Do you think bullying is a problem?
- Have you shared or liked anything mean on social media?
- What mean things have you heard or said in school?

The second survey asked for bullying experiences and stories kids could share anonymously.

23. Based on the questions in the survey, the author believes which of the following?
    A. All students have taken part in bullying on social media.
    B. Students who spread rumors about other students are bullying.
    C. Students who bully do not think that bullying is a problem.
    D. Students who are bullied usually tell someone about it.

24. Describe the way the authors organize the article. What does each section add to the text, and how does each section develop the authors' ideas? Write a paragraph analyzing the structure, referring to the text for support. (6 points)

25. What claim do the authors make about bullying? How do they develop this claim? What reasons, evidence, or other support do they use? Do you agree or disagree with this claim? Write a short essay on a separate sheet of paper, supporting your response with details from the text. (12 points)

Unit 2 Summative Assessment

Name _____ Date _____

Vocabulary

Directions: Circle the letter of the word that best completes the sentence.

1. The hard-working doctor spent every Monday _____ at the community swimming pool.

    A. navigating   C. associating

    B. luxuriating   D. anticipating

2. The puffy cloud soon changed into only a thin white _____.

    A. hull   C. wisp

    B. prop   D. trench

3. The house of cards was so _____ that it fell as soon as I blew on it.

    A. hasty   C. captive

    B. flimsy   D. visible

4. The _____ face of the Navajo chief commanded honor and respect.

    A. terraced   C. patriotic

    B. artificial   D. wizened

5. I know my dog's habits _____; I can predict his every move.

    A. intimately   C. previously

    B. stubbornly   D. cautiously

6. The _____ of her cooking skills was that of an expert chef, but she was self-taught.

    A. appeal   C. caliber

    B. notion   D. vanity

7. My mother kept house so _____ that you could practically eat off the floor!

    A. defiantly   C. appropriately

    B. suspiciously   D. immaculately

8. Before you declare your cell phone lost, let's _____ every inch of your room.

    A. purify   C. accompany

    B. scrutinize   D. commission

9. Even when the thunder boomed, the president barely _____ and continued his speech.

    A. faltered   C. plundered

    B. concealed   D. snickered

10. My father _____ that no one could leave the house until our rooms were clean.

    A. bartered   C. decreed

    B. tinkered   D. regretted

11. Jane knew her daughter's promise was _____ because she had lied so often before.

    A. dubious   C. distinctive

    B. consistent   D. privileged

12. The boy stared _____ at the broken window, wishing he hadn't thrown the rock near the house.

    A. gratefully   C. solemnly

    B. delicately   D. ruefully

13. If you want to _____ the car's engine, just remove the battery.

    A. hesitate   C. incapacitate

    B. facilitate   D. premeditate

14. The person on the phone was obviously a _____, so I hung up immediately.

    A. bureau   C. monitor

    B. swindler   D. destination

15. Because neither country would compromise, progress toward ending the war was _____.

    A. static   C. patriotic

    B. forlorn   D. obedient

Directions: Read the following Dutch folktale. Mark the text as you read and then answer the questions that follow.

The Man Who Fell from Heaven

by G. J. Boekenoogen, translated by D. L. Ashliman

Once upon a time there was a peasant woman, a good, simple soul who was just returning from the market. She had almost reached home when she met a young man on the road who was continuously looking up toward heaven.

"What is the meaning of that?" thought the woman, and when she came closer to him, she asked, "My friend, why are you looking up into the air? Did something happen up there?"

"Dear woman," he said, "I just fell from heaven, and now I cannot find the hole again."

"So," said the old woman, "if you just fell from heaven, then you must know your way around up there pretty well?"

"Of course," said the young man.

"Then perhaps you know my son Kees, who died last year?"

"Kees," said the man. "Is he your son? And you ask me if I know him? My dear woman, he is my nearest neighbor!"

"That is wonderful," said the old woman, "and how is he doing?"

"Quite well! Quite well! But last week he was complaining that his stockings are worn out. And the sausage, the ham, and the butter are all gone, but other than that he is doing well."

"Oh, man, oh, man! Isn't there anyone there who can take care of his clothes?"

"No," said the man, "in heaven you have to take care of your own clothes."

"Can't he buy sausage and butter?"

"Yes, they are for sale, but everything is terribly expensive, and he cannot afford what is there."

"Oh dear, it is too bad that Kees still has to be in need now that he is dead. And I could well afford to give him something!"

Then the man told her exactly how Kees was doing, and what he was doing, and where he lived. Finally he said that he had to go, otherwise he would be late in returning to heaven.

"Are you going back to heaven now?" asked the old woman.

"Yes, indeed," he said.

"Then because you know Kees so well, would you be so kind as to do me a great favor? Come home with me, and I will pack a few things that you can give to him."

"Well," he said, "I will do it because it is for Kees, but I shall get my ears pulled for being away so long."

They went together to the farmhouse, and the old woman prepared two packages: one for the man who had fallen from heaven, because he had been so friendly, and one for Kees, but the package for Kees was the larger one. She also gave him a bag of money for her son. Then he took leave in order to make his return trip.

Thinking, "Kees will be so happy when his neighbor comes home, and Kees hears that he has been here," the old woman watched him until he was out of sight.

She never learned if Kees received her package. A short time ago someone told me that this was because the man still has not found the hole through which he had fallen from heaven.

16. Part A: Which statement best describes the peasant woman?
   A. She thinks that her son will return to earth someday.
   B. She wishes that the young man would come and live with her.
   C. She does not really believe that the young man fell from heaven.
   D. She cares so much about her son that she will believe anything.

   Part B: Which excerpt from the text **best** supports the answer to Part A?
   A. *"But last week he was complaining that his stockings are worn out."*
   B. *Finally he said that he had to go, otherwise he would be late in returning to heaven.*
   C. . . . *"Kees will be so happy when his neighbor comes home, and Kees hears that he has been here . . ."*
   D. . . . *the man still has not found the hole through which he had fallen from heaven.*

17. Part A: What inference can be drawn based on evidence in the text?

   A. It is difficult to return to heaven once someone has left.

   B. The woman's favorite foods were sausage and butter.

   C. The man is lying about falling from heaven to get money.

   D. The man knew Kees when they both were growing up.

   Part B: Which excerpt from the text **best** supports the answer to Part A?

   A. *"I just fell from heaven, and now I cannot find the hole again."*

   B. *Finally he said that he had to go, otherwise he would be late.*

   C. *"I shall get my ears pulled for being away so long."*

   D. *She also gave him a bag of money for her son.*

18. Write a paragraph summarizing the story. Include references to the events, the setting, and the characters. Be sure to include the beginning, middle, and end. (6 points)

19. How is the young man's point of view different from that of the peasant woman? Write a paragraph explaining your answer. Cite evidence from the text in your response. (6 points)

20. Describe how the young man tricks the woman into giving him what he wants without ever asking for anything. How does he respond to each thing she says and turn it to his own advantage? What lesson does the man's behavior convey? On a separate sheet of paper, write an essay about how the character affects the theme, referring to the text to support your analysis. (12 points)

(continued)

Reading Informational Text

Directions: Read the following report from a government agency about a company that tricked its customers. The name of the company has been omitted. Mark the text as you read. Then answer the questions that follow.

Direct Marketer Agrees to Pay $8 Million for Deceiving Consumers
by the Federal Trade Commission

A **direct marketing** company selling "as-seen-on-TV" type products . . . has agreed to pay $7.5 million to the Federal Trade Commission for consumer <u>restitution</u> to settle FTC charges in connection with its deceptive "buy-one-get-one-free" promotions.

The FTC's settlement . . . was reached alongside actions by the New York State Office of the Attorney General, which is announcing a separate state case today. In addition to the $7.5 million paid to the FTC, [the company] will pay $500,000 to the Attorney General's Office for penalties, costs, and fees to settle that action.

"Marketers must clearly disclose all costs. That includes processing fees, handling fees, and any other fees they think up," said Jessica Rich, Director of the FTC's Bureau of Consumer Protection. "Working with the New York Attorney General, we'll return millions of dollars to consumers that [the company] collected in undisclosed fees."

"This agreement returns money to thousands of consumers in New York and across the nation who believed they were buying items at the price advertised on television, but ended up with extra merchandise and hidden fees they didn't bargain for," Attorney General Eric T. Schneiderman said. "The settlement also brings much needed reforms to a major firm in the direct marketing industry. Those who use small print and hidden fees to inflate charges to unwitting consumers must be held accountable."

In a recent commercial for one product, for example, [the company] promised that it would "double the offer" for consumers, if they just paid "processing and handling fees." While consumers were led to believe that they would then be getting two $19.95 products for "less than $10 each," in fact, the total cost with the undisclosed $7.95 "processing and handling" fees jumped from the advertised price of $19.95 to $35.85, according to the complaint. . . .

As **alleged** in the FTC's complaint, consumers who called [the company] were often

---

direct marketing: selling to customers in their homes, without stores
alleged: accused

immediately instructed to enter their personal and billing information, and were charged for at least one "set" of products, based on the "buy-one-get-one-free" offer, before they had a chance to indicate how many products they wanted to buy. Because the sales pitch was often confusing, some consumers purchased more "sets" than they actually wanted.

[The company] then attempted to **upsell** consumers additional products via automated voice prompts that requested the consumer accept the offer. Many times, the only way a consumer could decline the offer was to say nothing. At the end of the calls, [the company] sometimes routed consumers to other third-party sellers who made additional sales pitches. Once all of the offers ended, consumers were not told the total number of items they'd "agreed" to buy, or the total amount they would be billed, according to the complaint. The Commission has alleged that [the company] even charged those consumers who hung up mid-call, not intending to complete a sale.

According to the FTC's complaint, consumers who opted to buy [the company's] products online faced similar problems, including separate "processing and handling" fees which were only disclosed in very fine print at the bottom of the page, and a barrage of upsell offers. Consumers were not provided with the total price of their purchases, and despite a "30-day money-back guarantee" (less processing and handling fees) full refunds were difficult for consumers to obtain.

Based on this alleged conduct, the FTC's complaint charges [the company] with two violations of the FTC Act and three violations of the agency's Telemarketing Sales Rule (TSR), including the following:

- Billing consumers without their express informed consent;
- Failing to make adequate disclosures about the total number and cost of products before billing consumers;
- In connection with the up-selling of goods and services, violating the TSR by failing to disclose material information about the total cost of the products and that the purpose of the call is to sell goods or services; and
- During telemarketing, illegally billing consumers without first getting their consent.

The settlement order imposes a monetary judgment of $7.5 million, which, in consultation with the New York Attorney General's Office, may be used to provide refunds to defrauded consumers.

---

upsell: persuade a customer to buy extra or more expensive items

21. Part A: What statement best expresses the author's overall purpose?

    A. to praise the good work of the New York Attorney General

    B. to summarize and uphold the agency's Telemarketing Sales Rule

    C. to expose one dishonest company and warn others of the consequences

    D. to describe the reasons that a company might mislead its own customers

    Part B: Which excerpt from the text is the **best** evidence for Part A?

    A. *"Those who use small print and hidden fees to inflate charges to unwitting consumers must be held accountable."*

    B. *. . . consumers were led to believe that they would then be getting two $19.95 products for "less than $10 each" . . .*

    C. *. . . consumers who called [the company] were often immediately instructed to enter their personal and billing information . . .*

    D. *Many times, the only way a consumer could decline the offer was to say nothing.*

22. For what reason did this company agree to pay $7.5 million to the Federal Trade Commission? Why did the company pay another $500,000 to the New York Attorney General? Write a paragraph explaining your answer, referring to the text for support. (6 points)

23. What phrase from the text would most help a reader determine the meaning of *restitution* in paragraph 1?

    A. *buy-one-get-one-free*

    B. *processing fees, handling fees, and any other fees*

    C. *the advertised price of $19.95*

    D. *return millions of dollars to consumers*

24. Analyze and describe the point of view expressed by Attorney General Eric T. Schneiderman in this article. How did his point of view likely differ from that of the owners of the company referred to in the text? Write a paragraph that shows how the points of view contrast, using evidence from the text. (6 points)

25. Describe the Federal Trade Commission's Bureau of Consumer Protection and its mission. Based on evidence in the text, how does the Bureau accomplish this goal? Are their methods effective? Explain three of the Bureau's actions in an essay written on a separate sheet of paper. (12 points)

Unit 3 Summative Assessment

Name _____ Date _____

Vocabulary

Directions: Circle the letter of the word that best completes the sentence.

1. Ross did not use a GPS but was able to sense his way home _____.

   A. quickly   C. intuitively
   B. slowly   D. accidentally

2. Because kids are worth our investment, I believe taxes should _____ early childhood education.

   A. eliminate   C. celebrate
   B. subsidize   D. invent

3. Frankie tied his ship to the _____, right beside his father's boat.

   A. beach   C. boardwalk
   B. ground   D. quay

4. Anita was sent to the principal's office for her _____ behavior.

   A. disruptive   C. puzzling
   B. noticeable   D. solid

5. The restaurant was _____ with streamers and banners for the birthday celebration.

   A. festooned   C. stuffed
   B. hidden   D. improved

6. The game's characters were so lifelike that Beatrice nearly forgot she was in a _____ world.

   A. familiar   C. virtual
   B. nonsense   D. wonderful

7. My dad always tells me to stop being _____ and find a cause I care about.

   A. clever   C. rebellious
   B. hesitant   D. apathetic

8. Matthias hated when people told him to hold back—it only made him more _____.

   A. aggressive   C. isolated
   B. inspired   D. confused

9. Olive _____ her running schedule with good eating habits to prepare for the marathon.

   A. excluded   C. augmented
   B. celebrated   D. decreased

10. I prefer to surround myself with positive people instead of a bunch of _____.

    A. enemies   C. supporters
    B. naysayers   D. acquaintances

11. It took me days to _____ the secret hidden in the symbols and numbers.

    A. decrypt   C. present
    B. discover   D. illustrate

12. Patrick wrote his paper on the _____ between school attendance and academic achievement.

    A. importance   C. wellness
    B. assumption   D. correlation

13. I had not _____ the distance properly and was now on the ground with my skateboard rolling away from me.

    A. jumped   C. performed
    B. gauged   D. practiced

14. Dillon always cries to _____ his parents into giving him what he wants.

    A. anger   C. sympathize
    B. manipulate   D. encourage

15. Alice was applauded for her _____, organizing the project in a totally new way.

    A. innovation   C. defiance
    B. dedication   D. education

Directions: Read the following poem published in 1860. As you read, mark the text. Then answer the questions that follow.

Song of the Sewing-Machine

by George Pope Morris

I'm the Iron Needle-Woman!
   Wrought of sterner stuff than clay;
And, unlike the drudges human,
   Never weary night or day;
Never shedding tears of sorrow,
   Never mourning friends untrue,
Never caring for the morrow,
   Never begging work to do.

Poverty brings no disaster!
   Merrily I glide along,
For no thankless, **sordid** master,
   Ever seeks to do me wrong:
No **extortioners** oppress me,
   No insulting words I dread—
I've no children to distress me
   With unceasing cries for bread.

I'm of hardy form and feature,
   For endurance framed aright;
I'm not pale misfortune's creature,
   Doomed life's battle here to fight:
Mine's a song of cheerful measure,
   And no under-currents flow
To destroy the throb of pleasure
   Which the poor so seldom know.

---

sordid: morally corrupt; nasty
extortioners: those who obtain something by force or threats

In the hall I hold my station,

    With the wealthy ones of earth,

Who commend me to the nation

    For economy and worth,

While unpaid the female labor,

    In the attic-chamber lone,

Where the smile of friend or neighbor

    Never for a moment shone.

My creation is a blessing

    To the **indigent** secured,

Banishing the cares distressing

    Which so many have endured:

Mine are sinews superhuman,

    Ribs of oak and nerves of steel—

I'm the Iron Needle-Woman

    Born to toil and not to feel.

---

indigent: needy; poor

16. Part A: How does the poet describe the sewing machine in the first two stanzas?

    A. by providing flowery words of praise

    B. by noting the types of tasks it can perform

    C. by contrasting it with human seamstresses

    D. by listing the materials from which it was made

    Part B: Which line from the poem best supports the answer to Part A? Choose two.

    A. *I'm the Iron Needle-Woman!*

    B. *Merrily I glide along,*

    C. *I've no children to distress me*

    D. *With unceasing cries for bread.*

17. Which lines from the poem use sound repetition to highlight the machine's durability? Choose two.

    A. Wrought of sterner stuff than clay;

    B. Mine's a song of cheerful measure,

    C. In the hall I hold my station

    D. In the attic-chamber lone,

    E. Mine are sinews superhuman,

18. Which of the following best describes the purpose of the fourth stanza on page 3?

    A. to suggest that only rich people can afford to buy their own sewing machines

    B. to show that the sewing machine is valued, while human seamstresses are not

    C. to explain that seamstresses had to do their work in secret because of harsh laws

    D. to raise awareness of the unsafe working conditions for people working at home

19. When sewing machines were introduced during the 1850s, they were embraced more rapidly than any other invention. According to the poem, how will the sewing machine benefit human workers? Does the poem imply any negative consequences to workers using these machines? (6 points)

20. Think about the ideas in each stanza of the poem, and how the speaker—the sewing machine—describes itself. What central idea does the poem convey? Explain how the poet uses repetition of similar sounds, including alliteration, to communicate key ideas. Write a short essay on a separate sheet of paper, using details from the poem to explain your analysis. (12 points)

Reading Informational Text

Directions: Read the following excerpt from a 2016 government report. Mark the text as you read. Then answer the questions that follow.

Artificial Intelligence, Automation, and the Economy
by the Executive Office of the President

The End of Work?

AI (Artificial Intelligence) could prove different from previous technological change because it has the ability to [duplicate] something previously exclusive to humans: intelligence. There have long been fears that technology—the machines, the assembly lines, or the robots—would replace all human labor. But AI-driven automation has unique features that may allow it to replace routine . . . tasks in which humans previously maintained a stark . . . advantage. Initial waves of technology, such as the wheel and lever, allowed humans to do more by replacing or augmenting physical strength. Other processes allowed work to take place faster or more efficiently in a factory. Computers allowed calculations or pattern recognition to take place faster and augment humans' capacity to think or reason.

AI, though, may allow machines to operate without humans to such a degree that they fundamentally change the nature of production and work. It may be that the question is no longer which segment of the population will technology [assist], but whether . . . AI will substitute completely for much of human work. The skills in which humans have maintained [an] advantage are likely to erode over time as AI and new technologies become more sophisticated. Some of this is evident today as AI becomes more capable at tasks such as language processing, translation, basic writing, or even music composition.

AI-driven technological change could lead to even larger [differences] in income between capital owners and labor. For example, [experts] argue that current trends in the labor market, such as declining wages in the face of rising productivity, are indicative of a more drastic change in the distribution of economic benefits to come. Rather than everyone receiving at least some of the benefit, the vast majority of that value will go to a very small portion of the population. . . . The . . . fortunate few are likely to emerge as victors of the market. This would [worsen] the current trend in the rising fraction of total income going to the top 0.01 percent.

In theory, AI-driven automation might involve more than temporary disruptions in labor markets and drastically reduce the need for workers. . . . Society as a whole may need to find an alternative approach to resource [distribution] other than [payment] for labor. . . .

Although this scenario is speculative, it is included in this report to foster discussion and shed light on the role and value of work in the economy and society. Ultimately, AI may develop in the same way as the technologies before it, creating new products and new jobs such that the bulk of individuals will be employed as they are today.

Modernize and Strengthen the Social Safety Net

Changes to how people work and the dislocation of some workers due to automation heightens the need for a robust safety net to ensure that people can still make ends meet, retrain, and potentially transition careers. . . .

In addition, with the rise of part-time and [temporary] work, and a more mobile workforce in which individuals do not spend their entire career at a single company, policymakers will need to ensure that workers can access retirement, health care, and other benefits whether or not they get them on the job. . . .

Strengthen Unemployment Insurance

Job [loss] is likely to be one of the most serious negative consequences of AI-driven automation, impacting entire industries and communities. Since its [beginning], unemployment insurance has been a powerful tool to prevent a job loss from hurtling a family into poverty. Last year alone, more than 7 million working Americans relied on the program to get by in tough times. Yet its protections have weakened over time, and today coverage by the program is at its lowest level in at least 50 years. Fewer than one in three unemployed Americans now receive unemployment insurance benefits, and benefits replace a smaller percentage of wages than before for those who do qualify. . . .

The program will need to be further strengthened, as laid out in a proposal to Congress from the President, to ensure that the program can offer a more secure safety net for workers [replaced] by AI-driven automation. . . .

21. Part A: What role does the first paragraph play in developing the central idea of the text?
    A. It argues that AI is no substitute for human intelligence.
    B. It suggests that people fear robots will control humans.
    C. It contrasts AI with previous technological upheavals.
    D. It lists AI as just one technological change among many.

Part B: Which sentence from the passage best supports the answer in Part A? Choose two.

A. *AI (Artificial Intelligence) could prove different from previous technological change because it has the ability to [duplicate] something previously exclusive to humans: intelligence.*

B. *There have long been fears that technology—the machines, the assembly lines, or the robots—would replace all human labor.*

C. *But AI-driven automation has unique features that may allow it to replace routine . . . tasks in which humans previously maintained a stark . . . advantage.*

D. *Computers allowed calculations or pattern recognition to take place faster and augment humans' capacity to think or reason.*

22. According to the report, who will benefit the most from AI technology? Support your answer with evidence from the text. (6 points)

23. What role do the authors believe the federal government should play as AI technology continues to increase?

    A. Wait to see whether AI will develop in the same way as other technologies.

    B. Intervene to make sure AI productivity increases are shared equally.

    C. Study how society responds to AI-driven increases in leisure time.

    D. Actively prepare for AI-related job losses and provide worker supports.

24. The authors of the report used the second and third sections of this excerpt to recommend ways to respond to increased AI technology. How well did the authors support their argument? Write a short essay below, using examples from the text to support your response.
    (6 points)

25. Compare and contrast the points of view communicated by "Song of the Sewing-Machine" and "Artificial Intelligence, Automation, and the Economy." How does each passage portray the effects of new technology on human workers? Support your conclusions with evidence from the texts. Write a short essay on a separate sheet of paper. (12 points)

Unit 4 Summative Assessment

Name _____ Date _____

Vocabulary

Directions: Circle the letter of the word that best completes the sentence.

1. Photographers _____ the young pop star, so her father called the police.

   A. witnessed   C. distracted

   B. harassed   D. lectured

2. Because of his _____ of the document, the boy discovered the author's identity.

   A. scrutiny   C. reference

   B. rehearsal   D. perfection

3. An honor guard _____ the prize winner to the podium.

   A. regarded   C. contacted

   B. escorted   D. congratulated

4. Because the mayor believes in the _____ of all, she hires people of different races.

   A. celebration   C. culture

   B. settlement   D. equality

5. The _____ lady would not take off her lacy white gloves, even at sports events.

   A. scornful   C. prissy

   B. sincere   D. mature

6. During the civil rights era, our governor promised _____ of every public facility.

   A. satisfaction   C. measurement

   B. independence   D. integration

7. During our school's _____, I learned about the requirements of my courses.

   A. publication   C. orientation

   B. debate   D. development

8. Her _____ to excel led to great achievements.

   A. determination   C. judgment

   B. intelligence   D. concentration

9. The king is the _____ ruler of the country, according to its laws.

   A. primitive   C. legitimate

   B. regretful   D. sufficient

10. He's so _____ about basketball that he plays a pickup game every day.

    A. mischievous   C. confident

    B. gung-ho   D. reckless

11. Because of our school's _____, we can't wear hats to class.

    A. influences   C. importance

    B. restrictions   D. broadcasts

12. My mother is _____ that I must be home by 10 p.m., even on weekends.

    A. doubtful   C. jubilant

    B. reliable   D. adamant

13. It's my _____ that we should treat each other kindly.

    A. defense   C. conviction

    B. generosity   D. enterprise

14. Our book club plans to _____ donations from our parents.

    A. establish   C. detect

    B. calculate   D. solicit

15. She made a _____ promise to her father to finish her homework.

    A. solemn   C. persistent

    B. superior   D. forlorn

Reading Literature

Directions: Read the following excerpt from a novel about the Civil War. Mark the text as you read, and then answer the questions that follow.

The Little Shepherd of Kingdom Come
by John Fox

The hour had come.

"I'm going away this morning, Major."

The Major did not even turn his head.

"I thought this was coming," he said quietly. Chad's face grew even paler, and he steeled his heart for the revelation.

"I've already spoken to Lieutenant Hunt," the Major went on. "He expects to be a captain, and he says that, maybe, he can make you a lieutenant. You can take that boy Brutus as a body servant." He brought his fist down on the railing of the porch. "God, but I'd give the rest of my life to be ten years younger than I am now."

"Major, I'm *going into the Union army.*"

The Major's pipe almost dropped from between his lips. Catching the arms of his chair with both hands, he turned heavily and with dazed wonder, as though the boy had struck him with his fist from behind, and, without a word, stared hard into Chad's tortured face. The keen old eye had not long to look before it saw the truth, and then, silently, the old man turned back. His hands trembled on the chair, and he slowly thrust them into his pockets, breathing hard through his nose. The boy expected an outbreak, but none came. A bee buzzed above them. A yellow butterfly zigzagged by. Blackbirds chattered in the firs. The screech of a peacock shrilled across the yard, and a ploughman's singing wailed across the fields:

Trouble, O Lawd!

Nothin' but trouble in de lan' of Canaan.

The boy knew he had given his old friend a mortal hurt.

"Don't, Major," he pleaded. "You don't know how I have fought against this. I tried to be on your side. I thought I was. I joined the Rifles. I found first that I couldn't fight *with* the South, and—then—I—found that I had to fight *for* the North. It almost kills me when I think of all you have done."

The Major waved his hand imperiously. He was not the man to hear his favors recounted, much less refer to them himself. He straightened and got up from his chair. His manner had grown formal, stately, coldly courteous.

"I cannot understand, but you are old enough, sir, to know your own mind. You should have prepared me for this. You will excuse me a moment." Chad rose and the Major walked toward the door, his step not very steady, and his shoulders a bit shrunken—his back, somehow, looked suddenly old.

"Brutus!" he called sharply to a black boy who was training rosebushes in the yard. "Saddle Mr. Chad's horse." Then, without looking again at Chad, he turned into his office, and Chad, standing where he was, with a breaking heart, could hear, through the open window, the rustling of papers and the scratching of a pen.

In a few minutes he heard the Major rise and he turned to meet him. The old man held a roll of bills in one hand and a paper in the other.

"Here is the balance due you on our last trade," he said, quietly. "The mare is yours— Dixie," he added, grimly. "The old mare is in foal. I will keep her and send you your due when the time comes. We are quite even," he went on in a level tone of business. "Indeed, what you have done about the place more than exceeds any expense that you have ever caused me. If anything, I am still in your debt."

"I can't take it!" said Chad, choking back a sob.

"You will have to take it," the Major broke in, curtly, "unless—" the Major held back the bitter speech that was on his lips and Chad understood. The old man did not want to feel under any obligations to him.

"I would offer you Brutus, as was my intention, except that I know you would not take him," again he added, grimly, "and Brutus would run away from you."

"No, Major," said Chad, sadly, "I would not take Brutus," and he stepped down one step of the porch backward.

"I tried to tell you, Major, but you wouldn't listen. I don't wonder, for I couldn't explain to you what I couldn't understand myself. I—" the boy choked and tears filled his eyes. He was afraid to hold out his hand.

"Good-by, Major," he said, brokenly.

"Good-by, sir," answered the Major, with a stiff bow, but the old man's lip shook and he turned abruptly within.

Chad did not trust himself to look back, but, as he rode through the pasture to the pike gate, his ears heard, never to forget, the chatter of the blackbirds, the noises around the barn, the cry of the peacock, and the wailing of the ploughman:

Trouble, O Lawd!

Nothin' but trouble—

16. Part A: Which statement best expresses the central theme of the passage?
    A. During the Civil War, many young men made the choice to enlist.
    B. War can put family members and friends at odds with each other.
    C. The victims of war include those whose loved ones leave to fight.
    D. Those who are too old to fight are no less patriotic than soldiers.

Part B: Which excerpt from the story best supports the answer to Part A?
    A. *"I cannot understand, but you are old enough, sir, to know your own mind."*
    B. *"God, but I'd give the rest of my life to be ten years younger than I am now."*
    C. *"You don't know how I have fought against this. I tried to be on your side. I thought I was."*
    D. *"I've already spoken to Lieutenant Hunt," the Major went on. "He expects to be a captain, and he says that, maybe, he can make you a lieutenant."*

17. Part A: Which of these best describes Chad's relationship with the Major?
    A. The Major uses his superior rank to push Chad around.
    B. They have just gotten to know each other before the war.
    C. Chad is resentful that the Major shows off his money.
    D. They share a close bond based on respect for each other.

Part B: Which detail from the story best supports the answer to Part A?
    A. *"I thought this was coming," he said quietly. Chad's face grew even paler, and he steeled his heart for the revelation.*
    B. *The keen old eye had not long to look before it saw the truth, and then, silently, the old man turned back.*
    C. *"It almost kills me when I think of all you have done."*
    D. *"We are quite even," he went on in a level tone of business.*

18. What is the effect of the author's use of figurative language and sensory details in paragraph 7? Describe the impact of this paragraph on the meaning of the story, referring to the text for support. (6 points)

19. What does this story reveal about life in the South during the Civil War? In addition to details about the setting, consider the interaction between Chad and the Major. Write a paragraph explaining the historical information, referring to the text to support your answer. (6 points)

20. How does the setting of the excerpt affect the characters and the conflict? Could the plot have occurred anywhere else? Write a short essay on a separate sheet of paper. Use evidence from the story to support your analysis, including paraphrasing and quoting directly from text. (12 points)

Reading Informational Text

Directions: Read the following excerpts from an article. Mark the text as you read. Then answer the questions that follow.

No Time for Games
by the National Park Service

The Civil War affected more than the soldiers on the battlefield. An entire generation was shaped by their perception of events during this critical chapter of American history and the weight of war was borne on little shoulders as well as large. Whether they snuck into the army, served as drummer boys, helped tend the wounded, or faced every day as a struggle to stay alive, the perspectives of children offer unique insight into the effects of the Civil War. . . .

The Weight of War on Little Soldiers

Many children spent the war worried about relatives and friends who were fighting far away. Some felt the effects of the war in their stomachs, as food supplies dwindled. Some boys lied about their ages and went off to fight. Those not killed or wounded became scarred nonetheless, as their young eyes witnessed the horrors of war.

Most of the boys who joined the army were assigned less dangerous positions, such as bugler or drummer boy. These jobs were important because their instruments were used as calls and signals for the troops. Still, in large battles, there was no place to hide. Charley King was one of the youngest soldiers killed in the war. He was only thirteen when he died at the Battle of Antietam.

Johnny Cook enlisted as a bugler with Battery B, 4th United States Artillery in 1862. During the Maryland Campaign, fifteen-year-old Johnny served as a messenger. At the Battle of Antietam, Johnny and his unit came under heavy fire from Confederate soldiers along the Hagerstown Pike near the **infamous cornfield**. When Johnny returned from helping his wounded commander to safety, he discovered that the soldiers serving on the cannon had been killed. Johnny began to load the cannon by himself until Gen. John Gibbon rode by, saw what was happening, jumped off his horse, and began to help the brave young cannoneer.

The Confederate soldiers came dangerously close, but Johnny and Gen. Gibbon were able to man the cannon and push them back towards the West Woods. For his bravery at Antietam, Johnny Cook became one of the youngest soldiers ever to receive the Medal of Honor. His

---

infamous cornfield: An especially ferocious part of the battle was fought in a cornfield.

official Medal of Honor citation reads: "Volunteered at the age of 15 years to act as a cannoneer, and as such volunteer served a gun under a terrific fire of the enemy." Johnny went on to serve at Gettysburg and several other battles. After the war, he moved back to his hometown of Cincinnati, Ohio. He died in 1915 and is buried in Arlington National Cemetery. . . .

Caught in the Middle

By the time the Maryland Campaign started, eighteen-year-old Jennie Chambers was already a seasoned "civilian veteran." She witnessed John Brown's raid in 1859, the destruction of the U.S. Armory in 1861, and was nearly arrested by Confederates for aiding Union troops. She watched her father go to prison instead and was sent to live with her uncle in Maryland for the winter to keep her safe.

From September 13 through 15, 1862, Jennie and her family lived in the middle of the war zone, as their farm was strategically important to "Stonewall" Jackson's plan to capture the federal garrison at Harpers Ferry. On the night of the 14th, Jackson's men snaked along the ravines dragging artillery into position to turn the Union's left flank, positioned adjacent to the Chambers Farm. As dawn broke, Confederate artillery pounded their farm.

Jennie's family escaped to the cellar. "One shell exploded in front of the cellar door; another cut a limb from a large tree at the corner of the house. At about 10:00 A.M. the firing ceased and we were called out to gaze upon the white flag on Bolivar Heights. The grape shot, shell, cannon balls were lying almost like hail over the barn and fields of the farm . . . it was literally torn to pieces by the shelling."

Following the Union surrender, Jennie saw soldiers from both sides come together on her farm. "I remember my father passing 'round a large basket of peaches to the blue and gray indiscriminately, as they sat conversing. I looked at them and said, 'See what you are doing, a while ago you were in deadly combat. Now you are friends.' The answer came 'When we are in war, we are in war. We are brothers. When the battles are over we are brothers.'"

21. Part A: Which is the best statement of the central idea of the article?
    A. Many children served heroically, and even lost their lives, during the Civil War.
    B. The Civil War had a deep effect on the lives of many young people.
    C. Families were left behind when fathers joined the army during the Civil War.
    D. The Civil War forced many people to make great sacrifices.

Part B: Select three pieces of evidence that best support the answer to Part A.

A. *Many children spent the war worried about relatives and friends who were fighting far away.*

B. *Most of the boys who joined the army were assigned less dangerous positions, such as bugler or drummer boy.*

C. *For his bravery at Antietam, Johnny Cook became one of the youngest soldiers ever to receive the Medal of Honor.*

D. *By the time the Maryland Campaign started, eighteen-year-old Jennie Chambers was already a seasoned "civilian veteran."*

E. *On the night of the 14th, Jackson's men snaked along the ravines dragging artillery into position to turn the Union's left flank, positioned adjacent to the Chambers Farm.*

F. *Following the Union surrender, Jennie saw soldiers from both sides come together on her farm.*

22. Write an objective summary of the article. Explain the central idea of each section, referring to details from the text for support. (6 points)

23. What structure does the author use to develop the two main sections of the article?

A. The author uses comparison and contrast to show the effects of war on different groups of Americans, the Union and the Confederacy.

B. The author uses cause and effect to show what led to the war and its long-term impact on Americans who grew up in that time.

C. The author uses an example of a young person to represent each idea about how the Civil War affected youth.

D. The author uses claims and support to argue that the most devastating effects of the Civil War were felt by children.

24. What is the author's point of view about life for young people during the Civil War? Write a paragraph answering this question, referring to the text for evidence. (6 points)

25. The excerpt from *The Little Shepherd of Kingdom Come* presents a scene about a young man who announces he is joining the Union army to his friend who supports the Confederacy. How does the novel's use of this historical period compare with the information in "No Time for Games"? Compare and contrast the way details are represented in each text. Support your analysis with direct quotations from the texts or by paraphrasing information. Write a short essay on a separate sheet of paper. (12 points)

End-of-Course Assessment

Name _____ Date _____

Reading Literature

Directions: Read the excerpt from a short story. Mark the text as you read and then answer the questions that follow.

Robbie

by Isaac Asimov

George Weston was comfortable. It was a habit of his to be comfortable on Sunday afternoons. A good, hearty dinner below the hatches; a nice, soft, dilapidated couch on which to sprawl; a copy of the *Times*; slippered feet and shirtless chest; how could anyone help but be comfortable?

He wasn't pleased, therefore, when his wife walked in. . . . Sunday afternoons just after dinner were sacred to him and his idea of solid comfort was to be left in utter solitude for two or three hours. Consequently, he fixed his eye firmly upon the latest reports of the Lefebre–Yoshida expedition to Mars . . . and pretended she wasn't there.

Mrs. Weston waited patiently for two minutes, then impatiently for two more, and finally broke the silence.

"George!"

"Hmpph?"

"George, I say! Will you put down that paper and look at me?"

The paper rustled to the floor and Weston turned a weary face toward his wife, "What is it, dear?"

"You know what it is, George. It's Gloria and that terrible machine."

"What terrible machine?"

"Now don't pretend you don't know what I'm talking about. It's that robot Gloria calls Robbie. He doesn't leave her for a moment."

"Well, why should he? He's not supposed to. And he certainly isn't a terrible machine. He's the best darn robot money can buy and I'm [quite] sure he set me back half a year's income. He's worth it, though—darn sight cleverer than half my office staff."

He made a move to pick up the paper again, but his wife was quicker and snatched it away.

"You listen to *me*, George. I won't have my daughter entrusted to a machine—and I don't care how clever it is. It has no soul, and no one knows what it may be thinking. A child just isn't *made* to be guarded by a thing of metal."

Weston frowned, "When did you decide this? He's been with Gloria two years now and I haven't seen you worry till now."

"It was different at first. It was a novelty; it took a load off me, and—and it was a fashionable thing to do. But now I don't know. The neighbors—"

"Well, what have the neighbors to do with it. Now, look. A robot is infinitely more to be trusted than a human nursemaid. Robbie was constructed for only one purpose really—to be the companion of a little child. His entire 'mentality' has been created for the purpose. He just can't help being faithful and loving and kind. He's a machine—*made* so. That's more than you can say for humans."

"But something might go wrong. Some—some—" Mrs. Weston was a bit hazy about the insides of a robot, "some little jigger will come loose and the awful thing will go berserk and—and—" She couldn't bring herself to complete the quite obvious thought.

"Nonsense," Weston denied, with an involuntary nervous shiver. "That's completely ridiculous. We had a long discussion at the time we bought Robbie about the First Law of Robotics. You know that it is impossible for a robot to harm a human being; that long before enough can go wrong to alter that First Law, a robot would be completely inoperable. It's a mathematical impossibility. Besides I have an engineer from U.S. Robots here twice a year to give the poor gadget a complete overhaul. Why, there's no more chance of anything at all going wrong with Robbie than there is of you or I suddenly going looney—considerably less, in fact. Besides, how are you going to take him away from Gloria?"

He made another futile stab at the paper and his wife tossed it angrily into the next room.

"That's just it, George! She won't play with anyone else. There are dozens of little boys and girls that she should make friends with, but she won't. She won't go near them unless I make her. That's no way for a little girl to grow up. You want her to be normal, don't you? You want her to be able to take her part in society."

"You're jumping at shadows, Grace. Pretend Robbie's a dog. I've seen hundreds of children who would rather have their dog than their father."

"A dog is different, George. We *must* get rid of that horrible thing. You can sell it back to the company. I've asked, and you can."

"You've asked? Now look here, Grace, let's not go off the deep end. We're keeping the robot until Gloria is older and I don't want the subject brought up again." And with that he walked out of the room in a huff.

1. Part A: What is the main reason Grace wants to get rid of Robbie?
    A. She worries that her daughter will fall in love with him.
    B. She is embarrassed that no other families have a robot.
    C. She is afraid that the robot is going to harm her daughter.
    D. She resents that her husband will not pay attention to her.

    Part B: Which dialogue from the story best supports the answer to Part A?
    A. *"A dog is different, George. We must get rid of that horrible thing."*
    B. *". . . some little jigger will come loose and the awful thing will go berserk and—and—"*
    C. *"I won't have my daughter entrusted to a machine—and I don't care how clever it is."*
    D. *"You know what it is, George. It's Gloria and that terrible machine."*

2. Part A: What is the main reason George wants to keep Robbie?
    A. He wants to protect his daughter from other people.
    B. He enjoys taking the opposite view to annoy his wife.
    C. He does not want the expense of a robot to go to waste.
    D. He believes a robot is best suited to care for his daughter.

    Part B: Which dialogue from the story best supports the answer to Part A?
    A. *"A robot is infinitely more to be trusted than a human nursemaid."*
    B. *"Why, there's no more chance of anything at all going wrong with Robbie than there is of you or I suddenly going looney—considerably less, in fact."*
    C. *"He's the best darn robot money can buy and I'm [quite] sure he set me back half a year's income."*
    D. *"You're jumping at shadows, Grace. Pretend Robbie's a dog. I've seen hundreds of children who would rather have their dog than their father."*

3. Part A: How does the setting of the story most impact its plot?

    A. Grace worries about the neighbors because of the rich area they live in.

    B. George reacts angrily because Sunday afternoons are important to him.

    C. The location inside a family home brings different characters together.

    D. The technology of the future creates the conflict between the Westons.

    Part B: Which detail from the text best supports the answer to Part A?

    A. *Sunday afternoons just after dinner were sacred to him and his idea of solid comfort was to be left in utter solitude for two or three hours.*

    B. *"You know that it is impossible for a robot to harm a human being; that long before enough can go wrong to alter that First Law, a robot would be completely inoperable."*

    C. *Consequently, he fixed his eye firmly upon the latest reports of the Lefebre–Yoshida expedition to Mars . . . and pretended she wasn't there.*

    D. *He made another futile stab at the paper and his wife tossed it angrily into the next room.*

4. Part A: Why has Grace's point of view about Robbie changed?

    A. The neighbors have criticized her for having a robot.

    B. She has recently seen Robbie attempt to hurt Gloria.

    C. Gloria spends time with Robbie instead of other people.

    D. A newer, better model of robot has been advertised.

    Part B: Which dialogue from the text best supports the answer to Part A?

    A. *"That's just it, George! She won't play with anyone else."*

    B. *"It has no soul, and no one knows what it may be thinking."*

    C. *"It was different at first. It was a novelty; it took a load off me, and—and it was a fashionable thing to do."*

    D. *"It's that robot Gloria calls Robbie. He doesn't leave her for a moment."*

5. Part A: Read this sentence from the story.

    Sunday afternoons just after dinner were sacred to him and his idea of solid comfort was to be left in utter solitude for two or three hours.

    What does the word *solitude* mean?

    A. being alone

    B. feeling full

    C. taking a nap

    D. having freedom

    Part B: Which detail from the text best supports the answer to Part A?

    A. *It was a habit of his to be comfortable on Sunday afternoons.*

    B. *A good, hearty dinner below the hatches . . .*

    C. *He wasn't pleased, therefore, when his wife walked in.*

    D. *. . . a nice, soft, dilapidated couch on which to sprawl;*

Directions: Read the poem, marking the text as you read. Then answer the questions that follow.

The Watcher
by James Stephens

A rose for a young head,
A ring for a bride,
Joy for the homestead
Clean and wide—
    Who's that waiting
    In the rain outside?

A heart for an old friend,
A hand for the new:
Love can to earth lend
Heaven's hue—
    Who's that standing
    In the silver dew?

A smile for the parting,
A tear as they go,
God's sweethearting
Ends just so—
    Who's that watching
    Where the black winds blow?

He who is waiting
In the rain outside,
He who is standing
Where the dew drops wide,
He who is watching
In the wind must ride
    (Tho' the pale hands cling)
    With the rose
    And the ring
    And the bride,
        Must ride

With the red of the rose,

And the gold of the ring,

And the lips and the hair of the bride.

6. The poet ends each of the first three stanzas with a question that begins, "Who's that . . . ?" How does this repetition affect the meaning of the poem?

   A. It suggests there are several watchers in many places.

   B. It emphasizes that the watcher is always present.

   C. It shows the sadness of not being invited to a wedding.

   D. It creates a reassuring feeling of being watched over.

7. Read the following lines from the poem.

   Love can to earth lend

      Heaven's hue—

   What do these lines mean?

   A. The colors of the earth are the same as the sky.

   B. Attending a wedding is like visiting the afterlife.

   C. The speaker is a ghost watching earthly events.

   D. Feeling love makes the world seem more beautiful.

8. Who is the watcher, and how does he affect the theme of the poem? Write a paragraph explaining who, or what, the watcher represents. Support your answer with evidence from the text. (8 points)

Reading Informational Text

Directions: Read the excerpt from an article in *Newsweek* magazine, marking the text as you read. Then answer the questions that follow.

Money for Morality
by Mary Arguelles

I recently read a newspaper article about an 8-year-old boy who found an envelope containing more than $600 and returned it to the bank whose name appeared on the envelope. The bank traced the money to its rightful owner and returned it to him. God's in his heaven and all's right with the world. Right? Wrong.

As a reward, the man who lost the money gave the boy $3. Not a lot, but a token of his appreciation nonetheless and not mandatory. After all, returning money should not be considered extraordinary. A simple "thank you" is adequate. But some of the teachers at the boy's school felt a reward was not only appropriate, but required. Outraged at the apparent stinginess of the person who lost the cash, these teachers took up a collection for the boy. About a week or so later, they presented the good Samaritan with a $150 savings bond, explaining they felt his honesty should be recognized. Evidently the virtues of honesty and kindness have become commodities that, like everything else, have succumbed to inflation. I can't help but wonder what dollar amount these teachers would have deemed a sufficient reward. Certainly they didn't expect the individual who lost the money to give the child $150. Would $25 have been respectable? How about $10? Suppose that lost money had to cover mortgage, utilities and food for the week. In light of that, perhaps $3 was generous. A reward is a gift; any gift should at least be met with the presumption of genuine gratitude on the part of the giver.

What does this episode say about our society? It seems the role models our children look up to these days—in this case, teachers—are more confused and misguided about values than their young charges. A young boy, obviously well guided by his parents, finds money that does not belong to him and he returns it. He did the right thing. Yet doing the right thing seems to be insufficient motivation for action in our materialistic world. . . . Modern communication has catapulted us into an instant world. Television makes history of events before any of us has even had a chance to absorb them in the first place. An ad for major-league baseball entices viewers with the reassurance that "the memories are waiting"; an event that has yet to occur has already been packaged as the past. With the world racing by us, we have no patience for a rain check on good deeds.

Misplaced virtues are running rampant through our culture. I don't know how many times my 13-year-old son has told me about classmates who received $10 for each A they receive on their report cards—hinting that I should do the same for him should he ever receive an A (or maybe he was working on $5 for a B). Whenever he approaches me on this subject, I give him the same reply: "Doing well is its own reward. The A just confirms that." In other words, forget it! This is not to say that I would never praise my son for doing well in school. But my praise is not meant to reward or elicit future achievements, but rather to express my genuine delight in the satisfaction he feels at having done his best. Throwing $10 at that sends out the message that the feeling alone isn't good enough. . . .

As a society, we seem to be losing a grip on our internal control—the ethical thermostat that guides our actions and feelings toward ourselves, others, and the world around us. Instead, we rely on external "stuff" as a measure of our worth. We pass this message to our children. We offer them money for honesty and good grades. . . . We call these things incentives, telling ourselves that if we can just reel them in and get them hooked, then the built-in rewards will follow. . . . Nothing is permitted to succeed or fail on its own merits anymore. . . .

The simple virtues of honesty, kindness and integrity suffer from an image problem and are in desperate need of a makeover. One way to do this is by example. If my son sees me feeling happy after I've helped out a friend, then he may do likewise. If my daughter sees me spending a rainy afternoon curled up with a book instead of spending money at the mall, she may get the message that there are some simple pleasures that don't require a purchase. I fear that in our so-called upwardly mobile world we are on a downward spiral toward moral bankruptcy. Like pre-World War II Germany, where the basket holding the money was more valuable than the money itself, we too may render ourselves internally worthless while desperately clinging to a shell of appearances.

9. Part A: Which of the following best describe the central ideas? Choose two of the statements below.

    A. When a boy returned lost money to the bank, his teachers chose to reward him.

    B. The author chooses not to reward her son for good grades because she would prefer that he enjoy success for its own sake.

    C. Today's society is so driven by rewards that people aren't satisfied with the good feelings that come with doing what is right.

    D. People are so greedy that, like the man whose money was returned, they are unwilling to offer great enough rewards to those who help them.

    E. Offering incentives such as money for good grades creates a society that values the appearance of success at school more than actual learning.

    F. To change society's emphasis on selfish pursuits, people should demonstrate the value of helping others and having fun without spending money.

    Part B: Choose two excerpts from the article that best support the answers to Part A.

    A. *But my praise is not meant to reward or elicit future achievements, but rather to express my genuine delight in the satisfaction he feels at having done his best.*

    B. *Television makes history of events before any of us has even had a chance to absorb them in the first place.*

    C. *About a week or so later, they presented the good Samaritan with a $150 savings bond, explaining they felt his honesty should be recognized.*

    D. *A reward is a gift; any gift should at least be met with the presumption of genuine gratitude on the part of the giver.*

    E. *The simple virtues of honesty, kindness and integrity suffer from an image problem and are in desperate need of a makeover. One way to do this is by example.*

    F. *As a society, we seem to be losing a grip on our internal control—the ethical thermostat that guides our actions and feelings toward ourselves, others, and the world around us.*

10. Part A: How does the story of the boy affect the author's relationship with her own children?

    A. Because the author found the teachers to be confused, she chose to take control of her children's education.

    B. Reading about the story caused the author to reflect on the values she wanted to encourage her children to have.

    C. The author saw that incentives did not help the boy in the story, so she stopped offering her son money for grades.

    D. Because the boy's parents taught him proper values, the author decided to raise her children the same way.

    Part B: Which statement from the article best supports the answer to Part A?

    A. *A young boy, obviously well guided by his parents, finds money that does not belong to him and he returns it.*

    B. *Outraged at the apparent stinginess of the person who lost the cash, these teachers took up a collection for the boy.*

    C. *Throwing $10 at that sends out the message that the feeling alone isn't good enough.*

    D. *What does this episode say about our society?*

11. Part A: Both the author and the teachers approve of the boy's honesty. How is the author's point of view different from that of the teachers?

   A. The author does not feel the reward for the boy should have been such a large amount.

   B. The author believes the boy should not have been rewarded for doing the right thing.

   C. The author thinks the teachers are more interested in appearances than in true morality.

   D. The author disagrees with the teachers that students should be rewarded for their grades.

   Part B: Which excerpt from the article best supports the answer to Part A?

   A. *After all, returning money should not be considered extraordinary. A simple "thank you" is adequate.*

   B. *I can't help but wonder what dollar amount these teachers would have deemed a sufficient reward.*

   C. *Throwing $10 at that sends out the message that the feeling alone isn't good enough.*

   D. *But some of the teachers at the boy's school felt a reward was not only appropriate, but required.*

12. Part A: Read this sentence from the article.

   Not a lot, but a token of his appreciation nonetheless and not mandatory.

   What does the word *mandatory* mean?

   A. important

   B. generous

   C. necessary

   D. welcome

   Part B: Which sentence from the article provides the best context clue to the word's meaning?

   A. *Outraged at the apparent stinginess of the person who lost the cash, these teachers took up a collection for the boy.*

   B. *Evidently the virtues of honesty and kindness have become commodities that, like everything else, have succumbed to inflation.*

   C. *As a reward, the man who lost the money gave the boy $3.*

   D. *But some of the teachers at the boy's school felt a reward was not only appropriate, but required.*

13. Part A: Which of the following best describes the article's overall structure?

   A. The author relates a story about rewarding honesty and offers her opinions.

   B. The author explains the causes of people's changing values and their effects.

   C. The author makes a claim about modern society and supports it with evidence.

   D. The author describes the problem of declining morals and proposes a solution.

   Part B: How does the final paragraph contribute to this structure?

   A. It completes the narrative by showing how the author teaches her children morals.

   B. It predicts that if values continue to worsen, people will become completely immoral.

   C. It suggests a way to address the issue of misplaced virtues by offering an alternative.

   D. It concludes the author's argument by presenting the strongest reason for taking action.

14. Part A: Which of the following best describes the author's values?

    A. The satisfaction of hard work and kindness are the greatest rewards.

    B. It is not important for children to get good grades as long as they try.

    C. Acts of honesty should never be rewarded with gifts of money.

    D. People should spend more time reading and less time shopping.

Part B: Which excerpt from the article best supports the answer to Part A?

    A. *If my son sees me feeling happy after I've helped out a friend, then he may do likewise.*

    B. *Whenever he approaches me on this subject, I give him the same reply: "Doing well is its own reward."*

    C. *This is not to say that I would never praise my son for doing well in school.*

    D. *Certainly they didn't expect the individual who lost the money to give the child $150.*

15. The author argues that "Misplaced values are running rampant through our culture." Write a paragraph that examines how the author supports this claim throughout the article. Explain whether the author provides enough evidence to support the claim. (8 points)

Directions: Read the excerpts from a short story and an article, marking each text as you read. Then answer the questions that follow.

How Arthur Fought with Rome
by Maude L. Radford

In the time of the great Roman, Julius Caesar, about five hundred years before King Arthur was born, the people of Rome conquered Britain. They made many improvements in the land, building roads and walls, the remains of which may be seen to this day. But they also forced the Britons to pay them much money. All the kings did this up to the time of Arthur. He, however, considered that England was his own. He had conquered the lesser kings, and made one realm of all the land, over which he ruled with wise government. So he refused to send any money to Rome.

Once King Arthur's knights were all together in the great hall. It was a time of peace, and they spent the days in riding and hunting. On this day, while the king was sitting on his throne, twelve old men entered, each bearing a branch of olive, as a sign that they came in peace. They were the messengers of the emperor of Rome, and, after bowing to the king, they said:

"Sir, our mighty emperor sends you greeting, and commands you to acknowledge him as lord, and to send him the money due him from your realm. Your father and his predecessors did this, and so must you. If you refuse, the emperor will make such war against you that it will be an example to all the world." . . .

Arthur bowed courteously to the messengers, and . . . said to them:

"Return to your emperor. Tell him that I refuse his command, for I owe him nothing. I have won this kingdom by my own strength. Tell him that I shall come with all my army to Rome and make him acknowledge me as lord."

Then Arthur told his treasurer to give the messengers gifts, and to take them safely out of the country. . . .

When they told the emperor of Rome their message, he said:

. . . "This is foolish talk. . . . Remember that we are Romans. We have ruled the world for centuries, and a little king of little England shall not make us fear. You say that he is coming to fight with us. We will take a few troops and go forthwith to France to meet him." . . .

Meanwhile, Arthur had gathered together all his troops. He bade farewell to Queen Guinevere, who was so grieved that she fell in a swoon. Then he rode off at the head of his men till they came to the sea, and there they embarked in ten thousand boats and sailed to France. . . .

King Arthur galloped up and down before the front rank of his men, looking at them carefully. He was on a beautiful white horse whose mane rose and fell in the wind like a wave of the sea. His soldiers cheered lustily for their beloved commander. Then King Arthur raised his hand for silence, and spoke in a loud, clear voice:

"My knights and men whom I love, remember that you are fighting today for your rights and for the independence of Britain. Strike well, and do not forget that great courage is as powerful as great numbers."

With that, he gave the signal for attack. . . .

Then the Romans, at the call of the trumpet, rushed forward, and in a moment the two great armies clashed together. . . .

All fought bravely, but no one did so well as Arthur and Sir Lancelot. The battle did not cease until it was dark. Each side had lost many men. . . .

But the next day the two armies began to fight again, and when the emperor finally saw that his men were losing . . . he said:

"This Arthur is a demon and not a man. I will fight with him myself and end this battle." And before anyone could stop him, he spurred up to King Arthur and said:

"You on the white horse who refuse to pay me tribute, come out that I may kill you."

Then Arthur rode quickly towards the emperor. The two men began to fight, and Arthur soon saw that he was contending with a powerful man. He gave the emperor many a stroke with **Excalibur,** but he himself received deep blows. At last the emperor pierced Arthur's helmet, and wounded him deeply in the cheek.

King Arthur raised his good Excalibur with a last effort and struck his enemy with it so fiercely on the head that the blow cleft the helmet . . .

At last, seeing themselves conquered, the Romans surrendered.

Excalibur: Arthur's magic sword

(p. 14)

Geoffrey's Tale—Fact, Fiction, or Both?

by Andrew Galloway

The earliest surviving "historical" evidence about a mighty British king that might have been Arthur (or might not!) comes from a short "history." The work is really a rant against the pride of the "British"—that is, the Celtic peoples of Wales—by a writer named Gildas from about the year A.D. 550. Gildas mentions a fierce battle at Mount Badon against invading pagan Saxons, a war that later writers claim Arthur fought. How long it took for the legend of Arthur to develop is not certain.

And So the Tale Grows

However, stories about King Arthur only really started flowing in the mid-1100s, almost 600 years after he was supposed to have lived! It began with a popular history by Geoffrey of Monmouth, writing about 70 years after the Normans had conquered England by defeating the Anglo-Saxons. Geoffrey, who came from Wales but spent most of his life near Oxford University, says he was given "a very ancient book in the British [i.e., Welsh] language." He claims that he simply translated the text into Latin, the common language of historical writing, for his English and Norman readers.

How much Geoffrey created and how much he somehow learned is as mysterious as King Arthur himself. Geoffrey's history, which was finished by 1138, describes a period of English and Welsh history that other historians barely covered: from about the year 1200 B.C. to about A.D. 689. . . .

Geoffrey first presented Arthur in "historical" terms, dating his reign to A.D. 542. He describes Arthur's birth, however, in amazing terms. He tells how Arthur's father, King Uther Pendragon, asked the magician Merlin to make him look like the husband of Igerna, a beautiful, married lady whom Uther loved. . . .

Luckily for Uther, Igerna's real husband died in a fight. According to Geoffrey, the new couple loved each other anyway, and Arthur was born. . . .

The "sword in the stone" story, and Lancelot's love for Arthur's wife, Guinevere, are well-known, but neither appears in Geoffrey of Monmouth's version. Instead, Geoffrey dryly relates how Arthur conquered all the kings of Britain, Europe, and even Rome. . . .

Most medieval writers treated Geoffrey's story as real—or real enough to use its dates and names. Kings claimed to be descended from him. Countless further romances about Arthur's

(p. 15)

knights were written in all languages spoken throughout medieval Europe. . . .

A Kernel of Truth?

Stories passed down from memory can contain truth, especially in a world where few people could read or write. But stories that are passed down in that manner usually are transformed to suit people's lives or ideals at the time. For all of its dry and simple style, Geoffrey's history certainly shows creative rewriting. It would be extremely interesting if someone could find the "very ancient book" he used—if it ever existed! Meantime, old medieval books fill special libraries, awaiting more investigation. The story of Arthur continues to give people a good reason to explore an ancient, lost past—just as it did in Geoffrey of Monmouth's day.

16. Write a one-paragraph summary of the story "How Arthur Fought with Rome," including its central idea and most important details. Do not include your opinions. (8 points)

17. Part A: Which of the following best describes the theme of "How Arthur Fought with Rome"?

    A. Treat messengers kindly to make sure your message is delivered.

    B. People should only pay others if they are unable to win a fight.

    C. Leaders succeed by standing with their people, not for themselves.

    D. Heroes are people who never lose, even when they are outnumbered.

    Part B: Which excerpt from the story best supports the answer to Part A?

    A. *Then Arthur told his treasurer to give the messengers gifts, and to take them safely out of the country.*

    B. *"My knights and men whom I love, remember that you are fighting today for your rights and for the independence of Britain."*

    C. *"We have ruled the world for centuries, and a little king of little England shall not make us fear."*

    D. *"Strike well, and do not forget that great courage is as powerful as great numbers."*

18. Part A: What is the central idea of the article "Geoffrey's Tale—Fact, Fiction, or Both?"

    A. There is little evidence that Geoffrey's stories about Arthur were real history.

    B. Writings about Arthur go back to the year 550, when he fought a great battle.

    C. Later writers invented legends about Arthur, but Geoffrey recorded history.

    D. People have changed the true stories about Arthur to serve their own needs.

    Part B: Which statement from the article best supports the answer to Part A?

    A. *Geoffrey first presented Arthur in "historical" terms, dating his reign to A.D. 542.*

    B. *Gildas mentions a fierce battle at Mount Badon against invading pagan Saxons, a war that later writers claim Arthur fought.*

    C. *But stories that are passed down in that manner usually are transformed to suit people's lives or ideals at the time.*

    D. *How much Geoffrey created and how much he somehow learned is as mysterious as King Arthur himself.*

19. Part A: How does the section "A Kernel of Truth?" develop the ideas in the article?

    A. It explains that the author finds the evidence for a historical Arthur convincing.

    B. It shows that even though Arthur stories are not true history, they have value.

    C. It concludes that Geoffrey of Monmouth's history was completely made up.

    D. It reveals that even though historians doubt the stories, people believe them.

    Part B: Which statement from the article best supports the answer to Part A?

    A. *The story of Arthur continues to give people a good reason to explore an ancient, lost past— just as it did in Geoffrey of Monmouth's day.*

    B. *It would be extremely interesting if someone could find the "very ancient book" he used—if it ever existed!*

    C. *Most medieval writers treated Geoffrey's story as real—or real enough to use its dates and names.*

    D. *For all of its dry and simple style, Geoffrey's history certainly shows creative rewriting.*

20. Read this sentence from "How Arthur Fought with Rome."

He was on a beautiful white horse whose mane rose and fell in the wind like a wave of the sea.

What is the impact of the figurative language in this sentence?
A. It shows that the horse is moving slowly as if underwater.
B. It helps readers understand the motion of Arthur's horse.
C. It creates an image of Arthur as a majestic, heroic figure.
D. It emphasizes the importance of the horse to Arthur.

21. Part A: Read this sentence from "How Arthur Fought with Rome."

"Your father and his predecessors did this, and so must you."

What does the word *predecessors* mean?
A. subjects of the emperor
B. rulers of other countries
C. servants of the king
D. those who came before

Part B: Which sentence from the article provides the best context clue to the word's meaning?
A. *All the kings did this up to the time of Arthur.*
B. *"Sir, our mighty emperor sends you greeting, and commands you to acknowledge him as lord, and to send him the money due him from your realm."*
C. *"Tell him that I refuse his command, for I owe him nothing."*
D. *They were the messengers of the emperor of Rome . . .*

22. Part A: What is author Andrew Calloway's point of view about Geoffrey of Monmouth?
A. Geoffrey was a boring writer who believed in ridiculous stories.
B. Geoffrey was a serious historian who only recorded what he read.
C. Geoffrey made up everything about Arthur, who never existed.
D. Geoffrey used his imagination to make history more interesting.

Part B: Which sentence from the article best supports the answer to Part A?
A. *It began with a popular history by Geoffrey of Monmouth, writing about 70 years after the Normans had conquered England by defeating the Anglo-Saxons.*
B. *How much Geoffrey created and how much he somehow learned is as mysterious as King Arthur himself.*
C. *Instead, Geoffrey dryly relates how Arthur conquered all the kings of Britain, Europe, and even Rome.*
D. *He claims that he simply translated the text into Latin, the common language of historical writing, for his English and Norman readers.*

23. Why does Andrew Galloway relate the story of Uther and Igerna?

   A. It shows that important parts of the history are accurate.

   B. He develops readers' interest with an entertaining tale.

   C. It shows that Geoffrey's history treated legends as fact.

   D. He uses it as an example of Geoffrey's dry, simple writing.

Directions: Answer the following question on another sheet of paper.

24. The story "How Arthur Fought with Rome" reflects a battle that Geoffrey of Monmouth included in his history. Yet the author of "Geoffrey's Tale—Fact, Fiction, or Both?" questions whether the events actually happened. How does this information affect readers' understanding of the story?

   Your task: Using evidence from both texts, write an essay about how Maude Radford drew on the history of Arthur and why she may have altered that history. In your essay, be sure to include the following:

   • what details Maude Radford, author of "How Arthur Fought with Rome," drew or changed from history

   • what Andrew Galloway, author of "Geoffrey's Tale," says about this history

   • why Radford chose to tell this story

   • how Radford's creative use of history serves her purpose

   Finally, proofread your essay for errors in grammar, punctuation, and spelling. (20 points)

Answer Key

Answer Key

Unit 1 Summative Assessment (pp. 451–459)

1. C.
2. A.
3. D.
4. A.
5. B.
6. B.
7. D.
8. C.
9. D.
10. B.
11. C.
12. A.
13. C.
14. D.
15. B.

Questions 1–15 (DoK 1)

16. Part A: D. (DoK 2)
Part B: Sample answer: *In the story, Tom Little has "seen a thousand George Willards go out of their towns to the city." It is a natural part of growing up. The narrator says that George's life in Winesburg "had become but a background on which to paint the dreams of his manhood." Following his dreams is what makes him a man.* (DoK 2)

17. Part A: B. (DoK 3)
Part B: A., B. (DoK 2)

18. Sample answer: *A large crowd comes to the train station to see George off, suggesting that they think highly of him. Everyone shakes his hand, and Gertrude wishes him "good luck," expressing the sentiments and hopes of the entire town for his success. These expressions of good will all point to the idea that George is well liked and admired by one and all.;* (6 points) (DoK 2)

19. Sample answer: *The story suggests that small-town people value supporting their community, holding close ties, and sticking together. The big crowd that comes to see George off shows that the people of Winesburg support and help each other. George's father advises him to act "sharp," pointing not only to his protectiveness and care for his son but also suggesting a contrast with stereotypical city people who are believed to be cold and possibly uncaring. The contrast with the city points to the small-town values of honesty and suggests the security and safety that comes with those values.* (6 points) (DoK 3)

20. Answers will vary. An exemplary answer will point out that the metaphor compares George's old life and his dreams for the future with an artist's canvas: the old life being the background of the canvas, and his dreams of the future the main scene that the artist will begin to paint. The story describes George's departure as he leaves behind his old life in Winesburg. George remembers many details of that life while he waits for the train to take off, but then his dreams come to the forefront with a "passion." The metaphor and the farewell he receives from his community suggest that George carries strong values and has an admirable character that will serve him well as he works to create a new life for himself. (12 points) (DoK 3)

21. Part A: A. (DoK 3)

Part B: Sample answer: *In the second paragraph, Emily explains "I started a bullying prevention project because I wanted to raise awareness among my fellow students that bullying is a problem and help them understand the huge impact that bullying can have on their peers. I wanted people to realize how damaging bullying is." Then she explains a school assembly on bullying that she organized. Finally, she says "I know that an assembly like this is just the first step to dealing with bullying at my school, but it was an important step to take—to begin to raise awareness and voice students' concerns about bullying."* (DoK 2)

22. Sample answer: *The article describes the author's efforts to raise awareness of bullying at her school. She held an assembly and asked students to take two surveys to assess their understanding of the problem of bullying. The author also explains her own hard experiences with bullying. She shows that it may involve physical abuse but may also consist of saying mean things and spreading rumors.* (6 points) (DoK 2)

23. B. (DoK 3)

24. Sample answer: *The article has a problem/solution structure. The first section explains the problem of bullying with Emily's experience as evidence. It helps readers understand why bullying is an important issue. The next section describes how Emily tried to solve the problem. She made students at her school aware of bullying and worked with younger students to prevent bullying. This section shows that readers can (and should) take action to stop bullying.* (6 points) (DoK 3)

25. Responses will vary. An exemplary answer will identify the authors' claim that students should stop all forms of bullying. Their reasoning is that bullying inflicts pain on its victims, and as evidence they cite Emily's own experience with bullying and the pain others have experienced

in her school. The evidence also includes the fact that bullying takes many forms, including physical, verbal, and online bullying. Most students will agree and should support this claim with evidence from the selection. (12 points) (DoK 3)

Unit 2 Summative Assessment (pp. 460–468)

1. B.
2. C.
3. B.
4. D.
5. A.
6. C.
7. D.
8. B.
9. A.
10. C.
11. A.
12. D.
13. C.
14. B.
15. A.

Questions 1–15; (DoK 1)

16. Part A: D. (DoK 2)
    Part B: C. (DoK 2)
17. Part A: C. (DoK 2)
    Part B: D. (DoK 2)
18. Sample answer: *A peasant woman meets a young man on her way home. The young man claims that he has fallen from heaven. She immediately asks if he knows her dead son. When he says he does, she gives him food, clothes, and money. The reader knows that he has tricked her, and the story says that the man doesn't return to heaven.* (6 points) (DoK 2)

19. Sample answer: *The young man is out to trick the woman. His point of view is likely that foolish people deserve to be taken advantage of. He lies when he says that he fell from heaven and lies again when he says that Kees is his "nearest neighbor." He lies when he says Kees's "stockings are worn out" and his food is gone. These lies reveal the peasant woman's point of view. She misses her son and wants to take care of him even though he is dead. "Oh dear," she exclaims and admits that she can "well afford to give him something." Her grief makes her believe the young man's lies.* (6 points) (DoK 3)

20. Answers will vary. An excellent answer will observe that the young man begins to trick the woman by claiming to have fallen from heaven and lets the woman supply the information about her son, Kees. Instead of telling her what he wants, he says that Kees does not have it. He even pretends that he is not interested

in taking anything, saying he is only doing it "because it is for Kees." At each step, he lets the woman feel that everything is her own idea. This character's actions are meant to teach readers how to recognize a con artist, to question extraordinary claims like, "I just fell from heaven." He illustrates the theme that what seems too good to be true probably is. (12 points) (DoK 3)

21. Part A: C. (DoK 3)
    Part B: A. (DoK 2)

22. Sample answer: *The company agreed to pay the FTC because it broke the FTC Act and the Telemarketing Sales Rule. It deceived consumers by "billing customers without their express informed consent" and "failing to make adequate disclosures about the total number and cost of products before billing consumers." This money will be used to give those customers refunds. The company also paid the New York Attorney General to reimburse the agency for the money it spent on court fees, lawyers, and "fees to settle" the lawsuit.* (6 points) (DoK 2)

23. D. (DoK 1)

24. Sample answer: *Schneiderman's point of view was that companies should be honest and fair. He wanted the company to "be held accountable," and he also wanted the entire direct marketing industry to stop using "small print and hidden fees to inflate charges." This point of view is likely the opposite of the company's owners. They must have considered these tactics a good way to make more money. The owners were greedy and dishonest; Schneiderman was protective and moral.* (6 points) (DoK 3)

25. Answers will vary. An excellent answer will explain that the Consumer Protection Bureau is a government agency that works to protect America's consumers from misleading or unfair business practices. The response may include actions such as these: enforcing laws that protect consumers; suing companies that cheat their consumers; working with state attorneys general to hold businesses accountable; publishing reports such as these to inform the public; and seeking to return money to consumers who have been affected by such businesses. It may go on to suggest that the bureau is successful in pursuing companies such as the one in the text, securing multi-million dollar settlements against them. (DoK 3)

Unit 3 Summative Assessment (pp. 469–476)

1. C.
2. B.
3. D.
4. A.

5. A.
6. C.
7. D.
8. A.
9. C.
10. B.
11. A.
12. D.
13. B.
14. B.
15. A.

Questions 1–15 (DoK 1)

Part A: C. (DoK 2)
Part B: B., C., D. (DoK 2)

17. A., E. (DoK 2)
18. B. (DoK 3)

19. Answers will vary. Sample answer: The poem suggests that the sewing machine transformed the lives of women—especially the poor. For example, the first two lines of the fifth stanza say, "My creation is a blessing / To the indigent secured." The stanza goes on to describe how hard women had to work to sew everything by hand: "the cares distressing / Which so many have endured." It also notes that a sewing machine is hardier than the human body: "Mine are sinews superhuman, / Ribs of oak and nerves of steel." So the sewing machine was a huge labor-saving device that was "Born to toil." However, the poem hints that machines will take the place of workers because they are much less trouble than human workers who have "children to distress" them. (6 points) (DoK 3)

20. Answers will vary. An exemplary answer should identify the central idea that the sewing machine has transformed women's lives because it is free of human weaknesses. For example, the first stanza notes the sewing machine is sturdier than a human and has no cares. Other stanzas further compare its advantages to human limitations, like the need for rest, money, or company. The poet also uses sound repetition to develop the central idea. The repetition of the words *never* and *no* in the first and second stanzas emphasizes the contrast between people and machines, and the type of relief it brings to women. Alliteration in the first, third, and fifth stanzas highlights the machine's toughness. The pattern of end rhymes (ABABCDCD) also highlights each image. (12 points) (DoK 3)

21. Part A: C. (DoK 3)
    Part B: A., C. (DoK 2)

22. Answers will vary. Sample answer: The report says that the owners of the AI would benefit more than the workers. If AI becomes as smart as people, it could replace many jobs currently

held by humans. Even if AI does not put everyone out of work, it "could lead to even larger [differences] in income between capital owners and labor." (6 points) (DoK 3)

23. D. (DoK 3)

24. Answers will vary. An excellent answer will describe the authors' argument as saying that AI-driven technology could be different from other technological changes because it would enable machines to take over cognitive tasks "to such a degree that they fundamentally change the nature of production and work." Therefore, they argue, the government should "strengthen the social safety net" and unemployment insurance. It should help people who are replaced by AI through retraining programs and economic support. The authors present evidence that these programs already need improvement. They cite the number of people who used unemployment insurance and describe its decline over time. The authors' reasoning is sound. However, some students may note that there is no direct evidence that AI will have the worst-case consequences the authors describe. (6 points) (DoK 3)

25. Answers will vary. An excellent answer will note that the poem is much more positive toward technology than the government report. The poem praises the sewing machine and details how it will benefit human workers. It created more jobs for people. However, the report notes that AI has become so advanced that it will take the place of human workers. There will be fewer jobs and will widen the gap between those who own the technology and the average worker. (DoK 3)

Unit 4 Summative Assessment (pp. 477–485)
1. B.
2. A.
3. B.
4. D.
5. C.
6. D.
7. C.
8. A.
9. C.
10. B.
11. B.
12. D.
13. C.
14. D.
15. A.

Questions 1–15 (DoK 1)

16. Part A: B. (DoK 2)
    Part B: C. (DoK 2)
17. Part A: D. (DoK 2)

Part B: C. (DoK 2)

18. Sample answer: *The effect of the figurative and sensory language is to heighten the feeling of loss and alienation experienced by Chad and the Major. The simile compares the emotional effect of the news on the Major to being punched. In other words, it is shocking, painful news. The sound and movement of insects and birds emphasizes the silence between the two men. At the end of the paragraph, the metaphor comparing the farmer's singing to wailing reinforces the sense of grief.* (DoK 2)

19. Sample answer: *One thing the story illustrates is how every personal decision involving the war might have profound complications. One character supports the Confederacy (the Major), the other supports the Union (Chad). This scene clarifies how the Civil War pitted friend against friend. Fighting a war is terrible enough, but in a civil war, an enemy might also be a family member or a friend; this makes the horror even worse. The reactions of Chad and Major highlight this heartbreak of the Civil War.* (DoK 2)

20. Answers will vary. An excellent answer will reflect that the setting of the American Civil War profoundly affects the characters and their conflict. Only in a civil war do people choose which side to fight on and end up on opposite sides from their friends or family. This makes Chad's decision to join the Union army more difficult, knowing he is taking sides against Major. Students may point out other effects of the Civil War setting, including the issue of slavery. The Major offers to send his slave, Brutus, to be Chad's servant, until he learns of Chad's loyalty to the Union. The Major suggests that Chad may oppose slavery when he says "I know you would not take him" and implies that Chad would let the slave run away. Their disagreement on this issue, one of the major causes of the war, creates a unique conflict for the characters. (DoK 2)

21. Part A: B. (DoK 2)
    Part B: A., B., D. (DoK 2)

22. Sample answer: *The article describes the effects of the Civil War on children. Some children, like Johnny Cook, served as soldiers. Cook started as a bugler but ended up taking over a cannon at Antietam when others were wounded or killed. With a general, he fought off Confederate soldiers. Other children, like Jennie Chambers, experienced many hardships of war as a civilian. Chambers saw her father imprisoned and was witness to death and destruction. Her family was in the war zone for several days, and their farm was hit by artillery. She also saw soldiers from both sides come together after the battle, showing brotherhood as Americans.* (DoK 2)

23. C. (DoK 2)

24. Sample answer: *The author seems sympathetic to young people living through the Civil War, as shown in expressions like "their young eyes witnessed the horrors of war." The author mostly presents facts about the war but occasionally uses emotional language like "felt the effects of the war in their stomachs" to dramatize the suffering. The author seems equally concerned for young soldiers and civilians. But no one gets blamed for creating the situation in the first place, and the author does not support the North or the South. The author's point of view is not that war is good or bad, but that its effects on children are important because they "offer unique insight."* (DoK 3)

25. Answers will vary. An excellent answer will point out that both the novel and the article illustrate the tension and bonds between family and friends who find themselves on opposite sides of the war. In the scene from the novel, Chad's announcement shocks and disappoints the Major, but their bond is not broken. The Major still offers Chad a horse, and Chad is heartbroken to hurt his old friend. The article touches on the same idea when it describes Jennie Chambers's conversation with soldiers after the battle. The men said they were brothers despite the war. Students may also contrast the novel and the article by noting that Chad is not a child, or that the characters in the novel have not yet been directly affected by the war. Students may observe that the details of the article, and the stories of individuals like Johnny Cook and Jennie Chambers inform a reader's understanding of what the characters in the novel may experience in the war. (DoK 3)

End-of-Course Assessment (pp. 486–503)
1. Part A: C. (DoK 2); Part B: B. (DoK 2)
2. Part A: D. (DoK 2); Part B: A. (DoK 2)
3. Part A: D. (DoK 2); Part B: B. (DoK 2)
4. Part A: C. (DoK 2); Part B: A. (DoK 2)
5. Part A: A. (DoK 2); Part B: C. (DoK 2)
6. B. (DoK 2)
7. D. (DoK 2)
8. Sample answer: *The watcher in the poem is death. The speaker uses creepy images to show that the watcher is the opposite of the joyful people he watches. He is "in the rain outside," "where the black winds blow," and he has "pale hands" that he uses to "ride." The poem means that death is always waiting, even when people are young and in their happiest moments.* (8 points) (DoK 2)
9. Part A: C., F. (DoK 2)
   Part B: E., F. (DoK 2)
10. Part A: B. (DoK 1); Part B: D. (DoK 2)

11. Part A: B. (DoK 2); Part B: A. (DoK 2)
12. Part A: C. (DoK 2); Part B: D. (DoK 2)
13. Part A: D. (DoK 2); Part B: C. (DoK 2)
14. Part A: A. (DoK 2); Part B: B. (DoK 2)

15. Sample answer: *The author supports the claim by telling stories about teachers rewarding a student's honesty and parents rewarding their children for grades. She says this is because modern society is focused on instant rewards, like buying things. This argument is not very well supported because the author only offers a few examples from the news and from her own life. The story of the boy returning the money shows that people still value honesty.* (8 points) (DoK 2)

16. Sample answer: *King Arthur decides not to send money to Rome, even though Britain has done this for centuries. The Roman emperor sends messengers to demand payment, and Arthur refuses. The emperor decides to go to war with Arthur, and the two armies meet in France. They battle for days until finally Arthur fights the emperor, and Arthur uses his magic sword to defeat him.* (8 points) (DoK 2)

17. Part A: C. (DoK 2); Part B: B. (DoK 2)
18. Part A: A. (DoK 2); Part B: D. (DoK 2)
19. Part A: B. (DoK 2); Part B: A. (DoK 2)
20. C. (DoK 3)
21. Part A: D. (DoK 2); Part B: A. (DoK 2)
22. Part A: D. (DoK 3); Part B: B. (DoK 2)
23. C. (DoK 3)

24. Answers will vary. An exemplary answer will explain that Radford drew the idea of Arthur defeating the Roman Empire from Geoffrey's history and used Geoffrey's dates to provide context to the setting. Radford most likely invented all other details of the story in order to serve her own purpose. As Andrew Calloway noted, stories about Arthur are "transformed to suit people's lives or ideals." Radford used the story of Arthur defeating the Romans to deliver messages about courage, independence, and greed using the historical elements to give the story weight and importance. At the same time, Radford can invent whatever details she imagines without worrying about accuracy. Readers who know that Arthur is more legend than history can still enjoy the story as an adventure in which a greedy emperor is defeated by a small, brave group fighting for independence. (20 points) (DoK 4)

Lesson Planner

Connections: English Language Arts Grade 7	Connections: Writing & Language Handbook	Time needed
Introduction to Course		
Close Reading and Annotating Texts, pp. xxii–6	Chapter 31: Close Reading SB: pp. 418–439 TG: p. 290	2 days (3 days with Writing and Language)
Unit 1		
Introduction to Unit 1, p. 7		1 day
Chapter 1 Chapter Opener and First Read, pp. 8–15 (Summarizing a Text)		2–3 days
Second Read, pp. 15–17 (Understanding Technical Terms)		1 day
Third Read, pp. 17–20 (Identifying Claims, Reasons, and Details)		2 days
Language: Prefixes, Suffixes, and Root Words, pp. 20–22	Chapter 30: Prefixes and Suffixes SB: pp. 413–416 TG: p. 282	
Project-Based Assessment: Roundtable Discussion p. 23 Argumentative Essay, p. 24 On Your Own, p. 25	Chapter 33: Speaking Effectively; Listening Actively SB: pp. 459–464 TG: p. 308 Chapter 6: Argumentative Writing SB: pp. 92–117 TG: p. 46	*2–4 days per project (3–5 days with Writing and Language)
Connect to Testing, pp. 26–28		½ day
		Total: 7½ days
Chapter 2 Chapter Opener and First Read, pp. 29–36 (Analyzing Plot and Conflict)		2–3 days
Second Read, pp. 36–37 (Identifying Theme)		1 day
Third Read, pp. 38–39 (Understanding Point of View)		1 day
Language: Using Commas To Set Off Nonrestrictive Phrases and Clauses, pp. 39–40	Chapter 27: Commas That Enclose SB: pp. 381–383 TG: p. 251	
Project-Based Assessments: Change the Point of View, pp. 40–41 On Your Own, p. 42	Chapter 7: Writing a Short Story SB: pp. 130–139 TG: p. 58	*2–4 days per project (4–6 days with Writing and Language)
Connect to Testing, p. 43–45		½ day
		Total: 5½ days

Guide to Abbreviations: SB = student book; **TWE** = teacher wraparound edition; **TG** = teacher guide
*NOTE: Extension activities, Project-Based Assessment, and On Your Own are not included in total of class time.

Lesson Planner

	Connections: English Language Arts Grade 7	Connections: Writing & Language Handbook	Time needed
Chapter 3	Chapter Opener and First Read, pp. 46–52 (Making Inferences)		2–3 days
	Second Read, pp. 53–55 (Understanding Structure and Purpose)		1 days
	Third Read, pp. 56–57 (Determining Point of View)		1–2 days
	Language: Sentence Structure, pp. 57–58	Chapter 20: Kinds of Sentence Structure SB: pp. 293–295 TG: p. 176	
	Project-Based Assessment: Digital Presentation, p. 58 Roundtable Discussion, pp. 59–60 On Your Own, p. 60	Chapter 10: Evaluating Sources SB: pp. 187–188 TG: p. 90 Chapter 33: Speaking Effectively; Listening Actively SB: pp. 459–464 TG: p. 308	*2–4 days per project
	Connect to Testing, pp. 61–63		1 day
			Total: 7 days
Chapter 4	Chapter Opener and First Read, pp. 64–71 (Summarizing Central Ideas)		2–3 days
	Second Read, pp. 71–72 (Understanding Figurative Language)		½ days
	Third Read, pp. 72–74 (Determining Points of View)		2 days
	Language: Connotations and Denotations, pp. 74–75	Chapter 32: Words That Communicate Clearly SB: pp. 456–457 TG: p. 296	
	Project-Based Assessment: Pictorial Presentation, p. 75 Literary Analysis, p. 76 On Your Own, p. 77	Chapter 8: Writing About Literary Texts SB: pp. 148–165 TG: p. 74	*2–4 days per project (4–6 days with Writing and Language)
	Connect to Testing, pp. 78–80		1 day
			Total: 6½ days

Guide to Abbreviations: SB = student book; **TWE** = teacher wraparound edition; **TG** = teacher guide
*NOTE: Extension activities, Project-Based Assessment, and On Your Own are not included in total of class time.

Lesson Planner

	Connections: English Language Arts Grade 7	Connections: Writing & Language Handbook	Time needed
Chapter 5	Chapter Opener and First Read, pp. 81–86 (Identifying Author's Purpose)		2–3 days
	Second Read, pp. 86–88 (Evaluating an Argument)		1–2 days
	Third Read, pp. 89–92 (Comparing and Contrasting Arguments)		2–3 days (3–4 days with Writing and Language
	Language: Consistent Verb Tenses, p. 93	Chapter 22: Tenses of Verbs SB: pp. 308–310 TG: p. 197	
	Project-Based Assessments: Awareness Speech, p. 94 Letter to the Editor, p. 94 On Your Own, p. 95	Chapter 33: Speaking Effectively SB: pp. 459–461 TG: p. 308 Chapter 9: Writing Business Letters SB: pp. 171–178 TG: p. 81	*2–4 days per project (3–5 days with Writing and Language
	Connect to Testing, pp. 96–98		1 day
			Total: 9 days (10 days with Writing and Language)
Writing an Argumentative Essay	Prepare to Write, p. 99 Brainstorm, pp. 100–101 Generate Ideas, pp. 102–104	Chapter 6: Argumentative Writing SB: pp. 93–109 TG: p. 46	2 days
	Organize Ideas, p. 105 First Draft, p. 105	Chapter 6: Argumentative Writing SB: pp. 106–111 TG: p. 46	3–4 days
	First Peer Review, p. 106 Second Peer Review, p. 107 Final Peer Review, p. 108 Final Essay, p. 108	Chapter 6: Argumentative Writing SB: pp. 112–117 TG: p. 46	2–3 days
			Total: 9 days (14 days with Writing and Language)
Assessment	Practice Performance Task, pp. 109–116		2 days
	Unit 1 Summative Assessment, TWE pp. 451–459		2 days
			Total: 4 days
Unit 1 Total			50½ days (56½ days with Writing and Language)

Guide to Abbreviations: SB = student book; **TWE** = teacher wraparound edition; **TG** = teacher guide
*NOTE: Extension activities, Project-Based Assessment, and On Your Own are not included in total of class time.

Lesson Planner

Connections: English Language Arts Grade 7	Connections: Writing & Language Handbook	Time needed
Unit 2		
Introduction to Unit 2, p. 117		½ day
Chapter 6 Chapter Opener and First Read, pp. 118–125 (Making an Inference)		2 days
Second Read, pp. 125–126 (Analyzing Point of View)		1 day
Third Read, pp. 127–131 (Comparing and Contrasting Presentations)		1½–2 days (2–3 days with Writing and Language)
Language: Understanding Context Clues, p. 131	Chapter 32: Context Clues SB: pp. 445–447 TG: p. 296	
Project-Based Assessment: Introducing Frank Abagnale, pp. 132–133 Character Analysis, pp. 133–134 On Your Own, p. 134		*2–4 days per project
Connect to Testing, p. 135–137		½ day
		Total: 6 days (7 days with Writing and Language)
Chapter 7 Chapter Opener and First Read, pp. 138–145 (Analyzing Central Ideas)		2–3 days
Second Read, pp. 146–148 (Determining Word Meanings)		2 days
Third Read, pp. 148–150 (Evaluating an Argument)		1–2 days
Language: Using Commas with Coordinate Adjectives, p. 150	Chapter 27: Adjectives Before a Noun SB: p. 377 TG: p. 251	
Project-Based Assessments: Response Essay, p. 152 Draw a Diagram, p. 153 On Your Own, p. 154	Chapter 4: Writing Effective Compositions SB: pp. 61–71 TG: p. 26	*2–4 days per project (4–6 days with Writing and Language)
Connect to Testing, pp. 155–156		½ day
		Total: 7½ days

Guide to Abbreviations: SB = student book; **TWE** = teacher wraparound edition; **TG** = teacher guide
*NOTE: Extension activities, Project-Based Assessment, and On Your Own are not included in total of class time.

Lesson Planner

	Connections: English Language Arts Grade 7	Connections: Writing & Language Handbook	Time needed
Chapter 8	Chapter Opener and First Read, pp. 157–164 (Making an Inference)		2–3 days
	Second Read, pp. 164–165 (Analyzing Text Structure)		1–2 days
	Third Read, pp. 166–167 (Determining Point of View and Purpose)		2 days
	Language: Correcting Misplaced Modifiers, pp. 167–169	Chapter 18: As You Revise: Check for Clarity SB: p. 272 TG: p. 158	
	Project-Based Assessments: Investigative Report, pp. 170–171 Compare and Contrast Essay, pp. 171–173 On Your Own, p. 173	Chapter 3: Writing Well–Structured Paragraphs SB: pp. 48–55 TG: p. 17 Chapter 10: Inquiry: Initial Research and Development SB: pp. 184–189 TG: p. 90 Chapter 4: Writing Effective Compositions SB: pp. 60–71 TG: p. 26	*2–4 days per project (9–11 days with Writing and Language)
	Connect to Testing, pp. 174–175		½ day
			Total: 7½ days
Chapter 9	Chapter Opener and First Read, pp. 176–183 (Analyzing Interactions of Ideas, People, and Events)		2–3 days
	Second Read, pp. 183–184 (Analyzing Structure and Purpose)		1 day
	Third Read, pp. 185–187 (Evaluating Reasons and Evidence)		2–3 days (3–4 days with Writing and Language)
	Language: Complex Sentences with Subordinating Conjunctions and Relative Pronouns, pp. 187–189	Chapter 20: Adverb Clauses; Complex Sentences SB: pp. 289–291; 294 TG: p. 176	
	Project-Based Assessments: Digital Presentation, p. 190 Brochure, p. 191 On Your Own, p. 191	Chapter 10: Evaluating Sources; Inquiry and Initial Research SB: pp. 186–189 TG: p. 90	*2–4 days per project (5–7 days with Writing and Language)
	Connect to Testing, pp. 191–194		½ day
			Total: 7½ days (8½ days with Writing and Language)

Guide to Abbreviations: SB = student book; **TWE** = teacher wraparound edition; **TG** = teacher guide
*NOTE: Extension activities, Project-Based Assessment, and On Your Own are not included in total of class time.

Lesson Planner

	Connections: English Language Arts Grade 7	Connections: Writing & Language Handbook	Time needed
Chapter 10	Chapter Opener and First Read, pp. 195–202 (Citing Evidence)		3 days
	Second Read, pp. 202–203 (Analyzing the Interaction of Story Elements)		1 day
	Third Read, p. 204–206 (Analyzing Points of View)		2 days (3 days with Writing and Language)
	Language: Expressing Ideas Precisely and Concisely, pp. 206–208	Chapter 2: Writing Concise Sentences SB: pp. 42–43 TG: p. 10 Chapter 32: Words That Communicate Clearly SB: pp. 455–457 TG: p. 296	
	Project-Based Assessments: Personal Essay p. 209 Roundtable Discussion, pp. 209–211 On Your Own, p. 211	Chapter 7: Writing a Personal Narrative SB: pp. 125–129 TG: p. 58 Chapter 33: Speaking Effectively; Listening Actively SB: pp. 459-464 TG: p. 308	*2–4 days per project (5–7 days with Writing and Language)
	Connect to Testing, pp. 212–213		½ day
			Total: 6½ days (7½ days with Writing and Language)
Writing a Informative Text	Prepare to Write, p. 214 Brainstorm, pp. 215–217 Gather Information, pp. 217–219	Chapter 5: Informational Writing SB: pp. 73–77 TG: p. 34	2 days
	Write a Central Idea Statement, p. 219 Organize Ideas, pp. 220–221 Provide Graphics, p. 221 First Draft, p. 221	Chapter 5: Informational Writing SB: pp. 78–85 TG: p. 34	2–4 days
	First Peer Review, p. 222 Second Peer Review, p. 223 Final Peer Review, p. 224 Final Essay, p. 224	Chapter 5: Informational Writing SB: pp. 86–91 TG: p. 34	2 days
			Total: 8 days (13 days with Writing and Language)
Assessment	Practice Performance Task, pp. 225–230		2 days
	Unit 2 Summative Assessment, TWE pp. 460–468		2 days
			Total: 4 days
Unit 2 Total			47 days (55 days with Writing and Language)

Guide to Abbreviations: SB = student book; **TWE** = teacher wraparound edition; **TG** = teacher guide
*NOTE: Extension activities, Project-Based Assessment, and On Your Own are not included in total of class time.

Lesson Planner

Connections: English Language Arts Grade 7	Connections: Writing & Language Handbook	Time needed
Unit 3		
Introduction to Unit 3, p. 231		½ day
Chapter Opener and First Read, pp. 232–239 (Analyzing Interactions of People, Ideas, and Events)		2–3 days
Second Read, pp. 239–241 (Analyzing Text Structure)		2 days
Third Read, pp. 241–242 (Analyzing Point of View and Purpose)		2 days
Language: Using Dashes, pp. 243–244	Chapter 29: Dashes, Ellipses, and Parentheses SB: p. 203 TG: p. 271	
Project-Based Assessments: Letter to the Principal pp. 244–245 Write a Narrative, pp. 245–246 On Your Own, p. 246	Chapter 9: Writing a Business Letter SB: pp. 171–179 TG: p. 81 Chapter 7: Writing a Personal Narrative SB: pp. 125–129 TG: p. 58	*2–3 days per project (7–8 days with Writing and Language)
Connect to Testing, pp. 247–248		½ day
		Total: 7½ days
Chapter Opener and First Read, pp. 249–255 (Determining a Central Idea)		2 days
Second Read, pp. 255–256 (Examining the Impact of Repeated Sounds)		1 day
Third Read, pp. 257–259 (Analyzing How Structure Helps Develop an Idea)		1–2 days
Language: Interpreting Figures of Speech, pp. 259–261		
Project-Based Assessments: Poem About Modern Technology, p. 261 Digital Presentation, pp. 262–263 On Your Own, p. 263–264	Chapter 7: Writing a Poem SB: pp. 143–147 TG: p. 58 Chapter 10: Evaluating Sources SB: pp. 187–188 TG: p. 90	*2–4 days per project (4–6 days with Writing and Language)
Connect to Testing, pp. 265–267		½ day
		Total: 5½ days

Chapter 11 labels the first group of rows; *Chapter 12* labels the second group of rows.

Guide to Abbreviations: SB = student book; **TWE** = teacher wraparound edition; **TG** = teacher guide
*NOTE: Extension activities, Project-Based Assessment, and On Your Own are not included in total of class time.

Lesson Planner

	Connections: English Language Arts Grade 7	Connections: Writing & Language Handbook	Time needed
Chapter 13	Chapter Opener and First Read, pp. 268–274 (Analyzing the Development of Central Ideas)		2 days
	Second Read, pp. 274–278 (Comparing Media Portrayals of a Topic)		2 days
	Third Read, pp. 278–280 (Analyzing Presentations of the Same Topic)		1–2 days (2–3 days with Writing and Language)
	Language: Subject and Verb Agreement, p. 280	Chapter 24: Subject & Verb Agreement SB: pp. 332–335 TG: p. 217	
	Project-Based Assessment: Op-Ed, pp. 281–282 Job Fair Pamphlet, pp. 282–283 On Your Own, p. 283	Chapter 6: The Rhetoric of Persuasion SB: pp. 97–101 TG: p. 46 Chapter 10: Evaluating Sources SB: pp. 188–189 TG: 90	*2–4 days
	Connect to Testing, pp. 284–285		½ day
			Total: 6½ days (7½ days with Writing and Language)
Chapter 14	Chapter Opener and First Read, pp. 286–293 (Comparing Points of View)		2 days
	Second Read, pp. 293–294 (Analyzing the Effects of Setting)		1 day
	Third Read, pp. 295–298 (Determining Theme)		1–2 days (2–3 days with Writing and Language)
	Language: Using Context Clues, p. 298	Chapter 32: Context Clues SB: pp. 445–447 TG: p. 296	
	Project-Based Assessment: Write a Protest Song, p. 299 Write a Book Chapter, p. 300 On Your Own, p. 301	Chapter 4: Writing Effective Compositions SB: pp. 60–71 TG: p. 26 Chapter 7: Writing a Short Story SB: pp. 130–139 TG: p. 58	*2–4 days per project (7–9 days with Writing and Language)
	Connect to Testing, pp. 302–303		½ day
			Total: 5½ days (6½ days with Writing and Language)

Guide to Abbreviations: SB = student book; **TWE** = teacher wraparound edition; **TG** = teacher guide
*NOTE: Extension activities, Project-Based Assessment, and On Your Own are not included in total of class time.

Lesson Planner

	Connections: English Language Arts Grade 7	Connections: Writing & Language Handbook	Time needed
Chapter 15	Chapter Opener and First Read, pp. 304–309 (Finding Supporting Evidence)		2 days
	Second Read, pp. 309–311 (Determining Point of View and Purpose)		1 day
	Third Read, pp. 311–317 (Analyzing Interpretations of Evidence)		2–3 days (3–4 days with Writing and Language)
	Language: Comma Usage, pp. 317–319	Chapter 27: End Marks and Commas SB: pp. 372–381 TG: p. 251	
	Project-Based Assessment: Develop a Public Service Announcement, pp. 319–320 Roundtable Discussion, pp. 320–321 On Your Own, p. 321	Chapter 6: The Rhetoric of Persuasion; Crafting an Argument SB: pp. 97–115 TG: 36 Chapter 33: Speaking Effectively; Listening Actively SB: pp. 459-464 TG: p. 308	*2–4 days per project (5–7 days with Writing and Language)
	Connect to Testing, pp. 322–323		½ day
			Total: 6½ day (7½ days with Writing and Language)
Writing a Fictional Narrative	Prepare to Write, p. 325 Brainstorm, p. 325 Generate Ideas, pp. 326–328	Chapter 7: Writing a Short Story SB: pp. 130–139 TG: p. 58	2 days
	Organize Ideas, p. 329 First Draft, pp. 329–330		2–3 days
	Group Peer Review, p. 330 Markup Review, p. 331 Individual Review, p. 332 Final Narrative, p. 332		2 days
			Total: 7 days (9 days with Writing and Language)
Assessment	Practice Performance Task, pp. 333–338		2 days
	Unit 3 Summative Assessment, TWE pp. 469–476		2 days
			Total: 4 days
Unit 3 Total			42½ days (47½ days with Writing and Language)

Guide to Abbreviations: SB = student book; **TWE** = teacher wraparound edition; **TG** = teacher guide
*NOTE: Extension activities, Project-Based Assessment, and On Your Own are not included in total of class time.

Lesson Planner

Connections: English Language Arts Grade 7	Connections: Writing & Language Handbook	Time needed
Unit 4		
Introduction to Unit 4, p. 339		½ day
Chapter Opener and First Read, pp. 340–347 (Analyzing How Setting Affects Conflict)		2 days
Second Read, pp. 347–350 (Analyzing How Point of View Affects a Story)		1–2 days
Third Read, pp. 350–356 (Comparing and Contrasting Historical Fiction and Nonfiction)		2–3 days (3–4 days with Writing and Language)
Language: Capitalization, pp. 356–357	Chapter 26: Capitalization SB: pp. 360–370 TG: p. 241	
Project-Based Assessments: Historical Background, pp. 357–358 Historical Fiction, pp. 358–359 On Your Own, p. 359	Chapter 10: Inquiry: Initial Research and Development SB: pp. 184–189 TG: p. 90 Chapter 7: Writing a Short Story SB: pp. 130–139 TG: p. 58	*2–4 days per project (5–7 days with Writing and Language)
Connect to Testing, pp. 360–362		1 day
		Total: 8½ days (9½ days with Writing and Language)
Chapter Opener and First Read, pp. 363–369 (Making Inferences)		2 days
Second Read, p. 370 (Analyzing an Author's Use of Language)		1 day
Third Read, pp. 371–374 (Analyzing a Fictional Account of a Historical Event)		2 days (3–4 days with Writing and Language)
Language: Spelling, pp. 374–376	Chapter 30: Spelling Strategies SB: pp. 404–417 TG: p. 282	
Project-Based Assessments: Response Essay, p. 376 Argumentative Essay, p. 377 On Your Own, p. 377	Chapter 4: Writing Effective Compositions SB: pp. 60–71 TG: p. 26 Chapter 6: Argumentative Writing SB: pp. 92–117 TG: p. 46	*2–4 days per project (3–5 days with Writing and Language)
Connect to Testing, pp. 378–379		½ day
		Total: 5½ days (6½ days with Writing and Language)

In the table, the left column "Chapter 16" spans the rows from Chapter Opener pp. 340–347 through Connect to Testing pp. 360–362, and "Chapter 17" spans the rows from Chapter Opener pp. 363–369 through Connect to Testing pp. 378–379.

Guide to Abbreviations: SB = student book; **TWE** = teacher wraparound edition; **TG** = teacher guide
*NOTE: Extension activities, Project-Based Assessment, and On Your Own are not included in total of class time.

Lesson Planner

	Connections: English Language Arts Grade 7	Connections: Writing & Language Handbook	Time needed
Chapter 18	Chapter Opener and First Read, pp. 380–386 (Analyzing Parallel Stories)		2 days
	Second Read, pp. 386–387 (Exploring Theme)		1 day
	Third Read, pp. 387–388 (Analyzing Figurative Language)		1 day (2 days with Writing and Language)
	Language: Word Meanings, pp. 389–390	Chapter 32: Determining Word Meanings SB: pp. 444–447 TG: p. 296	
	Project-Based Assessment: Letter, p. 390 Oral Presentation, p. 391 On Your Own, p. 391	Chapter 9: Writing Informal Letters SB: pp. 167–171 TG: p. 81 Chapter 33: Speaking Effectively SB: pp. 459-461 TG: p. 308	*2–4 days per project (3–5 days with Writing and Language)
	Connect to Testing, pp. 392–393		½ day
			Total: 4½ days (5½ days with Writing and Language)
Chapter 19	Chapter Opener and First Read, pp. 394–401 (Analyzing the Impact of Setting on Conflict)		2 days
	Second Read, pp. 401–403 (Making Inferences About Characters)		1 day
	Third Read, pp. 403–405 (Analyzing Author's Use of Humor)		1½–2 days (3–4 days with Writing and Language)
	Language: Using Phrases Effectively, pp. 405–407	Ch. 18: Prepositional Phrases; Appositives and Appositive Phrases SB: pp. 271–275 TG: p. 158 Chapter 19: Verbals and Verbal Phrases, pp. 277–282	
	Project-Based Assessment: Diary, p. 407 Personal Interview, pp. 407–408 On Your Own, p. 408	Ch. 7: Writing a Personal Narrative; Writing a Short Story SB: pp. 125–139 TG: p. 58 Chapter 33: Speaking Effectively; Listening Actively SB: pp. 459–464 TG: p. 308	*2–4 days per project (7–9 days with Writing and Language)
	Connect to Testing, pp. 409–410		1 day
			Total: 6 days (8 days with Writing and Language)

Guide to Abbreviations: SB = student book; **TWE** = teacher wraparound edition; **TG** = teacher guide
*NOTE: Extension activities, Project-Based Assessment, and On Your Own are not included in total of class time.

Lesson Planner

	Connections: English Language Arts Grade 7	Connections: Writing & Language Handbook	Time needed
Chapter 20	Chapter Opener and First Read, pp. 410–418 (Determining Theme)		2 days
	Second Read, pp. 418–421 (Analyzing the Unique Format of a Play)		1 day
	Third Read, pp. 421–424 (Analyzing the Purpose of a Scene)		1–2 days (2–3 days with Writing and Language)
	Language: Determining Word Meaning, pp. 422–424	Chapter 32: Determining Word Meanings SB: pp. 444–447 TG: p. 296	
	Project-Based Assessments: Dramatic Scene, p. 425 Documentary, p. 426 On Your Own, p. 426	Chapter 7: Writing a Scene for a Play SB: pp. 139–143 TG: p. 58	*2–4 days per project (3–4 days with Writing and Language)
	Connect to Testing, pp. 427–428		½ day
			Total: 5½ days (6½ days with Writing and Language)
Writing a Research Paper	Brainstorm, p. 430 Gather Ideas, pp. 430–431	Chapter 10: Inquiry: The Process of Inquiry; Inquiry and Initial Research SB: pp. 185–188 TG: p. 90	3 days
	Conduct Research, p. 432 Take Notes, p. 433 Organize Ideas, pp. 433–434 First Draft, p. 434	Chapter 10: Inquiry and Initial Research; Developing Evidence-Based Claims SB: pp. 185–197 TG: p. 90 Chapter 11: Organizing Your Findings; Writing the First Draft SB: pp. 203–212 TG: p. 96	5 days
	Revision, p. 434 Final Essay, p. 436	Chapter 11: Revising and Editing; Publishing SB: pp. 213–215 TG: p. 96	3 days
			Total: 11 days (16 days with Writing and Language)
Assessment	Practice Performance Task, pp. 437–442		2 days
	Unit 4 Summative Assessment, TWE pp. 477–485		2 days
	End-of-Course Summative Assessment, TWE pp. 486–503		2 days
			Total: 6 days
Unit 4 Total			47 days (58 days with Writing and Language)

Guide to Abbreviations: SB = student book; **TWE** = teacher wraparound edition; **TG** = teacher guide
*NOTE: Extension activities, Project-Based Assessment, and On Your Own are not included in total of class time.

Notes